the Unofficial Guide® to Bed & Breakfasts in New England

1st Edition

Also available from Macmillan Travel:

Beyond Disney: The Unofficial Guide to Universal, Sea World, and the Best of Central Florida, by Bob Sehlinger and Amber Morris

Inside Disney: The Incredible Story of Walt Disney World and the Man Behind the Mouse, by Eve Zibart

Mini-Mickey: The Pocket-Sized Unofficial Guide to Walt Disney World, by Bob Sehlinger

The Unofficial Guide to Branson, Missouri, by Bob Sehlinger and Eve Zibart

The Unofficial Guide to California with Kids, by Colleen Dunn Bates and Susan LaTempa

The Unofficial Guide to Chicago, by Joe Surkiewicz and Bob Sehlinger

The Unofficial Guide to Cruises, by Kay Showker with Bob Sehlinger

The Unofficial Guide to Disneyland, by Bob Sehlinger

The Unofficial Guide to Florida with Kids, by Pam Brandon

The Unofficial Guide to the Great Smoky and Blue Ridge Region, by Bob Sehlinger and Joe Surkiewicz

The Unofficial Guide to Las Vegas, by Bob Sehlinger

The Unofficial Guide to Miami and the Keys, by Bob Sehlinger and Joe Surkiewicz

The Unofficial Guide to New Orleans, by Bob Sehlinger and Eve Zibart

The Unofficial Guide to New York City, by Eve Zibart and Bob Sehlinger with Jim Leff

The Unofficial Guide to San Francisco, by Joe Surkiewicz and Bob Sehlinger with Richard Sterling

The Unofficial Guide to Skiing in the West, by Lito Tejada-Flores, Peter Shelton, Seth Masia, Ed Chauner, and Bob Sehlinger

The Unofficial Guide to Walt Disney World, by Bob Sehlinger

The Unofficial Guide to Walt Disney World for Grown-Ups, by Eve Zibart

The Unofficial Guide to Walt Disney World with Kids, by Bob Sehlinger

The Unofficial Guide to Washington, D.C., by Bob Sehlinger and Joe Surkiewicz with Eve Zibart

the Unofficial Guide® to
Bed & Breakfasts in New England
1st Edition

Lea Lane

An International Data Group Company
Foster City, CA • Chicago, IL • Indianapolis, IN
New York, NY • Southlake, TX

To Chaim:
  Great man, Great love

Every effort has been made to ensure the accuracy of information through-out this book. Bear in mind, however, that prices, schedules, etc., are constantly changing. Readers should always verify information before making final plans.

IDG Books Worldwide, Inc.
An International Data Group Company
919 E. Hillsdale Blvd., Suite 400
Foster City, CA 94404

Produced by Menasha Ridge Press

MACMILLAN is a registered trademark of Macmillan General Reference USA, Inc., a wholly owned subsidiary of IDG Books Worldwide, Inc.

UNOFFICIAL GUIDE is a registered trademark of Macmillan General Refer-ence USA, Inc., a wholly owned subsidiary of IDG Books Worldwide, Inc.

0-02-863074-2

1521-4931

Manufactured in the United States of America

10 9 8 7 6 5 4 3 2 1

Contents

List of Maps

About the Author and Illustrator

Lea Lane has written about New England inns and bed-and-breakfasts in consumer guidebooks including Birnbaum USA, *The Zagat Hotel Survey*, and trade publications including *Star Service* for Reed Travel Group. She was a columnist for Gannett Suburban Papers, managing editor of "Travel Smart" newsletter, has co-authored a book on cruises, and contributes to publications including *The New York Times*, *The Miami Herald*, *Fodor's Greece*, *Fodor's Naples and the Amalfi Coast*, *Fodor's Europe 2000*, and *The Unofficial Guide to New York City*.

Born and raised in New York City, *Giselle Simons* received her Bachelor of Fine Arts degree from Cornell University. She currently lives on Manhattan's Upper West Side, where she works as an illustrator, architectural design drafter, and graphic designer. She is caretaker to a dog, two cats, an increasing number of fish, and her husband, Jeff.

Acknowledgments

This first-edition book is a labor of love, with an emphasis on both words. Hundreds of lodgings have been visited numerous times over the past 25 years, culminating in the past year of research and writing.

This team effort starts with tourism departments and innkeepers who answered endless questions, patiently opening their properties for inspection. For this *Unofficial Guide,* I am especially grateful to research associates Dian Larkin and Allyson Shames for their diligence and skills. Deep appreciation to Bob Sehlinger, Molly Burns, Chris Mohney, and the staff at Menasha Ridge Press for gentle, effective, and wise editorial support. Also, thanks to Erin Willder, Caroline Carr, Harper Cossar, Barry Kerrigan, and Molly Harrison for helping getting the book in order. Thanks also to all those who assisted and provided leads on new and interesting properties whether or not they were chosen to appear in the book. These stalwart researchers include Jane Peters, Janine Thomson, Dave Feibusch, Susan Pavleck, Judy Jacobs, Stan Jacobs, Carol Levy, Steve Levy, Stuart Bussey, Gloria Meisel, Sylvia Erlich, Randall Lane, Jen Reingold, Gayle Conran, Cary Lane, Louise Shames, and Chaim Stern.

And a special thank you to my Aunt Hilda, an independent woman and lover of things beautiful and delicious for all of her 87 years. She introduced me to travel and the pleasures of New England inns and B&Bs, early on, ahead of the game. Because of her, I have been able to follow the development of some of these properties for decades.

x

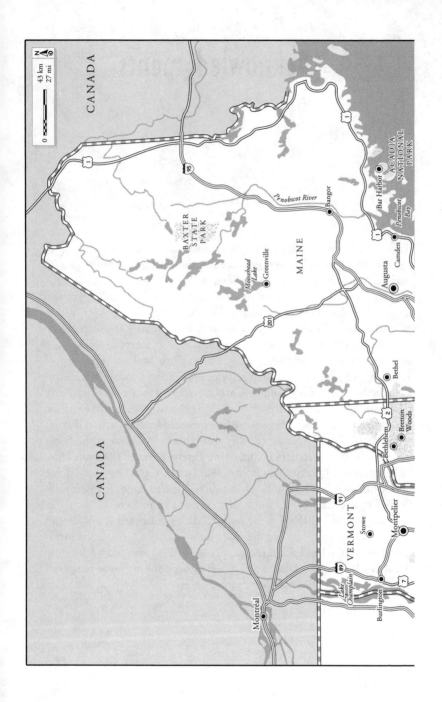

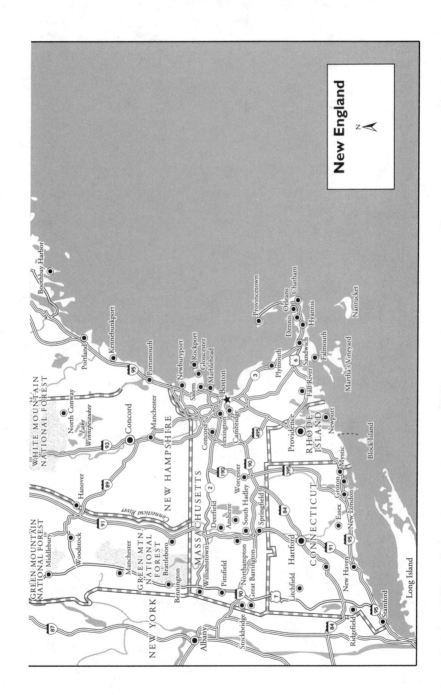

New England

the Unofficial Guide® to Bed & Breakfasts in New England

1st Edition

Introduction

How Come "Unofficial"?

The book in your hands is part of a unique travel and lifestyle guidebook series begun in 1985 with *The Unofficial Guide to Walt Disney World.* That guide, a comprehensive, behind-the-scenes, hands-on prescription for getting the most out of a complex amusement park facility, spawned a series of like titles: *The Unofficial Guide to Chicago, The Unofficial Guide to New Orleans,* and so on. Today, dozens of *Unofficial Guides* help millions of savvy readers navigate some of the world's more complex destinations and situations.

The *Unofficial Guides to Bed & Breakfasts* continue the tradition of insightful, incisive, cut-to-the-chase information, presented in an accessible, easy-to-use format. Unlike in some popular books, no property can pay to be included—those reviewed are solely our choice. And we don't simply rehash the promotional language of these establishments. We visit the good, the bad, and the quirky. We finger the linens, chat with the guests, and sample the scones. We screen hundreds of lodgings, affirming or debunking the acclaimed, discovering or rejecting the new and the obscure. In the end, we present detailed profiles of the lodgings we feel represent the best of the best, select lodgings representing a broad range of prices and styles within each geographic region.

We also include introductions for each state and zone to give you an idea of the nearby general attractions; these introductions also feature helpful phone numbers and websites for further, open-ended information. Area maps with the properties marked help you pinpoint your general destination. And detailed mini indexes help you look up properties by categories and lead you to places that best fit your needs.

With *The Unofficial Guides to Bed & Breakfasts,* we strive to help you find the perfect lodging for every trip. This guide is unofficial because we answer to no one but you.

LETTERS, COMMENTS, AND QUESTIONS FROM READERS

We expect to learn from our mistakes, as well as from the input of our readers, and to improve with each book and edition. Many of those who use the *Unofficial Guides* write to us to ask questions, make comments, or share their own discoveries and lessons learned. We appreciate all such input, both positive and critical, and encourage our readers to continue writing. Readers' comments and observations will contribute immeasurably to the improvement of revised editions of the *Unofficial Guides*.

How to Write the Author

Lea Lane
The Unofficial Guide to Bed & Breakfasts in New England
P.O. Box 43673
Birmingham, AL 35243

When you write, be sure to put your return address on your letter as well as on the envelope—they may get separated. And remember, our work takes us out of the office for long periods of research, so forgive us if our response is delayed.

What Makes It a Bed-and-Breakfast?

Comparing the stale, sterile atmosphere of most hotels and motels to the typical bed-and-breakfast experience—cozy guestroom, intimate parlor, friendly hosts, fresh-baked cookies, not to mention a delicious breakfast— why stay anywhere *other than* a bed-and-breakfast? But this isn't a promotional piece for the bed-and-breakfast life. Bed-and-breakfasts are not hotels. Here are some of the differences:

A bed-and-breakfast or small inn, as we define it, is a small property— from about 3 to 25 guestrooms (with a few exceptions), with hosts around, a distinct personality, individually decorated rooms, and breakfast included in the price (again, with a few exceptions). Many of these smaller properties have owners living right there; in others, the owners are nearby, a phone call away. **For our purposes, the only difference between a small inn and a bed-and-breakfast is that the inn serves dinner on a regular basis.**

Recently, the bed-and-breakfast and small inn trade has taken off— with mixed results. This growth, for the most part, has taken place on both fronts: the low and high end. As bed-and-breakfasts gain popularity, anyone with a spare bedroom can pop an ad in the Yellow Pages for "Billy's Bedroom B&B." These enterprises generally lack professionalism, don't keep regular hours or days of operation, are often unlicensed, and were avoided in this guide.

On the other end of the spectrum are luxury premises with more amenities than the finest hotels. Whether historic homes or lodgings built to be bed-and-breakfasts or inns, interiors are posh, baths are private and ensuite, and breakfasts are gourmet affairs. In-room whirlpool tubs and fireplaces are *de rigueur,* and extras range from in-room refrigerators (perhaps stocked with champagne) to complimentary high tea to free use of state-of-the-art recreational equipment to . . . the list goes on! (One long-time innkeeper, whose historic home was tidily and humbly maintained by hours of elbow grease and common sense, dubbed this new state of affairs "the amenities war.")

The result is an industry in which a simple homestay bed-and-breakfast with a shared bath and common rooms can be a budget experience, while a new, upscale bed-and-breakfast can be the luxury venue of a lifetime.

Who Stays at Bed-and-Breakfasts?

American travelers are finally catching on to what Europeans have known for a long time. Maybe it's a backlash against a cookie-cutter, strip-mall landscape, or longing for a past that maybe never was, and for an idealized, short-term interaction with others. Maybe it's a need for simple pleasures in a world over-the-top with theme parks and high-tech wonders. Who can say for sure?

The bed-and-breakfast trade has grown so large that it includes niches catering to virtually every need. Some bed-and-breakfasts and small inns are equipped to help travelers conduct business, others provide turn-down service and fresh flowers by the honeymooners' canopied bed, and still others offer amenities for reunions or conferences. Whatever your needs, there is a bed-and-breakfast or small inn tailored to your expectations. The challenge, and one this guide was designed to help you meet, is sifting through the choices until you find the perfect place.

Romantics

More and more, properties are establishing at least one room or suite with fireplace, whirlpool, canopied king, and the trappings of romance. Theme rooms can also be especially fun for fantasizing. Always check out the privacy factor. Sometimes a property that caters to families has a carriage house in the back, or a top-floor room away from the others. If an inn allows children under 16, don't be surprised if it's noisy; look for ones that are for older children or adults only.

Families

Face it Moms and Dads: rumpled surroundings will sometimes have to be accepted where children are welcome. You may have to give up pristine décor and breakfast tea served in bone china for the relaxed, informal mood, but on the upside, you won't have to worry as much about Caitlin or Michael knocking over the Wedgwood collection on the sideboard.

When an establishment says kids are "welcome," that usually means a really kid-friendly place. Check the age restrictions. If your children are under-aged but well-behaved, let the host know; often they will make exceptions. (But be sure it's true—other guests are counting on it.) On the flip side, honeymooners or other folks who might prefer common areas free of crayons, and breakfasts without sugar-frosted confetti, may want to look elsewhere.

Generally, bed-and-breakfasts are not ideal for high-action kids. But if your children enjoy games, puzzles, books, a chance for quiet pleasures and meeting others; if they don't need TVs, and can be counted on to be thoughtful and follow instructions ("whisper before 9 a.m.," "don't put your feet on the table"), you and your kids can have a wonderful experience together—and so can the rest of the guests.

Business Travelers

For individual business travelers, bed-and-breakfasts and small inns are becoming much more savvy at anticipating your needs, but in differing degrees. While phone lines and data ports are fairly common, they vary from one bed-and-breakfast to another. Some say they offer data ports when in fact they have two phone jacks in every room but only one phone line servicing the entire property. This can be fine for a three-room inn in the off-season, but if you're trying to conduct business, look for properties with private lines and/or dedicated data ports. If in doubt, ask. Rooms are often available with desks, but these also vary, particularly in surface area and quality of lighting. If this is an important feature, ask for specifics and make sure you secure a room with a desk when you reserve.

Some establishments even offer couriers, secretarial support, and laundry/dry cleaning. And for business travelers who don't have time to take advantage of a leisurely and sumptuous breakfast, hosts often provide an early-morning alternative, sometimes continental, sometimes full.

Finally, there are intangibles to consider. After the sterile atmosphere of the trade show, meeting hall, or boardroom, a small inn with a host and a plate of cookies and a personal dinner recommendation can be nice to come home to.

The atmosphere is also a plus for business meetings or seminars: the relaxed suroundings are quite conducive to easy-going give and take. During the week when guestrooms are often available, bed-and-breakfasts and small inns are usually eager to host business groups. Discounts are often included and special services such as catering and equipment are offered if you rent the entire property. But forget weekends; these properties are still tourist-oriented.

Independents

If you are on your own, small lodgings are ideal. Look for a place with single rates, and even if a special rate isn't listed, you can often negotiate a small discount. If you want some interaction, just sit in the parlor, lounge, or common rooms, and talk to people before meals. Most of the time if you're friendly and interested, you'll get an invite to join someone at a table. You could talk to the innkeepers about this even before you arrive, and they might fix you up with friendly folks. (And if you are traveling with others, invite a single to join you.) As for breakfast, communal tables are perfect for singles. Note our profiles to choose properties with that in mind.

Groups

Whether you are part of a wedding, reunion, or just a group of people who want to travel together, an inn or bed-and-breakfast is a delightful place to stay. The atmosphere is special, your needs are taken care of in a personal way, the grounds are most often spacious and lovely, and in the evening you can all retire in close proximity. (Remember the Alan Alda movie, *The Four Seasons*, filmed at one of our New England inns?) It's especially fun when you take over the whole place—so you may want to choose an especially small property if that's your goal.

Those with Special Needs

Look in our entries for mention of disabled facilities or access. Then call for details to determine just how extensive the accessibility is. Remember also that these houses are usually quite old, and owners of a small bed-and-breakfast will not have a team of accessibility experts on retainer, so be specific with your questions. If doorways must be a certain width to accommodate a wheelchair or walker, know how many inches before you call; if stairs are difficult for Great Aunt Agnes, don't neglect to find out how many are present outside, as well as inside. And if a property that seems otherwise special doesn't seem to have facilities, perhaps you can patch things together, such as a room on the first floor. Realistically, though, most of these properties were built with many stairs and steps, and are situated on hilltops or in rural terrain—so you will have to choose very carefully.

If you suffer from allergies or aversions, talk it over when you book and a good innkeeper will make every attempt to accommodate you. As for food, if you request a special meal and give enough notice, you can often get what you like. That's one of the joys of a small, personalized property.

You and Your Hosts

Hosts are the heart of your small inn or bed-and-breakfast experience and color all aspects of the stay. They can make or break a property, and sometimes an unassuming place will be the most memorable of all because of the care and warmth of the hosts. Typically, they are well versed in navigating the area, and can be a wealth of "insider information" on restaurants, sightseeing, and the like.

While many—most, in these guides—hosts live on the premises, they often have designed or remodeled their building so that their living quarters are separate. Guests often have their own living room, den, parlor, and sitting room; you may be sharing with other guests, but not so much with your hosts. The degree of interaction between host families and guests varies greatly; we try to give a feel for the extremes in the *Comments* section of each profile. In most cases, hosts are accessible but not intrusive; they will swing through the common areas and chat a bit, but are sensitive to guests' need for privacy. But sometimes hosts are in another building altogether; in the other extreme, you are intimately sharing living space with your hosts. This intimate, old-style bed-and-breakfast arrangement is called a "homestay." We try to note this.

In short, most bed-and-breakfast hosts are quite gracious in accommodating travelers' needs, and many are underpinning their unique small lodging with policies and amenities from hotel-style lodgings. But bed-and-breakfasts and small inns are not The Sheraton, and being cognizant of the differences can make your experience more pleasant.

Planning Your Visit

WHEN YOU CHOOSE

If you're not sure where you want to travel, browse through our listings. Maybe from an introduction or from a description of a property, you'll find something to spark your interest.

If you know you are going to a certain location, note the properties in that zone, and then read the entries. You can also call for brochures or take a further look at websites, especially to see rooms or to book directly.

We've provided a listing of some useful websites; others categorized by state and region are in their respective section introductions.

Helpful Websites

www.virtualcities.com
bbchannel.com
bbonline.com
bnbcity.com
bnbinns.com
epicurious.com
getawayguides.com
innbook.com
inns.com
innsnorthamerica.com
johansens.com
relaischateaux.fr/[name of inn]
travel.com/accom/bb/usa
travelguide.com
trip.com
triple1.com
virtualcities.com

WHEN YOU BOOK

Small properties usually require booking on your own. Some travel agents will help you out on this but may charge a fee, because many small properties don't give travel agent commissions. The fastest, easiest way to book is through the Internet or through a reservation service, but if you have special needs or questions, we suggest contacting properties directly to get exactly what you want.

Ask about any special needs or requirements, and make sure your requests are clear. Most of these properties are not designed for people in wheelchairs, so be sure to ask ahead of time if you need that accessibility. Specify what's important to you—privacy, king-size bed, fireplace, tub versus shower, view, first-floor access. A host won't necessarily know what you want, so make sure you decide what is important—writing it down will help you remember. Note the room you want by name, or ask for the "best" room, if you're not sure. Remember to ask about parking conditions—does the property have off-street parking or will you have to find a place on the street? And if air-conditioning is a must for you, always inquire—some bed-and-breakfasts do not have it.

Verify prices and conditions, and any factors or amenities that are important to you. The best time to call is in the early afternoon, before new guests arrive for the day and when hosts have the most free time. Book as soon as possible; for weekends and holidays, preferred properties could be filled a year or more in advance.

A Word about Negotiating Rates

Negotiating a good rate can be more straightforward at a bed-and-breakfast than at a hotel. For starters, the person on the other end of the line will probably be the owner and will have the authority to offer you a discount. Secondly, the bed-and-breakfast owner has a smaller number of rooms and guests to keep track of than does a hotel manager and won't have to do a lot of checking to know that something is available. Also, because the number of rooms is small, each room is more important. In a bed-and-breakfast with four rooms, the rental of each room increases the occupancy rate by 25%.

To get the best rate, just ask. If the owner expects a full house, you'll probably get a direct and honest "no deal." On the other hand, if there are rooms and you are sensitive about price, chances are you'll get a break. In either event, be polite and don't make unreasonable requests. If you are overbearing or contentious on the phone, the proprietor may suddenly discover no rooms available.

Some Considerations

Like snowflakes, no two bed-and-breakfasts are alike. Some are housed in historic homes or other buildings (churches, fraternal halls, barns, castles . . . !). Some are humble and cozy, some are grand and opulent. Some are all in one building, while others are scattered amongst individual, free-standing units. Some offer a breakfast over which you'll want to linger for hours, others . . . well, others make a darn good muffin. Bed-and-breakfasts are less predictable than hotels and motels, but can be much more interesting. A few bed-and-breakfast aficionados have discovered that "interesting" sometimes comes at a price. This guide takes the "scary" out of "interesting" and presents only places that meet a certain standard of cleanliness, predictability, and amenities. However, there are certain questions and issues common to bed-and-breakfasts and small inns that first-time visitors should consider:

Choosing Your Room

Check out your room before lugging your luggage (not having elevators is usually part of the charm). This is standard procedure at small properties, and saves time and trouble should you prefer another room. When a guest room has an open door, it usually means the proud innkeeper wants you to peek. You may just find a room that you like better than the one you are assigned, and it may be available, so ask.

Bathrooms

Americans are picky about their potties. While the traditional (sometimes referred to as "European-style") bed-and-breakfast set-up involved several bedrooms sharing a bath, this is becoming less common. Even venerable Victorians are being remodeled to include private baths. In fact, many bed-and-breakfasts offer ultra-luxurious bath facilities, including jetted tubs, dual vanities, and so forth. Our advice is not to reject shared bath facilities out of hand as these can be excellent values. Do check the bedroom-to-bath ratio, however. Two rooms sharing a bath can be excellent; three or more can be problematic with a full house.

Security

Many bed-and-breakfasts have property locks and room locks as sophisticated as hotels and motels. Others do not. For the most part, inns with 3½ stars or more have quality locks throughout the premises. (Many with lower rankings do as well.) Beyond locks, however, most bed-and-breakfasts provide an additional measure of security in that they are small properties, generally in a residential district, and typically with live-in hosts on the premises. Single female travelers might find a measure of security in coming "home" to a facility like this as opposed to a 150-room hotel with a cardlock system but God-knows-what lurking in the elevator.

Privacy

At a hotel, you can take your key and hole up in solitude for the duration of your stay. It's a little harder at a bed-and-breakfast, especially if you take part in a family-style breakfast (although many inns offer the option of an early continental breakfast if you're pressed for time or feeling antisocial, and some offer ensuite breakfast service—these options are noted in the profiles). Most bed-and-breakfast hosts we've met are very sensitive to guests' needs for privacy, and seem to have a knack for being as helpful or as unobtrusive as you wish. If privacy is hard to achieve at a given property, we've noted that in the profile.

Autonomy

Most bed-and-breakfasts provide a key to the front door and/or an unlocked front door certain hours of the day. While you might be staying in a family-style atmosphere, you are seldom subject to rules such as a curfew. (A few properties request that guests be in by a specific time; these policies are noted and rare.) Some places have "quiet hours," usually from about 10 or 11 p.m. until about 7 a.m. Such policies tend to be in place when properties lack sufficient sound insulation, and are noted in the profile. Generally, higher ratings tend to correspond with better sound insulation.

What the Ratings Mean

We have organized this book so that you can get a quick idea of each property by checking out the ratings, reading the information at the beginning of each entry and then, if you're interested, reading the more detailed overview of each property. Obviously ratings are subjective, and people of good faith (and good taste) can and do differ. But you'll get a good, relative idea, and the ability to quickly compare properties.

Overall Rating   The overall ratings are represented by stars, which range in number from one to five and represent our opinion of the quality of the property as a whole. It corresponds something like this:

★★★★★	The Best
★★★★½	Excellent
★★★★	Very Good
★★★½	Good
★★★	Good enough
★★½	Fair
★★	Not so good
★½	Barely Acceptable
★	Unnacceptable

The overall rating for the bed-and-breakfast or small inn experience includes all factors of the property including guest rooms and also public rooms, food, facilities, grounds, maintenance, hosts and something we'll called "specialness," for lack of a better phrase. Many times it involves the personalities and pesonal touches of the hosts.

Some properties have fairly equal star levels for all of these things, but most have some qualities that are better than others. Also, large, ambitious properties that serve dinner would tend to have a slightly higher star rating for the same level of qualities than a smaller property (the difference, say, between a great novel and a great short story; the larger it is the harder it is to pull off, hence the greater the appreciation). Yet a small property can earn five stars with a huge dose of "specialness."

Overall ratings and room quality ratings do not always correspond. While guest rooms may be spectacular, the rest of the inn may be average, or vice versa. Generally though, we've found through the years that a property is usually consistently good, or bad, throughout.

Room Quality Rating   The quality ratings, stated in the form of a letter grade, represent our opinion of the quality of the guest rooms and bathrooms only. For the room quality ratings we factored in view, size, closet space, bedding, seating, desks, lighting, soundproofing, comfort, bathrooms (or lack), style, privacy, soundproofing, decor, "taste," and other intangibles. A really great private bathroom with a claw-foot tub and antique table might bring up the rating of an otherwise average room. Conversely, poor maintenance or lack of good lighting will lower the rating of a spacious, well-decorated room. Sometimes a few rooms are really special while others are standard, and we averaged these, where possible. It's difficult to codify this, but all factors are weighed, and the grades seem to come up easily.

It corresponds something like this:

A = Excellent
B = Very Good
C = Good
D = Acceptable

Value Rating   The value ratings—A to D—are a combination of the overall and room quality ratings, divided by the cost of an average guest room. They are an indication rather than a scientific formulation—a general idea of value for money. If getting a good deal means the most to you, choose a property by looking at the value rating. Otherwise, the numbers and stars are better indicators of a satisfying experience. An A value, A room quality, five-star inn or bed-and-breakfast would be ideal, but most often, you'll find a C value, and you are getting your money's worth. If a wonderful property is fairly priced, it may only get a C value rating, but you still might prefer the experience to an average property that gets an A value rating.

Price   Our price range is the lowest-priced room in low season to the highest-priced room in high season. The range does not usually include specially priced times such as holidays and foliage season. It is a room rate, based on double occupancy, and assumes that breakfast is included. It does not assume that other meals are included in the rate. However, be sure to check the inn's Food & Drink category. If meals other than breakfast are included in your room rate, we will have noted MAP, which stands for the hotel industry's standard Modified American Plan, in the Food & Drink category. Lodgings where MAP is applicable offer breakfast and dinner in the room rate. Unless specifically noted, prices quoted in the formats do not include gratuities or state taxes, which can be fairly steep. Gratuities are optional; use your own discretion. Prices change constantly, so check before booking.

The Profiles Clarified

The bulk of information about properties is straightforward, but much of it is in abbreviated style, so the following clarifications may help. They are arranged in the order they appear in the profile format.

Many of the properties in this book have similar names or even the same name; for example, there are two Homestead Inns in Connecticut, one in New Milford and one in Greenwich. Town names, too, can be strikingly similar. Make sure you don't confuse properties or town names when selecting an inn.

Location

First, check the map for location. Our directions are designed to give you a general idea of the property's location. For more complete directions, call the property when you are in town.

Building

This category denotes the design and architecture of the building. Many of the properties in the *Unofficial Guides* are historically and architecturally interesting. Here are a few architectural terms you may want to brush up on, in no particular order: Painted Lady, hip-roof, Colonial, Federal, Queen Ann, Doric column, Shingle, King's Lumber, Pumpkin Pine, Bird's Eye Maple, Tiger Maple, Rumford fireplace, Georgian, Victorian, Arts and Crafts, English Aesthetic, Eastlake, Greek Revival, Gingerbread, 12-over-12 windows, claw-foot tub, and many more. The more you know the jargon, the better you can select the property you want.

Food & Drink

For food and drink, we offer a taste of the inn or bed-and-breakfast, so to speak. Most properties go all out to fill you up at breakfast, so that you could easily skip lunch (factor that into the value). In some areas, however, the tourist board regulates that properties can only serve a continental breakfast without a hot dish. Note whether we state "full breakfast," if that experience is paramount. In most cases, a bed-and-breakfast breakfast— even a continental—tends to include more homemade items, greater selection, and greater care in presentation.

In this category, what we call "specialties" are really typical dishes, which may not always be served, but should give you a good idea of the cuisine. And a very few bed-and-breakfasts and inns do not include the breakfast in the price. However, it is almost always offered as an option.

Many inns and bed-and-breakfasts offer afternoon tea, snacks or sherry or pre-dinner wine and cheese. If a property offers tea in the afternoon, we have noted so in this Food & Drink category by just stating "tea." Note that if an inn offers meals to the public as well as guests, the atmosphere becomes less personal. Also, if have noted MAP in this category, it means that the inn offers meals other than breakfast as part of the room rate.

Some inns provide alcoholic beverages to guests, some forbid consumption of alcohol—either extreme is noted in the inn's profile. The norm is that alcohol consumption is a private matter, and guests may bring and consume their own, if they do so respectfully. Glassware is generally provided. Bed-and-breakfasts are not well suited to drunkenness and partying.

A diet and a bed-and-breakfast or small inn go together about as well as a haystack and a lighted match. Come prepared to eat. If calories matter, a bed-and-breakfast will give you less guilt than an inn, as breakfast can easily last till an afternoon snack, and for dinner you can go lightly. Inns make that much, much harder, as often the prices for dinner are built in, and even when they aren't the aromas will lure even the most disciplined calorie-counter to the dining room. Dinners are usually served charmingly, with flowers, candlelight, crystal, silver, and so forth. Some bed-and-breakfasts will serve dinner on request, and we included that info when it was available.

Most bed-and-breakfasts are sensitive to dietary needs and preferences, but need to be warned of this in advance. When you make your reservation, be sure to explain if you are diabetic, wheat- or dairy-intolerant, vegetarian/vegan, or otherwise restricted. Many proprietors pride themselves on accommodating difficult diets.

Recreation

We do not usually spell out whether the activities noted in the format are on-site. With some exceptions, assume that golf, tennis, fishing, canoeing, downhill skiing, and the like are not on-site (since these are small properties, not resorts). Assume that games and smaller recreational activities are on the property. But there are some exceptions, so ask.

Amenities & Services

These blend a bit. Generally, amenities include extras such as swimming pools and games, or services such as business support and turning down beds in the evening. Business travelers should note if any services are mentioned, also if there are public rooms, group discounts, and so forth to back them up. Almost all bed-and-breakfasts and inns can provide advice regarding touring, restaurants, and local activities; many keep maps and brochures on hand.

Deposit

Unless otherwise noted, "refund" usually means "minus a service charge," which varies from $10 or so to 50 percent or more. The more popular the property, usually the more deposit you'll have to put down, and the further ahead. When canceling after the site's noted policy, most will still refund, less a fee, if the room is re-rented. Check back on this.

Discounts

Discounts may extend to singles, long-stay guests, kids, seniors, packages, groups and extra people in a room, even though not listed in the text. It doesn't hurt to ask, as these sorts of things are especially flexible in small establishments, mid-week, off-season, last-minute, when innkeepers may want to fill their rooms.

Credit Cards

For those properties that do accept credit cards (we note those that do not), we've listed credit cards accepted with the following codes:

V	VISA
MC	MasterCard
AE	American Express
D	Discover
DC	Diner's Club International
CB	Carte Blanche

Check-in/Out

As small operators, most bed-and-breakfast hosts need to know approximately when you'll be arriving. Many have check-in periods (specified in the profiles) during which the hosts or staff will be available to greet you. Most can accommodate arrival beyond their stated check-in period, but need to be advised so they can arrange to be home or get a key to you.

Think about it—they have to buy groceries and go to the kids' soccer games and get to doctors' appointments just like you. And they have to sleep sometime. Don't show up at 11:30 p.m. and expect a smiling bell-hop—the same person who lets you in is probably going to be up at 5 or 6 a.m. slicing mushrooms for your omelet!

Check-in times are often flexible, but, as with any commercial lodging, check-out times can be critical, as the innkeeper must clean and prepare your room for incoming guests. If you need to stay longer, ask and you'll often get an extension. Sometimes, a host will let you leave your bags and enjoy the common areas after check-out, as long as you vacate your room.

Please take cancellation policies seriously. A "no-show" is not a cancellation! If an establishment has a seven-day, or 72-hour, or whatever, cancellation policy, you are expected to call and cancel your reservation prior to that time, or you could be liable for up to the full amount of your reserved stay. After all, a four-unit bed-and-breakfast has lost 25% of its revenue if you arbitrarily decide not to show up.

Smoking

We've indicated in the inn's profile if smoking is banned outright, or if there are designated rooms where it's allowed. Usually it's fine to smoke outside, what with the excellent ventilation, but ask your hosts before you light up. Be mindful, too, of how you dispose of the butts—when you flick them into a nearby shrub, it's likely that your hosts, not some sanitation team, will be plucking them out next week.

Pets

We have not mentioned most of the inn-house pets in the profiles, as this situation changes even more frequently than most items. Many properties have pets on the premises. Don't assume that because an establishment does not allow guests to bring pets that pets aren't around. Dogs and cats and birds (and monkeys, pigs, goats, llamas, etc.) are often around. If you forsee a problem with this, be sure to clarify "how around," before booking. If properties allow pets, we have noted this, but most do not. And if you can't bear to leave your own beloved Fido or Miss Kitty for long periods, and want to stay in an inn that does not allow them, good innkeepers often know of reputable boarding facilities nearby.

Open

Properties often claim they are open all year, but they can close at any time; at the last minute for personal reasons or if business is slow. Similarly, properties that close during parts of the year may open specially for groups. If you can get a bunch of family or friends together, it's a great way to stay at

In this group of 300 profiled properties, our innkeepers include a former pro football player, an FBI agent, a soap opera actor, a former U.S. Congressman, feminists, a director of a New York ballet company, a mailman, opera singers, socialites, CEOs, poets, painters, musicians, sports enthusiasts, James Taylor's brother, Matt Damon's cousin, and so on. Their hobbies and collections and cooking abilities vary widely, and we've tried to mention them if we think you'd be interested. City folk, people from all over the country, and locals—all have the goal of hospitality, and some are truly gifted at it.

Returning to an inn after a crisp autumn day, welcomed by a friendly host; enjoying lobster soufflé and glass of chardonnay by a crackling fire; retiring to a canopied four-poster under hand-sewn down quilts; waking up to the smell of blueberry muffins, bacon, and brewing coffee; and the warmth of fellow travelers—these are as much a delight of a trip to New England as the blazing leaves or a steepled church on a village green. Indeed, the lodging at the end of the day can be an end in itself.

SOME BACKGROUND ON NEW ENGLAND SMALL LODGINGS

Venerable New England lodgings like The Hawthorne Inn have been around since Nathaniel Hawthorne himself (who lived across the road). But in the past, where you stayed wasn't why you went. People vacationed all summer at resorts in Maine or went to lodges in Vermont or motels on the Cape for a couple of weeks, but short getaways weren't in style, and "long weekends" were concepts of the future.

But many artisans and youth who traveled the world in the 1960s and '70s came back to New England and opened bed-and-breakfasts like the ones they stayed in overseas (maybe with a craft workshop in the attic or barn, in which to build handmade furnishings and art). Then there were the professionals who dropped out of the rat race to open an inn or bed-and-breakfast in a gentrified old house or building, with a goal of family togetherness and a laid-back life.

Today, the newest legion of bed-and-breakfast and small-inn owners—sophisticated and particular, many with hotel or cooking school backgrounds—are taking the small lodging experience to new, sophisticated, and even fantasy levels and creating an art form as varied as jazz. But the talent, artistry, and personality of the great innkeepers are a constant refrain.

Ten Reasons to Get out and Go

"Beauty is its own excuse for being," wrote local boy Ralph Waldo Emerson, who knew his way around these parts. We'd add, "The place to stay is its own excuse for going"—the only reason you need to drive around New England is to arrive at the place you are staying.

But some of you may need a more motivating prompt to get up and out in New England. State tourist boards offer free material about each area, and the Internet has much information as well. Here are a few more excuses to get going:

1. Shop. This part of the country is crammed with antiques, crafts, and discount outlets. Save your special-occasion, decorating, or holiday shopping for these excursions. Empty your car's trunk, and load up.

2. Retrace history. This is, after all, where the Pilgrims landed and the American Revolution began. This is where the Underground Railway hid slaves, and ship captains and merchants made fortunes and then created art colonies and wealthy enclaves, and where farmers and millworkers toiled. Read up on the history of the area, and visit historic sites.

3. Experience the full glory of seasons. Fall color here, one of the greatest concentrations in the world, is justly famous, and draws leaf-peeping visitors in crowds throughout late September and October. But summer in Maine and at the beaches of Connecticut, Rhode Island, and Massachusetts and winter in Vermont and New Hampshire are just as definitive. Spring is chancy and short in New England, with a spring mud season that is messy. But we love maple-sugar tapping in April and the hatchlings and buds and the roaring brooks and the empty trails and back roads. It's the best time for birding, fishing, biking, and shopping uncrowded stores. And the best time to get a room at popular bed-and-breakfasts and inns.

4. Make a college tour. Just for fun. Some of the most beautiful campuses in the world are in New England. From Harvard Yard to Bennington's artsy campus, from Amherst to UConn to Brown to Wesleyan, Smith, and Wellesley—just walking them gives you opportunity for nostalgia and dreams. The towns are charming. Museums are frequent: Williams and Yale are especially notable. Architecture on campuses is some of the

- Room diaries—comments from aspiring romance writers and star-crossed guests

- The Mallard Room at the Pitcher Inn, Warren, Vermont

- The Matisse Room at The Pomegranate Inn, Portland, Maine

- Gardens at Miles Country Inn, Hamilton, Massachusetts

- Wood-burning fireplaces that crackle, hiss, splatter, flare up, and die out

- Claw-foot tubs (bring your own bath gel, just in case)

Mini Indexes

Top 30 Overall

Five Stars
Adair Country Inn
Blantyre
Captain Lord Mansion
Cliffside Inn
Elm Tree Cottage
Inn at National Hall
Inn at Saw Mill Farm
Inn at Shelburne Farms
Inn at the Round Barn Farm
Inn on the Common
Jackson House Inn
Manor on Golden Pond
Mayflower Inn
Norumbega
Pitcher Inn
Rabbit Hill Inn
Twin Farms
White Barn Inn

Four-and-a-Half Stars
1661 Inn
Baldwin Hill Farm
Bay Beach Bed and Breakfast
Blue Hill Inn
Boulders Inn

Bufflehead Cove Inn
Bungay Jar Bed & Breakfast
Cornucopia of Dorset
Country Garden Inn
Eden Pines Inn
Edgewood Manor
Edson Hill Manor

Top 30 by Room Quality
1. Twin Farms
2. Blantyre
3. Inn at National Hall
4. Inn at the Round Barn Farm
5. Pitcher Inn
6. Rabbit Hill Inn
7. Adair Country Inn
8. Captain Lord Mansion
9. Elm Tree Cottage
10. Inn at Saw Mill Farm
11. Jackson House Inn
12. Mayflower Inn
13. White Barn Inn
14. Inn at Ormsby Hill
15. Lodge at Moosehead Lake
16. Manor on Golden Pond
17. Pomegranate
18. Wynstone
19. Bay Beach Bed and Breakfast
20. Cliffside Inn
21. Edgewood Manor

22. Field Farm Guest House
23. Ivy Lodge
24. Nannau-Seaside
25. Notchland Inn
26. Pilgrim's Inn
27. Angel Hill
28. Blue Hill Inn
29. Captain Jefferds Inn
30. Gibson House

Top Values

1661 Inn
Admiral Dewey Inn
Allen House Victorian Inn
Covered Bridge House
East Wind Inn & Meeting House
Edson Hill Manor
Hannah Davis House
Hartstone Inn
Hotel Manisses
Kingsleigh Inn 1904
Manor House
Nannau-Seaside
Wildcat Inn and Tavern

Boat-and-Breakfasts

Maine
Schooner Stephen Taber

Connecticut
Stonecroft

Budget Accommodations

At least some rooms rent for less than $75.

Maine
Alden House
Hartstone Inn
Homeport Inn
Island View Inn
Kingsleigh Inn 1904
Linekin Bay Bed & Breakfast

Pleasant Bay
Weston House

New Hampshire
Apple Gate Bed and Breakfast
Birchwood Inn
Carter Notch Inn
Covered Bridge House
Farm by the River
Hannah Davis House
Maple Hill Farm
Nereledge Inn
Ram in the Thicket
Wildcat Inn and Tavern

Vermont
Black Lantern Inn
Inn at Blush Hill
Siebeness
Willough Vale Inn

Massachusetts
Allen House Victorian Inn
Amelia Payson House
Harborview Inn
Manor House Bed and Breakfast
Martin House Inn
Morins Victorian Hideaway

Rhode Island
1661 Inn
1900 House
Hotel Manisses
Jailhouse Inn

Dinner Served

Maine
Blue Hill Inn
Captain Lindsey House
Crocker House Country Inn
East Wind Inn & Meeting House
Gosnold Arms
Greenville Inn

Maine (cont'd)
Hartstone Inn
Hartwell House
Inn on the Harbor
Keeper's House
Lake House
Lodge at Moosehead Lake
Newcastle Inn
Oakland House
Pilgrim's Inn
Schooner Stephen Taber
Telemark Inn
Weatherby's Fisherman's Resort
Weston House
White Barn Inn

New Hampshire
Adair Country Inn
Alden Country Inn
Bernerhof Inn
Birchwood Inn
Christmas Farm Inn
Colby Hill Inn
Darby Field Inn
Dexter's Inn and Tennis Club
Follansbee Inn
Foxglove
Hancock Inn
Inn at Crotched Mountain
Inn at Thorn Hill
Manor on Golden Pond
Notchland Inn
Ram in the Thicket
Red Hill Inn
Stafford's in the Field Inn
Sugar Hill Inn
Sunset Hill House
Wild Cat Inn and Tavern

Vermont
Black Lantern Inn
Edson Hill Manor

Four Columns Inn
Governor's Inn
Heermansmith Farm Inn
Inn at Ormsby Hill
Inn at Saw Mill Farm
Inn at Shelburne Farms
Inn at the Round Barn Farm
Inn at Weathersfield
Inn on the Common
Jackson House Inn
Juniper Hill Inn
Lilac Inn
Mountain View Creamery
North Hero House Country Inn
October Country Inn
Pitcher Inn
Rabbit Hill Inn
Reluctant Panther
Rowell's Inn
Shire Inn
Ten Acres Lodge
Tulip Tree Inn
Twin Farms
West Hill House
Wildflower Inn
Willough Vale Inn
Windham Hill Inn

Massachusetts
Blantyre
Deerfield Inn
Mary Prentiss Inn
Outermost Inn
Rhode Island
Hotel Manisses
Shelter Harbor Inn
Watch Hill Inn

Connecticut
Bee and Thistle Inn
Boulders Inn
Elms Inn

Gelston Inn
Homestead Inn (Greenwich)
Inn at National Hall
Lakeview Inn
Mayflower Inn
Old Lyme Inn
Roger Sherman Inn
Silvermine Tavern
Simsbury 1820 House
Three Chimneys Inn
Toll Gate Hill
Under Mountain Inn

Farm or Rural Setting

Maine
Bagley House
Cod Cove Farm
Pleasant Bay
Squire Tarbox Inn
Telemark Inn
Weatherby's Fisherman's Resort

New Hampshire
Apple Gate Bed and Breakfast
Bungay Jar Bed & Breakfast
Farm by the River
The Forest
Harrisville Squire's Inn
Inn at Crotched Mountain
Inn at Maplewood Farm
Maple Hill Farm
Nestlenook Farm
Olde Orchard Inn
Rosewood Country Inn
Sugar Hill Inn

Vermont
Cornwall Orchards
Edson Hill Manor
Heermansmith Farm Inn
Inn at Round Barn Farm

Inn at Shelburne Farms
Inn at Weathersfield
Inn at Woodchuck Hill Farm
Maple Leaf Inn
Mountain View Creamery
October Country Inn
Shire Inn
Strong House Inn
Ten Acres Lodge
Ten Bends on the River
Tulip Tree Inn
Twin Farms
Whitford House Inn
Wildflower Inn
Windham Hill Inn

Massachusetts
Amerscot House
Applegate
Baldwin Hill Farm
Blantyre
Field Farm Guest House
Historic Merrell Inn
Miles River Country Inn
River Bend Farm

Rhode Island
Historic Jacob Hill Farm
The Roost
Woody Hill

Connecticut
Angel Hill
Applewood Farms Inn
Boulders Inn
Elias Child House
Friendship Valley Inn
Hearthside Farm
Lord Thompson Manor
Mayflower Inn
Merrywood
Silvermine Tavern

Connecticut (cont'd)
Stonecroft
Toll Gate Hill
Under Mountain Inn

Family-Oriented

Maine
Goose Cove Lodge
Island View Inn
Keeper's House
Pleasant Bay
Schooner Stephen Taber
    (teenagers)
Telemark Inn
Weatherby's Fisherman's Resort

New Hampshire
Christmas Farm Inn
Covered Bridge House
Darby Field Inn
Dexter's Inn and Tennis Club
Goddard Mansion
Inn at Crotched Mountain
Maple Hill Farm
Nereledge Inn
Olde Orchard Inn
Ram in the Thicket
Sunset Hill House
Trumbull House Bed and Breakfast

Vermont
Cornwall Orchards
Edson Hill Manor
Heermansmith Farm Inn
Hickory Ridge House
Hugging Bear Inn
Inn at Shelburne Farms
Inn on the Common
Mountain View Creamery
North Hero House Country Inn
October Country Inn
Ten Bends on the River

Whitford House Inn
Wildflower Inn
Woodstocker

Massachusetts
Field Farm Guest House
Mary Prentiss Inn
Over Look Inn
Windflower

Rhode Island
1661 Inn
Jailhouse Inn
Shelter Harbor Inn
Watch Hill Inn

Connecticut
Brigadoon
Chester Bulkley House
Elms Inn
Gelston Inn
Homestead Inn (New Milford)
Inn at National Hall
Old Lyme Inn
Roger Sherman Inn
Silvermine Tavern
Toll Gate Hill

Ghosts
These inns boast friendly ghosts.

Maine
Crocker House Country Inn

Vermont
Willard Street Inn

Massachusetts
Deerfield Inn

Rhode Island
Stone Lea

Connecticut
Inn at Lafayette

Groups, Conferences, and/or Weddings Easily Accommodated

Check individual profiles for the one that suits your needs.

Maine
Bagley House
Captain Jefferds Inn
Captain Lord Mansion
Crocker House Country Inn
East Wind Inn & Meeting House
Five Gables Inn
Flying Cloud
Goose Cove Lodge
Hartwell House
Inn at Portsmouth Harbor
Lake House
Manor House
Oakland House
Old Fort Inn
Weatherby's Fisherman's Resort

New Hampshire
Adair Country Inn
Alden Country Inn
Buttonwood Inn
Carter Notch Inn
Christmas Farm Inn
Colby Hill Inn
Dexter's Inn and Tennis Club
The Forest
Foxglove
Gibson House
Goddard Mansion
Harrisville Squire's Inn
Highland Lake Inn
Inn at Crotched Mountain
Maple Hill Farm
Nestlenook Farm
Olde Orchard Inn
Pressed Petals Inn
Ram in the Thicket

Red Hill Inn
Rosewood Country Inn
Stafford's in the Field Inn
Sunset Hill House
The Inn at Thorn Hill
Trumbull House Bed and Breakfast
Wildcat Inn and Tavern

Vermont
Andrie Rose Inn
Four Columns Inn
Green Trails Inn
Hickory Ridge House
Inn at Ormsby Hill
Inn at Weathersfield
Jackson House Inn
Juniper Hill Inn
Lilac Inn
Maple Leaf Inn
North Hero House Country Inn
Northfield Inn
Somerset House
Strong House Inn
Ten Bends on the River
The Pitcher Inn
Thomas Mott Homestead
Tulip Tree Inn
Twin Farms
West Hill House
Whitford House Inn
Wildflower Inn
Windham Hill Inn

Massachusetts
Amerscot House
Augustus Snow House
Blantyre
Captain Freeman Inn
Clark Currier Inn
Cyrus Kent House Inn
Dunscroft-by-the-Sea
Harbor Light Inn
Hawthorne Inn

Massachusetts (cont'd)

Mary Prentiss Inn
Mary Rockwell Stuart House
Miles River Country Inn
Over Look Inn
Seagull Inn
Fernbrook Inn
Walker House
Wedgewood Inn
Whalewalk Inn
Windflower
Windsor House

Rhode Island

1855 Marshall Slocum Guest House
Admiral Dewey Inn
Four Gables
Francis Malbone House
Hotel Manisses
Ivy Lodge
Kismet on the Park
The Roost
Savana's Inn
Stone Lea
Victorian Ladies Inn
Watch Hill Inn
Woody Hill

Connecticut

Boulders Inn
Brigadoon
Copper Beech Inn
Elms Inn
French Bulldog Bed & Breakfast
    and Antiques
Gelston Inn
Hearthside Farm
Homestead Inn
Inn at Lafayette
Lord Thompson Manor
Manor House
Mayflower Inn
Old Lyme Inn

Old Mystic Inn
Roger Sherman Inn
Silvermine Tavern
Simsbury 1820 House
Stonecroft
Three Chimneys Inn
Toll Gate Hill
Under Mountain Inn
White Hart Inn

Historic

This list includes only those inns
that are 200 years old or older.

Maine

Bagley House
Captain Jefferds Inn
Flying Cloud
Harpswell Inn
Lake House
Pilgrim's Inn
Squire Tarbox Inn

New Hampshire

Amos A. Parker House
Birchwood Inn
Christmas Farm Inn
Colby Hill Inn
Dexter's Inn and Tennis Club
Farm by the River
Hancock Inn
Highland Lake Inn
Nereledge Inn
Olde Orchard Inn
Stafford's in the Field Inn
Sugar Hill Inn

Vermont

1811 House
Cornwall Orchards
Inn at Blush Hill
Inn at Ormsby Hill
Inn at Weathersfield
Inn at Woodchuck Hill Farm

Inn on Covered Bridge Green
Rabbit Hill Inn
Wildflower Inn

Massachusetts
Amerscot House
Clark Tavern Inn
Corner House
Harbor Light Inn
Historic Merrell Inn
Miles River Country Inn
River Bend Farm
Saltbox
Windsor House

Rhode Island
Bradford-Dimond-Norris House
C C Ledbetter
Clarkston
Francis Malbone House
Historic Jacob Hill Farm
Jailhouse Inn

Connecticut
Bee and Thistle Inn
Brigadoon
Cobbscroft
Elias Child House
Elms Inn
Friendship Valley Inn
Hearthside Farm
Homestead Inn
Old Mystic Inn
Red Brook Inn
Roger Sherman Inn
Silvermine Tavern
Toll Gate Hill

Island Setting

Maine
Keeper's House

Massachusetts
Corner House

Martha's Place
Martin House Inn
Outermost Inn
Pineapple Inn
Shiverick Inn
Thorncroft Inn
Tuscany Inn
Victorian Inn

Rhode Island
1661 Inn
Blue Dory Inn
Hotel Manisses
Sea Breeze Inn
Sheffield House
Weather Bureau Inn

Mountain Setting

Maine
Telemark Inn

New Hampshire
Adair Country Inn
Bernerhof Inn
Bungay Jar Bed & Breakfast
Darby Field Inn
Farm by the River
Foxglove
Inn at Crotched Mountain
Inn at Thorn Hill
Nereledge Inn
Notchland Inn
Sugar Hill Inn
Sunset Hill House

Vermont
Andrie Rose Inn
Black Lantern Inn
Cornwall Orchards
Edson Hill Manor
Inn at Blush Hill
Maple Leaf Inn
Mountain View Creamery
Pitcher Inn

Vermont (cont'd)
Rabbit Hill Inn
Siebeness
Strong House Inn
Ten Acres Lodge
Ten Bends on the River
Tulip Tree Inn
Twin Farms
West Hill House
Whitford House Inn
Willough Vale Inn
Windham Hill Inn

Massachusetts
Field Farm Guest House
River Bend Farm

Connecticut
Boulders Inn
Hilltop Haven
White Hart Inn

No Credit Cards

Maine
Harbor Hill
Keeper's House
Weston House

New Hampshire
Amos A. Parker House
Birchwood Inn
Inn at Crotched Mountain

Massachusetts
Bed and Breakfast of Sagamore Beach
Cliffwood Inn
Fernbrook Inn
Morins Victorian Hideaway
River Bend Farm
Seacrest Manor
Walker House

Rhode Island
1900 House
Elm Tree Cottage

Green Shadows
Kismet on the Park
Murphy's
One Willow By The Sea
Stone Lea
Woody Hill

Connecticut
Gibson House
Hilltop Haven
Palmer Inn

Pets Allowed
The following properties accept pets at least somewhere on their property. Many still have restrictions, so call ahead. Always let a host know ahead of time if you plan to bring a pet.

Maine
Balance Rock Inn By-The-Sea
Captain Jefferds Inn
East Wind Inn & Meeting House
Harbor Hill
Hartstone Inn
Inn at Bath
Island View Inn
Weatherby's Fisherman's Resort
White Hart Inn

New Hampshire
Ashburn House
Inn at Crotched Mountain
Olde Orchard Inn
Ram in the Thicket

Vermont
Four Columns Inn
Hugging Bear Inn
Inn on the Common
Ten Acres Lodge
Whitford House Inn

Massachusetts
Clark Tavern Inn
Field Farm Guest House

Harborview Inn
Over Look Inn
Victorian Inn
Walker House
Windsor House

Rhode Island
Four Gables

Connecticut
Applewood Farms Inn
Hearthside Farm
Silvermine Tavern
Sound Reach
Toll Gate Hill

Romantic

Maine
Balance Rock Inn By-the-Sea
Bufflehead Cove Inn
Lake House
Norumbega

New Hampshire
Gibson House
Hannah Davis House
Inn at Thorn Hill
Nestlenook Farm
Sugar Hill Inn

Vermont
Cornucopia of Dorset
Inn at Ormsby Hill
Juniper Hill Inn
Maple Leaf Inn
Rabbit Hill Inn
Shire Inn
Strong House Inn
Twin Farms
Willough Vale Inn

Massachusetts
Acworth Inn
Allen House Victorian Inn
Augustus Snow House

Captain Freeman Inn
Dunscroft-by-the-Sea
Martha's Place
Mary Rockwell Stuart House
Shiverick Inn
Spraycliff
Thorncroft Inn
Wildflower Inn

Rhode Island
Elm Tree Cottage
Hydrangea House Inn
Old Beach Inn
The Villa
Wynstone

Connecticut
Angel Hill
Boulders Inn
Elias Child House
House of 1833
Linden House
Lord Thompson Manor
Riverwind
Steamboat Inn
Stonecroft

Rustic

Maine
Goose Cove Lodge
Inn at Bay Ledge
Keeper's House
Lodge at Moosehead Lake
Telemark Inn
Weatherby's Fisherman's Resort

New Hampshire
Bungay Jar Bed & Breakfast
Stafford's in the Field Inn

Vermont
Heermansmith Farm Inn

Rhode Island
The Roost

Connecticut
Sound Reach

Solo-Oriented
These accommodations are good
for solo travelers because they
have communal breakfasts,
friendly hosts, and many activities
on site.

Maine
Admiral Peary House
Bagley House
Captain Jefferds Inn
Captain Lindsey House
Cod Cove Farm
Five Gables Inn
Flying Cloud
Harbor View Inn at Newcastle
Harpswell Inn
Hartwell House
Hawthorn Inn
Homeport Inn
Inn at Canoe Point
Linekin Bay Bed & Breakfast
Manor House
Oakland House
Pomegranate
Schooner Stephen Taber
Telemark Inn
Trellis House
Weston House
White House

New Hampshire
Ashburn House
Follansbee Inn
Glynn House Inn
Goddard Mansion
Hannah Davis House
Harrisville Squire's Inn
Highland Lake Inn
Meredith Inn

Olde Orchard Inn
Rosewood Country Inn
Wildcat Inn and Tavern

Vermont
Charleston House
Inn on Covered Bridge Green
Inn on the Common
Northfield Inn
Thomas Mott Homestead
Tulip Tree Inn
West Hill House
Windham Hill Inn

Massachusetts
Bay Beach Bed and Breakfast
Bed and Breakfast of Sagamore
    Beach
Field Farm Guest House
Hawthorne Inn
Honeysuckle Hill Bed and
    Breakfast
Manor House Bed and Breakfast
Martin House Inn
Mostly Hall
Pineapple Inn
River Bend Farm
Walker House

Rhode Island
1855 Marshall Slocum Guest House
Admiral Dewey Inn
Blue Dory Inn
Bradford-Dimond-Norris House
Cliffside Inn
Four Gables
Hotel Manisses
Ivy Lodge
Murphy's
The Roost
Savana's Inn
Victorian Ladies Inn
Woody Hill

Connecticut
Antiques & Accomodations
Applewood Farms Inn
Chester Bulkley House
Cobbscroft
Elias Child House
House of 1833
Lakeview Inn
Manor House
Merrrywood
Palmer Inn
Three Chimneys Inn

Smoking Allowed
These accommodations allow
smoking somewhere in the house.
Check the profiles for details.

Maine
Balance Rock Inn By-The-Sea
East Wind Inn & Meeting House
Goose Cove Lodge
Gosnold Arms
Greenville Inn
Oakland House
Weatherby's Fisherman's Resort

New Hampshire
Ashburn House
Christmas Farm Inn
Glynn House Inn
Harrisville Squire's Inn
Ram in the Thicket
Red Hill Inn

Massachusetts
Outermost Inn

Rhode Island
Blue Dory Inn
Hotel Manisses
Shelter Harbor Inn
The Villa

Connecticut
Applewood Farms Inn
Lakeview Inn
Roger Sherman Inn
Silvermine Tavern

Swimming Pool

Maine
Balance Rock Inn By-The-Sea
Inn at Bay Ledge
John Peters Inn
Old Fort Inn
White Barn Inn

New Hampshire
Bernerhof Inn
Buttonwood Inn
Dexter's Inn and Tennis Club
The Forest
Inn at Crotched Mountain
Inn at Thorn Hill
Manor on Golden Pond
Ram in the Thicket
Red Hill Inn
Sunset Hill House

Vermont
Edson Hill Manor
Four Columns Inn
Inn at Saw Mill Farm
Inn on the Common
Inn at Round Barn Farm
Juniper Hill Inn
October Country Inn
Siebeness
Ten Acres Lodge
Wildflower Inn
Windham Hill Inn

Massachusetts
Addison Choate Inn
Applegate
Baldwin Hill Farm

Massachusetts (cont'd)
Blantyre
Brook Farm Inn
Clark Tavern Inn
Cliffwood Inn
Field Farm Guest House
Gables Inn
Harbor Light Inn
Morins Victorian Hideaway
Windflower

Rhode Island
Historic Jacob Hill Farm
The Villa
Woody Hill

Connecticut
Mayflower Inn

Three Rooms or Less

Maine
Harbor View Inn at Newcastle
Pleasant Bay

Vermont
Birchwood Bed and Breakfast
Ten Bends on the River

Massachusetts
Amerscot House
Bed and Breakfast of Sagamore
    Beach
Bishops Bed and Breakfast
Clark Tavern Inn
Morins Victorian Hideaway
Saltbox
Seagull Inn

Rhode Island
1900 House
Four Gables
Green Shadows
Murphy's
One Willow By The Sea
The Roost

Connecticut
Elias Child House
Hearthside Farm
Hilltop Haven
Merrywood
Rosewood Meadow
Sound Reach

Twenty Rooms or More

Maine
Captain Lord Mansion
Castine Inn
East Wind Inn & Meeting House
Goose Cove Lodge
White Barn Inn

New Hampshire
Christmas Farm Inn
Manor on Golden Pond
Red Hill Inn
Sunset Hill House

Vermont
Andrie Rose Inn
Edson Hill Manor
Inn at Saw Mill Farm
Inn at Shelburne Farms
North Hero House Country Inn
Wildflower Inn
Windham Hill Inn

Massachusetts
Blantyre
Deerfield Inn
Harbor Light Inn
Mary Prentiss Inn

Rhode Island
1661 Inn
Jailhouse Inn
Shelter Harbor Inn

Connecticut
Homestead Inn
Mayflower Inn

Connecticut (cont'd)
Simsbury 1820 House
Toll Gate Hill
White Hart Inn

Waterside

Maine
Balance Rock Inn By-The-Sea
Bufflehead Cove Inn
East Wind Inn & Meeting House
Edward's Harborside Inn
Five Gables Inn
Greenville Inn
Goose Cove Lodge
Harbor Hill
Harpswell Inn
Inn at Bay Ledge
Inn at Canoe Point
Inn at Sunrise Point
Inn on the Harbor
Island View Inn
John Peters Inn
Keeper's House
Lake House
Lodge at Moosehead Lake
Nannau-Seaside
Oakland House
Pleasant Bay, Addison
Schooner Stephen Taber
Ullikana
Weatherby's Fisherman's Resort

New Hampshire
Covered Bridge House
Follansbee Inn
Highland Lake Inn
Manor on Golden Pond
Nestlenook Farm
Notchland Inn

Vermont
Green Trails Inn
Inn at Shelburne Farms

North Hero House Country Inn
Ten Bends on the River
Thomas Mott Homestead
Willard Street Inn
Willough Vale Inn

Massachusetts
Bay Beach Bed and Breakfast
Bed and Breakfast of Sagamore
  Beach
Bishops Bed and Breakfast
Diamond District Breakfast Inn
Dunscroft-by-the-Sea
Eden Pines Inn
George Fuller House
Harborview Inn
Historic Merrell Inn
Miles River Country Inn
Morins Victorian Hideaway
Outermost Inn
Scargo Manor Bed and Breakfast
Seagull Inn
Spraycliff

Rhode Island
1661 Inn
Cliffside
Elm Tree Cottage
Four Gables
Sea Breeze Inn
Stone Lea
Watch Hill Inn
Weather Bureau Inn

Connecticut
Bee and Thistle Inn
Boulders Inn
French Bulldog Bed & Breakfast
  and Antiques
Lakeview Inn
Silvermine Tavern
Stonecroft
Steamboat Inn

Maine

Maine is the first state to greet each day as the sun touches the summit of Cadillac Mountain in Acadia, and it reaches farthest into the icy Atlantic, inviting crystal waters into hundreds of bays, harbors, inlets and coves, with 33,000 square miles, 6,000 lakes, and 240 miles of dipping, curving Atlantic coastline, twisting and turning to equal 3,000 miles of oceanfront.

The state name derives from "mainland," and perhaps this rock-solid nature explains the legendary temperament of Maine's permanent residents: down-to-earth. Descendants of French, Acadian, Russian, Swedish, German, and Scottish settlers live here today, but the first residents were the Abnakis, woodland Algonquin Indians. Religious holidays, ethnic festivals, and fairs observe a variety of traditions and cultures.

Many summer visitors return for generations, dancing to the tune of the motto, "We're not here for a long time. We're here for a good time." Couples pulled by heartstring ties often return to marry in white-steepled churches or oceanfront inns, atop mountains or afloat on windjammers.

This "Pine Tree State" is indeed green throughout the year, and summertime colors of red-cracked lobster, gray rocks, and blue water are clichés come true. But locals treasure what the "summer people" never see—the golds, oranges, yellows, and reds of fall and the white grace and power of a Maine winter.

Quiet Aroostock County occupies the entire northern corner of the state bordering Canada. Residents celebrate their agrarian roots with festivals and fairs, and you can bike alongside flowering potato fields in this rural county with nearly 2,000 lakes, rivers and streams, and miles of wooded and cleared trails. You can also fish, canoe, and hike the northern Appalachian Trail, cross-country ski or snowmobile, or drive any portion of a five-hour, 204-mile fall foliage tour.

Inland is mountainous and wild, with excellent whitewater rafting on the Penobscot River and on The Forks in the state capital, Augusta. You can hike mile-high Mt. Katahdin or trails in White Mountain National Forest, view the largest moose population in the state around Baxter State Park and Moosehead Lake, or drive on scenic Route 201.

Acadia National Park on Mount Desert Island has streams, islands, lakes, mountains, and forests plus hiking and miles of carriage trails built and donated by the Rockefellers. Downeast coves protect authentic fishing villages such as Stonington; sleepy artist/native enclaves like Deer Isle, Isle au Haut, and the Cranberry Islands; quietly glamorous Bar Harbor; and quaint villages like Castine and Blue Hill, where antiquing and touring reign supreme.

Greater Portland and Casco Bay sparkle with Monhegan Island, historic forts, sandy beaches, lighthouses, and shopping at Freeport's L.L. Bean Outlet. The Southern Maine Coast and Midcoast tourism zones offer Atlantic-edge favorites: touring, antiquing, outlet shopping in Kittery, lobster pounds (where the crustaceans are hauled in, boiled and eaten on the spot), ocean activities and nature adventures on sandy beaches and rocky shores. Summering spots include the Yorks, Ogunquit, Kennebunkport, Bath, the Boothbays, Wiscasset, Searsport, Camden, and Camden Harbor.

April through October is traditionally visitors season; high season starts around mid-June. In early summer, arm yourself with a good insect repellent to ward off black flies and other biting bugs. September is a great month to get away. Peak prices and minimum-stay requirements may apply through foliage season, but you'll find fewer crowds and, usually, wonderful weather.

Much of tourist Maine closes or limits operation during winter months, particularly near the coast. Inland areas often offer winter activities, but check for lodging and dining availability. Walking deserted streets past closed restaurants and shops can be a letdown if you're expecting the full tourist experience. But the dramatic winter beauty offered by this most natural New England state compensates—if you bundle up.

For More Information

Maine State Ferry Service
(207) 596-2202
Many islands are accessible only through private boat operators

Maine Web Pages

www.state.me.us
www.visitmaine.com

www.mainetourism.com
www.maineguide.com

Maine Farm Vacation B&B Association
(207) 797-5540

Maine Innkeepers Association
(207) 773-7670

Zone I
Downeast/Acadia

Downeast is actually up north, coastally speaking, and Downeast Acadia occupies the large, northeastern coastal corner of the state. The term derives from the era of summer hotels, when guests arrived by the boat-load, literally. The prevailing coastal winds out of the northwest made the trip from Boston to Bar Harbor an easy voyage, with the wind at one's back traveling east. Over time, "downwind" translated into "downeast."

This easternmost point in the country has Maine's most striking coastline, with waves crashing against rocky precipices and wind whistling through stalwart pines. Peninsulas thrust into the Atlantic, sheltering harbors, coves, bays, and inlets. Ocean vistas are balanced by activities, including the "world's fastest lobster boat races" in Jonesport on Independence Day. You can enjoy fresh-off-the-boat lobster, look for whales and adorable puffins, sail, take a tour cruise, kayak, canoe, fish, hunt, climb, hike, bike, and more.

Writers and artists in the early 1800s were inspired by 22-square-mile Acadia National Park on ice-glacier-carved Mt. Desert Island. The morning sun rises first here, at Cadillac Mountain, on the highest point on the Atlantic north of Brazil. The ocean smashing against granite cliffs at Somes Sound and Thunderhole, and crescent-shaped Sand Beach are typical sights of the coast and tiny offshore islands. Horse-drawn carriages may no longer be allowed along the over 50 miles of carriage trails donated by the Rockefellers, but bikers and walkers are welcome.

To go international, ferry or drive across the bridge from Lubec, Maine, to New Brunswick, Canada, for Campobello Island, the longtime summer residence of Franklin D. Roosevelt. The 2,600-acre natural area includes the Roosevelt home, walking trails, gardens, scenic vistas and observation areas, and beaches. West Quoddy Head Lighthouse in Lubec can be visited by car and is one of 20 accessible lighthouses of the state's 63.

Blue Hill, Castine, Stonington, Northeast and Southwest Harbors, Hancock Point, Little Deer Isle and Deer Isle, the Cranberry Islands,

Vinalhaven Island, and Isle au Haut offer antiquing, lobster boats, fine dining, and several authentic fishing economies. The famous Haystack Mountain School of Crafts on Deer Isle has put the little island on the crafts lovers' map.

Finally, pricey, see-and-be-seen Bar Harbor on Mount Desert Island, still summer home to many rich and powerful, was part of the "Gilded Age" overflow. Cars are no longer banned within the town, which hosts throngs of summer visitors. The entrance to Acadia National Park, art galleries, museums, varied dining choices, concerts and fairs, the town pier, and the July and August Bar Harbor Music Festival are among the draws. Stick around long enough to walk from Bar Harbor to Bar Island at low tide.

Many of the mansions and summer retreats in this area have become exceptional small inns and bed-and-breakfasts. Summer bookings are hard to come by. Plan way ahead, especially for weekends, or come midweek and off-season when the crowds have thinned.

For More Information

Bar Harbor Chamber of Commerce
(207) 288-5103
fax: (207) 288-2565
email: bhcc@acadia.net
www.barharborinfo.com

Mt. Desert Chamber of Commerce
(207) 276-5040; Acadia (207) 288-3338

Deer Isle/Stonington Area
(207) 348-6124
email: deerisle@acadia.net
www.acadia.net/deerisle

East Penobscot Bay Association (East Penobscot, Deer Isle, Stonington)
(207) 359-8235
email: info@penobscotbay.com.

Ellsworth Area (Blue Hill, Castine, Deer Isle, Schoodic Peninsula)
(207) 667-5584
email: eacc@downeast.net
www.downeast.net/acadia or *www.ellsworthme.com*

Southwest Harbor Chamber of Commerce
(207) 244-9264 or (800) 423-9264
fax: (207) 244-4185

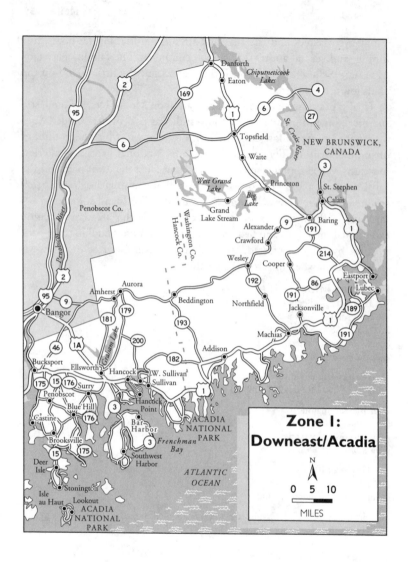

Zone I:
Downeast/Acadia

N

0 5 10

MILES

PLEASANT BAY, Addison

Overall: ★★★½	Room Quality: C	Value: B	Price: $55–$65

A really kid-friendly site, this informal bed-and-breakfast allows guests, young and old, to play with the wooly llamas and even take the them for walks. Here you are far from the crowds with water views, easy access to nature, and peace and quiet. Joan and Leon raised six children in New Hampshire and then traveled north, cleared this land, and built a comfortable, free-flowing house for themselves, family, and guests. They enjoy chatting about farming, canoeing, music, birding, gardening and, of course, their llamas.

SETTING & FACILITIES

Location: Follow signs from Rt. 1 in Columbia; overlooking water on tidal river
Near: Ocean, nature preserves, Pleasant River, vineyard and winery, aquarium, Acadia Nat'l Park, Campobello, Canada (international park, site of FDR's summer home)
Building: 1988 Cape/Colonial
Grounds: Rural; llama farm; water frontage; hiking trails
Public Space: Library, DR, family room, kitchen

Food & Drink: Full breakfast; specialties: popover fruit pancake, fresh farm eggs, homemade maple syrup or preserves; afternoon tea, fruit, and refreshments
Recreation: Beach activities, bird watching, puffin- and whale-watching cruises, canoeing, kayaking
Amenities & Services: Boat mooring, cots and cribs, trail maps, limited disabled access

ACCOMMODATIONS

Units: 3 guest rooms
All Rooms: Water view, spacious
Some Rooms: priv. bath (1), shared bath (2), carpet, hardwoods
Bed & Bath: Beds vary; full baths

Favorites: Room w/ priv. bath, upstairs, water view
Comfort & Decor: Art prints, quilts. Comfortable, pretty. Simple and family-friendly.

RATES, RESERVATIONS, & RESTRICTIONS

Deposit: 50%; must re-rent room for refund
Discounts: Singles, 3rd person
Credit Cards: V, MC
Check-in/Out: 12/11; noon w/ prior arrangement
Smoking: Outdoors only
Pets: No; inn has animals
Kids: Welcome

Minimum Stay: None
Open: All year
Hosts: Joan and Leon Yeaton
West Side Rd.
Addison, ME 04606
(207) 483-4490
Fax: (207) 483-4653
Pleasantbay@nemaine.com
www.nemaine.com/pleasantbay

BALANCE ROCK INN BY-THE-SEA, Bar Harbor

Overall: ★★★½	Room Quality: B	Value: C	Price: $95–$455

Overlooking the huge, precariously tipped rock it's named for, this hybrid seems a bit like a balancing act itself—an old-fashioned small hotel that's a bed-and-breakfast at heart. Set in a former summer house, with modern add-ons, it is on the fashionable, historic shore-path walk along the ocean, next door to residential mansions. The property seems isolated, but the busy Bar Harbor area is actually only a couple of blocks away. Furnishings are dramatic, decorated by a former theatrical manager. Focus is on stunning central pool and terrace, but when kids are splashing, things can get decidedly unromantic in this otherwise romantic setting.

SETTING & FACILITIES

Location: Rt. 3 to Bar Harbor, left on Main St., right onto Albert Meadow
Near: Ocean, Acadia National Park, 2-block walk to Bar Harbor
Building: Traditional 1903 mansion of the summer-cottage genre, refurbished and expanded
Grounds: Expansive oceanside gardens and lawns, heated ocean-water pool, Frenchman Bay views
Public Space: Entrance hall w/ grand staircase, parlor

Food & Drink: Full buffet breakfast in dining room, early-riser tea/coffee w/ paper; full afternoon tea; full bar
Recreation: Water sports, touring, hiking, biking, golf, tennis, whale watching, horseback riding, local cultural events
Amenities & Services: Gym in carriage house, cots, off-street parking, on-premises gift shop. Concierge, turndown service on request

ACCOMMODATIONS

Units: 14 guest rooms, 3 luxury suites
All Rooms: Bath, TV, phone, individual heat/AC control
Some Rooms: Water view, fireplace, sauna or whirlpool, sitting area, separate living area, kitchen, private deck/balcony
Bed & Bath: Luxury bedding, some canopy, four-poster beds; marble baths

Favorites: Rooms in original house, w/ deck and views
Comfort & Decor: Luxurious European ambiance. Plush carpet, reproduction wall and window coverings, English-print floral fabrics, Queen Anne furnishings. Good lighting and large window views. Rooms vary in size. Dramatic.

RATES, RESERVATIONS, & RESTRICTIONS

Deposit: Full payment 1–2 nights, 2 nights deposit for a 3-night stay, 50% longer stays; must cancel 10 days in advance
Discounts: Custom packages, off-season, 3rd person

Credit Cards: MC, V, AE, D
Check-in/Out: 3/11
Smoking: In certain rooms
Pets: Well-behaved pets in limited numbers; check

Kids: Over 12; infants and young children not permitted in busy season
Minimum Stay: None
Open: May–Oct.
Hosts: Nancy Cloud and Mike Miles
21 Albert Meadow
Bar Harbor, ME 04609

(800) 753-0494 or (207) 288-2610
Fax: (207) 288-5534
2barharbor@aol.com or
barhbrinns@aol.com
www.barharborvacations.com

INN AT BAY LEDGE, Bar Harbor

Overall: ★★★★½	Room Quality: A	Value: B	Price: $85–$260

Sipping a lemonade slush and nibbling homemade cookies on the sun porch overlooking Frenchman Bay, life looks pretty tranquil indeed. But 80 feet below the cliff are dramatic ledges and caves to explore. The decor is rustic-sophisticated and may seem more like Northern California than Maine, but whatever or wherever, this original bed-and-breakfast is romantic and beautiful—and unique in these traditional Downeast parts.

SETTING & FACILITIES

Location: half-mile off Rt. 3; 5 miles before Bar Harbor
Near: Penobscot Bay, Acadia Nat'l Park, Bar Harbor
Building: Lodge-style, 3 cottages
Grounds: Sun porch overlooks Frenchman Bay, stairs down cliff face to secluded rocky beach, heated outdoor pool w/ water view
Public Space: Common rooms, deck, sitting room w/ TV, VCR

Food & Drink: Full breakfast; specialties: cranberry and cashew granola, turkey, cheese and potato hash; refreshments; beer and wine for purchase
Recreation: Visiting caves, boating, biking, kayaking, touring
Amenities & Services: Common sauna and steam shower

ACCOMMODATIONS

Units: 7 guest rooms, 3 cottages
All Rooms: Bath
Some Rooms: Water view, priv. deck; cottage 1 has fireplace
Bed & Bath: Antique beds, sizes vary; feather bedding, down comforters, damask sheets; some whirlpool tubs
Favorites: Room 7—spacious, full view of bay, four-poster carved canopy king,

whirlpool; Room 10—most priv., queen canopy, view from deck; Cottages—privacy
Comfort & Decor: Designer fabrics, antiques in main building; cottages are casual country w/ wicker, very priv.; spacious, charming, immaculate.

RATES, RESERVATIONS, & RESTRICTIONS

Deposit: 2 nights; must cancel 14 days in advance
Credit Cards: MC, V
Check-in/Out: 3/11
Smoking: Outside only
Pets: No; B&B has dogs
Kids: Over 16
Minimum Stay: 2 nights in season

Open: May–mid-Oct.
Hosts: Jeani and Jack Ochtera
1385 Sand Point Rd.
Bar Harbor, ME 04609
(207) 288-4204
Fax: (207) 288-5573
www.maineguide.com/barharbor/bay/ledge

THE INN AT CANOE POINT, Bar Harbor

Overall: ★★★★½   Room Quality: B   Value: B   Price: $80–$245

What a gorgeous setting and view, with gray seal, fox, and bald eagle sightings common through big windows. The outside is wisely allowed to dominate the pale sophistication within. The affable hosts were formerly computer execs on Long Island and owned and operated the nearby Kingsleigh Inn. Their warmth has added oomph to this gabled, stucco-and-fieldstone fairytale cottage on the water's edge. Ask Maine innkeepers for a short list of their favorites, and it usually includes this bed-and-breakfast.

SETTING & FACILITIES

Location: Just past entrance to Acadia Nat'l Park on Mount Desert Island, 2 mi. from Bar Harbor on Frenchman Bay

Near: Bar Harbor, Acadia Nat'l Park
Building: 1889 Tudor-style home
Grounds: Rocky shoreline; 2 acres of wilderness; gravel beach

Public Space: LR, wraparound deck, 2nd common room
Food & Drink: 4-course communal breakfast, refreshments (e.g., chocolate chip cookies)
Recreation: Water sports, rock climbing, golf, carriage rides, X-C skiing, snowshoeing
Amenities & Services: Guest refrigerator, irons, rentals for activities, special occasions, recipes, can reserve entire property

ACCOMMODATIONS

Units: 3 guest rooms, 2 suites
All Rooms: Bath, water view, comp. port, radio
Some Rooms: 2 rooms share a deck, fireplace (1), priv. entrance (1), AC (2); suites: sitting area
Bed & Bath: Queens, 1 king; some shower only, robes, hairdryers
Favorites: Master Suite—sitting area, queen four-poster, view, shared deck; Garret Suite—sloped attic ceilings, 3rd-floor views; Garden Room—small, romantic, priv. entrance, whirlpool tub, window walls
Comfort & Decor: Uncluttered, comfortable, stylish. Mix of wicker, overstuffed love seats, eaves, contemporary w/ some antique pieces. Some rooms small, but views add dimension. Minimal decoration, maximal views.

RATES, RESERVATIONS, & RESTRICTIONS

Deposit: 1 night at least; refund w/ 21-day notice
Credit Cards: V, MC, D
Check-in/Out: 2–8/11
Smoking: No
Pets: No
Kids: Over 16
Minimum Stay: None

Open: Feb.–Dec.
Hosts: Nancy and Tom Cervelli
Rt. 3, Eden St., Box 216
Bar Harbor, ME 04609
(207) 288-9511
Fax: (207) 288-2870
Canoe.Point@Juno.com
www.innatcanoepoint.com

MANOR HOUSE, Bar Harbor

| Overall: ★★★★½ | Room Quality: A | Value: A | Price: $60–$185 |

Originally a summer home to several generations of Colonel Foster's family, this solid, many-gabled clapboard has a circular driveway and gingerbread cottages. It is a Victorian beauty without fussiness and clutter. Guests sign in on a stunning antique desk and are pampered from there. The talented innkeeper is a former banker with an eye for color and great period antiques. He keeps his bed-and-breakfast literally gleaming for first-timers and repeaters who appreciate dark woods, small prints, and constant care—and who don't need to put their feet up.

SETTING & FACILITIES

Location: On tree-lined residential street; from Ellsworth take Rt. 3 to Bar Harbor, left onto West St.
Near: Ocean, Bar Island, Porcupine Islands, Acadia Nat'l Park, Frenchman Bay
Building: 1887 22-room, 3-story Queen Anne Victorian; 2 garden cottages
Grounds: Parklike 1+ acres, gardens
Public Space: Veranda, foyer, DR, sitting room, 3rd-floor sitting room w/ TV

Food & Drink: Full communal buffet breakfast; a specialty: bread pudding w/ apple-cider sauce; afternoon tea
Recreation: Harbor, beach activities; kayaking, trails, rock climbing, fishing, antiquing
Amenities & Services: Fax, guest refrigerator, baby grand piano, irons, binoculars, special celebrations, beach towels, recipes, meeting facilities up to 20, entire property can be reserved

ACCOMMODATIONS

Units: 6 guest rooms, 8 suites
All Rooms: Bath, antiques, lace curtain
Some Rooms: Garden view, fireplace, sitting area, AC. Chauffeur's cottage: priv. entrance, fireplace, wet bar, sitting room, refrigerators. Garden cottages: priv., fireplace, sitting area, porch, TV
Bed & Bath: Bed sizes vary, some elaborate antique beds; some hall access, some showers only

Favorites: Room 5—largest, sitting area, charming, Oriental rug, fireplace
Comfort & Decor: Period wallcoverings, lighting fixtures. Victorian nooks and corners. Chauffeur's cottage w/ stained glass and skylights. Cottages w/ porches, small, BR/sitting area in one. Beamed cathedral ceilings, industrial-style carpet, wicker furnishings, minimal decoration.

RATES, RESERVATIONS, & RESTRICTIONS

Deposit: 2 nights; refund w/ 14-day notice.
Discounts: 3rd person
Credit Cards: MC, V, AE, D
Check-in/Out: 3–9/10:30; can stay till 11:30 w/ arrangement
Smoking: No
Pets: No; inn has dog, Sheltie, not permitted in guest rooms
Kids: Over 12

Minimum Stay: 2 nights
Open: April 15–Nov. 15
Hosts: Malcolm "Mac" Noyes
106 West St.
Bar Harbor, ME 04609
(800) 437-0088 or (207) 288-3759
Fax: (207) 288-2974
Manor@acadia.net
www.acadia.net/manorhouse

NANNAU-SEASIDE, Bar Harbor

Overall: ★★★★½	Room Quality: A	Value: A	Price: $75–$155

This lovely, secluded 20-room mansion was once home to the mother-in-law of the family who still lives next door. It's a solid example of an extravagant turn-of-the-century shingle-style summer cottage peculiar to the New England coastline. Vicki, an art history major, decorated this much-loved home in tasteful English Aesthetic furnishings, accented with imported William Morris fabrics and wallcoverings and deep, rich colors. Serene and private, the site is convenient to Bar Harbor restaurants and activities, and yet overlooks its own little rocky beach.

SETTING & FACILITIES

Location: Compass Harbor, Mt. Desert Island; in Bar Harbor south on Main St. (Rt. 3), 1 mi. south of town, small sign at head of long driveway on left
Near: 100 yards from Frenchman Bay, Acadia Nat'l Park hiking trails from property, short drive to Bar Harbor
Building: 1904 shingle-style mansion, Tudor overtones
Grounds: 4 wooded acres; screened porch, gardens; terrace, picnic area; fields; wooded path to bay, priv. rocky beach
Public Space: Entrance hall; LR, sitting area, TV area, games/writing table; parlor/library; DR
Food & Drink: Full breakfast; specialties: Danish fruit compote, almond French toast, personalized omelets, garden vegetables; early riser coffee
Recreation: Sailing, kayaking, cruises, biking, golf, tennis, whale watching, horses, beach activities, local events, hiking
Amenities & Services: Beach, games, croquet court, maps, fax

ACCOMMODATIONS

Units: 4 guest rooms, 2 suites
All Rooms: Bath, writing desk, water view, ambiance lighting
Some Rooms: Fireplace
Bed & Bath: Queen, twin beds; full baths, some claw-foot soaking tubs, hand-held showerheads, some marble vanities, 1 hall access, bathrobes provided
Favorites: Room 1—most spacious, views, bay window, fireplace, plush carpet; Room 4—best 2-BR suite for families, companions
Comfort & Decor: Spacious rooms, generous sitting areas. Reproduction turn-of-the-century wallcoverings, fabrics by William Morris. Some sponge-painted walls. Artwork. Elegant window treatments shove aside for views/light. 3rd-floor rooms smallest. Casual, stylish, luxurious, immaculate.

RATES, RESERVATIONS, & RESTRICTIONS

Deposit: 2 nights; refund w/ 21-day notice
Discounts: Singles, 3rd person
Credit Cards: MC, V
Check-in/Out: 4–7/11
Smoking: No
Pets: No
Kids: w/ prior arrangement

Minimum Stay: 2 nights; 3 nights holiday weekends in high season
Open: May–Oct.; weekends in spring;
check for limited winter availability
Hosts: Vicki and Ron Evers

396 Main St., Box 710
Bar Harbor, ME 04609-0710
(207) 288-5575
Fax: (207) 288-5421
www.nannau.com

ULLIKANA, Bar Harbor

| Overall: ★★★★½ | Room Quality: B | Value: C | Price: $140–$310 |

As offbeat as its mysterious name, this former summer cottage near
Balance Rock is seemingly isolated. Who knows what Alpheus Hardy, who
built and named it, would have thought of the magic of French-Canadian
host Helene, whose bold colors and decorative touches appear where you
least expect them. If you enjoy whimsy, surprise, and striking design you'll
love the mix-and-match—and not-match—that unfolds all around.
Breakfasts are just as creative. If you're more traditional, the talented and
warm hosts also own a lovely, newly refurbished mansion-turned-bed-and-
breakfast across the field. But this one is the tour de force.

SETTING & FACILITIES

Location: 1 block off Main St., behind
the Bar Harbor Banking & Trust, over-
looking the water
Near: Waterfront, town of Bar
Harbor, Acadia Nat'l Park
Building: 1885 Tudor-style mansion
Grounds: Minimal; fountain, terrace

overlooks harbor
Public Space: Huge foyer, parlors, DR,
terrace.
Food & Drink: Full breakfast;
specialties: raspberry soup w/ sorbet
and blueberries, apple popovers;
refreshments

Recreation: Water sports, biking, golf, tennis, whale watching, hiking

Amenities & Services: Art and book collection, games, French spoken

ACCOMMODATIONS

Units: 10 guest rooms
All Rooms: Bath, whimsical/offbeat decor
Some Rooms: Fireplace, priv. deck, sitting area; furnishings from France; add'l beds
Bed & Bath: Bed sizes vary; iron, brass beds; some soaking tubs, hall access
Favorites: Room 5—spacious, deck, fireplace, striking red-and-white wallpaper, coordinating fabrics, king and daybed, hall access to priv. bath
Comfort & Decor: Surprising color, design. Filled with original paintings, puppets, kilim rugs, wicker. Some rooms spacious, some under eaves, all comfy. Reading lamps.

RATES, RESERVATIONS, & RESTRICTIONS

Deposit: Refund w/ 14-day notice
Discounts: 3rd person
Credit Cards: MC, V
Check-in/Out: 3/11
Smoking: No
Pets: No
Kids: Over 8

Minimum Stay: None
Open: May–Oct.
Hosts: Helene Harton and Roy Kasindorf
16 The Field
Bar Harbor, ME 04609
(207) 288-9552

BLUE HILL INN, Blue Hill

Overall: ★★★★½   Room Quality: A   Value: C   Price: $140–$260

Delectable aromas wafting from the kitchen into the blue-stenciled, Colonial common rooms clue you in to the culinary delights that await. The inn was featured in a PBS cooking series (the chef grows 20 varieties of potatoes!), and it won the *Wine Spectator* Award for Excellence in 1998 for the second year. This understated winner is loaded with warmth and authentic, old-fashioned delights. Blue Hill is relatively quiet even at the height of summer, and this great, authentic inn is reputedly one of the oldest continuously operating in New England.

SETTING & FACILITIES

Location: Rt. 1 to Ellsworth to Blue Hill; on residential street 2 blocks from harbor
Near: Blue Hill Bay, kayaking center, artisan community, Acadia Nat'l Park, Castine, Blue Hill Falls, Deer Isle
Building: 1830 Federal clapboard; Cape House, contemporary annex
Grounds: 1-acre lawn, gardens, old elms, apple trees
Public Space: DR, small library, LR/parlor

Food & Drink: (MAP) Breakfast, communal on request; hors d'oeuvres; refreshments; 5-course prix fixe dinner open to public; liquor license, extensive wine list; Thanksgiving dinner, picnic lunches, food preferences noted
Recreation: Tennis, fishing, boating, summer chamber music in garden
Amenities & Services: Fax, copier, modem, irons, beach towels, postcards, twice-daily maid, meetings (25), group reservations, wheelchair access

ACCOMMODATIONS

Units: 10 guest rooms, 2 suites
All Rooms: Bath, sitting area, alarm clock
Some Rooms: Fireplace; phone; suites: sitting room, AC; wheelchair access; Cape House: priv. deck
Bed & Bath: Some antique beds, sizes vary, luxury bedding; some hall access, robes provided; hairdryers; some showers only

Favorites: Room 10—fireplace, antique queen bed; Cape House suite—open, airy, king canopy bed, fireplace, kitchen
Comfort & Decor: Attention to detail, good lighting. Hand-hewn beams, cathedral ceilings, pine floors, large windows. Add'l beds for families. Comfortable. Some rooms charmingly rustic, some formally Federal. All furnished w/ antiques.

RATES, RESERVATIONS, & RESTRICTIONS

Deposit: 1 night, 50% longer stays; refund w/ 14-day notice (Note: 15% gratuity added to price)
Discounts: Custom pkgs., off-season extended stays, singles
Credit Cards: MC, V, D
Check-in/Out: 2–5/10:30, possible to stay until 11:30
Smoking: No
Pets: No

Kids: Over 13
Minimum Stay: 2 nights
Open: Mid-May–Nov.
Hosts: Mary and Don Hartley
Union St., Box 403
Blue Hill, ME 04614
(800) 374-2844 or (207) 374-2844
Fax: (207) 374-2829
bluhilin@downeast.net
bluehillinn.com

JOHN PETERS INN, Blue Hill

| Overall: ★★★★½ | Room Quality: B | Value: B | Price: $105–$175 |

Neither TVs nor room keys are available at this romantic bed-and-breakfast at the water's edge, and you won't need them. You can walk down to the pebble beach, swim, sail away for the day, or just hole up with a book in front of a fire. Romantic and away from it all, in surroundings of meadows sloping to the sea, you can relax here, and mull about which breakfast delicacy Barbara will be preparing next in the glass-walled porch. Classical music, blue water, a quaint town—these are simple, deep pleasures to be savored.

SETTING & FACILITIES

Location: Rt. 1 to Rt. 15 to Blue Hill, follow signs
Near: Walk to Village of Blue Hill, 15 minutes to Deer Isle, 1 hr. to Acadia Nat'l Park, Camden, Bar Harbor
Building: 1815 plantation-style mansion, carriage house
Grounds: 25 shorefront acres on Blue Hill Bay
Public Space: LR, sun porch, deck
Food & Drink: Elaborate breakfast on sun porch or in DR; specialties: cantaloupe w/ strawberry sorbet, lobster omelet; honeymoon suite, breakfast in bed option
Recreation: Day excursions, biking, swimming, kayaking, canoeing, windjammer cruises, summer events, touring Blue Hill pottery and crafts shops, antiquing
Amenities & Services: In-ground pool, canoe and small sailboat for guest use, 2 boat moorings, chamber music recitals, grand piano

ACCOMMODATIONS

Units: 8 guest rooms in main house, 6 in carriage house
All Rooms: Bath
Some Rooms: Working fireplace, bay view, wet bar, kitchen, deck, sitting area, room for 3rd person, phone
Bed & Bath: Beds vary
Favorites: Westport Room—barn

beams, kitchen, living/dining area, deck; Surrey Room—elegant and comfortable w/ working fireplace and sitting area; Blue Hill Room—fireplace, priv. deck, king bed, wet bar
Comfort & Decor: Country comfort.

Rooms gracious and large. Colonial antiques, cherry hardwood floors, polished wood furnishings, rocking chairs. Quaint touches in wallcoverings, fabrics, and lace curtains. Fresh flowers. Good lighting.

RATES, RESERVATIONS, & RESTRICTIONS

Deposit: Will hold room w/ credit card; refund w/ 14-day notice
Discounts: 3rd person
Credit Cards: V, MC
Check-in/Out: 2–9/11ish
Smoking: No
Pets: No; inn has an aged Welsh terrier, DOC (DisObedientCanine)
Kids: Permitted, check

Minimum Stay: 2 nights weekends
Open: May–Oct.
Hosts: Barbara and Rick Seeger
Peters Point, Box 916
Blue Hill, ME 04614
(207) 374-2116
jpi@downeast.net
www.johnpetersinn.com

OAKLAND HOUSE, Brooksville

Overall: ★★★★	Room Quality: B	Value: B	Price: $75–$500

This venerable complex (also known as Shore Oaks Seaside Inn, Vacation Cottages & Country Dining) is the kind of old-fashioned New England resort that is dying out. The land was deeded to Jim's forebears by King George in the 1700s. Nanny and Gramp Herrick, Jim's great-grandparents, were the original hosts, over 100 years ago, when the property was a vacation stop for guests arriving by steamboat to Eggemoggin Reach. Groups, families, and vacationers who long for a comfortable seaside getaway with fine food won't go wrong. Families prefer cottages; couples and singles, the inn—which keeps everyone happy.

SETTING & FACILITIES

Location: On the shore of East Penobscot Bay in Brooksville; Rt. 15, 12 min. east of Blue Hill, follow Oakland House signs
Near: Blue Hill, Castine, Deer Isle, Acadia Nat'l Park
Building: Original mansard Victorian homestead, now restaurant; main building, the Seaside Inn, 1907 rustic; Arts and Crafts–style expanded cottage, recently renovated; vacation cottages;

barn
Grounds: 50 acres, .5 mile of oceanfront; dock, boat moorings, ocean and lake beaches, wooded areas, gardens, tidal pools
Public Space: Rustic parlor; well-stocked library; DR; front porch overlooks ocean, lighthouse
Food & Drink: (MAP) Full breakfast in high season, cont'l in off-season, communal or separate; 5-course dinner,

lunch for fee; specialty: lobster bake on beach, weekly in summer; wine and beer available

Recreation: Golf, biking, day cruises, trails, water sports; bald eagle, moose, and seal sightings

Amenities & Services: Fax, games, meetings, weddings, seminars

ACCOMMODATIONS

Units: 10 guest rooms; 15 cottages

All Rooms: Heat controls, local directory w/ stories, events, and attractions

Some Rooms: priv. bath (7), shared (3); view, fireplace or wood-burning stove; cottages w/ LR and kitchen; limited disabled access

Bed & Bath: Beds vary; some baths, showers only

Favorites: Lone Pine Cottage—log cabin, fully renovated w/ porch, fireplace, ocean views, kitchen, office, phone, satellite TV/VCR, housekeeping. At inn, Room 4, Annie's Room—artisan-crafted bed, 5 windows w/ views, large full bathroom; Room 6—moss and white room, 2 double beds, fireplace, views of sunset.

Comfort & Decor: Artisan, Mission, and Victorian pieces. Airy white window treatments. Cottages along shore vary in style and decor, w/ claw-foot tub, kitchen. All comfortable. TVs and phones deliberately excluded, but can request.

RATES, RESERVATIONS, & RESTRICTIONS

Deposit: Arranged at reservation; check cancellation policy

Discounts: Singles, 3rd person, pkgs.

Credit Cards: V, MC

Check-in/Out: 2 inn, 4 cottages/11

Smoking: Outside at inn, permitted in cottages

Pets: Not at inn; dogs on limited basis in cottages

Kids: Over 14 in inn; all ages in cottages unless specified; childcare available

Minimum Stay: 2 nights in inn; cottages, weekly

Open: All year, limited availability in winter

Hosts: Sally and Jim Littlefield
Herrick Rd., Box 400
Brooksville, ME 04617
(800) 359-RELAX(7352) or
(207) 359-8521
jim@oaklandhouse.com

CASTINE INN, Castine

Overall: ★★★★	Room Quality: C	Value: C	Price: $85–$210

This old-fashioned inn on a quiet peninsula in a pretty, sleepy sailing port is, like The Hartstone Inn in Camden (run by a similarly talented, young couple), worth a visit for the cuisine at least. Award-winning owner-chef Tom honed his skills at many great restaurants, including Bouley in New York City. The mural in the dining room and other original touches remain special. The ambitious hosts are slowly upgrading the faded guest rooms to match the sublime food, so when booking, ask for one that's been refurbished.

SETTING & FACILITIES

Location: In the heart of Castine village, a block from the water
Near: Penobscot Bay w/ offshore islands, Acadia Nat'l Park, Castine town square
Building: Built in 1898 as inn, late-Victorian clapboard
Grounds: Small Victorian gardens, brook w/ bridge, benches, walkways, stone walls, rose gardens
Public Space: Front hall, sitting room, pub, DR, wraparound porch
Food & Drink: Full breakfast: special-ties: goat-cheese omelets, apple bread French toast; creative dinners, including cheese course, focus on local, organic products; open to public, liquor license, pub
Recreation: Kayaking, sailing, island tours, beach activities, biking, whale watching, horses, fishing, local cultural events
Amenities & Services: Sauna, games, fax, modem, French spoken, maps, recipes, irons

ACCOMMODATIONS

Units: 17 guest rooms, 3 suites (up to 4 people)
All Rooms: Bath, fan
Some Rooms: Water view, reading chair
Bed & Bath: Queen/twin, some four-posters; robes, some showers only, cast-iron tub
Favorites: Room 11—cherry four-poster, views, antique tub, glass shower; 3rd-floor rooms facing water offer best views
Comfort & Decor: Bright, airy, functional, simply furnished. Small. Old-fashioned and uninspired, except for brighter refurbished rooms with floral coordinates, armoires, desks

RATES, RESERVATIONS, & RESTRICTIONS

Deposit: 1 night, checks only; refund w/ 10-day notice
Discounts: Singles, add'l person or cot
Credit Cards: MC, V
Check-in/Out: 3/11
Smoking: No
Pets: No
Kids: Over 8
Minimum Stay: 2 nights July–Labor Day, other holiday weekends, special event weekends
Open: May–Dec.
Hosts: Amy and Tom Gutow
Box 41
Castine, ME 04421
(207) 326-4365
Fax: (207) 326-4570
relax@castineinn.com

PILGRIM'S INN, Deer Isle

Overall: ★★★★½   Room Quality: B   Value: C   Price: $150–$215

This Pilgrim continues its progress, with new carriage-house accommodations and ever-changing menus from top chef Terry Foster. This artsy-craftsy village has provided inspiration within, and offers interesting browsing at numerous galleries. Built by Squire Ignatius Haskell in 1793 in fashionable Newburyport, Massachusetts, the house with spare, stylish rooms was transported up to this isolated fishing port at his demanding bride's request. Thank you, Mrs. Haskell.

SETTING & FACILITIES

Location: On Penobscot Bay; Rt 15 S to Deer Isle Village, turn right onto Main St. (Sunset Rd., 15A), drive 1 block; inn on left, opposite harbor

Near: Camden Hills State Park, nature conservatory, Northwest Harbor, ocean, Stonington fishing village, Acadia Nat'l Park, Islands, Haystack School of Crafts

Building: 1793 country home and cottage

Grounds: Lawns slope to large tidal pond, nature habitat

Public Space: Common room, DR

Food & Drink: Full breakfast; cocktails and hors d'oeuvre hour; dinner avail. in season; a specialty: rosemary tenderloin of pork in phyllo, w/ shiitakes, lentils, apricot chutney, and Dijon Cote Du Rhone sauce.

Recreation: Hiking, biking, kayaking, bird watching, touring

Amenities & Services: Gift shop, bikes, books, events sponsored by inn. Limited disabled access.

ACCOMMODATIONS

Units: 11 guest rooms, 2 apts.

All Rooms: Antiques, hardwood floors, luxurious furnishings. Cottage apts.: priv. deck, LR w/ sofa beds, BR, queen bed, kitchen, DR, full bath

Some Rooms: priv. bath (9), shared bath (2)

Bed & Bath: Beds vary

Favorites: Ginny's cottage—living area, cast-iron stove, kitchenette, TV,

deck; Room 5—four-poster, water views, hardwoods

Comfort & Decor: Main building, period luxury, antiques. Cottages, airy, romantic. Wainscot paneling, hardwoods, wicker, windows. Great water views from 3rd-floor rooms. Sizes vary widely from huge in cottages to cozy (Room 12, smallest).

RATES, RESERVATIONS, & RESTRICTIONS

Deposit: Check w/ inn

Discounts: Add'l person(s) in July/August, pkgs.; weekly rates for cottage apts.

Credit Cards: V, MC

Check-in/Out: 3/11

Smoking: No

Pets: No

Kids: All ages in cottage; limited in main building

No-No's: Dinner w/out reservations

Minimum Stay: Varies according to season

Open: All year

Hosts: Jean and Dud Hendrick
Box 69
Deer Isle, ME 04627
(207) 348-6615
Fax: (207) 348-7769
pilgrim@acadia.net
www.Pilgrimsinn.com

WESTON HOUSE, Eastport

| Overall: ★★★½ | Room Quality: C | Value: B | Price: $50–$70 |

John James Audubon stayed here on his way to Labrador, but most travelers don't get this far northeast. For breakfast, you may find a cute fish pastry filled with smoked salmon and dill (not surprisingly, Jett operates a catering business). The friendly innkeepers cater to guests' whims, and for holidays they love to decorate their classic house and prepare special fare and favors. If you can accept shared bathrooms and enjoy an out-of -the-way location, this sweet bed-and-breakfast offers good value and quiet pleasures.

SETTING & FACILITIES

Location: Rt. I to ME Highway 190, to Eastport, on a wooded hill
Near: Roosevelt's Campobello Island, St. Andrews by the Sea, St. Croix River, Moosehorn Nat'l Wildlife Preserve; Old Sow, world's second-largest whirlpool
Building: Stately 1810 hilltop Federal
Grounds: Country gardens, porch, gazebo, bay views
Public Space: Spacious; divided kitchen, sitting area; DR; LR
Food & Drink: Full breakfast, communal; a specialty: pancakes w/ hot apricot brandy sauce, bacon curls; seasonal brunch; sherry, tea; picnic lunches and candlelight dinners w/ reservation; setups for BYOB
Recreation: Whale or bird watching, beach/water activities, golf, biking, horses; summer events; ferry to Campobello; day trips
Amenities & Services: Irons, cordless phone, fax, lawn games; bike and boat rentals nearby

ACCOMMODATIONS

Units: 5 guest rooms
All Rooms: Shared bath
Some Rooms: Bay and/or garden view, fireplace and TV (1)
Bed & Bath: Antique beds, sizes vary; 2 full baths, 1 half-bath
Favorites: Weston Room—fireplace, king four-poster, views across bay
Comfort & Decor: Spacious, bright rooms simply but tastefully furnished. 1 luxurious. Muted colors. Robes for hall passage to bathrooms. Best when not crowded and bathrooms easily available. Good lighting.

RATES, RESERVATIONS, & RESTRICTIONS

Deposit: $50; refund w/ 24-hour notice
Discounts: None
Credit Cards: None; personal or travelers checks, incl. Canadian
Check-in/Out: Flexible
Smoking: No
Pets: No
Kids: No
Minimum Stay: None
Open: All year
Hosts: Jett and John Peterson
26 Boynton St.
Eastport, ME 04631
(800) 853-2907 or (207) 853-2907
Fax: (207) 853-0981
www.virtualcities.com/ons/me/e/mee8501. htm

WEATHERBY'S, THE FISHERMAN'S RESORT, Grand Lake Stream

Overall: ★★★½	Room Quality: C	Value: C	Price: $184+

Fisherpeople—and those who care about them—can't do much better. Charlene and Ken have operated this rustic inn, one of the country's oldest and best-known fishing lodges, for over 25 years, and grandchildren of original guests are now returning. The Grand Lake area—streams and rivers, and Wabassus, Pocumcus, and Sysladobsis lakes—is filled with lake trout, perch, landlocked salmon, and smallmouth bass. Partially accessible by road, the region is mainly wilderness, and much of it not yet fished extensively. Log cottages, comfy beds, fresh food, fresh air, birds, and woodsy beauty are pleasures for non-anglers as well.

SETTING & FACILITIES

Location: Interstate 95 N to Rt. 6 E to Rt. 1 S; or Rt. 9 E to Rt. 1 N; tucked in the St. Croix Valley, on Grand Lake Stream (one of the best salmon rivers in the country)
Near: Approximately 2 hrs. from Bangor; more than 32 productive waters surround fishing camp
Building: Large turn-of-the-century farmhouse
Grounds: Wooded acreage overlooking Grand Lake Stream
Public Space: LR, library, closed-in porch, DR
Food & Drink: (MAP) Breakfast and dinner; specialties: lobster stew, straw-berry-rhubarb pie; will cook catch to order; mealtimes according to individual guests' fishing schedule; lunch on request, cold picnic or hot fishing-site barbecue prepared by guide
Recreation: Stream and fly-fishing, boating, hiking, bird watching
Amenities & Services: Lawn games, basketball court, tennis court, piano, fishing-tour guides available, boat rentals, fishing licenses, air transportation available, L.L. Bean Introductory Fly-Fishing Schools offered, corp. retreats, daily maid service, ice and wood delivered daily

ACCOMMODATIONS

Units: 15 cottages
All Rooms: Bath, open brick or Franklin fireplace, screened porch
Bed & Bath: Beds vary; baths w/ sep. heaters, some showers only
Favorites: Cottages with extra BRs for families
Comfort & Decor: Rustic decor, antiques, wood paneled, airy, spacious and comfortable, priv. wooded settings.

RATES, RESERVATIONS, & RESTRICTIONS

Deposit: $100/person, refund w/ 21-day notice (Note: 15% gratuity added to room rate)
Discounts: Family rates, couples, children under 14, singles
Credit Cards: V, MC; add 4%
Check-in/Out: Flexible, check
Smoking: Limited, check

Pets: Limited, check
Kids: Welcome
Minimum Stay: None
Open: All year, except winter
Hosts: Charlene and Ken Sassi
Box 69
Grand Lake Stream, ME 04637

(800) 639-6353 or (207) 237-2911 or
(207) 796-5558
info@weatherbys.com
www.weatherbys.com

LE DOMAINE, Hancock

Overall: ★★★★	Room Quality: B	Value: C	Price: $225

You'll feel you're in the French countryside rather than rural Maine. The hostess, trained at the Cordon Bleu and in Switzerland, follows in her mother's footsteps, who opened this restorative restaurant with rooms in 1946, after fleeing France when it was learned she was hiding Jews. The pâté, café au lait, fresh honey and croissants, the copper bowls, French accents, and joie de vivre are delightful; and the dinners divine. The house may be unpretentious, but the restaurant is a local favorite, and it's hard to beat indulging on French cuisine and then falling into a comfy bed—awaiting breakfast.

SETTING & FACILITIES

Location: On the east side of rural stretch of Rt. 1, about 9 mi. north of Ellsworth.
Near: Pierre Monteux Conducting School across street, Hancock/Sullivan "singing" bridge; half-hour to Bar Harbor, Mt. Desert Island, Acadia Nat'l Park, ocean
Building: 1950s New England red shingle
Grounds: 100 acres; wooded areas, paths, pond, gardens, meadows
Public Space: Parlor/entrance hall w/ bar, sitting room, DR, sun porch
Food & Drink: (MAP) Cont'l breakfast; 4-course French dinner; specialties: rabbit w/ prunes; bread pudding w/ cream, orange syrup, and cognac-soaked raisins; vintage wine cellar
Recreation: Lawn games, rowing on pond; day trips, biking, boat tours, whale watching, beach activities, kayaking
Amenities & Services: Badminton, fresh fruit, fax, holiday gourmet gift pkgs. prepared to order

ACCOMMODATIONS

Units: 7 guest rooms
All Rooms: Bath, writing desk, seating, radio
Some Rooms: balcony (4) or priv. porch (4), AC
Bed & Bath: Bed sizes vary; some baths, showers only
Favorites: Rosemary—cozy, priv., balcony, locally made potter's sink
Comfort & Decor: Rooms named after herbs, smallish and hotel-like but comfortable and reliably immaculate. Sparse, some French Provincial touches and antique pieces, hardwood floors, large bright windows

RATES, RESERVATIONS, & RESTRICTIONS

Deposit: 1st and last nights; cancellation policy explained at reservation (Note: 15% gratuity added to room rate)
Discounts: Singles
Credit Cards: AE, V, MC, D
Check-in/Out: By 5/11
Smoking: Only in bar
Pets: By prior arrangement w/ extra charge
Kids: Under 5 by prior arrangement
No-No's: Unconfirmed dinner reservations

Minimum Stay: None
Open: June–Oct.
Hosts: Nicole Purslow, proprietor and chef
US 1, Box 496
Hancock, ME 04640
(800) 554-8498 or (207) 422-3395
Fax: (207) 422-2316
nicole@ledomaine.com
www.ledomaine.com

CROCKER HOUSE COUNTRY INN, Hancock Point

Overall: ★★★½	Room Quality: C	Value: C	Price: $90–$140

Reportedly haunted by the glamorous baroness who once owned it, the Crocker is not filled with glamour today, but a friendly staff makes up for the simple surroundings. The owner/chef serves large portions of good food, and enjoying it seems to be the major activity for many guests. This traditional inn, built during Hancock's shipbuilding era, is not much changed, and that has become a virtue. Though seemingly isolated, it is only three minutes from Frenchman Bay and boat moorings. Americana— the kind that's dying out fast — is its main feature. If you seek an old-fashioned, peaceful, unpretentious inn with a ghost, you've got it.

SETTING & FACILITIES

Location: From Ellsworth, 7.9 miles on Rt. 1; look for sign in Hancock; Right turn, 4.8 miles; inn on left, walk to Frenchman Bay
Near: Ocean, tennis, golf, horses; Acadia Nat'l Park; 15 miles Bar Harbor
Building: Gray–shingle Colonial, opened as inn in 1884
Grounds: Lawn w/ horseshoes, croquet
Public Space: Parlors, bar/check-in, DR
Food & Drink: Full breakfast; a la carte dinner open to public; American cuisine: grilled pepper quail, rack of lamb Crocker, Crocker House scallops; liquor license; picnic lunches (fee)
Recreation: Clay tennis courts, antiquing, crafts shopping, local events
Amenities & Services: Hot tub, bikes, kayak, boat moorings, irons, maps, business retreats, weekend live entertainment

ACCOMMODATIONS

Units: 11 guest rooms
All Rooms: Bath, out-calling phone

Bed & Bath: Varied bed sizes; small baths, showers only

Favorites: Room 7—2nd floor, king, alcove
Comfort & Decor: Simple, tasteful rooms, upstairs around a stairwell.

Decor a bit tired but neat and welcoming. Floral paper, lace curtains, and furnishings like those grandma had. Adequate lighting, tiny baths

RATES, RESERVATIONS, & RESTRICTIONS

Deposit: 1 night; must cancel 10 days in advance
Discounts: Off-season
Credit Cards: MC, V, AE, D
Check-in/Out: 2–7/11; call for later check-in
Smoking: Restricted
Pets: Restricted
Kids: OK
Minimum Stay: None

Open: Mid-April–Oct. 31, weekends mid-Nov. to New Year's Eve
Hosts: Richard and Elizabeth Malaby
HC 77 Box 171
Hancock Point, ME 04640
(207) 422-6806
Fax: (207) 422-3105
crocker@acadia.net
www.maineguide.com/downeast/crocker

KEEPER'S HOUSE, Isle au Haut

Overall: ★★★★   Room Quality: C   Value: C   Price: $255–$295/couple

This is the only property in this book with both a lighthouse and an outhouse. And what an exceptional experience for intrepid travelers and families seeking adventure in a wilderness area that is limited to a few dozen tourists a day. A restored lighthouse-keeper's inn is not for high-maintenance types, but indeed, shunning modern amenities is part of the charm. If you're prone to seasickness, beware, as the only access is via mailboat. Guests congregate in the simple kitchen; visit the town (possibly the smallest in America); watch the seals, minks, osprey, and porpoises; and top it off with a candlelight, wholesome dinner and a peaceful sleep.

SETTING & FACILITIES

Location: Rugged, tiny, appendage of Acadia Nat'l Park; Rt. 1 to Stonington fishing village, 40-min. mailboat cruise through islands to inn's dock on Isle au Haut
Near: Stonington, Deer Isle, Blue Hill Peninsula
Building: Turn-of-the-century, gambrel-roofed lighthouse keeper's home, suspended wooden bridge to lighthouse
Grounds: On Penobscot Bay, rocky coast; 3 other lighthouses

Public Space: LR, Shaker DR, country kitchen
Food & Drink: (MAP) Full breakfast; hearty lunch at inn, picnic on trail or shore; candlelight dinner; specialties: eggplant parmesan soup, chicken and fresh seafood (no red meat), apple charlotte, steamed lobsters on Sundays
Recreation: Hiking, biking 17 miles of Acadia trails, swimming pond
Amenities & Services: Bikes, links to civilization deliberately disconnected

ACCOMMODATIONS

Units: 4 guest rooms in main house, 1 guest room cottage
All Rooms: Shared bath, 1 outhouse
Some Rooms: Wood stove, sitting area
Bed & Bath: Some painted brass double beds, 1 trundle bed; 2 baths in main house; Oil House cottage w/ outhouse, outdoor sink, and shower
Favorites: Keeper's Room—wood stove, view of lighthouse; Horizon Room—best water view

Comfort & Decor: Minimal, but rugged delights. No phones, no electricity, no priv. baths. Illumination by gaslights, kerosene lanterns, and candles. Airy rooms, handpainted antique furnishings, island crafts, quirky nooks. Ceiling heights vary. Oil House, tiny 10-foot-square, w/ slate roof, double bed, potbellied stove, diminutive painted furniture, tiny deck overlooking water

RATES, RESERVATIONS, & RESTRICTIONS

Deposit: $100, full payment 30 days in advance; refund w/ 14-day notice
Discounts: 3rd person
Credit Cards: None
Check-in/Out: Coincides w/ mailboat schedule, varies seasonally
Smoking: No
Pets: No

Kids: Welcome
Minimum Stay: 2 nights July, August
Open: May–Oct.
Hosts: Judi and Jeff Burke
Box 26
Isle au Haut, ME 04645
(207) 367-2261, leave message
www.keepershouse.com

KINGSLEIGH INN 1904, Southwest Harbor

Overall: ★★★★	Room Quality: B	Value: B	Price: $55–$175

As sparkling as the Champagne in their name, the young hosts make you feel welcome in this comfortable, turn-of-the-century property on a residential street a short walk from the heart of Southwest Harbor. The dining room has lace curtains at the bay window, but the kitchen is where you enter, chat, and enjoy freshly baked cookies and drinks, and an open refrigerator to store whatever. This informal bed-and-breakfast is an especially good place to interact with others. Think down-home Downeast.

SETTING & FACILITIES

Location: Rt. 3 toward Bar Harbor, right on Rt. 102 to Southwest Harbor; in residential area
Near: Acadia Nat'l Park, on Mt. Desert Island, fishing and boat-building village of Southwest Harbor
Building: Stucco and clapboard w/ bay

windows, turrets, dormers, wraparound porch
Grounds: Overlooks harbor, minimal landscaping
Public Space: Country kitchen, LR, DR w/ library, sitting room, porch
Food & Drink: Full breakfast, candle-

light; specialties: marscapone-stuffed French toast w/ warm berry sauce, oatmeal toast; drinks and goodies
Recreation: Canoeing and kayaking, biking, rock climbing, whale watching,

golf, carriage rides, sailing, cruises, X-C skiing, snowshoeing, shopping, touring Bar Harbor, various seasonal events
Amenities & Services: Games, binoculars, reservations

ACCOMMODATIONS

Units: 8 guest rooms, 1 suite
All Rooms: Bath, ceiling fan, carpet, flowers, alarm clock
Some Rooms: Harbor view, sitting area
Bed & Bath: Antique beds, sizes vary; some robes, most shower-only
Favorites: Turret Suite—telescope, LR, TV, antique king, gas fireplace, tub;

2nd-floor rear rooms 3 and 5: quiet w/ harbor views
Comfort & Decor: Comfortable English country feel; Laura Ashley and Waverly fabrics, wallcoverings, and window treatments. Reading lamps at bedsides. Charming.

RATES, RESERVATIONS, & RESTRICTIONS

Deposit: 1 night; 50% longer stays
Discounts: 3rd person
Credit Cards: MC, V, D
Check-in/Out: 2/11
Smoking: Outside only
Pets: No
Kids: Over 12
Minimum Stay: None

Open: All year
Hosts: Cyd and Ken Champagne Collins
373 Main St., Box 1426
Southwest Harbor, ME 04679
(207) 244-5302
Fax: (207) 244-7691
www.bbchannel.com

INN ON THE HARBOR, Stonington

Overall: ★★★	Room Quality: C	Value: D	Price: $100–$130

This quirky, disjointed inn was formerly known as Captain's Quarters. Christina, a New Yorker who grew up here, returned and renovated the inn, especially the guest rooms. As common rooms are minimal, the guest rooms' renovation was vital, and now this is a fine place for a private getaway or secret romance. Stonington is a working fishing village with pluses (fresh fish, busy harbor, fog, atmosphere) and minuses (noise, crowds). The Inn on the Harbor is not an experience for everyone, but from the decks you'll get a close-up glimpse of real Maine.

SETTING & FACILITIES

Location: On Stonington Harbor; Rt. 15 SE to Deer Isle bridge, into Little Deer Isle; Stonington at tip; call inn for travel by air or sea
Near: Blue Hill, Deer Isle, Isle Au Haut,

Penobscot Bay, Haystack School of Crafts in Sunshine
Building: Waterfront Victorian, 4 buildings combined
Grounds: Decks built right over the

11-foot tide; inn restaurant, Café Atlantic, 2 buildings away
Public Space: Reception desk, formal dining tables; DR, decks
Food & Drink: Cont'l breakfast; espresso bar; informal lunch and dinner served at restaurant

Recreation: Walk to quaint village/harbor, biking, tennis, golf, day trips, boat cruises, fishing, ferry to islands, local artisan and crafts shopping, antiquing
Amenities & Services: Binoculars in each room; small gift shop, fax

ACCOMMODATIONS

Units: 13 guest rooms, 1 suite
All Rooms: Bath
Some Rooms: Priv. or semi-priv. deck, view, fireplace, ceiling fan, phone, TV, disabled access suite w/ sitting room (1), twin bed, large full bath, deck access
Bed & Bath: Bed sizes vary, new mattresses; all baths are full
Favorites: Victory Chimes—granite fireplace, picture window facing harbor,

sitting area, king bed, large bath, deck access
Comfort & Decor: Rooms recently renovated, named after Stonington Harbor sailing schooners. Original artwork. Stunning views, large decks, fireplaces. Comfortable, but decor not noteworthy. Overstuffed furnishings, sitting areas in front of bay windows. Harbor often noisy.

RATES, RESERVATIONS, & RESTRICTIONS

Deposit: 1 night; refund w/ 14-day notice
Discounts: Off-season, Oct. weekend dinner pkgs., Thanksgiving and Christmas pkgs., 3rd person
Credit Cards: V, MC, AE, D
Check-in/Out: 3–7/11
Smoking: On deck
Pets: No; board at nearby kennel
Kids: Over 12

Minimum Stay: None
Open: All year; Wed.–Sun. in winter
Hosts: Christina Shipps
Box 69, Main St.
Stonington, ME 04681
(800) 942-2420 or (207) 367-2420
Fax: (207) 367-5165
webmaster@innontheharbor.com
www.innontheharbor.com

ISLAND VIEW INN, Sullivan

Overall: ★★★½	Room Quality: C	Value: B	Price: $65–$100

For travelers who enjoy the isolated beauty of Downeast Maine, this friendly bed-and-breakfast on a private beach offers just that, at half the price of similar Bar Harbor properties, 30 minutes south. The namesake view is superb, encompassing Frenchman Bay and rugged Mt. Desert Island. How can you not take to a place that serves pancakes on Sunday, has a sailboat ready on a private beach, a moose head on the wall, and costs less than a motel?

SETTING & FACILITIES

Location: Just off Rt. I in Sullivan, on Frenchman Bay
Near: Hancock, Bar Harbor, Ellsworth, Mt. Desert Island, Acadia Nat'l Park, Schoodic Point, Maritime Canada
Building: Circa 1900 2-story "summer cottage"
Grounds: Lawn with pine trees, priv. beach

Public Space: Lodgelike LR, DR
Food & Drink: Full breakfast; specialties: French toast w/ berries, pancakes on Sundays
Recreation: Golf, tennis, fishing, beach, cruises, mountain biking/climbing
Amenities & Services: Canoe, rowboat, paddleboat; 18-foot day sailboat for exp. sailors

ACCOMMODATIONS

Units: 6 guest rooms
All Rooms: Bath
Some Rooms: Small priv. balcony, water views
Bed & Bath: Bed sizes vary; hall-access bath (1)
Favorites: Waterfront rooms—Bird Room w/ king bed, small balcony; Ships Room w/ twins, small balcony;

Lighthouse Room—a cozy, less expensive water-view alternative
Comfort & Decor: Simple, country antiques. Restored original summer home furnishings. TVs/phones deliberately excluded. Modest, clean. B&B interior renovated 1985–86. Back rooms have least road noise.

RATES, RESERVATIONS, & RESTRICTIONS

Deposit: I night, check w/ B&B for cancellation policy
Discounts: Singles, 3rd person/kids, children under 5 free
Credit Cards: MC, V, D
Check-in/Out: 3/11
Smoking: Restricted
Pets: Yes, if well behaved
Kids: Welcome

Minimum Stay: None
Open: Late May–Mid-Oct.
Hosts: Evelyn Joost
HCR 32, Box 24
Sullivan, ME 04664
(207) 422-3031
lph@acadia.net
maineus.com/islandview/

GOOSE COVE LODGE, Sunset

Overall: ★★★★	Room Quality: B	Value: B	Price: $90–$153

A relaxed waterfront retreat on a pristine bay, this is a great outdoors, family escape. The main lodge features a massive fieldstone fireplace, a mix of Southwestern and early American styles, a honey-toned paneled ceiling, whole log beams and posts, wide-plank pine floors, scattered Native-American rugs, and original split pine doors. Simple cabins and rustic guest rooms offer similar cozy appeal and comfortable furniture. Water views surround, activities abound, and this informal spot is surprisingly considered one of the best dining spots on coastal Maine.

SETTING & FACILITIES

Location: Goose Cove, Deer Isle, on sheltered piece of Penobscot Bay; Rt. 1 past Bucksport, right onto Rt. 15 to Deer Isle, right onto Main St. (Sunset Rd.), right at Goose Cove Rd.

Near: Haystack Mountain School of Crafts, Stonington, Blue Hill, Camden, nature conservancy, ocean and beaches, mail boat to Isle au Haut, Bar Harbor, Acadia National Park

Building: Log-and-shingle–style main lodge; rustic cottages on wooded hillside, sundecks

Grounds: Expansive water views; pine trees; pink granite rock, sand beaches; at low tide shore trail leads across sand bar to Barred Island

Public Space: Rustic common room, library, DR, deck cafe w/ water views; rec. hall

Food & Drink: (MAP) Hearty buffet breakfast; pre-dinner cocktails and hors d'oeuvres; 4–5 course candlelight dinners nightly May through Oct.; innovative American fare, fresh seafood; Sunday brunch; al fresco lunch and tea on deck June to Sept.; specialties: Fri. night beach lobster feast (high season), steamed lobsters, grilled steaks, free-range chicken; full liquor license

Recreation: Boating; art galleries, craft shops, museums, antiquing; hiking, biking; bird, seal and porpoise watching; cove swimming, golf, tennis; Ping Pong, games

Amenities & Services: Gift shop and nature center w/ educational activities; bikes, ocean kayaks, canoes, 24-foot sloop; firewood; naturalist-guided walks, star-gazing and instruction; evening child program (high season); massage; retreats, reunions, weddings low season); special events pkgs., including Columbus Day weekend Game and Wine Dinner

ACCOMMODATIONS

Units: 10 guest rooms/suites in main lodge; 7 cabins; 4 duplex cabins; 2 luxury cottages

All Rooms: Bath

Some Rooms: Fireplace/wood stove, ocean view, private or shared deck, game/dining table, sitting area, kitchenette, 1 handicapped accessible cabin

Bed & Bath: Queen/king beds; cabins w/ add'l twin and bunk beds, some sofa beds, cots available; many upgraded full baths, tile floors; some showers only, robes

Favorites: Cottages–Elm and Linnea, closest to water; Bayberry and Thistle fresh, newly built w/ state-of-the-art kitchens, French doors to decks, large stone fireplaces in great rooms; Lookout in Main Lodge–most spacious suite, ocean views, gas fireplace, full kitchen, living/dining room; cathedral ceiling, king bed, in master; 2nd bedroom w/ twins, full bath

Comfort & Decor: Rustic rooms chock-full of comfortable furniture. Paneled walls, beamed ceilings, country scatter rugs or Oriental rugs, quilts, framed prints, original artwork, antiques, collectibles, large windows capitalize views. Cabins basic, comfortable. More luxurious cottages w/ sleek, contemp. furnishings and design.

RATES, RESERVATIONS, & RESTRICTIONS

Deposit: $60 per adult per night, maximum $600 deposit per week; refund w/ 30-day notice. Note: rates are per person; 3-person minimum applies to some cabins, high season; 15% gratuity added

Discounts: Off-season, EP w/ dinner option low-season; children, according to age; 3rd person in room, events packages

Credit Cards: MC, V, AE, D

Check-in/Out: 3-5/10:30

Smoking: Permitted in limited areas

Pets: No

Kids: Welcome

No No's: Late arrival, early departure; deposit will be applied to canceled nights

Minimum Stay: 2 nights all units May–Oct.; week minimum for secluded cabins July and Aug.

Open: Mid-May–mid-Oct. all services; limited winter lodgings available without dining

Hosts: Joanne & Dom Parisi

Box 40

Sunset, Maine 04673

(800) 728-1963 or (207) 348-2508

Fax: (207) 348-2624

goosecove@hypernet.com

www.hypernet.com/goosecove.html

Zone 2
Midcoast Maine

Relatively flat, the Midcoast region has both sandy and rocky New England beaches, fishing villages, islands, historic sites, resort towns, and a relaxed attitude. While more exotic or more isolated surroundings can certainly be found, you may not find better summering.

Favorable cruising grounds attract private craft and yachts, and harbor watching is an honorable summer activity. Brunswick has U.S. naval and arctic explorer history, plus the Harriet Beecher Stowe house and historic homes. Bowdoin College hosts summer musical theater and festivals and features an art gallery that includes works by Andrew Wyeth and Winslow Homer. Eagle Island—summer home to Admiral Robert Edwin Peary, the first explorer to reach the North Pole—is crammed with arctic explorer accoutrements.

Labor Day sends folk traipsing to Thomas Point Beach to celebrate the Bluegrass Festival, right on the heels of the August Topsham country fair.

Wiscasset has been labeled the "prettiest village in Maine," and is home to the landmark Red's Eats—the shack at the corner of Route 1 (a line forms before the 11 a.m. opening). Wiscasset and Searsport are notable even among noted Midcoast antiquing towns. Bath is home to the famous Chocolate Church arts center, and the town encourages sun worship at nearby Reid State Park and Popham Beach State Park. Edgecomb is known for its pottery studios.

The Boothbays offer variety within themselves. Ocean Point is a favorite wedding area. Crowded Boothbay Harbor sports the Windjammer Festival in late June, Friendship Sloop Days in late July, the October Fall Foliage Festival and early December Harbor Lights Festival. (Don't leave Boothbay without a visit to King Brud's hot dog cart, a landmark since 1943.) The more peaceful little shipbuilding community of East Boothbay offers sitting on a dock on Linekin Bay and a good lobster dock.

Rockland, home to the world's largest fleet of sailing schooners, has the Farnsworth Art Museum, Andrew Wyeth exhibition, August Maine Lobster Festival, The Great Schooner Race in early July, and more.

Picturesque Rockport hosts year-round chamber concerts and the Maine Photographic Workshop. Authentic, 200-year-old Union heralds the harvest with the August Union Fair. The Belfast and Moosehead Lake Railroad takes nostalgic trips through the countryside. Pemaquid Point lighthouse and Fisherman's Museum at the end of the peninsula near Wicassett are must-sees for maritime buffs. Camden is the charming and popular gateway to Mount Battie in Camden Hills State Park and sponsors numerous winter festivals.

Finally, simple, whale-shaped Monhegan Island, with 510 acres of dramatic, natural scenery, is home to rugged lobstermen and inspired artists and is accessible by ferry from Boothbay, Porty Clyde, or New Harbor. A limit on construction and a ban on passenger cars help preserve the island.

Small lodgings are plentiful, competitive and excellent; usually homes converted to bed-and-breakfasts or sophisticated small inns. Many close in winter. Book far ahead, as this area fills up fast.

For More Information

Boothbay Chamber of Commerce
(207) 633-4924 or (207) 633-2353 or (207) 633-4743
email: seamaine@boothbayharbor.com

Camden Bed & Breakfast Association
(207) 230-0783 or (800) 813-5015
www.camdeninns.com

Camden-Rockport-Lincolnville Chamber of Commerce
(207) 236-4404
email: chamber@camdenme.org

Monhegan Island
(207) 372-8848

Rockland-Thomaston Area
(207) 596-0376

Searsport Area B&B Association
(207) 548-6575 or (800) 698-6575
email: SeapBB@SeapBB.SDI.Agate.net

Wiscasset
(207) 882-4600
email: wrba@gwi.net

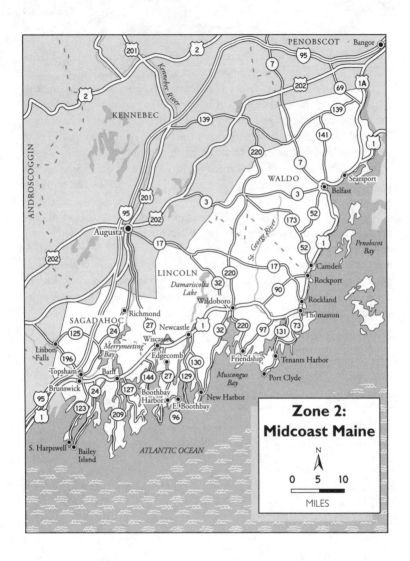

Zone 2:
Midcoast Maine

N

0   5   10

MILES

THE INN AT BATH, Bath

Overall: ★★★★½	Room Quality: A	Value: B	Price: $85–$330

House Beautiful featured this bed-and-breakfast in 1997, and it's easy to see why. Sophistication is evident in the collection of antiques and objets d'art. Oriental rugs over plank floors, ornate mantels, and numerous artistic touches add to the decor. Family photos and a local artist's whimsy in startling colors and unexpected detailing warm up the luxury. Host Nick was an investment banker in his previous life and enjoys both the quiet contemplation of books and art and active Maine endeavors, such as fly-fishing. He loves to talk about both.

SETTING & FACILITIES

Location: Rt. I to Bath, to Washington St., residential area
Near: Chocolate Church Arts Center; Bath Iron Works; Maine Maritime Museum; shops and restaurants; wildlife preserves; boat trips, incl. lighthouse tours; Kennebec River; day trips to Acadia Nat'l Park
Building: 1810 Greek Revival
Grounds: Small garden; porches; on distinguished street
Public Space: Twin parlors, DRs

Food & Drink: Full breakfast; specialties: blueberry pancakes, banana French toast; also cont'l breakfast; refreshments, boxed lunches
Recreation: Golf, tennis, river and deep-sea fishing, boat trips, skiing
Amenities & Services: Laundry, irons, bike storage, binoculars, fax, email, Internet access; beach towels, charters booked, trips planned, cots/portacribs, ice and glasses (BYOB), corp. facilities

ACCOMMODATIONS

Units: 8 guest rooms, incl. 1 disabled access room; 1 suite
All Rooms: Bath, TV, VCR, phone, alarm clock radio/cassette player
Some Rooms: 2-BR suites; fireplace w/ wood, desk, dbl. whirlpool, priv. entrance, AC
Bed & Bath: Firm/softer mattresses, some four-poster or canopy, sizes vary; dbl. whirlpools in BRs, hairdryers

Favorites: River Room—converted hay loft w/ beams, love seat; Lavender Room—antique fishnet-lace canopy double, sofa, bay window
Comfort & Decor: Spacious, furnished w/ 18th- and 19th-century antiques, designer fabrics. Elegant, but country touches: beams, brick/stone fireplaces, bookcases. Good lighting. Unexpected flair throughout. Immaculate.

RATES, RESERVATIONS, & RESTRICTIONS

Deposit: Credit card/check to hold for 1 night; special dep. for graduation weekends and priv. parties; refund w/ 14-day notice
Discounts: Off-season, June/July mid-week pkgs., longer stays, getaway pkgs., corp., 3rd and 4th person
Credit Cards: All accepted; pref. check or cash
Check-in/Out: In anytime (if ready), call after 10 p.m.
Smoking: On porch or in garden

Pets: Reservation req.
Kids: Over 6
Minimum Stay: 2 nights, but check for 1 night avail.
Open: All year
Hosts: Nick Bayard
969 Washington St.
Bath, ME 04530
(207) 443-4294
Fax: (207) 443-4295
inatbath@gwi.net
www.innatbath.com

ALDEN HOUSE, Belfast

Overall: ★★★½	Room Quality: B	Value: C	Price: $70–$110

USA Today rated Belfast "one of the top five culturally cool small towns in America," and this welcoming bed-and-breakfast is warm and pretty cool as well. Jess and Marla, former academics, restored the previously neglected mansion in 1997, and *The Oprah Winfrey Show* filmed it after renovation. It's not as grand as The White House down the block, but original details include Italian marble mantels and sinks, a handcarved cherry stair rail, tin ceilings, and plaster ceiling medallions. And it's not cluttered up, as many Victorians tend to be.

SETTING & FACILITIES

Location: I-95 to Rt. 1 to Belfast on residential street near The White House
Near: Belfast business and historic district, Penobscot Bay
Building: 1840 Greek Revival;

renovated 1997
Grounds: 1 acre, shade trees
Public Space: Double parlors, library, porches, circular staircase in entrance foyer

Food & Drink: Multi-course candle-light breakfast; special requests; special-ties: strawberry-rhubarb French toast, smoked trout cakes, poached eggs w/ Parmesan over baked tomatoes; refreshments

Recreation: Water/snow sports, antiquing, local events, lawn games
Amenities & Services: Rooms w/AC, grand player piano w/ 150 rolls, 400 videos; disabled access

ACCOMMODATIONS

Units: 7 guest rooms
All Rooms: Antiques; VCR available
Some Rooms: priv. (5) shared bath (2), fireplace
Bed & Bath: Antique pencil-posts or antique beds; marble sinks, showers only

Favorites: Hiram Alden—queen bed, 7-foot, handcarved cherry mantel; Centennial—red, white, and blue striped wallpaper, brass bed
Comfort & Decor: Emphasis on romance. Antiques, comfort. Immaculate. Good lighting.

RATES, RESERVATIONS, & RESTRICTIONS

Deposit: 50%; refund w/ 7-day notice
Discounts: Off-season, extended stay
Credit Cards: MC, V, AE, D
Check-in/Out: 4–8/before11
Smoking: Outside only
Pets: No
Kids: OK
No-No's: Kids under 16 in own room
Minimum Stay: None

Open: All year
Hosts: Jessica Jahnke and Marla Stickle
63 Church St.
Belfast, ME 04915
(207) 338-2151
Fax: Same as phone
alden@agate.net
bbonline.com/me/alden or
www.agate.net/~alden/

THE WHITE HOUSE, Belfast

Overall: ★★★★½	Room Quality: B	Value: A	Price: $80–$145

This White House, named for its white facade, actually hosted a vacationing Franklin Roosevelt on his way to Campobello. It is a much photographed, historic beauty with the largest copper beech tree in Maine and is wonderful within as well. The rich wallpaper, intricate ceiling medallions, marble mantels, hardwoods, Oriental rugs, crystal chandeliers, polished wood, and antique and reproduction touches are impressive. The young owners, formerly from Dallas, have worked hard to refurbish this landmark mansion, and offer its presidential-level pleasures at a bargain rate.

SETTING & FACILITIES

Location: At the head of Church St.
Near: Penobscot Bay, 6 state parks, Fort Knox, Warren Island, half-hour to Camden, 1 hour to Bar Harbor, walk to village and harbor
Building: Striking mid-1800s columned Greek Revival
Grounds: Triangular lawn, terrace, gardens, 1800s gazebo, harbor view
Public Space: Ornate DR, parlors, library

Food & Drink: Early riser coffee/tea; full breakfast, communal or separate; tea and refreshments, snacks, lunch baskets (fee)
Recreation: Golf, tennis, horses, antiquing, water/snow sports; day trips (car/boat)
Amenities & Services: Bicycle storage, irons, laundry service (fee); corp. facilities, games, celebrations (fee); videos

ACCOMMODATIONS

Units: 3 guest rooms, 2 suites; carriage house, spacious w/ priv. entrance, terrace
All Rooms: Bath, some hall access; flowers, plush rugs, phone
Some Rooms: Water view, TV, VCR w/ request at reservation
Bed & Bath: Some four-posters, sizes vary; robes for hall baths, hairdryers, 1 bath w/ fireplace

Favorites: Belfast Bay—king four-poster, fireplace, whirlpool, views
Comfort & Decor: Strikes a balance between elegant and country comfort. Sizes vary, but luxury level consistent. Overhead lighting, w/ table lamp augmentation. New, immaculate furnishings.

RATES, RESERVATIONS, & RESTRICTIONS

Deposit: 1 night
Discounts: 3 nights or more; seniors; off-season, pkgs., singles
Credit Cards: MC, V, D
Check-in/Out: 3–8/before 11; call for a check-in after 8
Smoking: No
Pets: No
Kids: Over 10
Minimum Stay: None

Open: All year
Hosts: Dianne Porter, Robert Hansen, Terry Prescott
1 Church St.
Belfast, ME 04915-6206
(888) 290-1901 or (207) 338-1901
Fax: (207) 338-5161
whitehouse@mainebb.com

ANCHOR WATCH, Boothbay Harbor

Overall: ★★★½	Room Quality: B	Value: C	Price: $106–$130

This is a host-driven little bed-and-breakfast: warm and welcoming with super breakfasts and views and appealing with its immaculate cottage-style accommodations. The former English teacher innkeeper and her daughter make guests feel right at home, with the run of the house. Feed the ducks, watch the birds and scudding clouds, or walk to the busy boating center. This inn seems far away from the tourist bustle.

SETTING & FACILITIES

Location: Rt. 1 to Edgecomb to Rt. 27, 12 miles to Oak St., to Commercial St., follow to dead end; left to Eames Rd.; residential area

Near: Shore in Boothbay Harbor, lighthouses, ferry to Monhegan and other islands; walk to town

Building: Late 19th-century sea captain's home

Grounds: Lawn down to fishing pier, float; views of islands, sunsets, and boats

Public Space: Sun porch, small parlor, open-air porch, kitchen, breakfast nook

Food & Drink: Full breakfasts; a specialty: egg-and-cheese pie; afternoon tea, microwave popcorn

Recreation: Boating, fishing; day trips on excursion boats owned by innkeeper's husband

Amenities & Services: Discounts for ferry trips to Monhegan Island; laundry and kitchen facilities

ACCOMMODATIONS

Units: 5 guest rooms

All Rooms: Bath, clock, radio

Some Rooms: Ocean view, balcony, TV, whirlpool, fireplace, AC

Bed & Bath: Some canopies, bed sizes vary

Favorites: Novelty—fireplace and whirlpool under stained-glass window,

3rd-floor balcony; May Archer—2nd-floor ocean view, queen bed, balcony

Comfort & Decor: Simple, but sweet. Each room named after a former Monhegan Island ferry. Country style w/ stenciling, old trunks, borders, quilts, skirted tables in small prints, painted dormers.

RATES, RESERVATIONS, & RESTRICTIONS

Deposit: 1 night; must cancel 7 days in advance

Discounts: Off-season, singles, pkgs., 3rd person

Credit Cards: MC, V

Check-in/Out: 2–6/before 11; call for later check-in

Smoking: No

Pets: No; house cat

Kids: Over 10

Minimum Stay: Holiday weekends

Open: 11 months; check for winter closing

Hosts: Diane Campbell and Kathy Reed
3 Eames Rd.
Boothbay Harbor, ME 04538
(207) 633-7565
diane@lincoln.midcoast.com
www.maineguide.com/boothbay/anchorwatch

EDGECOMBE-COLES HOUSE, Camden

Overall: ★★★½   Room Quality: C   Value: C   Price: $105–$185

This is a traditional house, crammed with antiques, toys, stuffed animals, and fine furniture. If you like "things," you'll feel right at home in this popular choice. If you prefer a more minimalist setting in the Camden area, try The Inn at Sunrise Point. You'll enjoy hanging out on the serene porch, with its rockers, swing, and telescope. The hosts are originally from California, and the laid-back atmosphere is intact.

SETTING & FACILITIES

Location: On Hwy 1A, .6 mile north of business district
Near: Ocean, lighthouses, Camden Hills State Park, Acadia Nat'l Park, Bar Harbor, Searsport, Rockport; short walk to Camden Harbor, on Penobscot Bay
Building: Sprawling 1891 clapboard farmhouse
Grounds: Priv.; overlooks Penobscot Bay

Public Space: Large common rooms, DR, front porch
Food & Drink: Full, elegant breakfast (in-room avail.); afternoon tea
Recreation: Sailing, biking, antiquing, day boat trips, golf, skiing
Amenities & Services: Baby grand piano, games, toys, chocolates, bicycles

ACCOMMODATIONS

Units: 6 guest rooms
All Rooms: Bath, TV, phone, clock, robe
Some Rooms: Water view, fireplace
Bed & Bath: Some canopy/four-poster, sizes vary, some "king" beds are twins together; small baths
Favorites: Star Sea—canopied bed, fireplace, view
Comfort & Decor: Atmosphere a mix of homey and stylish. Lots of books, artwork, cuddly collectibles, and crafts. Views calm overstimulated senses. Adequate lighting.

RATES, RESERVATIONS, & RESTRICTIONS

Deposit: 1 night; refund w/ 14-day notice
Discounts: Off-season, 3rd person
Credit Cards: MC, V, AE, D
Check-in/Out: Afternoon/before noon
Smoking: No
Pets: No; in-house dogs and cat
Kids: Over 7

Minimum Stay: None
Open: All year
Hosts: Louise and Terry Price
RR Box 3010, 64 High St.
Camden, ME 04843
(800) 528-2336 or (207) 236-2336
Fax: (207) 236-6227
edgcmcol@midcoast.com
www.CamdenBandB.com

HARTSTONE INN, Camden

Overall: ★★★★	Room Quality: C	Value: B	Price: $60–$140

A charming couple—an award-winning chef and his hotel-manager-wife—purchased this neglected inn in 1998 and has worked successfully to upgrade it. This inn glows with newness guised in Colonial style, but mostly it's a great restaurant with rooms to rest in between meals. Sumptuous breakfast may be lobster-and-asparagus quiche, or smoked salmon Benedict. Dinner? Perhaps sweet potato–crusted pheasant breast with a blueberry demi-glacé, ending with chocolate-Amaretto soufflé with an almond anglaise.

SETTING & FACILITIES

Location: Rt. 1 becomes Elm St.; inn on left near business district
Near: Camden Harbor, state park, Penobscot Bay, lighthouses, outlet shopping
Building: 1835 Mansard-style Victorian, barn
Grounds: Wooded in-town lot, wildflower gardens, patio, mountain views
Public Space: DR, parlor, library
Food & Drink: Gourmet candlelit breakfast; afternoon tea and coffee; 5-course candlelit dinner (reservations); wine, beer; picnic baskets; cooking classes; food festivals
Recreation: Schooner tours, antiquing, water sports, golf, day trips to Acadia Nat'l Park, skiing
Amenities & Services: Fax, refrigerator, irons, books, maps, special occasions, off-street parking

ACCOMMODATIONS

Units: 8 guest rooms, 2 suites
All Rooms: Bath, period furnishings
Some Rooms: Fireplace, sitting area, priv. entrance
Bed & Bath: Beds vary, lace canopy, iron, brass, four-poster; some antique tubs, robes for hall baths; some original marble sinks; some showers only
Favorites: Tea Cup—2nd floor, sitting area, quilt; Magnolia Room— fireplace, hardwoods, sitting area, canopy bed
Comfort & Decor: Romantic, some antiques, but still a bit underdecorated. Touches such as candlelight and fresh flowers soften edges. Immaculate.

RATES, RESERVATIONS, & RESTRICTIONS

Deposit: 1 night; must cancel 14 days in advance
Discounts: Seniors, special pkgs.; MAP available
Credit Cards: MC, V
Check-in/Out: 3/11
Smoking: No
Pets: OK in suites w/ priv. entrances
Kids: OK in suites w/ priv. entrances
Minimum Stay: None
Open: All year
Hosts: Mary Jo and Michael Salmon
41 Elm St.
Camden, ME 04843
(800) 788-4823 or (207) 236-4259
Fax: (207) 236-9575
info@hartstoneinn.com
www.hartstoneinn.com

HAWTHORN INN, Camden

Overall: ★★★★   Room Quality: B   Value: C   Price: $100–$195

Back from the main road, with a distinctive turret, bay windows, and porches, this handsome house is painted in Hawthorn yellow with red trim. The low-key hosts are former bankers: he's British, she's Texan. As they put it, they're "not on top of" guests, and they maintain a bed-and-breakfast of bright, comfortable elegance, with sheer white curtains and tall windows. Plans are to close the garden-level rooms and open luxury rooms on the third floor, with harbor views, whirlpools, and fireplaces—the big draws here.

SETTING & FACILITIES

Location: Rt. 1 into Camden, north of public library
Near: Bar Harbor, Acadia Nat'l Park, islands, Camden Hills State Park, Penobscot Bay
Building: 1894 Queen Anne Victorian mansion
Grounds: 1+ wooded acres; lawn slopes toward harbor; deck
Public Space: Parlors, DR

Food & Drink: Full breakfast, communal or separate; specialties: crème caramel French toast, crab strata; tea or coffee; picnic baskets
Recreation: Harbor/water activities, tobogganing, windjammer cruises, antiquing, museums
Amenities & Services: Fridge, irons, fax, meetings (up to 12), maps, toothbrush, hairdryer

ACCOMMODATIONS

Units: 6 guest rooms in main house; 4 in carriage house
All Rooms: Bath, phone, antiques

Some Rooms: "Keyhole" harbor view; carriage house: fireplace, TV, VCR, some w/ glass walls onto deck or patio, view

Bed & Bath: Some four-poster, iron, brass; queen, twin; some hall access, robes; some showers only in main house, some tubs in room, some dbl. whirlpools in carriage house
Favorites: Jillian—sitting room, queen four-poster, 5 windows; Rose—2 twins, lots of windows; in carriage house, Broughman—best views, gas fireplace, dbl. whirlpool, deck
Comfort & Decor: Casually elegant, pristine. Pine accents, botanical prints, floral wallcoverings, armoires. Good lighting, and lots of natural light. Varies widely from luxury to comfortable.

RATES, RESERVATIONS, & RESTRICTIONS

Deposit: 1 night for up to 3 nights stay, 25% on longer stays; refund w/ 10-day notice
Discounts: Longer stays, pkgs., 3rd person
Credit Cards: MC, V, AE
Check-in/Out: 3/11; till noon w/ arrangement
Smoking: No; violators pay cleaning fee
Pets: No; live-in aging spaniel (w/ restricted access)

Kids: Over 12
No-No's: Late check-in, leaving house w/out a key, front door locks at 9 p.m.
Minimum Stay: 2 nights on holidays for carriage house only
Open: All year
Hosts: Patty and Nick Wharton
9 High St.
Camden, ME 04843
(207) 236-8842
Fax: (207) 236-6181
hawthorn@midcoast.com

INN AT SUNRISE POINT, Camden

Overall: ★★★★½   Room Quality: A   Value: B   Price: $160–$350

The owner is a former travel writer, who obviously distilled his knowledge into this secluded bed-and-breakfast beauty. Penobscot Bay laps right up to the cottages, and beyond the expanses of glass are blue sky and water, peace and quiet. The afternoon snacks are especially lavish. Both the mood and the look are cool and serene, and this is one of the few New England properties in contemporary style. It's worth getting up at least once for the sunrise that gave the inn its name.

SETTING & FACILITIES

Location: 4 miles north of Camden Harbor, off Rt. 1 on Fire Rd. 9
Near: Camden Hills State Park, Camden Harbor, shopping, restaurants, galleries; abuts Penobscot Bay
Building: 1920s farmhouse, cluster of cottages; award-winning renovation in 1991

Grounds: Path from road to water, through 4 acres; priv. little stony beach, water views
Public Space: Domed conservatory, library, LR
Food & Drink: Full breakfast; a specialty: lobster hash; hors d'oeuvres, snacks

Recreation: Lake swimming and fishing, hiking, sailing

Amenities & Services: Some disabled access, books, videos

ACCOMMODATIONS

Units: 3 guest rooms, 4 cottages
All Rooms: Bath, near shore, fireplace, heat controls, TV, VCR, phone, view
Some Rooms: Deck; cottages: mini-refrigerator, wet bar, some w/ coffee maker
Bed & Bath: Queen or king, firm mattresses; some oversized tubs; some dbl. whirlpools, sep. showers, robes

Favorites: Fitz Hugh Lane Cottage— 10 yards from shore, every upgrade, cruise-cabin views
Comfort & Decor: Rooms named after Maine artists and writers, featuring their work. Understated, but upscale, w/ light pine furniture, emphasis on comfort, relaxation. Rooms in main house are smallish w/ cathedral ceilings.

RATES, RESERVATIONS, & RESTRICTIONS

Deposit: 50%; must cancel 20 days in advance
Discounts: June rates
Credit Cards: MC, V, AE
Check-in/Out: 3/11
Smoking: No
Pets: No
Kids: By prior arrangement

Minimum Stay: 2 nights on weekends
Open: Memorial Day–Oct. 31
Hosts: Jackie and Richard Diehl
Box 1344
Camden, ME 04843
(800) 435-6278 or (207) 236-7716
Fax: (207) 236-0820
www.sunrisepoint.com

NORUMBEGA, Camden

Overall: ★★★★½   Room Quality: B   Value: C   Price: $155–$450

"Norumbega" was a legendary 16th-century city of riches, and the name fits, as guest rooms are not discernibly better than those in nearby inns at half the price. Why stay? For the grandeur of this undeniably beautiful little "castle" built by the originator of the Western Union telegram after he toured the castles of Europe. Much photographed and admired, this stone, turreted showplace with leaded windows, high ceilings, and hidden passageways is the perfect place for Major Seduction. And if you want a "yes," spring for the penthouse, with wraparound water views.

SETTING & FACILITIES

Location: Off Rt. 1 N just past town overlooking the ocean
Near: Walk to Camden Harbor; Camden Hills State Park; drive to Acadia Nat'l Park, Bar Harbor, Searsport, Rockport

Building: 1886 stone, slate-roofed mansion
Grounds: Several landscaped acres, 2 summer gazebos, on Penobscot River
Public Space: DR, elegant parlors, billiards room, deck

Food & Drink: Full breakfast, tea or wine, evening wine and cheese, snacks
Recreation: Grounds games, sailing, antiquing, boat trips, golf, skiing

Amenities & Services: Murder Weekend w/ 2-night-stay prize, games, bikes, meeting facilities

ACCOMMODATIONS

Units: 9 guest rooms, 3 suites
All Rooms: Bath, phone, clock, robe
Some Rooms: Priv. or shared deck, view, fireplace, sitting area, TV; priv. entrance (1)
Bed & Bath: Some four-posters, all king, some are twins that may be separated; some showers only, 1 dbl. whirlpool

Favorites: Penthouse suite—up spiral staircase in turret, fireplace, wet bar, refrigerator, fold-out sofa, skylight
Comfort & Decor: Rooms named for English castles and are spacious and understated. Soft colors and a mix of antiques and reproductions. Good lighting.

RATES, RESERVATIONS, & RESTRICTIONS

Deposit: 1 night or 50%; refund w/ 21-day notice
Discounts: Off-season, pkgs.
Credit Cards: MC, V, AE, D
Check-in/Out: 3–9/11
Smoking: No
Pets: No
Kids: Over 7
Minimum Stay: 2 nights on weekends and holidays

Open: All year
Hosts: Kent Keatinge
61 High St.
Camden, ME 04843
(207) 236-4646
Fax: (207) 236-0824
Email form on website
www.acadia.net/norumbega

FIVE GABLES INN, East Boothbay

Overall: ★★★★½   Room Quality: B   Value: B   Price: $100–$170

The Southern, friendly, outgoing owners—he a trained chef, she an artist—purchased this peaceful, pretty property in 1995 far from the Boothbay tourist throngs after sailing to Polynesia. They describe their romantic, eclectically decorated bed-and-breakfast best: "It's not a 'poofy' place with 10,000 pillows, and swags and draperies everywhere. If your family had a summer cottage for several generations, it would look like this."

SETTING & FACILITIES

Location: Rt. 96 through east Boothbay; turn right at blinking light on Murray Hill Rd.; a mile or so on right
Near: Boothbay Harbor, Pemaquid Point Lighthouse, Ferry to Monhegan Island, Windjammer Schooners

Building: Gothic Revival Victorian
Grounds: Lawn to water, paths to shore, dock; overlooks Linekin Bay
Public Space: Common room, library, porch

Food & Drink: Buffet breakfast (in room by request or communal); specialties: grilled tomatoes w/ herbed cornmeal; afternoon refreshments; picnic lunches
Recreation: Whale watching; touring

harbor, kayaking, golf, swimming
Amenities & Services: 2 boat moorings for guests, irons, games, maps, recipes, celebrations; can reserve entire property

ACCOMMODATIONS

Units: 15 guest rooms
All Rooms: Bath, water view, sitting area, reading lamp
Some Rooms: Fireplace, built-in windowseat
Bed & Bath: Some, pencil-post or wrought-iron beds, sizes vary; most, showers only
Favorites: Room 14—biggest, king,

fireplace; Room 10—four-poster queen, sunrise bay views
Comfort & Decor: Traditional furnishings, softened w/ hand-crocheted afghans and artwork by owners. Casually elegant. Sheer curtains let in sun and water views. Good lighting. Immaculate, smallest rooms under gables are good deals.

RATES, RESERVATIONS, & RESTRICTIONS

Deposit: 50%; refund w/ 5-day notice
Credit Cards: MC, V
Check-in/Out: 2–8/11; can use facilities after vacating room
Smoking: In garden or on veranda
Pets: No
Kids: Over 12
Minimum Stay: None

Open: Mid-May–Oct. 31
Hosts: De and Mike Kennedy
Murray Hill Rd., Box 335
East Boothbay, ME 04544
(800) 451-5048 or (207) 633-4551
info@fivegablesinn.com
www.fivegablesinn.com

LINEKIN BAY BED & BREAKFAST, East Boothbay

Overall: ★★★½	Room Quality: C	Value: C	Price: $69–$149

The young hosts are really sweet: She is a special-education teacher; he, a retired policeman. They are still learning the ropes, and seasoning will soften the edges and add character to this modest but sparkling new property. His fresh-baked cookies are great with tea or cider, and their philosophy is "no one should leave the table hungry." By the time you read this, the downstairs luxury guest room and bath should be completed, as well as a deck off the dining room, for summer pleasure. Think of it as a work in progress.

SETTING & FACILITIES

Location: Rt. 27 toward Boothbay Harbor to Ocean Point Rd. (Rt.96) in East Boothbay, turn left at only traffic light, look for stained-glass sign

Near: Shipbuilding center of East Boothbay, Boothbay Harbor, Ocean Point, Railway Village, lighthouses, nature preserve

Building: 1850 Gothic Revival farm-house
Grounds: Gardens, porches
Public Space: Common room, DR
Food & Drink: Full communal breakfast; a specialty: baked peach oatmeal; early-riser coffee; afternoon tea, desserts
Recreation: Rail tours, day boat trips, antiquing, tours, boat rentals
Amenities & Services: Irons, games, maps, paper, recipes, off-street parking

ACCOMMODATIONS

Units: 3 guest rooms, 1 suite
All Rooms: Bath, reading lamp, crystal wine glasses and corkscrew
Some Rooms: Views of Linekin Bay, fireplace(1)
Bed & Bath: Sizes vary; hairdryers, 1 shower only; newly renovated
Favorites: Honeymoon suite—fireplace, king, love seat, bay views; Rhapsody in Blue—views, Laura Ashley
Comfort & Decor: Comfortable, clean. Underdecorated, as rooms are new, and hosts haven't accumulated objects. Should improve w/ age. Small, but cozy.

RATES, RESERVATIONS, & RESTRICTIONS

Deposit: 1 night; refund w/ 14-day notice
Discounts: Longer stays
Credit Cards: MC, V
Check-in/Out: 2–6/11
Smoking: On porch and grounds only
Pets: No; hosts own 2 miniature collies, not permitted on premises
Kids: Over 12
Minimum Stay: None
Open: All year
Hosts: Marti Booth and Larry Brown
771 Ocean Point Rd.
East Boothbay, ME 04544
(207) 633-9900

COD COVE FARM, Edgecomb

| Overall: ★★★★½ | Room Quality: B | Value: A | Price: $85–$105 |

Renovated and opened for business in 1997, this sparkling little property doesn't have a weak spot. It offers warm, helpful hosts; lavish, creative breakfasts; themed guest rooms of imaginative crafting; bucolic river views and gardens; and scrupulous attention to detail. Local artisans created everything from handmade soaps to murals, and Don and wife, Charley, fill Cod Cove Farm with true caring. This newcomer is a delightful winner and a real deal.

SETTING & FACILITIES

Location: Minutes from Rt 1, on right, on rural road
Near: Ocean, Camden, Rockport, Bath
Building: 1800s high-posted Cape, plus modernization
Grounds: Rural landscaping, gardens, pond
Public Space: DR, parlor, family room
Food & Drink: Full elegant breakfast, communal; a specialty: scones, fresh jams, omelets
Recreation: Antiquing, river cruises, sailing, fishing, golfing, biking, touring, outlet/boutique shopping

Amenities & Services: Priv. parties; games, grand piano, CD, VCR; house rental in Rangeley, ME

ACCOMMODATIONS

Units: 4 guest rooms
All Rooms: AC, sink
Some Rooms: Bath
Bed & Bath: Canopy, antique and artisan beds, varied sizes; 2 rooms share hall bath
Favorites: Moon and Stars Room—whimsical, willow queen canopy, celestial stencilings, bath mural; Adirondack Room—twig furniture, queen birch bed
Comfort & Decor: Handcrafted, handpainted furniture. Local artwork and crafts. Antiques, stencilings, lace. Smallish rooms, but impeccable and comfortable, with good lighting. All rooms surround hall and staircase.

RATES, RESERVATIONS, & RESTRICTIONS

Deposit: 50%; refund w/ 7-day notice
Discounts: Extended stay, group, off-season, third person
Credit Cards: MC, V, D
Check-in/Out: 4/11; Call to check in later than 6 p.m.
Smoking: No
Pets: No
Kids: Over 14

Minimum Stay: None
Open: "Most of the year"; check
Hosts: Charlene and Don Schuman
Box 94
Edgecomb, ME 04556
(207) 882-4299
codcovbb@biddeford.com
www.biddeford.com/~codcovbb

HARBOR HILL, Friendship

Overall: ★★½	Room Quality: C	Value: C	Price: $90–$110

This is really informal and down-home (clean, but a bit cluttered). We recommend our favorite room (Terrace Room) for couples and the cottage—basic, but a good deal—for a family. Mom and Pop are Latvian and outgoing (he was a civil engineer who climbed Mt. McKinley). The end-of-the-road location offers sunsets and close-up glimpses of Maine lobstermen at work at the tip of this rural peninsula. The owners are exceptionally friendly, and so is their golden retriever. The price here is friendly, too.

SETTING & FACILITIES

Location: Through town center, left at post office to Town Landing Rd., on left overlooking harbor
Near: Fishing village of Friendship, fishing sloops, Camden, Camden Hills State Park, Farnsworth Museum
Building: Century-old clapboard farmhouse
Grounds: Hillside lawn slopes to harbor, fieldstone terrace w/ views, gardens draw hummingbirds, butterflies

Public Space: Kitchen, common areas, LR/DR
Food & Drink: Full Scandinavian or Maine-style breakfast; specialties: black raspberry muffins, lingonberry preserves, Swedish pancakes, smoked sausage or smoked fish; coffee and tea; special diets
Recreation: Day trips, sailing, biking, sloop charters, kayaking, fishing
Amenities & Services: Lawn games

ACCOMMODATIONS

Units: 3 guest rooms; 2-BR cottage apt.
All Rooms: Bath, view, sitting area
Some Rooms: 2-BR cottage has kitchen, sun deck; priv. entrance (2); antiques, hardwoods
Bed & Bath: Down comforters; some showers only
Favorites: Terrace Room—spacious, Empire furnishings, priv. entrance, view
Comfort & Decor: Basic Americana with a dash of Europe, reflecting the hosts' Latvian heritage; original artwork showcases local artists, nautical touches

RATES, RESERVATIONS, & RESTRICTIONS

Deposit: 1 night; refund w/ 10-day notice
Discounts: Weekly cottage rental
Credit Cards: None
Check-in/Out: Afternoon/before noon
Smoking: On terrace only
Pets: W/ prior arrangement; inn has a dog
Kids: W/ prior arrangement
No-No's: Alcohol
Minimum Stay: None, but prefer 2 nights
Open: All year
Hosts: Liga and Len Jahnke
Town Landing Rd., Box 35
Friendship, ME 04547
(207) 832-6646

THE FLYING CLOUD, Newcastle

Overall: ★★★½	Room Quality: C	Value: C	Price: $85–$105

This unassuming old house is named after the clipper ship that still holds the world speed record, set in 1851, and the theme is carried throughout. But the pace is decidedly slower here, and the gracious hosts intend just that. Old-fashioned and homey, with a touch of style, this little bed-and-breakfast is on the same leafy street as the upscale Newcastle Inn. You can enjoy a fine dinner there, and walk a few steps back here, saving big bucks and getting some exercise. Warmth, charm, simplicity add up to a good deal here.

SETTING & FACILITIES

Location: Coastal Rt. 1; after Wiscasset turn right onto River Rd; .7 mile on left
Near: Shipyard, Pemaquid Lighthouse and Beach; day trips to Acadia Nat'l Park, Camden, Rockport, Boothbay Harbor, boat trips to Monhegan Island
Building: 1840 Greek Revival (added to 1790 Cape)
Grounds: Village yard, hammock, garden; overlooks Damariscotta River

Public Space: Common room, LR w/ library; sun porch
Food & Drink: Hearty communal breakfast; a specialty: sourdough pancakes and scrapple; refreshments

Recreation: Whale/bird watching, boat trips, day trips, antiquing, events, skiing
Amenities & Services: Board games, piano; groups can reserve entire property; celebrations

ACCOMMODATIONS

Units: 4 guest rooms, 1 suite
All Rooms: Bath, theme decor
Some Rooms: Water view, floor-to-ceiling windows, skylight; New York Suite: add'l beds in 2nd room
Bed & Bath: Some antique and four-poster beds, sizes vary; some hall access, robes, all shower, 1 w/ antique tub
Favorites: San Francisco— spacious,

river view, king four-poster, sitting area, large priv. bath down hall
Comfort & Decor: Rooms quirky w/ touches reminiscent of cities (Hong Kong, New York, London, Melbourne, San Francisco), ports of call for the namesake *Flying Cloud Clipper*. Smallish, warm, and cozy.

RATES, RESERVATIONS, & RESTRICTIONS

Deposit: Major credit card to hold; refund w/ 7-day notice
Discounts: Longer stays, groups, singles
Credit Cards: AE, V, MC
Check-in/Out: 3–7/11
Smoking: No
Pets: No
Kids: W/ prior arrangement

Minimum Stay: None
Open: All year
Hosts: Betty and Ron Howe
45 River Rd., Box 549,
Newcastle, ME 04553
(207) 563-2484
stay@theflyingcloud.com
www.theflyingcloud.com

HARBOR VIEW INN AT NEWCASTLE, Newcastle

| Overall: ★★★★ | Room Quality: B | Value: C | Price: $105–$140 |

This gracious bed-and-breakfast with pumpkin-pine floors, Oriental rugs, antiques, artwork, and fresh flowers is just a walk from antiques shops galore. Maureen is an avid sailor, and Joe a former corporate exec and avid chef. His gourmet breakfast menus, sometimes featuring guests' names, may be a bit precious, but the desire to please is evident. A sample: freshly squeezed orange juice, fresh fruit parfait, little corn pancake, spiral of eggs, riced parsley potato, tomato, baked ham, and almond sour cream coffee cake. That should hold you till evening, when twinkling window candles and lighted trees welcome you back.

SETTING & FACILITIES

Location: Take either Rt. 1 S or Rt. 215 S to Business Rt. 1; B&B is first driveway on left, off Bus. Rt. 1

Near: Boothbay Harbor, Pemaquid Point, Camden, Rockport, Popham and Reid state parks, Bath, L.L. Bean outlet,

lighthouses, Monhegan Island, Rockland
Building: Restored 1840s New England Cape
Grounds: Terraced lawn, gardens; overlooks Damariscotta/Newcastle Harbor
Public Space: LR, deck; DR; reading room; kitchen; common rooms wheel-chair accessible
Food & Drink: Gourmet breakfast, communal; friends welcome for fee; refreshments, tea
Recreation: Fishing, island cruises, golf, beach activities, bocce, croquet
Amenities & Services: Off-street parking, fax, irons, lawn games, maps, touring advice, sailing advice

ACCOMMODATIONS

Units: 1 guest room, 2 suites
All Rooms: Bath, sitting area, ceiling fan, TV, phone
Some Rooms: Gas fireplace, priv. deck, view; Garden Suite wheelchair accessible, shower w/ grab bar, not otherwise specially equipped
Bed & Bath: Beds vary; shower only (1)
Favorites: Damariscotta River Suite—views, beamed cathedral ceiling, fireplace, deck, king; Newcastle Square Room—views, gas fireplace, special antiques
Comfort & Decor: Traditional comfort, refined. Detail oriented. Spacious. Good lighting. Original art, antiques and period furnishings, luxurious accessories.

RATES, RESERVATIONS, & RESTRICTIONS

Deposit: 1 night; refund w/ 10-day notice
Credit Cards: MC, V
Check-in/Out: 3–7/11
Smoking: Grounds only
Pets: No; inn has dog (no access to inn except at guests' request)
Kids: Over 12
Minimum Stay: None
Open: March–Dec.
Hosts: Maureen Bates and Joe McEntee
34 Main St., Box 791
Newcastle, ME 04553
(207) 563-2900
Fax: Same as telephone
hrbvwinn@lincoln.midcoast.com
www.lincoln.midcoast.com/~hrbvwinn

NEWCASTLE INN, Newcastle

Overall: ★★★★	Room Quality: B	Value: C	Price: $145–$220

This unpretentious property with its colorful lupine flower gardens is a quiet retreat on the river. Come prepared to eat. Previous owners established its reputation for fine food, and the new owner/chefs are maintaining, with a bent now toward classic French, as in mussels in saffron cream; squash, zucchini, and roasted red pepper soup; duck breast with raspberry cassis; or grilled salmon Troisgros. The inn is being steadily upgraded to match the food (and the increased prices), and remains a glorious getaway for gourmands.

SETTING & FACILITIES

Location: 7 mi. past Wiscasset, turn right onto River Rd. and look for inn sign
Near: Lighthouses, fishing villages, Boothbay Harbor, Camden, Freeport; in residential area
Building: 1800s Colonial carriage house
Grounds: Lawn, gardens slope to Damariscotta River
Public Space: 2 LRs, porch, TV room; 2 DRs, deck; full-service pub
Food & Drink: Multi-course breakfast; afternoon coffee, holiday treats; open to public for dinner; lobster bakes; liquor license
Recreation: Touring, antiquing
Amenities & Services: Games, books, fax, paper, turndown

ACCOMMODATIONS

Units: 14 guest rooms
All Rooms: Bath
Some Rooms: River view, sitting area, fireplace, whirlpool, decks; priv. entrance (1), AC
Bed & Bath: Lace-canopy, sleigh or four-poster, sizes vary; some showers only, 2nd vanity sinks; hairdryers, robes
Favorites: Pemaquid Point—fireplace, queen canopy, sitting room, dbl.
whirlpool; Monhegan Island—king four-poster, fireplace
Comfort & Decor: Eclectic country furnishings, Waverly award for decor, renovations, and upgrades. Polished wood furniture, print wallpapers and patterned fabrics. Rooms small, but some being enlarged. Warm lighting and comfortable feel throughout.

RATES, RESERVATIONS, & RESTRICTIONS

Deposit: Half of reserved stay; cancel 14 days in advance
Discounts: Off-season, excludes holiday weekends and winter festivities
Credit Cards: MC, V, AE
Check-in/Out: 3–8/11; call if check-in after 8
Smoking: No
Pets: No
Kids: "Older" only
No-No's: Dinner w/out reservations; more than 2 people in room
Minimum Stay: None
Open: All year
Hosts: Rebecca and Howard Levitan
60 River Rd.
Newcastle, ME 04553
(800) 832-8669 or (207) 563-5685
Fax: (207) 563-6877
www.newcastle.com

THE GOSNOLD ARMS, New Harbor

Overall: ★★★½   Room Quality: C   Value: C   Price: $79–$150

Want to see whales and puffins? From this comfortable inn you can take a boat departing daily for Monhegan Island, where they are often spotted. And you can walk to many lobster pounds nearby for dinner. Since 1925, this unpretentious inn has been noted for congenial, family-style atmosphere and good American food. The harbor here is one of the prettiest in Maine, and not overrun with tourists. Laid-back is the mood, and the prices are right.

SETTING & FACILITIES

Location: Rt. 95 to Brunswick, Rt. 1 to Damariscotta, Rt. 130 S to New Harbor, Rt. 32, 1 mile to inn, across from harbor
Near: Islands, Pemaquid Point, lighthouse, Fort William Henry, archeological digs, Hog Island Nature Camp
Building: Large 1840 clapboard; attached barn, cottages
Grounds: On shores of Pemaquid Peninsula; rocky beach

Public Space: Lounge, DR, porch
Food & Drink: Full breakfast, dinner avail.; specialties: clam chowder, lobster; lobster pounds nearby
Recreation: Day boat tours to Monhegan Island, daily seal and puffin boat excursions, water activities, tennis, horses, golf, antiquing
Amenities & Services: Priv. wharf, boat moorings, board games

ACCOMMODATIONS

Units: 12 guest rooms; 14 cottages
All Rooms: Bath
Some Rooms: Water view, fireplace
Bed & Bath: Bed sizes vary, firm mattresses; some baths showers only
Favorites: Grey Cottage—fireplace,

LR, water view, deck
Comfort & Decor: Simple, comfortable, early American. Rooms in barn above gathering room, pine walls, pleasant furnishings. Cottages w/ water views, fireplaces

RATES, RESERVATIONS, & RESTRICTIONS

Deposit: 20%; call for cancellation policy
Discounts: 3rd person, weekly rates
Credit Cards: MC, V
Check-in/Out: 1–4/10
Smoking: Limited, check
Pets: No
Kids: In cottages, older kids; check
Minimum Stay: 1 week in cottages, summer

Open: May–Oct.
Hosts: The Phinney Family
146 State Route 32
New Harbor, ME 04554
(207) 677-3727
Fax: (207) 677-2662
www.gosnold.com

CAPTAIN LINDSEY HOUSE, Rockland

Overall: ★★★★	Room Quality: B	Value: C	Price: $100–$170

This solid, mustard-hued beauty with green awnings, a red door, and teal touches within is authentic and stylish. Released from its commercial incarnation as a utilities building, it is again filled with art, artifacts, and artful touches. Old photos, antiques, and international curios make it feel as if the captain himself may reappear from a world voyage any minute.

Charles, the assistant innkeeper, is especially helpful. The owners also have the schooner *Stephen Taber* and the motor yacht *Pauline,* docked in Rockland, so many sailors congregate here.

SETTING & FACILITIES

Location: In town, on side street, off main shopping artery; 2 blocks from water
Near: Ocean, Penobscot Bay, Rockland Harbor, Camden Harbor; Monhegan Island artists' colony, Farnsworth Museum, craft and antique shopping
Building: Solid 1832 brick Federal
Grounds: Small English garden, terrace
Public Space: Entrance lobby, LR, library, breakfast room, garden deck
Food & Drink: Cont'l breakfast; tea or sherry; lunch and dinner at inn's restaurant and communal-seating pub, open daily
Recreation: Live entertainment, darts/TV in pub, golf, tennis, X-C skiing, day boat trips, lighthouse, sailing
Amenities & Services: Guest refrigerator, irons, 2 vessels owned by inn can be reserved, tour itinerary, off-street parking in restaurant lot; computer port, fax, copier; reservations, pickup

ACCOMMODATIONS

Units: 7 guest rooms, 2 suites
All Rooms: Bath, phone, TV, radio, AC
Some Rooms: Wheelchair access (1)
Bed & Bath: Some four-posters, sizes vary; full baths, robes, sep. showers, some soaking tubs, hairdryers
Favorites: Room 4—art deco–style, spacious
Comfort & Decor: Tasteful seafaring theme, striped wallpapers, and colonial colors. Antique desks w/ reading lamps and comfortable seating. TVs in armoires.

RATES, RESERVATIONS, & RESTRICTIONS

Deposit: 1 night; must cancel 10 days in advance
Discounts: Seniors, longer stays, off-season, 3rd person, pkgs.
Credit Cards: MC, V, AE, D
Check-in/Out: After 3/before 11; later often OK
Smoking: In pub or garden only
Pets: No; nearby facilities
Kids: Over 10
Minimum Stay: None
Open: All year
Hosts: Lindsey@midcoast.com
5 Lindsey St.
Rockland, ME 04841
Captains Ellen and Ken Barnes
Fax: (207) 596-2758
(800) 999-7352 or (207) 596-7950
www.midcoast.com/-kebarnes/

SCHOONER STEPHEN TABER, Rockland

Overall: ★★★	Room Quality: C	Value: C	Price: $925/person

This is the oldest documented sailing vessel in continuous service in the United States and the only property in this book that moves. Captains Ellen and Ken Barnes, who also own Captain Lindsey House and Waterworks restaurant in Rockland, keep their inn shipshape, and this schooner as hospitable as an inn. As a bonus, Capt. Ellen's recipes are tasty enough to be published in *A Taste of the Taber* cookbook. BYOB and BYMI(musical instruments) to sing along. The schooner offers an unbeatable combination, especially for families with teenagers who might be bored at a more stationary site. Guests can combine a unique vacation visit to one or both of the Barnes' accommodations to appease landlubbers.

SETTING & FACILITIES

Location: Rt. 1 to Rockland, on Windjammer Wharf
Near: Prior to sailing, Rockland and Camden; after, hidden harbors along coastal Maine; docks at islands and fishing villages
Building: 68-ft. restored 1871 sailing ship
Public Space: Yacht deck, main cabin, galley w/ dining area, retractable awning

Food & Drink: All meals served daily; fresh fare; island lobster bake; BYOB
Recreation: Whale watching, swimming, jogging, rowing when anchor drops; evening singalongs
Amenities & Services: Indoor parking, games, books, ice and glasses for drinks, charters, sailing instruction

ACCOMMODATIONS

Units: 2 singles, 4 dbls, 6 twin (holds 22 guests)
All Rooms: Windows for light and air
Bed & Bath: Minimal bed space; sinks and electricity in cabins; heads and showers above deck
Favorites: The pilot berths, in foc'sle

Comfort & Decor: Bright and attractive cabins, but not much bigger than closets at some New England inns. Gleaming decks. Well designed and clean. Relatively comfortable berths.

RATES, RESERVATIONS, & RESTRICTIONS

Deposit: $300, balance paid in full prior to cruise; must cancel 5 weeks prior
Discounts: Off-season, 3-day cruises at beginning/end of season, Captain Lindsey House pkgs., 10% discount if reserve prior to February 1
Credit Cards: MC, V, A, D
Check-in/Out: Sunday after 4/Saturday 11; Ship departs Monday after breakfast
Smoking: In limited areas on deck only

Pets: No
Kids: Over 14
No-No's: Portable radios, TVs; hard luggage (must be stowable)
Minimum Stay: 6 days, 3 days
Open: Memorial Day–fall foliage
Hosts: Ellen and Ken Barnes
Windjammer Wharf, 70 Elm St.
Camden, ME 04843
(800) 999-7352 or (207) 236-3520 or (207) 596-7950
Fax: (207) 596-2758

HOMEPORT INN, Searsport

Overall: ★★★½	Room Quality: C	Value: B	Price: $55–$85

Searsport is one of Maine's antique centers, and the opulence of The Homeport Inn puts guests in the mood to rummage. Highway traffic roars by, but the building is solid and quiet inside. This house is a beautiful reminder of a time when Searsport was filled with ship captains, their prosperous homes, and their treasures from around the world. Other mansions in the area are in bad shape, but this bed-and-breakfast is a shining example of taste and upkeep.

SETTING & FACILITIES

Location: On Rt. 1 in Searsport
Near: Penobscot Bay, Penobscot Marine Museum, Fort Knox, Acadia Nat'l Park, Castine, Camden Harbor, Owl's Head Transportation Museum
Building: Hilltop 1861 ship captain's mansion w/ cupola, wraparound porch
Grounds: Extends to shore of E Penobscot Bay in rear; fronts on Rt. 1

Public Space: Front parlor; publike room
Food & Drink: Full communal breakfast
Recreation: Boat tours, steam-train tours, golf, water/snow sports, shore walks, antiquing
Amenities & Services: Bicycle rentals, lawn games

ACCOMMODATIONS

Units: 10 guest rooms; 2 cottages
All Rooms: Fairly spacious, flowers
Some Rooms: Priv. bath, priv. deck, view; cottages have 2 BRs and kitchen.
Bed & Bath: Some canopy beds, antique headboards
Favorites: 1st floor back rooms: sunny, quiet, decks, views

Comfort & Decor: Floor-to-ceiling windows. Fleur-de-lis wallpaper in some rooms, period decor, 19th-century antiques. Two-BR cottages, charming, gingerbread-trimmed mini-Victorians, work well for families.

RATES, RESERVATIONS, & RESTRICTIONS

Deposit: $25; non-refundable
Discounts: Singles, 3rd person, kids, off-season, weekly; $600 weekly for cottages
Credit Cards: V, MC, AE, D
Check-in/Out: Flexible, check
Smoking: Limited areas only
Pets: No; B&B has 1 cat and 1 dog
Kids: Over 3 OK in cottages

Minimum Stay: None currently; check
Open: All year
Hosts: Edith and George Johnson
Rt. 1, E. Main St.
Searsport, ME 04974
(800) 742-5814 or (207) 548-2259
Fax: 508-443-6682
www.bnbcity.com/inns/20015

HARPSWELL INN, South Harpswell

| Overall: ★★★★ | Room Quality: B | Value: B | Price: $75–$165 |

Harpswell has more coastline than any other town in America, and this handsome bed-and-breakfast has a long history involving the coastal waters. The kitchen and dining room were once the cookhouse for the nearby shipyard, and the bell on top of the three-story house—which you can still ring—called shipworkers to lunch. Within are collectibles, family photos, a warm hearth and windows overlooking the water and lobster boats. Bill is a longtime local of this area, where Longfellow lived. A comfortable, homey feel is evident throughout.

SETTING & FACILITIES

Location: On Lookout Point knoll overlooking Middle Bay lobster boat harbor
Near: Admiral Peary's Eagle Island, Freeport outlet, Boothbay Harbor, Portland, Brunswick, colleges, winery, state parks, lighthouses
Building: 1761 Federal Georgian columned clapboard, outbuildings; renovated in 1995

Grounds: 3 acres, lawns, gardens to water's edge, stone walls
Public Space: Great room, DR, porch
Food & Drink: Full communal breakfast; refreshments
Recreation: Boat/day trips, beach, tennis, golf, trails, hunting, kayaking
Amenities & Services: Bikes, dock, irons, guest refrigerator, daily paper

ACCOMMODATIONS

Units: 12 guest rooms and suites
All Rooms: Antiques
Some Rooms: Priv. bath, views, sitting area, desk
Bed & Bath: Some four-poster, brass; some baths, some showers only
Favorites: Lilac Room— love seat, desk, views, full bath

Comfort & Decor: Warm and inviting. Some handpainted faux murals, toile, decorator fabrics, Oriental rugs. 2 large suites w/ kitchens, dramatic decor, cathedral ceilings, fireplace, whirlpools; 1 suite, 2-story, window wall, can accommodate 3rd person; 2nd floor antique ceilings

RATES, RESERVATIONS, & RESTRICTIONS

Deposit: 1 night, 50% longer stays
Discounts: 3rd person, 14+ days
Credit Cards: V, MC
Check-in/Out: 4/10:30
Smoking: Porch only
Pets: No; B&B has 3 cats
Kids: Over 10
Minimum Stay: Req. on weekends

and holidays, July–Oct.; check
Open: All year
Hosts: Susan and Bill Menz
RR 1, Box 141
South Harpswell, ME 04079
(800) 843-5509 or (207) 833-5509
Prefer guests to call 800 number
www.gwi.net/~harpswell

EAST WIND INN & MEETING HOUSE, Tenants Harbor

Overall: ★★★★	Room Quality: C	Value: A	Price: $38–$260

Sailing and relaxing at an authentic country inn in a pretty fishing village are a true Maine combo you can enjoy here, as a sloop sails regularly from the inn's pier. This main inn, renovated captain's house, and cottage are owned and operated by a Tenants Harbor native, who has put much effort into restoring and maintaining the informal property. The furnishings are a mix of Victorian and whatever, and the food relies on local seafood such as fish chowder and crab cakes. The harbor view from the porch and rooms is peaceful and lovely.

SETTING & FACILITIES

Location: Rt. 1 N to Thomaston, right onto Rt. 131, to Rt. 131 S, bear left at post office; inn 200 yards at water's edge
Near: Village shops, Rockland, Farnsworth Art Museum, Rockport, Camden, Lincolville, Marshall Point Lighthouse, Monhegan Island Ferry, Montpelier, Owls Head Transportation Museum, Penobscot Bay
Building: 1890 New England–style clapboard
Grounds: Oceanfront; overlooks islands
Public Space: 3 buildings, common rooms; main house common room

Food & Drink: (MAP) Full breakfast, dinners in restaurant; specialties: baked haddock and horseradish mashed potatoes, strawberry-rhubarb pie; open daily, April–Nov., sporadically and by reservation Nov.–March
Recreation: Sailing, biking, nature trails, island trips, lighthouse tours, beach activities, touring, canoeing, horses
Amenities & Services: Sailing seminars, conference facilities, deepwater anchorage, piano

ACCOMMODATIONS

Units: 26 guest rooms: 15 in main house, 8 in Meeting House, 3 in cottage
All Rooms: Antiques, phone
Some Rooms: TV, priv. bath (19), view, suites/apts., singles
Bed & Bath: Some antique, brass; sizes vary
Favorites: Front Rooms—2-story apt.

in cottage, king, full kitchen, deck
Comfort & Decor: Early American–style brass bedsteads and pine chests. Oak and mahogany furnishings. Rooms appealingly plain. Larger rooms in Meeting House (originally captain's mansion). Wheeler Cottage houses 3 apts. w/ full kitchens/kitchenettes, 2 w/ fireplace

RATES, RESERVATIONS, & RESTRICTIONS

Deposit: 1 night, credited to last night; refund w/ 14-day notice; 50% refund 3-day notice
Discounts: 7 nights or more, 3rd person

Credit Cards: MC, AE, D, DC
Check-in/Out: 3/noon
Smoking: Permitted, except in DR
Pets: Permitted, limited
Kids: Over 12

No-No's: Early departure forfeits
deposit
Minimum Stay: 2 nights in suites or
apts.
Open: All year (check)
Hosts: Timothy L. Watts

Box 149
Tenants Harbor, ME 04860
(800) 241-VIEW or (207) 372-6366
Fax: (207) 372-6320
info@eastwindinn.com
www.eastwindinn.com

SQUIRE TARBOX INN, Wiscasset

Overall: ★★★★½   Room Quality: B   Value: B   Price: $85–$175

Observe morning and evening milkings at this stylish, sophisticated working farm, which produces a ton of cheese annually from 14 award-winning,
scene-stealing Nubian goats. You can also enjoy the company of two don-
keys, a horse, two barn cats, and several egg-laying chickens. A swing hanging from the rafters, an honor bar, a player piano, and a screened porch
overlooking pastures are added amenities. Bill is a pilot, Karen a quilter, and
both innkeepers worked in the hotel business. They create stylish, gracious
touches and proudly share gentlefolk farming and fresh, fine food.

SETTING & FACILITIES

Location: Rural Westport Island, 8.5
mi. down Rt. 144, which joins Rt. 1
between Bath and Wiscasset; at end of
country road
Near: Bath, Wiscasset, 30-min. drive to
Reid State Park ocean beaches, harbors,

L.L. Bean outlet, shipbuilding, art museums, craft shops, and lobster shacks
Building: New England Colonial farmhouse (1763–1825); barn w/ add'l rooms
Grounds: Fields, stone walls, woods,
path to saltwater marsh

Public Space: Parlors, barn room, music room, rustic DR
Food & Drink: (MAP) Buffet cont'l breakfast; cookies and beverages, goat cheese in evening; set dinner, by reservation; liquor license; specialties: pear

soup, apple-and-pecan salad w/ daylilies, whey buns
Recreation: Antiquing, biking, beach, horses, cruises, farm animals
Amenities & Services: Rowboats, bikes, beach towels

ACCOMMODATIONS

Units: 11 guest rooms
All Rooms: Bath, heat control, window fan or AC
Some Rooms: Fireplace
Bed & Bath: Some four-posters, sizes vary; showers only
Favorites: Main House Room 1— huge, king; Barn Room 11—priv., spa-

cious, pasture view
Comfort & Decor: Antiques, rocking chairs, candles, quilts, books. Main house more spacious than barn rooms w/ formal decor, fireplace. Seven rustic barn rooms have exposed beams, 4 have priv. entrances. Good reading lights.

RATES, RESERVATIONS, & RESTRICTIONS

Deposit: $100, 50% longer stay; refund w/ 14-day notice
Discounts: 3rd person
Credit Cards: MC, V, AE, D
Check-in/Out: 2/11
Smoking: Only on weather-protected deck
Pets: No
Kids: Over 12
Minimum Stay: 2 nights on some

weekends; check
Open: Mother's Day–Oct.
Hosts: Karen and Bill Mitman
1181 Main Rd., Box 1181, Westport Island
Wiscasset, ME 04578
(207) 882-7693
Fax: (207) 882-7107
squire@wiscasset.net

Zone 3
Southern Maine Coast &
Greater Portland

The southern Maine coast is a day at the beach. York, Ogunquit, Wells, Kennebunk, Saco, and Old Orchard have white sand not usually associated with New England's rocky shores. Lodgings are often just a block or so away from the beaches, or even directly accessible to them.

Kittery and Freeport—home of the famous L.L. Bean outlet—have hundreds of discount shops, and quaint Kittery is also famous for shipbuilding. Freeport's havens from the hectic outlets are Wolf Neck Woods State Park's hiking trails, nature sanctuaries, deep-sea fishing charters, bay cruises, and seasonal excursions to Eagle Island.

The Yorks offer a historical perspective, and the York Historic District features antique buildings still used today. The Cape Neddick Lighthouse (Nubble Light) is one of the oldest and most picturesque in the state.

Ogunquit, although it gets crowded, lives up to its Indian name, "beautiful place by the sea," and offers the historic Marginal Way footpath to Perkins Cove, a world-famous art colony, complete with New England's only foot drawbridge.

Bustling Wells is indeed bustling, blessed with seven miles of wide, white sand beaches. You can escape to Wells Estuaries Research Reserve and Laudholm Farm sanctuaries and wildlife refuge.

The Kennebunk area, with its rocky shoreline, protected harbors and own share of sandy beaches, is more like traditional New England and more crowded. Kennebunk's waterfront Dock Square offers an excuse to go shopping, as does the Brick Store Museum.

Portland, Maine's largest city with about 62,000 locals, is small enough to be comfortable, and yet has its share of cultural activities. Old Port Exchange and the Arts District overlook sparkling Casco Bay. Touring historic homes, relaxing to the strains of the Portland Symphony Orchestra, strolling through the Museum of Art and bringing kids to the Children's Museum of Maine can while away entire rainy days and nights.

On fine days, take a ferry trip on Casco Bay to various islands, and bring your bike for touring once you arrive. Area state parks have scenic lighthouses and sandy beaches—yes, even in Portland.

Winslow Homer once lived and painted in Scarborough, now a 3,000-acre wildlife refuge and marsh area. Just north of Portland is Falmouth, offering special events, classes, and displays at the Maine Audubon Society's headquarters at Gilsland Farm. Yarmouth also sponsors several seasonal fairs, including the Cumberland Fair and the United Maine Craftsmen Fair.

Southern coastal Maine has many small inns and bed-and-breakfasts from basic to ultra-luxurious, including some of New England's most beloved properties. But the season is short, and crowds are heavy, so reservations are a must to avoid disappointment.

For More Information
Convention and Visitors Bureau of Greater Portland
(207) 772-5800 or (207) 772-4994
Greater Portland Region: (207) 772-2811
Portland's Downtown District: (207) 772-6828

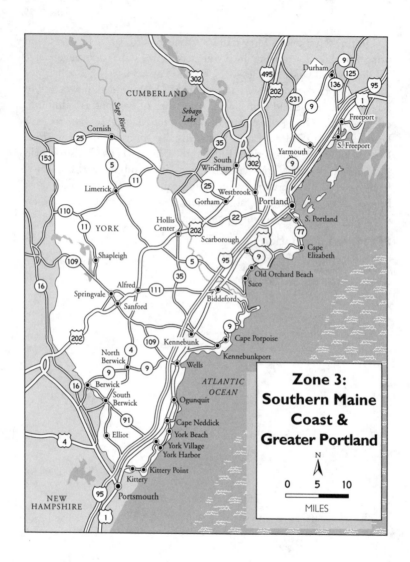

Zone 3:
Southern Maine
Coast &
Greater Portland

N

0   5   10

MILES

BAGLEY HOUSE, Durham

Overall: ★★★	Room Quality: C	Value: C	Price: $75–$135

This property has had many lives: church, schoolhouse, store, and public house. Today it is a modest bed-and-breakfast, a quiet option in an area not exactly brimming with accommodations. Antiques and handmade crafts are all around you, and here you are far from the crowds at nearby outlet shopping. The site is still evolving, and the enthusiastic hosts, one of them British, feel their considerable efforts are well received. Guests may prefer the main house, as the new Bliss Barn is still being decorated.

SETTING & FACILITIES

Location: 6 miles north of I-95, Exit 20 Freeport/Durham, on rural Rt. 136
Near: 10 minutes from Freeport, lighthouses, ocean and beaches, state parks, nature trails, Casco Bay Islands, X-C ski trails, outlets, Portland, colleges
Building: Built in 1772 as inn; 2nd building, Bliss Barn
Grounds: Rural, 6 acres of fields and woods

Public Space: LR, library, country kitchen; Bliss Barn, common room
Food & Drink: Full communal breakfast; specialty: sourdough pancakes
Recreation: Beach/water activities; lighthouse, island tours; day trips, trails
Amenities & Services: Books, games; portacrib; entire can be booked for events, lobster weekend (min. 5)

ACCOMMODATIONS

Units: 5 in main house, 3 in barn; 1 disabled access
All Rooms: Bath, custom pieces; heat controls
Some Rooms: Fireplace, reproduction Shaker beds, sitting area, carpet, hardwoods, add'l beds
Bed & Bath: Sizes vary; some shower only, some hall access

Favorites: The Cozy Nook—at top, sloping ceilings, 1 trundle and 1 3/4 bed, good for families; Emma's Room—woodburning fireplace; Pine Tree Room—in barn, queen, gas fireplace, sitting area, views
Comfort & Decor: Handsewn quilts, antique linens, flowers. Smallish rooms. Main house, less privacy.

RATES, RESERVATIONS, & RESTRICTIONS

Deposit: Hold credit card number
Discounts: 3rd person
Credit Cards: MC, V, AE, D
Check-in/Out: 3/11
Smoking: No
Pets: No; B&B has cat and dog
Kids: Welcome
Minimum Stay: 2 nights if reserve entire inn

Open: All year
Hosts: Susan Backhouse and Suzanne O'Connor
1290 Royalsborough Rd.
Durham, ME 04222
(800) 765-1772; (207) 865-6566 or (207) 353-6372
Fax: (207) 353-5878
bglyhse@aol.com

BUFFLEHEAD COVE INN, Kennebunkport

Overall: ★★★★½	Room Quality: B	Value: B	Price: $95–$250

You're a lucky duck, like the buffleheads who are attracted to this cove, if you get to stay here. The Gott family was raised here before the house recently turned into a bed-and-breakfast, and this special, homey property is becoming word-of-mouth-popular. Tranquil views of the tide's ebb and flow or blue heron in flight are just about everywhere, and it's hard to believe that this romantic little hideaway, a sensual treat, is only five minutes from the hubbub of town.

SETTING & FACILITIES

Location: Exit 3 (Kennebunk) from I-95, left onto Rt. 35 S, continue for 3.1 miles, on bank of the Tidal Kennebunk River
Near: Ocean, Dock Square, town
Building: Turn-of-the-century gambrel-roofed house
Grounds: Fields, apple trees, hammocks, decks
Public Space: Sunny LR, DR; wraparound porch; breakfast deck on water

Food & Drink: Full breakfast; specialties: ginger poached pears in English custard sauce, apple-stuffed French toast, maple-glazed sausage; early riser coffee; evening wine and cheese; teas
Recreation: Summer theatre, local events; beach/water activities, birdwatch from dock, antiquing
Amenities & Services: Beach permits, priv. dock

ACCOMMODATIONS

Units: 3 guest rooms, 2 suites
All Rooms: Bath
Some Rooms: Water view, gas fireplace, balcony, whirlpool; suites: sitting room, priv. entrance (1)
Bed & Bath: Bed sizes vary; robes, some dbl. whirlpools

Favorites: Balcony Room—mahogany dbl. armoire, large balcony; Hideaway—in cottage, dbl. gas fireplace, BR and LR, king, dbl. whirlpool
Comfort & Decor: Rooms sunny, quirky, and cozy-romantic. Americana quilts and artisan pieces, wicker and lace. Warm color and floral treatments.

RATES, RESERVATIONS, & RESTRICTIONS

Deposit: 1 night, 50% longer stay; refund w/ 14-day notice
Credit Cards: MC, V, AE, D
Check-in/Out: 3–8/11
Smoking: No
Pets: No; 1 cat
Kids: Limited, check
Minimum Stay: 2 nights on weekends June–Sept.

Open: April–Dec.; check for winter avail.
Hosts: Harriet and Jim Gott
Box 499
Kennebunkport, ME 04046
(207) 967-3879
Fax: Same as phone
bcove@dbanet.com

CAPTAIN JEFFERDS INN, Kennebunkport

Overall: ★★★★½	Room Quality: A	Value: C	Price: $105–$240

The gracious new owners lovingly redecorated this grand house, removing the kitsch and emphasizing the elegance, with a sophisticated mix of Americana and decorator touches. The spacious, high-ceilinged dining room, the heart of the house, is especially wonderful. Meticulously maintained, this stately white clapboard with picket fence is now an acceptable alternative to its more renowned neighbor, The Captain Lord Mansion.

SETTING & FACILITIES

Location: Rt. 9E to Main St; right onto Main, right on Pearl St; residential area
Near: Ocean, 2 nature preserves; Mt. Agamenticus; 1 block from Harbor
Building: 1804 Federal mansion, carriage house
Grounds: Smallish; gardens, fountain, terrace, screened-in sun porch
Public Space: Garden room, DR, LR

Food & Drink: 3-course candlelight breakfast, communal or separate; early coffee; tea
Recreation: Board games, sailing, fishing, dayboat trips, outlets/boutiques
Amenities & Services: Refrigerator, irons, recipes, paper, grand piano, holiday festivities, celebratory champagne, beach towels; entire facility may be reserved; fax, maps

ACCOMMODATIONS

Units: Main building, 2 jr. suites and 10 guest rooms; Carriage House, 3 suites and 1 guest room
All Rooms: Bath, ambiance lighting, AC

Some Rooms: Fireplace, porch, skylight, priv. entrance (1), fountain (1)
Bed & Bath: Four-poster, canopy, sleigh, varied sizes; some shower only, 1 hall access (robes), some soaking

tubs or oversized showers, bath w/
fireplace (1)
Favorites: Assisi Suite— king iron bed,
fireplace, large bath, indoor garden and
fountain, oversize Italian tiled shower;
Adare Suite—king sleigh, dbl. fireplace
(bed and bath), oversize shower

Comfort & Decor: Lower-priced
rooms are smallish, but all are pristine
and pretty w/ sophisticated touches.
New owners refurbished rooms in
1997 to reflect favorite places throughout the world.

RATES, RESERVATIONS, & RESTRICTIONS

Deposit: 1 night; refund w/ 14-day
notice
Discounts: Off-season, New Year's Eve
pkg.
Credit Cards: V, MC, AE
Check-in/Out: After 3/11. Call for
check-in after 7 p.m.; noon check-out
often OK
Smoking: No
Pets: Dogs w/ reservation and $20 fee;
not permitted alone in rooms.

Kids: Over 8
Minimum Stay: 2 nights on week-
ends, in-season (May–Oct.)
Open: Except Christmas week
Hosts: Pat and Dick Bartholomew
Box 691, 5 Pearl St.
Kennebunkport, ME 04046
(800) 839-6844 or (207) 967-2311
Fax: (207) 967-0721
captjeff@captainjefferdsinn.com
www.captainjefferdsinn.com

THE CAPTAIN LORD MANSION, Kennebunkport

| Overall: ★★★★★ | Room Quality: A | Value: C | Price: $130–$350 |

This imposing landmark, close to other neighborhood mansions, has a
"memory garden" crammed with inscribed stone blocks citing guests with
10 or more visits. Continually fine-tuned according to popular requests,
the stellar site is hard to book in season, and is perhaps losing a bit of its
charm because of its popularity. Still, this quintessential New England captain's house remains a great bed-and-breakfast, with a solid feel and great
authentic antique furnishings.

SETTING & FACILITIES

Location: 5th left off Ocean Ave., in
residential area
Near: Kennebunk River, ocean, waterfront, boutique and outlet shopping
Building: 1814 Federal clapboard mansion; in Nat'l Register of Historic
Places, 1807 Federal-style guesthouse
Grounds: Acre+ of lawns, flowers,
brick pathways

Public Space: Wide front hall, 4-story
staircase; gathering/DR; antique country
kitchen; 2nd floor common room
Food & Drink: Full breakfast;
refreshments
Recreation: Beach, touring, biking
Amenities & Services: Games,
books, maps, recipes, inn newsletter, gift
shop, beach towels, conf. rooms

ACCOMMODATIONS

Units: 16 guest rooms, 4 add'l in "Phoebe's Fantasy" guesthouse
All Rooms: Bath, fireplace, room diaries; all but 1, AC
Some Rooms: 2nd fireplace in bath, antique dolls/toys
Bed & Bath: Four-poster, lace canopy beds; Dana Suite—robes; dbl. vanities, some heated marble fls.; some dbl. whirlpools, bidets
Favorites: Ship Oriental and Ship Ophelia—large, lavish and lovely; room diaries explain why.

Comfort & Decor: Units named for Captain Lord's ships w/ themes. Federal decor w/ spirit, ambient lighting, sitting areas. Large fireplaces, Oriental rugs, oil paintings, gleaming woodwork, crystal chandeliers. Period colors, bold wallpapers, overstuffed chairs and loveseats, eye-catching draperies, antiques. Handmade pillows and whimsical touches.

RATES, RESERVATIONS, & RESTRICTIONS

Deposit: 2 nights, 50% of longer stay; refund w/ 15-day notice
Discounts: Off season, seasonal and theme pkgs. (e.g., New Year's, Winterfest, Brew Pub, Antique Lover's)
Credit Cards: MC, V, AE, D
Check-in/Out: After 3/11
Smoking: No, violators will pay cleaning fee
Pets: No
Kids: Over 12

No-No's: Returning after 11 p.m.
Minimum Stay: 2 nights on weekends, year round
Open: All year
Hosts: Rick Litchfield and Bev Davis
Box 800
Kennebunkport, ME 04046
(207) 967-3141
Fax: (207) 967-3172
innkeeper@captainlord.com

MAINE STAY, Kennebunkport

Overall: ★★★	Room Quality: B	Value: C	Price: $95–$225

This white-columned Italianate was once a taffy factory and later used by rum-runners. Today, lots of gleaming lace-curtained French doors, period wallpapers and carpets, restored stained glass, and antiques help create a romantic, classic bed-and-breakfast. It is a more informal alternative to the nearby grander ones, including The Captain Lord Mansion. The hosts are friendly, and the cottages, with their full kitchens to augment big breakfasts in the main house, are especially appealing for families.

SETTING & FACILITIES

Location: Traffic light at Rts. 35 and 9, left onto Rt. 9 to Kennebunkport, turn right at Main St.; in residential historic district

Near: Village, harbor
Building: 1860 Mansard Victorian w/ cupola

Grounds: Lawn, croquet area, playground
Public Space: Entrance hall, parlor, porch
Food & Drink: Full breakfast; tea

Recreation: Sailing; day trips to Camden, Boothbay; games
Amenities & Services: Covered bike rack, 2 phones in main house, papers, refrigerator, beach passes and towels, maps

ACCOMMODATIONS

Units: 6 guest rooms; 11 cottage rooms; 6 w/ 2 BRs, LR, kitchen
All Rooms: Bath, TV, clock/radio, AC
Some Rooms: Fireplace, deck, sitting area; cottage rooms: kitchen, coffeemaker, micro, refrigerator, VCR
Bed & Bath: Some antique, iron, brass, sizes vary; some whirlpools

Favorites: Room 14—deck, gas fireplace
Comfort & Decor: Victorian and Colonial colors. Romantic, flowery rooms. Cottages, English country charm. Good lighting. Immaculate.

RATES, RESERVATIONS, & RESTRICTIONS

Deposit: 1 night or 50%; full payment 2 weeks prior; refund w/ 14-day notice
Discounts: Off-season, midweek, add'l guests, kids under 4 free
Credit Cards: MC, V, AE; checks/cash pref.
Check-in/Out: After 3/11
Smoking: No
Pets: No
Kids: Welcome in cottages; over 5, main house

Minimum Stay: 2–3 nights, peak; check for 1 night avail.
Open: All year
Hosts: Carol and Lindsay Copeland 34 Main St., Box 500A
Kennebunkport, ME 04046
(800) 950-2117 or (207) 967-2117
Fax: (207) 967-8757
www.mainestayinn.com

OLD FORT INN, Kennebunkport

Overall: ★★★★   Room Quality: B   Value: C   Price: $95–$295

For those who enjoy recreation, this is the best game in town. You enter through an antiques store, and then into a super-size living room overlooking the pool. The imposing bed-and-breakfast's rustic exterior, with belfry, reflects a proud American heritage; its interior luxury reflects its sophisticated, well-traveled owners—he a former oil exec, she a flight attendant. Rooms at this secluded mini-resort are a mix of reliable comfort, amenities and romance. Christmas prelude activities, during the first week in December, are a big deal.

SETTING & FACILITIES

Location: I-95 to Kennebunkport, to Rt. 35, to Ocean Ave., to Old Fort Ave.; estate area at the edge of Kennebunkport
Near: Village, lighthouses, 2 golf courses; I block to ocean
Building: Colonial main building (converted barn); guest house
Grounds: 15 acres; 3 acres gardens, lawns; heated pool, tennis court
Public Space: Main lodge room, library, patio

Food & Drink: Full buffet breakfast; specialty: sticky buns
Recreation: Cruises, tennis, swimming, beach combing, horseshoes, shuffleboard
Amenities & Services: Antique/gift shop, laundry, storage, fax, copier, surf board, comp. tennis daily, beach towels, meetings (24); entire can be reserved

ACCOMMODATIONS

Units: 15 guest rooms, I suite
All Rooms: Bath, sitting area, TV, wet bar/mini-refrigerators, drinks, snacks, phone, iron, AC
Some Rooms: Fireplace (gas), canopy bed, dining area
Bed & Bath: Beds vary; some heated tile bath floors, some whirlpools

Favorites: Corner deluxe rooms—lace canopy beds, gas fireplaces, best baths
Comfort & Decor: Rooms spacious, tastefully and carefully appointed; Laura Ashley abounds. Period furnishings, armoires. Ample reading lights. Romantic ambiance w/ hotel-like amenities. Rooms in carriage house especially priv.

RATES, RESERVATIONS, & RESTRICTIONS

Deposit: I night, 2 nights for longer stay; refund w/ 15 day notice
Discounts: 3rd person
Credit Cards: MC, V, AE, D
Check-in/Out: 2–8/11
Smoking: Outside only
Pets: No
Kids: Over 12
Minimum Stay: 2 nights July–Aug., all weekends; 3 nights holiday weekends

Open: Mid-April–mid-Dec.
Hosts: Shelia and David Aldrich
8 Old Fort Ave., Box M-1
Kennebunkport, ME 04046
(800) 828-3678 or (207) 967-5353
Fax: (207) 967-4547
oldfort@cybertours.com
www.oldfort.com

THE WHITE BARN INN, Kennebunkport

| Overall: ★★★★★ | Room Quality: A | Value: C | Price: $190–$450 |

This dramatic, sophisticated inn on a busy Kennebunkport street has all things going for it, except perhaps for the grounds, which are limited. Antiques and country artifacts mix faultlessly with luxury detailing. The dining experience is especially delightful, not just because of creative cuisine, but also because of flawless, choreographed service, classical music, and a window wall on a lighted flower garden. The White Barn is a deserving member of the prestigious Relais & Chateaux.

SETTING & FACILITIES

Location: I 95 N to Maine Turnpike, Exit 3, follow Rt. 35 S 7 miles to Kennebunkport, straight to Beach St.; inn is .25 mile on the right
Near: Wildlife preserves, Dock Square, ocean
Building: Large, created from farmhouse and 170-year-old barn
Grounds: Lawns, courtyard, flower gardens
Public Space: Gracious parlors; sitting, breakfast, and DRs; Victorian porches, copper bar

Food & Drink: Full breakfast; tea; 4-course dinner (w/ res.), dinner menu revised weekly, prix fixe $65/person; specialties: Lobster dishes, incl. spring rolls, ravioli; full bar, fine wines
Recreation: Golf, coast/water activities, X-C skiing, horses, tennis, museums
Amenities & Services: Outdoor heated pool, massage therapy and spa treatments, canoe and biking equipment; turn-down, morning-evening valet, same-day laundry, business facil., gift cert.

ACCOMMODATIONS

Units: 12 guest rooms, 13 add'l rooms and suites in various contemp. annexes and Victorian cottages
All Rooms: Bath, fresh flowers and fruit, CD players, voice mail
Some Rooms: Deck, priv. entrance, fireplace, sitting area, pool access, entertainment armoire; TV/VCR on request where not standard
Bed & Bath: Four-poster, tapestry, contemp., sleigh, antique, handpainted beds, sizes vary; robes, some marble baths, whirlpools, sep. showers

Favorites: The Red Suite—dramatic and spacious, priv. porch; May's Annex—king four-posters, fireplaces, marble baths, whirlpools
Comfort & Decor: Formal New England period furnishings and Victorian touches, plush carpets, coordinated fabrics and wallcoverings. Room decor from traditional to whimsical. Rooms in May's Cottage most spacious and exclusive. Pool House, simplest rooms. Excellent lighting.

RATES, RESERVATIONS, & RESTRICTIONS

Deposit: Check w/ inn, must refund w/ 14-day notice; credit card req. to reserve dinner
Discounts: Off-season, holiday, various pkgs.
Credit Cards: MC, V, AE
Check-in/Out: 3/11
Smoking: No
Pets: No
Kids: Limited, check w/ inn
No-No's: Not cancelling dinner 24 hrs. in advance

Minimum Stay: Varies seasonally, check
Open: All year
Hosts: Laurence Bongiorno
37 Beach St., Box 560C
Kennebunkport, ME 04046
(207) 967-2321
Fax: (207) 967-1100
innkeeper@whitebarninn.com
www.whitebarninn.com

INN AT PORTSMOUTH HARBOR, Kittery

Overall: ★★★	Room Quality: C	Value: D	Price: $85–$150

This largely refurbished bed-and-breakfast, with new owners, was formerly The Gundalow Inn. The location, across from a lobster restaurant and shipyard, is picturesque or commercial, depending on your sensibilities. (The Portsmouth area hypes itself as the "restaurant capital of the world," and you can walk or bike from here to several good eateries.) The bed-and-breakfast has a hidden staircase, but everything else is right out in the open. The kitchen, with its big stoves, open shelves and home-baked smells, is the heart of this bright, homey house.

SETTING & FACILITIES

Location: From I-95 to Portsmouth or Kittery exits, to US 1, to Water St.; on Maine side of Memorial Bridge, Portsmouth Harbor
Near: Outlet shopping, University of New Hampshire, Phillips Exeter Academy, historic homes, Colonial Portsmouth
Building: 1890 brick Federal-style
Grounds: Privet hedge, roses, and flowers, patio; views of Portsmouth Naval Shipyard, Piscataque River

Public Space: DR, parlor, sun porch
Food & Drink: Full breakfast; p.m. wine and cheese, coffee or tea
Recreation: Beach activities, boating, day trips, touring
Amenities & Services: Games, pickup from Portsmouth bus or train stations, maps, beach towels, recipes, paper, reservations, meeting facilities for 25

ACCOMMODATIONS

Units: 6 guest rooms
All Rooms: Bath, ceiling fan, phone, TV, dataport, voice-mail, heat control
Some Rooms: Water/Portsmouth view, skylights

Bed & Bath: Bed sizes vary; some tubs w/ hand-held showers, claw-foot tubs
Favorites: Royal George—3rd floor, skylight decor, river view

Comfort & Decor: Antiques, Victorian decor. Bright rooms designed to maximize views. Some old-fashioned fixtures in baths. Good lighting. Comfortable, warm feeling throughout.

RATES, RESERVATIONS, & RESTRICTIONS

Deposit: 1 night or longer stay; refund w/ 14-day notice
Discounts: Mid-week stays Nov.–April, 3rd person
Credit Cards: MC, V
Check-in/Out: 3–7/11
Smoking: No
Pets: No; house golden retriever
Kids: Over 16
Minimum Stay: 2 nights weekends, high season, special events/weekends

Open: All year except Thanksgiving, Christmas; check in winter
Hosts: Kim and Terry O'Mahoney
6 Water St.
Kittery, ME 03904
(207) 439-4040
Fax: (207) 438-9286
innph@cybertours.com
innatportsmouth.com

HARTWELL HOUSE, Ogunquit

Overall: ★★★½	Room Quality: B	Value: C	Price: $85–$185

For groups, weddings, retreats, and business travelers who want the feel of an inn along with state-of-the-art business facilities, this is a fine choice. Spanning both sides of a busy road, the facade looks like a generic business retreat, but within, style and sophistication mixed with antiques and whimsy add up to surprisingly fetching public areas and accommodations, individually decorated in both country and contemporary decor.

SETTING & FACILITIES

Location: I-95 to York/Ogunquit Exit, left on Rt. 1, right onto Pine Hill Rd. to end, left on Shore Rd.
Near: Footpath along rocky shore, ocean beaches, Perkins Cove, lighthouses
Building: 5,200-sq.-ft. Colonial-style building (new); 2nd Colonial-style 1921 farmhouse
Grounds: 1.5 acre of landscaped grounds on 2 sides of road
Public Space: LR, DR, glassed-in front porch; conf. area (65)
Food & Drink: Cont'l breakfast, avail. to public, communal or separate; light p.m. fare, picnic lunches, full course dinners by arrangement, clam bakes for groups
Recreation: Beach, Windjammer cruises, golf, fishing, horses, X-C skiing, Christmas by the Sea celebration (2nd week in Dec.)
Amenities & Services: Golf privileges at Cape Neddick Country Club, conf. center and coordinator, papers; taxi and limo services, flowers on request, reservations made, spousal activities (for conf.), disabled access

ACCOMMODATIONS

Units: 13 guest rooms, 3 suites
All Rooms: Bath, antiques, AC
Some Rooms: Terrace/balcony; suites: LR/dining area, refrigerator, wet bar
Bed & Bath: Custom mattresses; full baths, some w/ 2nd sink

Favorites: Winslow Homer—floral tapestries, netted canopied bed, balcony
Comfort & Decor: European country style, mixed w/ Americana. Hotel-like comforts and sophistication. Crocheted coverlets. Fresh plants. Spacious, elegant.

RATES, RESERVATIONS, & RESTRICTIONS

Deposit: 50%, must cancel 14 days in advance; for meetings/functions, 50%, bal. due w/in 21 days of arrival, must cancel 21 days in advance
Discounts: "Inn-house Dining" week-end pkgs., New Year's Eve event, get-aways, weekly suites
Credit Cards: MC, V, AE, D
Check-in/Out: 3–9/11
Smoking: Outside only
Pets: No
Kids: Over 14

No-No's: Add'l people in rooms, late check-out (fee)
Minimum Stay: 3 nights July, Aug., hol-iday weekends
Open: All year
Hosts: Tracey and Chris Anderson
118 Shore Rd., Box 393
Ogunquit, ME 03907
(800) 235-8883 or (207) 646-7210
Fax: (207) 646-6032
hartwell@cybertours.com
hartwellhouseinn.com

NELLIE LITTLEFIELD HOUSE, Ogunquit

Overall: ★★★½	Room Quality: C	Value: C	Price: $75–$195

A hundred years ago this notable village house behind a picket fence was a center of summer social activity. Today, once again, the imposing, white-turreted village landmark sparkles within and without, and it has won 10 architectural awards for its remodeling. Nellie's hospitality continues today, a turn-of-the-century later, with warm hosts, hearty breakfasts, a fine location, and pretty period details.

SETTING & FACILITIES

Location: Rt. 1 to Ogunquit, turn onto Shore Rd., 1st Victorian on left
Near: Marginal Way Walk, Kittery out-let shops, Perkins Cove, ocean
Building: 1889 Victorian
Grounds: Minimal lawn, gardens
Public Space: LR, library, DR; 3 porches; all disabled access

Food & Drink: Full buffet breakfast; refreshments, wine and cheese
Recreation: Boating, biking, horses, diving, golf
Amenities & Services: Exercise room, hot tub, refrigerator, irons, maps, celebrations, books, beach towels, recipes, paper; fluent German.

ACCOMMODATIONS

Units: 6 guest rooms, 2 suites
All Rooms: Bath, TV, phone, AC
Some Rooms: Priv. deck; 3rd floor: keyhole ocean view; disabled access room (1)
Bed & Bath: Queen, twin beds; whirlpool (1), some showers only

Favorites: J.H.—LR, deck, ocean view, whirlpool, 2 TVs
Comfort & Decor: Comfortable and bright. Some period and antique touches. Plants. Framed art. Reading lamps. Feels like a small hotel.

RATES, RESERVATIONS, & RESTRICTIONS

Deposit: 1 night; refund w/ 14-day notice
Discounts: Longer stays
Credit Cards: MC, V, D
Check-in/Out: 3/11
Smoking: No
Pets: No
Kids: Over 12

Minimum Stay: 2 nights weekends, 3 nights holiday weekends
Open: May–Oct.
Hosts: Patty and Joerg Ross
9 Shore Rd., Box 1599
Ogunquit, ME 03907
(207) 646-1692
www.visit-maine.com/nellielittlefieldhouse/

TRELLIS HOUSE, Ogunquit

Overall: ★★★½	Room Quality: B	Value: C	Price: $85–$125

Trellises on the grounds give the name to this unpretentious house with a welcoming, wraparound wicker-filled screened porch, a mix of comfortable furnishings throughout, and a homey feel. Close to the action of the main shopping area, and to The Marginal Way walkway on the rocky shoreline, yet in an off-street atmosphere, you could almost feel that you are on a country lane. The carriage house and cottage are private and spacious, and a good deal for long stays. Pat and Jerry are hands-on hosts who know the area well.

SETTING & FACILITIES

Location: Rt. 1 to Ogunquit, on a side street off Shore Rd.
Near: Perkins Cove, Ogunquit Village, Marginal Way historic trail, ocean
Building: 1907 country summer cottage
Grounds: Gardens, flower arbors and trellises

Public Space: Common rooms, LR
Food & Drink: Full breakfast, communal; a specialty: ginger pancakes; tea
Recreation: Trolley, boat tours, harbor and crafts shops, walking tours, horses, XC skiing
Amenities & Services: Off-street parking

ACCOMMODATIONS

Units: 8 guest rooms, carriage house, Barbary Cottage
All Rooms: Bath, AC, clock
Some Rooms: Fireplace, alcove, deck, sitting area, kitchen, views
Bed & Bath: Antiques beds, sizes vary
Favorites: The Main Suite—spacious, sitting alcove, ocean view, queen brass bed

Comfort & Decor: Eclectic, early American pieces mingled w/ current collectibles. Comfortable, homey, unpretentious. Barbary Cottage priv., romantic. Carriage house w/ fireplaces, priv. decks.

RATES, RESERVATIONS, & RESTRICTIONS

Deposit: 1 night; refund w/ 10-day notice
Discounts: 3rd person, pkgs., weekly (apt.)
Credit Cards: MC, V
Check-in/Out: 2/11
Smoking: No
Pets: No; innkeepers have 1 dog
Kids: Over 13

Minimum Stay: 2 nights weekends; 2 nights, busy season, holidays; check w/ B&B
Open: All year
Hosts: Pat and Jerry Houlihan
2 Beachmere Place, Box 2229
Ogunquit, ME 03907
(800) 681-7909, (207) 646-7909
www.trellishouse.com

POMEGRANATE, Portland

Overall: ★★★★½	Room Quality: A	Value: B	Price: $95–$175

Artistic, sophisticated and witty, this now-beloved city charmer is imbued with flair and faux fun. Artists were given freedom to interpret throughout, and the combination of classic architecture and modern sensibilities works amazingly. Some favorite touches: the Matisse floral interpretations, the yellow and orange walls and checkerboard floor of the landing, the marbleized columns separating parlor and dining room, the painted irises in Bathroom #5, the painted swags in the dining room, etc. This immaculate postmodern bed-and-breakfast is loved most by those who enjoy the surprising pleasures of the offbeat and unexpected, and the hostess' name is appropriate.

SETTING & FACILITIES

Location: Historic Victorian Western Promenade area
Near: Casco Bay, midtown Art District, downtown Portland
Building: Italianate Colonial Revival townhouse
Grounds: City gardens, patio w/ seating

Public Space: Common rooms, DR
Food & Drink: Full communal breakfast; refreshments
Recreation: Museums, bay cruises, events, colleges
Amenities & Services: Books, games

ACCOMMODATIONS

Units: 6 guest rooms, 1 suite; 1 guest room in carriage house
All Rooms: Bath, TV, phone, clock, radio
Some Rooms: Fireplace, AC
Bed & Bath: Artisan-crafts beds, sizes vary; tiled, porcelain sinks
Favorites: No. 7—carriage house, floral motif, priv. patio

Comfort & Decor: Guest rooms big, w/ oversize, vivid florals, brash patterns. Bold colors from eggplant to Matisse red to black and white. Artistically interpreted decor. Luxurious, surprising, unique.

RATES, RESERVATIONS, & RESTRICTIONS

Deposit: Check w/ inn
Discounts: Check w/ inn
Credit Cards: V, MC, AE, D
Check-in/Out: 4–6/11
Smoking: No
Pets: No
Kids: Over 16 OK
Minimum Stay: 2 nights, busy season and holidays

Open: All year
Hosts: Isabel Smiles
49 Neal St.
Portland, ME 04102
(800) 356-0408 or (207) 772-1006
Fax: (207) 773-4426
www.pomegranateinn.com

EDWARDS' HARBORSIDE INN, York

Overall: ★★★½   Room Quality: B   Value: C   Price: $90–$250

Jay, a certified Coast Guard captain, bought and began renovating the bed-and-breakfast in 1985 and has been working and upgrading it since. Sailboats ply by, lobstermen unload their delectable catch by the dock, and the tiny, sandy beach is good for a (short) walk. Aside from that, check out the salty environs, read a book or chat up your fellow guests. A modern building across the water on one side mars the view a bit, but the pace here remains relaxing. Sunlight streams through the porch windows, and sunsets from the pier are especially nice with sherry.

SETTING & FACILITIES

Location: Rt. 1A through York Village into York Harbor, right onto Stage Neck Rd.; on ocean and Harbor
Near: Portsmouth, Kennebunkport; beach across street w/ rocky cliff path
Building: Gray/white, originally Victorian; completely refurbished
Grounds: Lawn slopes to water

Public Space: Sunporch, parlors
Food & Drink: Breakfast, sherry and cheese in p.m.
Recreation: Golf, tennis, boating, fishing, L.L. Bean outlet
Amenities & Services: Board games, books, hot tub, refrigerator, books, fax, pickup at Portland airport, groups

ACCOMMODATIONS

Units: 7 guest rooms, 3 suites
All Rooms: TV, AC, clock, radio, dataport
Some Rooms: Bath, priv. deck
Bed & Bath: Bed sizes vary; priv. or semi-priv., some whirlpools

Favorites: The York Suite—view, four-poster, dbl. whirlpool
Comfort & Decor: Hotel-style American country charm. Comfortable. Water views though large windows Rooms vary widely.

RATES, RESERVATIONS, & RESTRICTIONS

Deposit: 1 night or 50% of longer stay; refund w/14-day notice; groups: full payment at reserv.
Discounts: Off-season, 3rd person, pkgs.
Credit Cards: MC, V
Check-in/Out: 3/11
Smoking: Outside porches only
Pets: No
Kids: No

Minimum Stay: 2 nights, weekends; 3 nights, peak season
Open: All year
Hosts: Jay Edwards
Stage Neck Rd., Box 866
York, ME 03911
(800) 273-2686 (207) 363-3037
Fax: (207) 363-1544

Zone 4
Maine—Inland & Lakes

This so-called "quiet corner" (louder during snowmobile and hunting seasons) extends west/east from Fryeburg to Houlton and north/south from Madawaska and Edmunston to Bangor and New Gloucester. Although an inland portion of the state, this enormous land of loons, pines and covered bridges is nearly flooded with lakes, large ponds, waterways, streams, and white-water rivers.

Maine's extensive snowmobile Interconnecting Trail System (ITS) and the impending International Lakeland Trail running from New Brunswick, Canada, may threaten the pristine atmosphere, but the attraction remains simply the "great outdoors." Wildlife is really in the wilds. Baxter State Park, a 200,000-acre wilderness, has the state's highest population of moose and deer and quite a few bears.

The peaks of mile-high Mount Katahdin in the Longfellow Range of Mountains are the second in the state to be touched by the morning sun and are the terminus of the Appalachian Trail. Bike, hike or drive designated scenic Route 201 past farmlands and forest landscapes. Skowhegan has the largest Wooden Indian in the state. Crossing over to Maritime Canada, the nineteenth-century local-granite-built railway station in McAdam is worthy of a visit. Foliage season arrives here in September, perhaps the earliest in New England.

Photography, year-round camping, seasonal hunting, fishing, boating, biking, mountain biking, hiking, dog sledding, snowshoeing, cross-country skiing, golf, tennis, and some downhill skiing are popular pastimes. Penobscot River, St. Croix, and The Forks offer beginner to extreme white-water rafting complete with falls, and any kind of reasonable water or ice-water sport is possible on huge Moosehead Lake, including summer water-skiing. White-water rafting runs from mid-April through October, because of dam-controlled water release, and in the long winter season, salmon and trout are caught through the ice. Heated ice huts are available for rent.

Snowmobiling, however, appears to win the popularity contest. Miles and miles (and miles) of groomed snowmobile trails cross the region and connect to the ITS, and there are snowmobiling festivals, balls, fairs, and contests.

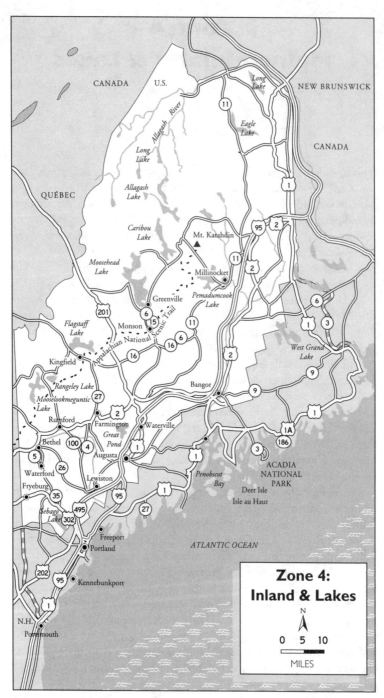

CANADA   U.S.

*Long
Lake*

NEW BRUNSWICK

Allagash River

⑪

QUÉBEC

*Long
Lake*

*Allagash
Lake*

*Eagle
Lake*

CANADA

*Caribou
Lake*

Mt. Katahdin ▲

�995 ②

*Moosehead
Lake*

⑪

②

Millinocket

Greenville

*Pemadumcook
Lake*

⑥

⑥

②01

Monson

⑮

⑥

③

⑪

*West Grand
Lake*

*Flagstaff
Lake*

Appalachian National Scenic Trail

⑯

⑥

⑨

Kingfield

⑯

②

Rangeley Lake

Bangor

⑨

*Mooselookmeguntic
Lake*

㉗

Rumford

②

①

Farmington

Bethel

⑩0

④

*Great
Pond*

Waterville

①A

⑤

Waterford

㉖

Augusta

①

⑱⑥

③

*Penobscot
Bay*

ACADIA
NATIONAL
PARK

Fryeburg

Lewiston

③

*Sebago
Lake*

㉟

④95

302

①

Deer Isle

Isle au Haut

㉗

Freeport

ATLANTIC OCEAN

Portland

②02

㊸5

Kennebunkport

Zone 4:
Inland & Lakes

N

①

N.H.

Portsmouth

0   5   10

MILES

And for "extreme" activities, the lakes region has an abundance of state-certified outfitters and guides ranging from those who go with you, cook for you and pitch your tent, to those who provide a map and just leave you alone.

Homespun, colorful celebrations abound in towns such as Caribou, Moosehead, Fort Kent, and Presque Isle, including the Maine Potato Blossom Festival, Winter Festival, Northern Maine Festival, Fall Arts & Crafts Festivals, Acadian Festival, Canoe Race & Scarecrow Festival, Dog Sled Races and Festivals, and Logging Days.

The bad news is that small lodgings up here—often rustic, converted lodges or camps usually near a lake or stream—are few and coveted, and drives to and between are long. Often you'll be eating all your meals at the inn, and you'll probably have to book for longer than one night. The prevailing atmosphere is outdoorsy, basic, informal, friendly, family-style and hearty. Unlike the more crowded coastal areas, with loads of choices and hotel options, you absolutely must have a reservation in hand or you may find yourself driving all night back to Bangor.

For More Information

Androscoggin County
(207) 783-2249

Greater Bangor Chamber of Commerce
(207) 947-0307

Greater Farmington Area
(207) 778-4215
email: info@farmingtonchamber.org

Greater Lincoln Area Chamber of
Commerce
(207) 794-8065 or (888) 794-8065

Jackman-Moose River Chamber of
Commerce
(207) 668-4171

Katahdin Area Chamber of Commerce
(Millinocket)
(207) 723-4443

Kennebec Valley
(207) 623-4559 or (800) 393-8629

Upper Kennebec Valley (The Forks)
Augusta: (207) 672-4100

Moosehead Lake Region
(207) 695-2702
email: moose@moosehead.net

Rangeley Lakes Region
(207) 864-5571 or (800) MT-LAKES
email: mtlakes@rangeley.org

Skowhegan
(207) 474-3621
email: skowman@skowhegan.org

Sugarloaf Area
(207) 235-2100

Windham Chamber of Commerce
(207) 892-8265
email: wincc@gwi.net

TELEMARK INN, Bethel

Overall: ★★★★	Room Quality: C	Value: A	Price: $95; $425–$825

Like to try new adventures? How 'bout skijoring (skiing while being pulled by a dog), llama trekking, or sweating in an authentic Indian lodge and then plunging into a snowbank? More traditional adventurers can enjoy mountain hiking trails, swimming hole excursions, canoeing, mountain biking, and exploring lakes, waterfalls, and beaver dams. This rustic eco-educational inn, formerly a millionaire's wilderness estate, creates its own electricity, offers healthy meals, and can be challenging or relaxing. You can just sit on the porch, listen to the birds, and twiddle your thumbs. So what if you have to share a bathroom.

SETTING & FACILITIES

Location: 10 miles from Bethel Village, 3 miles up a road in a stand of white birches at base of Caribou Mountain, the eastern fringe of the White Mountains
Near: Surrounded by White Mountain Nat'l Forest
Building: Turn-of-the-century Adirondack-style lodge
Grounds: 5 cleared acres inside 360 acres of wilderness, gardens, meadows, lakes, llama farm
Public Space: Restored lodge rooms; LR, DR, comfortable porch

Food & Drink: Organic fruit, vegetable and herbs; all meals provided; a specialty: rhubarb crepes
Recreation: Pkg. activities, hiking w/ gear carried by llamas, swimming holes w/ waterfalls and buffet lunch; skiing, snowshoeing, sleigh rides, skating, sledding, ski and skijoring lessons, horses, camping in teepee
Amenities & Services: Outside sauna, campfires, learning pkgs., nature talks, picnics, int'l travel tips

ACCOMMODATIONS

Units: 6 guest rooms
All Rooms: Handcrafted cabinetry, rustic furnishings
Some Rooms: Overlook grazing llamas, nat'l forest, mountains
Bed & Bath: Some bunk beds; rooms share 3 baths, sinks in each room

Favorites: Bunk-bed room—especially fun for kids
Comfort & Decor: All rooms comfortable, none outstanding. Some artisan pieces. TVs and phones deliberately excluded. Clean, basic, attractive.

RATES, RESERVATIONS, & RESTRICTIONS

Deposit: Typically 50%, varies according to pkg.; refund w/ 30-60–day notice, according to season and pkg.; prices include. meals, lodging and guided activities

Discounts: Children, singles, 3rd person
Credit Cards: MC, V
Check-in/Out: Varies/4
Smoking: No
Pets: No

Kids: Welcome
Minimum Stay: 3-, 5- and 7-day pkgs.
Open: All year except April; groups only in Nov.

Hosts: Steve Crone
RFD 2, Box 800
Bethel, ME 04217
(207) 836-2703

ADMIRAL PEARY HOUSE, Fryeburg

Overall: ★★★　　　Room Quality: B　　　Value: B　　　Price: $55–$128

Once the residence of arctic explorer Admiral Robert E. Peary, discoverer of the North Pole, this bed-and-breakfast lets you discover something too: that this is a fine stop, especially for tennis lovers and skiers. Geared toward quiet indoor time as well, the house offers books, paintings, a woodstove, a constantly hot tea pot in the big, country kitchen, and lots of good conversation in any of the nooks and crannies.

SETTING & FACILITIES

Location: Mt. Washington Valley; Rt. 302 W to Fryeburg (oldest village in White Mountains); block from center
Near: White Mountains, walk to Saco River, Lake Kazur; 6 miles to New Hampshire outlet shopping; 1 hr. to Maine coastline
Building: Sprawling 1865 Colonial, barn
Grounds: 10 acres; wooded, lawns, gardens
Public Space: LR; library; screened porch

Food & Drink: Full breakfast, communal; a specialty: Penguin Pie, turkey or ham w/ potatoes or homemade baked beans
Recreation: Boating, skiing, golf, Fryeburg Fair, antiquing
Amenities & Services: Hot tub, snowshoe rentals/trails, billiards; bikes, boat rides on Lake Kezur (fee); red clay tennis, lessons, rackets, ball machine; conf. facilities

ACCOMMODATIONS

Units: 6 guest rooms
All Rooms: Bath, sitting area, heat controls, AC, carpet, bright
Some Rooms: 3rd person
Bed & Bath: Queen/king; 1 king can sep. to twins; four-poster, brass, unique antique; showers only, recently remodeled

Favorites: North Pole—spacious, large window, country view, brass bed
Comfort & Decor: Spacious, comfortably furnished, formal Colonial decor, antique mahogany, decorator fabrics, wallcoverings, ambient lighting. Soothing, tasteful. Good lighting, workspace.

RATES, RESERVATIONS, & RESTRICTIONS

Deposit: 1 night, 50% longer stays; pkgs. paid in full at res.; refund w/ 14-day notice
Discounts: 3rd person, 5+ days, pkgs., contracts, midweek, business
Credit Cards: V, MC, AE
Check-in/Out: 3/11
Smoking: No
Pets: No; inn has border terrier dog, cockatiel
Kids: Permitted w/ limitations, check w/ inn

Minimum Stay: None
Open: All year
Hosts: Nancy and Ed Greenberg
9 Elm St.
Fryeburg, ME 04037-1114
(800) 237-8080 or (207) 935-3365
Fax: Same as telephone
admpeary@nxi.com
www.mountwashingtonvalley.com/admiral-pearyhouse

GREENVILLE INN, Greenville

Overall: ★★★★½	Room Quality: B	Value: A	Price: $75–$165

Built by a logging baron, this grand mansion is set in an equally grand location on a pristine lake in the northern Maine woods. Ship carpenters worked 10 years to complete the interior, which has a glorious leaded-glass window painted with a spruce tree. Dining is also grand, with heavy silver. A sample three-course dinner might be smoked rainbow trout with capers, grilled swordfish Provençal, and chocolate truffle tart with pecan crust. This inn would be exceptional anywhere, but up here in the middle of nowhere—along with The Lodge at Moosehead Lake—it's a real surprise.

SETTING & FACILITIES

Location: Rt. 15 N to Greenville, 2 blocks after blinking yellow light, turn right; overlooking New England's largest lake
Near: Bangor, Penobscot, Kennebec, Dead Rivers; Mt. Kineo, Mt. Katahdin,

Rip Gorge, state parks, lake beaches; half hr. drive to Bar Harbor, ocean, Acadia Nat'l Park
Building: 1895 hilltop Victorian mansion
Grounds: Spacious porch; overlooking lake

Public Space: Grand entrance stair
Food & Drink: Cont'l buffet breakfast;
dinner avail.; specialties: popovers,
snails, veal; full bar
Recreation: Float plane rides, boat
tours, water/snow sports; Moosemania

(spring), International Seaplane Festival
(Sept.)
Amenities & Services: Disabled
access

ACCOMMODATIONS

Units: 5 guest rooms, 6 cottages
All Rooms: Bath
Some Rooms: Fireplace, sitting area,
TV, lake view
Bed & Bath: Bed sizes vary, some
antique beds; some shower only
Favorites: Spacious Master Suite—sitting room, fireplace, large bath, views

Comfort & Decor: Main building
rooms romantically Victorian, without
fussiness. Airy lace curtains and bed
covers, period furnishings, muted wallcoverings, carpet. Cottages in meadow
setting, mountain view, wicker, floral
fabrics, French doors.

RATES, RESERVATIONS, & RESTRICTIONS

Deposit: 1 night, 50% longer stays
Discounts: 3rd person, children
Credit Cards: MC, V, D
Check-in/Out: 3/11
Smoking: In limited areas
Pets: No
Kids: Over 7; all ages welcome in
cottages
Minimum Stay: 3 nights, Seaplane Fly-
in (Sept.)

Open: DR and cottages, June 28–Oct.
14; main building, all year
Hosts: The Schnetzer Family
Norris St., Box 1194
Greenville, ME 04441-1194
888-695-6000 or (207) 695-2206
Fax: Same as phone
gvlinn@moosehead.net
www.greenvilleinn.com

LODGE AT MOOSEHEAD LAKE, Greenville

Overall: ★★★★½	Room Quality: A	Value: B	Price: $175–$350

Yes, this rustic inn has extensive outdoors activities, luxurious accommodations, endless lake views, and hearty food. But what you'll most remember are the four-poster beds, carved by a local artist. Totem poles, bears, nuzzling mooseheads, fish—you've got to see them to believe them. This decidedly over-the-top and far-north lodge is not for those who insist on refinement. But the enthusiastic hosts, relying on their extensive hospitality backgrounds, run this fantasy environment with a sure hand and a sense of fun. It's worth a detour.

SETTING & FACILITIES

Location: Rt. 15 N to Greenville, go
through blinking light, 2.5 miles up
steep hill, 3rd building on left, at top

Near: Bangor, Penobscot, Kennebec,
and Dead rivers; Mt. Kineo, Mt.
Katahdin, Rip Gorge, state parks, lake

beaches, half-hour to Bar Harbor, ocean, Acadia Nat'l Park
Building: 1917 Lodge-style building
Grounds: Unbroken view, pine-treed hills, pristine Moosehead Lake
Public Space: Common rooms, library; DR/restaurant; deck
Food & Drink: (MAP) Full buffet breakfast; candlelight dinner, 3

nights/week; specialty: Salmon in a Moose Suit; lunches; full bar
Recreation: Beach/water/snow activities, float plane rides, jet skiing, moose safaris, dogsled trips; Moosemania (spring), International Seaplane Festival (Sept.)
Amenities & Services: Equip. rentals, billiards, games, guided activities, lessons

ACCOMMODATIONS

Units: 5 guest rooms, 3 suites
All Rooms: Bath w/ whirlpool, gas fireplace, unique, TV/VCR
Some Rooms: Retreat Suites: spacious, whirlpool w/ chandelier, sunken LR, patio overlooking lake; 2nd fireplace in bath (1)
Bed & Bath: Unique four-poster/ canopied, 2 suites w/ hammock beds, sizes vary; dbl. whirlpools w/ TV, VCR
Favorites: Majestic Bear Room—lake view, four-poster w/ carved bears; Trout

Room—four-poster w/ leaping, painted trout, bath mirror framed w/ trout
Comfort & Decor: Artistic, eclectic, rustic. Beds set theme of room. Comfort and design prioritized. Whole log posts and beams, rough-hewn or handcarved bedposts mixed w/ period, Mission, Southwestern furnishings, rich fabrics. Dramatic, luxurious, unique. Some rooms—such as Moose Room w/ huge, nuzzling mooseheads—border on gaudy.

RATES, RESERVATIONS, & RESTRICTIONS

Deposit: 50%; refund w/ 21-day notice
Discounts: 3rd person; off-season room rates include dinner Fri./Sat. nights
Credit Cards: V, MC, D
Check-in/Out: Flexible, check w/ inn
Smoking: No
Pets: No; inn has 1 dog
Kids: No
Minimum Stay: 2 nights

Open: Dec. 28–Mar. 15; May 10–Oct. 25; check—may revise; summer/fall is high season
Hosts: Jennifer and Roger Cauchi
Upon Lily Bay Rd.
Greenville, ME 04441
(207) 695-4400
Fax: (207) 695-2281
lodge@moosehead.net
www.LodgeatMooseheadLake.com

LAKE HOUSE, Waterford

Overall: ★★★★	Room Quality: A	Value: C	Price: $140–$185

Once a stagecoach stop, then a hotel where Judy Garland, Mickey Rooney, Claudette Colbert, and other stars frolicked by the lake, today the inn is noted for elegant lodging, outdoor activities, and affordable prices. The host is the chef as well, and gourmet food and wine are as lovingly realized as the historic property itself, in this delightful rural village of 19th-century

white clapboard houses. Lakeside and mountains beckon from eight windows in the most romantic guest room: a 600-square-foot former ballroom, with curved ceilings and a claw-foot tub on a dramatic raised dais.

SETTING & FACILITIES

Location: On Rt. 35, 18 miles from Rt. 302, in tiny, pretty town
Near: Lakes, Mt. Washington Valley, White Mountains, L.L. Bean outlet, Shaker Village
Building: Gracious 1787 Greek Revival
Grounds: Gazebo; focus on lake and beach across street
Public Space: Sitting room, DR

Food & Drink: (MAP) Full breakfast; romantic dinner, creative menu; specialty: chicken Scala; award-winning wine cellar, wine-tasting events
Recreation: Water/snow sports, tennis, golf, hunting, horses, mountain and trail biking
Amenities & Services: Books, games, parties, event planning, disabled access

ACCOMMODATIONS

Units: 4 guest rooms, 1 single-room cottage
All Rooms: Bath, antiques, coffee maker
Some Rooms: Sitting area, desk, porch access
Bed & Bath: Antique beds, sizes vary; some claw-foot tubs, hairdryers, robes
Favorites: Grand Ballroom Suite—

spacious and airy, four-poster, tub open to room; Dudley House—cozy, romantic, cathedral ceiling, screened porch
Comfort & Decor: Room recently redone. Contemp. or mission furnishings w/ authentic Colonial, gleaming hardwoods, Oriental rugs. Original, spacious, romantic, airy.

RATES, RESERVATIONS, & RESTRICTIONS

Deposit: 1 night; refund w/ 14-day notice
Discounts: EP, 3rd, corp., group, longer stay

Credit Cards: MC, V, AE
Check-in/Out: Flexible/11
Smoking: No
Pets: No

Kids: Over 6
Minimum Stay: 3rd weekend in July and foliage weekends
Open: All year, except April and Nov.

Hosts: Michael Myers
Box 82, Routes 35 and 37
Waterford, ME 04088
(800) 223-4182 or (207) 583-4182
Fax: (207) 583-6078

New Hampshire

The Granite State's first settlers were the Algonquins, whose ancient names—Sunapee, Winnipesaukee, Ammonnoosuc—remain in many New Hampshire locales, lakes, and lodgings. These enlightened natives later instructed Europeans on basic survival tips to survive the rough winters and wilderness terrain of this ruggedly beautiful, mountainous area. (No guidebooks and no bed-and-breakfasts then.)

In 1775, fledgling independent New Hampshire sent three regiments of "Continentals" to fight with Washington for independence. New Hampshire was the first state to both declare its independence and adopt a state constitution. The 1819 state capitol in Concord is still in use. And New Hampshire remains the state with the first presidential primaries, a proud rite of early spring, every four years.

New Hampshire's motto, "Live Free or Die," is reflected not only in its history and tough spirit, but also in its outdoor resources and activities. From the small stretch of seacoast in the south, just above the Boston area, to the White Mountains, to the northern wilderness, there is much to help you live free—and easy. Recreation ranges from quiet fishing on a lake on one of the more than 100,000 state-owned acres, to skiing at more than 20 alpine resorts. Opportunities abound as well for hikers, hunters, golfers (86 courses!), traditional and off-road cyclists, and cross-country skiers.

Southern New Hampshire encompasses classic New England villages with commons and steepled churches in addition to busy, gritty towns. Here you'll find the still-bustling mid-seventeenth-century settlement of Portsmouth; the capital, Concord; outlet shopping in Manchester; and pretty Peterborough, which was Thornton Wilder's model for *Our Town*.

Heading slightly north to the Central New Hampshire/Lakes region, you'll find esteemed Dartmouth College in Hanover, the Newport Opera

House, and Mt. Sunapee State Park, with noteworthy skiing, hiking, and fishing. The region has more than 270 lakes and ponds for water recreation, and the Barnstormers, New Hampshire's oldest summer theater, for evening fun.

The northernmost third of the state is our Northern New Hampshire/White Mountains zone. As its name suggests, the region is dominated by the 780,000-acre White Mountain National Forest. Drive the Kancamagus Highway, ski from resort towns like Jackson, and view the turn-of-the-century summer grand hotels. The Great North Woods, at the top of the state, is a spectacular wilderness area of fishing, hunting, small-town pleasures, and wildlife watching.

Plenty of small accommodations range from basic lodges in the north to established inns in the mountains and lakes area, and historic properties and farmhouses scattered in villages and rural areas throughout New Hampshire. Costs remain generally low in this no-nonsense state, where the motto makes sense: The scenery is to die for, and although you may not live free, you can live cheap.

Zone 5
Southern New Hampshire

Southern New Hampshire delivers the charms of classic New England, with steepled white churches and village greens, and a short but sweet seacoast that may remind you of Maine's coast.

Start your visit in the east, just above the Massachusetts border, maybe cracking bright red lobster claws on a wooden table by the ocean. You can watch bobbing boats haul in their catch, walk for miles on breezy beaches, and set out into the cold Atlantic for deep-sea fishing. Or take in a bit of history: Odiorne Point State Park, in Rye, was the first European settlement in the state (founded in 1623, by Scottish fishermen). While there, leave some time for the Seacoast Science Center.

Fort Constitution Historic Site, in New Castle, was built in the 1600s and captured by the Revolutionary colonists in 1774. Nearby Fort Stark Historic Site also dates to the mid-eighteenth century. Make sure to save some time for antiquing (check out Route 4), shopping, going to the theater, biking, golfing, hiking, or whale watching.

A bit farther west, you'll find New Hampshire's most populated areas. Concord, the state capital, is home to the Museum of New Hampshire History and the State House. Manchester is the site of the See Science Center, the New Hampshire Philharmonic Orchestra, and the New Hampshire Symphony Orchestra.

In Derry, visit the Robert Frost Homestead with a romantic poet's path where you can stop and read a Frost poem at various spots as you stroll along. The 694-acre Canterbury Shaker Village dates to 1792. And this area has opportunities for boating, biking, swimming, fishing, and hiking.

In New Hampshire's southwest corner, you'll find the classic New England of movies and pictorial calendars. Hike up Mt. Monadnock, cross-country ski, or go for sleigh rides in the many state parks. Try out the summer theater, visit the children's museum, or spend time in one of the many historical museums. This is quiet, dreamy New England and is especially gorgeous in the fall.

Small lodgings are mainly in bed-and-breakfasts, homey and varied, from town mansions to rural old farmhouses.

For More Information

Monadnock Lodging Association
www.nhweb.com/monadnocklodging

Monadnock Travel Council
(603) 355-8155
fax: (603) 357-3529
www.virtualnh.com

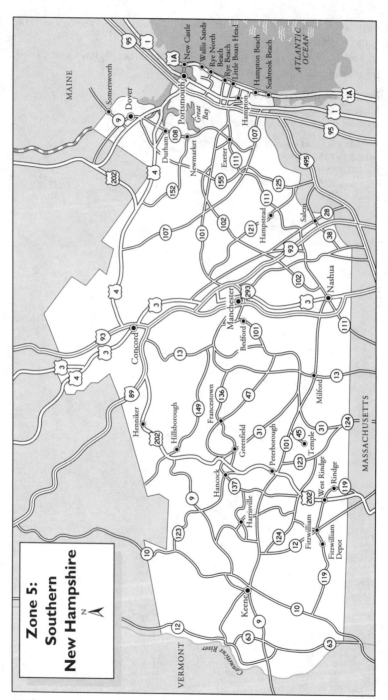

Zone 5:
New Hampshire

Fitzwilliam
Amos A. Parker House, 134
Ashburn House, 135
Hannah Davis House, 136

Francestown
Inn at Crotched Mountain, 137

Hancock
Hancock Inn, 138

Harrisville
Harrisville Squire's Inn, 139

Henniker
Colby Hill Inn, 141

Hillsborough
Inn at Maplewood Farm, 142

Milford
Ram in the Thicket, 143

Peterborough
Apple Gate Bed and Breakfast, 144

Temple
Birchwood Inn, 145

AMOS A. PARKER HOUSE, Fitzwilliam

Overall: ★★★★	Room Quality: B	Value: B	Price: $85–$95

The liberty pole out front designates that Revolutionaries once plotted on the site of this gray clapboard that has six wood-burning fireplaces and high-style, low-key decor. But it's the acre of gardens surrounded by marsh and woods that you'll remember most, with stone walls and walks, lily ponds, and hundreds of multi-hued annuals and perennials beckoning everything from butterflies to blue herons. Inside, the handpainted murals by local artists are also lovely. Almost-next-door neighbor Hannah Davis House is a big rival. Amos is friendlier, Hannah more refined, but both represent creative innkeeping.

SETTING & FACILITIES

Location: NH 119 to Fitzwilliam, less than .25 mi. from Rt. 12
Near: Sharon Arts Center, Fry's Measure Mill, Apple Hill Chamber Players, N.E. Marionette Theater, Mt. Monadnock, Cathedral of Pines
Building: 18th-century clapboard Colonial
Grounds: Extensive gardens, water lily pond, Oriental/Dutch features, unique plantings

Public Space: Parlor, DR, borning room, great room (c.1700), library, game room **Food & Drink:** Full formal breakfast; specialties: soufflés, puff-pancakes w/ caramelized apples, crepes; snacks: cookies, tea sandwiches, cheese, fruit
Recreation: Mt. Monadnock hiking, X-C skiing, tennis, swimming, water sports
Amenities & Services: Beach towels, hairdryers, maps, special requests

ACCOMMODATIONS

Units: 2 guest rooms, 2 suites
All Rooms: Bath, spec. toiletries (incl. razors)
Some Rooms: Fireplace, refrigerator (1), stove (1)
Bed & Bath: Beds vary, some four-posters; tubs
Favorites: Rear 2nd floor room—stenciled garden wall, brass/iron bed,

sitting room, view; 1st floor suite—fireplace, sitting area, Pullman kitchen
Comfort & Decor: Bright and immaculate. Designer touches, such as paper-doll collection. Elegant, tasteful, comfortable. Good lighting. A sure hand in decor and detailing.

RATES, RESERVATIONS, & RESTRICTIONS

Deposit: 1 night w/in 10 days of res.; refund w/ 14-day notice
Discounts: None
Credit Cards: None
Check-In/Out: 3–6/11

Smoking: No
Pets: No
Kids: OK
Minimum Stay: 2 nights some fall weekends

Open: All year
Hosts: Freda B. Houpt
146 NH Rt. 119 West, Box 202

Fitzwilliam, NH 03447
(603) 585-6540

ASHBURN HOUSE, Fitzwilliam

Overall: ★★★½	Room Quality: C	Value: C	Price: $80–$90

As these enthusiastic new innkeepers put it, in 1996 they "came to New England from Old England." And they brought with them some quirky, unusual collectibles, such as a wall of antique English insurance company firemarks, and a dining room table from the House of Commons. Back in London, Tina was a children's theatrical agent, and David an insurance executive. With the accents, the pub, the breakfasts of porridge, tomatoes, mushrooms, eggs, fried potatoes, toast, and marmalade, and the antiques and furnishings, you may think that you are far from this pretty village, across the Atlantic.

SETTING & FACILITIES

Location: 200 yds. off Rt. 119, in village center
Near: Fitzwilliam Inn (Old English-style bar, English beer); Old England Enterprises Antiques, performing arts, state forests, covered bridges, crafts, historic societies
Building: 1845 Colonial post-and-beam home
Grounds: Half-acre garden; lookout from Upper Troy Rd.

Public Space: 2 lounges (1 smoking), DR
Food & Drink: Early morning tea, coffee; English breakfast, communal or separate; specialties: jams; grilled bacon sausages, eggs; hot drinks and juices
Recreation: Mt. Monadnock trails, golf, water sports, fishing, hunting (w/ license), sleigh rides, berry picking
Amenities & Services: Fridge, irons, books, phone, fax, maps

ACCOMMODATIONS

Units: 3 guest rooms, 1 suite
All Rooms: Private or en suite bath
Some Rooms: Antiques
Bed & Bath: Queen, 2 twin beds; Country Room and Rose Room combine for suite; 2, showers only, 1 tub/shower combo

Favorites: Blue Room—English Victorian antique queen bed, en suite bath, fireplace; Rose Room—similar w/ priv. bath
Comfort & Decor: English antiques and paintings. 2 baths w/ stenciling. Modest, neat, smallish, cheerful.

RATES, RESERVATIONS, & RESTRICTIONS

Deposit: Refund w/ 7-day notice
Discounts: Singles

Credit Cards: V, MC
Check-In/Out: 3:30/11; flexible

Smoking: Lounge
Pets: Dogs; ask on others; gentle in-house St. Bernard restricted if nec., off-limits in guest rooms
Kids: Depends on age and number
Minimum Stay: None
Open: Closed Christmas Eve/Day, Boxing Day

Hosts: Tina and David Ashton
20 Upper Troy Rd.
Fitzwilliam, NH 03447
(603) 585-7198
Fax: (603) 585-6919
ash@top.monad.net

HANNAH DAVIS HOUSE, Fitzwilliam

Overall: ★★★★	Room Quality: B	Value: A	Price: $60–$115

This lovely little village is filled with renovated historic homes such as this one. Guest rooms surprise with unexpected pleasures, and although public space may be limited, the breakfasts aren't. Solo travelers may especially appreciate the spicy aromas and casual environment in the big kitchen, as warm, helpful Kaye chats with guests while preparing new recipes or old favorites. You might be served sourdough French toast stuffed with peaches and cream or with blueberry-strawberry sauce or perhaps scrambled eggs, country ham, potatoes with Portobello mushrooms and chives, and green beans from the garden. Or perhaps stir-fried chicken in crepes, or . . .

SETTING & FACILITIES

Location: S of Keene on NH 119 W, near town common
Near: Antiquing, beach, nature areas, historic district
Building: Restored 1820 Federal clapboard
Grounds: Smallish; overlooks beaver pond
Public Space: Open-kitchen entrance, breakfast area; small parlor; dining area; screened porch

Food & Drink: Extravagant breakfast; specialties: homemade sausage, homemade granola w/ chunky applesauce, lemon-poppy seed or cinnamon-raisin bread; afternoon tea; spec. diets accom.
Recreation: Canoeing, golf, hunting, horses, skiing, swimming
Amenities & Services: Some disabled access (visual, hearing impaired), maps, turndown, billiards

ACCOMMODATIONS

Units: 3 guest rooms, 3 suites (1 in Carriage Barn)
All Rooms: Bath, clock, radio
Some Rooms: Wood-burning fireplace, sitting room, sofa bed, extra bed, priv. entrance, porch

Bed & Bath: Mostly queens, one king, double beds, antique iron beds, some canopy; most w/ tubs and showers, pedestal sinks, footed tubs; some oversize showers

Favorites: Popovers—above garage, vaulted ceiling, antique cannonball bed, 2-sided fireplace, deck and walkway "pop over" backyard and bog; The Loft—former carriage house, spacious duplex, beams, barn siding, fireplace

Comfort & Decor: Room size and decor vary, many w/ antique iron and cannonball beds, high ceilings, pedestal porcelain sinks, footed or iron tubs. Some exposed timbers, Southwest feeling. Airy and bright. Natural woodwork.

RATES, RESERVATIONS, & RESTRICTIONS

Deposit: 50% w/in 5 days of res., or credit card; refund w/ 10-day notice
Discounts: 3rd person, singles
Credit Cards: MC, V, D
Check-In/Out: 3–6/11; call for late arrival
Smoking: Outside porches only
Pets: No; in-house cat, 2 dogs
Kids: No

No-No's: No shows (pay full cost of rooms)
Minimum Stay: 2 nights, some college weekends, some holidays, fall foliage
Open: All year
Hosts: Kaye and Mike Terpstra
Route 119, 186 Depot Rd.
Fitzwilliam, NH 03447
(603) 585-3344

INN AT CROTCHED MOUNTAIN, Francestown

Overall: ★★★★	Room Quality: B	Value: B	Price: $75–$120

On the north side of Crotched Mountain, 1,300 feet above sea level at the end of a winding path, is this way-out-of-the-way inn, built as a farmhouse in 1822. The builder was an Abolitionist who dug a tunnel from the cellar to the road and sheltered slaves on their escape north. Today, you can escape here (without political consequences) to relax, swim, play tennis, meander, and enjoy the flowers, the Indonesian-influenced food and the panoramic view. Crotched Mountain, by the way, takes its name from the shape of the twin peaks to the south.

SETTING & FACILITIES

Location: Rt. 136 to Francestown, 3.5 mi. from center of Francestown, on side of Crotched Mountain.
Near: Mt. Monadnock, Sharon Arts Center, Petersborough Players, Franklin Pierce Homestead, antiquing, outlet shopping, summer theater
Building: Colonial 1822 private farmhouse estate, rebuilt mid-1930s after fire

Grounds: Expansive, walking/X-C ski trails; vegetable, herb, flower gardens; 40-mile view of Piscataquog Valley
Public Space: 2 sitting rooms, 2 DRs, cocktail lounge; most disabled access.
Food & Drink: Full breakfast; specialties: fruit, French toast; hot drinks; cookies; dinner holidays, Fri., Sat. (extra) open to public w/ seasonal

menu; specialties: cranberry Port pot roast, plum chicken; liquor license
Recreation: Ice-skating, 2 clay tennis courts, wading and 30′ x 50′ pool on site; downhill skiing, mountain climbing nearby

Amenities & Services: Irons, games, wheelchair access, meetings (18), fax, maps

ACCOMMODATIONS

Units: 13 guest rooms
All Rooms: Radio/alarm clock
Some Rooms: Fireplace, wheelchair access (2)
Bed & Bath: Queen, double, 2 twin beds; 8 priv. baths, 6 full, 5 shower only, 2 half baths

Favorites: Room 9—fireplace, door to backyard w/ pool access, great views
Comfort & Decor: Country decor w/ antiques and Colonial reproductions. Worn but comfortable. Many w/ great views. Quiet.

RATES, RESERVATIONS, & RESTRICTIONS

Deposit: Full, 1 night; 2–4 nights, 1st and last; 50% other; all w/in 7 days of booking; refund w/ 14-day notice; other w/ rerental (fee)
Discounts: Midweek 3+ nights; May–Aug., 3+; 3rd person, singles
Credit Cards: None
Check-In/Out: 2/11; call for arrivals after 11
Smoking: Rooms nonsmoking
Pets: OK w/ $5 fee; in-house English cockers, off-limits in guest rooms

Kids: OK
Minimum Stay: Prefer 2 nights on weekends, 3 on holiday weekends
Open: Closed 3 weeks in Nov., April
Hosts: Rose and John Perry
534 Mountain Rd.
Francestown, NH 03043
(603) 588-6840
Fax: (603) 588-6623
www.Innbook.com

HANCOCK INN, Hancock

Overall: ★★★★½	Room Quality: B	Value: B	Price: $106–$172

The oldest inn in the state, it has been in continuous operation since 1789, when George Washington first became president. Back then, guests arrived in Concord coaches and often in sleighing parties. Named the Jefferson Tavern until the late 1800s, the inn enlarged when the railroad came in. TV cozies (like tea cozies), hand-sewn quilts, and superb 19th-century wall paintings are authentic charms. The American cuisine is satisfying, and theirs is a test kitchen for the *Old Farmers Almanac*. Named after founding father John, who once owned much of the land here, both the inn and the whole town (with a steeple bell by Paul Revere) are on the National Register of Historic Places.

SETTING & FACILITIES

Location: Across the street from the general store on Main St.

Near: Walk to Meeting House w/ Paul Revere bell, orig. schoolhouse, cemetery, Norway Pond; Mt. Monadnock, Pitcher Mountain, shopping, Marionette Theater, MacDowell Artists Colony, antiquing, Harrisville, Audubon Sanctuary, Gibson Pewter, Frye's Measure Mill, crafts, galleries, music, theater

Building: 1789 columned clapboard inn

Grounds: In-town, small, landscaped

Public Space: Parlor, LR, garden

room, tavern, DR

Food & Drink: Full breakfast; specialties: granola, apple-cheddar breakfast pie, Whispering coffee cake; dinner specialties: Shaker cranberry pot roast, roasted maple duck; pre-/post-dinner drinks in the tavern

Recreation: Boating/swimming in pond, beach, skiing, blueberry/apple picking, golf, tennis

Amenities & Services: 24-hour entry, map of local attractions, kayak rental nearby, online newsletter, packing picnics

ACCOMMODATIONS

Units: 11 guest rooms

All Rooms: Bath, AC, TV, phone, cassette player

Some Rooms: Wood stove, fireplace, mural, 19th-century stencils

Bed & Bath: 2 twins, doubles, most queens, some antique, some four-posters, some canopies; soaking tubs, tub/showers, showers only

Favorites: Moses Eaton Room—full, orig. Moses Eaton wall stencil, queen four-poster, gas stove, fireplace, tub, shower

Comfort & Decor: Period details like stencils and wall paintings, wood stoves and antique tubs. Size varies from cozy to spacious. Some handmade quilts; most full baths.

RATES, RESERVATIONS, & RESTRICTIONS

Deposit: Full payment 1 night, others 50%; refund w/ 15-day notice (30 days, stays of 6+ nights)

Discounts: Corporate; check

Credit Cards: V, MC, AE, D

Check-In/Out: 2/11

Smoking: No

Pets: No; in-house springer spaniel

Kids: 12 and up

Minimum Stay: Some weekends

Open: All year

Hosts: Linda and Joe Johnston
33 Main St.
Hancock, NH 03449
(800) 525-1789, (603) 525-3318
Fax: (603) 525-9301
innkeeper@hancockinn.com
www.hancockinn.com

HARRISVILLE SQUIRE'S INN, Harrisville

Overall: ★★★½	Room Quality: C	Value: C	Price: $80–$90

This working mill town is a National Historic Landmark, one of the few in New Hampshire, and this bed-and-breakfast is a fine example of a nineteenth-century farm complex. You won't need lunch—or maybe even dinner—after the five-course farm breakfast, starting with fresh fruit and ending with a dessert such as apple crisp. Some special features at this comfortable bed-and-breakfast: Monadnock Bicycle Touring, which plans bike tours, and a three-story barn that houses a gallery, studio, and gift shop, featuring paintings by host Pat, local artists, and former guests. Oh, and Pat is a justice of the peace in case you want to wed.

SETTING & FACILITIES

Location: Rt. 101 in Dublin, right at fire station; follow 3 mi.; left at fork; inn .3 mi. on right
Near: Antiquing, Appalachian Mt. Trail, Mt. Monadnock, theaters, museums
Building: 15-room 1842 farmhouse, barn
Grounds: 50 acres: gardens, meditation/wedding garden, hot tub, fields, trails, woods
Public Space: DR, LR, 2nd floor sitting area

Food & Drink: Family-style communal breakfast; specialties: quiche w/ tomato, peach cobbler, pears Rosamonde; refreshments, cheese and crackers
Recreation: 10K of groomed X-C skiing, hiking on site; winter sports, sleigh rides, golf, beach, nearby
Amenities & Services: Hot tub, catering, weddings, special events, custom day and overnight bike tours

ACCOMMODATIONS

Units: 5 guest rooms; 2 houses on lake (weekly, summer; 2+ nights spring/fall)
All Rooms: Bath, sitting area, heat control, garden view, clock, radio
Some Rooms: Bath w/ skylight (2), disabled access (1)
Bed & Bath: Beds vary, some antique, iron/brass; 1 dbl. shower, 1 whirlpool; 1 bath outside room

Favorites: Room 3—English-style paper/furnishings, skylight, whirlpool, beams; Room 5—queen and twin, large, TV, spacious, bath skylight
Comfort & Decor: Like grandma's: spacious and uncluttered w/ views of fields, gardens, forest. Comfortable, styles from Colonial to modern. Floral prints, wicker. Modern baths.

RATES, RESERVATIONS, & RESTRICTIONS

Deposit: Refund w/ 7-day notice
Discounts: No
Credit Cards: V, MC
Check-In/Out: 3/11; call for arrival after 10 p.m.
Smoking: Some areas
Pets: No
Kids: 8 and up
Minimum Stay: Some weekends

Open: All year
Hosts: Pat and Doug McCarthy
Keene Rd., Box 19
Harrisville, NH 03450
(603) 827-3925
Fax: (603) 827-3622
squiresinnbb@top.monad.net
www.nhweb.com/squires_inn

COLBY HILL INN, Henniker

Overall: ★★★½	Room Quality: B	Value: C	Price: $85–$330

This comfortable, informal inn, operated by the Days, is a family endeavor about as far as you can get from a chain motel. Son-in-law Michael Mack is a Culinary Institute of America graduate, and the cuisine features lots of fish, seafood, and homemade desserts. Easter and Thanksgiving feasts are offered. The wood-paneled dining room takes on a romantic glow in candlelight, and both the food and the view seem endless at breakfast, with a glass wall overlooking the meadowlike lawn of this former farmhouse and stage coach stop. The Days are gracious innkeepers who enjoy gabbing and helping out.

SETTING & FACILITIES

Location: 17 mi. W of Concord off Rt. 202/9; .5 mi. from center of town
Near: Covered bridge, river, Canterbury Shaker Village, New England College
Building: Circa 1800 white country inn, tavern, farmhouse
Grounds: 6 acres of barns, fields, gardens, pool, skating rink, carriage house, gazebo, fountains, statuary
Public Space: Spacious parlor, game room, DR
Food & Drink: Full country breakfast; a specialty: scrambled eggs w/ Boursin cheese in puff pastry. Dinner (extra), American w/ cont'l flair; a specialty: chicken Colby Hill w/ lobster; hot drinks, cookies; full beverage service, wine list
Recreation: Outdoor pool, lawn games on site; tennis, skiing, kayaking, biking nearby
Amenities & Services: Lobby and DR have disabled access, irons; group functions (32); business services: fax, overhead, easels

ACCOMMODATIONS

Units: 16 guest rooms, 2 suites
All Rooms: Bath, AC, phone, fan, dataport, some toiletries
Some Rooms: Wood-burning fireplace
Bed & Bath: Queens, kings, two twins; some canopies, new mattresses; some tubs
Favorites: Room 3—large upstairs corner room, king brass/iron bed, wood-burning stove, tub/shower combo
Comfort & Decor: Rooms indiv. decorated w/ antiques, wallpaper. Decorated as a gentleman's farm. Each room w/ different color linens. Comfortable rather than luxurious.

RATES, RESERVATIONS, & RESTRICTIONS

Deposit: Credit card holds room; 3-day cancel. policy; travel agency booking OK
Discounts: Singles, 3rd person
Credit Cards: MC, V, AE, D, DC
Check-In/Out: 2/11
Smoking: Outdoors
Pets: No; in-house dogs
Kids: 7 and up

Minimum Stay: Some holiday
weekends
Open: All year
Hosts: Ellie and John Day, Laurel Day-
Mack
3 The Oaks, Box 779

Henniker, NH 03242
(603) 428-3281, (800) 531-0330
Fax: (603) 428-9218
info@colbyhillinn.com
www.colbyhillinn.com

INN AT MAPLEWOOD FARM, Hillsborough

Overall: ★★★★	Room Quality: B	Value: B	Price: $75–$135

This must be the only bed-and-breakfast in the world with a collection of
old radios—and its very own station, Radio Maplewood Farm. Jayme collected cassettes of over 1,000 vintage shows like "The Shadow" and broad-
casts them throughout the house on a low-power transmitter. Other specialties? Laura's breakfast fantasies, featured in cookbooks—cantaloupe and
strawberry soup, orange-oatmeal flan with maple caramel sauce, goat
cheese frittata. Old-fashioned touches, such as milk in glass bottles (the
milk perhaps produced from the cows grazing beyond), and stylish faux-
painted rugs add more flavor to the inn. There's an antique store on the
property, homemade chocolates are provided in suites . . . and so on.

SETTING & FACILITIES

Location: 89N to 9W; .5 mi. from
Historic Hillsborough Center; 30 min.
from Concord
Near: Fox State Forest, historic area,
beaches, antiquing, auctions
Building: Pretty 1794 early Federal;
restored 1998; listed w/ National
Historic Register
Grounds: 14 acres, forest, fields,
organic garden, cows, brook, patio

Public Space: Entrance, LR, DR
Food & Drink: Basket Big Band
Breakfast; specialties: scones, cream-
basil shirred eggs; tea; special diets
Recreation: Golf, hunting, horseback
riding, water sports, horseshoes
Amenities & Services: Some disabled
access (hearing impaired), fruit basket,
stocked refrigerator, Port, tennis rackets,
bike rental; fax, copier, small meetings.

ACCOMMODATIONS

Units: 4 suites
All Rooms: Bath, vintage radio, sit-
ting/writing area, mini-library, phone,
amenities basket, robes
Some Rooms: Fireplace (all but 1),
deck (2), 4-person capacity (2)
Bed & Bath: King/queen beds,
wrought-iron, canopies; 2 tubs
Favorites: Front suite, main house—
canopied iron bed, fireplace, skylights;

Upstairs suite, barn—2 BRs, cathedral,
spindle bed, views
Comfort & Decor: Antiques.
Homemade candies, cordials by bed.
Environmentally green rooms available.
Radio Maplewood Farm accessible in
rooms. Skylights, views. Barn suites spacious. Thoughtful, stylish, special. Good
lighting, seating areas.

RATES, RESERVATIONS, & RESTRICTIONS

Deposit: Credit card or 50%; full refund w/ 14-day notice
Discounts: 3rd person, corp., longer stays, pkg. weekends incl. free instruction in orienteering and skiing
Credit Cards: MC, V, AE, DC, D
Check-In/Out: 2–6/11; late arrivals call ahead
Smoking: No
Pets: No
Kids: With advance notice

Minimum Stay: Holidays, special weekends
Open: May 1–early Dec.
Hosts: Jayme Henriques Simoes and Laura Simoes
447 Center Rd.
Hillsborough, NH 03244
(603) 464-4242, (800) 644-6693
Fax: (603) 464-4242
jsimoes@conknet.com
www.conknet.com/maplewoodfarm

RAM IN THE THICKET, Milford

Overall: ★★★	Room Quality: C	Value: B	Price: $60–$75

Sheep are here and a couple of horses, but the inn's name refers to the owners' quest for a substitute to their life in the Midwest; the Old Testament story is that Abraham finds "a ram caught in a thicket" and sacrifices it instead of his son, Isaac. Andrew and Priscilla bought the mansion in 1977, restored and renovated it, adding an indoor pool, and as a nod to their Dutch heritage, Delft tiles in the dining room (where the cuisine is international). Andrew enjoys a quip: "We have shared baths, but you don't have to share them at the same time." And as for the decor, "We don't call it Victorian. We think Queen Victoria was quite stuffy."

SETTING & FACILITIES

Location: 200 feet off Rt. 101, just W of Milford; 10 mi. from Nashua
Near: Flea markets, antiquing, beach, nature areas, Mt. Monadnock, American Stage Festival, film, galleries
Building: 1870 Victorian mansion
Grounds: 8 acres, gardens
Public Space: Lounge, sitting room, 4 DRs, porch, screened porch

Food & Drink: Cont'l breakfast; dinner; homemade breads, pasta, veal, pork; changes frequently; spec. diets accom.; full bar
Recreation: Canoeing, golf, hunting, horses, skiing, balloon rides
Amenities & Services: Fridge access, irons, hairdryers, tennis racket rental; unheated indoor pool, whirlpool; meetings (30), business lunches (10+)

ACCOMMODATIONS

Units: 9 guest rooms
All Rooms: Original detailing, period pieces
Some Rooms: Bath (3), fireplace

Bed & Bath: Beds vary, most doubles, some canopies, four-posters; some tubs
Favorites: Canopy Room—floral paper, canopy bed, claw-foot tub, good sun

Comfort & Decor: Some rooms combine for families. Many turn-of-the-century details, antiques. Size varies. Old-world European charm. Basic, old-fashioned.

RATES, RESERVATIONS, & RESTRICTIONS

Deposit: 50%; refund w/ 1-day notice, unless full
Discounts: Singles, 3rd person
Credit Cards: AE; checks preferred
Check-In/Out: No specified check-in/12
Smoking: Lounge, some rooms
Pets: OK ($10); in-house cat and dog
Kids: OK

Minimum Stay: None
Open: All year
Hosts: Andrew and Priscilla Tempelman
24 Maple St.
Milford, NH 03055
(603) 654-6440
aretee@jlc.net
www.jlc.net/~aretee/ram

APPLE GATE BED AND BREAKFAST, Peterborough

Overall: ★★★	Room Quality: C	Value: C	Price: $65–$80

Across from an orchard, with a gated picket fence, this little bed-and-breakfast's name was an obvious choice, but another could be "The Little Apple." The theme is carried out sweetly and crisply (sorry) with apple pancakes on apple-patterned plates and room names, including Granny Smith and Cortland. All rooms have apple chips to munch, the dog is named Macintosh, and there are apple games and wooden apples in the window. In the spring the orchards are especially beautiful, and you can pick apples in the fall. But thankfully, the basic, comfortable rooms are decorated in decidedly non-fruity country furnishings and fabrics.

SETTING & FACILITIES

Location: 2 mi. from downtown Peterborough, by country road; across from apple orchards
Near: Concerts in the Park, theater, country fairs, harvest festivals, antiquing, auctions, Cathedral in the Pines, 6 covered bridges, Peterborough Basket Company, Pickity Place in Mason, Mt. Monadnock State Park, Sharon Arts Center
Building: 1832 Colonial farmhouse
Grounds: 3 acres, gardens, woods, hammock

Public Space: DR, parlor, music/reading room, porch
Food & Drink: Full candlelight breakfast; specialties: baked pancakes, French toast w/ sautéed apples; special meals avail.; coffee area
Recreation: Fishing, maple sugaring, berry/apple picking, skiing, sleigh rides
Amenities & Services: Irons, refrigerator, games, books, maps, bikes, canoe, ski rental nearby

ACCOMMODATIONS

Units: 4 guest rooms
All Rooms: Bath, sitting area
Some Rooms: Stenciling, nonworking fireplace
Bed & Bath: 2 twins, queens, ¾ bed; 1 tub, 1 tub/shower, 2 showers, robes

Favorites: Granny Smith—large front corner, overlooks orchard, built-in desk, Laura Ashley fabrics
Comfort & Decor: Period farmhouse decor. Braided rugs, dried wreaths, ruffled curtains, wide floorboards. Front rooms sunniest. Macintosh, smallest.

RATES, RESERVATIONS, & RESTRICTIONS

Deposit: 1 night; refund w/ 7-day notice
Discounts: Singles
Credit Cards: MC, V
Check-In/Out: 3/11
Smoking: Porch, outside only
Pets: No; in-house dog, cat
Kids: Over 12
No-No's: More than 2 to a room

Minimum Stay: 2 nights summer and fall weekends
Open: All year
Hosts: Dianne and Ken Legenhausen
199 Upland Farm Rd.
Peterborough, NH 03458
(603) 924-6543
Fax: (603) 924-1633

BIRCHWOOD INN, Temple

Overall: ★★★   Room Quality: C   Value: C   Price: $60–$79

Thoreau stayed here (escaping the solitude of Walden Pond, perhaps), and the inn has housed the Temple post office, a general store, the town meeting hall, and an antique shop. In one form or another it has been the centerpiece of this pretty village since around the time of the Revolution. Judy and Bill haven't been innkeepers here quite that long (more like 20 years), but their touch is reflected in the way things hum and the tales they can tell.

SETTING & FACILITIES

Location: 1.5 mi. off Rt. 101, on Rt. 45, on Common in center of village
Near: Antiquing, Mt. Monadnock, summer theater, Monadnock Music Series, Cathedral of the Pines
Building: 1775 Federal brick inn; addition
Grounds: Porch, woods incl. birches, lilacs
Public Space: DR, 2 sitting areas, TV room

Food & Drink: Full country breakfast; dinner, blackboard menu, (extra; reservations), BYOB, open to public, country American cuisine w/ homemade soups, breads, desserts
Recreation: Skiing, horses, hayrides, antiquing, trout fishing, hunting
Amenities & Services: Puzzle table, games, toy trains, antique Steinway grand piano

ACCOMMODATIONS

Units: 7 guest rooms
All Rooms: TV
Some Rooms: Priv. baths (5)
Bed & Bath: Twin, queen, double beds; showers only
Favorites: Seashore—overlooks village; Thoreau—because he reputedly stayed here

Comfort & Decor: Rooms decorated by theme: music, train, editorial, library, general store, school, seashore, w/ coordinated furnishings. Braided rugs on hardwood floors. TVs a plus for most. One ground floor, disabled accessible room. Comfortable, basic, and homey.

RATES, RESERVATIONS, & RESTRICTIONS

Deposit: 1 night; refund w/ 14-day notice
Discounts: 3rd person (1 room only)
Credit Cards: None
Check-In/Out: 2/11
Smoking: No
Pets: No
Kids: Over 10
Minimum Stay: 2–3 days, weekends Sept./Oct.

Open: All year except 2 weeks in Nov. and April
Hosts: Judy and Bill Wolfe
Box 197
Temple, NH 03084
(603) 878-3285
Fax: (603) 878-2159
wolfe@birchwood.mv.com
virtualcities.com

Zone 6
Central New Hampshire
& Lakes

Stretching from the Connecticut River to the Maine border, the Central New Hampshire/Lakes region is home to rural retreats, water sports, skiing, and hills. The Dartmouth/Lake Sunapee area, stretching to the west near the Vermont border, is filled with rural villages and farming areas, now often catering to tourists or weekenders. The best-known town around is Hanover, home to Dartmouth College, with its world-class cultural offerings and seasonal festivities such as Winter Carnival.

The area is also known for Mount Sunapee State Park, with skiing, and nearby Lake Sunapee's fishing and water sports. Northwest of the lake lie New London and the Barn Playhouse, well known for summer theater. Enfield has a Shaker settlement. In Newbury, check out the Fells Historic Site at the John Hay National Wildlife Refuge, or visit Charlestown's Fort at No. 4 with its reconstructed stockade.

To the east are almost 300 lakes and ponds, providing opportunities for all sorts of water sports. Open vistas of hills reflect in the water; climb up for fabulous views or drive around the lakes for the scenery. Swim, boat, fish, ski, or take a lake cruise. And if you don't mind winter weather, try ice fishing or ice sailing, or if you're really adventurous, ice auto-racing.

But the area isn't all water or winter. Milton houses the New Hampshire Farm Museum, and there's Wakefield's Museum of Childhood where adults as well as children will discover how to uncover some of the mysteries of life. The region also has plenty of craftspeople and galleries with unique gifts.

Lodging is plentiful and unpretentious in this part of the state, with a large proportion of inns. People have been coming here for decades, spending a week or so enjoying the natural assets, eating good food, and getting away from crowds. Bed-and-breakfasts, mostly refurbished Victorians, are clustered near towns, where the proud homeowners once went to work.

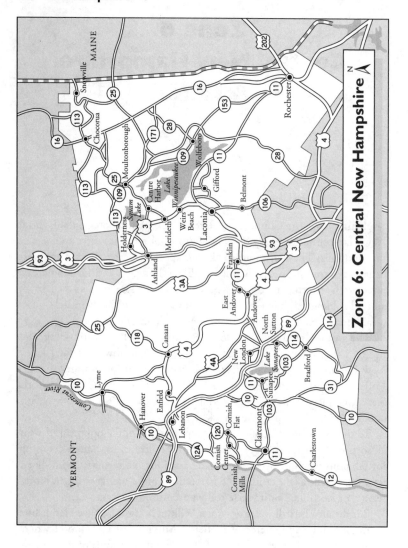

Zone 6: Central New Hampshire

You can feel the personal history of these places, no matter how many layers of paint have been applied.

For More Information

Lakes Region B&B Association
www.virtualcities.com/nh/lakesregion.htm

Sunapee Vacations
Sunapee Lodging Bureau
Box 400
Sunapee, NH 03782
(800) 258-3530
www.sunapeevacations.com
email: sunapeevacations@sugar-river.net

GLYNN HOUSE INN, Ashland

Overall: ★★★★	Room Quality: B	Value: C	Price: $85–$165

If you like Victoriana, you'll love Glynn House, which is quintessentially so, inside and out, from the top of the turret to the expansive, wraparound porch, and within every cozy nook and cranny. But the hosts are decidedly modern, with experience in the food business and in marketing, and their skills shine through at breakfast and in the little touches that make a place memorable. They love to collect antiques, and the oak-paneled rooms are filled with treasures massive and tiny. Savvy care and attention to detail make a fine transition from this turn-of-the-century to the last.

SETTING & FACILITIES

Location: About a mile off I-93 Exit 24, on quiet, tree-lined street on the edge of town
Near: Franconia State Park, White Mountains, Squam Lake (*On Golden Pond* lake), Lake Winnepesaukee, Science Center of NH, Lakes Region Summer Theatre, Keepsake Quilting, antiquing, outlets
Building: 1896 Queen Anne Victorian
Grounds: 1.5 acres, carriage house, garden, flowers

Public Space: Sitting room, DR, foyer, porch
Food & Drink: Morning coffee/tea; full communal breakfast; specialties: eggs Benedict, apple strudel, Belgian waffles, stuffed French toast, omelets; snacks, wine, sherry avail.
Recreation: Board games, canoeing, boating, skiing, snowshoeing
Amenities & Services: Video library, microwave, beach towels, fax, dataports; Polish, Russian spoken

ACCOMMODATIONS

Units: 5 guest rooms, 4 suites
All Rooms: Bath, AC, TV/VCR, clock/radio/tape player, zone heating
Some Rooms: Mountaintop views, fireplace, sitting room
Bed & Bath: Mostly queen beds, some canopies, four-posters; some tub/shower combos, some dbl. whirlpools

Favorites: Room A—2nd floor, half circle, queen canopy, whirlpool; Room H—1st floor, lace-canopied bed, fireplace, dbl. whirlpool; Carriage House suites
Comfort & Decor: Rooms indiv. decorated in Victorian style; not too fussy, but not for minimalists. Chocolates, romantic touches. Ornate florals. Immaculate.

RATES, RESERVATIONS, & RESTRICTIONS

Deposit: 50%; 14-day cancel. policy; travel agency booking except during foliage
Discounts: Seniors, off-season, 3rd person, singles

Credit Cards: MC, V
Check-In/Out: 3–11/11
Smoking: Not in bedrooms
Pets: No; in-house dog and 2 cats (never in inn)

Kids: Quiet, well-behaved, in some rooms
No-No's: Check-out after 11 a.m.
Minimum Stay: 2 nights most weekends, holidays, foliage
Open: All year

Hosts: Karol and Betsy Paterman
43 Highland St., Box 719
Ashland, NH 03217
(603) 968-3775, (800) 637-9599
Fax: (603) 968-3129
glynnhse@lr.net
www.nettx.com/glynnhouse/

ROSEWOOD COUNTRY INN, Bradford

Overall: ★★★½	Room Quality: B	Value: C	Price: $75–$175

Once a summer resort hosting celebs such as Jack London, Gloria Swanson, Mary Pickford, and Charlie Chaplin, it was abandoned for years until Leslie and Dick renovated it into an all-year property with stenciled walls and a country tavern. Special here are the creative packages, holiday, and annual events. For example: Mother and Daughter Weekends; The Intimate Escape (champagne, fruit, cheese, and crackers in room on arrival); Weekend Getaway for Gourmet Cooks; and Dickens Christmas Weekend with horse-drawn wagon rides, a homemade liquor demonstration, a Christmas floral workshop, and dinner and fireside storytelling with a professional storyteller.

SETTING & FACILITIES

Location: Rt. 114 through Bradford, to Pleasant View Rd, on a hill
Near: Mt. Sunapee skiing, Lake Sunapee cruise boats, Shaker villages, NH Int'l Speedway, Kearsarge Indian Museum, John Hay Estate, summer theater, concerts, Dartmouth College
Building: Country Victorian
Grounds: 12 acres: meadows, woods, gazebo, pond, award-winning gardens, wild deer and turkeys, organic garden
Public Space: Tavern Room: BYOB bar; 2 formal LRs, DR; reception room

(85); all public rooms and 1 public bath disabled-accessible
Food & Drink: "Candlelight and crystal" breakfast; specialties: ham/asparagus quiche, Belgian waffles w/ bananas Foster and praline sauce, plum pudding; wine, hors d'oeuvres; soda, water
Recreation: Winter sports, fishing; nearby downhill skiing, golf, swimming, boating, antiquing
Amenities & Services: Fridge, irons, picnic baskets, papers, fax, weddings

ACCOMMODATIONS

Units: 3 guest rooms, 8 suites
All Rooms: Bath, clock, radio
Some Rooms: AC, fireplace, TV/VCR, hairdryer, thermostat, sitting area, separate dressing room (1)

Bed & Bath: Twin, double, queen, some canopies, four-posters, Old Hickory; some tub/shower, some dbl. showers and whirlpools, some dbl. sinks

Favorites: Dreamcatcher—3rd floor, Lake Placid Lodge decor; beamed cathedral, fireplace, dbl. whirlpool, AC, TV/VCR; Mary Pickford Suite—2nd floor corner, fireplace, views

Comfort & Decor: Emphasis on suites, whirlpools, fireplaces. Upgrading continuous. Views from all rooms; country-Victorian decoration. Comfortable rather than luxurious.

RATES, RESERVATIONS, & RESTRICTIONS

Deposit: Full payment 1–2 nights, 50% for 3+ nights; refund w/ 14-day notice
Discounts: 3rd person, long stays
Credit Cards: MC, V, AE
Check-In/Out: 3–8/11
Smoking: Outside porch and deck only
Pets: No; in-house collie (in owners' quarters)
Kids: Over 10
Minimum Stay: None

Open: All year, closed 2 weeks after Easter
Hosts: Lesley and Dick Marquis
67 Pleasant View Rd.
Bradford, NH 03221
(603) 938-5253, (603) 938-5220, (800) 938-6273
Fax: (603) 938-5253
rosewood@conknet.com
www.bbonline.com/nh/rosewood/

RED HILL INN, Centre Harbor

Overall: ★★★½	Room Quality: C	Value: C	Price: $105–$175

This comfortable country inn on a hill hosted the Duke of Bavaria in the 1940s, but usually caters to just plain folks who want to relax and play. Rooms are spread among an 1850 farmhouse, the main inn, and adjacent cottages. Decor is a mix, with beams, oak paneling and picture windows—culminating in a bar constructed from half a boat and a wall of license plates. A swimming pool is due by the summer of 2000, to add to the many water sports already enjoyed at nearby Squam Lake. Chef Stefan Ryll serves what he calls "New England gourmet" cuisine, based on local, seasonal products, and herbs from the garden. Sunday Brunch is lavish, with everything from omelets to duck to lamb chops.

SETTING & FACILITIES

Location: 2 hrs. N of Boston on I-93, 5 mi. from Lake Winnipesaukee
Near: Canterbury Shaker Village, antique/craft/factory stores, Lake Winnipesaukee, Squam Lake, covered bridges, Mountains and Kancamagus Hwy., Red Hill climbing
Building: 100-year-old brick mansion

Grounds: 60 acres: nature preserve, sports field, pond, 4-person outdoor hot tub, herb garden
Public Space: Lounge; spacious LR, DR
Food & Drink: Full country breakfast; buffet or a la carte, candlelight dinner; specialties: shrimp scampi, lemon-

meringue pie; wine list; lighter dinner in lounge, cocktails
Recreation: X-C skiing, swimming on site; nearby water sports, downhill skiing

Amenities & Services: Maps; weddings/events; X-C ski rental

ACCOMMODATIONS

Units: 16 guest rooms, 5 suites, in inn, farmhouse, and cottage
All Rooms: Bath, phone
Some Rooms: AC, fireplace, priv. balcony, sitting area, desk
Bed & Bath: Beds vary; some dbl. whirlpools, some tubs

Favorites: Fireplace rooms—spacious, views of mountains and lakes, 5 w/ whirlpools
Comfort & Decor: Rooms vary in size and decor. Named after mountains. Antiques, wood floors; some high ceilings, exposed beams. Some gorgeous views.

RATES, RESERVATIONS, & RESTRICTIONS

Deposit: 50% w/in 10 days; 14-day cancel. policy w/ fee or rerental
Discounts: 3rd person, singles; theme pkgs
Credit Cards: MC, V, AE, D
Check-In/Out: 3/11
Smoking: OK (not in DR)
Pets: No
Kids: 10 and older
Minimum Stay: 2 nights weekends,

some holidays longer
Open: All year
Hosts: Rick Miller, Don Leavitt
RFD #1, Box 99M
Centre Harbor, NH 03226
(800) 5REDHILL, (603) 279-7001
Fax: (603) 279-7003
info@redhillinn.com
www.redhillinn.com

STAFFORD'S IN THE FIELD INN, Chocorua

| Overall: ★★★★ | Room Quality: C | Value: B | Price: $80–$160 |

These devoted innkeepers came from sunny California to cold, rural Yankeeland about 35 years ago, and with hard work and love have kept this special, peaceful place going. Fred has dry wit that not everybody gets (those who do have a ball). Sweet Ramona is a marvelous cook and turns out a different French-based menu each night. Photos of their family and the development of the property are in the parlor. This is a bucolic, isolated, rambling inn—great for a wedding—with rustic charm and well-worn beauty. It's one of the last of its old-fashioned kind, with character and characters, a true original based on two originals.

SETTING & FACILITIES

Location: Off Rt. 113, between Chocorua and Tamworth

Near: Nature preserves, Lake Winnipesaukee, Squam Lake, rivers,

waterfalls, antiquing, summer theaters
Building: 1700s Federalist-style main building; red barn for large events
Grounds: 36-acre estate w/ view, rolling fields, brook, garden, orchard, sugar house
Public Space: Entrance, library, taproom, DR, veranda
Food & Drink: Early bird tea cart; full breakfast; specialties: blueberry pancakes w/ maple syrup, cheddar and salsa omelet; cocktails; candlelight dinner (charge; reservations); specialties: mock turtle soup, pork tenderloin, brandied bread pudding; liquor license, wine list, ice avail.; special diets accom.
Recreation: Climbing, swimming, boating, fly fishing, X-C skiing
Amenities & Services: Welcome fruit/cookies, climbing maps, snowshoes; receptions (250), meetings (30), pickup from bus, picnic (fee), canoe, Steinway grand piano

ACCOMMODATIONS

Units: 13 guest rooms, cottages
All Rooms: Good view, fan
Some Rooms: Fireplace, bath (5), wheelchair accessible (1)
Bed & Bath: Double beds in shared-bath rooms; queens/king in rooms w/ priv. baths; some canopies; 2 large clawfoot tubs, 3 shower/tub
Favorites: Hearthroom—large fireplace, canopy bed, windows on 3 walls; Orchard room—beam ceiling, wicker and green oak furniture; both w/ 16-inch mattresses
Comfort & Decor: Rooms eclectic and individually decorated. Some signs of wear, but acceptable. Sizes vary but all comfortable, w/ useable antiques. Tasteful, some whimsy.

RATES, RESERVATIONS, & RESTRICTIONS

Deposit: 50%; refund w/ 14-day notice
Discounts: Long stays
Credit Cards: MC,V
Check-In/Out: 11/3
Smoking: No
Pets: No
Kids: Over 12
Minimum Stay: 2 days some weekends

Open: All year; usually closed April
Hosts: Ramona and Fred Stafford
Box 270
Chocorua, NH 03817
(603) 323-7766, (800) 446-1112
Fax: (603) 323-7531
ramona@ncia.net
www.staffordsinthefield.com

GODDARD MANSION, Claremont

Overall: ★★★½	Room Quality: C	Value: B	Price: $65–$125

Remember Buster Brown shoes and Tige? (If not, your parents will.) This turn-of-the-last-century, 18-room mansion was built by the shoe manufacturer, who obviously profited grandly from shodding our little feet. Debbie has a good sense of humor, sets a low-key tone, and loves to chat about the extensive restorations and the history of the house and town. Interesting elements abound, including a Tiffany lamp in the dining room, a working

Wurlitzer organ from the 1930s, a wraparound screened porch and a tea house set among the gardens.

SETTING & FACILITIES

Location: 30 min. S of Hanover; 10 min. from VT; 1.5 mi. from town center
Near: Dartmouth College, St.-Gaudens Nat'l Hist. Site, The Fort at #4, Simon Pearce Glass Blowing and Ceramics, Catamount Brewery and Tours, antiquing, theater
Building: 1905 English Manor Victorian shingled mansion
Grounds: Porches, teahouse, gazebo, lawn

Public Space: LR, sitting room, library, TV room, DR
Food & Drink: Full communal breakfast; specialties: muffins, jam from mansion's gardens; tea; spec. diets accom.
Recreation: Skiing, golf, horses, tennis, boating, mountain biking
Amenities & Services: Baby grand piano; receptions, celebrating spec. occasions

ACCOMMODATIONS

Units: 10 guest rooms
Some Rooms: Bath, environmentally green rooms, panoramic mountain view, TV, AC
Bed & Bath: Beds vary, some canopies, four-posters; tub (2)
Favorites: Former MBR—large corner

room, airy, mountain view; Cloud Room—papered in whimsical clouds
Comfort & Decor: Decor varies; incl. country French, Colonial, Laura Ashley, Victorian. Airy, light-filled, natural woodwork, light papers. Corner room good for families.

RATES, RESERVATIONS, & RESTRICTIONS

Deposit: $50 check or credit card, full payment on arrival; refund w/ 7-day notice
Discounts: Seniors, corp., longer stays, 3rd person
Credit Cards: MC, V, AE, D
Check-In/Out: 4/11; call for late arrival
Smoking: Porches and tea house only
Pets: No
Kids: Welcome; toy corner, swing, croquet for children

Minimum Stay: 2 nights holidays
Open: All year
Hosts: Debbie Albee
25 Hillstead Rd.
Claremont, NH 03743-3317
(603) 543-0603, (800) 736-0603
Fax: (603) 543-0001
goddardmansion@usa.net
www.turbont.net/goddardmansion

HIGHLAND LAKE INN, East Andover

Overall: ★★★½	Room Quality: B	Value: C	Price: $85–$125

The winding road leading to this nineteenth-century house is classic rural New Hampshire, with roughly stacked fieldstone and leafy maples bordering green fields, farms and red barns beyond. The porch with its swing is old-fashioned and welcoming. Living room walls are yellow, decorated with old plates and accented with blue and white Delft tiles. The rooms upstairs are similarly charming, done up with antiques, Oriental rugs and quilted coverlets. The atmosphere will make you feel less stressed, one of the great bonuses of a good bed-and-breakfast.

SETTING & FACILITIES

Location: I-91 exit Rt. 11 or I-93 Exit 17 to Rt. 11; opposite Andover Congregational Church
Near: Canterbury Shaker Village, Ruggles Mine, Proctor Academy, Mt. Sunapee Ski Resort, Ragged Mountain Ski, factory stores, Norsk Cross-Country Skiing, antiquing, auctions, nature preserve
Building: Private home, c.1767
Grounds: 12 acres on hill, overlooks lakes, mountains; 2 porches
Public Space: Gathering room, DR, porch

Food & Drink: Breakfast, communal or separate; specialties: waffles w/ fresh fruit sauces, featherbed eggs; cookies; snacks, sodas
Recreation: Boating, golf, ice skating, horseback riding, boat cruises, priv. beach
Amenities & Services: Books, beach towels, meeting space for 30-40; business services: fax, phone, laptop modem; touring advice/maps, making reservations

ACCOMMODATIONS

Units: 10 guest rooms
All Rooms: Bath, period pieces
Some Rooms: Fireplace, wheelchair access (not bathrooms) (2)
Bed & Bath: King, queen, 2 twin beds; some four-posters; showers only

Favorites: Highland—antiques, fireplace, window seat, lovely view; Andover—fireplace, four-poster
Comfort & Decor: Elegant country decor w/ floral shades, wood floors. Immaculate. Refined/feminine but not fussy. Bright and airy.

RATES, RESERVATIONS, & RESTRICTIONS

Deposit: Credit card, 1 night or 50% w/in 7 days of booking; refund w/ 14-day notice
Discounts: None
Credit Cards: MC, V, AE, D
Check-In/Out: 3/11
Smoking: No
Pets: No; call for alternate arrangements
Kids: 8 and older

Minimum Stay: 2 days some weekends
Open: All year
Hosts: Mary and Peter Petras
Box 164, 32 Maple St.
East Andover, NH 03231
(603) 735-6426
Fax: (603) 735-5355
www.highlandlakeinn.com

TRUMBULL HOUSE BED AND BREAKFAST, Hanover

Overall: ★★★★   Room Quality: B   Value: C   Price: $120–$210

Spacious rooms and luscious breakfasts are features at this Dartmouth-area bed-and-breakfast that obviously caters to college families but is a pleasant stop for any traveler. You can wake up to a cheese omelet with Portobello mushrooms and Brie, French toast made with English muffins, and scrambled eggs with smoked salmon, cream cheese and chives. Colors are vivid. The dining room has red walls and white trim, and guest rooms are aptly named "Green," "White," "Blue" and so on. The helpful innkeeper is colorful, too. She sold her business in Connecticut and renovated a wing of the house for her five kids, in her spare time of course.

SETTING & FACILITIES

Location: I-89 Exit 18 or I-93 Exit 13; 4 mi. E of Dartmouth College; 3 mi. from Dartmouth-Hitchcock Medical Center
Near: Dartmouth cultural and sports events, Hanover shopping, sightseeing
Building: White 1919 Colonial, remodeled 1995
Grounds: 16 acres w/ swimming pond, meadow, woods; link to Appalachian Trail

Public Space: LR, DR, reading nook, porches
Food & Drink: Breakfast; specialties: fresh-baked pastry; tea; fruit; low-fat, veg. meals
Recreation: Hiking, X-C skiing on site; water/snow sports, golf, horses, tennis
Amenities & Services: Cordless phones, iron, paper, CDs, copier, fax, conf. center, internet, celebrating occasions

ACCOMMODATIONS

Units: 4 guest rooms, 1 suite
All Rooms: Sitting area, TV, desk, clock, radio
Some Rooms: Window seat, whirlpool, dataport
Bed & Bath: King, queen, four-poster (1), sleigh (1); tubs (4), whirlpool (1), bath in suite (2)

Favorites: Yellow room—cheerful, romantic, sleeping alcove, window seat
Comfort & Decor: Spacious rooms, wood furniture, some with details like sleeping alcoves, dormers, built-ins. 3rd floor cozy w/ eaves.

RATES, RESERVATIONS, & RESTRICTIONS

Deposit: Full payment 1 night or 50%
Discounts: 3rd person, corporate. rates avail.
Credit Cards: MC, V, AE, CB
Check-In/Out: 4–8/11

Smoking: No
Pets: No; in-house 2 cats, 2 dogs
Kids: Welcome; babysitting on-site
Minimum Stay: 2 nights weekends, foliage season

Open: All year
Hosts: Hilary A. Pridgen
40 Etna Rd.
Hanover, NH 03755
(603) 643-2370, (800) 651-5141

Fax: (603) 643-2430
bnb@valley.net
www.valley.net/~trumbull.bnb; soon to be
TrumbullHouse.com

MANOR ON GOLDEN POND, Holderness

Overall: ★★★★★	Room Quality: A	Value: C	Price: $210–$350

As close as you can get to an English country manor in New England, this imposing property was built in 1907 by a wealthy Brit who made a fortune in Florida land deals. In the 1930s it became a photographers' colony. The mansion is nestled among tall pines on rolling lawns and overlooks "Golden Pond," of movie fame. With a pool, tennis court, sightseeing boat, and rooms with TVs, VCRs, and numerous luxuries, many guests book for a week. Bambi and David are warm hosts. You can dress up for the grand dinners, with hushed, formal service in the paneled dining room, candle and firelight reflecting in the original mirrors.

SETTING & FACILITIES

Location: On Squam Lake, 4.7 mi. off I-93 Exit 24
Near: Squam Lake, White Mountains, Science Center, *On Golden Pond* boat tours, outlets, glassblowing, crafts, quilt shop, gorge at Lost River, beach
Building: Large 1907 English country manor-style showplace; renovated 1992
Grounds: 14 acres on a hill; pool, tennis court, porch; 3 frontage acres on Squam Lake, boathouse
Public Space: 2 sitting rooms, registration area, pub, 2 DRs, terrace
Food & Drink: Buffet breakfast w/ hot entree; specialties: buttermilk pancakes, omelet of the day; tea; prix fixe dinner: New American cuisine nightly mid-May–end Oct. and holidays, other Wed.–Sun. (extra, res. req.); specialties: seared Rainbow trout w/ champagne vinaigrette, pumpkin ravioli w/ sauteed apples and hazelnut cream sauce; menu changes nightly; award-winning wine list
Recreation: Skating, canoeing, fishing on-site; horses, skiing, sleigh rides, ice fishing, golf, boat cruises
Amenities & Services: Boathouse, rec. facilities, sightseeing boat, turn-down, transportation to outdoor Sunday services on island

ACCOMMODATIONS

Units: 17 guest rooms in main inn, 4 cottages
All Rooms: Bath, AC, TV, VCR, CD, phone
Some Rooms: Wood-burning fireplace, priv. deck, refrigerator, wet bar
Bed & Bath: Mostly king beds, some canopies; lavish baths, some dbl. whirlpools
Favorites: Stratford—trapper's lodge motif w/ bearskin rug, barnboard walls, king canopy, fireplace; Dover-cottage by

lake—2 BRs, kitchen, fireplace (rented by week, no breakfast)
Comfort & Decor: Spacious rooms and designer fabrics in tasteful, luxury mix. Something for everyone. Many lake view, some w/ decks. Good lighting. Well-appointed, extremely comfortable. Theme rooms are fun.

RATES, RESERVATIONS, & RESTRICTIONS

Deposit: Full payment, 1 night; other 50%; refund w/ 14-day notice (30 for holidays)
Discounts: 3rd person, pkgs.; check on weekly cottage rentals
Credit Cards: MC, V, AE
Check-In/Out: 3–6/11; call for early/late check-in
Smoking: No
Pets: No
Kids: 12 and up

No-No's: Children in Manor House
Minimum Stay: 2 nights holiday/fall foliage weekends
Open: All year; some accom. seasonal
Hosts: Bambi and David Arnold
Box T, Route 3
Holderness, NH 03245
(800) 545-2141, (603) 968-3348
Fax: (603) 968-2116
manorinn@lrnet.com
www.manorongoldenpond.com

PRESSED PETALS INN, Holderness

Overall: ★★★★	Room Quality: B	Value: C	Price: $85–$120

Pretty as a flower, this immaculate, modest bed-and-breakfast across from the renowned Manor on Golden Pond, is a reflection of innkeeper Ellie, who carries out the namesake theme with framed pressed flowers on each guest room door, matching key rings, and a charming gift of a pressed-flower bookmark. The dried florals are her creation, the result of a childhood hobby. Simple, understated guest rooms, including Azalea, Forget-Me-Not, Mock Orange, and Wisteria, are colorfully furnished. For a great deal, you can have a fabulous meal at the luxury neighboring inn, a five-minute walk away, and then fall into bed under an embroidered coverlet at this neat, sweet haven.

SETTING & FACILITIES

Location: About 5 mi. off I-93 Exit 24, near Citgo station
Near: White Mt. Nat'l. Forest, Franconia Notch, Squam Lake, The Flume, Weir's Beach, Lake Winnipesaukee, Castle Springs, Science Center of NH, covered bridges
Building: Century-old farmhouse w/ gingerbread trim

Grounds: Wraparound porch, floral highlights
Public Space: Entry parlor, upstairs parlor, DR
Food & Drink: Candlelight breakfast; specialties: oven-baked French toast w/ apple cider sauce, egg casserole; finger desserts and hot drinks; hors d'oeuvres Sat. nights

Recreation: Golf, horses, boating, snowmobiling, skiing

Amenities & Services: Refrigerator, irons, disabled access; meetings (20), fax

ACCOMMODATIONS

Units: 6 guest rooms, 2 suites
All Rooms: Bath, fan, clock, hairdryer, luxury linens
Some Rooms: Disabled access (1)
Bed & Bath: Queen, twin, robes; shower/tub (2)

Favorites: Blue Hydrangea—Victorian headboard, rocking chair, china cabinet
Comfort & Decor: Simple, comfortable rooms, each decorated w/ a floral theme. Smallish. Good lighting.

RATES, RESERVATIONS, & RESTRICTIONS

Deposit: 1 night or 50%; refund w/ 14-day notice
Discounts: Off-season, 3rd person in suites
Credit Cards: V, MC, D
Check-In/Out: 3–7:30/11
Smoking: Outside porch only
Pets: No
Kids: Over 10

Minimum Stay: 2 days, Oct.; peak weekends; weddings
Open: Closed Thanksgiving, Christmas
Hosts: Ellie Dewey
Shepard Hill Rd.
Holderness, NH 03245
(800) 839-6205 (outside NH); (603) 968-4417
Fax: (603) 968-3661
www.Traveldata.com/inns/data/pressed.html

THE ALDEN COUNTRY INN, Lyme

| Overall: ★★★½ | Room Quality: C | Value: C | Price: $85–$165 |

Next to the glorious Lyme Congregational Church, with a bell cast by Paul Revere that rings hourly, this former tavern, stagecoach stop, and ballroom has been hosting guests for almost 200 years and counting. In the mid-nineteenth century, tiny Lyme was the most successful sheep-raising village in New England. The only flocks evident today are Dartmouth families, canoeing enthusiasts on the nearby Connecticut River, fisherpeople, and antiquers. The old tavern with its fireplace and original tables is especially cozy on a cold night, and the tasty American cuisine is complemented by an extensive wine list.

SETTING & FACILITIES

Location: On the far end of town green
Near: Dartmouth College, shopping in Hanover, Hopkins Center

Building: 1809 inn, 1820 tavern
Grounds: Lawn, field, gardens
Public Space: Common rooms, tavern, small DRs, library

Food & Drink: Full country breakfast; specialty: Portuguese toast w/ maple syrup; Sunday brunch; lunch, dinner nightly (extra); specialties: N.E. chowders, rack of lamb; veg. options, holiday meals; liquor license

Recreation: Skiing, golf, biking, fishing, canoeing
Amenities & Services: Live entertainment: Tues. (folk), Thurs. (blues); spec. occasions, function rooms, conf., business services, weddings

ACCOMMODATIONS

Units: Units: 15 guest rooms
All Rooms: Bath, phone, AC
Some Rooms: Extra bed, fireplace
Bed & Bath: Mostly king/queen, some twins; full baths

Favorites: Governor's Quarters—spacious suite, TV, refrigerator, king, full bath
Comfort & Decor: Country decor, antiques. Views of green, woods. Church bells a distraction to some. Small rooms. Authentic, spare feeling.

RATES, RESERVATIONS, & RESTRICTIONS

Deposit: 1 night, refund w/ 14-day notice
Discounts: Seniors (dining), 3rd person
Credit Cards: MC, V, AE, D
Check-In/Out: 3/11
Smoking: No
Pets: No
Kids: OK
Minimum Stay: 2 nights foliage, summer weekends

Open: All year
Hosts: Mickey Dowd
Box 60, On the Common
Lyme, NH 03768
(800) 794-2296, (603) 795-2222
Fax: (603) 795-9536
info@aldencountryinn.com
www.aldencountryinn.com

MEREDITH INN, Meredith

Overall: ★★★½	Room Quality: B	Value: C	Price: $99–$139

This new bed-and-breakfast near the center of Meredith has been an integral part of this small town's life for over 100 years. The original owner was a doctor who birthed a lot of the local kids; their grandchildren still come by now and then. The second owner was a popular dentist. The Carpenters, warm and helpful, are the third owners, and they're still working, adding whirlpools and beautifying this kid-friendly, rose-colored "Painted Lady." The Victorian house is not laden and overstuffed; the decor is actually rather light and airy, and a handsome staircase, handcrafted detailing and high ceilings add to the overall effect.

SETTING & FACILITIES

Location: 9.5 mi. off I-93, Exit 23 at the corner of Main and Waukewan Sts.

Near: Lake Winnipesaukee, White Mountains, arts, festivals, theater, craft shows, Science Center, historic district, shopping

Building: 100-year-old Gothic Victorian "Painted Lady"; restored 1997

Grounds: .5 acre in town, some gardens, small lawn

Public Space: LR, dining area, porch

Food & Drink: Full communal breakfast; specialties: French toast, frittata w/ ham and Monterey Jack, vegetable frittata, pancakes

Recreation: Water/snow/mountain activities, skating, go-karting, archery, berry/apple picking, beaches, bike/horse/carriage/train rides

Amenities & Services: Menus, tour guidance, reservations, bike and boat rentals

ACCOMMODATIONS

Units: 8 guest rooms

All Rooms: Bath, heat controls, TV, phone

Some Rooms: Wheelchair access, sitting area, bay windows, window seats, fireplace, desk

Bed & Bath: King, queen, twin bed (2); whirlpool/shower (6), some shower only, some shower seat

Favorites: Room 7—king bed, deep dbl. whirlpool, fireplace, 2nd floor

Comfort & Decor: Some turret sitting areas. Special antiques such as oak bureaus, hand-carved Chapman rocker.

RATES, RESERVATIONS, & RESTRICTIONS

Deposit: 1 night w/in 7 days of booking; refund w/ 14-day notice

Discounts: Off-season, 3rd person

Credit Cards: MC, V, AE, D

Check-In/Out: 3/11

Smoking: No

Pets: No

Kids: OK

Minimum Stay: 2 nights weekends, most rooms

Open: All year

Hosts: Janet, Ed, and Fay Carpenter

2 Waukewan St., Box 115

Meredith, NH 03253

(603) 279-0000

Fax: (603) 279-4017

inn1897@meredithinn.com

www.meredithinn.com

OLDE ORCHARD INN, Moultonborough

Overall: ★★★★	Room Quality: B	Value: B	Price: $75–$140

This inn comes by its name honestly. The property, acquired by Batchelder Brown for his wife in the late 1700s, is planted with hundreds of apple, cherry, plum and pear trees, so from the first flowerings in May to the last of the apple harvest in November, you can enjoy the beauty and the (literal) fruits of the innkeepers' efforts. Mary and Jim spent 26 years in the Foreign Service, and the old house is filled with international treasures such as Russian dolls, Afghan rugs, and Indian chests, mixed with a beehive oven, antique candlesticks, and other colonial remnants. And, of course, there are modern luxuries such as whirlpool tubs.

SETTING & FACILITIES

Location: Rt. 25 to Old 109 in Moultenborough, .25 mi. to Lee Rd., turn right; in foothills of White Mountains.
Near: Castle in the Clouds, Loon Center, Lake Winnipesaukee, Mt. Washington, antiquing; walk to The Old Country Store (opened c. 1800)
Building: 1790 farmhouse; brick addition, 1812; major renovation 1996
Grounds: 13 acres; mountain, brook; orchards, pond w/ paddleboat, gazebos
Public Space: LR, game room, DR, breakfast room
Food & Drink: Candlelight country breakfast, communal or separate; specialties: apple crisp, scones, cherry-berry coffeecake, frittata; soft drinks; special diets
Recreation: Exercise room, sauna, spa, golf, lake sports, antiquing
Amenities & Services: Antique shop, hot tub, videos, refrigerator, irons, beach towels, microwave meeting area (40), fax; weddings; events; bikes, fishing equip., croquet, boat rental

ACCOMMODATIONS

Units: 9 guest rooms
All Rooms: Bath, AC, TV
Some Rooms: Fireplace, coffee maker, clock, radio
Bed & Bath: Queen, double, twin; some tub/shower, whirlpools, robes
Favorites: Upper and Lower pond rooms—queen, fireplace, whirlpool
Comfort & Decor: Antiques and Oriental carpets collected during owners' diplomatic travels. Varied trunks at foot of beds. New wing w/ fireplaces and whirlpools.

RATES, RESERVATIONS, & RESTRICTIONS

Deposit: 1 night; refund w/ 14-day notice
Discounts: Long stays, off-season, 3rd person, kids (crib $5)
Credit Cards: MC, V, D
Check-In/Out: 3/11; call for arrival after 8
Smoking: Outside
Pets: Kennel space in barn if arranged; in-house dogs
Kids: Welcome
Minimum Stay: 2 days on certain summer/fall foliage weekends
Open: All year, may close for week in winter, spring
Hosts: Mary and Jim Senner
RR Box 256
Moultonborough, NH 03254
(800) 598-5845, (603) 476-5004
Fax: (603) 476-5419
innkeep@oldeorchardinn.com
www.oldeorchardinn.com

MAPLE HILL FARM, New London

Overall: ★★★	Room Quality: C	Value: C	Price: $60–$100

Generations of the same family lived here from 1824–1976, when the farm produced maple sugar, butter, and eggs. Today you can still sleep in their stenciled beds, and do gentle farm-related chores that most young children love. This informal, lakeside inn hasn't changed much, and has tin walls and ceilings, painted wooden floors, and quilts that Roberta crafted. She also spins yarn from resident lambs—and yarns of the past. Dennis cooks hearty breakfasts of blueberry pancakes and biscuits and sausage. From 1880–1950 you could stay here for $11 a week. With all meals. You'll have to pay a bit more now, but this simple place is still good value, especially for families and groups.

SETTING & FACILITIES

Location: 1 block off I-89, Exit 12, on pastures
Near: Antiquing, country fairs, theater, museums
Building: 1824 farmhouse
Grounds: Little Lake Sunapee .25 mi. behind barn, farm animals, pasture, sandbox, playground, beach
Public Space: LRs, DR, porches, barn, dance floor, basketball court, BYOB beverage bar

Food & Drink: Early bird coffee; breakfast; specialty: wild blueberry pancakes (once voted finest in NH); dinner for groups of 10 or more
Recreation: Swimming, snowshoeing on site; X-C and downhill skiing, ice skating, golf, tennis, boating, health club, fishing
Amenities & Services: 6-person hot tub, canoe and bikes, games, books, CDs; small conf., receptions, dinners, hayrides for groups

ACCOMMODATIONS

Units: 10 guest rooms
All Rooms: Good lighting, indiv. decorated
Some Rooms: Priv. bath (6), priv. entrance, pull-out loveseat, extra bed
Bed & Bath: Beds vary, but firm; sofa beds; basic baths, some vintage fixtures
Favorites: Room 1—double, bath, tin ceiling, antique mahogany sleigh bed;

Room 4—double, bath, closet, 2nd floor; Room 6—queen, pull-out loveseat, bath, Chippendale cherry bed
Comfort & Decor: Farmhouse decor. Many with indiv. details like 104-year old master bed (owned by orig. farm family), mahogany chests, homemade curtains. Basic, clean, simple.

RATES, RESERVATIONS, & RESTRICTIONS

Deposit: Credit card; refund w/ 7-day notice
Discounts: Stays of 3+ nights, children, packages w/ hayride for 10 couples or more, incl. meals
Credit Cards: MC, V, AE, D
Check-In/Out: Flexible
Smoking: No
Pets: No; 2 in-house large dogs
Kids: Welcome

Minimum Stay: 2 nights Jan.–Mar., July, Aug., Oct., weekends
Open: All year
Hosts: Roberta and Dennis Aufranc
200 Newport Rd.
New London, NH 03257
(800) 231-8637, (603) 526-2248
Fax: (603) 526-4170
daufranc@kear.tdsnet.com
www.maplehillfarm.com

FOLLANSBEE INN, North Sutton

Overall: ★★★½   Room Quality: C   Value: B   Price: $85–$120

By this inn on Kezar Lake there's a pier where you can sun and swim, and an island that you can canoe to and picnic on, with lunch packed by the hosts. You can hike up Mt. Kearsarge, and in winter, there's skiing, ice fishing, and reading by the fire. And this comfy former farmhouse, filled with informal furnishings such as an old school desk and cast-iron stove, is especially good for singles and people-people—you help yourself to breakfast and join the group at the table or hang around the piano. The whole experience is relaxed and unpretentious. Sandy and Dick contribute part of the earnings to Habitat for Humanity.

SETTING & FACILITIES

Location: About 2 mi. off I-89, Exit 10; lakeside; follow signs
Near: Summer stock theater, outdoor band concerts, antiquing, art galleries, beach, farm museum, St. Gaudens Nat'l Hist. Site (sculpture), nature area
Building: 1840 New England Cape farmhouse
Grounds: Porch w/ views; overlooks Kezar Lake; near pier, priv. beach
Public Space: Wide hallways, 2 sitting rooms, bar

Food & Drink: Full breakfast; specialties: granola, sunshine egg casserole; tea, wine/cheese; dinner by request ($20); specialties: crab-and-shrimp casserole, baked Alaska; spec. diets; beer and wine license
Recreation: Tennis, golf, water/snow sports, table tennis, horses
Amenities & Services: Bikes, boats (rowboat, canoe, paddleboat) windsurfing gear, maps

ACCOMMODATIONS

Units: 23 guest rooms; cottage
All Rooms: Indiv. decor
Some Rooms: 11 baths, lake views; cottage: priv. lake access, kitchen, fireplace, LR/DR
Bed & Bath: Beds vary; some shower/tub combos, some showers only

Favorites: Ira's Room (#11) and Ichabod's Room (#9)—overlook lake, queens, priv. baths
Comfort & Decor: Low ceilings, papered walls. Rooms named after town's ancestors. Cottage is intimate, secluded. Third floor rooms share bath. Good deal. Neat and basic.

RATES, RESERVATIONS, & RESTRICTIONS

Deposit: Cred. cd.; 1 night's rent if canceling and others turned away
Discounts: Singles, 3rd person, longer weekday stays; cottage $625/week
Credit Cards: V, MC; pref. checks

Check-In/Out: 2–10/11; call for other check-in
Smoking: No
Pets: No; in-house dog; kennel recomm.
Kids: Over 8 (not in cottage)

Minimum Stay: 2–3 nights, peak weekends
Open: Except April, Nov.
Hosts: Sandy and Dick Reilein
Box 92

North Sutton, NH 03260
(603) 927-4221, (800) 626-4221
follansbeeinn@conk.net
www.follansbeeinn.com

DEXTER'S INN AND TENNIS CLUB, Sunapee

Overall: ★★★★	Room Quality: B	Value: C	Price: $135–$400

Do you hanker for a love game? Have it both ways: a tennis serve on cushioned courts and eggs Benedict served at 10 a.m. in an antique bed. A daily pro and three USTA/NE tournaments a year please tennis buffs; others can enjoy the pool, fly-fishing, lawn games, hiking, or skimming hundreds of books. The inn is family-friendly, and kids will enjoy a recreation room in the barn and good, basic food. Originally the inn was a farmhouse, built in 1801 by a craftsman who carved bowls for ships' compasses from on-site maples. Restored by an advisor to President Herbert Hoover, it was run by Holly's parents from 1969–87, and by the next generation.

SETTING & FACILITIES

Location: I-89 Exit 12; left on Rt. 11; 5.5 mi. to Winn Hill Rd.; take a left, 2 mi. to inn, on steep back road
Near: Mt. Sunapee State Park, beach, antiquing, historic sites, St. Gaudens Museum, Lake Sunapee, *MV Mt. Sunapee II* cruise boat, dinner cruises, New London barn playhouse, Fells Nature preserve, Hopkins Center for the Arts, outlets, New London indoor tennis, Mt. Kearsarge
Building: 1801 clapboard Colonial, barn; remodeled 1998
Grounds: Gardens, pool, view of lake, mountains

Public Space: DR, LR/library, FR, scr. porch
Food & Drink: (MAP) Full breakfast; dinner Thurs.–Sun.; specialty: Sam Lord's Sunrise Salmon; special diets accom.; liquor license
Recreation: Water sports, downhill skiing, golf, billiards, table tennis, basketball, Foosball
Amenities & Services: Tennis pro 6/1–9/1, racket rental, lessons, 3 courts; weddings, family reunions; limited disabled access; conf. rooms, fax, dataport; piano; grill

ACCOMMODATIONS

Units: 19 guest rooms: 10 in house, 7 in annex, 2 in cottage
All Rooms: Bath, AC
Some Rooms: LR, kitchen, priv. entrance, antiques
Bed & Bath: Antique beds, four-posters; tubs

Favorites: Room 12—four-poster, good view, in annex
Comfort & Decor: Individually decorated w/ mix of modern and antique furnishings. Large, airy, bright. Fresh fruit, flowers. Some oddly shaped rooms. Cottage w/ LR, fireplace, kitchen, 2 BRs

RATES, RESERVATIONS, & RESTRICTIONS

Deposit: 2 nights; refund w/ 14-day notice

Discounts: Singles, kids, 3rd person, off-season, groups, longer stays, tennis pkgs., weekly cottage rates

Credit Cards: MC, V, D

Check-In/Out: 3/11

Smoking: No

Pets: OK ($10/day) in cottage, annex

Kids: Welcome; arrange prior for babysitting

Minimum Stay: Usually 2 nights on weekends

Open: Memorial Day–Nov. 1

Hosts: Holly and Michael Durfor
258 Stagecoach Rd.
Sunapee, NH 03782
(603) 763-5571, (888) 205-5120
dexters@kear.tds.net
www.bbhost.com/dextersinn

Zone 7
Northern New Hampshire
& White Mountains

If scenic grandeur interests you, this is your region. Here you will find perhaps the most dramatic vistas in New England. The Kancamagus Highway is northern New England's only National Scenic Byway, and its mountain views are worth the trip alone. The scope, height and quiet, granite ridges, rushing waters, and tiny isolated villages are invigorating to mind, body, and spirit.

Before air-conditioning was invented, well-off New England and New York families came here for the entire summer to avoid the city heat, and the grand hotels and vacation homes of that era still remain. Today the area is a year-round, short-stay destination offering abundant recreational opportunities in the 780,000-acre White Mountain National Forest, considered New Hampshire's home of outdoor activity.

From cross-country and downhill skiing, fishing, hiking, and mountain climbing to picnicking by a waterfall or just gazing in solitude at the snow-frosted peaks, you won't have to worry about being bored, despite the fact that there is little to do after sundown except in the town of Jackson during ski season. The bustling ski town is filled with activities, lodgings and restaurants, and is the hub of nightlife, so to speak, with live music every night during ski season. The village of Jackson features a covered bridge, waterfall, and spectacular cross-country ski trails.

For those who prefer indoor pursuits, there is plenty of tax-free shopping, including the North Conway outlets. In the Mt. Washington Valley, drive the eight miles to the summit of the highest peak in the Northeast (6,288 feet), or leave your car behind and try the Mt. Washington Cog Railway. There are seven downhill ski areas and six ski touring areas in the Valley alone.

Story Land, near Glen, is a pint-size, fairy-tale world for little ones; nearby Heritage, New Hampshire tells the story of the past 350 years of the state's history.

Small inns and bed-and-breakfasts center in ski areas and are relatively scarce otherwise. Not surprisingly, the atmosphere of these inns tends to be geared to families and activities, often with ski storage, hearty meals, and basic décor—style-conscious travelers with sophisticated palates be forewarned. In ski season and on weekends, be sure to reserve well in advance.

For More Information

Country Inns in the White Mountains
(603) 345-9460
email: stay@white-mountains-inns.com
www.white-mountains-inns.com

New Hampshire's Connecticut Lakes Region
(603) 538-7118
www.nhconnlakes.com

North Country Chamber of Commerce
(800) 698-8939, ext. 1

The Open Door Bed and Breakfasts
Box 1178
N. Conway, NH 03860
(800) 300-4799
www.mountwashingtonvalley.com/opendoor

White Mountains B&B Association
White Mountains Attractions
Box 10
North Woodstock, NH 03262
(603) 745-8720 or (800) 346-3687
www.VisitWhiteMountains.com

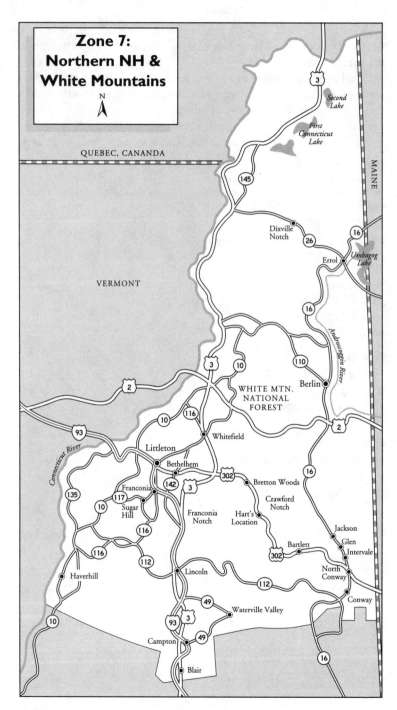

Zone 7:
Northern NH &
White Mountains

N

QUEBEC, CANANDA

VERMONT

MAINE

Second Lake

First Connecticut Lake

145

Dixville Notch

26

Errol

Umbagog Lake

16

16

16

110

Berlin

Androscoggin River

3 10

WHITE MTN. NATIONAL FOREST

2

93

Connecticut River

10 116

Whitefield

Littleton

2

16

Bethelhem

302

Bretton Woods

135

Franconia

142 3

Crawford Notch

117

Sugar Hill

Franconia Notch

Hart's Location

Jackson

10

116

Bartlett

Glen

Intervale

116

112

Lincoln

302

North Conway

Haverhill

112

Conway

10

49

Waterville Valley

93 3

49

16

Campton

Blair

COVERED BRIDGE HOUSE, Bartlett

Overall: ★★★½	Room Quality: C	Value: A	Price: $54–$89

This Colonial bed-and-breakfast's name refers to a restored 1850 trestle bridge, part of the property and the only one privately owned in the U.S. The inn has a gift shop at one end offering country crafts, including Nancy's jewelry designs. So homey that guests have come to breakfast in slippers and pajamas, the country-casual atmosphere has the innkeepers and their offspring much in evidence. With a private beach on the Saco River, and kids under 12 free in their parents' room, this pretty, well-maintained property offers a special environment for families with young children.

SETTING & FACILITIES

Location: 7 mi. N of North Conway, next to covered bridge
Near: Story Land, Heritage New Hampshire, Conway Scenic Railroad, Cog Railway, Covered Bridge Shop (on-site: N.E. crafts, antiques), outlet/specialty shops, Kancamagus Highway
Building: Circa 1900 Colonial
Grounds: 2 acres by Saco River w/ tubing, swimming holes

Public Space: LR, DR, outdoor hot tub
Food & Drink: Country breakfast; specialties: Belgian waffles w/ berry sauce, eggs any style; snacks: hot drinks, cookies
Recreation: Mini-golf, golf, canoeing, fishing, tennis, skiing
Amenities & Services: Roll-aways, cribs, tubing tubes, irons, kitchen privileges, maps

ACCOMMODATIONS

Units: 6 guest rooms
All Rooms: Clock/radio
Some Rooms: AC, bath (4)
Bed & Bath: Some queens; tub (1)
Favorites: Crawford Notch—featherbed, afternoon sun, bath; Carter Notch—Victorian, armoire, sofa, stenciling

Comfort & Decor: Antiques, colonial style. Bedside lighting. Some papered, some stenciled. Named for notches in White Mountains. Two rooms sharing bath connect, perfect for family.

RATES, RESERVATIONS, & RESTRICTIONS

Deposit: 50%; refund w/ 14-day notice
Discounts: Off-season, kids under 12, midweek, singles, 3rd person
Credit Cards: MC, V, AE, D
Check-In/Out: 3–10/11
Smoking: No
Pets: No
Kids: OK; call ahead
Minimum Stay: 2 nights holidays, fall

foliage, some weekends
Open: All year
Hosts: Nancy and Dan Wanek, Brian and Allison
Route 302
Bartlett, NH 03838
(800) 232-9109, (603) 383-9109
cbhouse@landmarknet.net
www.coveredbridgehouse.com

ADAIR COUNTRY INN, Bethlehem

| Overall: ★★★★ | Room Quality: A | Value: C | Price: $140–$285 |

The new hosts purchased this elegant hilltop inn in 1998. Bill, a former ad exec who enjoys gardening, and Judy, a caterer, apply their talents to this already renowned mansion, with grounds designed by the Olmsteds, who designed Central Park. You are treated as if you are visiting the original owner, Dorothy Adair, who was given the estate by her father, a famed trial lawyer, in 1927. Guests' names are written at the entry, as a welcome, and the quiet pampering continues. Rooms are named for the mountain ranges, which can be seen from many of the luxury guest rooms. And the evolving dinner cuisine can reach lofty peaks as well.

SETTING & FACILITIES

Location: I-93 to Exit 40; 3 mi. W of center of Bethlehem
Near: Antiquing, museums, White Mountain Nat'l Forest, shopping in Littleton, summer theatre, summer lectures
Building: 1927 Georgian Colonial, remodeled 1996
Grounds: 200-acres: trails, tennis, gardens, patio, gazebo, pond, woods
Public Space: Huge LR, DR; tap room, library

Food & Drink: Coffee, tea, full breakfast; specialties: "egg blossoms" (soufflé in phyllo dough), popovers, French toast w/ Vermont cob-smoked bacon; dinner in season, Wed.–Sun. (extra, res. req., no cred. cds); tea, cakes; bar
Recreation: Tennis, skiing, golf, walking, boating, fishing
Amenities & Services: Priv. phone, newspapers, pool table; business retreats, family reunions, etc.

ACCOMMODATIONS

Units: 7 guest rooms, 2 suites; suite in cottage
All Rooms: Bath
Some Rooms: Fireplace; cottage: deck, fireplace, TV
Bed & Bath: Queen/king; baths recently renovated; some whirlpools
Favorites: Dalton—extra-large 2nd-floor room, view of Mt. Washington;

1,400 sq.ft. cottage w/ modern art, Oriental rugs, quilts.
Comfort & Decor: Spacious w/ antiques and reproductions, carpet, views. Feel of privacy in mansion. Good bedside lighting. Whimsical and warming touches. Quietly luxurious.

RATES, RESERVATIONS, & RESTRICTIONS

Deposit: 1 night; refund w/ 15-day cancel.
Discounts: 3rd person, groups
Credit Cards: MC, V, AE

Check-In/Out: 3–8/before 11
Smoking: No
Pets: No; in-house cat; boarding nearby
Kids: Over 12

Minimum Stay: 2 nights weekends,
foliage; 3, holidays
Open: All year
Hosts: Judy and Bill Whitman
80 Guider Lane

Bethlehem, NH 03574-0359
(603) 444-2600, 888-444-2600
Fax: (603) 444-4823
Adair@connriver.net
www.adairinn.com

DARBY FIELD INN, Conway

Overall: ★★★½	Room Quality: B	Value: C	Price: $140–$240

Named not after a meadow but after an Irishman named Darby Field, the
first white man to climb Mt. Washington (1642), this comfortable inn is
atop Bald Hill in the wilds of mountainous northern New Hampshire. The
hosts are an interesting combo: Marc has traveled the world and especially
enjoys chatting about golf and skiing; Maria is a proponent of natural heal-
ing, massage therapy, Buddhism, and meditation. After a day on the slopes,
in the pool, or hiking by a nearby waterfall, what could be better than a
tasty meal overlooking a valley sunset, and then a special inn nightcap, an
Irish Revolution, by the wood-burning stove in the pub?

SETTING & FACILITIES

Location: 2.5 mi. S of Conway; on the
border of White Mountain Nat'l Forest
Near: Antiquing, beach, Mt.
Washington, Kancamagus Hwy., Scenic
and Cog Railroads, covered bridges
Building: 1826 Colonial homestead
Grounds: Great views; gardens, forest,
outdoor pool, patio, X-C skiing trails,
hot tub; 1,000 feet above valley

Public Space: LR, tavern, DR
Food & Drink: (MAP) Full breakfast;
candlelight dinner; specialties: roast
duckling w/ raspberry Chambord,
Darby cream pie; low-fat/veg. meals
Recreation: Golf, horses, skiing, tennis,
rock/ice climbing, river sports
Amenities & Services: Access to
X-C ski trails, maps; full-service inn

ACCOMMODATIONS

Units: 6 standard, 3 deluxe, 6 premium
All Rooms: Bath, garden or mountain
view
Some Rooms: Bay window, whirlpool,
TV/VCR, AC, sitting room, daybed
Bed & Bath: Beds vary; tub/showers
in all

Favorites: Suite—AC, queen, bay win-
dow w/ views, whirlpool
Comfort & Decor: Casual, w/
antiques, collectibles, reproductions.
Charming. Four-posters, carpet.
Creative use of space to create baths.

RATES, RESERVATIONS, & RESTRICTIONS

Deposit: 50%; refund w/ 14-day notice
Discounts: Singles, groups, longer stays,
off-season; call for groups, weddings

Credit Cards: MC, V, AE
Check-In/Out: 2–6/9–11
Smoking: Tavern only

Pets: No; in-house dog
Kids: Welcome
Minimum Stay: Some weekends, fall foliage
Open: May–March
Hosts: Maria and Marc Donaldson

Box D, Bald Hill Rd.
Conway, NH 03818-4003
(603) 447-2181, (800) 426-4147
Fax: (603) 447-5726
marc@darbyfield.com
www.darbyfield.com

BUNGAY JAR BED & BREAKFAST, Franconia

Overall: ★★★★½   Room Quality: B   Value: B   Price: $105–$225

Benny Goodman's bathtub, a llama herd, a moosehead of vines on a massive stone fireplace, banisters created from lightning rods, salvage decor with old church doors and stained glass—it's whimsical and constantly surprising. Cluttered and off-beat, this converted four-level barn with the hayloft great room is not for traditionalists. But for those who enjoy artistic, hands-on originality, magazine-cover gardens with lily ponds and twig gates, and warm and enthusiastic hosts, it's a delight. Oh, and a Bungay Jar isn't a vessel for "bungays", it's a folksy term for an unusual spring wind that shakes things up. This place does just that.

SETTING & FACILITIES

Location: From NY, Rt. 112, 12 mi. to Rt. 116 N (left); B&B, about 5 mi. on right
Near: Robert Frost Museum, Franconia Notch Park, Cannon Mountain, Appalachian Trail, Lost River Echo Lake; Sugar Hill, Franconia

Building: Rustic 18th-century barn moved to site in 1967; sep. Plum Cottage in Franconia village
Grounds: 12 secluded areas, garden paths, pond, woods, llamas and horses, terraced gardens, pergola

Public Space: 2-story living area, DR, decks, small library
Food & Drink: Buffet-style country breakfast; specialty: popovers; tea, snacks

Recreation: Hiking, skiing, biking, antiquing
Amenities & Services: Sauna, garden shop, games, garden workshops (fee)

ACCOMMODATIONS

Units: 5 guest rooms, 1 suite, sep. Plum Cottage
All Rooms: Bath, ornate bed
Some Rooms: Priv. balcony, skylight, fireplace; Plum Cottage—fireplace, TV, whirlpool, kitchen
Bed & Bath: Some king, four-poster, canopy, sleigh, antique beds; unique baths, skylight showers, claw-foot tubs, Benny Goodman's 6-foot soaking tub

Favorites: Garden Suite—kitchen/dining area, fireplace, dbl. jacuzzi facing mountains, priv. garden; Stargazer—3rd floor, tiny, skylights, view, twig furniture, telescope, claw-foot tub
Comfort & Decor: Eclectic to the max, from small to large, traditional to unique. Rustic wide-plank floors, beams, leaded glass, whimsy, antiques. Mountain views all around.

RATES, RESERVATIONS, & RESTRICTIONS

Deposit: Check
Discounts: Kids, singles, 3rd person; weekly rates for cottage
Credit Cards: MC, V, AE
Check-In/Out: 3/11
Smoking: No
Kids: Over 5
Pets: In cottage only; inn has cats and dogs

Minimum Stay: 2 nights foliage, holiday weekends
Open: All year except some holidays
Hosts: Kate Kerivan and Lee Strimbeck
P. O. Box 15, Easton Valley Rd.
Franconia, NH 03580
(603) 823-7775
Fax: (603) 444-0100
info@bungayjar.com
www.bungayjar.com

SUGAR HILL INN, Franconia

Overall: ★★★★	Room Quality: B	Value: C	Price: $90–$155

Sweet as its name, this unpretentious, warm, and welcoming inn doesn't take itself too seriously, and the innkeepers have lavished it with love. Stone walls, buildings of white clapboard with black trim, flower borders, simple country furnishings—it's hard not to rest here, especially in the glow of fireplaces crackling away. The mountains loom, all seasons are spectacular, the skiing is grand, and the feeling is old-fashioned pleasure, much as when local Bette Davis used to stay here to relax. But two new suites with whirlpool tubs may be harbingers of things to come.

SETTING & FACILITIES

Location: From I-93, right on Rt. 18, right on Rt. 117, .5 mi. on right
Near: Robert Frost home, New England Ski Museum
Building: 1789 New England farmhouse, expanded
Grounds: 16 acres nestled in hills, woodlands, lawns
Public Space: DR, pub, large wraparound porch

Food & Drink: (MAP) Three-course country breakfast; specialty: Swiss eggs. Dinner specialty: rosemary-crusted rack of lamb; afternoon tea, scones, sweet bread; wine cellar; spec. diets accom.
Recreation: Skiing, skating, snowshoeing, golf, tennis, fishing
Amenities & Services: Packages, incl. Harvest Your Own Christmas Tree; sleigh rides, concert and lecture series

ACCOMMODATIONS

Units: 10 guest rooms, 2 suites; 6 cottage rooms
All Rooms: Bath, antiques
Some Rooms: Fireplace, mountain view
Bed & Bath: Varied bed sizes, some four-posters; small baths w/ soaking tubs; whirlpools in suites

Favorites: Bette Davis—views on three sides; Cottage rooms—w/ fireplace, more space
Comfort & Decor: Small, but cozy. Each room stenciled, w/ reproductions and modest antiques. Immaculate and sweet. Separate cottages w/ fireplaces more private and spacious.

RATES, RESERVATIONS, & RESTRICTIONS

Deposit: One night or 50%; two nights fall foliage, holiday weekends; refund w/ 14-day notice
Discounts: Packages, extra person;
Credit Cards: V, MC, AE
Check-In/Out: 3/11
Smoking: No
Pets: No
Kids: Over 12 in main house, OK in cottages
No-No's: Return of fee if arriving late or leaving early

Minimum Stay: 2 nights, foliage, holiday weekends
Open: Except April, Nov.
Hosts: Barbara and Jim Quinn
Route 117
Franconia, NH 03580
(800) 548-4748, (603) 823-5621
Fax: (603) 823-5639
info@sugarhillinn.com
www.sugarhillinn.com

BERNERHOF INN, Glen

Overall: ★★★★	Room Quality: B	Value: C	Price: $75–$150

Built in the 1880s as a traveling spot for people on their way to Mt. Washington, the inn was purchased in the 1950s by a Swiss couple, who named it after their native city of Bern. They yodeled, played the Alpine Horn, and loved this area, so similar to the Tyrol. The current hosts have modernized the rooms, but they maintain a bit of European atmosphere. If you would like a taste, so to speak, of cooking school in a mountain setting, "A Taste of the Mountains" includes lodging and wine seminars, instruction, and all meals. And on the fourth morning, you get a champagne breakfast in bed.

SETTING & FACILITIES

Location: 1 mi. W of Rt. 302 and Rt. 16 intersection, 1 mi. E of Attitash

Near: N Conway village, Mt. Washington, Saco River, Cog Railroad, Attitash Bear Peak, Black Mt., Cranmore Resort, Wildcat and Bretton Woods skiing, theater

Building: Large, like small hotel, w/ turrets; c.1880

Grounds: 10 acres: gardens, pool, playground

Public Space: Sitting room, restaurant, pub, lounge

Food & Drink: Full breakfast; fine dining, creative cont'l cuisine; specialties: weinerschnitzel, trout w/ almonds, pots de crème; wine list

Recreation: Snow/water sports, ice/rock climbing, sleigh rides, horses

Amenities & Services: Custom amenities for indiv. rooms (flowers, chocolate truffles)

ACCOMMODATIONS

Units: 7 guest rooms, 2 suites

All Rooms: Bath, AC, phone, TV

Some Rooms: Whirlpool, window alcove

Bed & Bath: Rooms disabled access. (baths not wheelchair access.); some kings, some brass; most w/ whirlpool, pedestal sinks

Favorites: 2 rooms in turret—angles, queens, spacious; Suite—iris stained-

glass window, tear drop shower, whirlpool, sauna, sitting room w/ day bed, TV/VCR; Room 9—3-leaf clover whirlpool, bath w/ shower, 3rd floor, great view

Comfort & Decor: Interesting lighting options—many windows, skylights, stained-glass windows, direct lighting, decorative lighting. Individually decorated w/ Victorian flavor.

RATES, RESERVATIONS, & RESTRICTIONS

Deposit: Refund w/ 14-day notice

Discounts: Longer midweek (not holidays)

Credit Cards: MC, V, AE, D

Check-In/Out: 2–10/10–11

Smoking: No

Pets: No

Kids: OK

Minimum Stay: 2–3 nights weekends, holidays; flexible

Open: All year

Hosts: Sharon Wroblewski
Box 240
Glen, NH 03838
(800) 548-8007, (603) 383-9132
Fax: (603) 383-0809
stay@bernerhofinn.com
www.bernerhofinn.com

NOTCHLAND INN, Hart's Location

Overall: ★★★★½	Room Quality: A	Value: C	Price: $190–$280

Nestled on 400 acres among mountain walls, this English manor house is a artful expression of enthusiastic innkeeping. Les was general manager of American Ballet Theatre in New York, so you can get an idea of the level of quality. The inn's front parlor was designed by Gustav Stickley, a founder of the Arts and Crafts movement, and there are tin ceilings, a dozen fireplaces, an outdoor hot tub, a school-house suite annex, and more. Interesting facts: *The Secaucus Seven* was filmed on the property, which is home to llamas, miniature horses, and a Belgian draft horse named Dolly. Hart's Location is New Hampshire's smallest town, and had the first votes ever reported in national elections.

SETTING & FACILITIES

Location: East of Crawford Notch, on Rt. 302, across from swimming holes and Saco River
Near: Mt. Washington, White Mountain Nat'l. Forest, Kankamagus Hwy., covered bridges, antiquing, ski areas, 5 golf courses, Conway Scenic RR, Cog Railway
Building: 1860s granite Tudor Revival
Grounds: 400 acres, award-winning gardens, wood-fired hot tub in gazebo, pond, swimming holes; 8,000 ft. of Saco River frontage; at base of Mt. Bemis

Public Space: DR , front parlor, music room, sun room, library
Food & Drink: (MAP) Early-bird hot beverages; full country breakfast; 5-course dinner; specialty: blackened swordfish, chicken roulade; spec. diets accom.; liquor license
Recreation: Trails, fishing, swimming, skating on-site; snow/water/mountain sports, strawberry picking, brewery tour nearby
Amenities & Services: Some disabled access., pkgs., online reserv. and availability, check

ACCOMMODATIONS

Units: 7 guest rooms, 5 suites
All Rooms: Bath, wood-burning fireplace, quilts, antiques
Some Rooms: Whirlpool, mountain view, AC, sitting area, porch/deck
Bed & Bath: King/queen, some extra beds, four-poster (1), some Eastlakes; some tub/shower, some whirlpools

Favorites: Mad River Premium Suite—king, queen fold-out sofa, French doors to deck, dbl. whirlpool, views
Comfort & Decor: Green and blue hues, designer fabrics. Lots w/ capacities of 2–4 people. Front rooms, more road noise. Good lighting. Airy, sunny, stylish, spacious. Two suites in adjacent former schoolhouse.

RATES, RESERVATIONS, & RESTRICTIONS

Deposit: 50% w/in 7-days; refund w/ 14-days notice; less than 14-days, refund only if room rebooked

Discounts: Singles, 3rd person, midweek

Credit Cards: MC, V, AE, D

Check-In/Out: 4/11

Smoking: No

Pets: No; in-house Bernese mountain dog

Kids: Over 10

No-No's: Kids under 3 at dinner

(they'll help find babysitters)

Minimum Stay: 2 nights most Saturdays, 3 in-season

Open: All year

Hosts: Ed Butler and Les Schoof
Route 302
Hart's Location, NH 03812
(603) 374-6131, (800) 866-6131
Fax: (603) 374-6168
notchland@aol.com
www.notchland.com

GIBSON HOUSE, Haverhill

Overall: ★★★★½	Room Quality: A	Value: B	Price: $110–$250

On the sleepy green of Haverhill Corners, this traditional house is anything but. Keita, the gracious owner and resident artist, provides an otherworldly feast of texture and color and spirit—yellow and lime in unexpected places in the breakfast room (where the food presentation is just as eye-opening), faux windows, tribal rugs, stained-glass moons that light up the night. An art gallery is in the basement—the former stable of a 1776 stagecoach inn. But the whole of this new bed-and-breakfast is an artwork. And the house pets include a manx cat and a gray parrot named Leroy Brown.

SETTING & FACILITIES

Location: Village Green, Haverhill
Near: Hanover (Dartmouth Coll.),
lakes, Conn. River, Appalachian Trail,
antiquing
Building: 1850 Greek Revival
Grounds: 1.5 acres, lily pond, rose gardens, gazebo, sculptures, pottery fireplace, sunset views
Public Space: Parlors, DRs, porches

Food & Drink: Full gourmet breakfast;
specialties: blueberry pancakes, maple
syrup, smokehouse bacon; refreshments
Recreation: Tennis, skiing, golf, boating, cycling, hiking, antiquing
Amenities & Services: Gallery, garden wedding facil., catering, hot-air balloon and horse/carriage rides, owner's
favorite painting locations w/ picnic

ACCOMMODATIONS

Units: 4 guest rooms, 1 suite
All Rooms: Bath, phone, ceiling fan
Some Rooms: Four-poster bed, fireplace
Bed & Bath: Varied bed sizes; some
murals, pedestal sinks, claw-foot tubs
Favorites: Avalon Suite—king antique
teak bed, Moravian starlight draped
daybed, fireplace, French doors to priv.

porch, beamed ceiling, whirlpool with
arched stained-glass window
Comfort & Decor: Creative theme
rooms, such as Taj North w/ stained-glass moon and night sky over walnut
bed; A Day at the Beach w/ hanging
rope chair. Hand-stamped walls. Lush
whimsy. Dramatic colors. Not designed
for comfort, but very romantic.

RATES, RESERVATIONS, & RESTRICTIONS

Deposit: Full refund w/ 7-day notice
Discounts: 3rd, groups, long stays,
singles
Credit Cards: None
Check-In/Out: 3/11
Smoking: No
Pets: No; cat and parrot at inn
Kids: No

Minimum Stay: None
Open: All year
Hosts: Keita Colton
RR 1 Box 193, Rt. 10
Haverhill, NH 03765
(603) 989-3125
Fax: (603) 989-5749
gibson.house@ConnRiver.net

THE FOREST, Intervale

Overall: ★★★½	Room Quality: B	Value: C	Price: $80–$170

You can see The Forest for the trees on the 25 acres are spread beyond.
Bikers especially enjoy this Country Victorian lodging, part of a route with
other inns and bed-and-breakfasts. The parlor was a general store from the
1830s, moved to enlarge the premises in the 1880s, and the stone cottage
was the office of one of New Hampshire's first female lawyers. Hearty
breakfasts feature apple pancakes and eggs with all the trimmings. Guest
rooms are comfortable and old-fashioned, the parlors look lived in, and the

feeling here is kick-your-shoes-off relaxed. Grounds adjoin a cross-country ski trail, and the swimming pool is a big plus.

SETTING & FACILITIES

Location: 1.5 mi. from North Conway on Rt. 16A, adjoining X-C skiing trails
Near: North Conway outlets, jazz festivals, equine festivals, local theater, concerts, White Mountain Nat'l. Forest
Building: 3-story Victorian, mansard roof; stone cottage
Grounds: 25 acres, woods, stream, gardens, heated outdoor pool, picnic tables, grill, trails
Public Space: 2 LRs, TV room, porch

Food & Drink: Full breakfast; specialties: blueberry pancakes, spiced Belgian waffles, Amaretto French toast, homemade jam; refreshments
Recreation: Swimming, snow/water activities, golf, horses, tennis, sleigh rides
Amenities & Services: Picnic area, gas grill, refrigerator, lawn games, after-ski wine/cheese in winter; celebrating spec. occasions, gatherings, inn-to-inn bike tours

ACCOMMODATIONS

Units: 8 guest rooms, 3 cottages
All Rooms: Bath, coordinated fabrics, plants
Some Rooms: Fireplace, ceiling fan
Bed & Bath: Queens, brass, sleigh beds, four-posters in cottage; whirlpool (1)

Favorites: Cottle Room—in cottage, fireplace, priv. veranda
Comfort & Decor: Quilts and comforters, antiques, country furniture. Flowered wallpapers. 3rd floor rooms largest. Cottages most romantic.

RATES, RESERVATIONS, & RESTRICTIONS

Deposit: 50%, refund w/ 14-day notice
Discounts: Off-season, 3rd person
Credit Cards: MC, V, AE, D
Check-In/Out: 2/11
Smoking: No
Pets: No
Kids: Over 6
Minimum Stay: 2 nights most weekends, 3 nights holidays

Open: May–March
Hosts: Lisa and Bill Guppy
Box 37
Intervale, NH 03845
(603) 356-9772, (800) 448-3534
Fax: (603) 356-5652
forest@ncia.net
www.forest-inn.com

CARTER NOTCH INN, Jackson

Overall: ★★★½	Room Quality: B	Value: B	Price: $69–$139

When last visited a few years ago, this former home of the owners of the old Eagle Mountain House next door (now a condo) was a homey, ho-hum little budget bed-and-breakfast with a dumbwaiter elevator. But a later visit shows that innkeepers can make or break a place. Still the kind of lodgings where you can put your feet up, current hosts Jim and Lynda stress that guests are considered company, and have upgraded all around. Breakfasts are now lavish, with favorites like whole-wheat blueberry pancakes, guest rooms have been freshened, and the third floor transformed into luxury units. Jackson Falls is still a walk away for picnicking, the golf course across the road is as pretty as ever from the porch, and the dumbwaiter remains.

SETTING & FACILITIES

Location: Half mi. from village on country road, across from golf course, near Jackson Falls
Near: Wildcat River Valley, Jackson Falls, White Mountain Nat'l. Forest, outlets, downhill skiing, golf courses, waterfalls
Building: Circa 1909 former inn, annex, and family homestead; renovated 1995
Grounds: Wraparound porch; outdoor hot tub
Public Space: Cottage-style LR, sitting area, orig. weighted elevator

Food & Drink: Country breakfast, specialties: pumpkin pancakes, Grand Marnier stuffed French toast, omelets; p.m. snacks: hot drinks, Carter Notch Inn cookies; special meals
Recreation: X-C skiing, hiking; 5 min. to skiing, golf, canoeing, pool, tennis
Amenities & Services: AC, hosts' foliage and touring maps, refrigerator, kitchen privileges, rec. facil. next door, celebrating spec. occasions

ACCOMMODATIONS

Units: 7 guest rooms
All Rooms: Bath, AC, clock, radio
Some Rooms: Fireplace, whirlpool (1)
Bed & Bath: Most queens/doubles, some extra beds; new baths
Favorites: Room 5—cozy, double, blue-hued, sun from bay window overlooking golf course

Comfort & Decor: Small. Light, airy, lots of white. Painted floors and furniture, dried flowers, straw hats. Simple and elegant. Great views of Wildcat River Valley. Third floor luxury rooms.

RATES, RESERVATIONS, & RESTRICTIONS

Deposit: 1 night; 14-day cancel. w/ fee
Discounts: Off-season, midweek, singles, 3rd person
Credit Cards: MC, V, AE, D
Check-In/Out: After 1/before 11
Smoking: No
Pets: No; in-house dog (mag.-cover dog—ask) and cat
Kids: 6 and up

Minimum Stay: 2 nights fall foliage, weekends; 3 nights 3-day weekends
Open: All year
Hosts: Lynda and Jim Dunwell
Box 269, Carter Notch Rd.
Jackson, NH 03846-0269
(800) 794-9437, (603) 383-9630
www.journeysnorth.com/carternotch

CHRISTMAS FARM INN, Jackson

Overall: ★★★★	Room Quality: B	Value: B	Price: $78–$135

If you like talking politics, you can debate with innkeeper Bill, who served in the U.S. House of Representatives. Cutesy Christmas references abound: Mistletoe Pub, Sugar Plum Dining Room, and guest rooms named Prancer, Blitzen, et. al. But there's much more at this family-oriented inn. The Jackson Ski Touring Federation was founded in their living room, and access to 80 kilometers of trails is easy. Accommodations vary from suites in an up-to-date function center and cozy old-fashioned rooms in the main house, to cottages with two bedrooms and baths. And for those who can't wait, the Christmas-in-July fete has a tree and Santa.

SETTING & FACILITIES

Location: .25 mi. from post office on Rt. 16B
Near: Antiquing, beach, historic sites, outlets, trails; walk to Jackson Falls
Building: 1778 homestead, barn, outbuildings
Grounds: 14 acres: award-winning gardens; rec. facil., sauna, hot tub
Public Space: Pub, LR, library, DR, wheelchair access
Food & Drink: (MAP) Full breakfast; specialty: homemade doughnuts; poolside lunch, beverages; candlelight dinner; specialty: medallions of pork w/ brandy; spec. meals avail.; liquor license
Recreation: Tennis, guided ski tours, sleigh rides, ice skating, wine tastings in season
Amenities & Services: Packing lunch, spec. events coord., banquets (80). Corp. functions: conf. center (50), dataports, a/v, VCRs, wide-screen TVs, fax, copier, overnight mail, flip charts

ACCOMMODATIONS

Units: 10 guest rooms in inn, 9 in Salt Box; 4 suites in barn, cottages, log cabin, sugar house
All Rooms: Bath, phone
Some Rooms: Whirlpool, TV, refrigerator, shared sauna, fireplace, mountain views, sundeck, 2 BRs, priv. entrance, LR, loft
Bed & Bath: Beds vary, some canopies, four-posters; most tubs; some whirlpools
Favorites: 2 Salt Box—2nd floor, alcove, great view
Comfort & Decor: Colonial w/ Laura Ashley, but varies by type of lodging. Country feel. Small in main house. Quietest in outbuildings.

RATES, RESERVATIONS, & RESTRICTIONS

Deposit: 1 night, 50% for foliage, holidays, school vacations; 14-day cancel. policy
Discounts: 3rd person, corp., longer stays, seniors, groups, kids under 12 sharing w/ parents; extra for singles, dbl. occupancy in cottage
Credit Cards: MC, V, AE
Check-In/Out: 3/11
Smoking: Some rooms

Pets: No
Kids: OK
Minimum Stay: 2 nights winter weekends
Open: All year
Hosts: Synda and Bill Zeliff

Route 16
Jackson, NH 03846
(603) 383-4313, (800) 443-5837
Fax: (603) 383-6495
info@christmasfarminn.com
www.christmasfarminn.com

THE INN AT THORN HILL, Jackson

Overall: ★★★★½   Room Quality: A   Value: C   Price: $170–$320

An old Victrola phonograph and Victorian mannequins in period clothes are nostalgic elements of this complete, premier Jackson inn. If you want romance, there's candlelight dining and private cottages with whirlpools and fireplaces. If you're with a group, you can rent out the carriage house with its seven guest rooms surrounding a central great room with fireplace. Foodies will savor dishes like lobster pie or seafood sausage with lemon-caper butter. And active types can swim in the pool, or cross-country ski from the doorstep to a 146-kilometer touring trail. Designed by famed architect Stanford White, well-managed and casual, Thorn Hill is much more a rose than a thorn.

SETTING & FACILITIES

Location: Just up the hill from town
Near: Antiquing, beach, historic sights, galleries, Jackson Falls, Wildcat River, White Mountain Nat'l. Forest, Mt. Washington Valley Theater Company, Mt. Washington Auto Rd., Story Land, Conway Scenic RR, Cog Railway, Attitash Bear Peak and Fields of Attitash
Building: Built 1895, designed by Stanford White
Grounds: 9 acres: fields, stream, pond, flower/herb gardens, pool, views of Mt. Washington
Public Space: Porch, pub, common rooms
Food & Drink: (MAP) Full breakfast of breads, muffins, entree choices, eggs; 3-course dinners (res.), specialties: shrimp-and-asparagus open lasagne, grilled cumin chicken breast; wine list; veg. meals avail.
Recreation: Canoeing, golf, tennis, skiing, tennis racket rental, glider flights
Amenities & Services: Books, games, hot tub; packing picnics, arranging massages, guided hikes; near canoe, mountain bike rentals; celebrating spec. occasions

ACCOMMODATIONS

Units: 12 guest rooms, 4 suites, 3 cottages
All Rooms: Bath, AC, hairdryer
Some Rooms: Extra bed, LR, fireplace, deck, skylight, coffeemaker, phone, wet bar

Bed & Bath: Most queens, some kings, some four-posters; some whirlpools, dbl. whirlpools
Favorites: Katherine's Suite—queen, dbl. whirlpool, LR w/ dbl. gas fireplace, TV

Comfort & Decor: Main inn rooms in Victorian decor, named after nearby mountains. Cottages, French country. Carriage house in Adirondack decor, named after local hills. Some fabulous views.

RATES, RESERVATIONS, & RESTRICTIONS

Deposit: 1 night, 50% 3 or more nights w/in 7 days; refund w/ 14-day notice
Discounts: Seniors, long stays, off-season, 3rd
Credit Cards: MC, V, AE, DC
Check-In/Out: 3/11
Smoking: No
Pets: No
Kids: Over 8
Minimum Stay: 2–3 nights most

weekends, holidays, some peak
Open: All year, except part of April
Hosts: Ibby and Jim Cooper
Thorn Hill Rd, Box A
Jackson, NH 03846
(603) 383-4242, (800) 289-8990
Fax: (603) 383-8062
thornhll@ncia.net
www.innatthornhill.com

NESTLENOOK FARM, Jackson

Overall: ★★★★	Room Quality: B	Value: C	Price: $125–$320

The name well describes this picturesque, hyper-romantic bed-and-breakfast with a bird cage filled with love birds, a little chapel for weddings, and an arched covered bridge, perfect to pop the question. Victoriana is celebrated in guest room decor and details, and each summer the staff dresses in period costume for a day, and leads Victorian games. Horse-drawn sleighs (summer on wheels) whisk you to a forest, where you can feed deer, and around the 65 acres with gardens and paths, a heated lakeside gazebo and farm animals. The Never-Never Land quality works, if you like it and let it.

SETTING & FACILITIES

Location: Rt. 16, .5 mi. past covered bridge, 1st right onto Dinsmore Rd.
Near: Beach, shopping, antiquing
Building: Gingerbread Victorian; parlor c. 1800
Grounds: 65 acres: forest, lake, pool, gazebo, Riverside Chapel, Angle Island
Public Space: Sitting room, game room, guest kitchen, DR

Food & Drink: Full breakfast; specialties: pumpkin bread, baked omelets; fruit, wine/cheese hour; diet, low-fat meals
Recreation: Downhill skiing, water sports, golf, horses, sleigh rides
Amenities & Services: Some disabled access for visual, hearing-impaired, refrigerator, turndown, celebrating spec. occasions; banquet facil., weddings

ACCOMMODATIONS

Units: 5 guest rooms, 2 suites
All Rooms: Whirlpool bath, antique radio, clock
Some Rooms: 19th-century parlor stove, AC, 1 fireplace
Bed & Bath: Queen/king, some four-posters, canopies; dbl. whirlpools in all
Favorites: Paskell Room—private, hand-carved king four-poster; Morton

Room—oldest, orig. beams, brick hearth, porch access
Comfort & Decor: Victorian feel. Rooms named after local artists, featuring their paintings. Antiques, wallpapers. Hand-painted, patterned radiators. All w/ stove or fireplace. Highly romantic. Most, views of river or lake; 3rd-floor suite, three-way views

RATES, RESERVATIONS, & RESTRICTIONS

Deposit: 50%; refund w/ 14-day notice
Discounts: AAA, longer stays, 3rd person
Credit Cards: MC, V, D
Check-In/Out: 3/11
Smoking: No
Pets: No
Kids: Over 12
Minimum Stay: 2 nights weekends, 3 holidays

Open: All year
Hosts: Linda Wagstaff
Dinsmore Rd.
Jackson, NH 03846
(603) 383-9443, (800) 659-9443
Email through web site
www.luxurymountaingetaways.com

WILDCAT INN AND TAVERN, Jackson

Overall: ★★★	Room Quality: C	Value: A	Price: $38–$78

This lively, basic inn offers in-town location, a real lunch, nightly entertainment in season, and a great price. The front porch dining room is a people-watching venue where you'll enjoy home-baked pastries at breakfast, bagels and lox for lunch, and for dinner, maybe Wildcat chicken in puffed pastry, and rhubarb-pudding cake or sour-cream apple pie (you can afford the calories after skiing, tennis or golf). Apres-ski and live entertainment go on most nights, in-season: Tuesday is open-mike night in the tavern; Thursdays, R&B and jazz. This informal inn has roaring fireplaces, funny rules on the tavern wall, commotion, and acceptable rooms. For romantics, or those seeking a bucolic escape, try the cottage—or another inn.

SETTING & FACILITIES

Location: Route 16A in center of Jackson Village
Near: Jackson Ski Touring Foundation across the street, near other ski centers, outlets in North Conway

Building: Blue Colonial house and annex
Grounds: Award-winning garden, smallish lawns

Public Space: Sitting, game rooms, tavern, glassed-in porch/DR w/ disabled access

Food & Drink: (MAP) Farm breakfast, brunch/lunch; tea, cocoa, cookies; dinner; homemade desserts; taking dinner to room OK, spec. diets accom.

Recreation: Snowshoeing, ice skating, golf, tennis, fishing

Amenities & Services: Live entertainment, maps, games; catering, celebrating spec. occasions, refrigerator, irons

ACCOMMODATIONS

Units: 7 guest rooms, 5 suites, 1 cottage for 6

All Rooms: AC, TV, phone

Some Rooms: Pull-out sofa; cottage: LR, kitchen, 1.5 baths, 2 BR

Bed & Bath: Twin, double, king beds; some tub/shower

Favorites: Room 14—relatively large, queen, faces 7 windows, sunny

Comfort & Decor: Colonial style w/ antiques, wallpaper, and prints in style of New England farm. Sunny, basic; can be noisy at night.

RATES, RESERVATIONS, & RESTRICTIONS

Deposit: 1 night; 14-day cancel. w/ fee

Discounts: Off-season, singles, pkgs. (e.g., horse shows); cottage

Credit Cards: MC, V, AE

Check-In/Out: 12/10:30

Smoking: Tavern

Pets: No

Kids: OK

Minimum Stay: 2 nights weekends; 3 on holiday weekends

Open: All year

Hosts: Pam and Marty Sweeney
Route 16A, Box 7, Main St.,
Jackson, NH 03846
(603) 383-4245, (800) 228-4245
Fax: (603) 383-6456
wildcat@ncia.net
www.journeysnorth.com/mwv/wildcat.html

BUTTONWOOD INN, North Conway

Overall: ★★★★	Room Quality: B	Value: B	Price: $75–$200

Creativity abounds, cute as a button. Sample breakfast entrees: "Sunrise Puff," topped with spicy orange sauce, and "To Die for French Toast," baked caramel apple slices and egg-soaked bread topped with spiced applesauce. But get serious. An on-site meeting planner takes care of conference details, and candlelight dinners highlight winter Saturdays. Other pluses: The pool has a backdrop of old barn foundations. A New England scene borders the walls in the downstairs game room, the upstairs reading room has clouds on the ceiling and a box full of amenities, and the hosts provide day packs for hikers.

SETTING & FACILITIES

Location: 16 N to North Conway, 2 mi. from town, on dead-end road
Near: Antiquing, beach, museum; 2 hrs. from Dartmouth, 1.5 from Portland
Building: 1820s Cape-style farmhouse
Grounds: 17 acres on Mt. Surprise: award-winning gardens, pool, trails
Public Space: LR, FR, conf. rooms, DR, reading room

Food & Drink: Full breakfast; hot drinks; spec. diets avail.
Recreation: Horses, water/snow sports, tennis, billiards, golf, hunting
Amenities & Services: Fridge, day packs, guidebooks, picnic blankets, X-C skiing trails, theme weekends; meetings/events (20); fax, dataport, sep. phone line, on-site meeting planner

ACCOMMODATIONS

Units: 10 guest rooms
All Rooms: Individual decor, quilts
Some Rooms: Bath, fireplace, living area, whirlpool, AC
Bed & Bath: Queens, many Shaker-style headboards; some claw-foot tubs
Favorites: Garden room—tub/shower, garden/pool views, sitting area, AC;

Room 9—bright, yellow/white wide-striped paper
Comfort & Decor: Country style, wide-pine floors, Shaker furniture, period stenciling, antiques, reading lamps.

RATES, RESERVATIONS, & RESTRICTIONS

Deposit: 50%
Discounts: Singles, 3rd person, family; packages
Credit Cards: MC, V, AE, DC
Check-In/Out: 3/11
Smoking: No
Pets: No; in-house dog
Kids: No
Minimum Stay: 2 nights winter/holiday weekends

Open: All year
Hosts: Claudia and Peter Needham
Box 1817, Mt. Surprise Rd.
North Conway, NH 03860-1817
(603) 356-2625, (800) 258-2625
Fax: (603) 356-3140
button_w@moose.ncia.net
www.buttonwoodinn.com

FARM BY THE RIVER, North Conway

Overall: ★★★★	Room Quality: B	Value: B	Price: $65–$135

King George III deeded this property on the river to Rick's ancestors in 1771, and it was a dairy farm until 30 years ago. As a kid, Rick helped his grandmother run a boarding house here, so it was a natural for him to create a bed-and-breakfast. The past is evident not just in the beamed barn built in 1772, but in family treasures and old photos, and guest rooms named after ancestors or former guests. Charlene is a landscape architect and artist, and both talents are evident. Today, you can savor Belgian waffles with strawberries and cream by a crackling fire in the dining room, or on the deck overlooking 65 acres and the White Mountains. Then saddle up, or climb up nearby Cathedral Ledge.

SETTING & FACILITIES

Location: Rt. 16 to Conway; 2 mi. from village on Saco River, .5 mi. from Echo Lake State Park, on sandy beach
Near: Cathedral Ledge, N Conway shopping, Conway Scenic Railroad, Mt. Washington, Story Land, Heritage N.H.
Building: White clapboard farmhouse land-granted by King George III; in family since 1771
Grounds: 65 acres: forest, pasture, gardens, barns, deck, sugar maple orchard

Public Space: 2 common rooms, DR, deck
Food & Drink: Breakfast; specialties: blueberry pancakes, French toast amandine
Recreation: Water sports, stables, wagon/sleigh rides, X-C skiing, show-shoeing onsite; near rock climbing, golf, downhill skiing
Amenities & Services: Snowshoes, dinner reservations, maps

ACCOMMODATIONS

Units: 2 guest rooms; 5 deluxe rooms; 2 suites
All Rooms: Flowers, high ceiling, view
Some Rooms: Bath, whirlpool, fireplace, AC
Bed & Bath: King/queen, 1 full; 1 bath outside room (sink in room), some tubs

Favorites: Mrs. Carrol's—dbl. whirlpool, fireplace, pedestal sink, mountain view
Comfort & Decor: Family heirlooms, views of mountains/pastures. Mix of colonial and Victorian. Maple and walnut furniture, Oriental rugs. Good cross-ventilation. Two-room suites.

RATES, RESERVATIONS, & RESTRICTIONS

Deposit: Full payment 1-2 nights; 1st and last nights for 3+; refund w/ 14-day notice
Discounts: Singles, 3d person
Credit Cards: MC, V
Check-In/Out: 4–9/before 10:30
Smoking: No
Pets: No; in-house dog and horses; kennel 1 mi.
Kids: In rooms w/o fireplaces

Minimum Stay: Some rooms some weekends
Open: All year
Hosts: Charlene and Rick Davis
2555 West Side Rd.
North Conway, NH 03860-5925
(603) 356-2694, 888-414-8353
Fax: (603) 356-2694 (call first)
info@farmbytheriver.com
www.mountwashingtonvalley.com/thefarm

NERELEDGE INN, North Conway

Overall: ★★★½	Room Quality: C	Value: B	Price: $59–$119

Old-fashioned, inexpensive, and informal, this bed-and-breakfast by the river, built in 1787—and an inn for over 100 years—is noted mainly for its hospitality. And then, for its farmhouse breakfasts. The dining room is a cheery cherry-red and white, and you get to choose from a menu including creative omelets—maybe tomato, basil, and ricotta—or chocolate chip pancakes, and definitely dessert: English apple crumble topped with vanilla ice cream. To work this off, rock climbers and fly-fishers take note: Some of the best rock climbing in the East is nearby, and a fishing school is on site on seasonal weekends. The rest of us can bike, hike, canoe, chat with Val and Dave by the spinning wheel, or just wait eagerly until the next morning's repast.

SETTING & FACILITIES

Location: Rt. 16 into North Conway; 3 min. walk from town, on a quiet road near the Saco River
Near: Summer theater, 4 downhill ski resorts, and 1000km X-C skiing, 1 hr. away
Building: 1787, built by Moses Randall; inn since c.1880
Grounds: 2 acres; lawn; small herb, vegetable, flower gardens
Public Space: Entry, breakfast room, old pub room, large sitting room, old DR

Food & Drink: Country breakfast; specialties: blueberry pancakes w/ maple syrup, muffins; hot drinks, cookies; spec. diets accom.
Recreation: River sports; near rock/ice climbing, golf, tennis, amusement parks, mountain biking
Amenities & Services: Grand piano, irons, refrigerator, hairdryer, microwave, X-C ski rental nearby; bus pickup/drop-off; bike/canoe rental; fax, phone, dataport

ACCOMMODATIONS

Units: 11 guest rooms
All Rooms: Individual country decor
Some Rooms: AC, bath
Bed & Bath: Mostly queens, extra beds; firm beds; some half-baths
Favorites: 5-dormer, country decor and floral paper, queen and single beds

Comfort & Decor: Simple rooms. Cathedral ledge, mountain views. Informal, but immaculate. Set up especially for groups/families w/ multiple beds in rooms. Reading lights.

RATES, RESERVATIONS, & RESTRICTIONS

Deposit: 2 nights; 2-week cancel. policy
Discounts: Off-season, midweek, singles, 3rd person, kids ($1 extra for each year)

Credit Cards: MC, V, AE, D
Check-In/Out: 3/10:30; call for arrival after 10 p.m.

Smoking: No
Pets: No; will arrange local boarding
Kids: Welcome
Minimum Stay: Call; generally 2
nights weekends
Open: All year
Hosts: Valerie and Dave Halpin

River Rd., Box 547
North Conway, NH 03860-0547
(603) 356-2831
Fax: (603) 356-2831
nereledge@landmarknet.net
www.nettx.com/nereledge/index.html

FOXGLOVE, Sugar Hill

Overall: ★★★★	Room Quality: B	Value: B	Price: $85–$165

Details, details, details—nine Christmas trees, typed-up day trips, special bedding, extensive lupine gardens—and Janet and Walter are sophisticated and hands-on. Let some of the breakfasts speak for the bed-and-breakfast experience: scrambled eggs with chives, corn cob–smoked ham, and fried apples and walnuts; sunflower toast with homemade marmalade; cornmeal pancakes with scallions and corn, sour-cream dill topping, and smoked salmon; lemon-zest popovers; banana-pecan buttermilk pancakes with smoked turkey and mango. Janet is an interior designer with a sensual touch and soft palette, so the look is unusual and eclectic. And she'll cook dinner.

SETTING & FACILITIES

Location: I-93 Exit 38, right on Rt. 18, .25 to Rt. 117 turn left, 2.3 mi. on right, in hilly residential area
Near: Franconia Notch, Upper Conn. River, Mt. Washington Valley, cog railway to top of Mt. Washington, summer theater, concerts, museums, covered bridges, Robert Frost's cottage
Building: 1898 New England gabled
Grounds: 3 acres, lush woodland, quiet glades, terrace, gardens, fountains
Public Space: LR, sitting area, DR, 2 glassed-in porches; porch and DR w/ views

Food & Drink: Full breakfast; specialties: puffy baked cinnamon-apple pancakes; lunch and dinner by special request (extra); specialties: Belgian carrot soup, grilled salmon fillet, white chocolate tart; spec. diets accom.; wine, champagne
Recreation: Golf, tennis, water/snow sports, balloon/glider/sleigh rides, rock/wall climbing
Amenities & Services: Games, 3D puzzles; recipes (cookbook in progress); Internet news daily (European news), meetings (15), fax, dataports; weddings, cycling tours, planned day trips

ACCOMMODATIONS

Units: 6 guest rooms
All Rooms: Bath
Some Rooms: Sitting area
Bed & Bath: 1 double, 2 queens, 2 kings, excellent mattresses, some

upholstered or antique headboards; some claw-foot tubs, pedestal sinks, glass-enclosed showers
Favorites: Mrs. Harmes' Room—turret, 4 lace-curtained windows, maple

table from Parisian boudoir; Gingham Room—pastel palette, handpainted beds, antique armoire, "large and creamy" bath

Comfort & Decor: Individually decorated, in sophisticated, eclectic style. Attention to detail. Meticulous. New carriage house most private.

RATES, RESERVATIONS, & RESTRICTIONS

Deposit: 50%; refund w/10-day notice
Discounts: Longer stays, groups, singles
Credit Cards: MC,V
Check-In/Out: 3/10
Smoking: No
Pets: No; in-house cat (not in guest areas)
Kids: Over 12

Minimum Stay: None
Open: All year
Hosts: Janet and Walter Boyd
Route 117 at Lovers Lane
Sugar Hill, NH 03585
(603) 823-8840
Fax: (603) 823-5755
Foxglovelnn@compuserve.com
www.foxgloveinn.com

SUNSET HILL HOUSE, Sugar Hill

Overall: ★★★★	Room Quality: B	Value: C	Price: $90–$220

Bought at a foreclosure auction, this once-decrepit inn is a real success story. The family has transformed the old lady, if not again into a grand hotel, at least into a fine inn. Continuous upgrading is turning simple rooms into luxury units, now appealing to romantics as well as to families, golfers, skiers, and conference attendees. The heated pool faces the mountains, where lunch is served in summer. Golf is across the road, and in winter you can cross-country ski or take a horse-drawn sleigh ride over the course. There's lots to do, good food, and comfortable digs—plus, that sunset.

SETTING & FACILITIES

Location: Rt. 117 to the top of Sugar Hill, turn on to Sunset Hill Rd.; straddles a 1,700-foot ridge
Near: Major downhill ski areas
Building: 1882 annex to grand hotel; refurbished 1993
Grounds: Lawns, gardens, panoramic views
Public Space: Three airy fireplace parlors, DRs, tavern, art gallery in hall

Food & Drink: Full country breakfast buffet; a specialty: French toast stuffed with cream cheese and seasonal fruit; 4-course dinner; informal meals in tavern
Recreation: Golf, X-C skiing, swimming, ice skating, sleigh rides
Amenities & Services: 9-hole course (fees), banquet room (120), pool, golf lessons/rentals, special events such as cooking school, artist workshop, fly-fishing instruction, maple sugar tours

ACCOMMODATIONS

Units: 27 guest rooms, 3 suites
All Rooms: Bath, view, coordinated fabrics
Some Rooms: Whirlpool, brass bed, fireplace
Bed & Bath: Varied bed sizes; new bath fixtures

Favorites: Jacuzzi Suite—whirlpool, king/queen; odd-numbered rooms have preferable views
Comfort & Decor: Simple, neat. Bay windows, hardwood floors. Refurbished rooms w/ fireplaces, whirlpools. Some rooms spartan, small.

RATES, RESERVATIONS, & RESTRICTIONS

Deposit: One night or 50%
Discounts: Packages, extra person, kids under 11, MAP
Credit Cards: V, MC, AE, D
Check-In/Out: 3/11
Smoking: No
Pets: No
Kids: OK
Minimum Stay: 2 nights, weekends/holidays

Open: All year
Hosts: Tricia and Michael Coyle, and family
Sunset Hill Rd.
Sugar Hill, NH 03585
(800) SUNHILL, (603) 823-5522
Fax: (603) 823-5738
sunsethh@aol.com

Vermont

Vermont is classic New England: village greens with white, steepled churches; dirt roads; covered bridges over rushing streams; flaming autumns and winter-wonderland settings; mountains and lakes; rolling farmland punctuated by red barns; maple-sugaring buckets hanging under spigoted trunks; hand-crafted products and fresh local foods. This state is aware that much of its revenue comes from tourism, and it zealously protects its still-undeveloped countryside and rural traditions. After all, neither Burlington nor Montpelier, its major towns, has even 50,000 residents.

Originally home to the Iroquois and Algonquin Indians, Vermont was settled by Europeans following the explorations of Samuel de Champlain in 1609. The area was a site of the French and Indian War and the American Revolution, where the Green Mountain Boys fought with Ethan Allen and Benedict Arnold. As an independent republic in 1777, the state was the first to prohibit slavery before becoming the fourteenth state in 1791. Presidents Chester Arthur and Calvin Coolidge were native Vermonters.

Vermont's mountains, lakes, and winding dirt paths offer bracing outdoor pleasures. The Green Mountains became the home of Eastern skiing and the birthplace of the ski tow at pretty Woodstock in 1934. With more than 200 inches of annual snowfall, the state caters to the winter sports crowd with vast condo complexes and world-class resorts. Seventeen ski areas include Killington, Stowe, Mt. Snow, Smuggler's Notch, Jay Peak, Stratton, Sugarbush, Mad River Glen, Okemo, Askutney, Burke, and Bromley. Nine mountains are over 2,000 vertical feet, and there more than 1,000 ski trails.

The state also has 60-plus cross-country centers, with more than 2,000 miles of marked trails over woods and open fields. And there are more than 5,000 miles of marked snowmobile trails. Other winter activities include snowboarding, horse-drawn sleigh rides, ice skating, ice fishing, and snowshoeing. Winter carnivals are popular; check before your visit to see if one is scheduled while you're here.

Lake Champlain, along the state's western border, is another exceptional source of recreation, with fishing, boating, and water activities. Throughout Vermont you'll find more than 400 lakes and ponds and over 5,000 miles of rivers and streams. You can spend a solitary afternoon in a canoe or race in a powerboat. Summer pursuits include camping, golfing, biking, horseback riding, hunting, kayaking, swimming, and tubing.

Artisans have flocked to Vermont for centuries, and the Hitchcock Chair and art glass—still being produced at the Simon Pearce factory in Quechee—are just two examples of the high level of craftsmanship. In the same tradition, the Vermont Teddy Bear Company has proudly used the state name as a symbol of quality, turning a cozy craft into a world-class business.

Fresh, good foodstuffs made from local products are points of pride, and industries are being developed on coffee, cheddar cheese, maple syrup, and most successfully, Ben & Jerry's Ice Cream. But stop at a general stores to sample other local products as well. The New England Culinary Institute near Burlington offers elaborate meals prepared by student star-chefs-to-be, who take Vermont cuisine to a new level.

At Shelburne Farms, south of Burlington, you can learn about historic farming, dairy farming, and cheesemaking, and visit the bakery. Vermont's official state animal is celebrated here at the National Museum of the Morgan Horse. The UVM Morgan Horse Farm in Weybridge is also worth a trip.

Lodging throughout the state is exceptionally charming and increas-ingly sophisticated, often set in ski areas or villages that are beauty spots. Many high-powered types dream of retiring to this lovely state and open-ing the perfect bed-and-breakfast or small inn—and their fulfilled dreams and hard work are yours to enjoy at the end of a glorious drive.

For More Information

Vermont Guide
vermontguide.com

Vermont Lodging Directory
vtweb.com/wheretostay.html

Zone 8
Southern Vermont

Bucolic, beautiful, old-fashioned, mountain-framed, artsy-craftsy, and relaxing, Southern Vermont stretches from the Massachusetts border in the south to the edge of the Green Mountains/Champlain region to the north. New York forms the western boundary, and New Hampshire lies to the east. I-91, the major thoroughfare, runs near the New Hampshire border and easily connects the Boston area. For Connecticut and New York visitors, Route 7 winds closer to the west, providing a more scenic trip through mountain and river terrain.

Although this southern part of the state is perhaps less revered by expert skiers than northern regions, it offers excellent, family-oriented skiing and snowboarding. Mt. Snow/Haystack, Magic Mountain, Bromley, and Stratton Mountain are major resorts here, focusing on superb teaching and accessible lifts. The Stratton Arts Festival, during the glorious fall leaf-peeping season, shows off Vermont arts and crafts, and offers cultural and pops performances.

For invigorating hiking, try Equinox Mountain, Putney Mountain, or Mount Ascutney. While in Manchester you can enjoy the Manchester Music Festival, held in July and August, and exceptional, year-round outlet shopping.

Near the Baltimore Covered Bridge, the Eureka Schoolhouse is an eighteenth-century throwback, complete with old textbooks and antique classroom materials. Throughout Southern Vermont are public libraries and municipal halls, steepled churches, village greens, general stores, small factories, and farmhouses that impart a feeling of a time long gone. Fast-food chains and strip malls are only in a few concentrated areas.

Bennington, with its three covered bridges, fine college, and tradition of arts is an excellent overnight destination. The Bennington Museum has an outstanding collection of Grandma Moses' paintings as well as regional

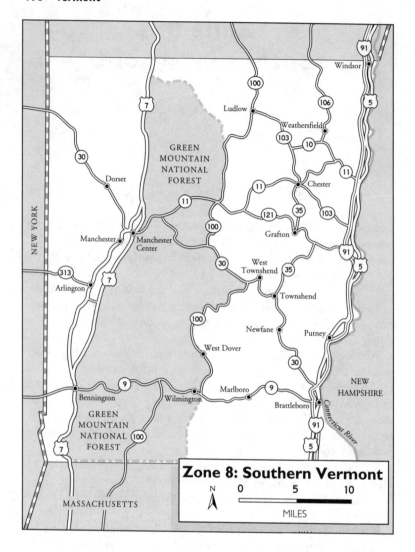

GREEN
MOUNTAIN
NATIONAL
FOREST

NEW YORK

Windsor

Ludlow

Weathersfield

Dorset

Chester

Manchester

Manchester
Center

Grafton

Arlington

West
Townshend

Townshend

Newfane

Putney

West Dover

NEW
HAMPSHIRE

Bennington

Wilmington

Marlboro

Brattleboro

Connecticut River

GREEN
MOUNTAIN
NATIONAL
FOREST

MASSACHUSETTS

Zone 8: Southern Vermont

N   0   5   10

MILES

exhibits, including Bennington pottery. The Bennington Center for the Arts offers first-rate, year-round exhibits and seasonal plays and musicals.

Nearby in Wilmington, you can learn about contemporary Vermont farming at the Adams Farm. Further east, visit Brattleboro, where Rudyard Kipling wrote the *Just So Stories*. Brattleboro was the first permanent European town in the state, settled in 1724. In Putney, a conservative place where summer residents couldn't wear shorts until the 1960s, the kids can check out Santa's Land, a Christmas village complete with petting zoo, open seasonally.

Regional foods are a big part of the menus at small restaurants and diners. Indulge at the Whitingham Sugar Festival in March, a celebration of maple syrup, or stop in general stores and take some cheese or syrup home.

Lodging in southern Vermont varies from five-star, sophisticated luxury inns to unpretentious family-oriented bed-and-breakfasts. Most lodgings cluster around towns like Manchester or near ski resorts. During ski season and in the fall, lodgings close to the mountains fill up fast.

For More Information

Lodging Association of Southern Vermont
www.lodgingvermont.com

INN ON COVERED BRIDGE GREEN, Arlington

| Overall: ★★★★ | Room Quality: B | Value: C | Price: $110–$165+ |

Whether or not you love Norman Rockwell's artistic vision of America, you can't help loving the idea of sleeping in his bedroom, with a view of the covered bridge that gives its name to the property. Rockwell's studio (where his bicycle hangs from the ceiling) also can be rented out as a two-bedroom apartment, and his son's former studio has a loft bedroom with a view. The great illustrator lived here from 1943 to 1954. Since 1987 warm and gracious Anne and Ron have filled this centuries-old farmhouse with antiques from their world travels. Not surprisingly, Rockwell worked on a series called *The Four Seasons* right here. It just doesn't get more New England.

SETTINGS & FACILITIES

Location: From Rt. 7 or 7A, take Rt. 313 W 4.5 mi.; left, through covered bridge

Near: Village church, Battenkill River, Rockwell Museum, East Arlington, shopping, restaurants

Building: 200-year-old farmhouse; studio

Grounds: Over 5 acres, on river; apple orchards, gardens, tennis court; mountain views

Public Space: Hall (Rockwell memorabilia), LR, DR

Food & Drink: Full communal breakfast; specialties: stuffed French toast w/ walnuts and maple syrup; herbed-baked tomato w/ egg

Recreation: Tennis, fishing, canoeing, biking, antiquing

Amenities & Services: Games, books, puzzles

ACCOMMODATIONS

Units: 5 rooms, 2 studios, weekly rentals

All Rooms: Bath, antiques

Some Rooms: Skylight, gas fireplace

Bed & Bath: Four-posters; some whirlpools

Favorites: Spooner Room—formerly Norman Rockwell's BR; four-poster

rice bed, fireplace, view of bridge

Comfort & Decor: Charm and a feel of historic interest. Good views. Fine antiques. Rooms adaptable for suites. Studio: rustic, former grain shed, with beams, ladder to loft.

RATES, RESERVATIONS, & RESTRICTIONS

Deposit: 1 night or 50%; refund w/ 14-day notice

Discounts: Long stay

Credit Cards: AE

Check-In/Out: 3/11

Smoking: No

Pets: No

Kids: In studios, preferably

Minimum Stay: None

Open: All year

Hosts: Ann and Ron Weber
Covered Bridge Rd. RD1, Box 3550
Arlington, VT 05250
(800) 726-9480, (802) 375-9489
cbg@sover.net
www.coveredbridgegreen.com

HUGGING BEAR INN, Chester

| Overall: ★★★½ | Room Quality: C | Value: C | Price: $85–$105 |

"Bearaphenalia" lolls on the porch, stares out the windows, pokes through the banisters, sits at the piano, grins from fabrics, and awaits on every bed. In firefighter costumes, as bride and groom, hanging on the antlers in the entry, perched on shelves and chairs—a veritable plethora of huggable stuffed ones. Over 6,000 bear-related items are in the shop, plus reading matter, ands accessories—and Georgette will try to order any they don't have. She says she's famous for "puppet acting during breakfast" in this relaxed, family-oriented Victorian on the green. Little kids and kids at heart will love it, but you may just have to grin and bear it.

SETTINGS & FACILITIES

Location: On the green, near a cemetery with Revolutionary War gravestones
Near: Summer theater, Vermont Stoneworks, galleries, shops
Building: 1850 Victorian w/ turret; transformed 1982
Grounds: Small, green as front yard; backyard w/ croquet, badminton; carriage house shop

Public Space: Entry, turret room, breakfast room, library, LR, front porch
Food & Drink: Full breakfast in DR, communal; specialties: blueberry pancakes, French toast
Recreation: Golf, fishing, tennis, swimming, biking, skiing, sledding, games, shopping
Amenities & Services: Games, puzzles, books, player piano, lawn games, gift shop

ACCOMMODATIONS

Units: 6
All Rooms: Bath, bears
Some Rooms: AC, extra bed
Bed & Bath: Kings, queens, doubles, twins; cots if needed
Favorites: Tower Room—queen, roundish room, views of Main St. and village green; Pooh Room—furnished

with fabric of Winnie the Pooh characters
Comfort & Decor: Teddy bears everywhere. Bears in every bed, bear motifs for rooms. Combination of 19th century and modern decor, original woodwork. Comfortable, child-friendly. Bright, airy.

RATES, RESERVATIONS, & RESTRICTIONS

Deposit: Credit card for deposit, refund w/ 14-day notice
Discounts: Singles, long stays, gift shop (good for 30 days after departure)
Credit Cards: MC, V, AE, D
Check-In/Out: 2/11

Smoking: No
Pets: Sometimes with prior notice
Kids: Welcome
Minimum Stay: 2 nights weekends
Open: All year except Thanksgiving, Christmas Day

Hosts: Georgette Thomas
244 Main St.
Chester, VT 05143
(802) 875-2412, (800) 325-0519

Fax: (802) 875-3823
georgette@huggingbear.com,
inn@huggingbear.com (reservations)
www.huggingbear.com

ROWELL'S INN, Chester

Overall: ★★★★	Room Quality: B	Value: C	Price: $160–$175

Built in 1820 as a stagecoach stop called The Simonsville Hotel by Major Edward Simon (for whom the hamlet also was named), this handsome brick building was later a general store and post office. When F. A. Rowell came along 100 years ago, he added the tin ceiling and cherry and maple flooring. Beth and Lee, Midwest transplants, proudly continue the tradition. They are natural hosts and cooks, and the preset, five-course dinners are superb, and charmingly presented. (Are Beth's famed applesauce and apple pie so good because she's supposedly related to Johnny Appleseed?) A shoeshine chair, an old Coke machine, and soda-fountain stools are typical of the charming Americana throughout.

SETTINGS & FACILITIES

Location: 7 mi. east of Chester on Rt. 11, in tiny hamlet
Near: Brook, country road, museums, summer theater, shopping, Weston Priory; Okemo, Stratton, Magic, and Bromley mountains
Building: 1820 brick Federal stagecoach hotel, 2nd- and 3rd-floor porch; Nat'l Register of Historic Places
Grounds: Gardens, mature trees, on road
Public Space: Sunroom, parlor, DR, tavern, front porch, patio

Food & Drink: (MAP) Full breakfast; specialties: coffee cake, oatmeal pie; tea; 5-course dinner, set menu w/ 1 entree; beer and wine list; specialties: mushroom strudel, Fiddlehead fern soup, cheddar-cheese pie
Recreation: Trail riding, golf, tennis, fishing, skiing
Amenities & Services: Games, piano, shop on site (antiques/country things), 1960s limo

ACCOMMODATIONS

Units: 6 guest rooms
All Rooms: Bath, quilts, hooked rugs
Some Rooms: Fireplace, porch
Bed & Bath: Double, queen, king; some brass, some extra beds; sinks in rooms, some soaking tubs
Favorites: #1—queen, wood-burning fireplace, soaking tub, no shower; 3rd

floor room—largest, 2 beds, claw-foot tub, once part of ballroom
Comfort & Decor: Individually decorated w/ antiques in period style. Rooms in back quietest. Homey, comfortable, unpretentious. Good lighting. Country charm.

RATES, RESERVATIONS, & RESTRICTIONS

Deposit: 1 night; refund w/ 14-day notice
Discounts: Meal credits for late arrivals, 3rd person
Credit Cards: MC, V; checks preferred
Check-In/Out: 3/11
Smoking: Restricted
Pets: No
Kids: 12 and up

Minimum Stay: 2 nights weekends
Open: May–March, closed 1st 2 weeks in Nov.
Hosts: Beth and Lee Davis
RR 1, Box 267D
Chester, VT 05143
(802) 875-3658, (800) 728-0842 reservations
Fax: (802) 875-3680

CORNUCOPIA OF DORSET, Dorset

| Overall: ★★★★½ | Room Quality: A | Value: B | Price: $125–$255 |

In a gracious, idyllic village where the sidewalks are made of marble and the former quarry—the country's oldest—is now a swimming hole, this late-nineteenth-century house fits right in. Its patio is made of marble, but more special than its surfaces are its services—a bouquet of thoughtful touches to make guests feel truly pampered. You can have coffee in your room, a cooked-to-order breakfast whenever you want, deluxe baths, and help with touring, finding restaurants for dinner, and other needs. The cottage suite is especially luxurious, but all rooms are lovely, and true to its name, this inn is brimming with good things.

SETTINGS & FACILITIES

Location: 6 mi. N of Manchester on Rt. 30, near village church

Near: Galleries, shops, antiquing, theater, Robert Todd Lincoln's "Hildene,"

Hunter Park (Vermont Symphony summer home), Southern Vermont Art Center, outlets
Building: 1880 Colonial, white clapboard, plus additions
Grounds: 3-season lush gardens, marble patio
Public Space: Library, LR, solarium, covered porch
Food & Drink: Wake-up tray of tea, coffee, flowers; candlelight breakfast; specialties: pear-almond breakfast pudding, cinnamon-apple puff pancakes; wines, champagnes; sweets/hot drinks; wine, champagne (extra)
Recreation: Winter and water sports, hay/sleigh rides, horseback riding
Amenities & Services: Champagne welcome; cookies, chocolates, fruit in rooms on arrival; kitchen privileges; video library, iron; daily papers, books, recipes, fax, turn-down; pick-up at bus, bike rental nearby

ACCOMMODATIONS

Units: 4 guest rooms, 1 cottage suite
All Rooms: Bath, AC, sitting area, deluxe toiletries, magnifying mirror, robes, phone, dataport, clock/radio and/or cassette player, hairdryer, area guides
Some Rooms: fireplace (4); stereo, cable, desk, loft, skylight, LR, kitchen, patio, French doors, cathedral ceiling
Bed & Bath: Queen, king, some four-posters, canopies; full baths
Favorites: Green Peak—great garden view, country decor, pencil-post queen, sitting area, corner stove fireplace; Cottage Suite—beamed cathedral, loft BR, skylight, kitchen, patio
Comfort & Decor: Spacious, comfortable rooms named after Dorset Mountains. Some built-in bookshelves. Good lighting. Blend of antiques, fine reproductions, and art. Handpainted touches, fresh flowers.

RATES, RESERVATIONS, & RESTRICTIONS

Deposit: 50% or 1 night w/in 5 days; refund w/ 14- or 30-day notice
Discounts: Off-season, midweek, longer stays
Credit Cards: MC, V, AE
Check-In/Out: 3–10/11
Smoking: No
Pets: No; nearby boarding
Kids: Over 16
Minimum Stay: 2 nights weekends, peak periods; 3 nights holidays
Open: All year; closed Christmas Eve/Day, 3 days following Labor Day, part of April
Hosts: Linda and Bill Ley
Box 307, Rt. 30
Dorset, VT 05251
(802) 867-5751, (800) 566-5751
Fax: (802) 867-5753
cornucop@vermontel.com,
Innkeeper@CornucopiaofDorset.com
www.cornucopiaofdorset.com

INN AT WOODCHUCK HILL FARM, Grafton

Overall: ★★★★   Room Quality: B   Value: C   Price: $89–$275

Gabriel family members grew up in this understated hilltop house, built in 1790 for the town's first minister. An antique shop was once in the barn, which is now restored into rustically elegant suites. The main house is a beauty, filled with antiques, books, family belongings, and art pieces. Two other outbuildings offer more private accommodations. The porch overlooks miles of Vermont countryside, and a swimming pond beyond the barn has a dock for sunning. Nearby are a gazebo and a sauna, heated by wood cut from orchards on the 200-acre spread. This is a special retreat in a truly lovely New England village.

SETTINGS & FACILITIES

Location: About 2 mi. up the hill from village, at end of country road, on left
Near: Shopping in historic Grafton Village, galleries
Building: Restored 1790 Colonial farmhouse
Grounds: 200 acres: woods, fields, country lanes, barn, pond, swimming area, gazebo, sauna/steam room, apple orchard

Public Space: Open porch, large lounge
Food & Drink: Breakfast specialties: French toast, homemade jams; wines, local beers on porch or in lounge; Grafton cheddar cheese, crackers
Recreation: Tennis, sledding, ice-skating, snow shoeing, X-C skiing
Amenities & Services: Bike rental, books, menus, play equipment

ACCOMMODATIONS

Units: Main House: 6 guest rooms, 1 studio suite, 1 suite; Barn: 1 suite, 1 guest room, 1 residence (4 person max.); 1 cottage (7 person max.)
All Rooms: Sitting area
Some Rooms: Bath, fireplace, kitchen (rooms with kitchens, breakfast en suite), corner rooms, priv. entrance, coffee maker, deck, multiple rooms, parking

Bed & Bath: Beds vary, some canopies, extra beds; tiled baths
Favorites: Frank Gabriel's room—2nd floor, window walls, twin beds, fireplace, secretary w/ boyhood books
Comfort & Decor: Light and airy w/ country antiques, some meadow and mountain views. Barn has original beams. Some skylights. 3rd floor room smaller, under eaves.

RATES, RESERVATIONS, & RESTRICTIONS

Deposit: 1 night or 50% (3+ nights); refund w/ 14-day notice
Discounts: 1 night free w/ weekly rental
Credit Cards: MC, V, AE, D
Check-In/Out: 1/11
Smoking: No
Pets: No
Kids: OK

Minimum Stay: Varies; call for info
Open: All year; dates closed varies
Hosts: Marilyn and Mark Gabriel
Middletown Rd.
Grafton, VT 05146
(802) 843-2398
info@woodchuckhill.com,
mmggabri@sover.net
www.woodchuckhill.com

ANDRIE ROSE INN, Ludlow

Overall: ★★★½	Room Quality: B	Value: C	Price: $80–$500

You enter through the granite-countered kitchen, which emphasizes the informality of this bed-and-breakfast complex. For groups, there's a conference room; for those in the main house, a full breakfast in the cheerful pink-and-blue dining room. For skiers at Okemo Mountain who want informal atmosphere and an in-town location, this is the best bet, especially for those staying a week or so. You can walk easily to the shops, entertainment, and restaurants of this popular ski town. There is a frequent, free shuttle to the mountain; and hot chocolate and snacks are waiting when you come back from a day on the slopes. The street name is appropriate.

SETTINGS & FACILITIES

Location: Quiet street .25 mile from Okemo Mountain; off Rt. 131, a block N of only stoplight in town
Near: Arts and crafts fairs, 5 ski resorts, antique shows, music festivals, shopping and outlets, lakes, waterfalls w/ swimming holes
Building: 4 early 1800s buildings at base of Okemo Mountain; Greek Revival, Federal style, Victorian
Grounds: Multilevel rose garden, flower boxes; small area
Public Space: LR, sunroom, porches, kitchen entrance

Food & Drink: Full candlelight breakfast; specialties: buttermilk waffles w/ Ben & Jerry's ice cream, cinnamon walnut French toast w/ maple syrup; cookies, snacks, hot/cold drinks; cocktail hour w/ local cheese, grapes, breads, crackers; full liquor license
Recreation: Golf, tennis, horseback riding, ice-skating, sleigh rides
Amenities & Services: Personal welcome notes, chocolate mints, maps, turn-down, shuttle to Okemo Mountain, weddings, functions

ACCOMMODATIONS

Units: 9 guest rooms in main lodge; 4 luxury, family suites in guesthouse; 3 suites in Victorian townhouse; 7 solitude luxury suites
All Rooms: Bath, toiletries, local information
Some Rooms: Skylight, library, fireplace, kitchen, AC

Bed & Bath: King (suites), hairdryer; some whirlpool/showers, pedestal sinks
Favorites: Solitude Luxury Suites—fireplace, CDs, VCR, whirlpool, refrigerator
Comfort & Decor: Antiques, skylights, whirlpools. Main house rooms small but cozy.

RATES, RESERVATIONS, & RESTRICTIONS

Deposit: 50% w/in 7 days; $200 deposit for family suites; refund w/ 14-day notice

Discounts: Midweek, off-season, seniors; family suites $200–400, sleep 4–6; townhouses $200–500, sleep

10–12; breakfast not included for family suites, Victorian suites (w/ kitchens)
Credit Cards: MC, V, AE
Check-In/Out: 3/11
Smoking: No
Pets: No
Kids: Guest house, Victorian buildings
Minimum Stay: 2 nights winter, summer, fall

Open: All year
Hosts: Ellen and Jack Fisher
13 Pleasant St.
Ludlow, VT 05149
(802) 228-4846, (800) 223-4846
Fax: (802) 228-7910
andrie@mail.tds.net
www.bbonline.com/vt/andrierose

THE GOVERNOR'S INN, Ludlow

Overall: ★★★★	Room Quality: B	Value: C	Price: $95–$325

Indeed, this award-winning bed-and-breakfast was once the home of Governor Stickney, and a marbleized slate fireplace dominating the parlor harkens to the turn of the century. Today, this small inn is renowned for "Vermont's Best Apple Pie" (often a fruit course at breakfast) and for fabulous food, including gourmet picnics. Both hosts trained in Europe and give cooking classes. The dining area is the epicenter: tables set formally, augmented by classical music, candlelight, crystal, and linen. The six-course dinners have been consumed by residents of the White House, Paul Newman, and Robert Redford, and none have complained.

SETTINGS & FACILITIES

Location: 1 mi. from Okemo Mountain, where Rt. 100 and 103 intersect, in village just off Main St.
Near: Calvin Coolidge birthplace, antiquing, shopping, theater
Building: 1890 Victorian; Nat'l Historic Register
Grounds: Small yard
Public Space: Foyer, LR, lounge, DRs
Food & Drink: (MAP) Full breakfast; a specialty: rum raisin French toast w/ apple-smoked bacon; tea; dinner Wed.–Sun., 6-courses; a specialty: blue fish flambéed w/ gin; picnics; specialties: braised quail, beef paté; special meals; full bar
Recreation: Canoeing, golf, hunting, horses, skiing, front porch rocking
Amenities & Services: House chocolates, games, recipes, gifts, cordials, turn-down

ACCOMMODATIONS

Units: 7 guest rooms, 1 suite
All Rooms: Bath, AC, robes, toiletries, butler's basket
Some Rooms: Whirlpool, sitting area
Bed & Bath: Doubles, queens, 1 king; some brass; showers/tubs
Favorites: #5—tranquil, garden view, queen w/ large head/footboard, sitting area
Comfort & Decor: Individually decorated. Lace curtains, antique armoires, bedside lamps. Smallish, stylish. Suite w/ living area.

RATES, RESERVATIONS, & RESTRICTIONS

Deposit: 50%; partial refund w/ 20-day notice

Discounts: Singles, longer stays, 3rd person

Credit Cards: MC, V

Check-In/Out: 2/11

Smoking: No

Pets: No

Kids: Over 8

Minimum Stay: Holiday weekends

Open: All year

Hosts: Deedy and Charlie Marble

86 Main St.

Ludlow, VT 05149

(802) 228-8830, (800) GOVERNOR

Fax: (802) 228-8830, call first

www.vermontlodging.com/governor.htm

1811 HOUSE, Manchester

Overall: ★★★★	Room Quality: B	Value: C	Price: $120–$230

Except for the 30 years when it was the home of President Lincoln's granddaughter, Mary Lincoln Isham, the main house has been an inn since 1811. It was built in 1770 and retains a dark, low-ceilinged look, with wainscoting, Oriental rugs over hardwood floors, and an outstanding array of Early American furnishings. The beamed tavern offers a dartboard and a wide selection of Scottish malt whiskies, and you can chat with Marnie and Bruce while they tend bar, or you can pick up cookies in the kitchen. Named after prominent Manchester residents including Charles Orvis of fly-fishing fame, the guest rooms vary widely in size, but all are meticulous and decorated in fine period style. The terraced gardens and the view of golf greens and mountains beyond are also exceptional.

SETTINGS & FACILITIES

Location: Center of village opposite Equinox Hotel; adjacent to church
Near: Antiquing, historic sites, museums, nature areas, Southern Vermont Art Center, Fly Fishing Museum
Building: 1761 Colonial; Nat'l Historic Register
Grounds: 7.5 acres, gardens, terraces, pond, herb garden
Public Space: Pub, 2 sitting rooms, rec room
Food & Drink: Full breakfast; a specialty: 1811 House French Toast, full English breakfast; chocolate chip cookies; sherry; special meals
Recreation: Water/snow sports, golf, hunting, horseback riding, tennis
Amenities & Services: Kitchen privileges, videos, use of Equinox Hotel's spa and facilities

ACCOMMODATIONS

Units: 13 guest rooms, 1 suite
All Rooms: Bath, AC, period pieces, seating area, reading light
Some Rooms: Fireplace; sitting room (1), porch (1), priv. staircase (1)
Bed & Bath: Doubles, queens, kings, canopies, four-posters; claw-foot tubs, sep. showers, large showerheads
Favorites: Robert Todd Lincoln—canopy four-poster, fireplace, slate mantel; Henry and Ethel Robinson—marble shower, claw-foot tub, porch, great view of gardens/mountains
Comfort & Decor: Elegant yet relaxed w/ Oriental rugs, fireplaces, period antiques, paintings. Some original windows, beams. Some mountain views. Can be cramped, but cozy under eaves. Good lighting.

RATES, RESERVATIONS, & RESTRICTIONS

Deposit: 1 night; refund w/ 14-day notice
Discounts: Corp., off-season
Credit Cards: MC, V, AE, D
Check-In/Out: 2/11
Smoking: No
Pets: No; 2 in-house cats
Kids: Over 16
Minimum Stay: 2 nights weekends
Open: All year
Hosts: Marnie and Bruce Duff
Rt. 7A, Box 39
Manchester, VT 05254
(802) 362-1811, (800) 432-1811
Fax: (802) 362-2363
info@1811house.com
www.1811house.com

THE INN AT ORMSBY HILL, Manchester Center

Overall: ★★★★½	Room Quality: A	Value: C	Price: $160–$305

History resonates throughout this superb bed-and-breakfast, named after Gideon Ormsby, local Revolutionary War hero. The basement contains one of the earliest jail cells in Manchester, bars intact. Ethan Allen hid in the smoke room during the Revolutionary War, and it may have been a safe house for the Underground Railroad. More? A former owner was in law practice with Lincoln's son, and President Taft stayed here. Today, you can enjoy rare books, classical music, hooked rugs made by Ted's mother, and a gourmet breakfast in the dramatic, sunny conservatory—with dessert from renowned chef Chris (who also cooks informal dinners on weekends).

SETTINGS & FACILITIES

Location: Historic Rt. 7A S, 2 mi. W of town center
Near: Bromley and Stratton mountains, shopping, barn sales, auctions, Southern Vermont Art Center, antiquing
Building: 1764 restored Manor house
Grounds: 2.5 acres: gardens, mountain views
Public Space: LR, gathering room, conservatory, TV room, porch w/ hammock
Food & Drink: Breakfast, either full or buffet, breakfast dessert; specialties:

risotto w/ bacon and egg, baked pancakes, scrambled eggs in puffed pastry, basil scrambled eggs on Portobello mushrooms; dinner Fri. ($30/2) in kitchen: soup, stew, or pasta, homemade bread, dessert; advance notice for special diets
Recreation: Swimming, golf, horseback riding, fly-fishing, all winter sports
Amenities & Services: Homemade cookies on arrival, irons, refrigerator, bike/X-C ski rental nearby; small conferences, weddings (20) if whole inn reserved

ACCOMMODATIONS

Units: 10 guest rooms
All Rooms: Bath, fireplace, AC, clock/radio, phone, dataport, hairdryer, robe, guest journal
Some Rooms: Priv. entrance, deck, disabled access
Bed & Bath: Queens, kings, most canopy; all rooms dbl. whirlpools, some showers w/ seat
Favorites: Tower Room—newest, turret, desk, views, sitting area, queen bow-

top canopy, tiled bath, dbl. shower, multileveled; Taft—largest room, vaulted wooden ceiling, brass chandelier, king canopy, afternoon sun, desk, sitting area, dbl. shower
Comfort & Decor: Romantic and comfortable, w/ rubber duckies and candlelight for whirlpools, details like beamed ceiling from 1764. Fireplaces seen from beds, whirlpools. Not much missing.

RATES, RESERVATIONS, & RESTRICTIONS

Deposit: 1 night; refund w/ 7-day notice
Discounts: Midweek, corp.
Credit Cards: MC, V, D
Check-In/Out: 3–9/11
Smoking: No; $100 fee for smoking
Pets: No
Kids: No
Minimum Stay: 2 nights weekends, some holidays

Open: All year
Hosts: Chris and Ted Sprague
Historic Rt. 7A
Manchester Center, VT 05255
(802) 362-1163, (800) 670-2841
Fax: (802) 362-5176
ormsby@vermontel.com
www.ormsbyhill.com

THE RELUCTANT PANTHER, Manchester Village

Overall: ★★★★	Room Quality: B	Value: D	Price: $168–$450

Upgrading continues at this popular, purple-hued inn, originally home to the village blacksmith. Common rooms are few, but the focus is on dining and guest rooms. Lavish suites with two-way gas fireplaces, terra-cotta and marble floors, and a marble terrace are especially sought-after, and more suites are on the way. Swiss-born Robert was food and beverage director at The Plaza in New York City, and the ambitious restaurant is in a trio of rooms, including a greenhouse. If you're a traditionalist, you'll prefer nearby 1811 House; sybarites who like the feel of a small, luxury hotel will seek this Panther, and with no reluctance.

SETTINGS & FACILITIES

Location: About 1 block from village green
Near: Bromley and Stratton mountains, shopping, barn sales, auctions, Southern Vermont Art Center, antiquing
Building: 1850s 3-story purple-hued main house
Grounds: Annuals/perennials, old maples, marble sidewalks
Public Space: Panther bar, restaurant, greenhouse, marble patio
Food & Drink: (MAP) 3-course breakfast; specialties: pancakes, French toast; dinner (reservations) Thurs.–Mon., 7 days foliage/holidays, weekends only in winter; American, Swiss specialties: raclette, osso buco, Wiener schnitzel; wine list
Recreation: Swimming, horses, fly-fishing, tennis, golf, X-C skiing (extra)
Amenities & Services: Welcome gifts (wine), in-room safety deposit boxes, access to Equinox Hotel spa facilities, turn-down, concierge, priv. DR (25)

ACCOMMODATIONS

Units: 18 guest rooms, suites
All Rooms: Bath, phone, TV, climate controls, soft colors
Some Rooms: Fireplace, whirlpool (some dbl.), AC, Vermont Castings stove, desk
Bed & Bath: Kings, queens; luxury baths

Favorites: Mark Skinner Suite—fireplaces in bed and bath, 2-person whirlpool
Comfort & Decor: Antiques, some luxury-papered, size varies. Locally handcrafted furnishings. Reading lamps. Mainly village views. Plush.

RATES, RESERVATIONS, & RESTRICTIONS

Deposit: Full payment 1 night; refund w/ 10-day notice
Discounts: $40 when restaurant closed in-season; $110–325 winter, Sun.–Thurs
Credit Cards: MC, V, AE
Check-In/Out: 3/11; extended checkout to 6 p.m.
Smoking: No
Pets: No
Kids: Over 14

Minimum Stay: 2 nights most weekends, 3 nights holidays
Open: All year
Hosts: Maye and Robert Bachofen
1 West Rd.
Manchester Village, VT 05254-0678
(802) 362-2568, (800) 822-2331
Fax: (802) 362-2586
panther@sover.net
www.reluctantpanther.com

FOUR COLUMNS INN, Newfane

Overall: ★★★★½	Room Quality: A	Value: C	Price: $110–$270

Washington may not have slept or dined here, but Henry Kissinger, Mick Jagger, Tom Cruise, Michael Douglas, Paul Newman, Nicole Kidman,

John Irving, Ron Howard, and John Kenneth Galbraith have, among many others. Star chef Greg Parks is constantly tweaking the renowned menu, which features delectable dishes from venison loin and sweetbreads to Chilean sea bass. Snow tubing, a swimming pool, and a stream beckon guests on breaks from dining in the beamed barn. Not much is newfangled at Newfane. It's just old-fashioned pleasures and surprising warmth in this uncommonly good columned inn on the most photographed village common in Vermont.

SETTINGS & FACILITIES

Location: 12 mi. N of Brattleboro on Rt. 30, behind courthouse, on historic town common
Near: Shopping in Newfane, antiquing, beach, museum, outlets, theater
Building: 1832 Greek Revival manor; Nat'l Historic Register
Grounds: 150 acres, pool, stream, 2 ponds, trails, woods, gardens
Public Space: Restaurant; LR; tavern w/ full-service pewter bar, deck; 3 porches
Food & Drink: Expanded cont'l breakfast, coffee cake, oatmeal in winter, fresh OJ; dinner, blend of New

American, French, Asian; specialties: Black Angus sirloin w/ horseradish Portobello sauce, seared rare tuna w/ greens and cardamom-scented sushi rice; wine list online; special meals accom.
Recreation: Winter/water sports, sleigh rides, golf, mountain biking, board games
Amenities & Services: Computer, videos, some disabled access, bike rental nearby, weddings, special occasions, fax, secretarial services, conferences, copier

ACCOMMODATIONS

Units: 5 standard rooms, 6 deluxe, 4 suites
All Rooms: Bath, AC, alarm clock, radio, phone
Some Rooms: Fireplace, sitting room, couch, wide pine floors, vaulted ceiling, fireplace in bath, skylight, ceiling fan
Bed & Bath: Queens, kings, 2 twins, canopies, four-posters, irons; bath and a half, dbl. whirlpools, some showers only, dbl. sinks
Favorites: Deluxe Suite 3—queen, 2

rooms, Rice four-poster, pink marbled bath, gas fireplace in bath, dbl. whirlpool; #16—Queen brass, tub, in garden wing, sliding glass doors, reading area, gas fireplace
Comfort & Decor: Lots of antiques. Plants, bedside lights, lots of natural light. Former parlor turned into huge suite. Top floor suite, porch w/ wicker above columns, overlooking common. Handmade rag rugs.

RATES, RESERVATIONS, & RESTRICTIONS

Deposit: 1 night or credit card; refund w/ 14-day notice
Discounts: Off-season, 3rd person
Credit Cards: MC, V, AE, DC

Check-In/Out: 2/11
Smoking: No
Pets: OK w/ prior approval
Kids: Welcome

Minimum Stay: None
Open: All year, except Christmas Day
Hosts: Pam and Gorty Baldwin
Box 278, West St.
Newfane, VT 05245

(800) 787-6633, (802) 365-7713
Fax: (802) 365-0022
frcolinn@sover.net
www.bbhost.com/fourcolumnsinn,
www.fourcolumnsinn.com

HICKORY RIDGE HOUSE, Putney

| Overall: ★★★½ | Room Quality: C | Value: C | Price: $95–$300 |

Once a college president's home, this Federal manor with a Palladian window and acres of country lawns is filled with music: Steve plays strings and brass, and there's a piano for guests. Despite many shared baths, it offers quiet pleasures at a good price. A few minutes' walk away is an old-fashioned swimming hole (more special than a heated pool). The Connecticut River is a short drive down a country road, where you can canoe, fish, walk along the shores, or loll in the sun. Good restaurants are nearby, and you can ski the fields under moonlight. One of the bedrooms has an original fireplace and a headboard created from a choir stall.

SETTINGS & FACILITIES

Location: 2 mi. from Putney on country hillside; 3 mi. off I-91 Exit 4
Near: Shopping in Putney and Brattleboro, theater, antiquing, crafts, music festival; 2 mi. from Connecticut River; 45 min. to Stratton
Building: 1808 brick Federal country manor; Nat'l Register of Historic Places
Grounds: 8 acres on hillside: country, quiet road, meadows, gardens
Public Space: Common rooms, upstairs sitting room, deck

Food & Drink: Full breakfast, home-grown herbs, local products; specialties: fresh egg dishes (from on-site chickens), hot applesauce, stollen
Recreation: Swimming, canoeing, kayaking, skiing
Amenities & Services: TV, refrigerator; weddings, receptions, small conferences, business services; disabled accessible room

ACCOMMODATIONS

Units: 6 guest rooms, 1 cottage
All Rooms: Individually decorated, antiques and reproductions
Some Rooms: Fireplace (5); cottage w/ 2 BRs, LR, deck, kitchen, fireplace
Bed & Bath: Queens, kings, sleigh beds, cribs, comforters, quilts, coverlets, line-dried sheets; 3 baths
Favorites: Federal rooms—4 original BRs, spacious, Rumford fireplaces,

antiques
Comfort & Decor: Individually decorated in period decor. Airy, comfortable, pretty colors. Rooms in original house preferred. Families can reserve newer wing. Lemon room w/ whimsical choir stall headboard. 1st-floor room disabled access, w/ fireplace. Well-maintained.

RATES, RESERVATIONS, & RESTRICTIONS

Deposit: Credit card number; refund w/ 10-day notice
Discounts: 3rd person, singles, long stays
Credit Cards: MC, V, AE
Check-In/Out: 3–7/11
Smoking: No
Pets: No
Kids: OK
Minimum Stay: 2 days cottage; call

for minimums for holidays or peak times
Open: All year
Hosts: Linda and Jack Bisbee
RR 3, Box 1410
Putney, VT 05346
(800) 380-9218, (802) 387-5709
Fax: (802) 387-5387
hickory@sover.net
www.hickoryridgehouse.com

THE INN AT WEATHERSFIELD, Weathersfield

| Overall: ★★★★ | Room Quality: B | Value: C | Price: $185–$225 |

Ghosts reside in this columned, country property filled with stenciled walls and family antiques. It was a stagecoach inn and a stop on the Underground Railroad—a hiding place for slaves fleeing to Canada before the Civil War. Today, you may just want to hide away for other reasons: poetry readings at breakfast, a wassail cup in a keeping-room cauldron, guest rooms named Wuthering Heights and Tara, with canopy beds, fireplaces, and mountain views. (Weddings are popular here.) But it's the food that is most notable—fresh, seasonal, and highly original—served by a warm staff, by candlelight flickering in the beamed, low-ceiling dining room.

SETTINGS & FACILITIES

Location: Half-mile S of Perkinsville on Rt. 106, set back on a tree-lined drive, off a hilly country road
Near: Conn. River, country stores, covered bridge, cheese and syrup factories, glass blowing; Springfield
Building: 1780s farmhouse, since expanded, w/ attached barn
Grounds: 21 acres, lawn, old lumber trails, pines, English gardens, pond, amphitheater
Public Space: Gathering room, keeping room, parlor, taproom, carriage house DR, game room, front porch, greenhouse

Food & Drink: (MAP) Full breakfast w/ poetry readings; p.m. tea, pastries, wine, fruit/cheese; 5-course dinner, menu changes nightly, open to public; specialties: farm-raised pheasant, salmon Wellington, sour cream blueberry pie; award-winning wine list; piano entertainment; tea, popcorn
Recreation: Skiing, golf, water sports, berry picking, sleigh/carriage rides
Amenities & Services: Pool table, exercise equipment, sauna, lawn games, movies, snowshoes; receptions, business events; turn-down, tour guidance, some disabled access, airport pickup

ACCOMMODATIONS

Units: 9 guest rooms, 3 suites
All Rooms: Bath, desk, Colonial trimmings, phone
Some Rooms: Fireplace (8); sitting room, balcony
Bed & Bath: Beds vary, some canopies; some claw-foot tubs, whirlpool, low ceilings, some tiny
Favorites: Tara—large corner room, main house, wide floorboards, four-poster; Bridal Suite—3rd floor, highly romantic and private
Comfort & Decor: Rooms, from Wuthering Heights to Tara, named and decorated after love stories. Handmade quilts, wide plank floors, antiques. Rooms in new wing smaller, more country style. Main house, more character, noisier during dinner; new wing, old tubs, fireplaces.

RATES, RESERVATIONS, & RESTRICTIONS

Deposit: 1 night; refund w/ 7-day notice
Discounts: Off-season, 3rd person, singles, groups, multiple nights, business, packages, B&B rates
Credit Cards: MC, V, AE, D, DC
Check-In/Out: 1/11
Smoking: No
Pets: No
Kids: Over 8
Minimum Stay: 2 or 3 nights some weekends and holidays
Open: All year
Hosts: Mary and Terry Carter
Rt. 106, Box 164
Weathersfield, VT 05151
(802) 263-9217, (800) 477-4828
Fax: (802) 263-9219
www.weathersfieldinn.com

INN AT SAW MILL FARM, West Dover

Overall: ★★★★★   Room Quality: A   Value: C   Price: $360–$495

These famed innkeepers bought the farm, so to speak, in 1967, on a whim and decided to create an inn. Rodney is an architect, Ione a decorator, and son Brill a chef—so how could they go wrong? The Williamses are pioneers in establishing the kind of elegant, expensive inn that sophisticated travelers now demand, such as The Mayflower in Connecticut or The White Barn in Maine. The atmosphere is mellow, with no TVs or phones in rooms, yet slightly formal, so that you can show off your casual designer clothes. Copper collections glow in candle and firelight, flowers accent chintz and beams, wine and food are divine, and Relais & Chateaux can book you.

SETTINGS & FACILITIES

Location: Rt. 100 N to West Dover; first left after village church, on the left after bridge
Near: Museums, antiquing, galleries, auctions, summer theatre, symphony, Mt. Snow

Building: Restored cluster of farm buildings, main barn w/ old posts, beams
Grounds: Set in woods; lawns, pool, tennis courts, gardens, 2 trout ponds
Public Space: Stairs up to common room, loft library, DRs, lounge w/ copper bar, terrace
Food & Drink: (MAP) Full breakfast; a specialty: fresh tomato juice; dinner, evening attire, cont'l/American cuisine; specialties: fresh sautéed foie gras, breast of pheasant, pork tenderloin; meals open to public; summer cocktails; 36,000–bottle wine list
Recreation: Fitness club, horseback riding, golf, winter and water sports, tennis, fishing
Amenities & Services: Baby grand piano, Godiva chocolates, A/V equipment, fishing lessons by Orvis, priv. airport 5 min., massage arrangements

ACCOMMODATIONS

Units: 20 guest rooms, suites, cottages
All Rooms: Bath, fireplace, carpet, antiques
Some Rooms: Balcony, sitting room w/ fireplace, reading area, desk
Bed & Bath: Canopied kings, fine linens, extra pillows, down duvets; dressing rooms, luxury baths, thick towels
Favorites: Farm house—pastel colors, fireplace, dressing room and bath; Cottage suites—sitting room w/ fireplace, coordinated papers and fabrics, canopied beds
Comfort & Decor: Lavish. Stylishly country, vivid florals. Antiques and reproductions. Spacious. King beds. Books, good reading lights. Large closets. Some Victorian decor, some English chintz. Decorator touches throughout.

RATES, RESERVATIONS, & RESTRICTIONS

Deposit: 1 night; refund w/ 14-day notice (30 for foliage, holidays)
Discounts: Corp. packages, off-season
Credit Cards: MC, V, AE, D
Check-In/Out: 3/12
Smoking: No
Pets: No
Kids: Not recommended
Minimum Stay: 2 nights on weekends; 3 on major holidays

Open: All year
Hosts: Rod, Ione, Brill Williams
Crosstown Rd. and Rt. 100, Box 367
West Dover, VT 05356
(802) 464-8131, (800) 493-1133
Fax: (802) 464-1130
sawmill@sover.net
www.vermontdirect.com/sawmill

WINDHAM HILL INN, West Townshend

Overall: ★★★★½	Room Quality: A	Value: C	Price: $245–$420

Panoramic views of the West River Valley envelop this hidden, hilltop beauty with all things going for it. Built in the early nineteenth century as a dairy farm, it was in the Lawrence family until the 1950s. Will Ackerman, who founded Windham Hill Records, worked here for a few summers in the 1960s and helped build what is now the music room, with an old Steinway grand and loads of CDs and games. The hayloft of the barn, guarded by a whimsical (fake) cow, has guest rooms with hand-hewn plank floors, skylights, and soaking tubs. Meals are delectably creative. You can swim, skate, and play tennis on site, and recreate wonderfully nearby.

SETTINGS & FACILITIES

Location: 1.5 mi. off Rt. 30, about 5 mi. S of Windham, at end of hilltop road
Near: Shopping, antiquing, outlets, crafts, state parks, Stratton Mountain, Mt. Snow, Bromley Mountain; auctions, Southern Vermont Art Center
Building: 1825, 3-story white farmhouse, converted barn
Grounds: 160 acres: hillside, forest, fields, pond, gardens, pool, tennis, trails, views
Public Space: Bar, check-in desk; music room, deck; parlor; pub room; DR
Food & Drink: (MAP) Full country breakfast, communal or separate; specialties: Belgian waffles, German soufflé

pancake w/ warm apple compote, cinnamon-raisin brioche; hors d'ouevres; 5-course candlelight dinner (reservations), seasonal menu; specialties: lamb w/ mustard-seed crust, strawberry-rhubarb soufflé; wine list, full bar; lunch for groups by arrangement
Recreation: Winter and water sports, mountain biking, golf, horseback riding, carriage/sleigh rides nearby
Amenities & Services: X-C skis, snowshoes, and toboggan rentals; 1888 Steinway grand piano; weddings, conf. center (50+), executive retreats, customized dining (corp.), full business equipment, computer access, tour guidance; floor plans of rooms on Web site

ACCOMMODATIONS

Units: 13 guest rooms in main house, 5 guest rooms and 3 loft rooms in White Barn
All Rooms: Bath, phone, sitting area, AC, writing table, great views
Some Rooms: Fireplace, Vermont Castings stove, priv. deck (10), daybed, window seat, porch, skylight
Bed & Bath: Most queens/kings, canopies/reproductions; some whirlpools, 2-person tubs, tub/showers, soaking tub

Favorites: Jesse Lawrence—king, bath, soaking tub near fireplace, window seat, stove, 3rd floor; Forget-Me-Not—porch-side, king, fireplace, soaking tub
Comfort & Decor: Antiques, locally made furniture. English country decor. Wallpapered. Good windows and reading lights. Stuffed animals on bed, but not kitschy. Barn rooms, rustically elegant, w/ skylights, tartan fabrics. Main house, country comfort. Baths smallish. One barn room wheelchair accessible.

RATES, RESERVATIONS, & RESTRICTIONS

Deposit: 1 night; refund w/ 14-day notice
Discounts: Off-season, B&B rates, singles, 3rd person, midweek/seasonal packages, corp.

Credit Cards: MC, V, AE, D
Check-In/Out: 2/11
Smoking: No
Pets: No; in-house pets
Kids: 12 and up

Minimum Stay: 2 nights most weekends, foliage; 3 nights some holidays; for weddings, must be rented in entirety, 2 nights
Open: All year except week of Christmas; check on April
Hosts: Pat and Grigs Markham

311 Lawrence Drive
West Townshend, VT 05359
(800) 944-4080, (802) 874-4080
Fax: (802) 874-4702
windham@sover.net
www.windhamhill.com

JUNIPER HILL INN, Windsor

Overall: ★★★★½	Room Quality: B	Value: B	Price: $95–$170

This elegant 1902 mansion at the end of a winding driveway was built for Maxwell Evarts, CFO for Union Pacific Railroad and son of the U.S. Attorney General who defended Andrew Johnson from impeachment. Former Presidents Rutherford Hayes, Benjamin Harrison, and Teddy Roosevelt visited here. The woman who engineered trails on Mount Ascutney first opened the inn in the 1940s, and views of that mountain loom from rooms and pool. After biking in the valley, or paddling downriver to the covered bridge at Cornish, you'll return to a four-course candlelight dinner by the hearth. In this romantic haven the hosts pamper, from classical music in the library to chocolates, sherry, and a local history book in each room.

SETTINGS & FACILITIES

Location: Above Windsor, on small mountaintop overlooking Lake Runnemede and Mt. Ascutney; from Rt. 5 S about 3 mi.; right onto Juniper Hill; half-mile, another right; left at junction
Near: Vermont State Crafts Center, Old Constitution House, covered bridge, brewery, Dartmouth College, Raptor Center, historic sites, Woodstock, Quechee, state park, Calvin Coolidge birthplace, Killington, Okemo, country club, antiquing, galleries, village shopping, museums
Building: 14,500-sq.-ft. Georgian-style mansion, built 1902; Nat'l Historic Register
Grounds: 14 acres, pines, gardens, lake, mountain view, pool

Public Space: Great hall, floor-to-ceiling fireplace, huge 1,000-lb. table; gentleman's sitting parlor; library; DR
Food & Drink: Full country breakfast; refreshments w/ homemade pastries; 4-course dinner Mon.–Sat. ($30, reservations), 3 choices, candlelight; specialties: rack of lamb, poached salmon; vegetarian w/ prior notice; cocktails; fully licensed
Recreation: Skiing, golf, horseback riding, sleigh rides, skating
Amenities & Services: Irons, breakfast in bed, bike rentals; weddings, functions, business services, meetings (24; priv. conf. room), dinner parties; pickup from station, fax, bike routes

ACCOMMODATIONS

Units: 16 guest rooms
All Rooms: Bath, sherry, hairdryer, flashlight
Some Rooms: Desk; lake or mountain view; fireplaces (11, 2 gas), porch (1)
Bed & Bath: Four-poster, canopy, sleigh beds; some claw-foot tubs, marble sinks

Favorites: Corner queen deluxes—canopies, seating areas, fireplaces, beautiful views
Comfort & Decor: Period wallpapers, antiques, and reproductions. Comfortable, wingback chairs, period artwork and decorations. Small details: corkscrews and crystal glasses, fresh flowers and chocolates.

RATES, RESERVATIONS, & RESTRICTIONS

Deposit: 1 night, 50% long stays; refund w/ 14-day notice
Discounts: Midweek meetings, winter midweek, specials for returning guests
Credit Cards: MC, V, D
Check-In/Out: 3/11
Smoking: No
Pets: No; 3 in-house Welsh Corgis
Kids: No
Minimum Stay: 2 nights weekends, holidays, foliage

Open: All year except first 3 weeks of April
Hosts: Susanne and Rob Pearl
153 Pembroke Rd.
Windsor, VT 05089
(800) 359-2541, (802) 674-5273
Fax: (802) 674-2041
innkeeper@juniperhillinn.com
www.juniperhillinn.com

Zone 9
Midstate Vermont/Champlain

Vermont's Green Mountains/Champlain region starts at Lake Champlain, at the western border with New York, and is bordered on the north by Canada, on the east by the Upper Valley/Northeast Kingdom, and in the south by Vermont towns such as Ascutney and Ludlow.

The Lake Champlain area is highlighted by Burlington, Vermont's largest city, with a whopping 39,000 people. Burlington overlooks the lake and offers sailing, sea kayaking, and biking as well as ferries to the Adirondacks, across the water in New York. The Ethan Allen homestead, just north of town, commemorates the local revolutionary.

Downtown, the Church Street Marketplace is brimming with lively sidewalk cafes and shops. The discount-hungry can visit the South Burlington Outlet Center to fill up on bargains. Summer is when Burlington's cultural life shines: in June, at the Discover Jazz festival; in July and August at the Champlain Shakespeare Festival and the Vermont Mozart Festival. And the New England Culinary Institute offers a chance to dine with future star chefs.

Shelburne Museum, south of Burlington, is a repository of Americana and fine arts. Shelburne Farms gives visitors a taste of early farming, cheese making, and baking (pre-microwave life; we're talking churns). Educational programs, featuring chores with barn animals, will especially delight children.

The Middlebury area is surrounded by farms and orchards and is high-lighted by the handsome New England college town. Revolutionary War buffs can visit historical sites of Fort Ticonderoga, Mount Independence, and the Hubbarton Battlefield. Along uncrowded winding roads are antique finds as well as local crafts and foods.

The Green Mountains are a renowned ski and snowboard destination, with an annual snowfall of 250 inches. Killington, farther south in the region, is the largest of the resorts, and in addition to snow-related activities—which can run as late as June—it hosts a music festival in July and August and is a hiking draw for those seeking challenging terrain. Smuggler's Notch, another well-equipped ski resort, is farther north.

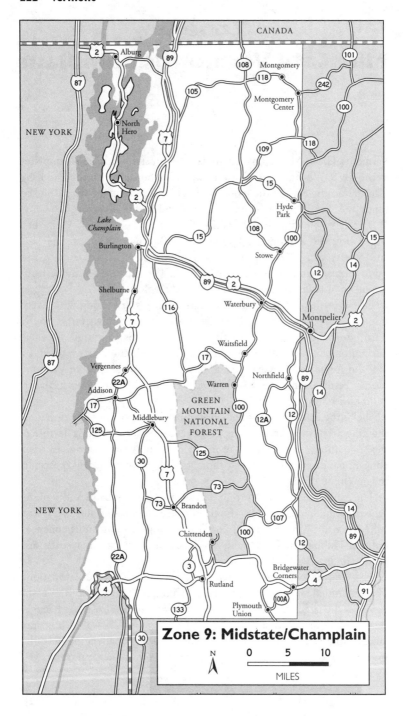

CANADA

Alburg

Montgomery

Montgomery
Center

NEW YORK

North
Hero

Lake
Champlain

Burlington

Hyde
Park

Stowe

Shelburne

Waterbury

Montpelier

Waitsfield

Vergennes

Northfield

Addison

Warren

GREEN
MOUNTAIN
NATIONAL
FOREST

Middlebury

NEW YORK

Brandon

Chittenden

Bridgewater
Corners

Rutland

Plymouth
Union

Zone 9: Midstate/Champlain

N   0   5   10

MILES

The Long Trail runs 270 miles from the Massachusetts border to Canada. Begun in 1910, it is part of the Appalachian Trail system in the south; in this region, it's maintained by the Green Mountain Club.

Along with maple syrup and cheddar cheese, Vermont is known for Ben & Jerry's Ice Cream, and a visit to the factory in Waterbury is a delicious experience; tours—and samples—are provided. At St. Albans, in northern Vermont by the lake, check out the Vermont Maple Festival in April.

Jedediah Hyde's log cabin in Grand Isle is one of the oldest log cabins in the country, dating to 1873. The round white church in Richmond and the New England Mountain Biking Festival in Randolph are good stops. In Plymouth Notch, history buffs can visit Calvin Coolidge's birthplace; it's well-maintained and more interesting than you'd expect with "Silent Cal's" reputation.

Lodging in this region caters to both romantics and families, skiers and active types, and ranges from small bed-and-breakfasts to larger inns, intimate to rustic. Many are clustered around Burlington, the Middlebury/Vergennes area, and the ski resorts, but there are plenty of worthy places in less-traveled areas. Summer, fall, and winter can be crowded on weekends, and many places close during early spring—aptly known as mud season.

THOMAS MOTT HOMESTEAD, Alburg

| Overall: ★★★★ | Room Quality: B | Value: A | Price: $75–$95 |

One of a kind, and an incredible deal. Pat fills his 1838 farmhouse on Lake Champlain with warmth and delights. Raspberries are planted for guests to "steal." The freezer is always stocked with Ben & Jerry's. Birds, including baby quails, abound. In mid-summer the famed Lipizzaner horses from Austria perform in a meadow down the road. Photos are snapped of all guests: a copy for you, one for the album in the family room; 27,000 so far, and Pat has pins representing hometowns in 90 countries and 50 states. No planes, no highway noise, just canoeing on a lake framed by mountains, cross-country skiing on the frozen lake in winter, and soaking in the pleasure.

SETTINGS & FACILITIES

Location: Follow signs off Hwy. 78
Near: Alburg Auction (Sat.), Mississquoi Wildlife Refuge, Shrine of St. Anne, Lake Champlain Islands; 1 hour, Montreal
Building: 1838 black-and-white farmhouse, barn
Grounds: 2.5 acres, 325 feet of lake frontage, dock, gazebo
Public Space: Original beams, floors; enclosed porch; 3 outdoor porches; full library, TV; game room, map w/ pins for all visitors' homes; DR

Food & Drink: Full breakfast at communal table from 16 choices; specialties: French toast with 5 kinds of nuts; Ben & Jerry's ice cream; tea and cookies
Recreation: Water activities, paragliding, golf, feeding quail, sky diving
Amenities & Services: Canoes, X-C ski trails, nearby ski rental, kitchen privileges with 5 room rental, refrigerator access, shop on premises, tour guidance/maps, weddings, nearby catering

ACCOMMODATIONS

Units: 5 guest rooms and suites
All Rooms: Bath, lake view, quilts, antiques
Some Rooms: Fireplace, balcony, daybed, sitting area, priv. entry
Bed & Bath: Queen shaker, some extra beds, 1 king; 2 full baths, 3¾ baths
Favorites: Honeymoon suite—fireplace, balcony overlooks lake; Corner

Suite—downstairs, larger, wraparound lake view, queen, daybed
Comfort & Decor: Built around quilts, individually collected. Papered. Some cathedral ceilings. Bedside lamps, reading chairs. Great lake views. Peaceful feeling. Bright decor.

RATES, RESERVATIONS, & RESTRICTIONS

Deposit: 1 night; refund w/ 7-day notice
Discounts: 3rd person, rental of entire property

Credit Cards: MC, V, AE, D, DC
Check-In/Out: 3/11
Smoking: No
Pets: No

Kids: Over 6
Minimum Stay: None
Open: All year
Hosts: Patrick Schallert
Blue Rock Rd. on Lake Champlain

Alburg, VT 05440-9620
(802) 796-3736, (800) 348-0843
Fax: (802) 796-3736
tmott@together.net
www.thomas-mott-bb.com

LILAC INN, Brandon

Overall: ★★★★	Room Quality: B	Value: C	Price: $120–$260

Albert Farr made a fortune in the Midwest, then built this huge Georgian Revival summer cottage in 1909. As Michael puts it, "We want it to seem you are visiting Farr at this vacation house, indulging in fine food and drink, relaxing on the grounds or in your room, and enjoying Vermont's attractions." They succeed. Dinners are sensual and creative—Loaf of Soup, baked Vermont cheddar haddock, chocolate-coffee crème brûlée. The coach entrance, grand staircase (with a time capsule from 1991 in the newel post), a putting green, tavern, library, and environs are at your disposal. But book weekdays in season: They have hosted 200 weddings and counting.

SETTINGS & FACILITIES

Location: .25 mi. E of Rt. 7 and center of Brandon, near village green
Near: Historical sites, gardens, covered bridges, arts and crafts, outlets, concerts, Middlebury College, brewery, Teddy Bear factory, museums, Shelburne Farms, Wilson Castle, UVM Morgan Horse Farm, waterfalls
Building: 1909 Greek Revival 10,000-sq.-ft. mansion, 5-arch facade; Nat'l. Historic Register
Grounds: Gardens, 2 ponds, waterfall, gazebo, courtyard: flower-lined cobblestone
Public Space: Grand ballroom, library (2,500 books), tavern, garden conservatory
Food & Drink: Breakfast, Sun. brunch; specialties: baked apple turnovers, grilled maple-glazed grapefruit, eggs Benedict w/ smoked ham, chocolate soufflés; dinner: contemp. New England cuisine; specialties: award-winning BBQ shrimp, banana-rum bread pudding w/ butter rum sauce; local products; Wed.–Sat.; reservations
Recreation: Lake Champlain boat tours, X-C skiing (rentals), golf, mountain biking
Amenities & Services: Irons, historic walking tour maps, turn-down; weddings, receptions (300); wedding specialists, cakes; cultural arts events: readings, concerts, art shows, cooking classes; conferences (75)

ACCOMMODATIONS

Units: 9 guest rooms

All Rooms: Bath, TV, iron, heat and AC controls

Some Rooms: Fireplace (3), breakfast area, bridal suite
Bed & Bath: 8 queens, two w/ 2 twins, four-posters, canopies; tile baths, whirlpools, some original 1909 tubs, pedestal sinks
Favorites: Albert's #7—step-up pine canopy bed, fireplace, wingback chairs, footboard

Comfort & Decor: Period decor, Ralph Lauren prints, Laura Ashley, American folk. TVs in armoires. Art collection and collectibles. Desks and wingback chairs in most rooms. Some rooms connect.

RATES, RESERVATIONS, & RESTRICTIONS

Deposit: Gift certificate w/ less than 30-day notice
Discounts: Frequent guests, tell-a-friend coupons, gov't, singles, multiple night stays, 3rd person
Credit Cards: MC, V, D
Check-In/Out: 3/11
Smoking: Outside only
Pets: No
Kids: When attending weddings only

Minimum Stay: 2 nights holidays and foliage
Open: All year
Hosts: Melanie and Michael Shane
53 Park St.
Brandon, VT 05733
(802) 247-5463, (800) 221-0720
Fax: (802) 247-5499
lilacinn@sover.net
www.lilacinn.com

OCTOBER COUNTRY INN, Bridgewater Corners

Overall: ★★★★	Room Quality: B	Value: C	Price: $124–$162

Glorious red-and-gold October may be the namesake, but the rest of the year around here isn't exactly mud. June brings the nearby Quechee Hot Air Balloon Festival; August, the Scottish Festival; winter has top skiing and Dartmouth's Winter Festival; spring, biking and maple sugaring. An outdoor summer deck nestles in the hillside, and the swimming pool is a sapphire in a meadow with a mountain view. This open, airy farmhouse with cozy hearths offers varying international cuisine, even Hungarian and African. Patrick and Richard love to talk theatre, and are exceptionally helpful—arranging just about anything your heart may desire.

SETTINGS & FACILITIES

Location: Near intersection of Rt. 100A and Rt. 4; up a back road, across from general store
Near: Summer theater; 8 mi. to Woodstock, Dartmouth College, Coolidge Homestead, 5 mi. to Killington, antiquing, shopping, museums

Building: Deep red 19th-century farmhouse
Grounds: 5 acres, pool, gardens, terraced hillside, meadows, apple trees; view of valleys and mountains
Public Space: Open LR, library; 2

DRs; deck

Food & Drink: (MAP) Early bird coffee; breakfast; specialty: blueberry pancakes; dinner, ethnic cuisine varying nightly; family-style, home-grown vegetables; special meals avail.; liquor

license; tea and cookies

Recreation: Skiing, fishing, golf, beach, horse shows, ballooning

Amenities & Services: Hot tub, boat rental nearby, irons, beer/wine refrigerator

ACCOMMODATIONS

Units: 10 guest rooms

All Rooms: Fan, antiques

Some Rooms: Bath (8), AC, extra bed, skylight

Bed & Bath: 6 queens, others vary; firm mattresses; some tubs, some showers only, some multiple sprayers

Favorites: Skylight rooms—light and well decorated

Comfort & Decor: Eclectic and individual. Good lighting. Some stenciling, some flowering, nothing like Laura Ashley. Views of gardens, hillside, trees. Well-maintained, airy.

RATES, RESERVATIONS, & RESTRICTIONS

Deposit: Check w/ inn; refund w/ 10-day notice

Discounts: 3rd person, singles, families, longer stays, weekends

Credit Cards: MC, V, AE

Check-In/Out: 2/11:30

Smoking: No

Pets: No; 2 in-house cats

Kids: Welcome

Minimum Stay: None

Open: Nov. 21–April 1, May 1–Oct. 31

Hosts: Patrick Runkel and Richard Sims

Upper Rd., Box 66

Bridgewater Corners, VT 05035

(802) 672-3412, (800) 648-8421 reservations

oci@vermontel.com

www.vermontel.com/~oci

WILLARD STREET INN, Burlington

Overall: ★★★★	Room Quality: B	Value: C	Price: $85–$200

Hurrah to restaurant owners Bev and Gordon, for reviving and converting this grand bed-and-breakfast on "The Hill" overlooking Lake Champlain. This cultural and all-around capital of Vermont prospered from lumbering fortunes in the late-nineteenth century, when State Senator Charles Woodhouse built this redbrick, gabled mansion. You'll adore the glorious solarium with its green-and-white flooring, three walls of paned windows overlooking the lake, and comfortable seating by a wood stove. Stay in the room named Martha's Memoirs to encounter the resident (friendly) lady ghost. Is she the one who leaves a cookie by your bed?

SETTINGS & FACILITIES

Location: I-89 Exit 14W, Left to Rt. 7S; 2 blocks, on right corner of Cliff St. in residential area, next to Champlain College
Near: Shelburne Farms, Shelburne Museum, Ben & Jerry's, Vermont Teddy Bear Co., Church Street Marketplace
Building: 1800s brick w/ slate roof, exterior marble staircase; Queen Anne, Colonial–Georgian Revival style
Grounds: Elaborate English gardens, fountain, summer lake view

Public Space: Large foyer, parlor, solarium
Food & Drink: Full breakfast in solarium; specialties: French toast, quiche; afternoon tea; coffee, tea avail. all day
Recreation: Burlington bike path, skiing, bocci, croquet
Amenities & Services: Irons, hairdryers, cable TV, piano; nearby banquet/meeting facility (100), culinary workshops; reservations at innkeepers' restaurants

ACCOMMODATIONS

Units: 15 guest rooms
All Rooms: Phone, cookies at night, clock, radio
Some Rooms: Bath (12), most AC, sitting area, nonworking fireplace
Bed & Bath: Kings, queens, canopies, iron beds, extra beds; some whirlpools
Favorites: Tower Room—cozy, priv. bath, queen, white wicker sitting area, enclosed widow's walk, best views

Comfort & Decor: Individually decorated, coordinated fabrics. Period antiques and reproductions, Victorian-style papers, armoires. Room colors vivid—creams, dark greens, blues, periwinkle. Varied sizes (some, previous servants' quarters). Third-floor rooms best deal, w/ best views of Lake Champlain, Adirondack Mountains.

RATES, RESERVATIONS, & RESTRICTIONS

Deposit: 1 night; refund w/ 7-day notice
Discounts: Corp., 2+ nights, 3rd person
Credit Cards: MC, V, AE, D
Check-In/Out: 3/11
Smoking: No
Pets: No; in-house 3 cats, 1 dog
Kids: OK
Minimum Stay: 2 nights summer/fall weekends

Open: All year
Hosts: Beverly and Gordon Watson
319 S. Willard St.
Burlington, VT 05401
(802) 651-8710, (800) 577-8712
Fax: (802) 651-8714
wstinn@vermontel.com
www.willardstreetinn.com

TULIP TREE INN, Chittenden

Overall: ★★★★	Room Quality: B	Value: C	Price: $99–$259

Thomas Edison's sidekick built this sprawling hilltop home to retire to, and you can see why. Private and peaceful, in woods by a babbling brook, it seems miles from anything, but you're on cross-country trails, near downhill skiing at Killington, and close to canoeing, swimming, and fishing in the nearby reservoir. Geared for quiet and romance, you'll find no kids, no phones, no TVs, no business services. You will find an award-winning wine list, a glowing pub, a four-course, candlelight dinner at a communal table (great for solo travelers), and rustically elegant rooms with whirlpools and fireplaces.

SETTINGS & FACILITIES

Location: From Rutland, N on Rt. 7; at Y in road (at country store), go right for 6 mi.; at fire station, half-mile more to inn, on left
Near: Shopping, antiquing, museums, galleries, Killington
Building: 1830s home of William Barstow, Thomas Edison's collaborator
Grounds: Lawns, flowers, surrounded by woods
Public Space: 2 common rooms, pub, library, large porch

Food & Drink: (MAP) Full breakfast buffet: apple, cheese, or blueberry pancakes; candlelight dinner; specialties: curried carrot soup, beef w/ Béarnaise sauce; menu changes nightly, vegetarian possible; wine list
Recreation: Golf, horses, tennis, plane flying, mountain biking, train rides
Amenities & Services: Refrigerator, irons, maps; small weddings, tour guidance/maps

ACCOMMODATIONS

Units: 9 guest rooms
All Rooms: Bath, antiques
Some Rooms: Whirlpool (5), fireplace (2), bay window
Bed & Bath: Mostly queens, some four-posters; most full baths
Favorites: Room 9—spacious, fireplace, dressing room, dbl. whirlpool, dbl.

shower, 2 vanities, fireplace in bath
Comfort & Decor: Antiques, reproductions, collectibles. Colors vary, in whites, creams, greens, blues. Some stenciling. 9th room new in 1999.

RATES, RESERVATIONS, & RESTRICTIONS

Deposit: 50%; refund w/ 21-day notice
Discounts: Midweek, off-season
Credit Cards: MC, V
Check-In/Out: 3/11
Smoking: No
Pets: No
Kids: No
No-No's: More than 2 to a room
Minimum Stay: Winter weekends, holidays

Open: Closed early April, early Nov.
Hosts: Rosemary and Ed McDowell
Chittenden Dam Rd.
Chittenden, VT 05737
(800) 707-0017, (802) 483-6213
Fax: (802) 773-2440
ttin@sover.net
www.tuliptreeinn.com

TEN BENDS ON THE RIVER, Hyde Park

| Overall: ★★★★ | Room Quality: B | Value: B | Price: $95–$115 |

What a find. You don't have to be a trout angler to love this refined, sophisticated little hideaway with knockout views of the river and mountains from the grounds, porch, and many of the rooms. (A great place for a small wedding!) The living room is awash in light, with white walls and furnishings, throw rugs, pillows, objets d'art, wide plank floors, and pretty rugs. Fishing lodges and drop-dead gorgeous don't often mix, but, happily, they do here. And Oatis and Madie, the two friendly labs, make you feel so much at home, you may never want to leave.

SETTINGS & FACILITIES

Location: 2 mi. N of Stowe on Rt. 100, left on Stagecoach Rd., left on Cady's Falls Rd., left on Main St. Bear left at Lute's Sales & Service to farmhouse on the riverbend
Near: Stowe, Snuggler's Notch, Jay Peak Ski areas
Building: 1859 New England farmhouse
Grounds: Rural, on banks of Lamoille River w/ mountain views
Public Space: LR, DR, library, porch, open kitchen
Food & Drink: Gourmet communal breakfast; specialties: granola, scones, blueberry pancakes
Recreation: Skiing, snowboarding, snowshoeing, river sports
Amenities & Services: Refrigerator w/ drinks; weddings

ACCOMMODATIONS

Units: 3 guest rooms
All Rooms: Antiques, down comforter
Some Rooms: Bath
Bed & Bath: Queen or double iron beds
Favorites: Violet Room—river view from bath, watercolors, old quilts

Comfort & Decor: Artwork, eclectic mix of furnishings, artful use of color.

Exceptionally tasteful, peaceful, lovely. Good lighting. Good everything.

RATES, RESERVATIONS, & RESTRICTIONS

Deposit: Credit card holds reservation
Discounts: None
Credit Cards: MC, V
Check-In/Out: 3/11; flexible
Smoking: No
Pets: No; two dogs at inn
Kids: OK

Minimum Stay: None
Open: All year
Hosts: Aimee B. Stearns
454 Black Farm Rd.
Hyde Park, VT 05655
(802) 888-2827
Rahboo@POP.State.Vt.Us
www.mt-mansfield.com/tenbends

CORNWALL ORCHARDS, Middlebury

Overall: ★★★½	Room Quality: C	Value: C	Price: $85

Sparkling, homey, breezy, this understated property on a country road has a long history; the sons of the second owner, Elisha Hurlbutt, were in the War of 1812. Juliet is English and was an assistant to a musician and composer; Bob was a lawyer. Both are warm and helpful innkeepers. In the hills near a fine college town offering crafts and cultural attractions, this uncluttered, pleasurable bed-and-breakfast prepares healthy and bountiful breakfasts from a coal stove, using corn flour for pancakes, seasonal fruits, and free-range eggs from a neighbor. As it's minutes from cross-country trails and right off a famed hiking trail, you at least can work the breakfast off.

SETTINGS & FACILITIES

Location: 2 mi. from Middlebury College on Rt. 30, next to and across from orchards
Near: Vermont State Craft Center, state park, Fort Ticonderoga, Mount Independence, Hubbarton Battlefield, Lake Champlain, antiquing, trails, public golf course; 45 min. to Burlington or Sugarbush
Building: 1783 Vermont farmhouse, expanded Cape; barn; restored, 1994
Grounds: 14 acres, on ridge w/ mountain views

Public Space: Kitchen entry, LR, DR, porch
Food & Drink: Full breakfast, all organic; specialties: granola, multigrain blueberry pancakes, strawberry-rhubarb compote, free-range eggs; refreshments
Recreation: Biking, skiing, golf, tennis, fishing, canoeing
Amenities & Services: Discount to Shelburne Museum, flowers, basketball equipment, public rooms all disabled accessible

ACCOMMODATIONS

Units: 5 guest rooms
All Rooms: Bath, country pieces
Some Rooms: Disabled access
Bed & Bath: Queens, twins, firm mattresses; tub/shower (3), showers (2); 2nd floor, tiled, wainscoted baths

Favorites: Gov—first-floor corner, off LR, quiet, largest, view of Adirondacks
Comfort & Decor: Mountain views. Simple, clean, tasteful, country look. Wide board floors, ruffled white curtains, lots of light, breezy. Baths updated. Immaculate.

RATES, RESERVATIONS, & RESTRICTIONS

Deposit: 1 night; refund if room rerented
Discounts: 3rd person (2 rooms)
Credit Cards: None
Check-In/Out: Flexible/noon
Smoking: No
Pets: No
Kids: Welcome; crib avail.

Minimum Stay: 2 days summer, foliage, holiday weekends
Open: All year
Hosts: Juliet and Bob Gerlin
Box 428
Middlebury, VT 05753
(802) 462-2272
Cornorch@together.net

BLACK LANTERN INN, Montgomery Village

Overall: ★★★½	Room Quality: B	Value: B	Price: $60–$145

Almost touching the Canadian border, this 1803 former stagecoach stop once catered to salesmen purveying to local mill workers—and the pub bar, recycled from an Ohio hotel, was the center of activities. Not today. You can travel internationally—skiing Canadian mountains—-or ski nearby Jay peak, and swim, canoe, and fish in the nearby reservoir. Rooms are simply decorated but offer luxury amenities. Four-course dinners by candlelight are surprisingly sophisticated. Bob and Rita live in the converted barn in back: He's an avid biker (lots of cyclists stay here and join him); Rita's warmth is a special pleasure in this sparsely populated North Country.

SETTINGS & FACILITIES

Location: On Rt. 118, center of village, near Trout River
Near: Jay Peak, covered bridges, auctions, antiquing, shopping in Canada, Hazen's Notch
Building: 1803 white-pillared former stagecoach stop; Nat'l. Historic Register
Grounds: Backyard; gazebo w/ hot tub
Public Space: Sitting room, TV room, bar, DR

Food & Drink: (MAP) Full breakfast; candlelight dinner nightly (reservations); specialties: spinach stuffed mushrooms, shrimp w/ salmon mousse, filet mignon
Recreation: Skiing, snowmobiling, fishing, golf, tennis
Amenities & Services: Hot tub for 6–7, games, bike route advice/maps

ACCOMMODATIONS

Units: 10 guest rooms, 6 suites
All Rooms: Bath, individual heat, fans
Some Rooms: Fireplace, whirlpool
Bed & Bath: Beds vary; some whirlpools
Favorites: Room 10—queen, gas fireplace, dbl. whirlpool, deck w/ mountain view; Suite 12—3 BRs, LR w/ wood stove, TV/VCR, whirlpool

Comfort & Decor: Individual decorated w/ Vermont antique furniture. Continually renovated. Main house rooms small.

RATES, RESERVATIONS, & RESTRICTIONS

Deposit: Daily rate, refund w/ 15-day notice
Discounts: Off-season, groups, singles, kids (half price), 3rd person, 5-night stay
Credit Cards: MC, V, AE
Check-In/Out: Any time in afternoon/11; check-out flexible
Smoking: None in common areas downstairs
Pets: No; in-house springer spaniel on grounds

Kids: OK
Minimum Stay: None
Open: All year
Hosts: Rita and Allan Kalsmith
Rt. 118
Montgomery Village, VT 05470
(802) 326-4507, (800) 255-8661
Fax: (802) 326-4077
blantern@together.net
www.blacklantern.com

NORTHFIELD INN, Northfield

Overall: ★★★½   Room Quality: C   Value: C   Price: $85–$220

Once occupied by an Asian princess, this pretty, pristine property on a hill is now owned by another formidable lady, of Greek origin. Host Aglaia is an independent, interesting woman who loves to suggest outings or talk by the fire. She hosts many business travelers. Cookies, fruits, and drinks are always available on the sideboard by the open kitchen; the dining room table is elaborately set with a lace cloth and crystal; and breakfasts are decadent, with courses such as warm, apple bread pudding. Charming, immaculate rooms are small, some of them with sinks by the bed, and showers and toilets in separate (literal) water closets. Resourceful, but not great for privacy.

SETTINGS & FACILITIES

Location: Exit 5 off Rt. 89, past Norwich College
Near: State capital, granite quarries, Ben & Jerry's, Shelburne Farms & Museum, Norwich College, Stowe, Sugarbush, covered bridges

Building: 1901 Queen Anne Victorian
Grounds: 2 acres of gardens, apple orchards, meadows, woods, pond; gazebo, hammock in the woods; views
Public Space: Parlors, sitting room, library, porches

Food & Drink: Full, formal breakfast, communal; specialty: eggs Florentine; evening wine; fruit, snacks, beverages
Recreation: Winter sports, lawn/board games, videos

Amenities & Services: Picnic baskets, binoculars, fitness room; group dinners and special events by arrangement; fax, overhead projectors, computer hook-up, Greek spoken

ACCOMMODATIONS

Units: 8 guest rooms, 2 suites
All Rooms: Sink, clock, Victorian decor, phone (out)
Some Rooms: Bath, brass or carved-wood bed
Bed & Bath: Brass or carved-wood beds; baths created from closets within rooms; two rooms share bath, mostly showers

Favorites: 2nd floor corner rooms—deluxe furnishings, more space and privacy
Comfort & Decor: Victorian charm w/ lace, dolls, dark woods, but not overdone. Pristine. Smallish rooms, w/ little storage. Some rooms a bit cool in winter.

RATES, RESERVATIONS, & RESTRICTIONS

Deposit: Full; request 14-day notice; deposit forfeited, less than 3-day notice
Discounts: AAA, extended stays, groups; 7th night comp.
Credit Cards: MC, V
Check-In/Out: 3–6/11
Smoking: No
Pets: No
Kids: Over 15

No-No's: Staying after checkout
Minimum Stay: 2 nights Sept. 15–Nov.1; 4 nights for special events
Open: All year
Hosts: Aglaia Stalb
27 Highland Ave.
Northfield, VT 05663
(802) 485-8558
www.pbpub.com/inn/northfieldinn

NORTH HERO HOUSE COUNTRY INN, North Hero

Overall: ★★★★½	Room Quality: A	Value: B	Price: $145–$300

A recent million-dollar-plus renovation turned this flagging island property around, big time. The illusion of old-fashioned Americana almost hides the elegance and comfort (so unpretentious it is almost pretentious). Lake Champlain practically laps against the nineteenth-century buildings and stretches to the horizon like an ocean; guests used to arrive by steamship, but today often drive between the Vermont and New York sides of the lake. The town is a New England gem, general store and all, and is summer home of the White Lipizzan stallions of Austria. Dining is in a reworked greenhouse with water views, of course, and creative American cuisine. Some say Champ, cousin of the Loch Ness monster, resides in the lake.

SETTINGS & FACILITIES

Location: On Grand Isle, in Lake Champlain: Take I-89 N to Exit 17, to Rt. 2 W to North Hero Island; connected to mainland by bridges, on Rt. 2 or take ferry from Plattsburgh
Near: Ski areas, Grand Isle Ferry, Plattsburgh, Burlington, Univ. of Vermont, St. Michael's College Playhouse, Shelburne Museum, St. Anne's Shrine, Ausable Chasm; state parks; working waterside farms, Revolutionary War villages; Montreal
Building: 1891 Colonial, fieldstone/clapboard; verandas on 2 floors; 3 other buildings; restored, 1997
Grounds: Big trees, trails, pier, sandy Lake Champlain beach, swim platform, lakeside sauna, large spa tub; boat rentals nearby, mountain views

Public Space: Main common room, library, sitting room
Food & Drink: (MAP) Buffet breakfast w/ hot entree selection; specialties: house-cured salmon with corn blini, mint-crusted rack of lamb; osso buco w/ saffron risotto. The Pub, specialties: buffalo wings, meat loaf, venison chili, flatbread pizza; weekend buffets; closed Mon. and Tues. in winter
Recreation: Water and winter sports, tennis, golf, duck hunting, vineyards
Amenities & Services: French spoken; boat slips, live entertainment, moonlight snowshoeing, sleigh rides, tennis privileges nearby, disabled access (check w/ inn); irons, hairdryers; cribs, cots; weddings, conferences; movies in room

ACCOMMODATIONS

Units: 26, 3 lakeside annexes/ only 12 open in winter
All Rooms: Bath, phone/dataport, TV
Some Rooms: Priv. deck/porch, fireplace, lake view, sitting area, window seat
Bed & Bath: Four-poster, antique, canopy, half-canopy, or handcrafted artisan beds; all sizes, deep mattresses, add'l beds; some marble baths, some whirlpools; 1 w/ claw-foot soaking tub under moon window overlooks lake

Favorites: Main House Room 203—artisan-crafted wrought iron canopy under transom window, muslin side curtains, sitting room, fireplace, priv. porch, green marble bath, large whirlpool; Cove House Cobbler's Room—lakeside suite, rustic, 3-foot interior stone walls, sitting room, stone fireplace, sleeper sofa, BR w/ handhewn pine bed, screened patio
Comfort & Decor: Unusual, special, extremely attractive. Many w/ fantastic

views, luxury touches. Carpet. 2 attic rooms rather small. Striped wallpapers pretty, old-fashioned, or almost contemporary. Homestead building notably newer, summer-cottage style. 1800s Cove House: some suites, exposed brick walls, sliding doors to lakeside porches, best for water lovers.

RATES, RESERVATIONS, & RESTRICTIONS

Deposit: Credit card; no charge w/ 14-day notice
Discounts: B&B meal plan; kids, midweek rates; specials and packages: Murder Mystery, ice fishing, cooking classes, pair skating, more (check w/ inn)
Credit Cards: MC, V, AE, DC
Check-In/Out: After 2/11
Smoking: No
Pets: Restricted, check
Kids: Welcome; free for 5 and under;

reduced rates 5 and up
Minimum Stay: 2 nights summer weekends
Open: All year
Hosts: Walter Blasberg
P.O. Box 155
North Hero, VT 05474
(888) 525-3644 or (802) 372-4732
Fax: (802) 372-3218
nhhlake@aol.com
www.northherohouse.com

THE INN AT SHELBURNE FARMS, Shelburne

Overall: ★★★★★	Room Quality: B	Value: B	Price: $95–$350

Though this grand mansion on the lake is magnificent enough for a Vanderbilt, the property was always a working dairy farm. The on-site plant is where award-winning cheddar is made by hand from the raw milk of brown Swiss cows. Children can milk the cows, gather eggs, groom sheep, and do chores. The focus is public education and promotion of conservation ethics, and programs include field trips, summer camps, and professional development workshops. Spare, spacious rooms seem frozen in time: Check out the attic dollhouses. You feel like a socialite farmer here. The unique experience and many weddings and groups means high occupancy.

SETTINGS & FACILITIES

Location: On Lake Champlain; from Burlington Rt. 89 to Exit 13, travel S on Rt. 7 approximately 5 mi., turn left at stop light in center of Shelburne, drive 1.6 mi. to entrance of farm, past gate house, follow signs along 2 mile driveway to hilltop
Near: Shelburne Museum, state parks; 8 mi. to Burlington; 30 mi. to Stowe

Building: 1886 mansion, eclectic w/ Tudor, Queen Anne, Gothic Revival features
Grounds: 1,400 lakeside acres, working dairy farm and nonprofit environmental education center; castlelike stone barn, gardens by Olmsted, paths, pastures, view of mountains

Public Space: Tea room, main hall, billiards room, library; porches (2)

Food & Drink: Cont'l breakfast and afternoon tea; dinner avail. in 2 elegant, orig. DRs; full breakfast (add'l charge) served in marble DR, specialties: bread from on-site bakery, fresh eggs, pancakes w/ homemade syrup; picnic lunches avail.; Sun. brunch; dinners, regional fare, home-grown produce, extensive wine list

Recreation: Special events, museum, tennis, croquet, boating

Amenities & Services: Priv. rocky lake beaches; farm tours and special events comp. to overnight guests incl. July Mozart Festival, Sept. art auction, July draft-horse field days, Sept. Harvest Festival; other farm special events, house tours; turn-down, maps, forgotten necessities, refrigerator storage; cribs, cots

ACCOMMODATIONS

Units: 24 guest rooms, 2 cottages

All Rooms: Decorative tiled fireplace, seating, phone, clock

Some Rooms: Priv. bath (14), 10 rooms share 5 baths; cottages w/ kitchens

Bed & Bath: Four-poster, canopy, antique beds; many baths w/ orig. soaking tubs, marble fixtures, tile floors

Favorites: Overlook Room—Lila Vanderbilt-Webb's BR, large corner room w/ window wall, views, king bed, orig. writing desk

Comfort & Decor: Huge rooms, spare luxury. Elegant, elaborate Vanderbilt pieces original to mansion. Carpet. Rich color schemes. Rustic cottage bungalows are honeymoon favorites, 1 w/ working fireplace. Can be warm in summer, cool in fall. Former servant's rooms Spartan but best deal. Public rooms spacious, w/ furnishings original to Webbs and Vanderbilts.

RATES, RESERVATIONS, & RESTRICTIONS

Deposit: 1 night; refund w/ 15-day notice

Discounts: 3rd person, kids; packages, workshops; check w/ inn

Credit Cards: MC, V, AE, D

Check-In/Out: 3/11

Smoking: No

Pets: No

Kids: Welcome; under 2, free

Minimum Stay: 2 nights weekends

Open: Mid-May to mid-Oct.

Hosts: Karen Polihronakis
1611 Harbor Rd.
Shelburne, VT 05482
(802) 985-8686
Fax: (802) 985-8123
www.shelburnefarms.org

EDSON HILL MANOR, Stowe

Overall: ★★★★½	Room Quality: B	Value: A	Price: $75–$175

A former gentleman's estate, Edson Hill Manor remains horsy, woodsy, and romantic—and surprisingly family-friendly. The pool is striking, and the public areas quietly elegant, with pine paneling, beams hewn from Ethan Allen's barn, Delft tiles around the fireplace, needlepoint-covered chairs, and fine paintings. You can catch a trout in the stocked ponds and have it for breakfast or dinner, ride guided trails, and cross-country ski practically from the door. (No wonder Alan Alda filmed the winter scenes here for *The Four Seasons*.) Food and wine are tops, views are panoramic, and of the two fine properties owned by laid-back Eric, we prefer the isolation and special amenities here, over nearby Ten Acres.

SETTINGS & FACILITIES

Location: Halfway between Stowe and Mt. Mansfield, 1,500 feet up, off Rt. 108
Near: Mt. Mansfield and village, Ben & Jerry's, Camel's Hump
Building: Brick/wood manor house, completed in 1940
Grounds: Rolling countryside, 225 forested acres; free-form pool, stocked ponds, red barn stable, trails, mountain views
Public Space: LR, DR, lounge

Food & Drink: Full country breakfast, buffet style; candlelight dinner, open to public; specialties: chilled melon soup w/ honey and lime, grilled Vermont rabbit; tea/coffee
Recreation: Snowshoeing, sleigh/carriage rides, skiing, canoeing, tennis, horseback riding
Amenities & Services: Stables, pool, trout ponds, trails, games X-C ski rental, fax, catering, French spoken, some disabled access

ACCOMMODATIONS

Units: 9 guest rooms in manor, 16 in carriage house
All Rooms: Bath, phone, artwork
Some Rooms: Fireplace, TV, sitting area, canopy bed
Bed & Bath: Pencil-post canopy beds, varied sizes; whimsically painted bathrooms, most tubs, some showers only

Favorites: Manor house rooms—special fabrics, charming accents
Comfort & Decor: Antiques throughout. Carriage house rooms larger, more subdued, w/ fireplaces, pine paneling, and beams. Manor house rooms more romantic w/ coordinated fabrics and wallcoverings.

RATES, RESERVATIONS, & RESTRICTIONS

Deposit: 1 night; refund w/ 15-day notice
Discounts: 3rd party in room, groups, off-season, extended stays, kids under 4 free
Credit Cards: MC, V, AE, D
Check-In/Out: 2/11
Smoking: No
Pets: No

Kids: OK
Minimum Stay: 1 night; 5 nights, holidays
Open: All year
Hosts: Eric Lande
1500 Edson Hill Rd.
Stowe, VT 05672
(800) 621-0284, (802) 253-7371
www.stowevt.com

SIEBENESS, Stowe

Overall: ★★★½	Room Quality: C	Value: C	Price: $70–$200+

The German name of this cozy, cheery bed-and-breakfast mystifies many guests—it means "seven S's" for the seven S-curves on a nearby Stowe ski trail. This world-class resort town gives this bed-and-breakfast a mix of sophisticated, international clientele and informal sports enthusiasts. New innkeeper Bill plans to upgrade accordingly, but maintain the relaxed atmosphere and hearty breakfasts that have garnered praise in the past. Big pluses are access to cross-country trails right from the property, and the outdoor pool, which keeps summer guests happy.

SETTINGS & FACILITIES

Location: 3.5 mi. from village, 2 mi. from Mt. Mansfield; in heart of downtown Stowe, turn toward mountain on Rt. 108; B&B on left
Near: Ski resorts, Mt. Mansfield—Vermont's highest peak, Stowe and Craftsburg villages, Ben & Jerry's, Cabot Cheese Creamery, Shelbourne Museum, sugarhouses
Building: 1952 Colonial, bay windows, front porch
Grounds: Adjacent to Stowe's recreation path; X-C ski to major trail systems or into village

Public Space: Lounge, DR
Food & Drink: Multicourse breakfast; a specialty: stuffed French toast; BYOB bar w/ snacks and soft drinks, hot cider
Recreation: Winter and water sports, sleigh rides, horseback riding, golf, antiquing, spa visits
Amenities & Services: Outdoor hot tub, village-mountain shuttle stop at inn, pool w/ mountain views; snow reports, maps, fax, dataport

ACCOMMODATIONS

Units: 12 guest rooms
All Rooms: Bath, AC
Some Rooms: Gas fireplace, deck, whirlpool, TV, refrigerator, 3rd person/family
Bed & Bath: Some canopy, four-poster, antique, feather beds, sizes vary; some shower-only, some 2-person whirlpools
Favorites: Mountain View Suites—gas fireplaces, decks, queen featherbeds, 2-

person whirlpools, TVs, refrigerators, private
Comfort & Decor: Country pine furnishings, quilts, hand stenciling. Some awkwardly designed rooms, some more spacious. Light and bright. Phones and TVs deliberately excluded. Being upgraded w/ more whirlpools, fireplaces, amenities.

RATES, RESERVATIONS, & RESTRICTIONS

Deposit: 50%; refund w/ 14-day notice; 1 month notice for holidays/special weekends

Discounts: Singles, 3rd person; holiday or midweek packages, ski packages, many others (10% gratuity and Vermont

taxes; expect increases for millennium holiday season)
Credit Cards: MC, V, AE
Check-In/Out: 3/10
Smoking: No
Pets: No
Kids: Over 12
No-No's: Early departure

Minimum Stay: 2 nights weekends; 3 holidays
Open: All year
Hosts: William Kern Ruffing
3681 Mountain Rd.
Stowe, VT 05672
(800) 426-9001 or (802) 253-8942
Fax: (802) 253-9232

TEN ACRES LODGE, Stowe

Overall: ★★★★	Room Quality: B	Value: B	Price: $75–$220

This Stowe favorite, well known for its fine food and wines, was bought by the owners of nearby Edson Hill Manor in 1993. It offers a more traditional, less rarified atmosphere of comfortable Americana, with paneled walls, slate floors, and paintings by Walt Whitman's brother-in-law, Charles Heyde. Hill House units here are preferable to the Edson Hill Manor carriage house units, but the main house rooms don't measure up to those in the main house at EHM. Guests can use both facilities, and eat at both excellent restaurants, so budget-conscious travelers can stay here and enjoy the grounds and facilities at its lovely sibling up the mountain road.

SETTINGS & FACILITIES

Location: 2 mi. N of Stowe on Rt. 108 to Barrows Rd. Left for half-mile.
Near: Mt. Mansfield, Ben & Jerry's, Trapp Family Lodge
Building: 1835 farmhouse; recent addition
Grounds: 10 acres, pastures, mountain views
Public Space: LR, DR, library, lounge

Food & Drink: Full country breakfast; dinner w/ New American cuisine, open to public; tea/snacks; extensive wine list
Recreation: Horseback riding, snow-shoeing, canoeing, skiing
Amenities & Services: Outdoor hot tub, tennis, pool (unheated), X-C ski trails, massage, trail/sleigh rides, fax, French-speaking host

ACCOMMODATIONS

Units: 16 guest rooms, 2 cottages
All Rooms: Bath, phone, AC
Some Rooms: TV, four-poster, fire-place, sitting area, kitchenette, balcony
Bed & Bath: Queen/king, some four-poster, brass; most baths with tub
Favorites: Hill House—fireside seat-ing area, balcony, AC, TV

Comfort & Decor: Rooms in main lodge more traditional, smaller, w/ country antiques. Hill House, fireplaces, balconies. Cottages w/ kitchenettes, 2 BRs. All comfortable.

RATES, RESERVATIONS, & RESTRICTIONS

Deposit: 1 night; 2 during foliage, Christmas, and Presidents' week
Discounts: Extended stay, groups, kids, 3rd person, off-season
Credit Cards: MC, V, AE, D; prefer final bill paid in cash or check
Check-In/Out: 2/11
Smoking: Only in Hill House units
Pets: Check
Kids: OK

No-No's: "Staying longer than a week without settling bill"
Minimum Stay: None
Open: All year
Hosts: Eric Lande
14 Barrows Rd.
Stowe, VT 05672
(800) 327-7357, (802) 253-7638
Fax: (802) 253-4036

STRONG HOUSE INN, Vergennes

Overall: ★★★★½   Room Quality: B   Value: B   Price: $75–$270

A banking bigwig named Strong created this distinguished home in the nineteenth century, and its appeal is stronger than ever. His portrait looms over the living room, but the house has been enhanced with Mary's award-winning innkeeping talents. If you're peckish, you can raid the guest refrigerator in the kitchen, and dinner baskets, prepared by a local French restaurant, can be in your room on arrival. (Why don't more bed-and-breakfasts offer this option?) Activities include winter quilting seminars, with a quilt teacher on-site ("sewing and eating," as Mary puts it). The luxury country house addition, opened in 1999, is loaded with amenities.

SETTINGS & FACILITIES

Location: Rt. 22A, 1 mi. S of Vergennes Center
Near: Antiquing, covered bridges, crafts, historic sites, Middlebury College, Yale

Building: 1834 Federal, cottage; Nat'l. Historic Registry; country house addition, 1999
Grounds: 6 sloping acres; meadow, forest, trails, gazebo, gardens; mountain views

Public Space: Freestanding stairway in entry, LR, DR, library
Food & Drink: Full breakfast; specialties: Grand Marnier French toast, eggs Benedict, apple dumplings, crepes; 4-course tea monthly, open to public, Nov.–May (reservations); appetizers, desserts; dinner baskets, picnic baskets, sandwiches and salads for late-arrivals (prearranged, extra); liquor license
Recreation: Snowshoeing, sledding, ice-skating on site, skiing
Amenities & Services: AC, refrigerator, irons, daily paper, boutique, turndown (suites), packing picnics, wedding arrangements; quilting and wellness pkgs.

ACCOMMODATIONS

Units: 12 guest rooms (6 in country house), 2 suites
All Rooms: Bath, AC, thermostat, TV, phone
Some Rooms: Fireplace, library, sunroom; dbl. whirlpool (1), balconies (2), porches (2), garden (1); coffee niche, coffeemaker; breakfast option: delivered or in main house for country house rooms
Bed & Bath: Doubles, queens, kings, some canopies; tubs and showers
Favorites: Adirondack—twig furniture, king canopy, stone fireplace, breakfast area, wet bar, refrigerator, dbl. whirlpool, dbl. vanity; Plantation—Southern style, 2nd floor, king four-poster, fireplace, balcony; Vermont room—French doors, views, pine queen four-poster
Comfort & Decor: Mountain views and wonderful sunsets. Green Mountains in front, Adirondacks in back. Names match decor. Rooms individually decorated, from coastal theme to 18th-century English to Provence. Luxury and creative style. Country house, w/ coffee niches, breakfast areas, doors out to garden.

RATES, RESERVATIONS, & RESTRICTIONS

Deposit: 1 night; refund w/ 14-day notice
Discounts: Off-season, 3rd person, corp.
Credit Cards: MC, V, AE
Check-In/Out: 3/11
Smoking: No
Pets: No; in-house cat
Kids: Well-behaved over 8
Minimum Stay: 2 nights summer weekends, holidays
Open: All year
Hosts: Mary and Hugh Bargiel
82 West Main St.
Vergennes, VT 05491-9531
(802) 877-3337
Fax: (802) 877-2599
innkeeper@stronghouseinn.com
www.stronghouseinn.com

WHITFORD HOUSE INN, Vergennes

Overall: ★★★★½   Room Quality: B   Value: C   Price: $110–$175

On a little-traveled road by Dead Creek sits a sophisticated country home in the midst of meadows, cornfields, and mountains. Slate, wool, wood, glass, multi-paned and picture windows, a stone hearth, Morris chairs,

wideboard floors, Southwest touches, and artwork from daughter Katie create a casually elegant ambiance. Breakfasts are comparable to the understated, striking style of the property. Bruce estimates that almost half of their guests are references or returns, and they "get lots of notes saying thanks." This open, informal house is contemporary country—and the former Californian hosts are a big part of things without being intrusive.

SETTINGS & FACILITIES

Location: 25 mi. from Adirondack High Peaks, 2 mi. E of Lake Champlain, on a dirt road with meadows and fields; hosts consider themselves in Addison, in spite of Vergennes address
Near: Adirondack Mountains, Middlebury College, Revolutionary War sites, antiquing, Shelburne American Folk Art Museum, wildlife preserves, Lake Champlain
Building: 1790s post-and-beam Cape Cod farmhouse; modernized without changing its look; cottage
Grounds: 37 acres: fields, woods, organic garden, recycling; views of mountains

Public Space: Dramatic LR, library, DR, veranda, decks
Food & Drink: Full breakfast; specialties: homemade bread, eggs Florentine, frittatas, stewed apples; wine/cheese, hors d'oeuvres; dinner w/ prior reservation; special meals accom.
Recreation: Boating, skiing, golf, kayaking, horseshoes, swimming, tennis, horseback riding, fishing, lawn games, flying kites
Amenities & Services: Games, books, baby grand piano, canoes, bikes; limited disabled access; weddings, receptions, conferences

ACCOMMODATIONS

Units: 3 guest rooms in main building, 1 suite, cottage
All Rooms: Bath, alarm clock, antiques
Some Rooms: Sitting room, wet bar
Bed & Bath: 2 twins, doubles; king; tubs, glass showers; radiant heat slate floors
Favorites: Suite—spacious, king, sitting room, bath, pull-out bed, large windows

Comfort & Decor: Great mountain views. Dramatic mix of country and contemporary. Old windows, few curtains or drapes. Oriental rugs, mostly antique, many collected on travels. Fresh flowers. Cottage separated by brick path.

RATES, RESERVATIONS, & RESTRICTIONS

Deposit: 1 night; refund w/ 14-day notice
Discounts: Off-season, 3rd person
Credit Cards: MC, V
Check-In/Out: 1/11; flexible
Smoking: Outside only
Pets: OK, arrange prior; in-house cat, 2 beagles
Kids: Welcome

Minimum Stay: None
Open: All year
Hosts: Barbara and Bruce Carson
912 Grandey Rd.
Vergennes, VT 05491-8851
(802) 758-2704, (800) 746-2704
Fax: (802) 758-2089
whitford@together.net

THE INN AT THE ROUND BARN FARM, Waitsfield

Overall: ★★★★★   Room Quality: A   Value: B   Price: $135–$240

The nineteenth-century farmhouse and attached barns were part of a dairy farm until the 1960s, and the idyllic setting remains. Resident ducks such as Huey, Dewey, and Lucy waddle from the pond; black-and-white cows look like they are painted on the green hills by the carton artist at Ben & Jerry's. You also get classical music, farm breakfasts, swimming into a greenhouse filled with hibiscus, acres of trails, maybe an apple tart and sherry by the fire, and similar delights. The big, rare barn is extremely popular for weddings and conferences, and skiers are only a few minutes from great slopes. This bed-and-breakfast is deluxe yet friendly, truly elegant and original—a deserved classic.

SETTINGS & FACILITIES

Location: From Rt. 100 in Waitsfield, turn onto Bridge St., through covered bridge, bear right at fork onto East Warren Rd; 1 mi. to B&B, in heart of farm country
Near: Pastures with cows, covered bridge, Sugarbush, Mad River Glen
Building: 1910 former farm buildings; newer wing attached to huge round barn, used for functions
Grounds: 85 acres of hills, gardens, lily ponds, terraces, mountain views

Public Space: Eat-in breakfast area off kitchen, traditional parlors, library, barn
Food & Drink: Lavish full breakfasts; specialty: French toast w/ sautéed fruits; afternoon goodies, sherry; some weekend dinners in winter
Recreation: Swimming, bird watching, skiing, golf
Amenities & Services: 60-foot lap pool; groomed X-C skiing trails, rentals and instructions; snowshoe rentals and tours

ACCOMMODATIONS

Units: 11 guest rooms
All Rooms: Bath, fresh flowers, heat

controls, reading lamp, lighted makeup mirror, clock

Some Rooms: Fireplace, cathedral ceiling, steam shower, oversized whirlpool tub
Bed & Bath: Varied bed sizes, canopied beds and four-posters; inviting baths with views, skylights, robes
Favorites: Sterling Room—1st floor, stenciled walls, handpainted headboard, skylight, fireplace; window wall vistas

make up for small size; all rooms have special appeal
Comfort & Decor: House rooms more traditional, w/ antiques, some fireplaces and enlarged baths. New wing in former barn, canopied beds, cathedral ceilings, beams, gas fireplaces, steam showers, whirlpools. Sumptuous.

RATES, RESERVATIONS, & RESTRICTIONS

Deposit: 1 night, full; 2 or more, 50%
Discounts: Singles, 3rd person, mid-week packages
Credit Cards: MC, V, AE, D, DC
Check-In/Out: 3/11, call if arriving after 7 p.m.
Smoking: No
Pets: No
Kids: Over 16
Minimum Stay: Varies

Open: All year
Hosts: Doreen and AnneMarie DeFreest
RR1 Box 247, E. Warren Rd.
Waitsfield, VT 05673
(802) 496-2276
Fax: (802) 496-8832
roundbarn@madriver.com
www.inattheroundbarn.com

THE PITCHER INN, Warren

Overall: ★★★★★   Room Quality: A   Value: C   Price: $200–$425

Fantasy lovers and fast-trackers, you ain't seen nothing till you see the revolving fowl in the Mallard Room. Or the whimsical, luxurious details throughout. Ask to see other units, if humanly possible, or peek in while the maid is cleaning. (My evil twin must have said that!) Completely rebuilt on the site of a burned-down landmark, this beauty has already become another, and each unique habitat is astoundingly designed with a Vermont theme, by a different top architect. The dining is divine, the baths, to die for. Coolish atmosphere can't compete with the decor, but who cares?

SETTINGS & FACILITIES

Location: North of Rutland on Rt. 100, along the Mad River; one hour from Burlington Airport in hamlet across from general store and antique stores
Near: River, antiques-filled villages, skiing, Mad River Glen, Sugarbush

Building: 1997 replica of 19th-century inn
Grounds: Minimal, with gardens, grape arbor, decks overlooking waterfall; mountain views
Public Space: Porch, reception area, common room, library dedicated to

Robert Frost, lounges, basement game room, 1,200-bottle wine cellar, DRs, decks

Food & Drink: Full breakfast; creative American cuisine from star chef; dinner, breakfast open to public, dining in wine cave; tea/pastries; brunch included on weekend

Recreation: Snowboarding, skating, sleigh rides, golf, tennis, horseback riding, shuffleboard

Amenities & Services: Locker/storage rooms, ski boot and glove warmer, gift shop, 19th-century billiards table, elevator; preferences noted, spa treatments, business facilities, disabled access

ACCOMMODATIONS

Units: 8 guest rooms in main building, 2 suites in barn

All Rooms: Bath, concealed TV/VCR, phone, dataport, AC

Some Rooms: Fireplace, whirlpool, steam shower, balcony

Bed & Bath: Mix of styles, mostly kings; huge, lavish baths, some w/ dbl. whirlpools and showers, radiant heat floors

Favorites: Lodge Room—unique four-poster, star-studded ceiling, slate fire-

place, TV in lecturn; all rooms qualify for favorite

Comfort & Decor: Incredible detailing, luxury and wit. Many artifacts. Over-the-top themes include locals Calvin Coolidge (quiet, w/ two-wall handpainted mural), Chester Arthur (disabled access), a schoolroom (bed headboard a blackboard, w/ chalk), trout fishing (tie your own flies), etc.

RATES, RESERVATIONS, & RESTRICTIONS

Deposit: 50%

Discounts: Extra person, midweek winter

Credit Cards: MC, V, AE

Check-In/Out: 3/11

Smoking: No

Pets: No

Kids: OK

Minimum Stay: 2 nights weekends, 5 nights Christmas week; refund w/ 21-

day notice

Open: All year

Hosts: Heather and John Carino
P.O. Box 347
Warren, VT 05674
(888) TO-PITCHER, (802) 496-6350
Fax: (802) 496-6354
pitcher@madriver.com
www.pitcherinn.com

WEST HILL HOUSE, Warren

Overall: ★★★★	Room Quality: B	Value: B	Price: $90–$170

Dotty and Eric are exceptionally warm and thoughtful innkeepers, and their presence permeates every aspect of this outstanding little bed-and-breakfast. Built in the 1850s, and once a ski lodge, its "great room" addition was recently built by Eric, who was in the construction business. In winter, guests occasionally gather around the brick bake oven and build

individual pizzas for informal group dinners, and Dotty may cook a special Saturday night dinner or prepare a birthday cake. Close to Sugarbush resort, the mood here is personal and unassuming. This is a haven for solo travelers, and those who want to feel like part of a family.

SETTINGS & FACILITIES

Location: 1.5 mi. up from Rt. 100, on quiet road adjacent to championship golf course

Near: 1 mile to Sugarbush, Mad River Glen Ski, Ben & Jerry's, Cabot Cheese Creamery, Cold Hollow Cider Mill, Montpelier, Rock of Ages Granite Quarry

Building: 1850s farmhouse; recent addition

Grounds: 9 acres: woods, apple trees, meadows, gardens, beaver pond, mountain views; terraced rear yard w/ deck, screened gazebo coming

Public Space: Library, great room, DR, sunroom

Food & Drink: 3-course communal breakfast, specialties: sticky buns, streusel, ginger-lemon muffins, soufflés; après ski tea and refreshments; cocktail hour treats; wet bar and refrigerator in great room stocked w/ set-ups, soft drinks, beer and wine for purchase; family-style candlelight dinners served to minimum 6 guests Sat. nights in season or by reservation (add'l per-person charge), 4-course menu agreed on by guests at breakfast; holiday dinners/celebrations, birthday/wedding cakes; priv. label comp. champagne for honeymooners and anniversary couples

Recreation: Soaring, summer theatre/concerts, sleigh rides; Vermont Icelandic Horse Farm Trekking

Amenities & Services: Snowshoes, sleds, binoculars, beach towels; irons, guest phone line and number, daily paper, maps, refrigerator; videos; meetings, full wedding services, fitness center nearby

ACCOMMODATIONS

Units: 6 guest rooms, 1 suite

All Rooms: Bath, good reading lights, thermostat, AC or ceiling fans

Some Rooms: Fireplace; sitting room, TV, VCR on request, 3rd person

Bed & Bath: Comfortable beds, queen or king/twin; some showers only; some 2-person steam showers, whirlpools; hairdryers, some robes, new fixtures and tile

Favorites: Stetson Suite—ground floor, gas woodstove in sitting room w/ sofa bed, TV/VCR, tub, 2-person steam shower; Secluded Fireplace Room— priv. spiral staircase, fireplace, queen, beamed ceiling, lots of windows, large bath

Comfort & Decor: Room sizes vary, but all comfortable. Original artwork, sloped ceilings, handmade quilts, stenciling, sponge-painted walls. Good lighting. Carpet or original wide plank floors w/ handmade rugs, exposed beams, barn siding walls. Wreaths, candles, ambiance lighting, antiques.

RATES, RESERVATIONS, & RESTRICTIONS

Deposit: 1 night; refund w/ 14-day notice

Discounts: 3rd person; custom packages

Credit Cards: MC, V, AE

Check-In/Out: 3/11; flexible

Smoking: No

Pets: No

Kids: Over 12

Minimum Stay: 2 nights, weekends; 3 nights, holidays/foliage

Open: All year

Hosts: Dotty Kyle and Eric Brattstrom
West Hill Rd., RR1, Box 292
Warren, VT 05674
(800) 898-1427 or (802) 496-7162
Fax: (802) 496-6443
westhill@madriver.com
www.westhillhouse.com

INN AT BLUSH HILL, Waterbury

Overall: ★★★★	Room Quality: B	Value: B	Price: $65–$130

Originally a stagecoach stopover, and the oldest lodgings in Waterbury, this pristine bed-and-breakfast is up a steep hill off a busy road where horse-drawn carriages once clanked along, and yet it seems isolated. Window walls highlight sunrise over the mountaintops, and warm woodwork and greetings add to the sunshiny feel. Dieters will face a dilemma with breakfast temptations served in the rustic kitchen. How about cornmeal waffles with warm applesauce and bacon, or four-berry pancakes topped with maple syrup and ice cream from neighbor Ben & Jerry's? Pam and Gary were in the hospitality biz in Washington, D.C., and boy, does it show. You'll feel pampered.

SETTINGS & FACILITIES

Location: I-89 to Exit 10 N, left onto Blush Hill Rd., B&B is on right at top of hill; alternately, site is just off Rt. 100

Near: Stowe, Sugarbush Ski Resorts, Ben & Jerry's Ice Cream Factory, Cabot Cheese Creamery, Cold Hollow Cider Mill, Montpelier, Burlington, Lake

Champlain, state parks, shopping, quaint villages and antiques, covered bridges, Art Vermont, Maritime Museum, Shelburne Museum, Vermont Teddy Bear Co.
Building: Circa 1790 Cape; 1840 addition, broad veranda
Grounds: 5 rolling acres, gardens, Green Mountain views
Public Space: Parlor, DR, country kitchen

Food & Drink: Full country breakfast; specialties: dishes featuring Ben & Jerry's products: breakfast parfait, melon w/ sorbet; cont'l breakfast for late risers; refreshments
Recreation: Winter and water sports, soaring, summer theatre/concerts, guided snowmobile tours
Amenities & Services: Refrigerator, binoculars, irons, videos, discount ski lift tickets, maps, recipes

ACCOMMODATIONS

Units: 5 guest rooms
All Rooms: Bath, clock/radio
Some Rooms: Mountain views; fireplace (1), sitting area (1); accommodate 3rd person
Bed & Bath: Some antique brass, oak, canopy beds, queen or double; some shower only, whirlpool (1), hall access bath w/ robes (1)

Favorites: Sunflower—largest room, full canopy queen, 15-foot-wide window views
Comfort & Decor: Mixed styles, some colonial antiques. Each room includes special amenity or antique: fireplace, romantic bed, love seat, whirlpool, Laura Ashley prints. Some head-banging slanted ceilings. Adjoining rooms work for families, companions.

RATES, RESERVATIONS, & RESTRICTIONS

Deposit: 50%, min. 1 night; refund w/ 14-day notice
Discounts: Packages, 3rd person, family, long stays
Credit Cards: MC, V, AE, D
Check-In/Out: 3/11
Smoking: No
Pets: No
Kids: Over 6
No-No's: Changing length of stay

Minimum Stay: None
Open: All year, except Thanksgiving, Christmas Eve, Christmas Day
Hosts: Pam and Gary Gosselin
Blush Hill Rd., Box 1266
Waterbury, VT 05676
(800) 736-7522 or (802) 244-7529
Fax: (802) 244-7314
innatbh@aol.com
www.Blushhill.com

Zone 10
Vermont—Upper Valley/
Northeast Kingdom

The Northeast Kingdom ranges from the Green Mountains in the west to the Connecticut River on the east. Quebec is north. This is Vermont's wildest, quietest side, where you can hunt, trap, bike, fish, canoe, hike, and gaze at a sky full of stars.

The great outdoors here offers 50 public boat launch sites, remote lakes, and over a million forested acres. Cross-country and downhill ski trips at Jay Peak and Burke offer quieter, less-crowded venues than at more popular resorts. Stowe is one of the oldest and finest ski destinations in the country. Lake Willoughby has beaches, swimming, and fishing, with pretty lake views. With more dirt roads than paved ones, the northern corner is great for hiking and biking. And keep an eye out for moose—in some areas you're more likely to meet up with the formidable bearded beasts than with tourists (bearded or not).

Although truly rural, this northeast corner of Vermont is not without culture and family-centered activities. Craftsbury features the Craftsbury Chamber Players. You can enjoy a civilized, traditional tea at Perennial Pleasures in East Hardwick. The Caledonia County Fair in Lyndonville and the Orleans County Fair in Barton (both in August) are among the best in New England. Stop by church suppers, auctions, or fiddling contests. For kids, The Bread & Puppet Circus is based in Glover, and Circus Smirkus is in Greensboro.

The region is the birthplace of Ethan Allen furniture, and fine craftsmakers still choose to live and work here. Local galleries and workshops show blown glass, wood carvings, quilts, pottery, and photographs. And there's plenty of antiquing at good prices.

Noteworthy architecture is another plus. After admiring the 1878 church and 1856 courthouse in the old railroad town of St. Johnsbury, stop by the Fairbanks Museum and Planetarium, which has enough stuffed animals to keep tots happy. Covered bridges and barns also abound. In Burke, the Inn at Mountain View Creamery (one of our profiled lodgings), has outstanding old barns.

Agriculture is a cornerstone of Vermont, and the Billings Farm & Museum in Woodstock provides a history. Cabot Cheese, produced in the area, is good enough for star chefs to demand; the plant offers tours and samples. Restaurants serve mainly fresh, local fare, and country stores and general stores are a charming remnant of classic New England, with local crafts and foodstuffs crammed among the canned goods and mops.

Lodging in the Northeast Kingdom ranges from famed romantic inns to simple, inexpensive places. Crowds aren't a problem, but the farther north you go, the fewer accommodations you'll find. To be sure, reserve ahead.

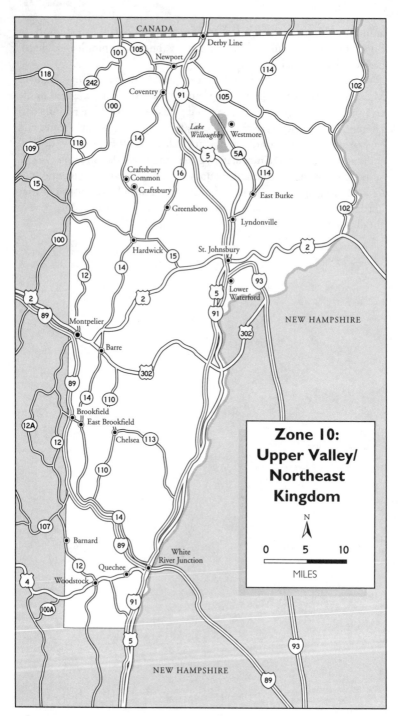

CANADA

Derby Line

101 105 Newport

118 242 114 102

Coventry 91 105

100

14 Lake Willoughby Westmore

109 118 5 5A

15 Craftsbury Common 16 114

Craftsbury East Burke

Greensboro 102

Hardwick 15 Lyndonville

100 14 St. Johnsbury 2

12 5 93

2 Lower Waterford

2 5 NEW HAMPSHIRE

89 91

Montpelier 302

Barre

302

89

14 110

12A Brookfield

East Brookfield

12 Chelsea 113

110

**Zone 10:
Upper Valley/
Northeast
Kingdom**

N

0   5   10

MILES

107

14

Barnard 89

12 Quechee White River Junction

4 Woodstock

100A 91

5

NEW HAMPSHIRE

93

89

MAPLE LEAF INN, Barnard

Overall: ★★★★½	Room Quality: B	Value: B	Price: $115–$190

Built around 1990, this divine, gabled bed-and-breakfast was created by Gary and Janet with romance in mind, and it seems in many ways 100 years older than it really is. Old-fashioned octagonal bath tiles cover heated floors. Vintage-looking pedestal sinks and wainscoting contrast with soaking tubs for two. King-size beds face fireplaces salvaged from an old Boston house. A maple leaf welcome card waits at arrival, and chocolates are placed by your turned-down bed. Breakfast is at tables for two, surrounded by "Love" postage stamp samplers cross-stitched by Janet. As for the videos for the in-room VCRs, forget Stallone—chick-flicks reign.

SETTINGS & FACILITIES

Location: Rt. 12, 9 mi. N of Woodstock; .25 mile S of Barnard General Store

Near: Woodstock, arts/crafts galleries, Silver Lake, Billings Farm & Museum, Vermont Institute of Natural Science, Raptor Center, Pentangle Council on the Arts, Quechee Gorge, Calvin Coolidge birthplace, glassblowing, Appalachian Trail, Long Trail, covered bridges

Building: Victorian-style farmhouse; built 1990s

Grounds: 16 acres, mountain/lake views, gazebo

Public Space: Parlor; library, Middle East artifacts; DR; wraparound porch, gazebo

Food & Drink: Breakfast, 3 courses; specialties: buttermilk scones, sautéed bananas w/ ice cream, stuffed French toast w/ maple sausage; dinner by arrangement, food allergies/special diets accomm.; tea

Recreation: Skiing, biking, golf, tennis, fishing, horseback riding, games, puzzles

Amenities & Services: Refrigerator, irons, bike rental nearby, romantic movies; small weddings, maps, dinner reservations

ACCOMMODATIONS

Units: 7 guest rooms
All Rooms: Bath, sitting area, TV, VCR, phone
Some Rooms: Wood-burning fireplace, disabled access
Bed & Bath: Kings, 1 iron bed, most oak, some Victorian, 1 four-poster; most whirlpools, dbl. whirlpools, soaking tubs, heated floors
Favorites: Winter Haven—2nd floor, oak Victorian rolltop panel bed, dbl.

whirlpool, fireplace; Country Garden—picket fence–style headboard, mini-garden on mantel, fresh flowers
Comfort & Decor: Bright lace curtains. Maple and birch views. Victorian Country look. Handmade quilts, room themes, stenciled walls. Lots of cross-stitching, needlework by host. Excellent reading lights.

RATES, RESERVATIONS, & RESTRICTIONS

Deposit: 50%; refund w/ 14-day notice, longer notice for multiple reservations
Discounts: Midweek off-season
Credit Cards: MC, V, AE, D, DC
Check-In/Out: 3–6/11; prior arrangement for late arrival
Smoking: No
Pets: No
Kids: No

No-No's: 3rd person in room
Minimum Stay: 2 nights weekends, holidays, foliage
Open: All year
Hosts: Janet and Gary Robison
Box 273
Barnard, VT 05031
(802) 234-5342, (800) 51-MAPLE
www.mapleleafinn.com

TWIN FARMS, Barnard

Overall: ★★★★★	Room Quality: A	Value: C	Price: $800–$1,500

In a class by itself, Twin Farms is worth what it costs. Novelist Sinclair Lewis built it for his bride, journalist Dorothy Thompson, in 1928. Today, it's one of the world's greatest small properties, with sumptuous, themed rooms and cottages and incredibly pampering yet casual luxury. Service, beauty within and without, food, recreation—all are close to perfection. Acres of wildflowers, private ski runs (with perhaps a mountaintop picnic lunch), Hockney and Avery paintings, a jukebox, a Japanese faro tub, a private covered bridge, mountain bike rides (pick-ups for uphill, with champagne, if desired)—anything goes, and you should, too. Bill Gates stayed here, but if it's more of a stretch for you, rooms in the main house are the best deal, almost as sublime as the "cottages."

SETTINGS & FACILITIES

Location: 1.5 mi. E of the general store on Rt. 12, in rural area overlooking mountain vista

Near: Covered bridges; 10 mi. to Woodstock

Building: Two 18th-century farm-houses renovated into main house; 9 widely scattered, large cottages and lodge, varied styles; game house/pub, faro tub building

Grounds: 235 acres: woods, meadows, gardens, orchards, lake, ski runs, covered bridge

Public Space: Main house: great room, wine cellar, rustic DR, parlor; porch; faro Japanese bathhouse; pub and game building, jukebox

Food & Drink: All meals and drinks included; breakfast, lunch, dinner, snacks served anywhere on property; star-chef Neil Wigglesworth, creative American cuisine; cocktails at 7; wine cellar

Recreation: Water sports, fly fishing, tennis, biking, downhill and X-C skiing, tennis, croquet, ice-skating; golf nearby

Amenities & Services: Fitness center, skates, toboggans, bikes, Steinway piano; massage (fee), turn-down, food delivered anywhere, shuttles; business/group support; 2:1 staff/guest ratio

ACCOMMODATIONS

Units: 4 suites, 8 cottages, 2 suites in lodge

All Rooms: Bath, fireplace, phone, TV/VCR/CD, AC, mini-refrigerator, antiques, sitting area, custom furnishings

Some Rooms: Porch, loft, skylight, collections

Bed & Bath: King beds, four-posters, antique; huge, lavish baths w/ soaking tubs, whirlpools, steam showers, antique fixtures, stone/natural materials, skylights

Favorites: Cottages are all remarkable; Tree Tops—beams, four-poster, stone fireplace, heated slate floor in bath, screened porch; Studio—largest, loft BR, splatter-paint floor, orig. art (incl. Stella, Hockney)

Comfort & Decor: Breathtaking beauty, space, style, luxury. Whimsical. Fantasy themes, w/ no expense spared, include 19th-century Log Cabin, Moroccan tented palace, Scandinavian farmhouse, Tuscan cottage in woods. Disabled access in main house, Washington Room. House rooms huge, lavish, more traditional, best deal for budget-conscious. $26+ million spent. Decor by Jed Johnson, designer who died in TWA 800 crash.

RATES, RESERVATIONS, & RESTRICTIONS

Deposit: Paid in full, 30 days in advance, 90 days foliage and holidays; Note: Rates are all-inclusive.

Discounts: None; entire property, $14,500/night

Credit Cards: MC, V, AE, D

Check-In/Out: 3/11

Smoking: No

Pets: No

Kids: Over 18, unless renting entire property

No-No's: Daytrippers

Minimum Stay: 2 nights weekends, 3 nights holidays

Open: All year except April

Hosts: Beverley and Shaun Matthews
P.O. Box 115
Barnard, VT 05031
(800) TWINFARMS, (802) 234-9999
Fax: (802) 234-9990
www.twinfarms.com

GREEN TRAILS INN, Brookfield

Overall: ★★★★½   Room Quality: B   Value: C   Price: $79–$130

Overlooking the longest pontoon bridge east of the Mississippi, this oddly shaped bed-and-breakfast was home to one of Rutgers University's first women professors, a botanist who invited friends and students to join her horseback riding on the namesake trails. The 1790 guest house has a corner room with floor-to-ceiling stencils from those days—and now, a whirlpool tub. Brookfield's few white clapboard houses haven't changed much, and the entire village is on The National Historic Register. But time passes, as Mike, an avid clockmaker, is well aware. The house is filled with about 50 working timepieces, some of them 175 years old, and a shop on the property sells, repairs, and restores antique clocks.

SETTINGS & FACILITIES

Location: Center of village, across the road from Sunset Lake, by former riding trails
Near: Floating bridge, Chandler Music Hall, New England Culinary Institute restaurants, Ben & Jerry's
Building: Marcus Peck House (c.1840); 18th-century guest house
Grounds: 17 acres behind inn, on Sunset Lake by floating bridge, trails; front of inn faces village
Public Space: Common rooms, sitting area, dining area, formal DR, parlor; parlor in guest house

Food & Drink: Early bird coffee; full breakfast 8–9, cont'l after 9; specialties: rhubarb coffee cake, baked omelets, buttermilk waffles; hot drinks; MAP plan w/ restaurant across street; wine and beer
Recreation: Fishing, canoeing, swimming, 35km X-C skiing trails, snowshoeing, downhill skiing nearby
Amenities & Services: Weddings/functions (175), maps, refrigerator use, iron, forgotten toiletries, music collection, canoes, bikes, X-C skis, snowshoes; concierge service, mountain bike deliveries

ACCOMMODATIONS

Units: 9 guest rooms, 4 suites
All Rooms: Individually decorated
Some Rooms: Bath (9 priv.), fireplace, extra room; some rooms can join
Bed & Bath: Doubles, queens, twins; some whirlpools, some tubs; 1, tub only

Favorites: Stencil suite—wingback chairs, dbl. whirlpool, 1830s stenciling
Comfort & Decor: Comfortable. Mix of antiques, reproductions, Oriental rugs. Excellent lighting. Most with reading chairs. Constantly being updated. Guest House most luxurious.

RATES, RESERVATIONS, & RESTRICTIONS

Deposit: 1 night; refund w/ 14-day notice
Discounts: Package discounts

Credit Cards: MC, V, D
Check-In/Out: 3/11; call for late check-in

Smoking: Outdoors
Pets: No; boarding nearby
Kids: Over 10
Minimum Stay: 2 nights holidays, some weekends
Open: All year

Hosts: Sue and Mike Erwin
By the Floating Bridge
Brookfield, VT 05036
(802) 276-3412, (800) 243-3412
greentrails@quest-net.com
www.quest-net.com/gti

SHIRE INN, Chelsea

Overall: ★★★★	Room Quality: B	Value: C	Price: $105–$215

Set between the Connecticut Valley and Stowe, this out-of-the-way village is untouched by ski developers, factory outlets, or colleges. This inn of understated charms and pleasures fits perfectly into this environment of commons, Federal-era buildings, and not much else. Karen is an award-winning chef, and her multicourse candlelight dinners, punctuated with a sorbet intermezzo, are romantic and delicious. Attention to small details is evident; even the sheets are ironed. The innkeepers also rent out a separate two-bedroom cottage on 10 acres of woods, with a wood-burning stove, gas heat, and antiques. And check out the antique in the inn's backyard: a five-hole privy.

SETTINGS & FACILITIES

Location: Near center of village from VT 110, on White River
Near: 2 town commons, dairy farms, covered bridges, Rock of Ages, Woodstock, Cold Hollow Cider Mill, Montpelier, Ben & Jerry's, Dartmouth College
Building: 1832 brick Federal Davis House mansion; Nat'l Historic Register
Grounds: 23 hilly acres: stream, apple trees, wildflowers, gardens, river w/ farm bridge
Public Space: Circular stairway, parlor, porch, DR
Food & Drink: (MAP) Full breakfast; specialties: waffles, pancakes, asparagus omelets; tea; 6-course dinner, candle-light, inn guests only; 3 entrees, specialties: rainbow trout, chicken Boursin, eggplant ravioli, apple-cranberry crumble w/ vanilla ice cream; wine cellar: 1,000 bottles, many by glass
Recreation: Fishing, biking, X-C skiing, boating, ice skating
Amenities & Services: Tour books, games, hiking maps, bikes, X-C skis, Vintage Vermont tours

ACCOMMODATIONS

Units: 6 guest rooms, 1 cottage
All Rooms: Bath, antiques
Some Rooms: Wood-burning fire-places (4)
Bed & Bath: 3 queens, 1 king, 2 doubles, some canopies, hand-ironed cotton sheets, antique quilts, some extra beds
Favorites: Windsor—former master BR, canopy bed; Essex—yellow and green decor, canopy bed

Comfort & Decor: Rooms named after Vermont shires. 10-foot ceilings and large windows, wide-planked floors, super-soft sheets. Quilts, period antiques. High ceilings. Immaculate.

Deposit: Refund w/ 14-day notice
Discounts: Call for avail. discounts, weekly and monthly rates
Credit Cards: MC, V, D
Check-In/Out: 3/11
Smoking: Covered porch only
Pets: No
Kids: Over 6
Minimum Stay: 2 nights most weekends

Open: Except April, Nov., winter weekdays
Hosts: Karen and Jay Keller
Main St.
Chelsea, VT 05038
(802) 685-3031, (800) 441-6908
Fax: (802) 685-3871
Info@shireinn.com
www.shireinn.com

HEERMANSMITH FARM INN, Coventry

| Overall: ★★★½ | Room Quality: C | Value: C | Price: $75–$125 |

This unassuming, truly rural farmhouse is not for neatnicks. It is far north, hard to find, and so low-key that you might wonder, why bother? Maybe because it's about the closest you can come to life in these parts 50 years ago. And the delicious, reasonably priced, surprisingly sophisticated meals have earned a whopping reputation from locals. Home to generations of the same family, this rumpled inn offers a true value and a country escape with soft-spoken Vermont hosts. And it is worth the trip just to see the little covered bridge and the hidden waterfall down the road, and the brilliance of stars when you're miles from anything.

SETTINGS & FACILITIES

Location: Vermont 5 to Coventry; locate church-turned-antique store (Holy Cow); straight across street and up steep hill; B&B, just ahead
Near: Black River, Canadian border; Jay Peak, Burke Mountain ski areas, Crafstbury Village, Stowe
Building: 1807 Cedar Plank house; outbuildings (incl. "sugar shack")
Grounds: Nonworking farm, in quiet valley; rear deck
Public Space: Entry hall, bar; library; spacious DR

Food & Drink: Full breakfast; specialties: blueberry muffins, pancakes; 4-course dinners, candlelight table settings; specialties: hickory-smoked Vermont pheasant risotto, duck w/ strawberry Chambord sauce; wine list, full bar
Recreation: Hidden waterfall, covered bridge, snowmobile trails, Alpine skiing, groomed X-C ski trails
Amenities & Services: Fridge, bike storage, irons, cots (no cribs), 1 high chair, games

ACCOMMODATIONS

Units: 6 guest rooms; 1 fully equipped cottage, incl. kitchen
All Rooms: Bath
Some Rooms: Seating area, reading light
Bed & Bath: Some antique beds; most shower-only

Favorites: Room 1—largest; orig. pine flooring, high-post double bed, hand-made quilt, meadow views, only room w/ full bath
Comfort & Decor: Rooms small and modest. Homey comfort, not elegant or elaborate. Simple, clean charm. Cottage accommodates up to 8.

RATES, RESERVATIONS, & RESTRICTIONS

Deposit: 1 night
Discounts: Kids, 3rd person; cottage $500 weekly; $5 add'l per person/breakfast, cottage
Credit Cards: MC, V, AE
Check-In/Out: 2/11
Smoking: No
Pets: No
Kids: Welcome

Minimum Stay: None
Open: All year
Hosts: Louise and Jack Smith
Heermanville Rd.
Coventry, VT 05825
(802) 754-8866
hersmith@sovernet.com
www.scenesofvermont.com//heermansmith

INN ON THE COMMON, Craftsbury Common

| Overall: ★★★★★ | Room Quality: A | Value: B | Price: $220–$290 |

The Inn on the Common is anything but. After chocolates and coffee in the library, just before retiring to your canopied, quilt-covered bed by a flickering fireplace, you'll probably surmise that life really is grand. This inn complex with a white rose and wisteria-entwined pergola by the clay tennis courts welcomes families seeking great cuisine and wine. It offers elegant communal dining for singles, and even gives a conditional OK for pets. There's just no excuse not to splurge here, even though it is a bit of a drive, close to the Quebec border. The sleepy hamlet is the perfect setting to walk off a meal and dream of the next—perhaps designing your own omelet.

SETTINGS & FACILITIES

Location: Off Rt. 14 N, on left of village common
Near: Craftsbury Nordic Center, Big Hosmer Lake
Building: Three Federal-style buildings: large white 18th-century main house, south annex, north annex
Grounds: 10 acres: maple and cypress trees, trellised gardens, views
Public Space: Elegant DR, parlors, library/lounge
Food & Drink: (MAP) Full communal breakfast; hors d'oeuvres; family-style

candlelight gourmet dining; specialties: iced plum soup, vegetable baklava, roast pork loin w/ peaches and pecans; extensive wine list
Recreation: X-C skiing, swimming, croquet, boating
Amenities & Services: Pool, clay tennis courts, connected to Craftsbury Nordic Center, common TV, VCR w/ 250 movies, guest kitchen in south annex, refrigerator; baby-sitting, catering, bike/canoe rentals; meetings

ACCOMMODATIONS

Units: 14 guest rooms, 2 suites in 3 buildings
All Rooms: Bath, sitting area, clock
Some Rooms: Fireplace, canopy bed
Bed & Bath: Some canopies, brass and iron; varied tubs, showers
Favorites: Room 10, south annex—fishnet canopy, couch facing fireplace;

Room 7—2-BR suite with easy chairs, fireplace
Comfort & Decor: Elegantly appointed. Wallcoverings and fabrics blend. Each room different, from airy and simple to lavishly traditional. Good lighting. Lovely views.

RATES, RESERVATIONS, & RESTRICTIONS

Deposit: 1 night; snow guarantee or deposit returned
Discounts: Kids under 3 free; packages
Credit Cards: MC, V, AE
Check-In/Out: 1 (earlier by arrangement)/11
Smoking: Limited
Pets: With notice and $15
Kids: OK

Minimum Stay: 2 nights during peak
Open: All year
Hosts: Penny and Michael Schmitt
North Main St.
Craftsbury Common, VT 05827
(802) 586-9619, (800) 521-2233
Fax: (800) 521-2233, (802) 586-2249
info@innonthecommon.com
www.innonthecommon.com

BIRCHWOOD BED AND BREAKFAST, Derby Line

Overall: ★★★½	Room Quality: C	Value: C	Price: $75

You are so close to Canada here that in the nearby opera house the border runs down the middle of the hall. The audience sits in one country, the players in other! Other delightful spots in the area include The Old Stone House Museum, designed by Rev. Alexander Twilight, thought to be the United States' first black college graduate and first black legislator. Dick, an avid golfer, loves talking about music; Elizabeth is an antiques dealer and enjoys gardening in the pretty yard, although the summer season here on the Quebec border is short and sweet. For those traveling to Montreal, this neat little bed-and-breakfast is a good deal and a pleasant overnight stop.

SETTINGS & FACILITIES

Location: I-91 to Exit 29 (last U.S. exit), turn left, .75 mi. to Main St., turn left, B&B is half-mile on right, on quiet residential road in village
Near: Canadian border, lakes, mountain views, historic opera house, park, antiquing, outdoor concerts, museums; 90 min. to Montreal
Building: 1920 Colonial Revival; restored 1993

Grounds: Gardens behind house; panoramic view
Public Space: DR, LR, porch
Food & Drink: Full candlelight breakfast; specialties: homemade muesli, fruit-filled crepes; afternoon tea
Recreation: Water sports, golf, tennis, sleigh rides, maple sugaring
Amenities & Services: Flowers, chocolates, games, maps of Canada

ACCOMMODATIONS

Units: 3 guest room
All Rooms: Bath, on 2nd floor, individually decorated, fresh flowers, antiques
Some Rooms: Large
Bed & Bath: Twins, double, queen, I canopy, firm mattresses; showers
Favorites: Double room—former

maid's quarters, antique pineapple bed, marble dresser, Waverly fabrics, hooked throw rugs
Comfort & Decor: Individually decorated w/ antiques. Wonderful views. Rooms small to large. Immaculate. Basic.

RATES, RESERVATIONS, & RESTRICTIONS

Deposit: I night; refund w/ 5-day notice
Discounts: 3rd person
Credit Cards: None
Check-In/Out: 3/11
Smoking: No
Pets: No
Kids: No
No-No's: Alcoholic beverages

Minimum Stay: 2 nights on weekends
Open: All year
Hosts: Elizabeth and Dick Fletcher
48 Main St., Box 550
Derby Line, VT 05830-9203
(802) 873-9104
Fax: (802) 873-9121
birchwd@together.net
homepages.together.net/~birchwd/index.html

MOUNTAIN VIEW CREAMERY, East Burke

Overall: ★★★★	Room Quality: B	Value: C	Price: $115–$220

A century ago this farm provided meat and dairy products to a New York City hotel. Now it serves them only to happy guests, along with organically grown vegetables and beer from a local microbrewery. John is a cardiologist, and Marilyn is an avid skier who emphasizes that this bed-and-breakfast "loves children!" The views are great, and the colors, memorable: deepred barns, green-and-white-striped umbrellas on the patio, raspberry and apple-green interiors. It's good for families, conferences, and weddings. With an adjoining restaurant open to the public, the complex is surprisingly elegant despite the farm atmosphere, which includes a pet Holstein cow named Clover as well as an enormous oak icebox used to store cheese.

SETTINGS & FACILITIES

Location: Exit 23 off I-91, above the valley on a rural road
Near: Burke Mountain, Lake Willoughby
Building: 1890 redbrick Georgian Colonial creamery, butter churn cupola; restored/modernized in 1989
Grounds: 440 acres of hills, meadows, gardens; impressive barns, stable; mountain views
Public Space: Large hall, parlors, DR

Food & Drink: Full breakfast, communal or in-room; specialties: blueberry-lemon pancakes, breakfast polenta; dining on weekends, open to public; well-selected wine and beer; light lunches, picnic baskets; tea, punch, après ski wine
Recreation: Trout/ice fishing, skiing, table tennis, lawn bowling, croquet
Amenities & Services: Function room, VCR, videos, farm animals; catering; sleigh/hay rides, bike/canoe rentals

ACCOMMODATIONS

Units: 8 guest rooms, 1 suite, 1 cottage
All Rooms: Bath, alarm clock, coordinated fabrics
Some Rooms: Sitting area; cottage w/ fireplace, whirlpool
Bed & Bath: Antique beds; tiled baths, coordinated w/ BR
Favorites: The Westmore—corner room w/ green sleigh bed, cranberry florals

Comfort & Decor: Authentic and special, with a spare, country feel. Rooms smallish, but comfortable and pretty with botanicals and chintz. Reading lamps, skirted tables, artwork. Small windows. Unique sense of farmhouse living.

RATES, RESERVATIONS, & RESTRICTIONS

Deposit: One night on credit card
Discounts: Packages, singles, more than 2 nights
Credit Cards: MC, V, AE

Check-In/Out: 3/11
Smoking: No
Pets: No
Kids: OK

Minimum Stay: Appreciate 2 days on weekends
Open: All year; restaurant on weekends, winter and summer
Hosts: Marilyn and John Pastore
Box 355, Darling Hill Rd.

East Burke, VT 05832
(800) 572-4509, (802) 626-9924
Fax: Same as phone
innmtnview@kingcon.com
www.innmtnvu@plainfield.bypass.com

LAKEVIEW INN, Greensboro

Overall: ★★★½	Room Quality: C	Value: D	Price: $85–$230

Like fine wine and cheese, a good bed-and-breakfast grows more interesting and wonderful with age. And this new one, set in a carefully refurbished historic inn in this tiny, white-clapboard village, will undoubtedly ripen well. The young hosts are locals who lovingly care about historical detailing, and intend to carefully grow this into a more evocative property. It will take time, and cash, but the heart is already there. The "excellent fishing, repose, delightful scenery, healthful food, bracing air," extolled in a publication from 1885, still apply.

SETTINGS & FACILITIES

Location: From south, on the right, on Greensboro's main street
Near: Lake Caspian, Stowe, Burke Mountain, Morgan Horse Farm, Vermont Historical Society Museum
Building: 1872 former boarding house
Grounds: 2 acres, bird sanctuary, gardens, mountain views
Public Space: Common rooms, beamed DR, porch

Food & Drink: Full breakfast; specialties: vanilla-almond French toast, mango pancakes; light meals until 7 p.m., baked goods and takeout
Recreation: Skiing, boating, fishing, golf, tennis, antiquing
Amenities & Services: Cafe/bakery, gift shop; big-screen TV, puzzles, maps, irons; disabled access, catering, packed lunch

ACCOMMODATIONS

Units: 9 guest rooms, 1 suite
All Rooms: Bath, antiques, heat
Some Rooms: AC
Bed & Bath: Varied sizes, queens and twins; small baths
Favorites: Rooms on the backside—expansive views

Comfort & Decor: Some antiques, mainly reproductions. Rooms in historic colors, but seem underdecorated. Comfortable, good lighting. Size varies. Needs seasoning, more sense of place.

RATES, RESERVATIONS, & RESTRICTIONS

Deposit: One night or 50%; refund w/ 14-day notice

Discounts: Long stays, singles, groups
Credit Cards: MC, V

Check-In/Out: 4/11
Smoking: No
Pets: No
Kids: Well-behaved
No-No's: Check-in after 6:30
Minimum Stay: 2 nights, weekends in season
Open: All year

Hosts: Kathryn Unser and John Hunt
Box 180, Main St.
Greensboro, VT 05841
(802) 533-2291
Fax: Same as phone
lkview@her.net
www.her.net/lakeview

SOMERSET HOUSE, Hardwick

Overall: ★★★½	Room Quality: C	Value: C	Price: $80–$90

Walkways through a hedged "secret garden" are a special treat at this economical bed-and-breakfast far from crowds and the stress of daily life. British Ruth was inspired by a stay in Somerset and incorporates an English country-house atmosphere in Vermont-style lodgings. This politically correct operation won an environmental award, and upgrading continues, creating private baths for all rooms. Hardwick has population of a mere 1,800, and the innkeepers put it best: "We're an old-fashioned small town in Vermont's remote Northeast Kingdom, with friendly people and beautiful surroundings." The village has a good bookstore, so you can find a nook and read in peace.

SETTINGS & FACILITIES

Location: 1 block from intersection of Vermont Rts. 14 and 15, in a quiet, residential neighborhood, 1 block from river
Near: Village, operational covered bridge, hiking trails, lakes, X-C ski areas, Stowe, Montpelier, Canadian border
Building: 1894 unusual plantation style/Queen-Anne Victorian
Grounds: Village lawn, porch, fish pond, adult swing, gardens, butternut trees
Public Space: Sitting room, DR, writing alcove

Food & Drink: Full breakfast; free-range eggs, B&B garden produce, English tea; specialties: omelet w/ fresh pesto, garden tomatoes/herbs; egg/cheese tortilla w/ avocado and salsa, waffles or pancakes w/ cinnamon apples; refreshments on arrival; tea
Recreation: Mountain/trail biking, canoeing, fishing, sailing, swimming
Amenities & Services: Fans in rooms, irons, bike storage, cots (no cribs), maps; small meetings, groups

ACCOMMODATIONS

Units: 4 guest rooms
All Rooms: Fresh flowers, carpet, seating, reading light
Some Rooms: Bath, balcony

Bed & Bath: Iron, brass beds; firm bedding, queen and twin sizes; some shower only; some hall access, robes

Favorites: Room 4—Light, airy room w/ bay window and balcony
Comfort & Decor: Rooms vary: large, cozy, bright. All w/ pretty wallpa-per, antique furnishings, artwork. Large round tower room, queen bed, con-nects w/ cozy twin bed room. Bay win-dows, collectibles.

RATES, RESERVATIONS, & RESTRICTIONS

Deposit: 1 night; refund w/ 5-day notice
Discounts: 5+ days, singles, 3rd per-son, children over 2
Credit Cards: MC, V
Check-In/Out: By arrangement/11 or by arrangement
Smoking: Outside only
Pets: No
Kids: Check

Minimum Stay: None
Open: All year
Hosts: Ruth and David Gaillard
24 Highland Ave., Box 1098
Hardwick, VT 05843-1098
(800) 838-8074 or (802) 472-5484
gaillard@plainfield.bypass.com
www.obs-us.com/chesler/somersethouse/

RABBIT HILL INN, Lower Waterford

Overall: ★★★★★	Room Quality: A	Value: C	Price: $210–$370

Gentle, warm, exquisite, welcoming, pampering, luxurious, and romantic don't begin to define this inn. Hosts Leslie and Brian, the Ginger and Fred of innkeeping, make it look easy. They rightly call it "a paradise for the senses, vacation for the soul." Whatever the magic "it" is, the award-winning hospitality, refined cuisine, and perfectionism established by the former owners continue, unabated. Sweet and sophisticated, lively and peaceful, carefully orchestrated with appreciative management and skillful care, this is truly an award-winning, 24-carrot inn experience. Can the "it" be love?

SETTINGS & FACILITIES

Location: Edge of tiny historic white village, off Rt. 18
Near: Franconia Notch State Park, Fairbank's Museum, Cabot Cheese Creamery, antiques, art galleries
Building: Restored 1795 white-columned Greek Revival inn
Grounds: 15 acres, gardens, spring-fed swimming pond, waterfall, gazebo, shuf-fleboard, horseshoes; mountain views
Public Space: Common rooms, library, pub, video and TV room, DRs, oil lamp–lit porches, phone rooms, all in period, w/ antiques, art
Food & Drink: (MAP) Lavish, candle-light buffet breakfast; 5-course dinner, open to public, harpist on Sat.; a spe-cialty: warmed sweet potato and red cabbage salad w/ toasted walnuts and spiced apple cider vinaigrette; tea/snacks; light meals and drink in pub
Recreation: Sledding, snowshoeing, X-C skiing, golf, swimming, stave puzzles, games

Amenities & Services: VCR library, full concierge services, gift popcorn with videos; candle, soft music at turn-down; 1:1 staff to guest ratio, preferences noted; disabled accessible room

ACCOMMODATIONS

Units: 9 guest rooms, 12 suites
All Rooms: Bath, seating, hairdryer, coffee maker, climate controls, tape player and radio, robes
Some Rooms: AC, gas fireplace, sundeck, porch, enlarged sitting area, skylight
Bed & Bath: Mostly kings, canopies, four-posters; some whirlpools in BR
Favorites: Jonathan Cummings Suite—queen canopy, 2nd fireplace in sitting room, whirlpool for 2, porch, mountain views
Comfort & Decor: Rooms vary in size, decor, and luxury. All w/ romantic touches and attention to smallest detail, each w/ a theme, a room diary to record thoughts, and romantic lighting. Rugs, antiques, murals and stenciling, photos. Rooms in inn less private.

RATES, RESERVATIONS, & RESTRICTIONS

Deposit: 1 night, more for extended stay; refund w/ 14-day notice (28 days, holidays)
Discounts: Single, 3rd person, packages
Credit Cards: MC, V, AE
Check-In/Out: 2/11
Smoking: No
Pets: No
Kids: Over 12
No-No's: Jeans at dinner, tipping

Minimum Stay: 2 nights on weekends, holidays
Open: Except first two weeks of April and Nov.
Hosts: Leslie and Brian Mulcahy
Box 55
Lower Waterford, VT 05848
(800) 76-BUNNY, (802) 748-5168
Fax: (802) 748-8342
info@rabbithillinn.com
www.rabbithillinn.com

WILDFLOWER INN, Lyndonville

Overall: ★★★½   Room Quality: C   Value: C   Price: $115–$230+

Children are pampered at this sprawling 1796 farmhouse complex on 500 acres, once part of an estate. Kiddie amenities include a playroom with dress-up clothes, bumper pool, a separate swimming pool, nightly games and movies, baby-sitting, a children's theater, a petting farm, pony rides, early family-style meals, a teen rec center, and more. Families have the run of the place except during school, when couples and conferences reign. Lovers can retreat to the former one-room schoolhouse suite with a two-person whirlpool, and enjoy the sunset view along the ridge, in peace.

SETTINGS & FACILITIES

Location: 4 mi. from I-91, same road as Mountain View Creamery, on Darling Hill

Near: Burke Mountain Ski Resort, over 50 lakes and ponds, 4 golf courses, covered bridges, museums, dairy farms, maple sugar houses, antiquing, Cabot Cheese Creamery; 2 hrs. to Montreal

Building: Large farm (settled in 1796); several farmhouse-style buildings, barns, and outbuildings

Grounds: 500+ farm acres, gardens, trails

Public Space: Sitting rooms

Food & Drink: Full breakfast; specialties: eggs w/ ham, bacon or sausage, pancakes, blueberry muffins; p.m. snack; simple dinner avail. in public restaurant, open all year/days vary, reservations recommended; breads, soups, children's menu

Recreation: Golf, winter and water sports, horseback riding, fall foliage tours

Amenities & Services: Gift shop, art gallery; sauna, hot tub; indoor/outdoor play areas, petting barn, pool; hay/sleigh rides; tennis, basketball, batting cage, soccer, skating, X-C/snowshoe trails, summer children's programs/theater, add'l cots/cribs, guests may use grounds after check-out

ACCOMMODATIONS

Units: 15 guest rooms, 8 suites in main farmhouse, carriage house, 1 cottage

All Rooms: Bath, endless country view

Some Rooms: Priv. deck/balcony/patio, priv. stairway, dining/sitting area, bunk bed, sofa bed, kitchenette, washer/dryer; disabled access (1)

Bed & Bath: Some canopy, four-posters; some shower-only, some 1- and 2-person whirlpools

Favorites: Yellow Room—upstairs, main farmhouse, twin and double beds in 1 room, double canopy in 2nd, full bath; School House Cottage—private, queen, dbl. whirlpool, deck, kitchenette, dining/sitting area.

Comfort & Decor: Vary from family units to secluded cottage. Touches including stenciling, antique or reproduction beds, country quilts. Simple but comfortable. Can be noisy when school not in session.

RATES, RESERVATIONS, & RESTRICTIONS

Deposit: 1 night; refunds w/ 14-day notice (check for holiday rate increases; add 10% gratuity, Vermont taxes)

Discounts: Various packages, midweek, longer stays, singles, 3rd person, kids (under 5 free)

Credit Cards: MC, V

Check-In/Out: 3/11

Smoking: Outdoors only

Pets: No

Kids: Welcome

Minimum Stay: 2 nights, weekends

Open: All year

Hosts: Mary and Jim O'Reilly
Darling Hill Rd.
Lyndonville, VT 05851
(800) 627-8310 or (802) 626-8310
Fax: (802) 626-3039
wldflwrinn@aol.com
www.wildflowerinn.com

COUNTRY GARDEN INN, Quechee

Overall: ★★★★½	Room Quality: B	Value: B	Price: $110–$180

Have you ever waded in a nineteenth-century, waterfall-fed rock pool? That is only one of many special parts adding up an extra-special whole at this sophisticated, ever-delightful bed-and-breakfast. Other examples: bathrooms with nineteenth-century chamber-pot seats and modern massaging shower heads; breakfast and afternoon tea in a brick-floored, plant-filled greenhouse; and a den with hundreds of videos and an old safe recycled into a complimentary minibar. Amid the decor you'll find Russian decorated eggs, musical instruments, stained glass, stenciling, Oriental rugs and sleigh beds. Shelly decorates with objects from her travels, but even better, knows how to please and surprise.

SETTINGS & FACILITIES

Location: Left after covered bridge; 1st driveway past church
Near: Theaters, brewery, glassblowing, museums, antiquing, art galleries, Dartmouth College
Building: Circa 1819, w/ original beams, ceilings; Victorian (and later) additions
Grounds: Garden, 1840 wading pool w/ waterfall, BBQ, picnic tables
Public Space: Greenhouse, common rooms, lounge, parlor, DR
Food & Drink: 3-course country breakfast; a specialty: French toast w/ walnuts; tea by appt.; hot and soft drinks; evening cocktails
Recreation: Games, exercise equipment, fly-fishing, sleigh/hay rides
Amenities & Services: Breakfast concerts some summer Sundays; fire, security system; turn-down, pick-ups from airport; privileges at Quechee Club: golf, pool, tennis, skiing, boating, fishing, health club, seasonal polo (Sat.), bike/canoe rentals nearby

ACCOMMODATIONS

Units: 4 guest rooms
All Rooms: Bath, AC, robes, clock/radio, phone on request
Some Rooms: Extra bed, unusual artifacts
Bed & Bath: Beds vary, some canopy, sleigh; massage shower heads, curling irons, hairdryers
Favorites: Rose room—queen brass bed, Tiffany-style lamps, window seat, chandelier, huge bath
Comfort & Decor: Details, details. Embroidered pillow cases, handmade quilts. Flower themes, Oriental rugs. Sophisticated touches. Thoughtful amenities. 1 family-oriented w/ daybed and priv. entrance.

RATES, RESERVATIONS, & RESTRICTIONS

Deposit: 1 night; refund w/ 14-day notice (30 days, multiple rooms)
Discounts: Off-season
Credit Cards: MC, V

Check-In/Out: 3–7/10
Smoking: No
Pets: No
Kids: 12 and up
No-No's: Check-in after 11 p.m.
Minimum Stay: 2 nights weekends, all nights Sept. 15–Oct. 31, some holidays, events; 3 nights holiday weekends, Dartmouth graduation

Open: All year
Hosts: Shelly Gardner
37 Main St.
Quechee, VT 05059
(802) 295-3023
Fax: (802) 295-3121
innkeeper@country-garden-inn.com

WILLOUGH VALE INN, Westmore

Overall: ★★★½	Room Quality: C	Value: C	Price: $69–$129

Location, location, location. This isolated area has been designated a registered national landmark by the National Park Service. If you can't get to Norway, a fjord-like lake high up in Vermont will suffice quite nicely. After staying at the inn in 1909, Robert Frost wrote about it in his poem "A Servant to Servants." More prosaically, if you enjoy large Victorians, front porches, hanging baskets, and breathtaking views, this spacious, informal property will appeal. Cottages are more private than rooms in the main house, and the atmosphere is casual throughout.

SETTINGS & FACILITIES

Location: Rt. 5A, facing Lake Willoughby
Near: Burke Mountain, Jay Peak
Building: Circa 1900 Victorian farmhouse
Grounds: Lawn to shore of lake; views of granite cliffs beyond lake; gazebo
Public Space: Common room, DR, taproom, porch, cozy DR

Food & Drink: Cont'l breakfast for inn guests; creative American cuisine at lunch, dinner, brunch; served seasonally; open to public
Recreation: Swimming, (ice) fishing, boating, skiing
Amenities & Services: Books, puzzles, games; snowmobile/snowshoe rentals

ACCOMMODATIONS

Units: 7 guest rooms, 1 suite; 4 lakefront cottages (heated)
All Rooms: Bath, TV, handcrafted furnishings, heat
Some Rooms: Queen four-poster, whirlpool, fireplace, kitchen
Bed & Bath: Vermont furnishings, queen beds; cottages, 1- or 2-BR; some whirlpools

Favorites: The Angler—lakefront cottage for 2 w/ French doors on water, sunken LR, fireplace, kitchen
Comfort & Decor: Casual furnishings, spare, almost hotel-like feel. Bright, clean, contemporary. Wall sconces and table lamps. Heated cottages have fireplaces, priv. docks, decks, screened porches. Good lake views.

RATES, RESERVATIONS, & RESTRICTIONS

Deposit: Check or credit card w/in 10 days; refund w/ 14-day cancellation
Discounts: Packages, extra person, singles, kids under 12, free; 6th night free; half off Green Mountain Inn, Stowe
Credit Cards: MC, V, AE
Check-In/Out: 2/11
Smoking: No
Pets: $5/ night, $25/week
Kids: OK

Minimum Stay: None
Open: All year
Hosts: Green Mountain Inn, Stowe
RR 2 Box 403
Westmore, VT 05860
(800) 594-9102, (802) 525-4123
Fax: (802) 525-4514
info@willoughvale.com
www.willoughvale.com

ARDMORE INN, Woodstock

Overall: ★★★★	Room Quality: B	Value: B	Price: $85–$150

International influence defines this Greek Revival bed-and-breakfast with a red slate roof. The Tullys from Ireland, the original owners, gave the guest rooms their family names, and Ardmore means "Great House" in Gaelic. Current host Giorgio, born in Peru, creates healthy breakfasts such as multigrain pancakes, but his specialty is "Woodstock Sunrise," a baked concoction of Vermont flatbread filled with eggs, peppers, mushrooms, and cheddar. The house was previously a general store, but rooms of shelves and cracker barrels have been completely transformed with furnishings such as Oriental rugs, an antique sideboard once owned by Governor Winthrop, and local artwork.

SETTINGS & FACILITIES

Location: On Woodstock's main street in historic district
Near: Galleries, arts/crafts shops, covered bridges, glassblowers, potters, Dartmouth College, antiquing, theater, Killington
Building: 1850 Victorian Greek Revival; renovated, 1994
Grounds: Back lawn, garden, maple trees
Public Space: Parlor, DR, screened veranda
Food & Drink: Full breakfast; specialties: berries in maple wine sauce,

sautéed eggs, truffle butter and veggies on flat Vermont bread w/ cheddar, asparagus, or Hollandaise sauce; p.m. tea, espresso; wine/cheese, fruit; special diets accom.
Recreation: Sleigh/carriage rides, skiing, biking
Amenities & Services: Chocolates, fresh flowers; concierge, tour guidance/maps, limited disabled access (vision, hearing)

ACCOMMODATIONS

Units: 5 guest rooms
All Rooms: Bath, fireplace, clock, radio
Some Rooms: Sitting area
Bed & Bath: Queens, king, double; I four-poster, cannonball; whirlpools, marble baths
Favorites: Sheridan—1st floor, hand-carved French walnut queen, marble shower, whirlpool; Maggie's Room—

2nd floor, smallest, morning sun, antique carved oak double, Victorian feel
Comfort & Decor: Rooms named for owner's family members. Spacious, graceful, comfortable. Vary widely in size and style from Colonial to Victorian. Tara, former billiards room in back, quietest.

RATES, RESERVATIONS, & RESTRICTIONS

Deposit: I night; refund w/ 14-day notice
Discounts: Off-season, seniors (30% except foliage)
Credit Cards: MC, V, AE, DC
Check-In/Out: 3–7/11
Smoking: No
Pets: No
Kids: No

Minimum Stay: During Sept. 20–Oct. 20
Open: All year
Hosts: Giorgio Ortiz
23 Pleasant St.
Woodstock, VT 05091-0466
(802) 457-3887, (800) 497-9652
Fax: (802) 457-9006
ArdmoreInn@aol.com
www.ardmoreinn.com

CHARLESTON HOUSE, Woodstock

Overall: ★★★½	Room Quality: B	Value: C	Price: $110–$195

Hosts Willa and Dixi have been married 40 years and counting and seem to love innkeeping—and having as much fun as their guests. This in-town bed-and-breakfast is less pricey and stylish than other Woodstock properties noted in the book, yet offers a warm, traditional, and comfortable stay. After a candlelight breakfast of Swiss soufflé you can easily stroll to most shops and restaurants in this classic town, then hole up in your room by the fire or soak in a whirlpool tub. Nearby restaurants are numerous, and the hosts are happy to give recommendations. The third-floor room is especially large and suitable for families.

SETTINGS & FACILITIES

Location: 10 mi. W of I-89 and I-91, at edge of village
Near: Nature area, galleries, museums, Woodstock Village Green, auctions
Building: 1835 brick Greek Revival townhouse; Nat'l Register of Historic Places

Grounds: Small, landscaped lawn
Public Space: LR, porch
Food & Drink: Full candlelight breakfast, communal or in room; specialties: Charleston French toast, Swiss soufflé; tea; wine, cheese

Recreation: Canoeing, golf, horseback riding, skiing, swimming, sleigh rides

Amenities & Services: Irons, access to kitchen refrigerator, limited disabled access (visual, hearing)

ACCOMMODATIONS

Units: 7 guest rooms
All Rooms: Bath
Some Rooms: TV, fireplace, sitting area, porch, adjoining rooms
Bed & Bath: Queens and kings, some twins, some headboards, 4 four-posters, canopies; some claw-foot tubs, whirlpools

Favorites: Summer Kitchen—queen bed, whirlpool, fireplace
Comfort & Decor: Colonial decor or more formal. Drapes, carpet, coordinated bedspreads. Village views, great reading lights. Each room decorated differently, from country to traditional.

RATES, RESERVATIONS, & RESTRICTIONS

Deposit: 1 night; refund w/ 14-day notice
Discounts: Longer stays, off-season
Credit Cards: MC, V, AE, D
Check-In/Out: 2:30/11
Smoking: No
Pets: No; 1 in-house cat
Kids: Depends; check w/ B&B
No-No's: Cots or 3rd person in room
Minimum Stay: 2 nights in season

weekends
Open: All year
Hosts: Willa and Dieter (Dixi) Nohl
21 Pleasant St.
Woodstock, VT 05091
(802) 457-3843, (888) 475-3800
Fax: (802) 457-2512
NOHL@together.net
www.charlestonhouse.com

JACKSON HOUSE INN, Woodstock

Overall: ★★★★★	Room Quality: A	Value: C	Price: $180–$290

Have you ever seen a pond with a tiny marble beach? Expect the unexpected. The bed-and-breakfast is gleaming with Chef Brendan Nolan, formerly of The Four Seasons in Boston, turning out meals to match the surroundings: elegant, superb, sensual, refined, memorable. If you're not about to spring for nearby Twin Farms, you won't be exactly slumming at this 1890 clapboard with great gardens, fine antiques, themed guest rooms, and basement spa. Gloria and Juan are Argentinian, and speak French, Spanish, and Italian, so expect an international clientele to interact with at breakfast and evening nibbles. Viva!

SETTINGS & FACILITIES

Location: 1.5 mi. W of Woodstock on Rt. 4, in semi-residential area at edge of village

Near: Art and craft galleries, antiquing, theater
Building: 1890 Victorian clapboard,

copper roof; Nat'l Register of Historic Places

Grounds: 5-acre garden, huge trees, meadow, pond, arched bridge, brook

Public Space: Parlor, library, DR, front veranda; wheelchair access

Food & Drink: Full breakfast; specialties: fresh smoked salmon and shallots in scrambled eggs, fruit compote w/ peach schnapps; evening cocktails and hors d'oeuvres; dinner; specialties:

grilled venison tenderloin w/ chestnut spaetzle, Maine lobster, Maine scallops; pastry chef; open to public

Recreation: Horseback riding, canoeing, swimming, golf, tennis, skiing, sleigh rides, hot-air ballooning

Amenities & Services: Refrigerator, irons, on-site spa w/ exercise equipment, big-screen satellite TV; weddings, business services, nearby bike and ski rental

ACCOMMODATIONS

Units: 9 guest rooms, 6 suites

All Rooms: Bath, AC, hairdryer

Some Rooms: Desk, chair, French doors, balcony, fireplace, wheelchair access, skylight

Bed & Bath: Twins, queen; four-posters, some brass, iron, spool, cannonball, sleigh, antique; marble, whirlpools, massage tubs for 2

Favorites: Half-a-Six Pence—New England country, queen, desk, French doors, balcony, small and cozy; Wales

Johnson—queen cherry sleigh bed, antique English desk, gas fireplace, French doors to patio/gardens, whirlpool

Comfort & Decor: Themed decor, w/ period antiques, detailing. Styles from Napoleonic to Victorian to New England country. Oriental rugs, ceiling fans, wide plank floors, art. New suites: especially luxurious baths. French doors to views of gardens.

RATES, RESERVATIONS, & RESTRICTIONS

Deposit: 50%; refund w/ 10-day notice

Discounts: Midweek seasonally

Credit Cards: MC, V, AE

Check-In/Out: 3/11

Smoking: No

Pets: No

Kids: 14 and up

No-No's: 3rd person in room

Minimum Stay: 2 nights weekends

Open: All year

Hosts: Gloria and Juan Florin
37 Rt. 4W
Woodstock, VT 05091
(802) 457-2065, (800) 448-1890
Fax: (802) 457-9290
innkeeper@jacksonhouse.com
www.jacksonhouse.com

WOODSTOCKER, Woodstock

Overall: ★★★½	Room Quality: C	Value: C	Price: $85–$155

With a low-key atmosphere, cheery rooms, and a convenient location at the edge of the village, this former farmhouse and attached barn (with suites) is a good choice for budget travelers and families. Like so many bed-and-breakfast owners, sociable Nancy and Tom left their former lives, seeking togetherness and a chance to stay home and raise their family. They moved from Cleveland in 1996, and have been tweaking the property since. Tom, an accountant, does the maintenance; Nancy, a former English teacher, sets out a bountiful buffet breakfast in the comfortable family room filled with country furnishings, warmth, cookies, and a big-screen TV.

SETTINGS & FACILITIES

Location: Just over Rt. 4 (River St.) bridge, at western edge of Woodstock
Near: Covered bridge, galleries, crafts, shopping, Marsh-Billings Nat'l Park, Historical Society Museum
Building: 1830s 2-story Cape-style farmhouse, attached barn
Grounds: Gardens, small lawn, picket fence
Public Space: Common room

Food & Drink: Buffet breakfast; specialties: puffed pancakes w/ banana-walnut topping, eggs w/ Vermont cheeses, apple-berry crisp w/ raspberries from garden; tea; cookies
Recreation: Skiing, fishing, maple sugaring, ice-skating, sleigh rides
Amenities & Services: Refrigerator, 5-person whirlpool (winters), local bike rental, pick-up from train/bus

ACCOMMODATIONS

Units: 7 guest rooms, 2 suites
All Rooms: Bath, individual heat
Some Rooms: Kitchen, TV (1), extra bed, AC, sitting room, balcony (1)
Bed & Bath: 2 doubles, queens, 1 canopy; tub/showers; cribs/roll-aways
Favorites: Canopy room—roses, cherry floors, antique Victorian chairs; Room 6—wicker, Shaker-style furnishings, sunflower print fabrics

Comfort & Decor: Individually decorated. Spacious suites w/ TV, kitchen, great for families. Antiques and reproductions, floral coordinates, braided rugs, skirted tables. Comfortable and casual. Rooms in back, quietest. Well-maintained.

RATES, RESERVATIONS, & RESTRICTIONS

Deposit: Full payment 1 night; others 50%; refund w/ 14-day notice
Discounts: Off-season
Credit Cards: MC, V
Check-In/Out: 3–6/11; call for late arrival
Smoking: No
Pets: No; in-house dog (lab/greyhound mix)
Kids: OK

Minimum Stay: Some weekends and holidays; check
Open: All year
Hosts: Nancy and Tom Blackford
61 River St., Rt. 4
Woodstock, VT 05091
(802) 457-3896
Fax: (802) 457-3897
thomas.blackford@valley.net
www.scenesofvermont.com/woodstocker/

Massachusetts

Every school kid knows that Massachusetts's history goes back to the Pilgrims who landed at Plymouth on the *Mayflower*, sharing Thanksgiving with the Native Americans who accepted them. The state was home to the opening skirmishes of the American Revolution, from the Boston Tea Party to Lexington and Concord, and it was a major manufacturing center during the Industrial Revolution, 100 years later.

With a third technological revolution now upon us, Massachusetts is again a major player, which makes historical buildings and sites fascinating places to visit—the real deal, not virtual—and the state's great universities, arts groups, and museums offer world-class cultural opportunities.

Martha's Vineyard's beaches, Fenway Park, Sturbridge Village, cranberry bogs, the Berkshires hills scenery. Massachusetts' varied pleasures include beaches and whale watching in the east, historic villages with classic commons and hilly terrain for skiing in the west. And fairs, festivals, exhibits, and just about everything in between keep visitors busy throughout the year. This is an all-season state in all ways.

Massachusetts reveals much of its history in its architecture, including red brick townhouses in Boston and rows of eighteenth-century homes in historic Deerfield, on the other side of the state. Foliage season runs from mid-September to late October throughout the varied landscapes—figure on peak color around Columbus Day.

In the Boston area, spend a day walking the Freedom Trail through the city, visiting Old North Church and Faneuil Hall (once a planning spot for the Revolution, it's now a shopping mecca). Take in a Red Sox game. Check out the new exhibits at the Museum of Fine Arts. Listen to the Boston Pops, or tour Harvard University.

When you are ready to escape, head just north to Marblehead's rocky beaches or to Salem's witch sites. Or head to the quiet area south of Boston and take a trip to the New Bedford Whaling Museum or to Plimoth Plantation, a re-creation of the 1627 community.

About an hour's drive from the southern Boston area is Cape Cod, with its dune-backed, sandy ribbon of beaches and the art scene in Provincetown at the tip. The Cape is also home to the John F. Kennedy Memorial and Museum in Hyannis, the Woods Hole Oceanographic Institute and the National Marine Fisheries Aquarium in Woods Hole, and to summer theater and antiquing.

Ferries can take you to Martha's Vineyard or Nantucket Island. The Vineyard is home to several communities: Edgartown is among the most bustling, while Gay Head provides a serene preserve among colorful cliffs. Nantucket Island is a National Historic District for its 800 buildings built before 1850. After walking or biking around the island, visit the specialty shops or the Whaling Museum in Nantucket Town.

Central/Western Massachusetts may not have beaches, but its delights include Old Sturbridge Village, which re-creates life in 1830s New England; the Worcester Art Museum in the state's second-largest city; and colleges including Smith, Mt. Holyoke, University of Massachusetts at Amherst, and Hampshire near the western border south of the Berkshires.

Bordered by Connecticut to the south, Vermont to the north, and New York to the west, the glorious Berkshire Hills are home to Tanglewood Music Festival and Williamstown, with its great college and museums. This refined area of arts, villages with grand mansions, and camps and farms with rural vistas seems far from the bustle of Boston but offers similar cultural delights in a setting of much-photographed New England beauty.

Small lodging is plentiful throughout Massachusetts, from Berkshire mansions to Cape Cod sea captains' homes, many beautifully restored. The tradition of wayside inns is another part of this state's pleasures and continues in fine form.

For More Information

Bed and Breakfast Associates, Bay Colony, Ltd.
(781) 449-5302 or (800) 347-5088
info@bnbboston.com

Massachusetts B&B Association
Box 352
Chesterfield, MA 01012

Massachusetts Lodging Association
(617) 720-1776
fax: (617) 720-1305
email: info@massachusettslodging.com
www.massachusettsloding.com

Zone 11
Boston Region

From Plymouth Rock and Plimoth Plantation (a re-creation of the 1627 Plymouth settlement), to the New Bedford Whaling Museum, Boston Harbor, and the fishing villages of Rockport, Gloucester, and Newburyport, the history of the Boston region seems defined by the Atlantic Ocean it borders.

South of Boston, visit the Buzzards Bay villages and Horseneck State Reservation, plus more recent historical sites with Battleship Cove, home to U.S. Navy ships. Try whale watching, visit a vineyard or a park, or attend a concert at the Great Woods Center for the Performing Arts in Mansfield. There are plenty of period homes to visit, as well as museums that highlight the shipbuilding, sea-captain, and early settlement histories of the region.

Boston is New England's great city and one of the finest concentrations of our history and culture. The Freedom Trail, with 16 textbook-familiar sites, includes Paul Revere's House, Old North Church, and Faneuil Hall—with its shops, entertainment, and restaurants. The USS *Constitution* (the navy's oldest ship), the New England Aquarium, Museum of Science, Museum of Fine Arts, Isabella Stewart Gardner Museum, Kennedy Library and Museum, and Boston Tea Party Ship and Museum are just a few more worthy stops.

You can stroll through Harvard Square in Cambridge, glide on a swan boat in the Public Garden, listen to the Boston Symphony Orchestra, or catch the Red Sox in action. And the Black Heritage Trail highlights Boston's nineteenth-century black community on Beacon Hill.

North of the city, eighteenth- and nineteenth-century fishing, sailing, and whaling towns have become suburbs with character. Salem, site of the 1692 witch-hunting trial, now has museums and a village dedicated to the pointy-hatted, broom-flying ladies in black.

Rockport, Marblehead, and Gloucester—working ports and artists' colonies, blue collar and artsy—are full of homes and bed-and-breakfasts with notable architecture. Newburyport is an undiscovered gem of nineteenth-century architecture. On the north edge of the Atlantic coast, Salisbury and Plum Island are worthy beach destinations, where you can sea kayak, canoe, and whale watch.

Lexington and Concord, in the Merrimack Valley just to the west, are where the first shots of the Revolution rang out in 1775. Louisa May Alcott and Ralph Waldo Emerson, among others, had homes here that are now open to visitors. Buckman Tavern, where the Minute Men once met, is also open seasonally, as is the Hancock-Clarke House, to which Paul Revere rode, warning of the British. The Concord Museums, housing treasures like Revere's signal lantern, is open year-round in Concord.

Check out nearby Lowell's Sports Museum of New England, and relive the city's mill history at the Lowell National Historic Park. Lowell, a center of the industrial revolution, has canal footpaths by many of the brick mills.

The city of Boston has few small lodgings—hotels and motels naturally dominate. But many old homes in surrounding areas, especially to the north, have become bed-and-breakfasts, and to the west are a few inns dating back 200 years. If you want to stay in the Boston region, book early and be prepared to commute to the city.

For More Information

A Bed & Breakfast Agency of Boston
(617) 720-3540 or (800) 248-9262
fax: (617) 523-5761

Citywide Reservation Services, Inc.
(617) 267-7424 or (800) 468-3593
fax: (617) 267-9408
www.cityres.com

Just Right Reservations
(617) 423-3550
www.ziplink.net/~jimwells/

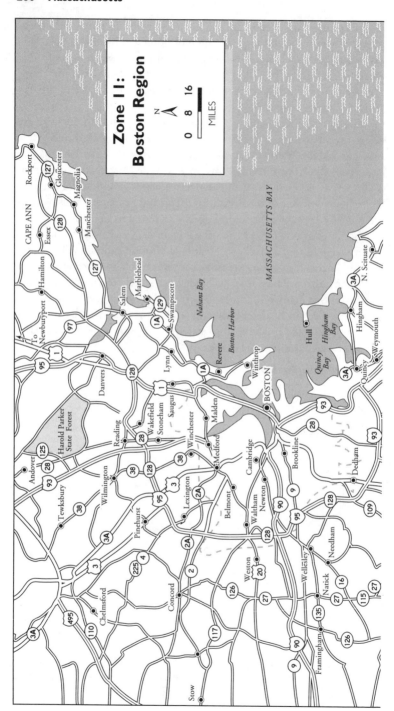

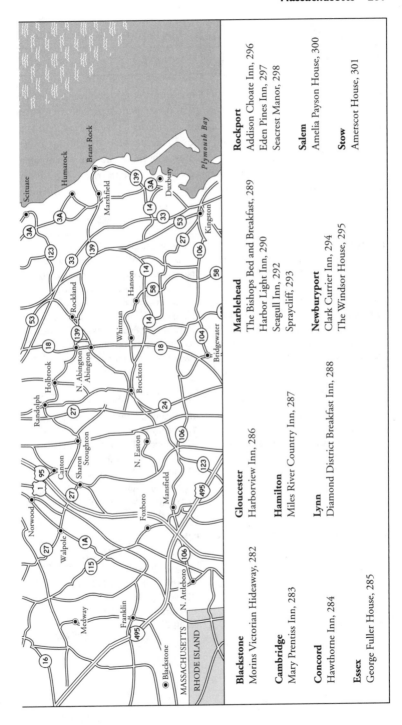

MORINS VICTORIAN HIDEAWAY, Blackstone

Overall: ★★★	Room Quality: C	Value: C	Price: $65–$75

This big white clapboard, built in 1844, is on the midpoint of a 27-mile canoe tour on the Blackstone River. Canoeists paddle along, then stop here, maybe take in a movie and a meal in nearby Providence, spend the night in a comfortable room, and enjoy breakfast before paddling away. The bed-and-breakfast is also near a major bike trail. The inn is in an area on the Rhode Island border not exactly known for tourism. A billiards room and swimming pool await, walls are stenciled or rag-painted, and a fireplace is marbleized in mid-nineteenth-century style.

SETTING & FACILITIES

Location: Off Rt. 122 (Main St.)
Near: Walk to Blackstone River and Gorge; zoo, historic Quaker Meeting House, boat tours, state park, Providence, restaurants, outlets; hour to Newport, commuter rail to Boston
Building: 1844 19-room Victorian
Grounds: 3.5 acres, woods, lawn, pool
Public Space: Entrance foyer, sunny gathering room, library area, billiards room, guest kitchenette
Food & Drink: Cont'l breakfast buffet; guest refrigerator; kitchen always stocked w/ refreshments, snacks
Recreation: Providence activities, antiquing, day trips, extensive trails
Amenities & Services: Exercise room, TV, cordless phone, iron, rollaway bed, train schedule, maps

ACCOMMODATIONS

Units: 3 guest rooms
All Rooms: Spacious, bright
Some Rooms: Priv. bath, decorative mantel
Bed & Bath: Some antique beds; double, queen, twin; add'l bath on 3rd floor, some orig. fixtures
Favorites: Rose Room—romantic, handpainted furnishings, priv. tile bath, large shower
Comfort & Decor: Almost Heaven Room w/ cherubs, 3 beds, mantel. Shares old-fashioned bath w/ Lilac Room. Bay window w/ river, sunset views; queen bed, original in-room sink. Comfortable, basic.

RATES, RESERVATIONS, & RESTRICTIONS

Deposit: 1 night; refund w/ 7-day notice
Discounts: 7+ day stays
Credit Cards: None
Check-in/Out: 2/11
Smoking: No
Pets: No
Kids: Limited, check w/ B&B
Open: All year
Hosts: Lynn and Chip Morin
48 Mendon St.
Blackstone, MA 01504
(508) 883-7045

MARY PRENTISS INN, Cambridge

Overall: ★★★★	Room Quality: B	Value: C	Price: $99–$229

There were no traffic jams in 1843 when Mary Prentiss' father-in-law built this Greek Revival home as a country house outside of Boston for the newly-weds. Mary's ancestors were among Cambridge's founding families in the 1600s, and their graves are in the nearby Historic Old Burying Ground. The innkeepers have preserved the essence of the old and added artful touches while bridging to a new wing of rooms and updating with phones, air-conditioning, and other high-tech conveniences. It's no longer rural here, so breakfast on the sunny deck among the flowers is about as close as you'll get to a country getaway.

SETTING & FACILITIES

Location: Off Massachusetts Ave. between Harvard Square and Porter Square, on a residential street
Near: Harvard Univ., Lesley College, Christ Church, museums, subway, bus line to Boston
Building: 1843 Greek Revival; Nat'l Register of Historic Places
Grounds: Side yard, pear trees, front planters, deck
Public Space: Entry, curved stairway; DR; conservatory; 1,000-sq.-ft. deck
Food & Drink: Full breakfast; specialties: quiche and potatoes, raisin scones, apple pancakes; tea and cookies; summer lunch, outdoor cafe; weekend dinners (extra); specialties: cream of broccoli soup, chicken or fish; comp. wine
Recreation: Tennis, gym, pool, golf, rowing, rollerblading, sports fields nearby
Amenities & Services: Hot tub, refrigerator, irons, books, daily paper, fax, limited underground parking, flowers/chocolates in rooms (extra); meetings (4–5), weddings (20–25)

ACCOMMODATIONS

Units: 15 guest rooms, 5 suites
All Rooms: Bath, phone, cable, dataport, individual heat/AC
Some Rooms: Wheelchair access, fireplace, wet bar, refrigerator
Bed & Bath: Varied sizes, four-posters, cannonballs; tiled, tubs, dbl. whirlpools, makeup mirrors, hairdryers
Favorites: Garden Room—priv. deck, fireplace, whirlpool
Comfort & Decor: Oversized armoires, antique wingchairs and desks. Oriental rugs, vaulted ceilings, original moldings, 1800s wood floors, exposed beams. Some rooms dark. Twin beds for parents and kids sharing room.

RATES, RESERVATIONS, & RESTRICTIONS

Deposit: 1 night when making reservation; refund w/ 14-day notice
Discounts: Seniors, longer stays, singles, off-season, 3rd person

Credit Cards: MC, V, AE
Check-in/Out: 3–9/11; bags OK until 4; arrange late check-in
Smoking: No
Pets: No
Kids: Welcome
Minimum Stay: 2 nights holidays, weekends; 3 nights graduation, events

Open: All year
Hosts: Jennifer and Nicholas Fandetti
6 Prentiss St.
Cambridge, MA 02140
(617) 661-2929
Fax: (617) 661-5989
maryprentissinn.com

HAWTHORNE INN, Concord

Overall: ★★★½	Room Quality: C	Value: C	Price: $95–$225

History drifts all around this traditional, comfortable property off the Battle Road of 1775, on land where Emerson, the Alcotts, and Hawthorne once lived. Popular yet not really commercial, it caters midweek to conferences, weekends to families. Gregory, whose ancestors settled here in 1637, paints and sculpts. Marilyn quilts and is a hospice volunteer. These helpful and informative hosts donate money to Habitat for Humanity every time they rent a room. The spiritual nature of the nineteenth-century literary greats and the American Revolution remain.

SETTING & FACILITIES

Location: Near Exit 30B (Rt. 2A W) off Rt. 128-95, across from Hawthorne's home (The Wayside)
Near: Sleepy Hollow Cemetery, Old North Bridge; homes of Emerson, Alcott, Hawthorne, Thoreau; 30 min. from Boston, 20 min. from Cambridge
Building: Built 1870 as priv. home
Grounds: 1.5 acres of maples, pines, ornamental trees, eclectic perennials bordered by Mill Brook; seating nooks throughout yard; tree house, swing for children; view of Wayside, home of Alcotts and Hawthornes; large parking lot
Public Space: Common room, DR
Food & Drink: Cont'l breakfast, communal; a specialty: honey-molasses bread; tea, coffee, snacks at check-in by request
Recreation: Swimming at Walden Pond, bike rentals, birding, museums, antiquing
Amenities & Services: Daily paper, books, piano, irons; meetings off-season (10), fax, early breakfast; pick-up at train; whole property rental

ACCOMMODATIONS

Units: 7 guest rooms
All Rooms: Bath, AC, toiletries, snacks, hairdryer, iron/board, books, clock/radio
Some Rooms: Skylight
Bed & Bath: 3 queens, 3 doubles, 1 double with fold-out; 3 cots; tubs in 4
Favorites: Bay window—overlooking gardens; Wayside—lace canopy queen w/ fireplace, antique artwork

Comfort & Decor: Eclectic, antique furnishings; extensive artwork: African, Asian, island masks, paintings, sculpture; Oriental rugs, handmade quilts, wood floors

RATES, RESERVATIONS, & RESTRICTIONS

Deposit: 1 night, 1–2 nights; other 50%; refund w/ 2-week notice; can book through travel agency
Discounts: Long stays
Credit Cards: MC, V, AE, D
Check-in/Out: After 3/11
Smoking: No
Pets: No; 3 in-house dogs and 4 cats
Kids: OK
Minimum Stay: 2 nights, Sept–Oct.

Open: All year
Hosts: Gregory Burch and Marilyn Mudry
462 Lexington Rd.
Concord, MA 01742
(978) 369-5610
Fax: (978) 287-4949
hawthorneInn@concordmass.com
www.concordmass.com

GEORGE FULLER HOUSE, Essex

Overall: ★★★   Room Quality: C   Value: D   Price: $100–$155+

If you like water views, you have them here. The salt marsh reaches the border of the lawn during high tide. Most of the time though, this modest bed-and-breakfast in this historic shipbuilding town by the river is high and dry. George Fuller was a shipbuilder (what else?), and both Bob and Cindy are knowledgeable about the nearby Essex Shipbuilding Museum and all things local. An easygoing, family feel pervades here—Cindy's mom caned the chairs, and her aunt provided the braided rugs and handmade quilts. And then there's a cruising sailboat that the family maintains if you want to get right on the water.

SETTING & FACILITIES

Location: 30 mi. N of Boston near I-95
Near: Salem, Gloucester, Rockport, Boston
Building: 1830 Federal home
Grounds: 3 porches, balcony, small lawn
Public Space: LR, DR
Food & Drink: Full breakfast; special-ties: gingerbread pancakes, French toast with brandied lemon butter; afternoon coffee, tea, cold drinks
Recreation: Sailing (lessons) on site; antiquing, tennis, golf, beach nearby
Amenities & Services: Bikes, gift certificates, fax, cruising sailboat

ACCOMMODATIONS

Units: 7 guest rooms
All Rooms: Bath, individual heat/AC, TV, phone

Some Rooms: Working fireplace (4)
Bed & Bath: Brass and canopy beds; showers only

Favorites: 3rd-floor room—king, fireplace, wet bar, kitchenette, river view, sun deck
Comfort & Decor: Antiques and period reproductions. Braided rugs, hand-caned Boston rockers. Colonial feel. Pretty, simple, modest, clean. Some rooms small.

RATES, RESERVATIONS, & RESTRICTIONS

Deposit: One night, refunded w/ 14-day notice
Discounts: Nov.–mid-May, except holidays; 3rd person
Credit Cards: V, MC, AE, D
Check-in/Out: 3–6/11
Smoking: Outdoors only
Pets: No; in-house cat
Kids: OK

Minimum Stay: 2 nights holidays, in-season weekends
Open: All year
Hosts: Bob and Cindy Cameron
148 Main St., Rt. 133
Essex, MA 01929
(978) 768-7766, (800) 477-0148
Fax: (978) 768-6178
www.cape-ann.com/fuller-house

HARBORVIEW INN, Gloucester

Overall: ★★★½	Room Quality: C	Value: C	Price: $49–$149

Once a guest house owned by descendents of the Gortons (famed for fish sticks), this comfortable, unassuming little bed-and-breakfast near the famous Gloucester Fisherman Memorial statue reemerged if not as a swan, then at least as pretty ducky after a 1994 *Better Homes and Gardens* makeover. Its main attractions are the location—facing the sea and a walk to America's oldest fishing harbor—and a cozy, shipshape feel, with nautical paintings and other original trinkets interspersed among the coordinated fabrics and wallcoverings. John is a local shopowner and Marie runs a daycare center—in her spare time.

SETTING & FACILITIES

Location: Near Exit 14 off Rt. 128 by fisherman statue, in residential neighborhood across the road from water
Near: Galleries, shops, restaurants, beaches, harbor, art colony, Salem witchcraft exhibits, Rockport
Building: 1839 3-story clapboard
Grounds: Small yard, porch, patio

Public Space: Small entrance area, LR, DR
Food & Drink: Cont'l buffet breakfast until 11
Recreation: Whale watching, sailing, sight-seeing, museum
Amenities & Services: Books, games

ACCOMMODATIONS

Units: 3 guest rooms, 3 suites
All Rooms: AC, TV, phone
Some Rooms: View, fireplace, priv. entrance, reading room, French doors, seating area, priv. bath, futon, sofa bed, murals
Bed & Bath: Beds vary; robes for shared baths

Favorites: Magnolia Studio—blue decor, queen, futons, priv. bath; view of water and on clear days, Boston
Comfort & Decor: Room size varies. Country-style decor, floral paper in most. Modest, but tasteful, well-coordinated. Good lighting. TVs and phones a plus for many. Rooms in back, quietest.

RATES, RESERVATIONS, & RESTRICTIONS

Deposit: None
Discounts: Off-season, senior citizens, business travelers
Credit Cards: MC, V, AE, D
Check-in/Out: 3/11
Smoking: No
Pets: Check
Kids: Over 12

Open: All year
Hosts: Marie and John Orlando
Stacy Blvd., 71 Western Ave.
Gloucester, MA 01930
(800) 299-6696, (978) 283-2277
info@harborviewinn.com
www.harborviewinn.com

MILES RIVER COUNTRY INN, Hamilton

Overall: ★★★★½	Room Quality: B	Value: B	Price: $80–$210

Ever want to stay over at a sophisticated friend's gorgeous country estate set among acres of landscaped lawns and flower beds, rare birds and wildlife? Sleep in a room with a fireplace and windows overlooking marshlands and river? Walk in a secret garden with an iron gate, then enjoy a breakfast of fresh-laid eggs, homemade preserves, and honey from the estate's bees? You can, at this sprawling home, which the hosts didn't leave when their kids grew up. It's yours for the taking (and you don't have to bring a gift—just some cash). A townhouse can be rented weekly during the summer, monthly during winter, like a private country estate. Greta speaks French, Spanish, and German fluently. The rooms are named after the hosts' children.

SETTING & FACILITIES

Location: 2.5 mi. N of center of Hamilton off Rt. 1A, halfway between Boston and North Shore; in estate and horse country
Near: Beaches, Cape Ann, shopping/galleries in Newburyport, Rockport, Manchester-by-the-Sea; historical sights in Salem, Ipswich, Gloucester
Building: 200-year-old Colonial farmhouse estate; 24 rooms, 12 fireplaces
Grounds: 30+ acres: terraces, woodland walkways, 12 gardens, fountain, 2 ponds; Miles River on property

Public Space: Garden terraces, glassed-in porch, common rooms, study
Food & Drink: Full buffet breakfast; specialties: estate-produced fresh fruit, honey, eggs; early riser coffee; afternoon tea
Recreation: Sailing, X-C skiing, whale watching, horse competitions
Amenities & Services: Hiking trail maps, bike maps, birder's reference book; weddings

ACCOMMODATIONS

Units: 8 guest rooms
All Rooms: Elegantly furnished, books, artwork
Some Rooms: Priv. bath (6), fireplace (4), four-poster, desk, sitting room
Bed & Bath: Beds vary; some claw-foot tubs, tub/shower

Favorites: Liesl's room—garden view, fireplace, four-poster, claw-foot tub
Comfort & Decor: Colonial, much authentic, inherited from host's family. Wooden bedsteads are 19th century. Some views of garden, river, waterways.

RATES, RESERVATIONS, & RESTRICTIONS

Deposit: Credit card; refund w/ 14-day notice, otherwise re-rental and $15 fee
Discounts: Weekly rates, off-season
Credit Cards: MC, V
Check-in/Out: After 3/11; call with arrival time
Smoking: No
Pets: No
Kids: OK

Open: All year
Hosts: Gretel and Peter Clark
823 Bay Rd.
Hamilton, MA 01936
(978) 468-7206
Fax: (978) 468-3999
milesriver@mediaone.net
milesriver.com

DIAMOND DISTRICT BREAKFAST INN, Lynn

Overall: ★★★★	Room Quality: B	Value: C	Price: $110–$245

The once-fashionable neighborhood on the North Shore was designed by the same architect who built the Schubert Theater in Boston, and the homes have the dramatic flair of turn-of-the-century prosperity. This elegant bed-and-breakfast was built for a worldly shoe manufacturer who had factories in Paris and Moscow—hence the guest rooms' whimsical footwear names. The friendly and easygoing hosts, who once lived in another house on the block, now reside in the huge basement floor. And when it comes to attention to details, they are anything but easygoing.

SETTING & FACILITIES

Location: Just N of Boston in Diamond District, 300 feet to 3-mi. beach, in residential neighborhood
Near: Beach, shops, restaurants, Boston, Salem, Marblehead, 2,000-acre nature area; bus to Boston
Building: 21-room 1911 Georgian-style estate
Grounds: Manicured lawn, gardens,

gazebo, 36-foot veranda w/ ocean views
Public Space: Banquet-size DR, formal parlor, 3rd floor cozy guest area, meeting space for 6–8
Food & Drink: Candlelight breakfast; specialties: lobster quiche, eggs Caron, apple puff pancakes, breads and muffins; early-morning coffee; special diets accom.; chips and soda

Recreation: Whale watching, jogging, croquet, heated outdoor spa
Amenities & Services: Fax, maps, videos, refrigerators, iron, beach towels and umbrellas; theater

ACCOMMODATIONS

Units: 9 guest rooms, 2 suites
All Rooms: AC, TV, phone w/ voice-mail, dataport
Some Rooms: Bath, fireplace, whirlpool, deck, VCR, CD player
Bed & Bath: Bed and room size varies; some canopies; 2 orig. claw-foot tubs/shower, 1 shower/whirlpool, 4 tub/showers, 1 orig. built-in tub/shower, 1 shower

Favorites: Gaiter—2nd floor, fireplace; Slipper—1st floor, antique English four-poster canopy, gel fireplace, VCR
Comfort & Decor: Formally deco-rated w/ antiques, collections, Oriental rugs. Good reading lights. Some ocean views. Highly individualized rooms. Feel of grand house, w/ quirky corners, per-sonality.

RATES, RESERVATIONS, & RESTRICTIONS

Deposit: Credit card or deposit; refund w/ 14-day notice
Discounts: Off-season
Credit Cards: MC, V, D, DC
Check-in/Out: After 3/11
Smoking: No
Pets: No
Kids: Well-behaved (they're "not child-proof")
No-No's: Leaving w/ keys ($25 fee)

Minimum Stay: 2 nights, summer–Nov.
Open: All year
Hosts: Sandra and Jerry Caron
142 Ocean St.
Lynn, MA 01902
(781) 599-4470, (800) 666-3076
Fax: (781) 599-5122
Diamonddistrict@msn.com
www.bbhost.com/Diamonddistrict

THE BISHOPS BED AND BREAKFAST, Marblehead

Overall: ★★★	Room Quality: C	Value: D	Price: $85–$135

This is a new property with minimal public facilities. Why stay here? Because it is quiet, and has the feel of a real house sitting on the water, and indeed it has been the home of the innkeepers' family for generations. For those who like to feel like a local rather than a visitor, this house by the sea off a quiet residential street makes you feel just that. You can walk to the center of Marblehead, or just hang out in your pleasant room, with two things to view: the in-room TV or the boats and waves and birds of Little Harbor. It's especially good for families or friends, who could rent out the entire house.

SETTING & FACILITIES

Location: Peach's Point and Little Harbor, in residential area 5 min. from center
Near: Shops, restaurants, walk to historic area; 25 mi. north of Boston
Building: Mid-1800s cottage, renovated 1997
Grounds: Seawall just outside inn

Amenities & Services: Ample parking

Public Space: Minimal; entry area, kitchen, sitting room
Food & Drink: Cont'l breakfast of fresh, seasonal fruit, tea, coffee, juice, baked goods
Recreation: Walk to Brown's Island for swimming, walk to Marblehead's historic old town

ACCOMMODATIONS

Units: 2 guest rooms, 1 suite
All Rooms: TV, views
Some Rooms: Priv. bath, priv. entrance, dressing room, sitting area
Bed & Bath: 2 queens and 1 double; suite has priv. bath
Favorites: Landfall Suite—1st floor, priv. entrance through greenhouse, sitting area, dressing room, full bath, queen bed
Comfort & Decor: All rooms close enough to hear waves on the shore. Rooms pleasant, smallish on 2nd floor. Sunny, immaculate.

RATES, RESERVATIONS, & RESTRICTIONS

Deposit: 1 night w/in 1 week of reserving; refund w/ 7-day notice
Credit Cards: MC,V
Check-in/Out: 2–5/10:30; flexible if necessary
Smoking: No
Pets: No; 2 resident cats
Kids: 6 and up

Minimum Stay: 2 nights on weekends
Open: Most of year; check
Hosts: Hugh and Judy Bishop
10 Harding Lane
Marblehead, MA 01945
(781) 631-4954
Fax: (731) 631-2102

HARBOR LIGHT INN, Marblehead

Overall: ★★★★½	Room Quality: A	Value: B	Price: $95–$245

Luxurious and stately, this twin-Federal building on a narrow street in the historic district retains a formal hush of the past. Deep red and Wedgwood blue walls, old paintings, softly chiming mantel clocks, brass touches, and arched doorways create an elegant ambiance. The innkeeper is a sailor, as are many of the residents and visitors to this historic seaport town whose harbor is filled with bobbing sail masts, as it was in Washington's time. If you climb up to the roof walk, you can see the Marblehead Light for which the bed-and-breakfast was named and much the same view as when the house was built.

SETTING & FACILITIES

Location: On narrow street in historic harbor district, 15 mi. N of Boston, Logan; 15 mi. from I-95 and Rt. 128

Near: Marblehead's historic district, downtown Boston; walking distance to harbor, antiques, galleries; zoo, aquarium, nature area, winery

Building: 1720 Colonial, 19th-century wing, annex next door

Grounds: Rooftop walk; heated pool

Public Space: Formal sitting rooms, DR, conf. room

Food & Drink: Cont'l buffet breakfast; a specialty: smoked salmon; tea, wine and cheese

Recreation: Canoeing, golf, hunting, table tennis, swimming

Amenities & Services: AC, fax, tennis rackets (fee) for midweek seminar/retreat meetings to corp. groups

ACCOMMODATIONS

Units: 21 guest rooms
All Rooms: Bath
Some Rooms: Fireplace (11), whirlpool (5), skylight
Bed & Bath: Pencil-post or carved mahogany canopy beds; spacious, modern baths, some whirlpools

Favorites: Poolside room—2nd floor, priv. deck

Comfort & Decor: Rooms individually decorated. Fireplace rooms special. Oriental carpets, pine floors, chandeliers, carvings, small-paned windows. High ceilings, spacious and luxurious. Good baths.

RATES, RESERVATIONS, & RESTRICTIONS

Deposit: 1 night or 50% for 2+ nights, w/in 7 days; refund w/ 14-day notice; early departures treated as partial cancellations
Credit Cards: MC, V, AE

Check-in/Out: After 1/10. Call for check-in after 10 p.m.
Smoking: No
Pets: No; 1 in-house cat

Kids: Over 10; others by special arrangement
Minimum Stay: 2 nights, weekends; 3 nights, holiday weekends
Open: All year

Hosts: Peter C. Conway
58 Washington St.
Marblehead, MA 01945
(781) 631-2186
Fax: (781) 631-2216

SEAGULL INN, Marblehead

Overall: ★★★	Room Quality: B	Value: C	Price: $85–$225

This "host with the most"(according to *Boston* magazine) has turned his family's rambling house on the water, long ago a small hotel, back into a welcoming respite for travelers. Skip is a former corporate guy who worked on the furniture and painted murals, and has a great sense of humor and gift of gab. (His reported description of the sitting room: "a blend of hand-crafted furniture and antiques, including the owner.") While the rooms and breakfast are fine, this is a prime example of innkeepers' impact at small properties such as bed-and-breakfasts and inns. They can and do make or break them.

SETTING & FACILITIES

Location: Marblehead Neck, a residential peninsula, 18 mi. N of Boston
Near: Beach, lighthouse, fishing fleets, sailboat races
Building: Restored, shingled century-old summer hotel
Grounds: Gardens, decks, water views
Public Space: Sitting room

Food & Drink: Cont'l breakfast; specialties: homemade granola, freshly ground coffee
Recreation: Water sports, golf, antiquing
Amenities & Services: Local info in rooms, use of nearby health club, books, videos, games; meeting space, fax

ACCOMMODATIONS

Units: 3 guest rooms
All Rooms: Bath, TV/VCR, phone, coffee maker, AC
Some Rooms: Kitchen, deck, ocean views, Victorian artifacts
Bed & Bath: Queen beds, four-posters; hairdryers
Favorites: Lighthouse Suite—duplex apt. w/ priv. entrance, grill, hammock,

kitchen, bath and roof deck w/ views, sofa bed and daybed in LR, 4-poster queen in upstairs BR
Comfort & Decor: Rooms sunny and individually decorated w/ cherry floors, Shaker furniture, and original paintings. Two multiple rooms. Tasteful. Much of furniture crafted by innkeeper.

RATES, RESERVATIONS, & RESTRICTIONS

Deposit: Refund w/ 14-day notice
Discounts: 3rd person
Credit Cards: MC,V
Check-in/Out: Check-in 2 p.m. or arranged
Smoking: No
Pets: Check
Kids: Check

Minimum Stay: 2 night min. some weekends and holidays
Open: All year
Hosts: Skip Sigler
106 Harbor Ave.
Marblehead, MA 01945
(781) 631-1893
Fax: (781) 631-3535

SPRAYCLIFF, Marblehead

Overall: ★★★★   Room Quality: B   Value: C   Price: $175–$200

The name fits, as this bright and breezy Tudor is set within the salty spritz of the Atlantic, the only oceanfront bed-and-breakfast in Marblehead. Color accents are knockout aspects within. Wicker in red, blue, and yellow, and bright pottery and art, all painted by talented interior designer Sally, are set against vividly against white walls, and the pretty guest rooms are filled with bold hues as well. This romantic property is popular with gay and lesbian travelers, among others.

SETTING & FACILITIES

Location: 15 mi. N of Boston on the ocean (B&B)
Near: Old Town Marblehead, beach, Logan International Airport, shopping
Building: Large 1910 Tudor, redecorated 1995

Grounds: Oceanfront atop a seawall, courtyard and gardens
Public Space: Patio on the water; Gathering Room
Food & Drink: Cont'l breakfast; afternoon libations

Recreation: Hiking, biking, antiquing

Amenities & Services: Daily papers, library, beach towels, bikes, fresh flowers, special requests

ACCOMMODATIONS

Units: 7 suites

All Rooms: Bath, sitting area

Some Rooms: Fireplace, ocean view, bay window

Bed & Bath: Queen or king, some full; some tubs

Favorites: Winnetka—king, fireplace, priv. oceanfront patio,

Comfort & Decor: Antique and handpainted furnishing. Styles vary, and evoke locations where hosts resided (Athens, Winnetka, Little Rock, etc.). Fresh flowers. Windows and water views. Immaculate and refreshing.

RATES, RESERVATIONS, & RESTRICTIONS

Deposit: 1 night's stay; cancellations w/ 7-day notice and $25 fee

Discounts: Off-season (Nov.–April)

Credit Cards: AE, V, MC

Check-in/Out: 3–7/11

Smoking: No

Pets: No; 2 in-house schnauzers

Kids: No

Minimum Stay: 2 nights most weekends, 3 nights some holiday weekends

Open: All year

Hosts: Sally and Roger Plauche
25 Spray Ave.
Marblehead, MA 01945
(800) 626-1530, (781) 631-6789
Fax: (617) 639-4563
spraycliff@aol.com
www.marbleheadchamber.org/spraycliff

CLARK CURRIER INN, Newburyport

Overall: ★★★★	Room Quality: B	Value: C	Price: $100–$150

This elegant three-story bed-and-breakfast reflects the classic grace and beauty of this still-wonderful port town—which was the country's fourth-largest city in 1803, when the house was built. Today it is filled with world treasures from that era. Pretty and well-maintained, with decorative moldings and classical music, it has an informal sitting room and a charming little garden to lighten the formality.

SETTING & FACILITIES

Location: 2 mi. off I-95, Exit 57, in historic downtown district

Near: Market Square historic district, performing and visual arts, museums, Historical Society of Old Newbury, waterfront park, shopping, nature areas, beach, zoo, aquarium, ruins, winery, rodeo

Building: 1803 Federal 3-story; remodeled 1994; Nat'l Historical Register

Grounds: Restored garden w/ gazebo, roses, tiny pond

Public Space: Wide entrance hall, parlor, sitting room, DR, library

Food & Drink: Cont'l breakfast; a specialty: low-fat brownies; can take tray to room; afternoon tea in garden room, sherry
Recreation: Deep-sea fishing, whale/bird watching, harbor cruises, hay/sleigh rides, ice-skating, X-C skiing
Amenities & Services: Small weddings, seminars, other engagements; arranging baby-sitting

ACCOMMODATIONS

Units: 5 guest rooms, 1 suite
All Rooms: Bath, AC
Some Rooms: Fireplace, enclosed porch, deck, priv. entry, Franklin stove
Bed & Bath: Queen, double, twin, 1 canopy; tubs
Favorites: Currier—pencil-post bed, fireplace, enclosed porch

Comfort & Decor: Rooms named for prominent locals, such as John P. Marchand, Pulitzer Prize–winning author; individually decorated w/ antiques, period furnishings.

RATES, RESERVATIONS, & RESTRICTIONS

Deposit: 1 night; refund w/ 5-day notice
Discounts: Corp. rates
Credit Cards: MC, V, AE, D
Check-in/Out: 3–4/11
Smoking: Outside
Pets: No; in-house cat
Kids: No
No-No's: Arriving after 7 p.m. without special arrangement

Minimum Stay: 2 nights weekends, in-season
Open: All year
Hosts: Mary and Bob Nolan, daughter Melissa
45 Green St.
Newburyport, MA 01950
(800) 360-6582, (978) 465-8363
clarkcurrierinn.com

THE WINDSOR HOUSE, Newburyport

Overall: ★★★	Room Quality: C	Value: D	Price: $135

As English as its name, this bed-and-breakfast has the feel of a modest English country house and was built in the eighteenth century—before the house of Windsor came to be. Host John was in the Royal Navy and lived in a cottage by King Arthur's castle in Tintagel; Judith writes about Neolithic Britain, and it's not surprising that they run a tour company specializing in Great Britain. Check out the details of the guest room dedicated to Princess Di.

SETTING & FACILITIES

Location: 45 min. N of Logan Airport off I-95, on quiet residential street across from a church, 2 blocks from center

Near: Plum Island, Parker River Wildlife Refuge, Custom House Maritime Museum, Historical Society, state park

Building: 1786 3-story brick Federal mansion, remodeled 1998

Grounds: Across from brick church, courtyard, garden

Public Space: Common room, DR, meeting space (20), eat-in kitchen

Food & Drink: Full two-course English breakfast; tea; special diets accom.

Recreation: River cruises, whale watching, deep-sea fishing, antiquing; local events, architecture

Amenities & Services: Fax, copier, washer/dryer, some disabled access

ACCOMMODATIONS

Units: 4 guest rooms

All Rooms: Priv. bath, AC, alarm clock, phone, tea/coffee maker

Some Rooms: Priv. entrance, library, sleigh or four-poster bed, fireplace

Bed & Bath: Beds vary, king or queen

Favorites: English Rose—in memory of Princess Diana, rose wallpaper, photos, mementos, king bed

Comfort & Decor: Rooms restored to memory of original use w/ some original features. Old-fashioned, pluses and minuses of English style. A bit fussy.

RATES, RESERVATIONS, & RESTRICTIONS

Deposit: 1 night or credit card

Discounts: Singles, corp., 1 night free w/ 7-day stay, 3rd person

Credit Cards: MC, V, AE, D

Check-in/Out: 4/11

Smoking: No

Pets: By arrangement; in-house cat

Kids: Over 6

Minimum Stay: 2 nights weekends, 3 on holidays

Open: All year

Hosts: Judith and John Harris
38 Federal St.
Newburyport, MA 01950
(888) TRELAWNY, (978) 462-3778
Fax: (978) 465-3443
Tintagel@greennet.net
www.bbhost.com/windsorhouse

ADDISON CHOATE INN, Rockport

Overall: ★★★½	Room Quality: C	Value: B	Price: $95–$140

This is a bed-and-breakfast without luxury touches, but with a pleasant old-fashioned atmosphere, a throwback to a time before whirlpools and fireplaces and themes became popular. The look is summery and eclectic, and the perennial borders and outdoor pool are especially inviting. Knox is a landscape architect and architectural designer who enjoys birding and photography; Shirley is an interior designer, weaver, and gardener. Both are friendly and helpful. Waking to the smell of freshly baked muffins and brewed coffee in the morning is one of this bed-and-breakfast's simple but comforting pleasures.

SETTING & FACILITIES

Location: Hour N of Boston, tip of Cape Ann; on main residential street
Near: Town center, state park, ocean, walking trails
Building: 1851 late Greek Revival
Grounds: Wraparound porch w/ seating overlooking garden
Public Space: Living room, DRs, TV room

Food & Drink: Buffet breakfast: baked goods, granola, fresh fruit; in-room possible; tea; restaurants 5 min. walk
Recreation: Outdoor pool; nearby bird/whale watching, sea kayaking
Amenities & Services: Binoculars, irons, maps, recipes, daily papers, phone, fax, copier; pick up from train

ACCOMMODATIONS

Units: 5 guest rooms; 3 suites
All Rooms: Bath, reading lamp, hairdryer, sitting area, toiletries
Some Rooms: TV; refrigerators in suites, AC (all but one), kitchen, dining area, loft, skylight, ceiling fan
Bed & Bath: King, queen, twin, tub/shower combo
Favorites: Chimney Room—sunny, chimney through it, queen canopy,

antique bureau, tub/shower. Celebration Suite—BR, sitting room, view of Rockport and ocean, pine queen canopy
Comfort & Decor: Rooms mix antique and reproduction furniture in homey style. Suites in the Stable House include loft bedrooms, kitchen, and dining areas. Individually and tastefully decorated with attention to detail.

RATES, RESERVATIONS, & RESTRICTIONS

Deposit: One night, refund w/ 10-day notice or re-rental; can book through travel agency
Discounts: Singles, 3rd person (suites); Stable House suites $800 weekly, not incl. breakfast
Credit Cards: MC, V, D; cash or check preferred
Check-in/Out: 3/11
Smoking: No
Pets: No; 2 in-house cats
Kids: 12 and older

Minimum Stay: 2 nights mid-June–mid-Sept., Valentine's Day, Memorial Day, Columbus Day, 3 nights July 4 weekend
Open: All year, except 2 weeks in Nov.
Hosts: Shirley and Knox Johnson
49 Broadway
Rockport, MA 01966
(978) 546-7543, (800) 245-7543
Fax: (978) 546-7638
www.cape-ann.com/addison-choate

EDEN PINES INN, Rockport

Overall: ★★★★½   Room Quality: B   Value: B   Price: $120–$170

The house is decorated in casually elegant style, and the breathtaking view from the deck and most rooms is mesmerizing day and night: ocean and rocky cove, Thatcher island with twin lighthouses, lobstermen tending traps, seagulls hovering over boats, sea cormorants surface diving, sunrise and moonrise. And you can hear the waves lapping. The charming innkeeper agrees with Emerson: "Make acquaintance with the sea." And this is the place.

SETTING & FACILITIES

Location: 1.5 mi. from downtown Rockport, in residential area overlooking water
Near: Beaches, Rockport tourist attractions
Building: 1900 Federal-style home
Grounds: Rock garden, croquet, porch, brick sun deck

Public Space: LR, DR
Food & Drink: Breakfast; a specialty: homemade cake; tea and cookies, snack
Recreation: Swimming, golf, tennis, whale watching, fishing trips
Amenities & Services: Daily papers, refrigerator, irons, maps

ACCOMMODATIONS

Units: 7 guest rooms; one in sep. house, weekly rental only
All Rooms: Bath, AC, sitting area
Some Rooms: Marble or tile bath, sep. showers and tubs, priv. deck (6)
Bed & Bath: Queen, king, or 2 double beds, most canopy; robes for long stays
Favorites: #2—blue/yellow decor, decks w/ view, soaking tub, marble

bath; #6—canopy queen, pink/green florals; 3rd floor penthouse—king canopy, balcony, large wicker sitting area
Comfort & Decor: Priv. decks overlook the sea, California colors and styles, especially blues and yellows. Casually elegant.

RATES, RESERVATIONS, & RESTRICTIONS

Deposit: 1 night; refund w/ 14-day notice; booking through travel agent OK (in-house preferred)
Discounts: 3rd person
Credit Cards: MC, V
Check-in/Out: 2/11
Smoking: Outside and porches only
Pets: No
Kids: Teenagers

Minimum Stay: 2 days, 3 on holiday weekends—paid in full
Open: Mid-May–Oct.
Hosts: Inge Sullivan
48 Eden Rd.
Rockport, MA 01966
(978) 546-2505; winter (978) 443-2604
Fax: (978) 546-1157 mid-May–Oct. only
www.rockportusa.com/edenpines/

SEACREST MANOR, Rockport

Overall: ★★★★½	Room Quality: B	Value: B	Price: $92–$146

"Decidedly small, intentionally quiet" is the way the Seacrest Manor describes itself, and that seems true. There's only one phone line—in the office—and this is not a place for Frisbee throws on the lawn. Gentility,

propriety, elegance come to mind, in the style of an English country house. The spacious living room features a gilt mirror from the old Philadelphia Opera House. A red oak tree out front dates from the nineteenth century, and the mood does, too. Leighton is a retired NBC exec; Dwight is a retired college professor who looks like an older cousin of movie star Matt Damon. He is.

SETTING & FACILITIES

Location: Less than 5 mi. from northern end of Rt. 128, 1 mi. from center of Rockport, in residential area
Near: Beach; across the street from 9-acre John Kiernan Nature Preserve
Building: 1911 brick structure, pedestaled portico
Grounds: 2 acre corner lot: gardens, statues, fountain; 2nd story deck w/ ocean view
Public Space: DR, library, spacious LR
Food & Drink: Full, formal breakfast; specialties: spiced Irish oatmeal w/ chopped dates, corn fritters w/ hot syrup; early bird coffee and tea; afternoon tea, snacks
Recreation: Golf, deep-sea fishing, boat trips, tennis, whale watching nearby
Amenities & Services: Safe, stationery, daily papers, Sun. papers (fee), notecards (fee), beach towels, gift cert., bike rental, turn-down, men's shoe polishing, BYOB set-up (dry town)

ACCOMMODATIONS

Units: 6 guest rooms, 1 suite
All Rooms: TV, radio, fan, fresh flowers
Some Rooms: Priv. bath (6), priv. entrance, nonworking fireplace
Bed & Bath: Most queen or king, some double; suite shares bath

Favorites: Carpeted rooms. Shakespeare quotes on pillows w/ mints.
Elegant.
Comfort & Decor: Rooms 7, 8— open directly on deck, ocean views

RATES, RESERVATIONS, & RESTRICTIONS

Deposit: 1 night; 2 nights for weekends, 7+ days; refund w/ 14-day notice
Discounts: Singles, 2-week or longer stay
Credit Cards: None
Check-in/Out: 2/11
Smoking: Outside only
Pets: No
Kids: Over 12
No-No's: Groups; check-in after 9 p.m.; 3 people in a room; incoming calls after 9 p.m.; bare feet in public rooms

Minimum Stay: 2 nights mid-May–Oct., 3 nights holiday weekends
Open: April–Nov.
Hosts: Dwight B. MacCormick Jr. and Leighton T. Saville
99 Marmion Way
Rockport, MA 01966
(978) 546-2211
seacrestmanor@rockportusa.com
www.rockportusa.com/seacrestmanor/

AMELIA PAYSON HOUSE, Salem

| Overall: ★★★½ | Room Quality: C | Value: C | Price: $65–$125 |

Witches are welcome (as well as non-witches) in this little homestead located north of Boston near the site of the Witch Trial and other historic happenings. The blue-painted, columned facade is a prelude to a formal but friendly in-town bed-and-breakfast, which allows you to easily visit the museums in this historic town without having to get in a car. Pink and mauve and other pastels are the colors of choice, and the atmosphere is delicate, with swag drapes and marble mantels. Halloween is when the town gets crowded, and the town is jumping with people wearing black.

SETTING & FACILITIES

Location: Half-hour N of Boston on IA N
Near: Boston; walk to Salem shopping, restaurants, Salem Witch Museum, House of the Seven Gables, Peabody Essex Museum, Nat'l Maritime Site, ferry, Amtrak station
Building: 1845 Greek Revival
Grounds: City backyard garden, deck area

Public Space: Parlor, DR
Food & Drink: Cont'l-plus, family-style breakfast with baked goods
Recreation: Tennis, swimming, sailing, whale watching, dinner and music cruises
Amenities & Services: Fridge, baby grand piano, microwave, beach towels, irons, books; pickup from train and ferry

ACCOMMODATIONS

Units: 4 guest rooms
All Rooms: Bath, AC, hairdryer, TV, clock/radio

Some Rooms: Tub, canopy bed
Bed & Bath: Queens, some twins in addition, antique frames; full baths

except one shower only
Favorites: The Canopy—canopied
four-poster, antiques, Oriental rugs

Comfort & Decor: Sunlit spacious
rooms, floral paper with soft rose and
blue accessories, lace and antiques.

RATES, RESERVATIONS, & RESTRICTIONS

Deposit: 1 night; refund w/ 7-day
notice; 30 days for Halloween. Travel
agent booking OK (prefer in-house).
Discounts: None
Credit Cards: MC, V, AE, D
Check-in/Out: 4/11
Smoking: Outdoors
Pets: No
Kids: Over 12

Minimum Stay: 2–3 days for week-
ends/holidays; 4 days during Halloween
Open: March–Nov.
Hosts: Ada and Donald Roberts
16 Winter St.
Salem, MA 01970
(978) 744-8304
bbamelia@aol.com
www.salemweb.com/biz/ameliapayson

AMERSCOT HOUSE, Stow

Overall: ★★★★	Room Quality: B	Value: C	Price: $100–$125

If you enjoy rural life and dream of owning a farm or just spending some
time on one, you'll especially enjoy this authentic, charming farmhouse
with a dollop of Scottish influence. The fields stretch out beyond this
warm house, and the hearth, rustic parlor, and open kitchen are comforting and restful. You can retire to the luxury of a suite with a whirlpool or a
combined room and loft. Apple picking in nearby orchards or an evening
of Scottish Country dancing are charming diversions, and business travelers are well-supported with services. As Doreen and Jerry would say it, *cead
mille fialte:* a hundred thousand welcomes.

SETTING & FACILITIES

Location: Rural, 5 mi. from Rt. 495
and Rt. 2, near Concord
Near: Shopping in Boston and
Concord, Mayard, Sturbridge; 4 golf
courses
Building: Early American (c.1734)
farmhouse
Grounds: 2.5 acres: gardens, greenhouse, side porch
Public Space: Colonial DR, FR; function room (25–30)

Food & Drink: Full breakfast; specialty:
homemade granola; tea and scones,
sherry.
Recreation: Canoeing, trails, apple
picking; Scottish country dancing with
hosts
Amenities & Services: Copy, fax,
dataports; secretarial services for business travelers

ACCOMMODATIONS

Units: 2 guest rooms, I suite
All Rooms: Bath, fireplace, phone, cable TV
Some Rooms: Sitting room, adjoining lofts with twin beds, whirlpool, desk
Bed & Bath: 2 queens, I king with twin option

Favorites: The Lindsay Suite—Queen canopy bed, sitting room, whirlpool
Comfort & Decor: Rooms decorated with antiques, handmade quilts, and fresh flowers. Paned windows, bedside lighting.

RATES, RESERVATIONS, & RESTRICTIONS

Deposit: I night; 7-day cancellation policy
Discounts: Singles, corp. rates, 3rd person
Credit Cards: MC, V, AE, D
Check-in/Out: 4–9/11
Smoking: No
Pets: No
Kids: OK

Open: All year
Hosts: Doreen and Jerry Gibson
61 West Acton Rd., P.O. Box 351
Stow, MA 01775
(978) 897-0666
Fax: (978) 897-6914
doreen@amerscot.com
www.amerscot.com

Zone 12
Central/Western
Massachusetts

Central Massachusetts, with meadows, ponds, farms, and low mountains, is highlighted by Worcester, the second-largest city in the state and home to the Worcester Art Museum and the New England Science Center.

Old Sturbridge Village, which re-creates 1830s New England, is south of the city and has two covered bridges, staff in period costumes, farming with ox teams, and crafting of products you can buy. Hardwick also has a covered bridge. In Sutton, Purgatory Chasm runs 70 feet deep and makes for wonderful sightseeing.

Shoppers can load up in outlet malls in both Worcester and Gardner ("Chair City of the World") as well as at roadside stands for corn and tomatoes in summer, pumpkins and apples in fall. This region is the home of Johnny Appleseed, and the trail named after this legendary planter starts in Lancaster and winds through 25 communities in the north-central area, with orchards, galleries, antique centers, wineries, microbreweries, and furniture outlets. Nearby Wachusett Mountain offers skiing and panoramic views.

Hoop fans will want to stop at the Naismith Memorial Basketball Hall of Fame in the city of Springfield, where the game began. The first U.S. armory is here as well. The colleges of Smith, Mt. Holyoke, Hampshire, and the University of Massachusetts at Amherst are nearby. In summer you can waterslide 400 feet down Mount Tom's Pipe Dream, where you can also ski or snowboard in winter.

Fans of history won't want to miss the town of Deerfield, complete with period architecture and decor and 14 museum-houses open to the public. Horses clippity-clopping by, pulling carriages along the cobblestones, carry you back two centuries. Check out Yankee Candle to watch how beeswax tapers were traditionally made.

Western Massachusetts may be best known for the Berkshire region, at the far end of the state, bordered by New York. It's a bucolic area of

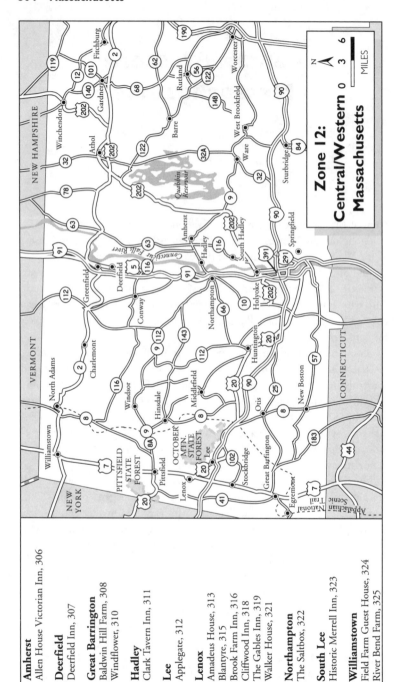

Zone 12: Central/Western Massachusetts

low-mountain landscape and art-filled villages. This was an area where artists, writers, and many of New England's wealthiest families created an alternative to Newport in the late-nineteenth century. Mansions remain, some converted to bed-and-breakfasts or museums, their facades highlighting pretty village greens and backroads.

In addition to strolling through gardens and estates, and biking, hiking, and skiing the mountains, there's an array of summer cultural events—music, dance, theater, and more. Popular sites are the Norman Rockwell Museum in Stockbridge; Tanglewood (summer home to the Boston Symphony Orchestra) near Lenox; the Hancock Shaker Village; Williams College in charming, museum-filled Williamstown; and the evocative new Massachusetts Museum of Contemporary Art (Mass MoCA) in a restored mill complex in North Adams.

Bed-and-breakfasts and small inns in this area are sophisticated and choice, often in old famous taverns and coach stops, former mansions, or historic homes. Many are clustered in the western end of the state.

For More Information
Southern Berkshire Chamber of Commerce
(413) 528-4006
www.berkshirelodging.com

ALLEN HOUSE VICTORIAN INN, Amherst

Overall: ★★★★	Room Quality: B	Value: A	Price: $45–$155

Even if you're not a fan of ornate Victoriana, a mélange of peacock feathers, Eastlake furnishings, and William Morris prints, you can't help admire the dramatic effect of this award-winning bed-and-breakfast, re-creating the "Aesthetic period" of the 1880s, when Emily Dickinson still lived in town. Both hosts love to create romantic touches when requested, such as roses on pillows, chocolates, and champagne, and they serve special dishes on holidays and special occasions. Alan stayed here first as a student and was thrilled to own this Painted Lady. Today, he and Ann are renovating barns and expanding gardens to include a Japanese tea house. Continual improvement is a sign of a really fine property.

SETTING & FACILITIES

Location: About 6 mi. from Exit 19 off I-91

Near: Walk to Emily Dickinson Homestead, Amherst, Hampshire College, UMass, Nat'l Yiddish Bookcenter, Yankee Candle, Historic Deerfield, Old Sturbridge Village, Hancock Shaker Village, Norman Rockwell Museum, galleries, theaters, shopping

Building: 1886 Queen Anne Stick–style Victorian

Grounds: 3.5 landscaped acres, shade trees, gardens, meadow

Public Space: DR, LR

Food & Drink: Full formal, 5-course Victorian breakfast in room, communal or separate tables; specialties: eggs Benedict, soufflés, quiche, Belgian waffles; can be in-room; afternoon and evening tea, pastries, cookies, lemonade in summer, hot cider in fall. Special diets accom. Nearest restaurant, 5-min. walk.

Recreation: Concerts, tennis, golf, X-C skiing, Hampshire Fitness (fee); bike rental nearby

Amenities & Services: Daily papers, fax, refrigerator, irons; shuttle to town, to and from local colleges, pick-up from train/bus; storage, concierge service

ACCOMMODATIONS

Units: 7 guest rooms
All Rooms: Bath, AC, ceiling fan, antique-style radio, clock, phone, dataport, fine Swiss chocolates, English toiletries
Some Rooms: Larger, space for add'l guests
Bed & Bath: 4 full and 3 queen beds, some add'l twin beds; tile baths, some deep claw-foot tubs
Favorites: The front rooms, such as

Louis Comfort Tiffany—large, filled w/ Victoriana, silk-screened wallpapers, extra bed
Comfort & Decor: Rooms spacious in front, smaller in former maids' rooms in back. Individually decorated w/ antiques, period art. Museum-quality restorations. Feels like 1880s, but dataports and modern comforts. Meticulous attention to detail.

RATES, RESERVATIONS, & RESTRICTIONS

Deposit: Within 7 days of reserving; refund w/ 14-day notice
Discounts: Off-season, long stays, extra person
Credit Cards: MC, V, D
Check-in/Out: 3/11
Smoking: Outside verandas only
Pets: No
Kids: 10 and older

Minimum Stay: Holiday, graduation, and Oct. weekends: 3 nights; high season weekends: 2 nights
Open: All year
Hosts: Alan and Ann Zieminski
599 Main St.
Amherst, MA 01002
(413) 253-5000
allenhouse@webtv.net
www.allenhouse.com

DEERFIELD INN, Deerfield

Overall: ★★★★½   Room Quality: B   Value: D   Price: $147–$242

Bonafide ghosts Cora and Herschel haunt this award-winning bed-and-breakfast on "The Street," filled with a dozen historic eighteenth- and nineteenth-century clapboard and brick houses. This fine house is one of the original New England inns and is well aware of that history, abounding in antiques, decorative arts fabrics, and wallcoverings. Popular with the public, it can get busy during dining hours but is a complete, traditional New England experience. It's especially lovely to retire for the evening with the clip-clop of horse-drawn carriages outside the window.

SETTING & FACILITIES

Location: Exit 24 off I-91 N, Exit 25, S on "The Street"

Near: Museum houses, Memorial Hall museum, historical sights, Williamstown

Building: 1884 Federal-style inn; large double porch with pillars
Grounds: Fronts old Main St.; flower beds, small lawns; village view, on-street parking and behind inn
Public Space: LRs, DRs, refurbished tavern, coffee shop, porches, terrace
Food & Drink: Full country breakfast; dinner open to public; a specialty: mussels steamed with chorizo sausage, coconut milk, and lime; light fare in Terrace Cafe; tea/snack
Recreation: 3-mi. loop walk, boating, X-C skiing, whitewater rafting, tennis
Amenities & Services: Elevator, refrigerator, wheelchair access, catering, business support

ACCOMMODATIONS

Units: 23 rooms
All Rooms: Bath, climate controls, phone, TV with cozy, quilts, hairdryer, lighted mirrors, robes
Some Rooms: Queen, four-poster, cannonball beds
Bed & Bath: High beds with steps; tub and shower
Favorites: Room 43—ultra-traditional w/ charming details
Comfort & Decor: Antique and reproduction mix. Rich draperies and furnishings. Authentic period patterns. Historic, comfortable.

RATES, RESERVATIONS, & RESTRICTIONS

Deposit: One night; refund w/ 7-day notice
Discounts: AAA seniors, off-season, groups, extended stays, midweek
Credit Cards: MC, V, AE, D
Check-in/Out: 2/noon
Smoking: Porch or terrace only
Pets: No
Kids: "Well-behaved" welcome
No-No's: Late check-out, $50 charge; entry after 11 p.m., inappropriate attire in DR
Minimum Stay: 2 nights, busy weekends
Open: All year except Dec. 23–26
Hosts: Jane and Karl Sabo
81 Old Main St.
Deerfield, MA 01342-0305
(800) 926-3865, (413) 774-5587
Fax: (413) 773-8712
frontdesk@deerfield inn.com
www.deerfieldinn.com

BALDWIN HILL FARM, Great Barrington

Overall: ★★★★½	Room Quality: C	Value: B	Price: $85–$110

Once a working dairy farm, this truly rural bed-and-breakfast retains almost 500 acres of its original farmland, and another 190 acres across the way has been purchased for the State Agricultural Project and will remain undeveloped. The quiet Berkshire Hills countryside seems to stretch forever in a 360-degree panorama so striking it was featured in *Travel & Leisure*. The breezy property has been in the Burdsall family for three generations. At "retirement" in 1989, Dick and Priscilla added a swimming pool and turned the unpretentious, comfortable house into a bed-and-breakfast. As a kid, Dick slept in the same simple rooms and ate at the same breakfast table guests now enjoy.

SETTING & FACILITIES

Location: Rt. 71 to Baldwin Hill Rd. E/W, left for 1 mi.; turn left at crossroad, B&B is 200 yards further on the right, on rural dirt road
Near: Tanglewood, Berkshire School Choral Festival, Berkshire Summer Theatre Festival, Shakespeare at the Mount, Jacob's Pillow, Norman Rockwell Museum, Egremont Country Club, French Park, Prospect Lake, Appalachian Trail, Mount Everett (highest Berkshire peak), Monument Mountain, ski areas
Building: Civil War–era country hilltop Victorian farmhouse, Gothic overtones; barn and outbuildings
Grounds: Hundreds of acres: Catalpa trees, gardens, 3-state views; ungroomed X-C skiing trails, heated pool
Public Space: Twin parlors, DR, screened porch
Food & Drink: Full breakfast; preferences from menu for next morning; a specialty: creamed dried beef; afternoon snack
Recreation: Picnics, antiquing, golf, tennis, trails, lake boating
Amenities & Services: Outdoor pool, refrigerator, heat adjusted according to guests' preferences

ACCOMMODATIONS

Units: 4 guest rooms
All Rooms: Seating, reading lighting, alarm clock, rural view
Some Rooms: Priv. bath (2), some heirloom Victorian pieces
Bed & Bath: Queen, king/twin beds, new mattresses every 2 years; 2 rooms share 1.5 baths, robes, 1 w/ sink/vanity in room
Favorites: Bay Window Room—sitting area in window, extensive views
Comfort & Decor: Marble-topped dressers, antique mirrors—at least 1 piece per room. Country floral wallpapers, soothing color schemes. Quilts. Small, authentic, old-fashioned feel, well-maintained.

RATES, RESERVATIONS, & RESTRICTIONS

Deposit: 1 night; refund w/ 10-day notice
Discounts: 4+ night stays
Credit Cards: MC, V, AE, D
Check-in/Out: 3–6/ 11
Smoking: No
Pets: No, nearby facilities
Kids: Over 10
Minimum Stay: 2 nights high-season weekends, holidays
Open: All year
Hosts: Priscilla and Richard Burdsall
121 Baldwin Hill Rd.
Great Barrington, MA 01230
(888) 528-4092 or (413) 528-44092
Fax: (413) 528-6365
rpburds@aol.com

WINDFLOWER, Great Barrington

Overall: ★★★½	Room Quality: B	Value: C	Price: $120–$200

A kid-friendly, people-friendly environment awaits in this comfortable, established bed-and-breakfast. Two decades ago Barbara and Gerry opened the Tulip Tree Inn in Vermont. Five years later daughter Claudia, an experienced chef, and husband, John, with a degree in arbor culture and lots of handyman experience, came to co-innkeep here in the Berkshires. Accommodating is the word, in every way: For an allergic guest, they removed carpeting and used special supplies—he stayed three months. A Polish visitor with dietary problems was given special foods, and Barbara shopped with him before he left. A party of 80 paid to have all furnishings removed and replaced (the party went fine).

SETTING & FACILITIES

Location: Across road from Egremont Country Club; to Rt. 23 & 41 to Egremont for 3 mi., follow signs to Country Club and B&B
Near: Berkshires mountains, Tanglewood, Jacob's Pillow, theatre festivals, Shaker Village, Clark Art Institute, Norman Rockwell Museum, Edith Wharton's home, 400-acre John Drummond Kennedy park, ski areas, walk to dining and shops
Building: 1850 Colonial, columned front porch
Grounds: 10 acres: perennial gardens, organic berry, vegetable, and herb gardens

Public Space: LR, reading room
Food & Drink: Full breakfast; specialty: cottage cheese soufflé pancakes; tea, cookies; B&B chef caters for groups, events
Recreation: Antiquing, tennis, golf, boating, horseback riding
Amenities & Services: Pool, discounted ski tickets; cribs, roll-aways; ltd. disabled access, BYOB set-ups, refrigerator, iron; fly-fishing, biking equipment and lessons; weddings, meetings, etc. (150), catered, planned; recipes

ACCOMMODATIONS

Units: 13 guest rooms
All Rooms: Bath, good lighting, radio alarm clock, TV, AC
Some Rooms: Fireplace, seating, access to common porch, add'l bed, window seat, bay window
Bed & Bath: Some four-poster, canopy, elaborately carved beds, sizes vary; baths vary: modern, claw-foot tub/shower, shower only; extra-large tile showers(1), pedestal sinks

Favorites: Room 12—fieldstone fireplace, Laura Ashley, stocked bookshelves, door to common porch; Room 1—MBR—fireplace, queen and twin bed, dressing room
Comfort & Decor: Rooms 4 and 5, sunny, four-poster canopies, but some traffic noise. Fairly spacious rooms, constant maintenance and upgrades. Carpet or hardwood floors. Some small, Duralog-only fireplaces. Some bold pattern combinations.

RATES, RESERVATIONS, & RESTRICTIONS

Deposit: 1 night, applied to last night stay; refund w/ 21-day notice
Discounts: Seasonal packages; 3rd person/children, infants, corp. and midweek
Credit Cards: AE
Check-in/Out: 2/11
Smoking: Restricted to 1 LR w/ efficient air-purifier, no pipes or cigars
Pets: No
Kids: Welcome

Minimum Stay: 2 nights weekends; 3 nights weekends July, August, holidays
Open: All year
Hosts: Barbara and Gerry Liebert; Claudia and John Ryan
684 South Egremont Rd.
Great Barrington, MA 01230
(800) 992-1993 or (413) 528-2720
Fax: (413) 528-5147
wndflowr@windflowerinn.com
www.windflowerinn.com

CLARK TAVERN INN, Hadley

Overall: ★★★★   Room Quality: B   Value: C   Price: $95–$155

Minutemen stayed here en route to the Battle of Concord, and one of the many Early American antiques is a chair from poet Emily Dickinson's estate. The swimming pool is set among flowers, birdsong, and a shimmering water garden. Hearty breakfasts (optionally in your room), evolve from a local organic farm. This bed-and-breakfast is authentic Americana, moved and saved from demolition when the I-91 expressway was built—and lovingly, meticulously restored. The young innkeepers are a big plus: gentle, helpful former health caregivers who not only dote on guests, but on animals wild and domesticated.

SETTING & FACILITIES

Location: I-91 Exit 19, Rt. 9 E 25 mi. to Bay Rd., 1.1 mi. on left
Near: Live music and performances, antiquing, historic Deerfield, Univ. of Mass., 4 colleges
Building: 1742 New England Colonial inn
Grounds: 1+ acres, gardens, priv. garden nooks, hammock, water garden w/ goldfish, pool
Public Space: Keeping room, common room, circular screened patio

Food & Drink: Full breakfast, make choices night before; early breakfast OK; specialties: hot spiced apples, orange French toast, hash browns and ham; vegetarian sausage avail.; beverages all day
Recreation: Bird watching, trails, Conn. River marinas, hot-air balloon or glider rides
Amenities & Services: Binoculars, videos, refrigerator, irons, books, beach towels, recipes, daily papers, (lawn) games, fax

ACCOMMODATIONS

Units: 3 guest rooms
All Rooms: Bath, TV, VCR, table/chairs, phone, dataport
Some Rooms: Fireplace (2), vaulted ceiling w/ chandelier (1)
Bed & Bath: Queens, 2 canopies, high-grade mattresses, roll-aways; baths new, large; showers, tubs, handheld shower, antique sink vanities; hairdryer, forgotten toiletries

Favorites: Gardenview Room—vaulted ceiling, back of inn, large bath; Fireplace Room—fireplace, canopy bed, 4 windows, front of inn, large bath
Comfort & Decor: Colonial decor, yet comfortable and relaxed with modern conveniences. Upholstered chairs. Attractive comforters. Simple, authentic feel. TV nice option. Most queens.

RATES, RESERVATIONS, & RESTRICTIONS

Deposit: 50%; refund w/ 14-day notice
Discounts: Longer stays, singles, off-season
Credit Cards: MC, V, AE, D, DC
Check-in/Out: 3–8/11; call for late arrival
Smoking: Outdoors
Pets: OK w/ prior approval; in-house cats

Kids: Over 12
Open: All Year
Hosts: Ruth and Mike Callahan
98 Bay Rd.
Hadley, MA 01035-9688
(418) 586-1900
Fax: (413) 587-9788
MRCallhn@aol.com
members.aol.com/mrcallhn

APPLEGATE, Lee

Overall: ★★★★	Room Quality: B	Value: C	Price: $120–$240+

In 1929 this was the summer home of a New York surgeon. Indeed, it feels as if you are a guest at a gracious house that hasn't changed much at all—still comfortable, tasteful, and serene, with lots of space, classical music in the air, and a double-size, lived-in living room with built-in bookshelves, and family and guest photos. The screened porch overlooks a swimming pool, and golf is across the street—a rarity at a bed-and-breakfast. Godiva chocolates and brandy awaiting in your room, a game room and a grand piano are other pleasures, and Nancy and Rick pamper ceaselessly. The pillared portico seems grand, but the unpretentious beauty within is grander.

SETTING & FACILITIES

Location: .5 m from center of town; take I-90 to Exit 2, bear right on Rt. 20 into town, pass 1st stop sign to inn on left, across from golf course

Near: Albany Berkshire Ballet; homes of Herman Melville and Edith Wharton; Contemporary Artists Center, Bidwell House, ski area, Mass MoCa Modern

Art Museum, Marionette Theatre; unique Santerella in Tyringham, Sculpture House and Museum; Pittsfield Players, other performing arts, quaint villages, parks, antiquing
Building: 1920s pillared Jeffersonian-style Colonial
Grounds: 6 acres: pines, gardens, rose arbors, old apple trees, croquet
Public Space: Entryway, carved stair-case; spacious LR, TV room, large screened porch
Food & Drink: Cont'l candlelight breakfast; specialty: sour-cream walnut muffins; evening wine and cheese
Recreation: Tennis, golf, boating, horseback riding
Amenities & Services: Pool, baby grand piano, refrigerator, bike storage, pay phone, bikes

ACCOMMODATIONS

Units: 6 main house guest rooms; 1 carriage house apt. (services/rates vary from B&B)
All Rooms: Bath, seating, luggage rack, closet, AC
Some Rooms: Fireplace, garden views
Bed & Bath: Four-poster, canopy, iron and brass, sleigh beds; some shower only, extra-large steam shower (1), pedestal sinks
Favorites: Room 1—largest, most expensive, huge sitting area, steam shower for 2, king four-poster bed, fireplace; Room 6—may be best value, smallest, carved Russian Victorian double bed; Room 5—sunny corner, illusion canopy draped over four-poster bed, garden view
Comfort & Decor: Guest rooms small/average to almost enormous. Stylish elegance, pretty Victorian or romantic touches. Antiques. Some wallpapers detract from otherwise lovely rooms. Fresh flowers, guest journals, brandy and chocolates in room. Two-bedroom carriage suite: living room, TV/VCR, kitchen facilities, priv. deck, whirlpool. Check for minimum stay

RATES, RESERVATIONS, & RESTRICTIONS

Deposit: 1 night, 50% 2+ nights; refund w/ 14-day notice, 30 days July/August
Discounts: Pkgs., 3rd person, mid-week, weekly; carriage house $1,000 weekly
Credit Cards: MC, V
Check-in/Out: 2/11
Smoking: No
Pets: No
Kids: Over 12
Minimum Stay: 2 nights weekends June, Sept., Oct.; 3 nights weekends July, Aug., holidays
Open: All year
Hosts: Nancy Begbie and Rick Cannata 279 West Park St.
Lee, MA 01238
(800) 691-9012 or (413) 243-4451
Fax: (413) 243-4451
nancy@applegateinn.com
www.applegateinn.com

AMADEUS HOUSE, Lenox

Overall: ★★★½	Room Quality: B	Value: C	Price: $80–$225

Books line the walls floor to ceiling, there's a large CD collection, and guests are encouraged to "pick up a baton and conduct a symphony in the living room." Mary and John opened this comfortable, refined turn-of-the-last-century site in 1993. John was a deputy foreign editor for National Public Radio, and Mary is a freelance editor. Like Walker House, rooms are named after composers, and you can sleep in a bird's-eye maple four-poster in namesake Mozart, with his bust staring back at you. Guests rave about the cleanliness and personal service, and the feeling is indeed more like a Mozart concerto here than at the village's other music-oriented bed-and-breakfast (more Brahmsian, perhaps).

SETTING & FACILITIES

Location: At edge of village, near Cliffside B&B; residential side road off village main street
Near: Near center of Lenox Village; Berkshire mountains, Tanglewood, Jacob's Pillow, Theatre Festivals, Hancock Shaker Village, Clark Art Institute, Norman Rockwell Museum, 400-acre John Drummond Kennedy park, ski areas, wildlife sanctuary
Building: Rustic 1820 Colonial farmhouse, Victorian touches

Grounds: .5 acre, lawns
Public Space: Parlor, library, DR
Food & Drink: Full breakfast; specialties: orange waffles, "no-cal" yogurt pancakes; tea
Recreation: Edith Wharton's home, antiquing, boating, horseback riding
Amenities & Services: Extensive recording and book collections, background music, refrigerator, phone, lawn games, chocolate violins, fax

ACCOMMODATIONS

Units: 7 guest rooms, 1 suite
All Rooms: Antiques, clock/radio, fan
Some Rooms: Priv. bath, sitting area, space for add'l guests, priv. porch (1); suite: phone, desk, refrigerator, AC
Bed & Bath: Some antique or four-poster beds; robes for shared bath and suite

Favorites: Sibelius—hostess' favorite, most cozy, shared bath
Comfort & Decor: Sparsely yet richly furnished w/ antique wicker, Shaker and Colonial pieces. Muted wall colors, floral and pastel fabrics. Wreaths, quilts, artwork. 4 room types: small, shared bath; medium, priv. bath; larger, priv. bath; suite, 2 BRs, small living room, kitchen, bath.

RATES, RESERVATIONS, & RESTRICTIONS

Deposit: Full payment summer and fall, weekends and holidays; 1 night midweek off-season; refund w/ 14-day notice
Discounts: 3rd person, midweek rates, weekly rates, special pkgs., off-season dinner pkgs.; spa services
Credit Cards: MC, V, AE, D
Check-in/Out: 2/11:30
Smoking: Not inside or on porches

Pets: No
Kids: Over 10
Minimum Stay: 2 nights weekends and holidays; 3-4 nights weekends late June–Labor Day and some holidays, 2 nights some midweek stays
Open: All year
Hosts: Mary Gottron and John Felton
15 Cliffwood St.
Lenox, MA 01240

(800) 205-4770 or (413) 637-4770
Fax: (413) 637-4484

info@amadeushouse.com
www.amadeushouse.com

BLANTYRE, Lenox

Overall: ★★★★★	Room Quality: A	Value: C	Price: $270–$685

Baronial halls, velvet chairs, antelope heads, rocking horses, turrets, tapestries, whites for tennis, gargoyles, grilled loin of lamb with lemon-thyme-braised turnips, a harpist, fragrant flowers, gentility, friendliness: Blantyre. This estate sanctuary is a cross between a small inn and a luxury hotel, but the level of personal attention here tips it toward inn. A deserving member of Relais & Chateau, this ever-better property does not have the icy attitude of some wannabes. And that, in the end, is why guests feel they get their money's worth. The Fitzpatricks also own the Red Lion Inn in Stockbridge, a classic country hotel.

SETTING & FACILITIES

Location: From Stockbridge, take Rt. 7 N to 2nd light (5 mi.), right onto Rt. 20, .5 m to Blantyre; from Lee, take Exit 2 off Mass. Pike, take Rt. 20 W to inn on right
Near: Botanical gardens, mountains, Tanglewood, Jacob's Pillow, theatre festivals, Hancock Shaker Village, Clark Art Institute, Norman Rockwell Museum, 400-acre John Drummond Kennedy park, ski areas
Building: 1901 mansion reminiscent of Edwardian "castle" w/ Tudor features
Grounds: Nearly 100 acres: lawns, lightly wooded areas, meadows, gardens, trails
Public Space: Museum-quality common rooms, huge hearthed fireplaces; music room; terrace

Food & Drink: Cont'l breakfast; full breakfast, add'l fee; hors d'ouevres in main hall, prix-fixe 3-course dinner; maitre d', over 400 wines, candlelight, harpist; seasonal menu; specialties: grilled squab, pan-roasted black sea bass, warm plum-almond tarts with plum compote and crème fraiche ice cream.
Recreation: Skeet shooting, Lenox fitness center, arts centers and events, museums, historical home tours
Amenities & Services: Tennis, pool, whirlpool, sauna, croquet, newspapers; tennis instruction, ltd. wheelchair access; comp. beverage/snack baskets in rooms, turn-down; corp. and priv. events

ACCOMMODATIONS

Units: 23 total; 3 suites and 5 guest rooms in main house; others in carriage house, cottage suites; 1 secluded 2-BR cottage

All Rooms: Antiques, sitting area, phone, TV, AC
Some Rooms: Fireplace, dressing room, sitting room, 2 baths, 2 double

beds, refrigerator, sliding doors to patio, balcony

Bed & Bath: Antique brass, canopy, four-poster beds, sizes vary; robes, towel warmers

Favorites: Main House rooms—high ceilings, 5 w/ working fireplaces; Windside Carriage House Suite—loft ceiling w/ mural, balcony, spiral staircase to queen bed

Comfort & Decor: Large, grandly elegant rooms. Carriage House located poolside. Grandfather clocks, secretaries, armoires, leather-covered desks. Finely upholstered furnishings. Antique beds, some in bay window alcoves. Large, comfortable conversation areas. Rooms vary from masculine mahogany, to summery wicker, to feminine, romantic. Paterson Suite fit for royalty.

RATES, RESERVATIONS, & RESTRICTIONS

Deposit: 1 night for 1–2 night stay; 1st and last night for longer stays; refund w/ 21-day notice; 10% gratuity added to price

Discounts: 3rd person, special packages

Credit Cards: MC, V, AE, D

Check-in/Out: 3/noon

Smoking: Restricted

Pets: No

Kids: Over 12

Minimum Stay: 2 nights weekends, Sept. 24–Oct. 17

Open: May 14–Nov. 7

Hosts: Senator John Fitzpatrick and family

16 Blantyre Rd.

Lenox, MA 01240

(413) 637-3556

Fax: (413) 637-4282

hide@blantyre.com

www.blantyre.com

BROOK FARM INN, Lenox

Overall: ★★★★	Room Quality: B	Value: C	Price: $90–$210

"There is poetry here," is the credo of this artsy, Victorian bed-and-breakfast, named for a nearby literary commune that celebrated 50 years in 1999. The seasonal newsletter, "Brook Farm Bard," always includes a new poem. Anne and Joe present informal poetry readings at Saturday tea (guests can join in), and offer a daily poem on a podium in a library of 1,500 books. There's music, too. A piano, light opera, show tunes, and classical music on CD, and live chamber music at Sunday breakfasts during Tanglewood season. You can even hear festival practice sessions from the pool area. Oh, and maestro Leonard Bernstein stayed here, when it was a boarding house.

SETTING & FACILITIES

Location: Massachusetts Turnpike to Exit 2 (Lee), turn onto Rt. 183, towards Lenox, bear left at monument in Lenox, left onto Old Stockbridge Rd., right onto Hawthorne St., residential road, walk to village

Near: Dining and shops; walk to Tanglewood, near Berkshires, Jacob's Pillow, theatre festivals, Hancock Shaker Village, Clark Art Institute, Norman Rockwell Museum, 400-acre John Drummond Kennedy park, ski areas
Building: 100-year-old Colonial farmhouse, Victorian touches
Grounds: 1 acre: lawn, garden, hammock
Public Space: Large entry hall, library, DR
Food & Drink: Full buffet breakfast; specialties: egg strata, bread pudding; English tea; 2nd floor guest pantry always open, boiling water faucet, icemaker, beverages
Recreation: Edith Wharton's home, antiquing, tennis, golf, boating, horseback riding
Amenities & Services: Pool, ongoing library puzzle; large collection of poetry, fiction, and history; add'l 70+ poets on tape; guest refrigerator; hall basket of practical toiletries; writing desk in guest pantry; gift cert., recipes

ACCOMMODATIONS

Units: 12 guest rooms
All Rooms: Bath, reading lighting, phone, ceiling fan, AC, carpet
Some Rooms: Fireplace, seating, dormer, stained glass window
Bed & Bath: Some brass, canopy, fourposter beds; some shower only, some tiny baths, all newly tiled
Favorites: Room 1—Spacious, queen canopy, sitting area, fireplace, heartshaped checkers; Room 9—real attic space, skylights, beamed slanted ceilings, 1 queen and 2 twin beds; Bridal suite, Room 2—mahogany canopy bed, fireplace, hand-painted antique hope chest, balcony
Comfort & Decor: Cozy, warm, casually romantic. Quilts, stenciled walls, artwork. Wicker, oak. Lovely mantels, special antiques, rocking chairs. Pastel color schemes. Country, but not rustic. Five rooms remodeled 1998–99. Room sizes vary. Smaller Rooms A, C, 8, and tiny room 7 best values—most attractive, comfortable.

RATES, RESERVATIONS, & RESTRICTIONS

Deposit: 1 night, full payment Tanglewood, foliage season; refund w/ 15-day notice
Discounts: Specials include dinner, spa, sports, art, New Year's pkgs., 3rd person, 7+ night stays, midweek
Credit Cards: MC, V, D
Check-in/Out: 3–8/noon
Smoking: Outside only
Pets: No
Kids: Over 15
No-No's: Facilities and meals for guests only—guests may not bring guests
Minimum Stay: 2 nights most weekends; 3 nights holidays, Tanglewood, foliage season
Open: All year
Hosts: Anne and Joe Miller
15 Hawthorne St.
Lenox, MA 01240
(800) 285-POET or (413) 637-3013
Fax: (413) 637-4751
innkeeper@brookfarm.com
www.brookfarm.com

CLIFFWOOD INN, Lenox

Overall: ★★★★	Room Quality: B	Value: C	Price: $90–$240

Well-traveled Joy and Scottie lived in France, Belgium, Italy, and Canada and bring international flair to this former summer home built for McEvers Livingston, one-time U.S. diplomat to France. With 12-foot ceilings, inlaid floors, and a veranda overlooking the pool, it was built during the "Gilded Age," from 1880–1920 when Lenox became "inland Newport," as Vanderbilts, Morgans, and Carnegies grew bored with their Rhode Island favorite. The hosts are dealers for quality Eldred Wheeler Colonial reproduction furniture, and the atmosphere is stylish, but not standoffish; in fact, to get to the indoor lap pool and spa you have to go through the basement.

SETTING & FACILITIES

Location: I-90 E to Lee exit, take Rt. 20 to Rt. 7A N to Lenox, look for signs to B&B, on quiet, residential street
Near: 2 blocks from center of Lenox Village; Berkshire mountains, Tanglewood, Jacob's Pillow, theatre festivals, Hancock Shaker Village, Clark Art Institute, Edith Wharton's home, Norman Rockwell Museum, 400-acre John Drummond Kennedy park, ski areas, walk to dining and shops
Building: 1890s Stanford White–style Colonial Revival mansion, Belle-Epoque flourishes
Grounds: 1.5 acres: gardens, picnic gazebo, deck, pool

Public Space: Entry foyer; LR, music room; DR; common rooms
Food & Drink: Cont'l breakfast; p.m. wine and cheese; breakfast served most seasons; otherwise, coupon for breakfast locally
Recreation: Boating, golf, horseback riding, winter sports
Amenities & Services: Outdoor pool; indoor counter-current pool, whirlpool, winter robes for pool; refrigerator, BYOB set-ups; activities guidebook computer created by hosts, seat cushions/beach chairs for Tanglewood

ACCOMMODATIONS

Units: 6 guest rooms, 1 suite
All Rooms: Bath, seating, ceiling fan, AC
Some Rooms: Fireplace (6), small writing desk, small TV (4)
Bed & Bath: Some canopy, four-poster beds, antique double (1), queen (1), king/twin sizes; some shower only, hall access bath w/ robes (1); whirlpool (1), skylight; fireplace (1)

Favorites: Jacob Grosse Jr. Room—fireplace, seating, canopy king, full bath, balcony; Walker/Linton suite—king four-poster canopy, curtained partition sitting room w/ fireplace, hidden TV, shower bath
Comfort & Decor: Strong European influence. Contemporary art pieces, personal, period antiques. Corner fireplace in most expensive Helen Walker

room w/whirlpool bath. Best value: Karl Stimm room, hall access priv. bath, fireplace, four-poster double bed. Cozy

Catherine White room on 3rd floor w/ king bed, fireplace in bath, visible from bed.

RATES, RESERVATIONS, & RESTRICTIONS

Deposit: Full payment at reservation; refund w/ 14-day notice
Discounts: Midweek rates, except high season; 3rd person
Credit Cards: None
Check-in/Out: 2–10/11
Smoking: Gazebo only
Pets: No
Kids: Over 11
No-No's: Guests' guests using premises; personal food on-premises except gazebo or lower deck

Minimum Stay: 2 nights (some rooms 3) weekends foliage season; 3 nights (some rooms 4) all week Tanglewood season; 3 nights (some rooms 4) some weekends other seasons
Open: All year
Hosts: Joy and Scottie Farrelly
25 Cliffwood St.
Lenox, MA 01240
(800) 789-3331 or (413) 637-3330
Fax: (413) 637-0221
joy@cliffwood.com
www.cliffwood.com

THE GABLES INN, Lenox

Overall: ★★★★	Room Quality: A	Value: B	Price: $90–$225

Edith Wharton, author of *The Age of Innocence* among many other nineteenth-century novels, spent two productive years writing in the eight-sided library—while waiting for her nearby mansion, The Mount, to be completed. The Gables was then known as The Pines and was home to her mother-in-law. With its red damask paper, portrait of Edith above the parlor mantel, and florid furnishings, the bed-and-breakfast seems much as it must have in its glamorous heyday. Frank is a stage producer and knows and hosts many celebs, so the glamour continues. Warmth isn't the draw here; dramatic decor, luxury suites, history, and the tennis court and swimming pool are what sells.

SETTING & FACILITIES

Location: From south, follow Rt. 7 N through Stockbridge, bear left onto Rt. 7A to Lenox, look for signs to inn
Near: Berkshire mountains, Tanglewood, Jacob's Pillow, theatre festivals, Hancock Shaker Village, Clark Art Institute, Norman Rockwell Museum, 400-acre John Drummond Kennedy park, Edith Wharton's home, ski areas, walk to dining and shops
Building: Circa 1900 Queen Anne "cottage"
Grounds: Gardens, waterfall, patio

Public Space: Entrance hall, library, staircase, breakfast room
Food & Drink: Full breakfast; specialties: French toast, breads and pastries
Recreation: Shopping, antiquing, tennis, golf, boating, horseback riding, some bike rentals, skiing
Amenities & Services: Summer indoor pool, summer tennis court, grand piano, rare document/book collection, recorded music library features pre-Sondheim Broadway themes, BYOB setups; 1st floor rooms disabled accessible

ACCOMMODATIONS

Units: 12 guest rooms, 4 suites
All Rooms: Bath, seating, antiques, clock/radio, phone, AC
Some Rooms: Fireplace, sitting area, desk, balcony, TV/VCR, refrigerator
Bed & Bath: Antique beds, incl. quilted headboards, elaborately carved Edwardian-style headboards, canopy and four-poster beds; some shower-only
Favorites: Edith Wharton suite—fireplace, plush carpet, four-poster w/

charming quilt, seating area, artwork feminine and romantic; Teddy Wharton suite—most popular, masculine counterpart, boldly striped wallcoverings, leather sofa, carved bed
Comfort & Decor: Rooms smallish. Suites are 1 large room. TVs small, not hidden. High ceilings, carpet-on-carpet. Lushly decorated according to themes. Rose Room w/ bay window most romantic. President's Room, presidential photos, autographs, private balcony.

RATES, RESERVATIONS, & RESTRICTIONS

Deposit: 1 night, full payment Tanglewood season; refund w/ 14-day notice
Discounts: 3rd person
Credit Cards: MC, V, D
Check-in/Out: 2/noon
Smoking: Restricted, and no cigars
Pets: No
Kids: Over 12
No-No's: Others besides guests using facil., lingering too long over breakfast, taking NY Times out of library and

reading at breakfast table
Minimum Stay: 2 nights, Oct., all holiday weekends; 3 nights, Tanglewood season, some holidays
Open: All year
Hosts: Mary and Frank Newton
103 Walker St., Route 183
Lenox, MA 01240
(800) 382-9401 or (413) 637-3416
www.gableslenox.com

WALKER HOUSE, Lenox

Overall: ★★★★   Room Quality: C   Value: C   Price: $85–$220

This bed-and-breakfast has a doorbell that plays Beethoven's "Ode to Joy." Peggy was editor of *Performing Arts* magazine, and Richard was a music critic and arts administrator, so the conversation at this comfortable, cluttered, Federal-era house is lively and artsy. The library has hundreds of videos and a 12-foot movie-mogul-like screen. A third plus, depending on your preferences, is the pet-friendly environment. Four-legged guests may especially enjoy the giant stuffed animal "tea party" around an antique oak table and the animal-shaped doorstop collection on the stairs. And as for the rooms, Handel is airy, Verdi has lime-green wallpaper, and Puccini has a porch.

SETTING & FACILITIES

Location: Near center of Lenox across from Gables Inn
Near: Berkshires mountains, Tanglewood, Jacob's Pillow, theatre festivals, Shaker Village, Clark Art Institute, Norman Rockwell Museum, Edith Wharton's home, 400-acre John Drummond Kennedy park, ski areas, walk to dining and shops
Building: 1804 Federal Clapboard, Greek Revival touches
Grounds: 3 landscaped and natural, wooded, acres; picnics encouraged

Public Space: Parlor, library, DR, screened porch
Food & Drink: Generous cont'l breakfast, communal; homemade muffins; afternoon tea
Recreation: Golf, boating, horseback riding
Amenities & Services: Comp. summer tennis at Lenox Tennis Club, games, grand piano, extra beds avail., large-screen TV, refrigerator, bike storage; radio/tape recorders, old-time radio show tapes, quarterly B&B newsletter; weddings, reunions

ACCOMMODATIONS

Units: 8 guest rooms
All Rooms: Bath, clock/radio, AC
Some Rooms: Fireplace, sitting area, priv. small porch (1)
Bed & Bath: Antique, four-poster, canopy beds, sizes vary; some claw-foot soaking tubs, some shower only
Favorites: Mozart—Mahogany furnishings, antique loveseat, queen fishnet

canopy bed, antique harpsichord, fireplace
Comfort & Decor: Fairly spacious rooms w/ 1 exception, named for composers. Period furnishings, wallcoverings, artwork. Little touches of added comfort, wine, bubble bath. Not high style, but comfy.

RATES, RESERVATIONS, & RESTRICTIONS

Deposit: 1 night; 3 nights July, August, holidays; refund w/ 14-day notice
Discounts: 3rd person, weekly, mid-

week, packages
Credit Cards: None
Check-in/Out: 2/noon

Smoking: No
Pets: Well-behaved dogs by prior arrangement, dog sitting avail.
Kids: Over 12
Minimum Stay: 3 nights in July, August, holidays
Open: All year

Hosts: Peggy and Richard Houdek
64 Walker St.
Lenox, MA 01240
(800) 235-3098 or (413) 637-1271
Fax: (413) 637-2387
phoudek@vgernet.net
www.walkerhouse.com

THE SALTBOX, Northampton

Overall: ★★★★	Room Quality: B	Value: C	Price: $85–$130

College town inns and bed-and-breakfasts don't always have the incentive to sparkle because they can count on group- and student-related business much of the year. But this little property, right across from the Smith College campus, sparkles away. Craig is the president of a local hospital. Carol's background includes design, and her decorating flair is evident throughout. Rooms are refurbished to bring out history of this eighteenth-century house (named for its architectural style) with a light, welcoming touch. Unassuming, tasteful, comfortable, welcoming.

SETTING & FACILITIES

Location: Exit 18 from 91N (20 min. from Mass. Turnpike and Rt. 2); across the street from Smith College, Botanical Gardens, Paradise Pond, and Noll River
Near: UMass, Hampshire, Amherst, Mt. Holyoke, Deerfield, Williston, Conn. River, Berkshires, arts venues and outdoor recreation
Building: 1784–86 home; converted 1997
Grounds: Priv. backyard, flower gardens, seating areas
Public Space: Entry hall, small guest parlor and breakfast room; disabled access

Food & Drink: Buffet breakfast w/ fresh, seasonal ingredients; in room possible; specialties: coffee from local roaster, poached pears, crisps, baked apples; wine glasses, corkscrew, welcome snacks; special items avail. with advance notice; dozens of restaurants in walking distance
Recreation: Skiing, tennis, picnicking; walking distance to YMCA
Amenities & Services: Newspapers on weekends, maps/books, irons, cell phones; can reserve entire property (30-day cancellation policy)

ACCOMMODATIONS

Units: 3 suites
All Rooms: Bath, priv. entrance, heat controls, AC, TV, sitting area
Some Rooms: Efficiency kitchen, disabled access, daybed, priv. patio

Bed & Bath: 2 queens (one w/ add'l, quilted daybed in alcove), 1 double; excellent mattresses; heated towel racks; whirlpools for 2, oversized showers (w/seats), tub/showers

Favorites: Hester's Retreat—queen four-poster, seating/sleeping alcove, dbl. whirlpool; The Sabbatical—queen four-poster, wicker seating area, efficiency kitchen

Comfort & Decor: Upstairs rooms overlooking Holyoke Mountain Range, best in winter. Creative style. Comfortable and cheery. Ground-floor room, separate entrance and patio, especially good for smokers.

RATES, RESERVATIONS, & RESTRICTIONS

Deposit: 50%, refund w/ 14-day notice; can book through travel agency
Discounts: Long stays, 3rd person
Credit Cards: MC, V, AE, D
Check-in/Out: 2–6/11
Smoking: No
Pets: No; in-house cat and schnauzer
Kids: Older children OK

Minimum Stay: 2 nights, weekends; 3, holiday weekends
Open: All year
Hosts: Carol and Craig Melin
153 Elm St.
Northampton, MA 01060
(413) 584-1790
www.javanet.com/~saltbox

HISTORIC MERRELL INN, South Lee

Overall: ★★★½	Room Quality: C	Value: C	Price: $85–$225

Built in 1794 for a general in the Massachusetts militia, this columned building was turned into a stagecoach stop, and the framed visages of the original innkeepers stare out in the tavern room. The circular birdcage bar is the last extant example of its kind in this country. The sliding bars protected the liquor, the cash, and the bartender from rowdy highwaymen. Today's guests may not be as disorderly, but they do enjoy the same river views, beehive oven, candlebeam lighting, and seconds at breakfast. And the country guest rooms, while small and simple, are undoubtedly more romantic than when the Merrells presided.

SETTING & FACILITIES

Location: On Housatonic River; 1 mi. E of Stockbridge Village
Near: Quaint Stockbridge Village, Norman Rockwell Museum, Tanglewood, theater festivals, Jacob's Pillow Modern Dance Festival, outlets; Lee and Lenox Villages, ski areas
Building: 200 year-old plantation-style Federal
Grounds: 2 riverfront acres, parklike lawns, gazebo, hammocks

Public Space: Parlor; tavern room, rare birdcage bar; keeping room; TV room
Food & Drink: Full breakfast, choice of entrees; specialties: basil/cheese omelets, blueberry pancakes, sausage
Recreation: Picnics, mountain swimming, scenic drives, antiquing
Amenities & Services: Refrigerator, BYOB set-ups

ACCOMMODATIONS

Units: 9 guest rooms, 1 suite
All Rooms: Bath, phone, TV, AC
Some Rooms: Fireplace, desk, seating or sitting area
Bed & Bath: Some canopy, half-canopy beds; queen, king/twin sizes; most shower only
Favorites: Room 1—Emerald-green walls, paisley fabrics, canopy queen, fireplace, wood floors, sofa; Room 3—river view, country decor, fireplace;

Riverview Suite—sep. wing, fireplace, bookshelves, dining table, balcony overlooking river
Comfort & Decor: Rather small rooms, well furnished. Decor from Early American to country. Walls painted Federal colors or papered w/ romantic or country prints. Window swags, Oriental carpets. VCR. Some rooms dark. B&B is close to road, back rooms quietest.

RATES, RESERVATIONS, & RESTRICTIONS

Deposit: 1 night, refund w/ 14-day notice
Discounts: Off-season packages, corp. rates
Credit Cards: MC, V
Check-in/Out: 2–10/11
Smoking: No
Pets: No
Kids: Check w/ B&B, no cribs; no kids in summer season

Minimum Stay: 2 nights weekends; 3 nights July, August
Open: All year, except Christmas week
Hosts: Faith and Charles Reynolds
1565 Pleasant St., Rt. 102
South Lee, MA 01260
(800) 243-1794 or (413) 243-1794
Fax: (413) 243-2669
info@merrell-inn.com
www.merrell-inn.com

FIELD FARM GUEST HOUSE, Williamstown

Overall: ★★★★½	Room Quality: A	Value: C	Price: $125

Here's a chance to stay in a modern art museum set in almost 300 acres of unspoiled nature. Actually, it's the former house of art patron Lawrence Bloedel, and although much of his collection is now in museums, including the nearby Williams College Museum of Art, many of the sculptures and handmade furniture from this American modern 1948 cedar building do remain. The views of the countryside and mountains beyond are as beautiful as the artwork. Enjoy the pool, tennis, and the on-site Folly House, opened only for tours. This unique haven for modernists and nature-lovers is managed by a Massachusetts land conservation trust, started in 1891.

SETTING & FACILITIES

Location: At the foot of the Taconic mountain range in North Berkshire County; Rt. 7 S from Williamstown to
Rt. 43 S, right onto Sloan Rd., 1.2 mi. farther on right

Near: Williamstown Theatre Festival, Clark Art Institute, Williams College, Mountain Meadow Preserve, Jiminy Peak ski area, Pittsfield Players
Building: 1948 American modern-style contemporary 16-room main house; unique circular structure; 2nd building, Folly House, built as guest house, 1966
Grounds: 296 acres: mountain views, sculptures, gardens, beaver pond, corn fields, meadows, woods; 4 mi. of trails

Public Space: Large LR, DR, common terrace, kitchen and pantry
Food & Drink: Full breakfast, communal; specialties: Friendship bread, egg pie, granola, peach French toast
Recreation: Picnicking, bird watching, lake boating; natural activities, incl. Dinosaur Footprints, Ashley Falls
Amenities & Services: Heated summer pool, tennis court, pantry and refrigerator, phone, books, small nature center

ACCOMMODATIONS

Units: 5 guest rooms
All Rooms: Bath, reading lamps, alarm clock, fresh flowers, picture window
Some Rooms: Priv. deck, fireplace, writing desk
Bed & Bath: Some w/ Scandinavian-style bookshelf headboards, queen, twin sizes; some shower only, range from quite small to fairly spacious, 1940s vintage baths

Favorites: Master Room—most spacious, fireplace, large deck, views, large bath; North Room—queen, fireplace w/ butterfly tiles, mirrored dressing table, coziest
Comfort & Decor: Sparsely furnished, in keeping w/ museum-style contemporary theme. Top-quality 1950s spare furnishings. Graceful table light fixtures. Tile-bordered fireplaces. Original artwork. TVs, phones deliberately excluded.

RATES, RESERVATIONS, & RESTRICTIONS

Deposit: 50%; refund w/ 14-day notice
Discounts: 3rd person, singles
Credit Cards: MC, V, D
Check-in/Out: 2–10/11
Smoking: Outside only
Pets: Not inside house, welcome on grounds

Kids: Welcome—no cots or cribs
Open: All year
Hosts: Jean Marie and Sean Cowhig
554 Sloan Rd.
Williamstown, MA 01267
(413) 458-3135
Fax: Same as phone, call first

RIVER BEND FARM, Williamstown

Overall: ★★★½	Room Quality: C	Value: C	Price: $90

This truly historic, truly authentic Colonial house was built by one of Williamstown's original founders and commander of the victorious Massachusetts forces at the Revolutionary Battle of Bennington, which was planned in the Tap Room. Ethan Allen, Seth Warner, and Benedict Arnold all walked these wavy floors, in spare rooms with the same details today.

The chimney provides five fireplaces, two bake-ovens, an attic smoking chamber, and a cellar ash pit. Restoration is total throughout the house; there's no plastic anywhere, bread is fresh-baked, as it was for Revolutionary soldiers, and you feel transported 200 years back. Yes, bathrooms are shared, but the chamber pots are for decoration only.

SETTING & FACILITIES

Location: On Rt. 7, "intown" country setting
Near: 1 mi. from village and Williams College; Hoosic River adjacent to property, Appalachian Trail, Mount Graylock, ski areas, museum, Clark Art Institute, Mass MoCA, Williamstown Theater Festival, Pittsfield Players; 40 min. to Yale Summer Chamber Music Festival, Tanglewood, Jacob's Pillow, Shaker Village, Berkshire attractions; 15 mi. to Pittsfield; day trip to Saratoga
Building: Col. Benjamin Simonds House, c. 1770, river valley restored Georgian Colonial

Grounds: 5 acres, picnic area, gardens, patio, mountain views
Public Space: LR; orig. tap room, "funeral" or "casket" side door; keeping room, originally borning room and sick room, w/ open hearth fireplace and bake oven
Food & Drink: Cont'l breakfast, communal; granola, muffins, jam, honey; p.m. tea on request; fresh fruit
Recreation: Golf, tennis, horseback riding, bikes avail. for rent in town, sleigh/carriage rides
Amenities & Services: Refrigerator, phone, picnic area, canoe

ACCOMMODATIONS

Units: 4 guest rooms
All Rooms: Authentic Colonial furnishings
Some Rooms: Decorative mantel, wainscoting
Bed & Bath: Double, twin, four-posters, rope beds, feather mattresses; 1 room and shower bath on 1st floor; 3 rooms and bath w/ claw-foot tub on 2nd floor

Favorites: Parlor Room—decorative open hearth fireplace, double antique rope four-poster, Oriental rugs
Comfort & Decor: Rooms large. Not cozy or romantic in 20th-century sense. Early American simplicity, modernized. Wing-backed chairs, braided or Oriental rugs on wide-plank flooring, dried flowers, Colonial light fixtures, spinning wheels. Federal colors.

RATES, RESERVATIONS, & RESTRICTIONS

Deposit: 50%; refund w/ 14-day notice
Discounts: Add'l person, group rental
Credit Cards: None
Check-in/Out: Upon request
Smoking: Outside only
Pets: No
Kids: Welcome w/ prior arrangement

Minimum Stay: 2 nights some weekends in summer
Open: April–Oct.
Hosts: Judy and Dave Loomis
643 Simonds Rd., Route 7
Williamstown, MA 01267
(413) 458-3121

Zone 13
Cape Cod

Cape Cod—that flat, narrow, breezy peninsula that looks on a map like a flexed bicep—is an hour southeast of Boston, and a great place to relax. If you want to veg out on a ribbon of sandy beach, backed by undulating sand dunes (once substituted as the Sahara in silent movies), the Cape is still the perfect spot. But it isn't just a beach destination or the place to catch the Martha's Vineyard or Nantucket ferries.

When the sun is too intense, or for an off-season visit, there's still plenty to keep you occupied. You can drive, bike, or walk the 300-mile shoreline. The Cape Cod Rail Trail is 25 miles of former train tracks, and another path from the Salt Pond Visitor's Center passes dunes, sea grasses, and wooden bridges. Kite flying, whale watching, antiquing, shopping, golfing, theater-going, and slurping clam chowder are other pleasures.

The 27,000-acre Cape Cod National Seashore is the best place to explore wild flora and fauna. Woods Hole is home to the National Marine Fisheries Aquarium and the Woods Hole Oceanographic Institute. Lighthouses, as traditional as boats hauling catches on wooden wharves, dot the shoreline. The Highland Light, built in 1795, is in North Truro, and the Scargo Hill Observation Tower in Dennis has a view across Cape Cod Bay.

History, recent and not-so, is here, from the John F. Kennedy Museum in Hyannis to the 1797 Grist Mill in Chatham, at the "elbow" of this peninsula. Eastham has a one-room schoolhouse, and Brewster has the Cape Cod Museum of Natural History and Expedition. Pretty, old Sandwich, established in 1637, sparkles with a glass museum and restored homes at Heritage Plantation. Whydah Sea Lab in Provincetown is the home of pirate treasure (in fact, the only such authentic place in the world).

Colors seem brighter in the sun of the Cape. Crimson sunsets, scarlet cranberry bogs, cherry-red lobsters and geraniums, burgundy chrysanthemums—these hues, and blue, yellow, and green as well seem to come into focus in the clear air. And the night, pierced by silver sprinkles, seems black velvet.

Gabled, gray-shingled homes—many of them built by sea captains—are scattered along Route 6A, the Old King's Highway and still Cape Cod's main road, which can get mighty congested in summer. Many homes have

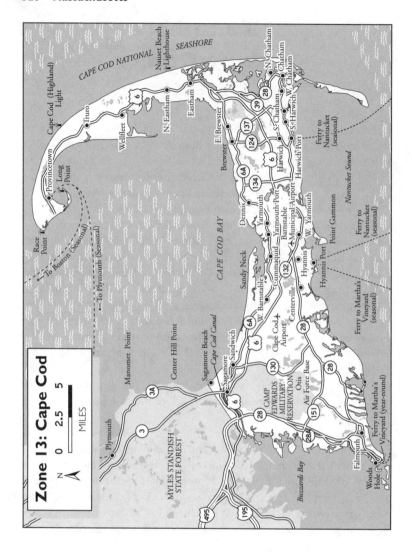

Zone 13: Cape Cod

been turned into alluring bed-and-breakfasts and small inns. Some stay open throughout the year, though most close in the dead of winter. Summer weekends need to be booked way ahead, but in September, still warm here but delightfully uncrowded, rooms are often available last minute, especially midweek.

For More Information
Bed & Breakfast Cape Cod
Nantucket: (800) 686-5252
fax: (508) 775-2884
email: bedandb@capecod.net

Harwich Acommodations Association (HAA)
(508) 432-7166 or (800) 321-3155
email: lionhead@capecod.net

Orleans Bed & Breakfast Associates
Bed & Breakfast Cape Cod: (508) 225-3824 or (800) 541-6226
fax: (508) 240-0599
email: orleansbnb@capecod.net
www.capecod.net/bb

THE CAPTAIN FREEMAN INN, Brewster

Overall: ★★★★	Room Quality: B	Value: C	Price: $100–$220

Carol is a gourmet chef with her own cooking classes and Tom raises orchids and creates stained glass. Their talents are put to obvious use in this award-winning bed-and-breakfast. Breakfasts and snacks are lavish and fresh, in good weather served on the screened porch or by the herb and perennial gardens surrounding the pool. The careful restoration of this captain's mansion is recorded in photos, fun to study by the fireplace. The feeling of romance is evident, perhaps because the innkeepers themselves were married here.

SETTING & FACILITIES

Location: Exit 10 off Rt. 6, faces "Currier and Ives" town green
Near: Cape Cod Nat'l Seashore, theater, Museum of Natural History and Exhibition, Cape Cod Bay, antiquing, galleries
Building: 1866 Victorian
Grounds: 1.5 acres: woods, gardens, pool
Public Space: Parlor, screened dining porch, DR, sitting room
Food & Drink: Full breakfast, freshly squeezed juice, fruit; specialties: French sausage pastry, eggs Benedict, lemon–wild rice pancakes; tea, lemonade, mulled cider, baked goods, fruit
Recreation: Whale/bird watching, golf, tennis, biking, all water sports, horseback riding
Amenities & Services: Badminton, croquet, bikes, binoculars, videos, refrigerator, beach towels, recipes, daily papers; meetings (25–30), fax, e-mail, flipchart, overhead; laundry, ironing, pick-up from plane/train; winter cooking school, weekends

ACCOMMODATIONS

Units: 6 guest rooms, 6 luxury rooms
All Rooms: Bath, sitting area, hairdryer, antique desk, large closet or armoire, dresser
Some Rooms: AC, refrigerator, TV/VCR, phone w/ answering system, fireplace, dbl. whirlpool
Bed & Bath: Queen canopies; 2-person whirlpools or tub/shower combo
Favorites: The Eastham Room—2nd floor, fireplace, large sitting area, sunset view from balcony whirlpool
Comfort & Decor: Antique Victorian furnishings, wood floors, period decorating. Baths: marble and tile or original wood floors with plaster detail. Wicker, lace canopies. Two rooms disabled accessible. Luxury rooms just that.

RATES, RESERVATIONS, & RESTRICTIONS

Deposit: Full payment, 1–3 nights; 50% others; for stays of 4+ nights, balance due 14 days before arrival; cancellations within 14 days refunded only if room rerented
Discounts: Add-on pkgs. for special occasions: champagne and two 45-min. massages in-room by masseuse, 3rd person
Credit Cards: MC, V, AE

Check-in/Out: 2–8/11
Smoking: No
Pets: No
Kids: Over 10
Minimum Stay: 2 nights
Open: All year

Hosts: Carol and Tom Edmondson
15 Breakwater Rd.
Brewster, MA 02631
(508) 896-7481, (800) 843-4664
Fax: (508) 896-5618
visitus@capecodnet
www.captainfreemaninn.com

FERNBROOK INN, Centerville

| Overall: ★★★★ | Room Quality: B | Value: C | Price: $110–$150 |

Built in 1881 by a hotelier from Boston's Parker House, this gabled Queen Anne has landscaping and a heart-shaped rose garden designed by F.L. Olmsted of Central Park fame. The next owner co-invented Technicolor, and hosted Disney, DeMille, and other Hollywood types. Left to the Catholic church, the grand house became a retreat, and later a summer home for Boston's Cardinal Francis Spellman, whose guests included John Kennedy Sr. and Richard Nixon. Recent guests have been Bill Murray and Alec Baldwin, visiting the nearby Kennedy Compound. Friendly new owner Mary Anne is a European-trained art historian. You can stay in the former chapel, amid stained glass and real cathedral ceilings.

SETTING & FACILITIES

Location: Exit 5 Mid-Cape Highway, cross Route 149; first right on Old Stage Rd.; continue to lights at Route 28, continue straight; road turns into Main St., B&B on left

Near: Antiquing, beaches, boat/ferry trips, Kennedy compound in Hyannis, JFK Museum
Building: 1881 Queen Anne Victorian; Nat'l Register of Hist. Places

Grounds: Landscaping by Frederic Law Olmsted in 1881; heart-shaped sweetheart—1 acre (out of orig. 18), rose garden, ponds, unusual trees and plantings

Public Space: Ballroom, LR, DR all formal; sitting room/orig. library; 2 large covered porches

Food & Drink: Full breakfast; specialty: crabmeat/cheese quiche; afternoon tea, cakes

Recreation: Skeet shooting, whale watching; Fourth of July parade watching; Christmas stroll on Main St., Centerville Old Home Week in August

Amenities & Services: Refrigerator, irons, books, beach towels; meetings (80), weddings

ACCOMMODATIONS

Units: 7 guest rooms, 1 cottage

All Rooms: Bath, individual furnishings

Some Rooms: Fireplace, refrigerator, priv. entrance, TV, sitting room

Bed & Bath: Twins, queens, kings, some canopies, four-posters; full baths, new baths

Favorites: The Cardinal Room—formerly chapel, cathedral ceiling, stained glass, TV, exquisite antiques, sweetheart garden view; Cottage—cathedral ceiling, living area, TV, cooking facil., balcony, flowers

Comfort & Decor: Rooms named after events in the inn's history. Oriental rugs. Hardwood floors. Antiques, sitting rooms, sundeck, suite in turret.

RATES, RESERVATIONS, & RESTRICTIONS

Deposit: 50%; refund w/ 14-day notice

Credit Cards: None

Check-in/Out: 1/11; flexible

Smoking: Porches only

Pets: No

Kids: Over 12

No-No's: More than 2 to a room

Open: All year

Hosts: Mary Anne Wuthrich
481 Main St.
Centerville, MA 02632
(508) 775-4999

CYRUS KENT HOUSE INN, Chatham

Overall: ★★★★	Room Quality: B	Value: C	Price: $95–$280

The bright and elegant innkeeper, a long-time local, has created, not unexpectedly, a bright and elegant inn. "I remember walking past the house when it was being restored, but I never would have believed I'd own it," Sharon has said. Her previous career as fashion buyer reflects itself throughout the property, with taste and style. White carpets within echo the white clapboard exterior of the inn and adjoining carriage house. The cozy kitchen has a brick hearth, which you can see through the wainscoted dining room's Dutch door. Modern amenities and tradition, past and present, mingle throughout.

SETTING & FACILITIES

Location: Close to downtown Chatham, in residential neighborhood, 1 block from Main St.
Near: Galleries, dining, shopping, beach; whale watching, Cape Cod Nat'l Seashore
Building: White Victorian Clapboard, carriage house
Grounds: Landscaped yard, parking area
Public Space: LR, DR, deck, porch overlook gardens

Food & Drink: Homebaked cont'l breakfast; specialties: hot fruit compote, granola; afternoon tea and coffee
Recreation: Fishing, whale watching, beach, bike trails
Amenities & Services: Beach towels, recipes, daily paper, baby grand piano, refrigerator, irons, kitchen privileges; meetings (12), weddings/groups (20)

ACCOMMODATIONS

Units: 11 guest rooms, 3 suites
All Rooms: Bath, phone, TV
Some Rooms: AC (9), priv. entrance
Bed & Bath: Queen and full beds, canopies, four-posters; baths w/ showers only (4)
Favorites: Room 10—large BR w/ fireplace and canopy bed; Room 8, in Carriage House—2nd floor, canopy

bed, fireplace, cathedral ceiling, sitting area
Comfort & Decor: Each room unique. Many antiques. Bedrooms restored to preserve original character. 4 w/ parlor beds. Deluxe rooms in Carriage House, sitting rooms and fireplaces. Real flair.

RATES, RESERVATIONS, & RESTRICTIONS

Deposit: One night; refund w/ 10-day notice or charge 1 night as future stay credit; can book through travel agency
Discounts: Long stays, seniors; groups can reserve entire, 3rd person
Credit Cards: MC, V, AE
Check-in/Out: 2–8/11–12
Smoking: No
Pets: No
Kids: Over 6

Minimum Stay: 2 nights
Open: All year
Hosts: Sharon Mitchell Swan
63 Cross St.
Chatham, MA 02633
(800) 338-5368; (508) 945-9104
Fax: (508) 945-9104
info@cyruskent.com
www.cyraskent.com

MARY ROCKWELL STUART HOUSE, Chatham

| Overall: ★★★½ | Room Quality: B | Value: C | Price: $110–$275 |

It's fun to watch an emerging property ripen. Opened in 1998, this former private mansion is very much a work in progress, and the enthusiastic owners are still wallpapering, replacing windows, and upgrading patios, outdoor furniture, and landscaping. They are delighted that people stop to admire their efforts, and plan to restore with function, warmth, history, and romance in mind. "The porch, with its pillars and railings, seems to define the house," says Deborah, who met hubby, Ron, at an inn, and knows the power of romantic ambiance. As for local color, the three-hour Fourth of July parade passes in front, and band concerts are nearby.

SETTING & FACILITIES

Location: Rotary through town to 314 Main St., at end
Near: Lighthouse Beach, shopping, Nantucket/Martha's Vineyard ferries, fishing pier, Monomoy Island wildlife refuge
Building: Prestigious-looking Victorian Cape, 1823–1901
Grounds: 1 acre set off from Main St., ocean views, mill pond across street; porches, patio
Public Space: Large LR, breakfast room, wraparound porch
Food & Drink: Full breakfast; specialties: Stuart Scrambler w/ ham and cheese, sourdough French toast, blueberry pancakes, baked goods, fresh fruit; hors d'oeuvres w/ hosts Sat. evenings; afternoon tea
Recreation: Fishing, whale watching, boating, tennis, antiquing
Amenities & Services: Irons, books, daily papers, disabled access, meetings (12), picnic lunches (extra)

ACCOMMODATIONS

Units: 4 guest rooms, 2 suites
All Rooms: Bath, gas fireplace, ceiling fan, phone, hairdryer, toiletries
Some Rooms: Deck, disabled access
Bed & Bath: Queens, some four-posters, iron, brass, cherry spindle; new, large baths, spacious counters, Corian sinks, tile floors, tub (1)
Favorites: Large 3rd floor room—wonderful views, deck, fireplace; 1st floor suite—spacious, priv. porch, priv. entrance
Comfort & Decor: Individually decorated. Spacious rooms with antiques, comfortable chairs, pine floors, quilts. Light and airy w/ big windows. Four rooms on second floor. Fireplaces nice touch.

RATES, RESERVATIONS, & RESTRICTIONS

Deposit: 1 night by check or credit card; refund w/ 7-day notice
Discounts: Off-season
Credit Cards: MC, V, AE
Check-in/Out: 3/11
Smoking: No
Pets: No; in-house indoor white Persian cat
Kids: Over 14
No-No's: More than 2 people in a room
Minimum Stay: 2 nights holidays, season weekends
Open: All year
Hosts: Deborah and Ron McClelland
314 Main St.
Chatham, MA 02633
(508) 945-4634
Fax: (508) 945-8012
www.axs.com/mrshouse

ACWORTH INN, Cummaquid

Overall: ★★★★	Room Quality: B	Value: C	Price: $85–$185

This small, typical Cape house displays flowers within and without, and its all-white look is fresh and pretty. But the warmth and cheerfulness of the innkeepers is the real strength. They love to recommend jazz clubs and bird-watching spots, and greet guests as if they were forever friends. Classical music, a crackling fire, ribbons and greenery on breakfast tables, heart-shaped waffles—no charming detail is overlooked. (Even embossed toilet paper!) Guest journals reflect the appreciation of happy visitors.

SETTING & FACILITIES

Location: 4.6 mi. E of Rt. 6A off Rt. 132N; N side of Mid-Cape
Near: Cape Cod Nat'l Seashore, Hyannis Airport, antiquing, galleries, historic landmarks, beaches, ferries to Nantucket and Martha's Vineyard, summer theatre
Building: Secluded 1860 Greek Revival
Grounds: .3-acre flower and herb garden
Public Space: Sitting room, library, dining area, deck

Food & Drink: Buffet breakfast; specialties: low-fat granola, seasonal fruit w/ edible flowers, fresh pastries, hot entrees; cranberry spritzers on arrival; afternoon tea; nearest restaurant 2 min.
Recreation: Whale watching, golf, tennis, boating, horseback riding
Amenities & Services: Daily papers, recipes, beach towels, bikes, irons, fax, books, fluent German

ACCOMMODATIONS

Units: 4 guest rooms, 1 suite
All Rooms: Bath, triple sheeting, fresh flowers, toiletries
Some Rooms: AC, fireplace, tub and shower, sitting area; suite: whirlpool, gas fireplace, mini-refrigerator
Bed & Bath: Queens, some canopy; some tubs, robes

Favorites: Cummaquid Room—1st floor, fireplace, French doors, full bath; Yarmouth Port Room—2nd floor, TV, full bath, sitting area
Comfort & Decor: Light, airy rooms with a romantic feel accentuated by painted floors and furniture, lace and decorator fabrics. Fresh flowers and turn-down service.

RATES, RESERVATIONS, & RESTRICTIONS

Deposit: 50% or one night's stay
Credit Cards: MC, V, AE, D
Check-in/Out: 3–9/11
Smoking: No
Pets: No
Kids: Over 12

No-No's: Canceling w/out 15-day notice; $20 cancellation fee
Minimum Stay: 2 nights weekends and holidays
Open: All year, except Christmas week

Hosts: Cheryl and Jack Ferrell
Box 256
Cummaquid, MA 02637

(508) 362-3330, (800) 362-6363
Fax: (508) 375-0304
www.acworthinn.com

SCARGO MANOR BED AND BREAKFAST, Dennis

Overall: ★★★	Room Quality: C	Value: C	Price: $80–$160

You can relax on the 55-foot dock on freshwater Scargo Lake, attend a play at The Cape Playhouse, or go in just about any direction from here, the center of the peninsula. Summer festivals and Christmas holiday tours are popular. This, another peak-roofed nineteenth-century captain's house, is relatively new and unheralded in the press, yet a nice place to unwind. It's one of the many mid-level, mid-range bed-and-breakfasts in New England that line main roads and byways, edge lakes and woods. No high style, no whirlpools, just comfortable king or queen canopy beds, private baths, ample breakfasts, and warm atmosphere.

SETTING & FACILITIES

Location: Near Sagamore Bridge off Rt. 35, overlooking Scargo Lake.
Near: Summer theater, Cape Cinema, Scargo Pottery, Dennis Antique Center, museums
Building: 1895 Victorian
Grounds: 3 manicured acres, gazebo, 30′ of sand beach and 55′ dock on the lake; Scargo Tower on top for observation
Public Space: Enclosed porch, large sitting room, LR, DR; 3rd floor sitting room

Food & Drink: Cont'l breakfast; specialty: freshly baked bread; coffee self-service
Recreation: Public golf course, Cape Cod bike trail (Dennis-Provincetown), 25-mi. ocean beach, whale watching, deep-sea fishing, sunset/sightseeing cruises, tennis courts, swimming in fresh and ocean water
Amenities & Services: Beach towels/chairs, recipes, daily papers, irons, refrigerator

ACCOMMODATIONS

Units: 4 guest rooms; 2 suites
All Rooms: Bath, AC, hairdryer
Some Rooms: TV, iron; large suite: working fireplace
Bed & Bath: king (1) and queen canopy (2), queen spool beds (2), queen four-poster; tub/shower (1), glass showers (5)
Favorites: Hydrangea—at the back of 3rd floor, vaulted ceilings, ceiling fan

and skylight; overlooks Scargo Lake
Comfort & Decor: Designer bedding, down pillows and comforters, Amish quilts, crochet canopies. Individually designed rooms w/ period furniture, sitting areas, extra bed in suites, painted wide floorboards, wingback chairs. Ceramic tile floors in bathrooms.

RATES, RESERVATIONS, & RESTRICTIONS

Deposit: 1–2 nights: full payment, 3–4 nights: 2 nights payment, 5+ nights: 50% payment. Refund w/ 14-day notice
Discounts: 3rd person (suites)
Credit Cards: MC, V, AE, D, DC
Check-in/Out: 2–9/11
Smoking: No
Pets: No; inn has golden retriever
Kids: Over 10
No-No's: Use of property for func-

tions (but can rent all six rooms)
Minimum Stay: 2 nights on in-season weekends
Open: April–Dec.
Hosts: Jane and Chuck MacMillin
909 Main St., Route 6A
Dennis, MA 02638
(800) 595-0034; (508) 385-5534
Fax: (508) 385-3992
www.virtualcapecod.com/scargomanor

OVER LOOK INN, Eastham

Overall: ★★★½	Room Quality: C	Value: C	Price: $75–$165

This popular nineteenth-century house is a family-run operation. The warm internationally influenced hosts are Scottish and fluent in Portuguese, French, and Spanish. Nan is President of the Eastham Chamber of Commerce; Ian is a chartered surveyor who takes guests out in his vintage London taxicab and plays bagpipes at afternoon teatime. The sons have lived in the Amazon region and Canada. At holiday time you can ring in the New Year with a Scottish traditional dinner package, and Scottish woolens are always on sale at the shop onsite. Then there's the Hemingway billiard room, the Churchill library, and lots of comfortable fun.

SETTING & FACILITIES

Location: Heart of the Outer Cape between Chatham and Provincetown
Near: Cape Cod Nat'l Seashore, Salt Pond Visitor's Center, Wellfleet Audubon Sanctuary
Building: 1869 Queen Anne Victorian
Grounds: 3 well-treed acres w/ garden, porch
Public Space: Parlor, tea room, library, billiard room, DR
Food & Drink: Full Scottish breakfast; specialties: kedgeree-smoked cod, rice, raisins, porridge; scones for afternoon; walk to nearest restaurant
Recreation: Bike trails; kayaking, horseback riding, windsurfing, antiquing
Amenities & Services: Daily papers, refrigerator, irons, beach towels, recipes, Scottish woolens shop; meetings (20), weddings (50); fax, easel and flipcharts; reserving entire property

ACCOMMODATIONS

Units: 14 guest rooms, 4 BR lodge, cottage
All Rooms: Bath, AC, hairdryer, alarm clock, sitting area

Some Rooms: Cathedral ceiling, claw-foot bathtub, fireplace
Bed & Bath: Twin, double, queen brass beds; baths w/ pedestal sinks, robes

Favorites: The Garden Room—priv. porch, log fireplace
Comfort & Decor: Rooms decorated w/ Victorian antiques, original artwork by hosts' artist-son. Cottage w/ kitchenette. Comfortable, not elegant.

RATES, RESERVATIONS, & RESTRICTIONS

Deposit: Full payment for 3 nights or less, other 50%; refund w/ 10-day notice
Discounts: 3rd person, packages
Credit Cards: MC, V AE, D, DC
Check-in/Out: 2–5/11
Smoking: Library only
Pets: Cottage only; in-house basset hound and beagle
Kids: Welcome

Open: All year
Hosts: Ian and Nan Aitchison, Mark and Clive
PO Box 771
Eastham, MA 02642
(508) 255-1886
Fax: (508) 240-0345
stay@overlookinn, winstonsc@aol.com
www.overlookinn.com

WHALEWALK INN, Eastham

Overall: ★★★★½	Room Quality: A	Value: C	Price: $125–$250

The Lorillards of tobacco fortune lived here in the 1920s as gentleman farmers (the luxury saltbox cottage was once a chicken coop). But originally, like so many others in this region, this was a whaling captain's house. The friendly hosts, both former advertising executives, keep working hard to maintain this exceptional, airy, elegant retreat. Its reputation is formidable, but in reality it is a warm and fuzzy bed-and-breakfast in sophisticate's trappings. Dick creates tempting breakfasts—how about walnut-raisin crepes with vanilla ice cream?—and Carolyn wins awards for decorating. But we're the real winners.

SETTING & FACILITIES

Location: Rock Harbor Rd. exit off Orleans Rotary; left on Rock Harbor, right on Bridge Rd.; in residential neighborhood

Near: Hyannis ferries, Wellfleet Wildlife Sanctuary
Building: Enormous 1830 Federal; outbuildings
Grounds: 3 acres: lawns, meadows, gardens
Public Space: 2 parlors: 1 formal, 1 informal; formal DR; guest pantry; sunporch; garden patio
Food & Drink: Full imaginative breakfast, in-room by request; specialties: cranberry/blueberry Cape-Cod pancakes, granola pizza w/ fresh fruit, Belgian waffles; refreshments, cookies; evening hors d'oeuvres
Recreation: Cape Cod Nat'l Seashore, bike to Cape Cod Rail Trail Bike Path, whale watching
Amenities & Services: Refrigerator, irons, books, beach towels, bikes; meetings (8–10), fax, e-mail, bike storage

ACCOMMODATIONS

Units: 11 guest rooms, 5 suites; rooms in the inn, barn, guest house, carriage house, saltbox
All Rooms: Bath, AC, iron, clock/radio, hairdryer
Some Rooms: Fireplace, wet bar, TV/VCR, coffee/tea service
Bed & Bath: 2 twins, queens, kings, most antiques; some dbl. whirlpools, some tubs, some sep. showers
Favorites: Room w/ king antique fourposter, sitting area w/ fireplace, priv. entrance off patio; room w/ queen fourposter, large sitting area w/ fireplace, tub for 2, garden view
Comfort & Decor: Soft colors, contemporary, spacious. Mix of country antiques and reproductions, some country cottage. Bed skirts, coverlets, and decorative pillows. Light-filled, airy, fresh flowers. Suites exceptionally spacious, w/ kitchens; good for families. Cape saltbox: priv. patio.

RATES, RESERVATIONS, & RESTRICTIONS

Deposit: 50%; refund w/ 14-day notice
Discounts: Off season, extra persons in West Suite
Credit Cards: MC, V
Check-in/Out: 2/11
Smoking: No
Pets: No
Kids: Over 12
Minimum Stay: 2 nights in-season, weekends; 3 nights holiday weekends
Open: April 1–Nov. 30
Hosts: Carolyn and Dick Smith
220 Bridge Rd.
Eastham, MA 02642
(508) 255-0617
Fax: (508) 240-0017
whalewak@capecod.net
www.whalewalkinn.com

MOSTLY HALL, Falmouth

Overall: ★★★★	Room Quality: B	Value: C	Price: $95–$135

The name comes from a child who visited over 100 years ago; he walked in, looked at the 35-foot foyer, and exclaimed, "Why Mama, it's mostly

hall!" Halls or not, it feels like a home, and a distinctive one. Built by a sea captain for his New Orleans bride, this plantation-style "raised cottage" is the oldest summer house in Falmouth. The 13-foot windows and wraparound porch seem more Bayou than Back Bay. Convenient to the historic district, it is nonetheless private, set back from the busy road on sweeping lawns. Caroline and Jim are warm hosts, breakfasts are creative, the enclosed widow's walk den is special, so mostly, it's delightful.

SETTING & FACILITIES

Location: Just off Falmouth Village Green
Near: Beaches, trails, harbors, Woods Hole (marine science), Cape Cod Nat'l Seashore, train rides, galleries, ferries, theaters
Building: 1849 plantation-style house; Nat'l Hist. Register
Grounds: 130 ft. from road, gardens, 1.3 acres; lush, secluded setting; gazebo
Public Space: Enclosed Widow's Walk, den sitting space; wraparound porch; LR; LR/DR; library wall 2nd floor

Food & Drink: Full breakfast, communal; specialties: stuffed French toast, cheese blintz muffins w/ blueberry sauce, eggs Benedict soufflé; refreshments and sherry
Recreation: Golf, whale watching, canal cruises, Shining Sea bikeway, antiquing
Amenities & Services: Bikes and helmets, AC, inn cookbook, irons, hairdryers, use of host refrigerator, beach towels/passes, daily papers, rides to ferry or shuttle bus

ACCOMMODATIONS

Units: 6 guest rooms
All Rooms: Bath, AC, ceiling fan, reading chairs, antiques
Bed & Bath: Queen four-poster canopies; showers only, some small, some marble-topped sink outside bath
Favorites: Downstairs—13-foot ceilings, floor-to-ceiling windows

Comfort & Decor: Floral papers, Oriental rugs. Reading chairs. Antique and traditional furniture. All corner rooms w/ garden views. Bright and airy, big, shuttered windows. Rooms in back, second floor most private.

RATES, RESERVATIONS, & RESTRICTIONS

Deposit: Full payment 1 night, other 50%; refund w/ 14-day notice
Discounts: Off-season, honeymoon package (ferry tickets w/ 3 nights)
Credit Cards: MC, V, AE, D
Check-in/Out: 3–7/11
Smoking: No
Pets: No; kennel nearby
Kids: Over 16
Minimum Stay: 2 nights May–Oct.,

weekends; 3 nights holidays, Falmouth Road Race Weekend
Open: Mid-Feb.–Dec.
Hosts: Caroline and Jim Lloyd
27 Main St.
Falmouth, MA 02540
(800) 682-0565, (508) 548-3786
Fax: (508) 457-1572
mostlyhl@capecod.com
www.mostlyhall.com

WILDFLOWER INN, Falmouth

Overall: ★★★★	Room Quality: B	Value: C	Price: $80–$195

Lavender poached pears, lemon flower pancakes, rose petal morning cakes, sunflower crepes, pansy butter, ten-fruit compote sprinkled with chopped marigolds—sound yummy? Not for you? Never fear, the edible flowers grown at this homey bed-and-breakfast are optional, and you could have plain old eggs overeasy as part of your five-course breakfast. Phil is a barber, Donna a former social worker and quilting teacher, and between them they have eight children and ten grandchildren, who probably prefer pickles to candied violets.

SETTING & FACILITIES

Location: .5 mi. from 1st set of lights after divided highway ends on Rt. 28; in Falmouth's historic district
Near: Martha's Vineyard ferry, aquarium, nature area, Woods Hole, Plimoth Plantation, beaches, winery
Building: Pre-1898 Victorian, wrap-around porch
Grounds: Award-winning; herbs and edible flower gardens, sitting area, fish pond, gazebo
Public Space: Gathering room, 3rd floor TV room

Food & Drink: Breakfast in-room, picnic, or in gathering room; specialties: cooked w/ edible flowers: frozen fruit smoothies, fresh fruit w/ herbs; hot drinks, wine, snacks avail. 24 hours; afternoon tea; dessert; special diets accom.
Recreation: Water sports, sports center, antiquing, billiards, X-C skiing
Amenities & Services: Piano, grill, washer/dryer, phone, games, bikes, computer, fax; comp. champagne for special occasions

ACCOMMODATIONS

Units: 5 guest rooms, 1 cottage
All Rooms: Bath, AC, ceiling fan, dataport, alarm clock, radio, shower

Some Rooms: Skylight, robes, window seat, priv. entrance, sitting area

Bed & Bath: Queens, some four-posters, sleigh, iron, canopies, feather-bed (1); some tub/showers, dual shower heads, claw tubs, whirlpools **Favorites:** Third-floor room—bed w/ skylight, whirlpool, 2-head shower

Comfort & Decor: Unique decors are comfortable and elegant: antiques, floral, garden effect furniture, wicker, tailored. Tasteful. Good light. Cottage: queen and twin beds, pull-out sofa, kitchen, spiral staircase, LR, loft bedroom

RATES, RESERVATIONS, & RESTRICTIONS

Deposit: 50%; refund w/ 14-day notice **Discounts:** Singles, 3rd person, gov't, 5-day stay (10%), theme packages: quilting, Christmas, antiques, lighthouse, etc.; cottage rented weekly, monthly **Credit Cards:** MC, V, AE **Check-in/Out:** 3/11 **Smoking:** No **Pets:** No **Kids:** No

Minimum Stay: 2 nights May 1–Oct. 31, weekends **Open:** All year **Hosts:** Donna and Phil Stone 167 Palmer Ave. Falmouth, MA 02540 (508) 548-9524, (800) 294-5459 Fax: (508) 548-9524 wldflr167@aol.com *www.bbhost.com/wildflowerinn*

AUGUSTUS SNOW HOUSE, Harwich Port

Overall: ★★★★	Room Quality: B	Value: C	Price: $105–$170

Gables, dormers, a screened gazebo, turrets, leaded windows, organs that don't work, pianos that do—this imposing Queen Anne mansion is filled with charms. The atmosphere has a decidedly feminine slant—from a cabinet brimming with Cabbage Patch dolls to the pretty guest rooms, named after Joyce and Steve's daughters. The romantic inn is a fine spot for a small wedding, as the landscaped lawn and patio with its white furniture are a lovely setting for ceremonies and cocktails. The Garden Room can hold 60 guests, with fine catering and all services, and that working piano is ready for the wedding march or swing music.

SETTING & FACILITIES

Location: Exit 10 off Rt. 6, S on 124/39; near Main St., Harwich Center **Near:** Martha's Vineyard ferry, shopping in Chatham, downtown Harwich; 1 block from priv. beach on Nantucket Sound; Nantucket ferry, 1 mi. **Building:** Large 1901 Queen Anne Victorian estate **Grounds:** 1+ acre; gazebo, porch, views, patio

Public Space: Entry, LR, porch, wraparound veranda **Food & Drink:** Breakfast; specialties: baked pears w/ raspberries and cream, cinnamon-pecan bread pudding w/ brandy-caramel sauce; refreshments **Recreation:** Swimming, golf, tennis, boating, whale watching, lawn games **Amenities & Services:** Gift cert., books, games, fax; weddings

ACCOMMODATIONS

Units: 5 guest rooms
All Rooms: Bath, AC, fireplace, TV, phone, ceiling fan
Some Rooms: Whirlpool, refrigerator, sitting area, orig. bathroom, bay window
Bed & Bath: Queen or king beds; full tubs and showers, whirlpools

Favorites: Melissa's Room—4-poster canopy, sitting area, bay windows, bath w/ ornate marble sink, dramatic wall-covering
Comfort & Decor: Rooms large. Victorian decor and modern amenities. Individually decorated. Baths in period style with imported European fixtures.

RATES, RESERVATIONS, & RESTRICTIONS

Deposit: 50%. Check deposits w/in 5 days of reserving. Refunded w/ 15-day notice
Discounts: Off-season, packages, 3rd person
Credit Cards: MC, V, AE, D
Check-in/Out: 2/11
Smoking: Outdoors
Pets: No
Kids: Over 12

Minimum Stay: 3 nights July/August weekends, 2 nights other weekends and July/August midweek
Open: All year except 3–4 weeks in Jan.
Hosts: Joyce and Steve Roth
528 Main St.
Harwich Port, MA 02646
(800) 320-0528, (508) 430-0528
Fax: (508) 432-7995 x15
SNOWHOUSE1@aol.com
www.augustussnow.com

DUNSCROFT-BY-THE-SEA, Harwich Port

Overall: ★★★½   Room Quality: C   Value: D   Price: $105–$250

Hearts and flowers are all around you at this weathered shingle Colonial—especially the former: heart-shaped pillows, picture frames, boxes, shells and rocks, a book called *Hearts*. At Valentine's Day, the bread may be heart-shaped and the farmer's cheese served in heart-shaped ramekins. Cupids, "love letter" info packets in each guest room addressed to Scott and Zelda and other lovers, roses, Hershey's Kisses—get the point? Alyce, the romantic-minded host, insists "it's not overdone." But be forewarned, it may be intoxicating: she and Wally were married here.

SETTING & FACILITIES

Location: Rt. 10 mi. E of Hyannis, on quiet tree-lined street between beach and village
Near: Cape Cod Nat'l Seashore, JFK Museum, Pilgrim Monument, Nantucket, Martha's Vineyard, Plymouth Rock and Plantation, shopping, galleries

Building: 1920 Beachside Colonial Revival
Grounds: Priv. mile-long beach on Nantucket Sound; sun and shade; patio, porch, water views; croquet
Public Space: LR, library, porch; DR

Food & Drink: Full country buffet breakfast, communal or separate; specialties: fried apples, blueberry buckle, cottage pudding, Caribbean French toast; juice and hot drinks, cookies avail. **Recreation:** Whale watching, horseback riding, golf, scuba; boat rental nearby

Amenities & Services: Baby grand piano, refrigerator, irons, beach chairs/towels, recipes, daily papers, picnic baskets; fax, copier; meetings (10–15), weddings off-season (30)

ACCOMMODATIONS

Units: 8 guest rooms, 1 cottage
All Rooms: Bath, robes, hairdryer, phone, toiletries
Some Rooms: AC, whirlpool, fireplace, TV/VCR, kitchenette, priv. entrance; disabled access (1)
Bed & Bath: King and queen, fourposters, canopies, sleigh beds; shower-only baths (4), tub/shower (2), whirlpool/shower (2)

Favorites: King suite, cottage, and Room 6—romantic beds, whirlpools
Comfort & Decor: Decidedly romantic, with heart pillows, lace window treatments. Feminine but not frilly, Laura Ashley fabrics and wallcoverings. Front upstairs rooms have water views.

RATES, RESERVATIONS, & RESTRICTIONS

Deposit: Full payment 1–3 nights; refund w/ 14-day notice; reservations w/in 14 days of arrival require full non-refundable payment
Discounts: Off-season, 3rd person
Credit Cards: AE, V, MC
Check-in/Out: 2/11; ask for late departures
Smoking: No
Pets: No
Kids: 14 and up

Minimum Stay: 3 nights July–Labor Day, 2 nights other in-season weekends, holidays
Open: All year
Hosts: Alyce and Wally Cunningham
24 Pilgrim Rd.
Harwich Port, MA 02646
(800) 432-4345, (508) 432-0810
Fax: (508) 432-5134
dunscroft@capecod.net;
alyce@capecod.net
www.virtualcities.com/ma/dunscroft.htm

BED AND BREAKFAST
OF SAGAMORE BEACH, Sagamore Beach

Overall: ★★★½	Room Quality: C	Value: C	Price: $95

A big painting of Carmen Miranda hanging in the living room? Grandma's bedspread brought from Italy? Omelets on tortillas with salsa, and cinnamon coffee? If these original, offbeat touches appeal, then you won't mind sharing a bath at this beach house on a hill, overlooking Cape Cod Bay. You can sit on the decks and porches and enjoy the serenity, then come in and enjoy John's eclectic talents. He is a well-known food stylist, chef, author, and former art director, and his cooking classes are renowned. So the food presentation is fabulous, accentuated by bright colors, and he may test out recipes with you. This bed-and-breakfast by the sea may be over the top for many, but for others, it's just tops.

SETTING & FACILITIES

Location: On a hill overlooking Cape Cod Bay, near Sagamore Rotary
Near: Beach, shops, restaurants, Sandwich, Cape activities; Boston
Building: Large 1900 Cape Cod beach house
Grounds: Large, outdoor enclosed shower; lawns, vegetable, herb, and flower gardens; hammock
Public Space: LR, large porches and decks

Food & Drink: Healthy breakfast, communal; specialties: theme breakfasts, such as all blueberry dishes or dairy-free
Recreation: Tennis courts, semi-priv. beach a short walk
Amenities & Services: Large porches for meetings; beach towels; cooking/decorating discussions

ACCOMMODATIONS

Units: 3 guest rooms
All Rooms: Fresh flowers, robes, on 2nd floor
Some Rooms: Water views
Bed & Bath: Double antique beds; 1 shared bath
Favorites: Four-poster room—white coverlet, blue walls, orig. paintings, two breezy window exposures

Comfort & Decor: Exciting use of fabric and color w/ eclectic furnishings and antiques. All beds different, antique. Original, quirky. Fresh flowers, plants. Ceiling fans. Smallish rooms.

RATES, RESERVATIONS, & RESTRICTIONS

Deposit: None
Discounts: Weekend packages, incl. cooking class
Credit Cards: Cash only
Check-in/Out: After 5/11
Smoking: No
Pets: No
Kids: No
Minimum Stay: 1 night

Open: All year
Hosts: John F. Carafoli
Box 205
Sagamore Beach, MA 02562
(508) 888-1559
Fax: (508) 888-1859
CARAFOLI@CAPE.COM
bbchannel.com

BAY BEACH BED AND BREAKFAST, Sandwich

Overall: ★★★★½   Room Quality: A   Value: C   Price: $175–$345

Less is more here, in the style of Japan or Sweden, but warmth is not the strong point at this award-winning beauty on a private beach. The hosts spent almost 30 years in the business, are well-traveled, and love good restaurants. They stay in the background, and the emphasis is on seclusion, understated luxury, and low-key elegance. Fresh flowers are everywhere inside and out, the water views are gentle through window walls, cookies are on the kitchen counter, a telescope looks out to the bay, and there is a sense of beauty and peace throughout. The closest cousin to fine inns such as The Inn at Sunrise Point in Camden, Maine, or The Inn at Canoe Point near Bar Harbor, Maine, this is a place for those who appreciate contemporary elegance, water views, privacy—and the pristine perfection of carpets vacuumed in concentric circles.

SETTING & FACILITIES

Location: Near Rt. 6A-E off the Sagamore bridge; residential area overlooking water on private road
Near: Plimoth Plantation, Plymouth Rock, Kennedy compound, Glass Museum, Heritage Plantation, other historical sites, waterfront, marina
Building: Contemporary inn, opened 1987
Grounds: Secluded priv. waterfront property, lots of flowers, gardens, boardwalk to priv. beach, view of Cape Cod Bay and Canal

Public Space: DR, LR, deck
Food & Drink: Full breakfast buffet, communal or separate; specialties: eggs Savory, pineapple French toast; afternoon tea; wine, fruit, cheese, crackers in room on arrival; nearest restaurant 5 min.
Recreation: Boating, golf, inline skating, whale watching
Amenities & Services: Exercise room, bike rentals, irons, daily papers, fresh flowers, daily faxing, books

ACCOMMODATIONS

Units: 4 guest rooms, 3 suites
All Rooms: Bath, priv. deck, phone, TV, cable, CD player, refrigerator, AC, ceiling fan, hairdryer, toiletries
Some Rooms: Whirlpool, fireplace, disabled access
Bed & Bath: Mostly king, some double; full baths

Favorites: Dune Caper and Canal Caper—oceanfront suites w/ marsh view, whirlpools, fireplaces
Comfort & Decor: Rooms are spacious and contemporary w/ wicker furniture, fresh flowers, mirrored walls, and views of ocean or marsh.

RATES, RESERVATIONS, & RESTRICTIONS

Deposit: Varies by length of stay; refunds w/ 21-day notice
Discounts: 3rd person
Credit Cards: MC, V
Check-in/Out: 2–6/12
Smoking: Outdoors only
Pets: No
Kids: 16 and older
No-No's: Sand on the carpets

Minimum Stay: 2 nights midweek, 3 on weekends, holidays
Open: All year except Halloween
Hosts: Emily and Reale Lemieux
1–3 Bay Beach Lane
Sandwich, MA 02563
(508) 888-8813, (800) 475-6398
Fax: (508) 888-5416
www.baybeach.com

HONEYSUCKLE HILL BED AND BREAKFAST, West Barnstable

Overall: ★★★½   Room Quality: B   Value: C   Price: $95–$185

Mary and Bill know their business—they were innkeepers in Vermont for a dozen years and lectured at seminars for prospective innkeepers. They cook together—parceling out parts of the original, lavish breakfasts in a kitchen built for two—and the results are original and delicious. Their bed-and-breakfast, furnished comfortably with antiques and family pieces, is on a former stagecoach path, and is fresh and pretty and unassuming, with a wicker-filled screen porch. The beds are fluffy featherbeds, the linens are ironed, and the new baths, gleaming marble.

SETTING & FACILITIES

Location: About 2 mi. from Exit 5 off Rt. 6 E, on former stagecoach path
Near: Beach, Cape Cod Nat'l Seashore, Sandwich Glass Museum, JFK Museum, Heritage Plantation, Cape Cod Rail Trail
Building: 1810 Queen Anne–style home; Nat'l Register of Hist. Places
Grounds: 1+ acre; lawns, gardens, waterfall, fish pond, view
Public Space: LR, DR, screened porch

Food & Drink: Full breakfast, communal or separate; specialties: "Dutch babies," Grand Marnier French toast, granola; early-riser coffee and papers; snacks, sherry, soda, coffee/tea; nearby restaurant
Recreation: Whale watching, golf, tennis, swimming, fishing, bird watching
Amenities & Services: Refrigerator, irons, books, beach towels/chairs/umbrellas, recipes, daily papers

ACCOMMODATIONS

Units: 4 guest rooms; 1 suite
All Rooms: Priv. bath, AC, clock/radio, drink set-up, English toiletries

Some Rooms: Writing desk, dressing tables, TV/VCR, priv. entrance (1)

Bed & Bath: Double and queen featherbeds; marble and brass baths, seats in oversize showers
Favorites: Magnolia—1st floor, queen four-poster, sitting area, dressing table

Comfort & Decor: Sunny, comfortable. Recently redecorated with antiques, white wicker, Battenburg lace. All rooms named after flowers, and all pretty.

RATES, RESERVATIONS, & RESTRICTIONS

Deposit: 1 night; 50% for longer stays; refund w/ 14-day notice
Discounts: Off-season
Credit Cards: MC, V, AE, D
Check-in/Out: 3–9/11
Smoking: Garden only
Pets: No; in-house labrador greets guests outdoors
Kids: 12 and over

Minimum Stay: 2 nights on weekends
Open: All year
Hosts: Mary and Bill Kilburn
591 Old King's Hwy., Historic Rt. 6A
West Barnstable, MA 02668
(800) 441-8418, (508) 362-8418
stay@honeysucklehill.com
www.honeysucklehill.com

MANOR HOUSE BED AND BREAKFAST, West Yarmouth

Overall: ★★★½	Room Quality: C	Value: C	Price: $68–$128

How can you not enjoy sleeping in a room named "Picket Fence," "Cranberry Bog," "Birdsong," or "Howling Coyote"? The young innkeepers have a toddling son and two kitties at this informal, friendly mid-Cape bed-and-breakfast in a quiet residential neighborhood in close proximity to Cape activities. A major landscaping project is part of general upgrading. The senses are teased and pleased, with salty breezes from nearby Lewis Bay, flickering candles, fresh flowers, classical music, and the feel of handcrafted quilts. This Dutch Colonial house is highly decorated for Thanksgiving and Christmas, quiet times on the Cape.

SETTING & FACILITIES

Location: Near Route 6, Exit 7; in seaside neighborhood near the beach
Near: JFK Museum and Memorial, beach, whale watching, Nantucket/Martha's Vineyard ferries
Building: 1920 Dutch Colonial
Grounds: Small grounds, flowers, view
Public Space: Large DR, LR, book nook

Food & Drink: Full candlelight breakfast, communal; specialties: cranberry-orange juice w/ raspberry sherbet, crab casserole; afternoon tea and cookies
Recreation: Bocci, trails, sailing, horseback riding, mini/regular golf
Amenities & Services: Daily papers, beach towels/chairs, irons, info

ACCOMMODATIONS

Units: 7 guest rooms
All Rooms: Bath
Some Rooms: AC
Bed & Bath: queen, double, and twin beds, some canopies; some showers only, modern tub/shower (1); antique tubs and showers
Favorites: Secret Garden—2nd floor, queen four-poster, sunny, partial view

Comfort & Decor: Country decor, scattered antiques, braided rugs. Modest, clean, comfortable accommodations, w/ armchairs, space for personal objects. Rooms named after Cape Cod area.

RATES, RESERVATIONS, & RESTRICTIONS

Deposit: Full payment for 1 night; other, 50%; 14-day notice or re-rental for refund
Discounts: Holiday packages; seniors, 3rd person, long stays, singles, off-season, AAA
Credit Cards: MC, V, AE
Check-in/Out: 3–8/11
Smoking: No
Pets: No; two in-house cats

Kids: 12 and over
Minimum Stay: 2 nights in-season
Open: All year, except Christmas Day
Hosts: Rick and Liz Latshaw
57 Maine Ave.
West Yarmouth, MA 02673
(508) 771-3433; (800) 962-6679
Fax: (508) 790-1186
manorhse@capecod.net
www.capecod.net/manorhouse

WEDGEWOOD INN, Yarmouth Port

Overall: ★★★★   Room Quality: B   Value: C   Price: $105–$185

Lots of interesting talk here: Gerrie was a professional dancer, Milt played pro football with the New England Patriots and was an FBI agent assigned to the notorious Bronfman kidnapping. Set among 200-year-old trees and extensive gardens, this first village house is classic Early Americana, built for a maritime attorney (fees were apparently huge in 1812, too). Public rooms in the main house are small, furnished formally with nineteenth-century antiques and interesting pieces like a blacksmith's bellows table. The rustic carriage barn, renovated in 1997, is great for groups, with its beamed common room and suites with soaking tubs, fireplaces, dataports, and private decks.

SETTING & FACILITIES

Location: Rt. 6, Exit 7, turn right on Willow St. to Rt. 6A; turn right, inn on right, 100 yards from corner, on knoll
Near: Beaches, antiquing, galleries, boutiques
Building: 1812 Greek Revival/Federal inn
Grounds: 2 acres, lawns, gardens, patios, gazebo, huge trees
Public Space: Entryway, common room, DR, carriage barn; wheelchair access

Food & Drink: Tea trays in rooms, early bird coffee, full breakfast, in room if requested; specialties: Belgian waffles w/ strawberries, pecan pancakes; special diets accom. w/ prior notice; afternoon tea
Recreation: Whale watching, golf, tennis, fishing, sailing, harbor cruises
Amenities & Services: Refrigerator, irons, beach towels, daily papers; pick-up from plane; 2 meeting rooms (15–20 each), fax

ACCOMMODATIONS

Units: 4 guest rooms, 5 suites (3 in Carriage House)
All Rooms: Bath, fresh fruit, wood for fireplace, hairdryer, evening tea tray, AC
Some Rooms: Working fireplace (7), screened porch, deck (2), phone (3), TV
Bed & Bath: Kings in carriage house, queen canopies in main house suites, others queens, pencil posts; most claw-

foot tubs, 3 oversized tubs, large baths
Favorites: Wedgwood Blue Room— spacious, canopy bed, porch w/ wicker
Comfort & Decor: Period design and detailing, stencils. Wide-board floors, Oriental carpets. Wing-back chairs, spacious sitting areas. Comfortable and truly Colonial. Antiques but not restrictive.

RATES, RESERVATIONS, & RESTRICTIONS

Deposit: Full payment, 1 night; others 50%; refund w/ 15-day notice
Discounts: Off-season
Credit Cards: MC, V, AE, DC
Check-in/Out: 2/11
Smoking: No
Pets: No
Kids: Over 10
Minimum Stay: None

Open: All year
Hosts: Gerrie and Milt Graham
83 Main St.
Yarmouth Port, MA 02675
(508) 362-5157, (508) 362-9178
Fax: (508) 362-5851
www.virtualcapecod.com/market/wedge-woodinn

Zone 14
Martha's Vineyard/
Nantucket

Nobody seems to be quite sure just who Martha was (for sure, not Stewart), but the Vineyard is named for the wild grapes that were abundant here in 1602, when explorer Bartholomew Gosnald discovered the little island (and did not, for sure, stay in a bed-and-breakfast or small inn!).

Most commonly accessed by ferry or boat from Cape Cod or Nantucket, Martha's Vineyard is an ever-popular beach destination and an increasingly stylish haven for the rich and famous, who for centuries have built huge summer mansions along the water. Presidents, moguls, heads of state, and celebs relax here in season, and you are likely to see a tanned and rested famous face at a local restaurant or hardware store.

The main towns have distinct personalities, and all have many shops and restaurants. Edgartown was a nineteenth-century whaling port; the 1843 Old Whaling Church is now a performing arts center. Vineyard Haven is the ferry port and retains vestiges of a turn-of-the-last-century community. For seafaring buffs, the Seaman's Bethel houses whaling artifacts.

Oak Bluffs, a mid-nineteenth-century Methodist campground, offers an enchanting photo opportunity: Teeny gingerbread cottages adorned in a rainbow of brightly colored facades that long ago replaced the original campground tents. Also in Oak Bluffs, Flying Horses is supposedly—like one in Rhode Island—the oldest working carousel in the country.

"Up island" West Tisbury and Chilmark are quieter destinations, with rolling farmland. Gay Head, at the tip of the Vineyard, has a secluded beach backed by multicolored clay cliffs, a wildlife preserve, and lighthouse. Check out the seasonal tours at Chicama Vineyards in West Tisbury, or the Cedar Tree Neck Wildlife Sanctuary, containing 300 acres on the northern part of the island.

Many small lodgings, most of them reconverted seamen's homes or established inns in or near the towns, will arrange transfers to the ferry. Make ferry reservations far ahead in summer season, when the island gets crowded, especially if you plan to bring your car. Martha's Vineyard is a haven for bicyclists, and a car is unnecessary for many parts of the island.

A bit farther out, 30 miles from Cape Cod, is crescent-shaped Nantucket Island, which still looks like a whaling-ship port from 1850. More quaint and low-key than the larger, trendy Vineyard, Nantucket is one entire National Historic District. In town you'll find cobblestone streets, shops and restaurants, as well as many captains' houses turned bed-and-breakfasts, showing off the widow's walk roofs and architectural detailing of centuries past. The decor and feel are traditional and period, simple and engaging.

Nantucket Town houses the Whaling Museum, and there are whale watching and fishing trips from the wharf. For the ecologically minded, Nantucket has a natural history museum, observatory, aquarium, the Maria Mitchell Science Center, and the Marine and Shellfish Laboratory, as well as the Nantucket Vineyard, open seasonally.

For More Information
Most sources for Cape Cod can also help with reservations and information for Martha's Vineyard and Nantucket (see page 329).

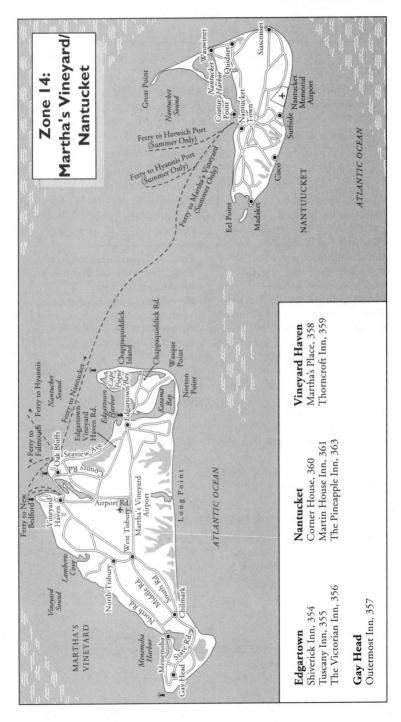

Zone 14:
Martha's Vineyard/
Nantucket

Great Point

Nantucket Sound

Wauwinet

Quidnet

Siasconset

Nantucket Harbor

Coatue Point

Nantucket Town

Surfside

Nantucket Memorial Airport

Ferry to Harwich Port
(Summer Only)

Ferry to Hyannis Port
(Summer Only)

Ferry to Martha's Vineyard
(Summer Only)

Cisco

 El Point

Madaket

NANTUUCKET

ATLANTIC OCEAN

Ferry to Nantucket →

Chappaquiddick Island

Chappaquiddick Rd.

Wasque Point

Cape Pogue Bay

Edgartown Bay

Edgartown Harbor

Edgartown

Katama Bay

Norton Point

Ferry to Hyannis

Ferry to Falmouth

Nantucket Sound

Ferry to Nantucket →

Oak Bluffs

Edgartown–Vineyard Haven Rd.

Seaview Ave.

County Rd.

Vineyard Haven

Airport Rd.

Martha's Vineyard Airport

West Tisbury

Long Point

ATLANTIC OCEAN

Ferry to New Bedford

Vineyard Sound

Lamberts Cove

North Tisbury

Middle Rd.

North Rd.

South Rd.

Chilmark

MARTHA'S VINEYARD

Menemsha Harbor

Menemsha

Gay Head

State Rd.

Edgartown
Shiverick Inn, 354
Tuscany Inn, 355
The Victorian Inn, 356

Gay Head
Outermost Inn, 357

Nantucket
Corner House, 360
Martin House Inn, 361
The Pineapple Inn, 363

Vineyard Haven
Martha's Place, 358
Thorncroft Inn, 359

SHIVERICK INN, Edgartown

Overall: ★★★½	Room Quality: B	Value: C	Price: $120–$270

Dr. Clement Shiverick was the town physician in 1840 when this gracious home with a mansard roof was built near the center of a thriving whaling center. Today, Edgartown is still thriving, and still a whale center, but the huge mammals attract people to watch them rather than catch them. Shiverick's house has been hosting visitors as a comfortable, refined bed-and-breakfast since 1981. Marty and Denny emphasize romance, and this three-story, white clapboard Victorian retreat is one of several fine properties here geared toward couples. The chandelier in the cupola casts a soft glow that has become a landmark on summer evenings.

SETTING & FACILITIES

Location: 1 block from Main St.
Near: Hist. Edgartown, antiquing, museums, summer events
Building: 1840 Greek Revival
Grounds: Small courtyard w/ fountain, wrought-iron furniture
Public Space: Entrance, terrace; 2nd-floor library, sundeck; parlor; DR

Food & Drink: Cont'l breakfast; specialty: island preserves; afternoon tea; low-fat breakfast avail.
Recreation: Biking, beaches, sailing, swimming, tennis
Amenities & Services: Refrigerator, irons

ACCOMMODATIONS

Units: 10 guest rooms
All Rooms: Bath, AC
Some Rooms: Fireplace
Bed & Bath: Kings, queens; canopies and four-posters; tubs
Favorites: 2 front rooms—1 canopy, fireplace, 1 on south side of house (bright)

Comfort & Decor: 18th–19th-century early American and English antiques, Oriental rugs, wood floors. Lighting varies. Romantic style. Stylish, tasteful, refined.

RATES, RESERVATIONS, & RESTRICTIONS

Deposit: Full payment 1–3 nights; other 50%; refund w/ 14-day notice
Discounts: Off-season, packages
Credit Cards: MC, V, AE, D
Check-in/Out: 2/11
Smoking: No
Pets: No
Kids: Over 12
Minimum Stay: 3 nights mid-June–end Sept; 2 nights off-season weekends

Open: Feb.–Dec.
Hosts: Marty and Denny Turnelle
5 Pease Point Way, Box 640
Edgartown, MA 02539
(800) 723-4292 (reservations only),
(508) 627-3797
Fax: (508) 627-8441
shiverickinn@vineyard.net
www.mvweb.com/shiv/

TUSCANY INN, Edgartown

Overall: ★★★★   Room Quality: B   Value: B   Price: $90–$375

Italian is not the most typical influence for an inn on the Vineyard, but this former sea captain's mansion in the heart of town evokes a hilltop farm in Tuscany—at least within. Laura is Tuscan and has decorated the house with stylish flair and sunny colors. The feel is sophisticated and sensual, a far cry from the New England/nautical atmosphere of many properties on the islands and Cape. She offers Northern Italian cooking classes weekends off-season, and in season, the restaurant serves filet mignon with Gorgonzola ravioli on the patio. Tutto bene.

SETTING & FACILITIES

Location: Downtown Edgartown
Near: Block from harbor, ferries, restaurants, shops; 2 blocks from beach, museums, galleries
Building: Grand, newly remodeled Victorian
Grounds: Pond, herb/flower gardens, hammock
Public Space: LR, library, common room, breakfast area off kitchen

Food & Drink: Breakfast; specialties: fresh bread, blueberry pancakes; afternoon biscotti, cappuccino; family-owned La Cucina restaurant, North Italian dinner seasonally
Recreation: Biking, nature trails, golf, tennis, fishing, sailing
Amenities & Services: Refrigerator, flowers

ACCOMMODATIONS

Units: 8 guest rooms
All Rooms: Bath
Some Rooms: Harbor view, whirlpool
Bed & Bath: Beds vary, some canopies; robes, some tubs

Favorites: Room 5—King bed under eaves, whirlpool
Comfort & Decor: Antique furniture, toile prints, sponge-painted walls. High style. Some rooms small, all attractive. Airy, fresh, sophisticated decor.

RATES, RESERVATIONS, & RESTRICTIONS

Deposit: Full payment 1–3 nights; others 50%; refund w/ 15-day notice
Discounts: Off season
Credit Cards: MC, V, AE
Check-in/Out: 2/11
Smoking: No
Pets: No
Kids: Over 10
Minimum Stay: 3 nights for summer weekends

Open: Except part of winter
Hosts: Laura Sbrana and Rusty Scheuer
22 North Water St.
Edgartown, MA 02539
(508) 627-5999
Fax: (508) 627-6605
70632.3363@compuserve.com
www.mvweb.com/tuscany

THE VICTORIAN INN, Edgartown

Overall: ★★★★	Room Quality: B	Value: C	Price: $100–$325

Across from the town's famous "Pagoda Tree" brought in a bucket from China in the nineteenth century, this award-winning bed-and-breakfast of the same era was a whaling captain's home. Like other fine properties in this book (not always noted as such) it is listed in the National Register of Historic Places. Karyn and Stephen are personable innkeepers and seem to enjoy polishing the hardwood floors and brass; in the half-dozen years since they bought the three-story, white-clapboard house, they have been constantly renovating. Breakfasts are exceptional, served in the wainscoted dining room or enclosed garden patio.

SETTING & FACILITIES

Location: Hist. Edgartown, 1 block from town dock, Main St., harbor
Near: Restaurants, museums, galleries, summer theater, wildlife sanctuaries, beaches
Building: Restored whaling captain's home
Grounds: English garden, walk to town
Public Space: Entry, common rooms, DR

Food & Drink: Award-winning 4-course breakfast; specialties: scrambled eggs w/ basil and feta cheese, banana-rum pancakes; afternoon tea in garden
Recreation: Tennis, golf, horseback riding, sailing, fishing, swimming
Amenities & Services: Games, books, advice

ACCOMMODATIONS

Units: 14 guest rooms
All Rooms: Bath, flowers, sherry, ceiling fan
Some Rooms: Priv. balcony (6), deck, balcony, sundeck, porch, harbor view, bay window, most AC
Bed & Bath: Beds vary, four-posters, canopies, pencil-posts; some baths

small, papered, laminate surfaces
Favorites: Third floor rooms—French doors to balconies, best views
Comfort & Decor: Individually decorated w/ family furniture, antiques, flowers. Bedside lighting. Floral papers and fabrics.

RATES, RESERVATIONS, & RESTRICTIONS

Deposit: Full payment 1–3 nights; other 50% w/ full payment 14 days before arrival; refund w/ 15-day notice
Discounts: Off-season, singles
Credit Cards: V, MC
Check-in/Out: 2–6/11

Smoking: Balconies and porches only
Pets: Dogs from Nov.–March: $20 fee
Kids: Over 8
Minimum Stay: 2 nights April–Oct.
Open: Valentine's Day–New Year's Day

Hosts: Karyn and Stephen Caliri
24 South Water St.
Edgartown, MA 02539

(508) 627-4784
victorianinn@vineyard.net
www.thevic.com

OUTERMOST INN, Gay Head

Overall: ★★★★½   Room Quality: B   Value: C   Price: $180–$320

Streaking sunsets over multicolored cliffs, a private beach, a flashing beacon, catamaran sails, and dunes filled with birds, rabbits and deer are among the natural delights just outside your door. The land by the lighthouse at the tip of the island was in Jeanne's family, and no other house can be built here. Surrounded by water and bluffs of bayberry and scrub oaks, this unique, understated house is understandably hard to book. Only drawback is the distance from restaurants, as dinner here isn't nightly. Hugh is brother to James and Livingston Taylor (you'll spot the resemblance immediately), and he's musical too.

SETTING & FACILITIES

Location: Western tip of Martha's Vineyard, on Gay Head Cliffs
Near: Beaches; 18 mi. from down-island towns
Building: Built 1971; gabled, wrap-around porch; recently renovated
Grounds: 6 acres: lawn, lounge chairs, hammocks; 20-plus acres: open land, wildlife; priv. beach; views of ocean, dunes, islands
Public Space: DR, 2 LRs, large porch, dining area, self-serve bar
Food & Drink: Early-bird coffee and tea; full breakfast; specialties: Belgian waffles, omelets, French toast; afternoon drinks on porch; prix fixe dinner option spring–fall (reservations needed); specialties: smoked bass chowder, grilled swordfish, stuffed free-range chicken breast; special diets accom.
Recreation: Sportfishing, windsurfing, sailing on hosts' catamaran, bike rental nearby, horseback riding
Amenities & Services: Daily papers, BYOB orders and delivery

ACCOMMODATIONS

Units: 7 guest rooms
All Rooms: Bath, phone, TV, water views
Some Rooms: Suite: LR, sep. BR; extra bed/sofa bed, hot tub (1)
Bed & Bath: Queens, 1 king; most shower/tub
Favorites: Oak Room—king, best space, large sun-porch; Lighthouse Suite—own entry, deck; Beech Room—hot tub
Comfort & Decor: Wood flooring. No curtains at picture windows. No frills, lace, or clutter. Light, white, airy, casually elegant. Wildflowers.

RATES, RESERVATIONS, & RESTRICTIONS

Deposit: Full payment 1–3 nights by credit card; 50% other; refund w/ 15-day notice
Credit Cards: MC, V, AE, D
Check-in/Out: 2/11
Smoking: In some areas, not in rooms
Pets: No; local kennels
Kids: Over 12
Minimum Stay: Usually 2 nights

Open: May–Oct.
Hosts: Jeanne and Hugh Taylor
RR1, Box 171, Lighthouse Rd.
Gay Head, MA 02535
(508) 645-3511
Fax: (508) 645-3514
inquiries@outermostinn.com
www.outermostinn.com

MARTHA'S PLACE, Vineyard Haven

Overall: ★★★★	Room Quality: A	Value: C	Price: $100–$395

This romantic new bed-and-breakfast with more than a harbor breeze of history and sophistication was built by Nathaniel Mayhew, descendent of a Martha's Vineyard founder who also built Seaman's Bethel and Sail Martha's Vineyard next door, which were originally The Tisbury School, and later a Congregational Church. A white Liberty Pole nearby commemorates the three teenage girls who blew up the town's liberty pole in 1776 so that the British couldn't use it as a mast. Richard and Martin are engaging innkeepers, yet know to respect your privacy. With antique fainting couches, crystal chandeliers, tasseled knobs, brass wall sconces and lush, detailed decor, this is, as Martha Stewart would say, "a good thing."

SETTING & FACILITIES

Location: Across from Owen Park, overlooking Vineyard Haven Harbor, next door to sailing school
Near: Ferry and town, beaches
Building: 1840s Greek Revival
Grounds: Small yard, surrounded by roses
Public Space: Large entry, LR, DR, reading room, porch, patio

Food & Drink: Expanded cont'l breakfast; in room or in bed on request; afternoon tea
Recreation: Tennis, biking, sailing, beach
Amenities & Services: Beach towels/chairs, coolers, tennis racquets/balls, bikes, sailing boats to charter, box lunches, daily papers, refrigerator, irons, turn-down, limited disabled access

ACCOMMODATIONS

Units: 6 guest rooms
All Rooms: Bath, antiques

Some Rooms: Chandelier, harbor view, most fireplace, most AC, sep. sitting room (1)

Bed & Bath: Full and queen; top-quality fixtures, tile and granite; many whirlpools, shower/tub (1), others showers only; hairdryer, robes
Favorites: Empire Room—whirlpool, bath fireplace, antique brass bed w/ half tester in blue velvet, Oriental rug
Comfort & Decor: Individually decorated in romantic style. Period antiques, custom window dressings, hardwood floors, Oriental rugs. Spacious and sunny.

RATES, RESERVATIONS, & RESTRICTIONS

Deposit: Full payment 1–3 nights, 50% other; refund w/ 14-day notice
Discounts: Off-season, longer stays during off-season, 3rd person (1 room only)
Credit Cards: MC, V
Check-in/Out: 1/10; call a day ahead with arrival time
Smoking: Outside
Pets: No
Kids: OK, 1 room best
No-No's: More than 2 to a room; no cots, roll-aways, or cribs

Minimum Stay: 2 nights weekends, 3 nights July/Sept. weekends, 3 nights August
Open: All year
Hosts: Richard Alcott and Martin Hicks
114 Main St., Box 1182
Vineyard Haven, MA 02568
(508) 693-0253
Fax: (508) 693-1890
marthas@vineyard.net
www.marthasplace.com

THORNCROFT INN, Vineyard Haven

Overall: ★★★★	Room Quality: B	Value: C	Price: $170–$450

Romance is emphasized at this shingled cottage on what was once the Thorncraft estate. You choose your breakfast menu the previous evening and can opt for a private breakfast in your room. Thoughtful room touches include earphones for TVs (so others don't have to listen to Leno if they have other ideas), lots of stacked wood for the fireplace, wine glasses and corkscrews, and a chocolate on the pillow. The super-organized hosts live nearby. If you're laid-back and don't need everything laid out, opt for the private cottage. And if you like soaking, book the room with a hot tub big enough for a dozen, but just for two.

SETTING & FACILITIES

Location: From ferry dock take right to Main St.; 1 mi. on left in residential area, 1 block from ocean
Near: Ferry dock, Main St.
Building: Craftsman bungalow, 2 add'l buildings; built 1908-18 as estate's guest house

Grounds: 3.5 landscaped acres
Public Space: 2 DRs, sunroom, LR
Food & Drink: Full country breakfast; specialties: buttermilk pancakes w/ blueberry honey sauce, almond French toast, burritos, quiche; afternoon tea, pastries

Recreation: Shopping, beaches
Amenities & Services: Bike storage, daily paper delivered, wood for fires

year-round; meetings (10), preparing fireplaces, evening turn-down

ACCOMMODATIONS

Units: 14 guest rooms, 1 guest cottage
All Rooms: Bath, AC, phone, TV, hairdryer, robes, iron/board
Some Rooms: Wood-burning fireplace, furnished balcony/porch, priv. entrance, skylight, refrigerator
Bed & Bath: Most canopies, high-back Victorian, four-posters; brass faucets, claw-foot tub, 2-person whirlpools, 300-gallon hot tub

Favorites: The Cottage—king-size canopy, porch w/ hammock, dbl. whirlpool in mirrored alcove, fireplace; Room 1—carved Victorian headboard, woodburning fireplace, 300-gallon hot tub
Comfort & Decor: Individually decorated, some 1900-style w/ antiques. Big windows, bedside lights. Carriage house in Colonial style, most spacious.

RATES, RESERVATIONS, & RESTRICTIONS

Deposit: Full payment 1–2 nights, 50% for 3+ nights; deposit by credit card only; refund w/ 21-day cancellation notice
Discounts: Off-season, on local car rental (call for info)
Credit Cards: MC, V, AE, D, DC
Check-in/Out: 3–9/11; arrange for check-in after 9 p.m.
Smoking: No, extra-tough smoking policy
Pets: No

Kids: No
No-No's: Roll-aways or cots, cash, TVs in main house without earphones
Minimum Stay: 3 nights in-season
Open: All year
Hosts: Lynn and Karl Buder
460 Main St., Box 1022
Vineyard Haven, MA 02568
(508) 693-3333, (800) 332-1236
Fax: (508) 693-5419
innkeeper@thorncroft.com
thorncroft.com/thorncroft/

CORNER HOUSE, Nantucket

Overall: ★★★½	Room Quality: C	Value: C	Price: $75–$235

Comfortable and authentic are adjectives that come to mind about this roomy eighteenth-century bed-and-breakfast complex. It's really a trio of houses on the corner of a residential block, an easy walk to the cobble-stoned center of Nantucket. British-born John is an actor, appearing in local productions; Sandy has run these relaxed lodgings since 1981, and both know the best of the many nearby shops and restaurants. History buffs will especially appreciate the original details of the main house, with its keeping room, hearths, uneven planked floors and Colonial colors. A full afternoon tea with scones and sandwiches by the fireplace is a real treat, and so is breakfast on the flower-rimmed patio.

SETTING & FACILITIES

Location: Across from Congregational Church on Centre St.
Near: Ferries, shops, museums, theaters, beaches
Building: Colonial, c. 1790
Grounds: Screened porch w/wicker furniture, garden terrace
Public Space: Cozy sitting rooms, patio

Food & Drink: Cont'l breakfast buffet; tea w/ sandwiches, cakes, scones, fruit breads, tea, mulled cider
Recreation: Tennis, beach, shopping, antiquing, walking
Amenities & Services: Beach towels, games, concierge service w/ international staff, bike racks

ACCOMMODATIONS

Units: 16 guest rooms, suites in 3 buildings
All Rooms: Bath, AC, reading lamps, antiques
Some Rooms: Kitchenette (1), sitting area, fireplace, TV, refrigerator, patio
Bed & Bath: Queens, doubles, some canopies; large towels; some shower only
Favorites: Elderberry—1st floor, main house, canopy bed, TV, fireplace, priv.

entrance; Lily—3rd floor, cozy, beams, harbor view
Comfort & Decor: Romantic w/ English and American antiques. Rich colors. Rooms range widely—tiny to spacious to suites. Main house most authentic, 3rd floor most private. Swan's nest—larger, same style and decor. Two rooms on floors above innkeepers' house smallish.

RATES, RESERVATIONS, & RESTRICTIONS

Deposit: 50%; refund w/ 15-day notice; late boat/plane arrivals don't jeopardize reservations
Discounts: Off-season, midweek
Credit Cards: MC, V
Check-in/Out: 1/10:30; can leave bags and come back for tea
Smoking: Outdoor sitting rooms only
Pets: No
Kids: Older children

Minimum Stay: Usually 2–4 nights weekends, 2–3 nights midweek; call for shorter stays
Open: Mid-April–mid-Dec.
Hosts: Sandy and John Knox-Johnston
49 Centre St., Box 1828
Nantucket, MA 02554
(508) 228-1530
cornerhs@nantucket.net
www.cornerhousenantucket.com

MARTIN HOUSE INN, Nantucket

Overall: ★★★½	Room Quality: C	Value: C	Price: $60–$195

Debbie is especially helpful and gracious and keeps this nearly 200-year-old mariner's home a warm and cozy house even in the windiest, wettest of Nor'easter storms. The open-plan living/dining area is inviting, with fireplace, piano, TV, and windowseats. Families will appreciate accommodations that can sleep four guests—hard to find on this pretty island. The convenient location by the cobblestoned streets of the village center by the ferry landing means more noise from crowds, but more convenience.

SETTING & FACILITIES

Location: Walk from ferry, 400 yards; historic district, near center
Near: Beaches, shopping, center
Building: Columned 1803 mariner's home; refurbished 1991
Grounds: Large yard w/ seating, hammock
Public Space: Large LR, opens to DR; side porch

Food & Drink: Communal cont'l breakfast; specialties: cranberry muffins, granola
Recreation: Swimming, boating, other water activities
Amenities & Services: Piano, 2 guest refrigerators, irons, books, daily papers, flowers; bike rental nearby

ACCOMMODATIONS

Units: 12 guest rooms; 1 suite
All Rooms: Sherry; individual, traditional decor; large
Some Rooms: Fireplace, bath, refrigerator
Bed & Bath: Most queens, some doubles, twins; canopies, four-posters, extra beds; baths tiled, some shared, some full, shower only (4)

Favorites: Room 21—priv. porch, canopy bed, wood-burning fireplace, sofa, refrigerator, huge but cozy
Comfort & Decor: Antique period pieces. Some rooms papered, some sponge-painted. Lots of old windows, so breezy. Large, bright. Rooms in back quietest.

RATES, RESERVATIONS, & RESTRICTIONS

Deposit: 1–3 nights full payment, 50% longer; refund w/ 14-day notice
Discounts: Singles, off-season (Nov.–May), extra person
Credit Cards: MC, V, AE
Check-in/Out: 3/11
Smoking: No
Pets: No
Kids: 9 and up
Minimum Stay: 2 nights off-season weekends, 3 nights in-season, 4 nights July/August weekends

Open: All year, closed 2nd week of Jan.–1st week Feb.
Hosts: Debbie Wasil
61 Centre St., Box 743
Nantucket, MA 02554
(508) 228-0678
Fax: (508) 325-4798
martinn@nantucket.net
nantucket.net/lodging/martinn

THE PINEAPPLE INN, Nantucket

Overall: ★★★★½   Room Quality: B   Value: C   Price: $110–$275

In the colonies, sharing a hard-to-acquire pineapple was the height of hospitality, so the name well fits this luxurious new bed-and-breakfast acquired by the gracious, former owners of Island Quaker House Inn and Restaurant. A total, architecturally sensitive renovation—reportedly for $1 million—has transformed Captain Uriah Russell's Greek Revival house into the island's most luxurious bed-and-breakfast. No hot breakfasts are allowed at Nantucket small properties (complicated tourist-board reasoning), but Caroline manages nicely: spinach and cheese tart with pecan pesto, nectarine and blueberry clafouti (custard tart), and other delectables.

SETTING & FACILITIES

Location: Steamship Authority or Hy-Line Cruises from Hyannis; ferry 3–4 blocks from B&B; heart of historic district
Near: Hist. waterfront, ferry, restaurants, galleries, theaters, museums
Building: Classic Clapboard, c. 1838, Federal Colonial, Greek Revival touches
Grounds: Bricked garden patio, small pineapple-topped fountain, privacy fencing
Public Space: Parlor, formal DR

Food & Drink: Cont'l breakfasts, communal and staff-served; espresso, cappuccino; specialties: cinnamon biscuits, currant scones w/ nutmeg cream, ciabatta bread
Recreation: Golf, tennis, shopping, cultural events, Christmas Stroll events
Amenities & Services: Classical music in DR, parlor; bike racks, 1 wheelchair equipped room, daytime concierge, DR/conf. room; fax, copier; recipes

ACCOMMODATIONS

Units: 12 guest rooms
All Rooms: Bath, good reading lights, desk, phone/voice mail/dataport, AC, alarm clock, temperature controls
Some Rooms: Ornamental fireplace, seating, French doors, priv. patio (1)
Bed & Bath: Hand-crafted Eldred Wheeler lace canopy or carved beds, queen/king sizes; white marble baths, some shower only
Favorites: Captain George Pollard Room—King canopy, priv. garden patio

Comfort & Decor: Most windows overlooking rear gardens. Victorian light fixtures. Oriental carpets. Quality reproductions and 19th-century antiques. TVs in highboys. Rooms named after Nantucket whaling captains. Comfort and quiet romance. Queen bed rooms, smallish; king rooms spacious.

RATES, RESERVATIONS, & RESTRICTIONS

Deposit: Full payment 1–3 night stays; 50% 4+ nights; refund w/ 15-day notice, earlier notice for holidays

Discounts: None

Credit Cards: MC, V, AE

Check-in/Out: 3/11

Smoking: No

Pets: No

Kids: No

No-No's: 3rd person in room

Minimum Stay: 2–3 nights weekends/holidays

Open: last weekend in April–Dec., after Christmas Stroll

Hosts: Caroline and Bob Taylor
10 Hussey St.
Nantucket, MA 02554
(508) 228-9992
Fax: (508) 228-9992
pineappl@nantucket.net
www.nantucket.net/lodging/pineappleinn

Rhode Island

It may be tiny, but a state whose flag's motto is "Hope," and which was founded by Roger Williams in 1636 on the principles of religious and political freedom, is indeed impressive. Rhode Island was the first colony to declare independence from British rule; the first to denounce its own profits and prohibit the importation of slaves; and the last to sign the Constitution—on May 4, 1776—holding out until the Bill of Rights was incorporated.

Merely 37 miles wide by 48 miles long (you could cover it in less than an hour), Rhode Island still packs a punch, with art museums, Brown University in booming Providence, historic sites, and performing arts centers. And this Ocean State has 100 miles of sandy beaches and 400 miles of ocean coastline.

The gem is Newport, a prominent New World shipping port that thrived on farming and sea trade. In the Gilded Age of the late nineteenth century, it provided the ultimate lifestyle for the rich and famous. It retains elaborate mansion "cottages," Ocean Cliff Walk, music festivals, shopping, fine dining, beaches—and some of the most authentic and luxurious bed-and-breakfasts in America.

In addition to Providence and Newport, down-to-earth Pawtucket is credited as the "Birthplace of American Industry," Bristol is known for shipbuilding, Blackstone offers river activities, Block Island is a fresh breath of the past, and Watch Hill has one of the oldest carousels in America.

Squeezed into the southeastern corner of New England, Rhode Island is 60 miles from Boston and 180 miles from New York City, so weekenders abound. Veer across Massachusetts or Connecticut and dip into its choice pleasures at wildly luxurious or basic small inns and bed-and-breakfasts— some among the best bargains in New England. Look for Victorian retreats on Block Island, reconverted mansions in Newport, the academic and quirky little houses in Providence, and industralists' former homes in seaside town and river valley bed-and-breakfasts.

For More Information

Anna's Victorian Connection
(401) 849-2469 or (800) 884-4288
email: annas@well.com

RI State Tourism Bureau
(888) 746-6835 or (800) 556-2484
email: riedc@ried.com

Rhode Island Tourism
www.visitrhodeisland.com
(links to area weather, tourism)

Zone 15
Newport & Little Compton, Rhode Island

A foremost shipping port in the 1700s, Newport became a synonym for luxury and ostentatious living as a summer resort in the late 1800s, catering to Vanderbilts, Carnegies, and hundreds of their nearest and dearest. Later, Jacqueline and John F. Kennedy were married in St. Mary's Church here in town, hosting a wedding reception at Jackie's home, Hammersmith Farm, the "summer White House" from 1961–1963.

Today the "City-by-the-Sea" is less elitist but still cultivates and glories in its image. Numerous grand cottages are open for tours. Some favorites: The Breakers residence, stables, and carriage house, a 70-room, ocean view, Italianate complex featuring Vanderbilt memorabilia and furnishings; Belcourt Castle, Louis XIII–style down to its full-size gold coronation coach; the Astors' Beechwood, with costumed actors; and Chateau-Sur-Mer, lavishly, dreamily Victorian.

Newport's historic trappings back up the mansions. Touro Synagogue, the oldest temple in America, was built in 1763; Pelham Street was the first in the country to install gas-illuminated streetlights. The White Horse Tavern, c. 1673, the oldest tavern building in the country, still dispenses suds.

You can sail or cruise, visit the International Tennis Hall of Fame or the yachting or doll museums, enjoy jai alai, a day spa, or even an aquarium. Summer theater is popular, and Newport hosts fairs, shows, and tournaments including music festivals in July and August, a boat show in September, and a 10-day Winter Festival in dreary February. A brisk walk along Newport's three-and-a-half mile Ocean Cliff Walk may put this bounty in perspective.

Easton's Beach is the beach, and Fort Adams State Park is the nature retreat among all this activity. The information center in the historical district operates as a transportation/activity/information hub. At Christmas, the town sponsors prizes for best seasonal decorations, right down to the symbolic luminaria candle lights.

Not surprisingly, the mansion bed-and-breakfasts in town maintain high standards and cut-above service. Many properties offer the option of packages that include dinner at a local restaurant and mansion-tour tickets.

The nearby, isolated island of Little Compton is far from the bustling crowds; it is rural and small townish with farms and vineyards and some simple bed-and-breakfasts. It couldn't be more of a contrast with Newport.

For More Information

Bed & Breakfast Newport
(800) 800-8765

Newport County Commerce & Visitors Bureau
(800) 976-5122
fax: (401) 849-0291
www.gonewport.com

Newport Inns Association
(401) 847-1355
email: nibbs@newport1.com

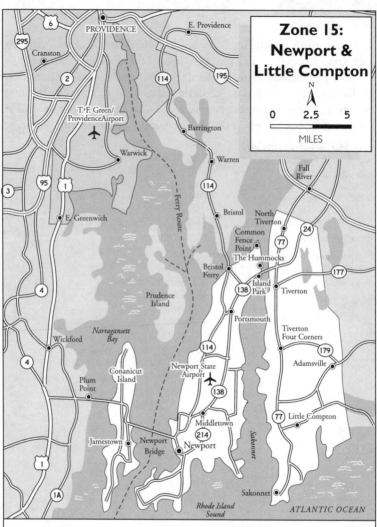

Zone 15:
Newport &
Little Compton

N

0   2.5   5

MILES

THE ROOST, Little Compton

Overall: ★★★★	Room Quality: C	Value: B	Price: $85–$95

This small bed-and-breakfast on an isolated peninsula at the entrance of the Sakonnet Vineyards is a haven for wine and food lovers—and great for friends traveling together, who could take over the premises and party among the vines. Fifty acres are planted with varietals including Chardonnay, Gewurztraminer, Pinot Noir, and Cabernet Franc, as well as Vidal Blanc, a French-American hybrid. Production here is over 50,000 cases annually, with many award-winners. As you bicycle along flat, rural roads toward the harbor, it almost seems you're in Bordeaux.

SETTING & FACILITIES

Location: Rt. 77 S, through traffic light at Tiverton Four Corners; Sakonnet Vineyards is on left, 3 mi. after the light
Near: Ocean; 30 min. to Newport, Providence; 1 hour to Boston
Building: Orig. rustic farmhouse, natural shingles, porches
Grounds: Over 50 acres of vineyards, founded in 1975
Public Space: Cozy common room, small dining area

Food & Drink: Communal cont'l breakfast; specialties: scones, muffins
Recreation: Antiquing, beach activities, tours, comp. winery tours/tastings
Amenities & Services: Phone avail.; monthly fall–spring Sakonnet Chefs program, cooking classes, dinner, appropriate wines served; Sakonnet House facil. avail. for business meetings, priv. dinners, weddings; rooms freshened daily

ACCOMMODATIONS

Units: 3 guest rooms
All Rooms: Bath, seating, reading light
Some Rooms: Skylight
Bed & Bath: 1 queen canopy bed, 1 double, 2 twins, trundle; 2 full, 1 shower bath
Favorites: Blue Room—queen canopy, largest room, pickled floor, shutters, tiled shower

Comfort & Decor: Guest rooms on 2nd floor. Recently renovated and decorated. Gray room quietest, back of house. Two twins can be fitted together. Cozy, small rooms.

RATES, RESERVATIONS, & RESTRICTIONS

Deposit: 1 night or 50% if longer; refund w/ 14-day notice; otherwise, credit
Discounts: Events packages
Credit Cards: MC, V, AE
Check-in/Out: 4/11
Smoking: No
Pets: No

Kids: Over 12
Minimum Stay: 2 nights weekends, Memorial Day–Columbus Day; 3 nights holiday weekends
Open: All year
Hosts: Susan and Earl Samson
162 West Main Rd.

Little Compton, RI 02837
(800) 91-WINES or (401) 635-8486
Fax: (401) 635-2101

sakonnetri.@aol.com
www.sakonnetwine.com

1855 MARSHALL SLOCUM GUEST HOUSE, Newport

Overall: ★★★½	Room Quality: B	Value: C	Price: $90–$165

Delightful Joan states that she has a large family of guests who make this pretty bed-and-breakfast their home away from home. "I love what I do, it truly is a wonderful life." And it's a family affair. Daughter Julie lends a hand with summer lobster dinners on the deck on Wednesdays, a real New England treat. Few owners have tampered with this nineteenth-century, gingerbread-trimmed structure, so there has been little modernization and loads of enhanced charm and comforts remain for you to enjoy, along with the lobster and the handcrafted antique beds.

SETTING & FACILITIES

Location: Kay-Catherine area of Newport; Victorian residential neighborhood

Near: Easton's Beach, ocean, historic mansions, Tennis Hall of Fame, Bowen's Wharf, cobblestone Marine District, Brick Market Place, Cliff Walk, state park, museums, aquarium, summer theater, White Horse Tavern

Building: 1855 Victorian

Grounds: Spacious rear yard, back deck, barbecue

Public Space: Traditional LR, lived-in parlor, DR

Food & Drink: Yankee-style 3-course breakfast, communal, separate or in room; a specialty: crepes w/ asparagus and ham in cheddar sauce; refreshments, hors d'oeuvres: homemade Boursin with Chardonnay; lobster dinner Wed. nights, comp. w/ 3-night midweek stay, summer only; beach picnics avail.; gourmet menu for priv. functions

Recreation: Shopping; harbor cruises, golf; summer classical music festival, jazz festival, and folk festival

Amenities & Services: Beach towels, irons, daily paper; fax, computer services; maps, recipes; catering, weddings, functions, groups

ACCOMMODATIONS

Units: 6 guest rooms

All Rooms: Bath, reading lights, clock/radio

Some Rooms: AC, ceiling fan, skylight, 3rd person, quilts

Bed & Bath: Antique, handcarved, brass beds, queen and twin sizes; some showers only, 1 claw-foot tub, robes

Favorites: Brass Room—brass queen, hunter green walls, white wicker, mirrored French doors

Comfort & Decor: Cozy and inviting. Under-the-eaves warmth. Some wall bunks, skylights. Comforting fabrics, wallpapers, rugs. Antique furnishings and period touches.

RATES, RESERVATIONS, & RESTRICTIONS

Deposit: 1 night or will hold w/ credit card; refund w/ 7-day notice
Discounts: 3rd person
Credit Cards: MC, V, AE
Check-in/Out: 2/noon
Smoking: No
Pets: No
Kids: Over 12
Minimum Stay: 2 nights weekends, 3 nights holidays

Open: All year
Hosts: Joan Wilson
29 Kay St.
Newport, RI 02840
(800) 372-5120 or (401) 841-5120
Fax: (401) 846-3787
marshallslocuminn@edgenet.net
www.marchallslocuminn.com

CLARKSTON, Newport

| Overall: ★★★★ | Room Quality: B | Value: C | Price: $95–$245 |

On one of Newport's first streets, this is one of the oldest inns anywhere in the states; the current dining room was the entire original one-story, one-room structure. History is much appreciated and venerated by Tamara and Rick, who named and decorated guest rooms after famous or infamous locals. This bed-and-breakfast wins the Newport town prize for holiday decorations every year, a reflection of their efforts throughout. The enthusiastic hosts love their antique home—renovated in the 1990s and decorated to provide updated comfort while retaining authentic Colonial charm.

SETTING & FACILITIES

Location: On America's Cup Ave. in Newport, turn left at the Marriott onto Marlboro St., right onto Thames, left onto Touro St., second right to Clarke St.; B&B is on left
Near: Tennis Hall of Fame, Yachting Museum; Bowen's Wharf, cobblestone Marine District, Brick Market Place, state park, museums, aquarium, summer theater, Hammersmith Farm, ocean, Cliff Walk, mansions; walk to harbor, restaurants
Building: 1705 Village Colonial; addition in late 1800s; renovated under aus-

pices of Parks Commission in 1993
Grounds: Minimal; parking lot
Public Space: Entry parlor, DR
Food & Drink: Full breakfast; comp. tea/coffee/soft drinks
Recreation: Tennis, golf, boating, harbor cruises, beach activities; Music Festival (July), Jazz and Folk Festivals (Aug.), Int'l Boat Show (Sept.) Christmas in Newport (Dec.), and Winter Festival (Feb.)
Amenities & Services: Refrigerator w/ refreshments, irons, phone, daily paper, maps, fax, dataport

Accommodations

Units: 9 guest rooms
All Rooms: Bath, fireplace or whirlpool, AC
Some Rooms: Orig. wide-plank or hardwood floors, Oriental rugs; sound/media system (1), sitting area (2), 3rd person (1)
Bed & Bath: Some four-poster, sleigh, canopy beds, queen or king, all featherbeds; luxury baths, marble, some dbl. sinks, tiled oversized showers, some showers only, some 2-person whirlpools

Favorites: Joseph Burrill—fireplace, king four-poster, blue/white decor, corner w/ 4 windows, dbl. shower; Harry Belmont Room—dbl. whirlpool, king sleigh bed, hunter green walls, dbl. marble vanity
Comfort & Decor: 3rd-floor rooms smaller but lots of Colonial character, antique wide-plank floors. Mrs. Oelrich Room, casual white-and-green–striped fabrics, wicker, summery decor, w/ all amenities: fireplace, 1-person whirlpool, sitting area

Rates, Reservations, & Restrictions

Deposit: 100%
Discounts: Midweek, dinner packages, AAA, seniors, corp./groups, longer stays
Credit Cards: MC, V, AE
Check-in/Out: 3/11
Smoking: No
Pets: No
Kids: Welcome in certain rooms only
Minimum Stay: 2 nights weekends, 3 nights holidays/festivals

Open: All year
Hosts: Tamara and Rick Farrick
28 Clarke St.
Newport, RI 02840
(800) 524-1386 or (401) 849-7397
Fax: (401) 847-7630
clarkeston@travelbase.com
www.innsofnewport.com

CLIFFSIDE INN, Newport

Overall: ★★★★★	Room Quality: A	Value: C	Price: $195–$480

Originally built for Maryland Governor Thomas Swann, Cliffside was purchased by American painter and eccentric recluse, Beatrice Turner, who dressed exclusively in Victorian garb, painted her house black and even painted her embalmed father. She created 3,000 paintings—over 1,000 self-portraits. Short-sighted executors burned most of her works in 1948, and in 1980 passersby rescued the rest from piles tossed on a rainy sidewalk. In 1996, savvy businessman Winthrop Baker—original producer of the *Oprah Winfrey Show*—spent over $1 million to restore Cliffside. Today, he offers a reward for Turner paintings, and continues to enhance this lush, evocative, dramatic property.

SETTING & FACILITIES

Location: Quiet residential neighborhood, 1 mi. from downtown Newport, on Seaview Ave.

Near: 1 block to ocean Cliff Walk, 5 min. walk to ocean beach, walk to Gilded Age mansions, Tennis Hall of Fame, shopping and restaurants, cobblestone Marine District, Brick Market Place, state park, museums, aquarium, summer theater

Building: 1880 Second-Empire Victorian summer mansion; Cliffside Cottage, purchased and renovated in 1996

Grounds: Garden, veranda; Seaview Cottage: semi-priv. patio, seating; 1 acre total

Public Space: Front hall, spacious parlor; breakfast alcove

Food & Drink: Gourmet breakfast communal or separate; specialties: red pepper cornbread, farmhouse eggs Benedict w/ rosemary Hollandaise, chocolate tart; wake-up coffee/tea delivered to rooms; Victorian afternoon tea, delicious standard fare; after-dinner treats

Recreation: Tennis, harbor cruises, golf, biking, summer music festivals

Amenities & Services: Hot tub, laundry, refrigerator, irons, bicycle storage, turn-down, maps, daily paper, videos, fax, beach towels; small meetings

ACCOMMODATIONS

Units: Main building: 6 guest rooms, 10 suites; Cliffside Cottage: 3 suites

All Rooms: Bath, antiques, TV, VCR, phone, heat/AC controls, alarm/radio, fireplace, whirlpool

Some Rooms: Ceiling fan, hardwood floors, dramatic architectural features, skylight, window seat, dataport, priv. entrance, priv. or semi-priv. outdoor space, ocean view (1)

Bed & Bath: Antique or handcrafted beds, queen or king; robes, hairdryers, some dbl. whirlpools, separate showers, some fireplaces, some showers only, some hand-held showers, 1 steam bath, 1 antique Victorian birdcage shower, 1 heated bath floor, fresh flowers

Favorites: Seaview Cottage Cliff Suite—study, LR, BR, obscured water views, king plantation bed, 3 fireplaces, stereo/media systems, bath skylight, large whirlpool, dataport, pine-paneled cathedral ceilings

Comfort & Decor: Oak and mahogany trim, antiques, stenciled walls, Laura Ashley florals. Victorian Tower Suite: 18 foot paneled cupola ceiling. Garden Suite: 2 levels. Beatrice's room: floral murals, preserved over 90 years.

RATES, RESERVATIONS, & RESTRICTIONS

Deposit: 50%; nonrefundable, 1 year credit for future stay w/ 15-day notice

Discounts: Packages Nov.–April, check; extra $25 charge high-season weekends, holidays/festivals

Credit Cards: MC, V, AE, D

Check-in/Out: 3–9/11; till noon by arrangement

Smoking: No

Pets: No

Kids: Over 13

Minimum Stay: 2 nights over Sat., 3 nights holidays/festivals

Open: All year

Hosts: Stephan Nicolas, innkeeper; Winthrop P. Baker, owner
2 Seaview Ave.
Newport, RI 02840
(800) 845-1811 or (401) 847-1811
Fax: (401) 848-5850
cliff@wsii.com
www.cliffside.com

ELM TREE COTTAGE, Newport

Overall: ★★★★★	Room Quality: A	Value: C	Price: $135–$325

Perfect hosts Priscilla and Tom, both trained artists and artisans, established a bed-and-breakfast evocative of the "casual ritziness" of Newport's gilded age—a time when local mansions were honestly called summer cottages. Tom's stained glass and Priscilla's watercolors are showcased, and they work in the basement producing magnificent windows, many for guests. The hosts continue to add glamour and glitz to rooms once owned by a railroad heiress. Cheeky touches includes a pub interior with portholes, and a bar inlaid with silver dollars. Luxury, romance, warmth, unexpected pleasures, and lavish comfort describe this wonderful bed-and-breakfast experience, perhaps the best in Rhode Island.

SETTING & FACILITIES

Location: In estate neighborhood; Rt. 138 to Newport Bridge, take Scenic Newport Exit, turn right onto Farewall St., right onto America's Cup Ave., the road becomes Memorial Blvd., left onto Gibbs Ave., B&B is 3rd house on right after stop sign
Near: Overlooks Easton Pond and First Beach; Cliff Walk, Easton's Beach, mansions, Tennis Hall of Fame, Bowen's Wharf, cobblestone Marine District, Brick Market Place, state park, museums, aquarium, summer theater
Building: 1882 Shingle-style summer mansion, 8,000 square feet
Grounds: 1 acre, landscaped lawns

Public Space: Sunroom; spacious LR, pub room, DR
Food & Drink: Cold buffet, hot entree breakfast; specialties: French toast soufflé w/ whipped maple cream, Chateau potatoes topped w/ poached egg and parmesan cheese sauce, Quiche Lorraine in crepe cups w/ broiled tomato; coffee always avail.; BYOB bar
Recreation: Tennis, golf, boating, harbor cruises, biking, summer music festivals
Amenities & Services: Grand piano, books, games, turn-down, gift cert.

ACCOMMODATIONS

Units: 6 guest rooms
All Rooms: Bath; French, English, and Newport estate antiques
Some Rooms: Fireplace, sitting area, AC, TV on request
Bed & Bath: Carved queen or Louis VX king beds, crown or half canopies; luxury appointments in baths, some showers only
Favorites: The Windsor—nearly 1,000 square feet; winter water views, crown

canopy king bed, 2 sitting areas, fireplace, stained glass, Victorian decor; sink w/ crystal legs
Comfort & Decor: Creatively coordinated fabrics/wallcoverings. Elaborately elegant pieces toned down by casual/country appointments. Original carved mantels. Dramatic, romantic beds. Playful props carry room themes. Abundance and comfort.

RATES, RESERVATIONS, & RESTRICTIONS

Deposit: 1 night or 50% with longer stay; refund w/ 30-day notice; credit w/ 15-day notice; deposits for multiple-room reservations nonrefundable
Discounts: Off-season; add 15% gratuity to price for groups and whole house rentals
Credit Cards: None
Check-in/Out: 2/11; will hold luggage for early arrival
Smoking: No
Pets: No

Kids: Over 14
Minimum Stay: 2 nights weekends; 3 nights weekends July–Oct./holidays/festivals
Open: Feb.–Dec.
Hosts: Priscilla and Tom Malone
336 Gibbs Ave.
Newport, RI 02840
(888) ELM TREE or (401) 849-1610
Fax: (401) 849-2084
elmtree@efortress.com
www.elmtreebnb.com

FRANCIS MALBONE HOUSE, Newport

Overall: ★★★★½	Room Quality: A	Value: C	Price: $155–$375

This house is attributed to America's first famed architect, Peter Harrison, who also designed Newport's Truro Synagogue. Legend is that the colonel, a wealthy shipping merchant, built an underground tunnel to the nearby waterfront to smuggle rum and avoid taxes. The house was later seized by the British Army to store gold, and in the 1800s was returned to the colonel's son, a U.S. senator. Today this historic bed-and-breakfast, now near shops and trendy restaurants, is little changed from when its forebears dined by the open hearth or slept in the high-ceilinged bedrooms (except maybe for the whirlpools and skylights—and the raspberry cream-cheese French toast).

SETTING & FACILITIES

Location: Downtown harborfront, Rt. 138 E into Newport; Scenic Newport Exit to downtown, to Thames St.
Near: Ocean, Tennis Hall of Fame, museums, Bowen's Wharf, cobblestone Marine District, Brick Market Place, Cliff Walk, state park, aquarium, summer theater, White Horse Tavern
Building: 1760 Colonial mansion; Mediterranean-style rear building exterior; 1996 addition
Grounds: Flagstone patio, gardens, fountain; French doors to 2nd secluded courtyard.

Public Space: Formal entrance foyer, guest parlor, library/sitting room, Colonial DR
Food & Drink: Gourmet breakfast, early riser coffee/tea, afternoon treats; specialties: peach ricotta pancakes, pear or almond crepes; guest pantry and coffee maker
Recreation: Tennis, golf, harbor cruises, biking; summer music festivals, incl. Jazz Festival
Amenities & Services: Separate phone line for incoming guest calls, TV, turn-down, comp. postcards mailed for guests, corp./priv. affairs, wedding facilities

ACCOMMODATIONS

Units: 16 guest rooms, 2 suites
All Rooms: Bath, antiques, hardwood floors, phone, AC
Some Rooms: Fireplace, sitting area, desk/table, whirlpool, TV, French doors to semi-priv. courtyard, 3rd-person bed, wet bar (1), mini-refrigerator (1), priv. entrance (1)
Bed & Bath: Queen Anne four-poster king and queen beds; plush towels, 1 dbl. whirlpool
Favorites: Courtyard Suite—fireplace, spacious sitting area, wet bar,
French doors to courtyard, king four-poster, whirlpool, TV; Counting House Suite—all amenities plus dbl. whirlpool, refrigerator, priv. entrance; rooms in addition are desirable for courtyard access
Comfort & Decor: Guest rooms in traditional Colonial style. High ceilings, spacious, hardwood floors, Oriental rugs, traditional mahogany furnishings. Window seats, period art prints, federal colors.

RATES, RESERVATIONS, & RESTRICTIONS

Deposit: 1 night or 50% with longer stay; refunds w/ 14-day notice
Discounts: 3rd night free in Dec. (exclusions), 2nd night free midweek off-season, corp. retreats, meeting planners, 3rd person
Credit Cards: MC, V, AE
Check-in/Out: 2/11; will hold luggage
Smoking: Courtyard only
Pets: No
Kids: Over 12
Minimum Stay: 3 nights weekends, July–Oct.; 2 nights weekends, Nov.–June; check for holidays
Open: All year
Hosts: Will Dewey and Mark Eads
392 Thames St.
Newport, RI 02840
(800) 846-0392 or (401) 846-0392
Fax: (401) 848-5956
innkeeper@malbone.com
www.malbone.com

HYDRANGEA HOUSE INN, Newport

| Overall: ★★★★ | Room Quality: B | Value: C | Price: $100–$280 |

This blooming beauty on top of Newport's historic hill is aptly named after the flowering plant beyond the veranda. (According to legend, mansion gardeners took cuttings from summer Gilded Age gardens, thereby spreading the luxury.) The owners are former antiques dealers, and the on-site art gallery showcases an extensive fine-art collection from all over the world. Breakfasting here amid the paintings is a real treat, and the magnificent suite is darkly, lushly romantic.

SETTING & FACILITIES

Location: Center of Newport's historic walking district

Near: Ocean, Tennis Hall of Fame, Yachting Museum; shopping and restaurants, cobblestone marine district; Brick Market Place, state park, museums, aquarium, summer theater, White Horse Tavern

Building: 1876 Victorian cottage-style; art gallery storefront; renovated, 1994

Grounds: Roof sun deck, rear deck, perennial gardens, hydrangeas

Public Space: Art gallery; faux marble entrance, drawing room

Food & Drink: Full buffet breakfast; specialties: raspberry pancakes, seasoned eggs, home-baked breads and granola; English tea; bedtime cookies and milk

Recreation: Tennis, harbor cruises, 3.2 mi. Cliff Walk, musical festivals

Amenities & Services: Refrigerator access, beach towels, maps, fax

ACCOMMODATIONS

Units: 6 guest rooms

All Rooms: Bath, antiques, orig. artwork, AC, crystal glasses, plush carpet, fresh flowers

Bed & Bath: Some four-posters, sizes vary; some showers only

Favorites: The Hydrangea Suite—fireplace, elegant king bed, sitting area, dbl. whirlpool in room, steam bath in mar-

ble bath, TV, VCR, phone, turn-down service

Comfort & Decor: Fresh flowers, plush carpet, and Oriental rugs, ambiance lighting, Federal colors, gleaming woodwork, rich fabrics. Formal romance—possibly too dramatic for some. Street-front rooms can be noisy. Some rooms tiny. Suite is super-deluxe.

RATES, RESERVATIONS, & RESTRICTIONS

Deposit: Greater of 1 night or 50%; refund w/ 14-day notice

Discounts: Midweek 2nd night free Nov.–April (exclusions)

Credit Cards: MC, V

Check-in/Out: 2–9:30/11

Smoking: No

Pets: No

Kids: No

No-No's: 3rd person in room

Minimum Stay: 2 nights high-season weekends, 3 nights all holidays and all

event weekends; but check for 1 night availability

Open: All year

Hosts: Dennis Blair and Grant Edmondson
16 Bellevue Ave.
Newport, RI 02840
(800) 945-4667 or (401) 846-4435
Fax: (401) 846-6602
BandBInn@ids.net
www.bestinns.net/usa/ri/hydr.html

IVY LODGE, Newport

Overall: ★★★★½	Room Quality: A	Value: C	Price: $125–$225

Considered one of Newport's most exciting bed-and-breakfasts, the property's original, remarkable paneled entry hall soars with a triple staircase and balconies with enough spindle balusters for every day of the year. The rest, designed by famed Stanford White, is decidedly anticlimatic, but still lovely. The dining room has a 20-foot table seating 16, and an antique sideboard is laden at breakfast with goodies such as popovers with peaches and Romanoff sauce. Maggie was a social worker, and her caring ways can be seen throughout. All the guest rooms are charming, but the turret room is, well, tops.

SETTING & FACILITIES

Location: Rt. 138 across Newport Bridge, Memorial to Bellevue to Narragansett, turn left at 1st light and left again onto Clay St., B&B is 1st large house on right, near the cottages
Near: Ocean Cliff Walk, Easton's Beach, Gilded Age mansions, Tennis Hall of Fame, Bowen's Wharf, cobblestone Marine District, Brick Market Place, state park, museums, aquarium, summer theater
Building: Large 1886 Shingle Victorian designed by Stanford White
Grounds: 1 acre: privacy hedge, lawn games, English-style specimen gardens

Public Space: 3-story entry hall; airy LR, floor-to-ceiling windows/arched doors to veranda; small sitting room; DR
Food & Drink: Communal buffet breakfast; specialties: smoked fish, bananas flambé, bread pudding; afternoon refreshments
Recreation: Tennis, boating, harbor cruises, biking, golf, summer music festivals
Amenities & Services: Baby grand piano, irons, beach towels, maps, recipes, small/medium meetings, small weddings

ACCOMMODATIONS

Units: 8 guest rooms
All Rooms: Bath, fresh flowers, carpet, AC
Some Rooms: Fireplace, whirlpool, balcony
Bed & Bath: Antique, four-poster beds, sizes vary; some showers only

Favorites: The Library—mahogany sleigh bed, fireplace, whirlpool; The Turret—great view, connecting room
Comfort & Decor: Striking Victorian feel, Laura Ashley fabrics/papers. Pretty decorative touches such as wicker birdcage, open parasol, bedside topiary. Configurations good for family or friends.

RATES, RESERVATIONS, & RESTRICTIONS

Deposit: 50%
Discounts: Singles, longer stays
Credit Cards: MC, V, AE, D

Check-in/Out: 2/11, later by arrangement
Smoking: On veranda only

Pets: No
Kids: Welcome
Minimum Stay: 2 nights weekends
Open: All year, except Thanksgiving
Eve, Christmas Eve, and Christmas Day

Hosts: Maggie and Terry Moy
12 Clay St.
Newport, RI 02840
(800) 834-6865 or (401) 849-6865

JAILHOUSE INN, Newport

Overall: ★★★	Room Quality: C	Value: C	Price: $45–$385

For those who relish the idea of a night in the pokey, this former jail will have to do. (An unnamed source mentioned handcuffs found in guest rooms over the years, presumably voluntary.) A reception area behind bars, cell doors leading to the breakfast room, and hallways created from the original cell blocks are a few of the fun touches, but a bit more decorative imagination would be a bonus. Kids might especially enjoy the idea of spending "time," here, near the wharf and shops, and it beats being incarcerated.

SETTING & FACILITIES

Location: Historic downtown Newport
Near: 1 block to Visitor's Center, shops and wharf, ocean, museums, aquarium, summer theater, historic White Horse Tavern
Building: 1772 white brick, columns, Colonial facade; restored jailhouse
Grounds: Front porch

Public Space: Reception area behind bars; orig. cell doors lead to breakfast room; cell blocks are now inn's hallways; breakfast room and airy lobby
Food & Drink: Cont'l breakfast; tea; MAP avail. (area restaurants)
Recreation: Tennis, boating, harbor cruises; music festivals, eating
Amenities & Services: Irons; hairdryers, sewing kits, masseuse avail.

ACCOMMODATIONS

Units: 17 guest rooms, 5 suites
All Rooms: Bath, TV, compact refrigerator, phone, AC
Some Rooms: Sitting area or 2nd BR, skylight, wheelchair access (1)
Bed & Bath: Queen or king beds; full baths

Favorites: 3rd floor walk-ups—sitting area, skylight; L-shaped corner room—partly obstructed harbor view
Comfort & Decor: Contemporary ambiance, austere, small rooms. Not romantic. Comfortable bedding, striped bedsheets, prints of Elvis in *Jailhouse Rock* on walls.

RATES, RESERVATIONS, & RESTRICTIONS

Deposit: 1 night; refund w/ 5-day notice

Discounts: Off-season corp., military and longer stay; children free; MAP

packages incl. 2 tickets to Newport
Mansions Tour
Credit Cards: MC, V, AE
Check-in/Out: 3/11
Smoking: Front porch only
Pets: No
Kids: Welcome
Minimum Stay: 2 nights weekends; 3
nights holidays and festivals

Open: All year
Hosts: Bob Briskin
13 Marlborough
Newport, RI 02840
(800) 427-9444 or 201-847-4638
Fax: (401) 849-0605

OLD BEACH INN, Newport

Overall: ★★★★   Room Quality: B   Value: C   Price: $100–$185

Originally a commodore's home, named The Anchorage, the 1879 property indeed has an anchor carved in the wood at the top of the house. The guest room names are more evocative, such as Ivy, with its dark green accents and cozy, masculine feel, and Forget-me-not, in blues and yellow, with a fireplace. But today, the name Old Beach Inn, after the road it's on, most reflects the interests of Newport's bed-and-breakfast guests: water pleasures, tradition, cottage architecture, and good times.

SETTING & FACILITIES

Location: Newport's Top of the Hill area of Historic Hill
Near: Tennis Hall of Fame, Yachting Museum; Bowen's Wharf, cobblestone Marine District; Brick Market Place, state park, museums, aquarium, summer theater, Hammersmith Farm; walk to ocean beach, Cliff Walk, Gilded Age mansions, restaurants
Building: 1879 Gothic Victorian, renovated in 1991
Grounds: Village yard: flower gardens, Japanese fish pond, gazebo, brick patio

Public Space: Entrance foyer, parlors, breakfast room
Food & Drink: Cont'l buffet breakfast, full breakfast on Sun.; guest pantry
Recreation: Harbor cruises, music festivals, Int'l Boat Show (Sept.) Christmas in Newport (Dec.), and Winter Festival (Feb.)
Amenities & Services: Refrigerator, irons, maps, beach towels, daily paper, small meetings, Dec. decorations

ACCOMMODATIONS

Units: 5 main house guest rooms, 2 carriage house rooms
All Rooms: Bath, carpet, AC
Some Rooms: Fireplace, TV, skylight, antique English wood stove (1)

Bed & Bath: Some handpainted antique beds, full and queen sizes; some showers only
Favorites: Romantic Rose Room—most spacious, creative queen canopy

bed, fireplace, oak armoire, wicker
Comfort & Decor: Main house guest
rooms: high ceilings, original moldings,
nooks and alcoves. Carriage house
rooms more private, separate
entrances. Whimsy in creative use of
laces, wreaths, flowers, artwork, stenciling, collectibles, coordinated fabrics.

RATES, RESERVATIONS, & RESTRICTIONS

Deposit: 1st 3 nights or 50%; refund
w/ 15-day notice (30 for multi-room
bookings); cancellations w/ less notice
receive future-stay credit if room is
re-rented
Discounts: Longer stays, midweek off-
season
Credit Cards: MC, V, AE, D
Check-in/Out: 2–8/11
Smoking: Outside only
Pets: No

Kids: Over 12
Minimum Stay: 3 nights holiday/festi-
val weekends
Open: All year
Hosts: Cynthia and Luke Murray
19 Old Beach Rd.
Newport, RI 02840
(888) 303-5033 or (401) 849-3479
Fax: (401) 847-1236
info@oldbeachinn.com
www.oldbeachinn.com

SAVANA'S INN, Newport

Overall: ★★★★½	Room Quality: B	Value: C	Price: $135–$275

No, the name has nothing to do with the city in Georgia. This new bed-
and-breakfast arrived in 1998, after perfectionists Ande and Phil had
delayed the opening for two years to complete the restoration to their sat-
isfaction. The Savanas are only the third owners of this historic property,
filled with parquet and hardwood floors, bold Oriental rugs, Victorian
mantels and woodwork, period wallpapers, and gilded finishes. Family
photos and other warm touches remind guests that this elegant bed-and-
breakfast is also a home, and guests are encouraged to chat in the kitchen.
Still evolving in a city filled with other wonderful properties, this diminutive one rises up to the challenge.

SETTING & FACILITIES

Location: Historic Hill District; on
Pelham St.
Near: Bowen's Wharf, Antique Row,
Cliff Walk, Easton's Beach, Gilded Age
mansions, Tennis Hall of Fame, cobble-
stone Marine District, Brick Market
Place, state park, museums, aquarium,
summer theater
Building: 1865 Second-Empire
Victorian

Grounds: English gardens, fountains,
walking paths, sitting areas, pergola,
secluded stone-encased hot tub
Public Space: Foyer, parlor, "Men's
club" library, DR
Food & Drink: Gourmet breakfast,
communal; specialties: puffed pancakes
w/ fruit garnish, vegetable frittatas,
salmon corn cakes; refreshments on
arrival; evening cordials and treats

Recreation: Tennis, golf, boating, harbor cruises, biking, summer music festivals
Amenities & Services: Hot tub, irons, hairdryers, fax, shuttle to town, maps, turn-down; videos; small/medium meetings, weddings and adjunct services, groups

ACCOMMODATIONS

Units: 3 guest rooms, 1 suite
All Rooms: Bath, TV, VCR, phone, voice mail, AC, heat controls
Some Rooms: Fireplace (1), keyhole harbor view (2)
Bed & Bath: Antique beds, sizes vary; showers only, heat fans, robes
Favorites: Louis XV Suite—quietly lavish, tapestry rugs, sitting room w/ keyhole harbor view, queen leather sleigh bed
Comfort & Decor: Restored theme rooms. Casino Room: brass bed, tartan wallpaper, tennis, yachting, and golf prints. English country garden Cottage Room: elaborate iron bed, lush tea-stained wallpaper. Special, immaculate.

RATES, RESERVATIONS, & RESTRICTIONS

Deposit: 50%; refund w/ 15-day notice; gift cert. for future stay issued thereafter
Discounts: Various packages w/ dinners, mansion tours
Credit Cards: MC, V, AE, D, DC
Check-in/Out: 3/11; will hold luggage, may use common rooms for late departure
Smoking: On porch or in gardens
Pets: No
Kids: Not encouraged, but check
Minimum Stay: 2 nights weekends high season, 3 nights holidays/festivals
Open: All year
Hosts: Andrea (Ande) and Phil Savana
41 Pelham St.
Newport, RI 02840
(888) 880-3764 or (401) 847-3801
Fax: (401) 841-0992
inquireries@savanas.com
www.savanasinn.com

THE VICTORIAN LADIES INN, Newport

Overall: ★★★★	Room Quality: B	Value: C	Price: $95–$205

These Painted Ladies on a busy road are not just another pretty facade. The eclectic, richly decorated guest rooms have been featured on the home-improvement show *Room by Room*, the gardens win annual awards, and local magazine readers named it "Favorite B&B" for three consecutive years. Helene and Donald, now involved with the Newport Restoration Foundation, opened the property after being struck by the lifestyle while at a California bed-and-breakfast, and have been going strong for 20-something years. Elaborate seasonal decorations and a New Year's Eve cocktail party are some of the holiday festivities at this decidedly stylish, somewhat feminine Victorian.

SETTING & FACILITIES

Location: On Memorial Blvd.;
Rt. 138 to Newport; look for "Area
Beaches" sign; left on Rt. 138A, left at
second light
Near: Museums; Bowen's Wharf,
Marine District; Brick Market Place,
state park, aquarium, summer theater;
Easton's Beach, Cliff Walk, Gilded Age
mansions
Building: 1851 Painted Lady Victorian;
2 carriage houses
Grounds: 3 award-winning garden/
courtyard areas; storybook brick walking paths to courtyards, Japanese garden; 2 goldfish ponds, 1 koi fishpond;
foot bridge, patio, seating
Public Space: LR, adjoining DR
Food & Drink: Full breakfast, communal, separate or in room; choice of 2
entrees; a specialty: Portuguese sausage
w/ marinated ham, poached eggs and
Hollandaise sauce
Recreation: Tennis, golf, boating, harbor cruises; music festivals
Amenities & Services: 1 car per
room comp.; irons, fax, maps, beach
towels, board games, recipes; small
meetings

ACCOMMODATIONS

Units: 11 guest rooms
All Rooms: Bath, chairs or love seat,
radio/alarm clock, TV, AC
Some Rooms: Sitting room,
desk/table, phone, hardwood floors, carpet
Bed & Bath: Some antique, four-
poster or sleigh beds, 9 queen beds, 1
room w/ 2 twins, 1 king bed; full baths
Favorites: Burgundy Canopy Room—
Romantic large room, second level
main house, w/ small sitting room,
queen-size canopy bed, burgundy wallpaper, coordinated bedding, telephone
Comfort & Decor: Eclectic combination of Oriental and modern accent
pieces, formal Victorian furnishings, English cottage-style floral fabrics. Romantic
beds, artwork. All pretty, some frilly. Colorful walls, coordinated patterns. Many
rooms overlook gardens. Carriage house
and rear rooms most quiet, spacious.

RATES, RESERVATIONS, & RESTRICTIONS

Deposit: 1 night, 50% longer stays, add
on tax; refund w/ 15-day notice
Discounts: Longer stays, groups, mid-
week stays
Credit Cards: MC, V
Check-in/Out: 2–8/11
Smoking: No
Pets: No
Kids: Over 10, only in certain rooms
Minimum Stay: 3 nights
July/August/holiday weekends
Open: Feb. 11–Jan. 1
Hosts: Helene and Donald O'Neill
63 Memorial Blvd.
Newport, RI 02840
(401) 849-9960
Fax: Same as telephone
info@victorianladies.com
www.victorianladies.com

WYNSTONE, Newport

Overall: ★★★★½   Room Quality: A   Value: D   Price: $195–$325

This lavish, romantic getaway calls to mind the gilded age in this evocative city. Luxury details are loaded into the property, including one bed so large it had to be built in the room. The bathrooms are especially notable, clad in colored marbles and swagged window treatments, with tapestries and sconces—sybaritic retreats where the towels are plush and the private sound systems can play Luther Vandross or Vivaldi while you soak, solo or duo.

SETTING & FACILITIES

Location: Newport's Historic Hill
Near: Antique row, ocean, Tennis Hall of Fame, Yachting Museum; shopping and restaurants, cobblestone Marine District; Brick Market Place, Cliff Walk, state park, museums, aquarium, summer theater, White Horse Tavern

Building: 1850 Greek Revival
Grounds: Small garden area w/ seating
Public Space: DR, halls
Food & Drink: Full breakfast
Recreation: Tennis, boating, harbor cruises, beach activities; music festivals
Amenities & Services: 2 small guest refrigerators, irons, large video library

ACCOMMODATIONS

Units: 5 guest rooms
All Rooms: Bath, fireplace, plush carpet or hardwoods, Oriental or tapestry rugs, stereo/CD system, TV, VCR
Some Rooms: Sitting area
Bed & Bath: Featherbeds; luxury marble baths, dbl. whirlpools, sep. showers, robes

Favorites: The Belcourt—enormous carved California pine king bed, hunter green walls.
Comfort & Decor: Custom fabrics and wallcoverings, antiques. Polished cherry, mahogany furnishings. Rich colors. Pampering baths. Elaborate ornamentation without clutter. Large beds, lots of pillows.

RATES, RESERVATIONS, & RESTRICTIONS

Deposit: Payment in full
Credit Cards: MC, V, AE
Check-in/Out: 3/11
Smoking: No
Pets: No
Kids: No
No-No's: 3rd person in room
Minimum Stay: 2 nights weekends; 3 nights holidays and festivals

Open: All year
Hosts: Cathy Darigan
232 Spring St.
Newport, RI 02840
(800) 524-1386 or (401) 849-7397
Fax: (401) 847-6071
wynstone@travelbase.com
www.innsofnewport.com

Zone 16
Block Island

The Native-American name for Block Island is Manisses, or "God's Little Island." Travel by private boat, ferry, or air to Block Island and you may agree—or not—with the Indians.

The "Little Island" part is accurate, only 11 square miles, with scenery often compared to Ireland—rolling hills, dramatic bluffs, but with panoramic water vistas. This island—seven miles long by three miles wide—comprises long stretches of sandy ocean beaches and 365 ponds—including the vast Great Salt Pond. Mopeds and bikes can be rented right at the ferry docks, and slips for private boats are available.

Shopping, dining, and people watching are respected and expected activities in restored Old Harbor. The Block Island Club sponsors sailing, windsurfing, tennis, swimming, and social activities for the entire family, and accepts memberships for a week or the entire season.

More isolated activities include a trek to Mohegan Bluffs, a stratospheric 200 feet above sea level, and Beacon Hill with a 360-degree view of the island and surrounding water. Tour the island cemetery, or glimpse rare birds protected in the island's Nature Conservancy. Walking and hiking nature trails will lead you across the shoreline and through meadows and woods.

During the 1800s Block Island was called the stumbling block of the New England coast, as ships floundered attempting to navigate its treacherous waters. Modern technology has solved this problem, and today the old lighthouses built to warn of the fog and rocky shoals are historical beauties. Poetic Southeast Light, built in 1875, perches at the pinnacle of Mohegan Bluffs; at the other end of the island, granite-and-iron North Light, from 1867, stands guard at Sandy Point.

Block Island was originally a Victorian retreat, and bed-and-breakfasts here reflect every variation of that era's accommodations—formal, summery, romantic, or a combination. June to Labor Day is the island season,

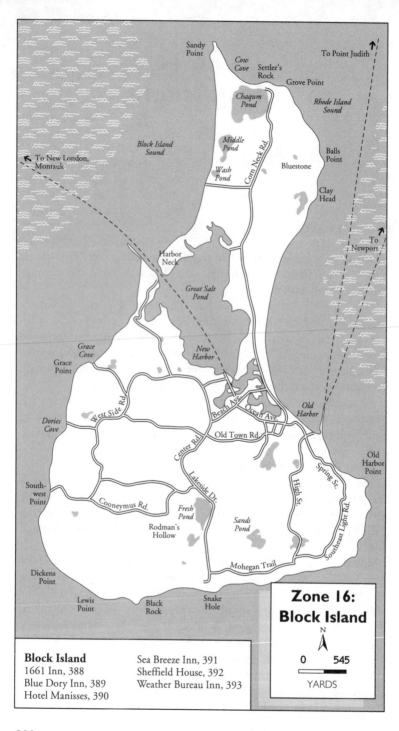

Sandy Point

Cow Cove

Settler's Rock

Grove Point

To Point Judith

Chaqum Pond

Rhode Island Sound

Block Island Sound

Middle Pond

Corn Neck Rd.

Bluestone

Balls Point

Wash Pond

Clay Head

To New London, Montauk

Harbor Neck

Great Salt Pond

To Newport

New Harbor

Grace Cove

Grace Point

West Side Rd.

Beach Ave.

Ocean Ave.

Old Harbor

Dories Cove

Old Town Rd.

Center Rd.

Southwest Point

Cooneymus Rd.

Lakeside Dr.

Fresh Pond

Rodman's Hollow

Sands Pond

High St.

Spring St.

Old Harbor Point

Southeast Light Rd.

Dickens Point

Lewis Point

Black Rock

Snake Hole

Mohegan Trail

Zone 16: Block Island

N

0   545

YARDS

Block Island
1661 Inn, 388
Blue Dory Inn, 389
Hotel Manisses, 390

Sea Breeze Inn, 391
Sheffield House, 392
Weather Bureau Inn, 393

but if you're willing to brave blustery winds and weather, some places remain open, and the ferry runs all year. For ferry information call Interstate Navigation, (401) 783-4613. For air service call New England Airlines, (800) 243-2460

For More Information

Block Island Chamber of Commerce
(401) 466-2982
fax: (401) 466-5286
email: Bichamber@BIRI.com

Block Island Tourism Council
(401) 466-5200 or (800) 383-BIRI
www.blockisland.com

Ferry Information
Interstate Navigation from Point Judith: (401) 783-4613
Viking Fleet from Montauk, Long Island: (516) 668-5700

1661 INN, Block Island

Overall: ★★★★	Room Quality: B	Value: B	Price: $55–$310

The Abrams family operates many of the best properties on the island, and one, the Hotel Manisses across the street, can provide dinner to all. Nearby, The Dodge Cottage, a pretty c. 1900 farmhouse, has 9 rooms, all with private baths, some with kitchenettes, and breakfast is at the 1661 Inn. The Dewey Cottage, a 1906 home renovated in 1994 and new to the group, has six rooms with modern furnishings. Continental breakfast is available at the cottage, or you can have a buffet breakfast at the 1661 Inn. Within this complex you can find luxury to budget accommodations.

SETTING & FACILITIES

Location: From the ferry, Water St. S, up hill on Spring St.
Near: Rest of the 1,500-acre island
Building: White clapboard 1870 mansion and outbuildings, incl. replica of church destroyed by hurricane in 1938
Grounds: Colorful gardens, big decks, ocean views
Public Space: Parlor w/ reception desk, DR, screened porch overlooking ocean
Food & Drink: Lavish buffet breakfast; specialties: whole baked bluefish, corned beef hash; afternoon wine and nibbles; dinner avail. w/ reservations in the Hotel Manisses; opt. champagne or cheese platter in room, boxed picnic lunches; refreshments/honor bar in each room
Recreation: Beach activities, horseback riding, harbor cruises; touring lighthouse, bluffs, Old Harbor
Amenities & Services: Access to farm animals, games, dinner at Hotel Manisses; comp. hour-long island tour, luggage storage for early arrivals/late departures

ACCOMMODATIONS

Units: 9 in main house, 9 in Guest House; 3 in Nicolas Ball Cottage
All Rooms: Antique furniture
Some Rooms: Priv. bath, loft, porch, stained-glass window, add'l/sofa bed; kitchenette (1)
Bed & Bath: Antique four-poster and canopy beds, sizes vary; some whirlpools, stained glass, showers for 2
Favorites: Edwards—spacious, king-size canopy bed, full ocean view, priv. deck and loft w/ spa tub; Staples—every upgrade and best view
Comfort & Decor: In main house, fantastic ocean views. Units vary widely. Rooms named after early settlers; Guest House rooms modest, minimal views. Cottage rooms romantic. Multiple levels.

RATES, RESERVATIONS, & RESTRICTIONS

Deposit: 50%; refund w/ 15-day notice
Discounts: Various packages
Credit Cards: MC, V
Check-in/Out: 1–2/11
Smoking: Most rooms nonsmoking; can request smoking, but will limit room choices
Pets: No

Kids: Welcome
Minimum Stay: 3 nights, weekends in July/August, holidays
Open: Hotel Manisses: all year; check specifically for availability in the 1661 Inn

Hosts: Joan and Justin Abrams
1 Spring St.
Block Island, RI 0280
(800) 626-4773 or (401) 466-2421
Fax: (401) 466-3162
BIRESORTS@aol.com

BLUE DORY INN, Block Island

Overall: ★★★½	Room Quality: B	Value: C	Price: $155–$425

Blue accents. A carousel horse and a flag snapping in the breeze, a blue paint job, and a back deck overlooking the (blue) sea. Dynamic owner Ann, a former New York legislator, purchased the bed-and-breakfast in 1989 after staying here for over 20 years, and has opened several others. The Adrian Inn is close to the old harbor. Waverly Cottage is the most luxurious with private decks, ocean views, whirlpools, and one apartment. Both have Blue Dory beach rights. The Sherman Cottage is a three-bedroom Victorian-contemporary home, and Harmony Cottage has four bedrooms, a stone fireplace, a view of the lighthouse and ocean from the upper deck, and two baths. All units are romantic, tasteful, casual.

SETTING & FACILITIES

Location: From ferry, up Dodge St., 3rd building on right
Near: Oceanfront, in historic/business district; backs onto ocean, fronts onto active village street; stroll to Crescent Beach
Building: Shingle, century-old Victorian
Grounds: Patio and garden, front door opens on island's main street
Public Space: Victorian parlor, basement breakfast room

Food & Drink: Cont'l breakfast; a specialty: frittata; coffee, juice, tea, fresh fruit always avail.; afternoon wine and cheese; evening cookies; Thanksgiving and Christmas dinners
Recreation: Boating, beachcombing, tennis, surfing, touring by moped
Amenities & Services: Grill for guest use, chess; tours, rentals arranged; extra persons in rooms, chef-prepared Thanksgiving dinner; Christmas decorations and dinner w/ guest participation

ACCOMMODATIONS

Units: 11 guest rooms and 3 suites; 4 cottages
All Rooms: Bath
Some Rooms: Ocean view, TV, VCR, AC, kitchenette
Bed & Bath: Sizes vary; some period brass or wooden, many w/out head-

boards or w/ wispy wicker backs; some whirlpools; newly renovated
Favorites: The Dodge Suite—Victorian sitting area, sleeps up to 4 comfortably, w/ refrigerator, TV, VCR, AC; The Doll House and The Tea House—aptly named 1-room cottages, cozy for couples

Comfort & Decor: Some rooms quite small. Victorian touches and colors, lots of pillows. Summery lie-about ambiance. Reproduction wicker; a few more substantial, genuine pieces. Back rooms quieter. Flowery borders, feminine feeling.

RATES, RESERVATIONS, & RESTRICTIONS

Deposit: 50%, full payment due at check-in
Discounts: Off-season (3 seasons), midweek
Credit Cards: MC, V, AE, D
Check-in/Out: 11/3; can stay later if room not needed right away
Smoking: Tolerated
Pets: Check for approval, limited to cottages and suites
Kids: Welcome in cottages and suites

No-No's: Not reserving ahead
Minimum Stay: June–Sept. 2 nights, 3 nights for holidays; 2 nights weekends rest of year
Open: All year
Hosts: Ann Law
Box 488, Dodge St.
Block Island, RI 02807
(800) 992-7290 or (401) 466-5891
Fax: (401) 466-9910
rundezvous@aol.com

HOTEL MANISSES, Block Island

Overall: ★★★★	Room Quality: B	Value: B	Price: $55–$260

This beautifully refurbished landmark hotel may not reflect the earliest settlers here, but instead the genteel pace of more than 100 years of tourism. It is the hub for the complex of five restored properties including the 1661 Inn and Cottages, all within a short walk, and it sparkles throughout as colorfully as its stained-glass windows. Attention to detail is apparent, from sherry glass decanters by the beds, to sun-filled, immaculate rooms. Dining is sophisticated and features fresh local ingredients.

SETTING & FACILITIES

Location: Spring St. across from 1661 Inn
Near: Rest of the 1,500-acre island
Building: 1872 Victorian summer hotel, refurbished exterior
Grounds: Deck in back, animal petting zoo, small garden, no special views
Public Space: Hotel parlor, bar; sun-filled DR, open to public; library/sitting room
Food & Drink: Full buffet breakfast in the 1661 Inn's breakfast room/porch; in winter in hotel DR; can be in room; afternoon wine and nibbles for guests; dinner avail. w/ reservations; can order champagne or cheese platter in room, boxed picnic lunches; refreshments and honor bar in each room
Recreation: Beach activities, harbor cruises; touring lighthouse, Bluffs, Old Harbor, beach horseback riding
Amenities & Services: Games, comp. hour-long island tour; library can be reserved for meetings

ACCOMMODATIONS

Units: 17 guest rooms
All Rooms: Bath, antique furniture
Some Rooms: Priv. porch, add'l bed
Bed & Bath: Bed sizes vary, some canopy beds; some whirlpools, 1 whirlpool in room

Favorites: Princess Augusta—in-room dbl. whirlpool, king bed
Comfort & Decor: Victorian, Victorian, Victorian. Wallpapers, carpets, and antique furnishing. Dark, understated, Old World elegant. Some rooms small. Immaculate.

RATES, RESERVATIONS, & RESTRICTIONS

Deposit: 50%; refund w/ 15-day notice
Discounts: Various packages, incl. kayaking, pig roast, visiting chef, Trimming the Tree, Valentine's Day, midweek, etc.
Credit Cards: MC, V
Check-in/Out: 1–2/11; will hold luggage
Smoking: Some rooms
Pets: No

Kids: 10 and older
Minimum Stay: 3 nights, weekends in July/August, holidays
Open: All year
Hosts: Joan and Justin Abrams
1 Spring St.
Block Island, RI 02807
(800) 626-4773 or (401) 466-2421
Fax: (401) 466-3162
BIRESORTS@aol.com

SEA BREEZE INN, Block Island

| Overall: ★★★½ | Room Quality: C | Value: C | Price: $90–$240 |

This serene little complex of cottages, with its swan pond and fields of roses and wildflowers, is wonderful for weddings or when you want to get away with a significant other. You can have breakfast on a porch in your room and not see anyone but your love and the ocean. Hosts are transplanted from Manhattan: she's an artist, he's a doctor, both are avid gardeners. They worked hard to restore these once-tired properties, and the resultant bed-and-breakfast now has a freshness, like salt-air.

SETTING & FACILITIES

Location: Crest of Spring St. hill
Near: Ferry, shops, Old Harbor
Building: White gambrel-roofed (Dutch) Colonial main house, 4 shingle cottages
Grounds: Hilltop ocean, coastline view, 2 acres of wildflower meadows, perennial gardens w/ over 100 varieties, swan pond

Public Space: Sitting room, writing/sitting area, library
Food & Drink: Cont'l breakfast; specialty: Viennese coffee, homemade preserves; served in sitting room or brought to room in basket (this option only for rooms w/ priv. bath)
Recreation: Beach/water activities, harbor cruises; touring lighthouse, Bluffs, Old Harbor

Amenities & Services: Kayak for use in pond, guest refrigerator, sink for guest kitchen use, beach towels, maps, bike rental, nature workshops

ACCOMMODATIONS

Units: 10, some suites
Some Rooms: Cathedral ceiling, water view (6), small priv. porch (4)
Bed & Bath: Double and twin beds; 5 priv. baths, 5 shared baths, all showers only

Favorites: Room 10—fabulous view
Comfort & Decor: Cottages low-key, befitting summer boarding-house origins. Eclectic decor mix of country, artsy, and summer seaside. Relaxing, understated. Winter rooms, no views.

RATES, RESERVATIONS, & RESTRICTIONS

Deposit: 50%; refund w/ 14-day notice
Discounts: Weekly rates, off-season rates
Credit Cards: MC, V
Check-in/Out: 2/11; will hold luggage
Smoking: No
Pets: No
Kids: Over 5

Minimum Stay: 2 nights; 3 nights over holidays
Open: All year
Hosts: The Newhouse Family
Spring St., Box 141
Block Island, RI 02807
(800) 786-2276 or (401) 466-2275

SHEFFIELD HOUSE, Block Island

| Overall: ★★★½ | Room Quality: C | Value: C | Price: $100–$160 |

Breakfast or evening cocktails in a small garden filled with golden daffodils is typical of the quiet delights at this homey, casual bed-and-breakfast near the beach. The McQueeny family has lovingly passed this property, formerly their summer home, from generation to generation, and personal heirlooms and mature flowerbeds are among the happy results. Rock on the front porch swing, watch the sunrise from the tower sitting room, or just relax with a book and gaze at the water. Here the outside is vintage, the interior modernized, and the welcome sincere.

SETTING & FACILITIES

Location: In historic district, near beach, ferry
Near: Old Harbor, ocean
Building: 1888 Victorian summer cottage
Grounds: Privacy, small yard, award-winning gardens
Public Space: Porch, sitting room; country-style kitchen

Food & Drink: Cont'l breakfast; afternoon refreshments; cookies always out
Recreation: Windsurfing, parasailing, boating, fishing, harbor cruises
Amenities & Services: Guest refrigerator, games, grill, bike rack, beach towels, island tour, pick-up at ferry or airport

ACCOMMODATIONS

Units: 7 guest rooms
All Rooms: Full-length mirror, ceiling fan
Some Rooms: Bath, antiques
Bed & Bath: New queen beds, 1 w/ add'l twin bed; 5 priv. baths, 2 shared
Favorites: 2nd floor rooms—water views and priv. baths

Comfort & Decor: Room sizes vary. Irish lace curtains, quilts, and hand-hooked rugs. Some heirloom and antique pieces. Airy and summery. Casually comfortable. Some water views.

RATES, RESERVATIONS, & RESTRICTIONS

Deposit: Full payment for 1–2 nights, 50% longer stays; refund w/ 14-day notice
Discounts: Off-season, midweek
Credit Cards: MC, V, AE
Check-in/Out: 2/11; will hold luggage
Smoking: No
Pets: No
Kids: No
No-No's: Mopeds on property
Minimum Stay: 3 nights for high-season weekends, 4 nights holiday weekends

Open: All year; reservations required for summer stays
Hosts: Molly McQueeny O'Neill and Chris O'Neill
High St., P.O. Box 1557
Block Island, RI 02807
(800) 466-8329 or (401) 466-2494
Fax: (401) 466-8890
info@sheffieldhouse.com
www.Sheffieldhouse.com

WEATHER BUREAU INN, Block Island

Overall: ★★★½	Room Quality: B	Value: C	Price: $95–$325

If you watch the Weather Channel, then you might especially enjoy this little bed-and-breakfast which, as its name denotes, was a weather bureau for most of its almost-100 years. In the early 1900s forecasts were provided by banners on the flagpole atop the pretty rooftop deck, seen by all on the island (just as you can see all of the island). Later, weather info was broadcast from here until the 1950s. Within are cozy rooms with great views and antique weather forecasting equipment, including an original barometer. The lawn slopes to New Harbor, where you can kayak. Breakfast or afternoon wine and cheese are on the back deck, overlooking the sound, and sunset is clearly "cool."

SETTING & FACILITIES

Location: Center of the island, on hilltop
Near: Ferry, shops, Old Harbor
Building: Former U.S. weather station, built 1903; 2 story, widow's-walk

rooftop deck, railing; Nat'l Register of Historic Places
Grounds: Lawns to harbor edge
Public Space: Common rooms, front and back porches

Food & Drink: Full breakfast; specialties: raspberries and cream granola w/ strawberries/blueberries, Portobello mushroom quiche, berry-filled biscuits, cinnamon buns; wine and cheese; chocolate-chip cookies
Recreation: Beach/water activities, harbor cruises, biking, croquet
Amenities & Services: Games, beach chairs/towels, bikes, kayaks

ACCOMMODATIONS

Units: 4 guest rooms
All Rooms: Bath, water view
Some Rooms: Woodburning fireplace, seating area
Bed & Bath: Queen and king beds, some brass; small, standard baths

Favorites: White Cap—fireplace, seating area, queen four-poster, most spacious
Comfort & Decor: Attractive, water views. Beds positioned for views. Bright, airy. Rooms in back quietest. Antiques, wood floors, some damask wallcoverings.

RATES, RESERVATIONS, & RESTRICTIONS

Deposit: Credit card number
Discounts: 4th day free, midweek
Credit Cards: MC, V
Check-in/Out: 1/11
Smoking: No
Pets: No
Kids: Over 10

Open: All year
Hosts: Brian Wright
Beach Ave.
Block Island, RI 02807
(401) 466-9977, (800) 633-8624
Fax: (401) 466-8899

Zone 17
Mainland Rhode Island/
Providence

With civic improvements and a brighter image, Providence now sparkles as Rhode Island's capital and primary metropolis. *Something About Mary* was filmed here, and the TV drama titled (what else?) *Providence* has filmed at outdoor cafes on Wickenden Street, in restored Colonial shops on South Main, and in boutiques and eateries on hip Thayer Street. Also featured on film are the arch leading to Little Italy at Federal Hill, Kennedy Plaza—the town square—complete with sculpture fountain, and a Bruins hockey game at the Civic Center.

Providence's other treasures include Brown University; the restored Mile of History on eighteenth-century Benefit Street, with shipping-magnate mansions next to modest sailor homes; the Rhode Island School of Design; and the Museum of Art.

Other options? William Rodgers Park, the zoo, the Museum of Natural History and Planetarium, Waterplace Park with its water taxis and gondolas, Rockefeller-Center–modeled Fleet Skating Center, the Performing Arts Center, India Point Park, the Children's Museum, or downtown itself—locals call it downcity.

Mainland attractions focus on the water. Watch Hill, famous for antiquing, has a good beach, an 1858 lighthouse and museum, and one of the nation's oldest carousels. Jamestown has both a lighthouse and a windmill. Bristol is noted for shipbuilding and Blithewold Mansion, 33 acres with gardens overlooking Narragansett Bay and Bristol Harbor. The Swamp Meadow covered bridge in Foster is worthwhile, as is the Butterfly Zoo in Middletown.

Narragansett Bay has Point Judith Lighthouse and The Towers beach, and icy New Year's Day Polar Bear and Penguin plunges—fun to watch if not to join. Woonsocket and Wakefield have notable performing arts and summer theater. And Wilcox Park at Westerly Town Hall, an 18-acre 1898

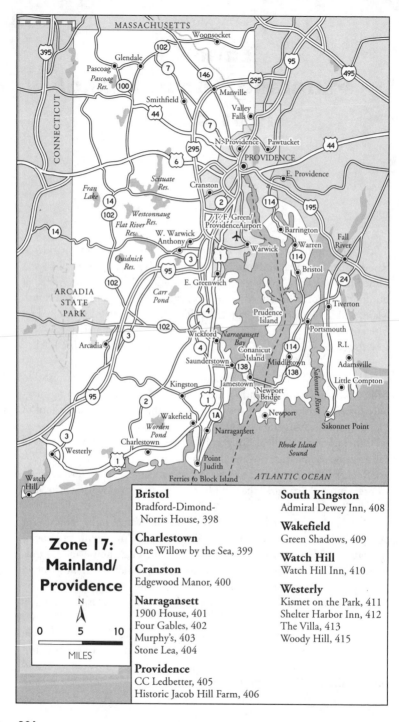

MASSACHUSETTS

CONNECTICUT

Woonsocket

395

102

Glendale

7

Pascoag
Pascoag
Res.

100

146

95

295

495

Smithfield

44

Manville

Valley
Falls

7

N. Providence

Pawtucket

PROVIDENCE

44

295

6

E. Providence

Fran
Lake

Scituate
Res.

Cranston

2

114

195

102

14

Westconnaug
Res.

Flat River
Res.

14

W. Warwick
Anthony

3

T.F. Green/
Providence Airport

1

Barrington

Warwick

Fall
River

Quidnick
Res.

95

Warren

114

Bristol

24

ARCADIA
STATE
PARK

Carr
Pond

E. Greenwich

4

Prudence
Island

Tiverton

102

3

Arcadia

102

Wickford

Narragansett
Bay

4

Conanicut
Island

Portsmouth

R.I.

Saunderstown

138

Middletown

114

Adamsville

Kingston

2

1

Jamestown

138

Little Compton

95

Wakefield

1

Newport
Bridge

Sakonnet River

3

1A

Worden
Pond

Charlestown

Newport

Narragansett

Sakonnet Point

Westerly

Point
Judith

Rhode Island
Sound

1

Watch
Hill

Ferries to Block Island

ATLANTIC OCEAN

Zone 17: Mainland/ Providence

N

0   5   10

MILES

Victorian park, features twentieth-century sculpture in trees and ponds along its walking trails, Colonial Theater's Shakespeare in the Park, and summer pops concerts.

Inland Pawtucket's Blackstone River State Park and Lincoln Woods State Park offer greenery as well as canoe portage, historic walking trails, and Colonial homesteads. The Blackstone River Bikeway, opened in October 1998, will ultimately provide a 17.1-mile, 12-foot-wide bikeway linked to both the East Coast Greenway—running from Florida to Maine—and the East Bay Bike Path.

Bed-and-breakfasts are not as numerous here as in Newport or on Block Island, but new ones are opening each year, many in nineteenth-century homes with fine detailing. Inns are few. Providence offers a few quirky bed-and-breakfasts. Coastal Rhode Island offers beachy New England complete with antiques and charm. Inland spots tend to be homey, with personal atmosphere and service.

For More Information

Bed-and-Breakfast Referrals of South Coast Rhode Island
(800) 853-7479

Blackstone Area Web
www.tourblackstone.com

Bristol County Chamber of Commerce
(888) 278-9948
email: bristolcountychamber@wsii.com
www.bristolcountychamber.org (for East Bay)

Providence Web
www.providenceri.com/home.html

Providence/Warwick Convention and Visitors Center
(401) 751-1177 or (800) 233-1636

South Country Web
email: kathleen@southcounty.com
www.southcounty.com

The Greater Westerly-Pawtucket Chamber of Commerce
(401) 596-7761 or (800) 732-7636

Warwick
(401) 738-2000 or (401) 739-9150
fax: (401) 738-6639
www.warwickri.com

BRADFORD-DIMOND-NORRIS HOUSE, Bristol

Overall: ★★★½	Room Quality: C	Value: C	Price: $80–$110

When Governor William Bradford's house was destroyed by British fire during a 1778 raid, the torched structure was replaced by this stately home. The third-floor exterior filigree balustrade added after the Civil War earned it the nickname "Wedding Cake House," and later additions gave it an even more distinctive appearance. You sense layers of history within as well, with Victorian marble mantels and furnishings such as camelback couches and bonnet-topped highboys. It is on the route of the oldest Fourth of July parade in American history and a real piece of America itself.

SETTING & FACILITIES

Location: In historic waterfront district; Hope St. in Bristol
Near: Roger Williams University, Providence, Newport, state park; 1 hour to Mystic; walk to bike trail, waterfront antiques shops, restaurants, museums, historical home tours, $1.99 movie theater
Building: 1792 Federal-style mansion; restored 1995
Grounds: Rear veranda overlooks gardens and huge purple beech tree

Public Space: Entrance foyer, sitting room, DR
Food & Drink: Full breakfast in DR, at Duncan-Fyfe communal table or on veranda
Recreation: Museums, shopping, antiquing, historic tours, performing arts, 15-mi. bike trail, walking trails, water sports, day trips
Amenities & Services: Bike storage, irons, hairdryers

ACCOMMODATIONS

Units: 4, all can be opened to suites for 3rd person
All Rooms: Bath, seating, reading lamps, TV, central AC
Some Rooms: Decorative orig. mantel
Bed & Bath: Queen lace-canopy beds; white tile shower baths, glass showers

Favorites: Pink Room—mantel, canopy bed, highboy, love seat, dressing table, soft colors
Comfort & Decor: Custom window treatments, hardwood floors w/ Oriental rugs. Comfortably formal decor. Antiques and reproductions

RATES, RESERVATIONS, & RESTRICTIONS

Deposit: Credit card holds room; no charge w/ 10-day notice
Discounts: 3rd person
Credit Cards: MC, V, AE
Check-in/Out: Flexible
Smoking: No
Pets: No

Kids: Over 12
Minimum Stay: 2 nights weekends; 3 nights holidays
Open: All year
Hosts: Suzanne and Lloyd Adams
474 Hope St.
Bristol, RI 02809

(888) 329-6338 or (401) 253-6338   bdnhouse@edgenet.net
Fax: (401) 253-4023   *www.edgenet.net/bdnhouse*

ONE WILLOW BY THE SEA, Charlestown

Overall: ★★★	Room Quality: C	Value: C	Price: $70–$80

Ever take a shower on a warm summer night under starry skies and sea breezes? You can here, at the bed-and-breakfast's outside facility. This is a simple, peaceful retreat with an interesting, feminist host who was once president of NYC National Organization for Women (NOW); the fascinating political photos scattered about the house tell the tale. Guaranteed stimulating conversation is yours for the asking, and bird watchers can watch the seasonal migrations. And the big breakfasts are outstanding (not so always in Rhode Island, where bed-and-breakfast continental breakfasts can be as small as the state).

SETTING & FACILITIES

Location: Residential area, bordered by nature area
Near: Bird migration flyways, ocean, restaurants; 25 min. to Newport, Mystic
Building: Split-level house
Grounds: Rural, peaceful; sun decks, gardens; outdoor shower
Public Space: LR, sun deck
Food & Drink: Full breakfast; specialties: French crepes, English scrambled eggs w/ ham, cheese and asparagus tips
Recreation: Beachcombing, whale watching, sailing, local cultural/crafts events, kayaking
Amenities & Services: Outside shower for beach; grill, refrigerator; parking for boat trailers, storage for kayaks, bicycles, beach gear; will meet trains

ACCOMMODATIONS

Units: 3 guest rooms
All Rooms: Bedside radio, ceiling and floor fans, reading lamps
Some Rooms: Priv. bath
Bed & Bath: Queen beds, cots; sun-dried sheets and towels
Favorites: Suite—sitting room, TV, VCR
Comfort & Decor: Ordinary, but bright and clean.

RATES, RESERVATIONS, & RESTRICTIONS

Deposit: 1 night; 2 nights longer stay; refund w/ 6-day notice
Discounts: Off-season, 3rd person
Check-in/Out: 1/12
Credit Cards: None
Smoking: Outside only
Pets: No; cat on premises
Kids: Considerate children welcome weekdays; 3 and under free; cots, playpens supplied
No-No's: Teenagers
Open: All year

Hosts: Denise Dillon Fuge
1 Willow Rd.

Charlestown, RI 02813-4162
(401) 354-0802

EDGEWOOD MANOR, Cranston

| Overall: ★★★★½ | Room Quality: A | Value: C | Price: $110–$225 |

Like the idea of sleeping in a former convent? You can here, but anyone would savor the luxury of this finest Rhode Island bed-and-breakfast outside of Newport. Five years of restoration have paid off handsomely. The turn-of-the-century, 18-room mansion is laden with showcase details such as a foyer staircase with three spindle types, handcarved oak paneling, silk tapestry wallcoverings, and original leaded and stained glass. The charming and enthusiastic hosts are justifiably proud of their considerable accomplishment, and word of this elegant newcomer near the capital should spread quickly.

SETTING & FACILITIES

Location: I-95 to Exit 18, right on to Allen's Ave.; look for Norwood Ave., right turn
Near: Walk to Roger Williams Park and Zoo, antiques stores, Narragansett Bay; 3 mi. from downtown Providence; 30 min. to Newport; 1 hour to Foxwoods Casino, Boston
Building: 1905 Greek Revival mansion, Rococo overtones
Grounds: .5 acre rear yard, sculptured lawns, fountain, patio, statuary

Public Space: Grand foyer, salon, DR; each common room presents a varied theme
Food & Drink: Full breakfast; afternoon tea; liquor for purchase, bar in pantry
Recreation: Activities in 430-acre park, museum, boathouse, zoos
Amenities & Services: Bike storage, priv. parking, daily paper

ACCOMMODATIONS

Units: 4 guest rooms, 3 suites
All Rooms: Bath, TV, antique furnishings
Some Rooms: Fireplace, seating, whirlpools, priv. porch (1)
Bed & Bath: Antique four-poster, canopy beds; king/queen sizes; marble baths, 2 w/ shower only, 4 w/ whirlpools/sep. shower, 1 full bath
Favorites: Scarlett's Retreat—king rice four-poster, carved fireplace inset

w/ Grueby tile, priv. porch, marble bath w/ whirlpool
Comfort & Decor: Victorian and Empire furnishings. Rooms elegant and romantic, although not enormous. Uncluttered. 18th- and 19th-century antique furnishings, fine art pieces throughout.

RATES, RESERVATIONS, & RESTRICTIONS

Deposit: 50%; refund w/ 7-day notice
Discounts: Seniors
Credit Cards: MC, V, AE
Check-in/Out: After 3/11
Smoking: Restricted
Pets: No
Kids: Limited; check w/ B&B
Minimum Stay: 2 nights weekends; 3 nights holidays; check

Open: All year
Hosts: Linda and Andrew Lombardi
232 Norwood Ave.
Cranston, RI 02905
(800) 882-3285 or (401) 781-0099
www.travelguides.com/inns

1900 HOUSE, Narragansett

Overall: ★★★½	Room Quality: B	Value: B	Price: $65–$95

Relaxed and approachable describe the hosts—and the feel—of this cozy bed-and-breakfast, where the window boxes, birdfeeders, gingerbread trim, flower gardens, and collectibles match their charming personalities. Touch the quilts and the dress from 1911, read the old postcards, open the boxes, pick up the 3-D stereoptic camera, and swap books: this is a hands-on bed-and-breakfast with personality. The strawberries, from Bill's garden, are served on Lusterware and Depression glass, and you can enjoy unlimited refills of freshly baked muffins and other goodies.

SETTING & FACILITIES

Location: Rt. 1 to Narragansett Exit, right at exit, left onto Rt. 108 N; enter rotary, exit to Narragansett; next light, right onto Kingstown Rd., residential street
Near: Ocean, village; short drive to fishing port, 11 golf courses, wildlife conservatories, horseback riding, Watch Hill, Wickford, Narragansett Towers, Newport; 1 hour to Foxwoods Casino
Building: Circa 1900 Victorian
Grounds: .5 acre yard, vegetable and flower gardens, shed

Public Space: Sitting room, DR, screened porch
Food & Drink: 3-course breakfast; specialties: French-dipped filled croissants, tarragon eggs and bacon, stuffed baked apple
Recreation: Boating, kayaking, fishing, surfing; local events, whale-watching cruises
Amenities & Services: Guest refrigerator, beach towels, outdoor post-beach shower and sep. changing room; pick-up from train

ACCOMMODATIONS

Units: 2 guest rooms, 1 suite
All Rooms: Bath, TV
Some Rooms: Canopy bed

Bed & Bath: Antique full-size beds; old-fashioned tubs

Favorites: Blue Room—canopy bed, claw-foot tub; Gable Room—new bath **Comfort & Decor:** Laura Ashley fittings and comforters. Not luxurious, but interesting artifacts, rugs, antiques. TVs a plus. Good lighting.

RATES, RESERVATIONS, & RESTRICTIONS

Deposit: 1 night; refund w/ 14-day notice
Discounts: Off-season, 7th night free, 3rd person
Check-in/Out: 3/11; may use shower and changing room after check-out
Smoking: Porch only
Pets: No; 2 resident cats
Kids: OK

Minimum Stay: 2 nights, but check for 1 night availability
Open: All year
Hosts: Sandra and Bill Panzeri
59 Kingstown Rd.
Narragansett Pier, RI 02882
(401) 789-7971

FOUR GABLES, Narragansett

Overall: ★★★	Room Quality: C	Value: C	Price: $80–$90

Narragansett has much of the charm and appeal of Newport, without the crowds, and this little bed-and-breakfast reflects that mood. Barbara is a landscape designer and has put her talent to obvious use in the perennial and herb borders. Savoring homemade preserves and cranberry-nut bread on the veranda, or in the dining room overlooking a breathtaking view of Narragansett Bay is the greatest delight here. Otherwise, full of nooks and crannies and great woodwork, it feels like a home away from home.

SETTING & FACILITIES

Location: Rt. 1 to Narragansett, right at ramp, straight to inn, in residential neighborhood
Near: Narragansett Pier; walk to ocean beaches, incl. historic Tower Beach; Newport, Mystic, Foxwoods Casino, Providence
Building: Small c. 1900 Shingle-style summer cottage
Grounds: 1 acre; small perennial gardens, quaint paths; brick patio
Public Space: LR; parlor; DR, opens to veranda

Food & Drink: Hearty communal breakfast; a specialty: cheese crepes w/ blueberry-ginger sauce; p.m. refreshments
Recreation: Seawall walks, boat trips, biking, kayaking, fishing, summer theater
Amenities & Services: Fax, computer, gym equipment, irons, common TV, board games, videos, binoculars; pick-up from train, turn-down, small meetings; Spanish spoken

ACCOMMODATIONS

Units: 2 guest rooms
All Rooms: Shared bath, antiques, ceiling fans
Some Rooms: TV on request
Bed & Bath: Antique four-posters, 1 queen, king converts to twins; robes, hairdryer

Favorites: King room—bay views
Comfort & Decor: Inviting, charming wallpapers and decorative pieces, arts and crafts. Ceiling fans. Good lighting. Quiet.

RATES, RESERVATIONS, & RESTRICTIONS

Deposit: 50%, refund w/ 7-day notice
Discounts: Midweek 3-night stay, longer stays, reserve both rooms
Credit Cards: MC, V, AE
Check-in/Out: 3–7/11, later OK
Smoking: On veranda/patio only
Pets: On approval; house dogs and cats
Kids: Over 12

Minimum Stay: 2 nights summer weekends, 3 nights holidays
Open: All year, except Christmas
Hosts: Barbara and Terry Higgins
12 South Pier Rd.
Narragansett, RI 02882
(401) 782-0961
Fax: Same as phone
TJHiggins@ids.com

MURPHY'S, Narragansett

Overall: ★★★½	Room Quality: C	Value: C	Price: $80–$100

Morning sun on Irish-linen tablecloths; antique silver table settings; warm, fragrant yeast bread and cinnamon rolls; thick preserves from the bed-and-breakfast's own berries—get the picture? In this small property, a walk from restaurants and a fishing pier, you will feel as pampered as a private guest. Martha wrote the book on breakfasts—literally (*The Bed & Breakfast Cookbook*). Kevin is a commercial fisherman, and carves scrimshaw on swordfish swords, some displayed. They do nice things like finding theater tickets and placing them on your pillow.

SETTING & FACILITIES

Location: Block from ocean, set back from street
Near: Narragansett Pier; Wickford antiques shops, drive to Newport, Mystic, Block Island Ferry, Foxwoods Casino, vineyards
Building: 1894 Victorian cottage
Grounds: Front porch, cafe tables

Public Space: Entrance hall, LR, upstairs reading nook, DR, large, renovated kitchen
Food & Drink: Lavish communal breakfast; seasonal menu, early riser coffee; specialties: peaches-and-cream French toast, eggs Benedict

Recreation: Seawall walks, beach activities, boat trips, kayaking, fishing, summer theater

Amenities & Services: Refrigerator, special occasion celebrations

ACCOMMODATIONS

Units: 2 guest rooms
All Rooms: Bath, fresh flowers, TV, AC, privacy (no common walls)
Bed & Bath: Queen or king/2 twins; robes, ocean views
Favorites: Queen room—good ocean view, chaise

Comfort & Decor: Under-the-eaves. Simple, handcrafted headboards, Laura Ashley wallpapers, traditional furnishings. Original honey-colored wide-pine floors. Bright, fresh. Good lighting. Comfortable and inviting.

RATES, RESERVATIONS, & RESTRICTIONS

Deposit: 50%; refund w/ 14-day notice
Discounts: Longer stays, various off-season specials including workshops on operating a B&B and baking at home
Credit Cards: None
Check-in/Out: 1/11
Smoking: On porch only
Pets: No
Kids: Over 8

Minimum Stay: 2 nights; 3 nights, holidays
Open: May–Oct.; Nov.–April weekends
Hosts: Martha and Kevin Murphy
43 South Pier Rd.
Narragansett, RI 02882
(401) 789-1824
Fax: (401) 788-0778

STONE LEA, Narragansett

Overall: ★★★★	Room Quality: C	Value: C	Price: $125–$175

The name of this grand "cottage" by famed architects McKim, Mead, and White derives from its stone construction, and the lea, or green meadow by-the-sea, on which it's built. Owner Guy is a surgeon, and his helpful parents help him run this breeze-filled place with the magnificent stairway and huge living room (and supposed ghost room). Peaceful, romantic, dramatic, and right on the lapping water, you'll feel like a nineteenth-century millionaire—when a million was a million.

SETTING & FACILITIES

Location: From South Pier Rd., south on Ocean Rd., towards ocean on Newton Ave., last house on left; in area formerly known as Millionaire's Row
Near: Oceanfront; 20 min. to Newport; 45 min. to Mystic; 10 min. to Block Island Ferry
Building: Imposing 1884 Victorian mansion w/ Tudor overtones

Grounds: 2 sprawling acres, 9,000 square feet of oceanfront
Public Space: Stunning entrance foyer w/ dramatic "Grand Piano" staircase and balcony, spacious LR, elegant DR, sitting room, breakfast room
Food & Drink: Full, chef-prepared breakfast; a specialty: ham and potato omelet

Recreation: Fishing, tennis, golf, summer theater, evening entertainment, jai alai

Amenities & Services: Guest refrigerator, irons, beach towels, gift cert., meetings (20)

ACCOMMODATIONS

Units: 5 guest rooms, 3 suites
All Rooms: Priv. bath, antiques, hardwood floors, ocean view, named after nearby islands
Some Rooms: Oceanfront, add'l bed; 1 suite w/ sitting room, sleeper sofa
Bed & Bath: Beds vary, all new, all-natural fibers; some hall access baths, 1 shower only

Favorites: The Block Island Room—blue decor, in-room bath, queen and double beds, 2-way ocean view
Comfort & Decor: Sizeable rooms, many hall baths. Comfortable, pleasant. Fresh flowers. Good lighting.

RATES, RESERVATIONS, & RESTRICTIONS

Deposit: 1 night; 50% longer stay; refund w/ 14-day notice
Discounts: Off-season, holidays and special event weekends excluded; extra person
Credit Cards: None; MC, V only to hold reservations
Check-in/Out: 3/11; may extend stay to 1 p.m.
Smoking: No

Pets: No
Kids: Over 10
No-No's: Check-in after 10 p.m.
Minimum Stay: 2 nights all weekends; 3 nights all holiday weekends
Open: April–end of Nov.
Hosts: The Lancellotti Family
40 Newton Ave.
Narragansett, RI 02882
(401) 783-9546

C C LEDBETTER, Providence

Overall: ★★★	Room Quality: C	Value: C	Price: $75–$125

This bed-and-breakfast is slightly down-at-the-heels but in the best area for college kids' parents. It's funkily stylish, and the innkeeper keeps it fresh. She speaks French and Italian, loves to chat about literature, art, cartography, and gardening—and growing David Austin English Roses—and corresponds with repeat guests to exchange books in between bed-and-breakfast visits. Make reservations a few years in advance (seriously). The site, on historic Benefit Street, across from the John Brown house in the charming Colonial area near Brown University is currently booked for graduation weekends into the millennium.

SETTING & FACILITIES

Location: Benefit St. between Charlesfield and Power, directly across from the John Brown House; no sign, look for building

Near: Museum, Supreme Court; 1 block to Brown University, Rhode Island School of Design, downtown Providence

Building: 1768 Colonial, Victorian-style mansard roof; renovated in 1997

Grounds: Double lot, extensive gardens, hammocks

Public Space: LR, DR

Food & Drink: "Cont'l Plus" communal breakfast, gourmet coffees/teas, fresh fruit; a specialty: coffee cake; afternoon tea, refreshments

Recreation: Waterfront gondolas, rent canoes, river walks, park activities, galleries

Amenities & Services: Lots of reading material

ACCOMMODATIONS

Units: 5 guest rooms

All Rooms: Good reading lights, TV, AC

Some Rooms: Priv. bath, decorative mantel

Bed & Bath: Bed sizes vary, 1 extra-long king; full baths

Favorites: The Twin Bed Room—coziest, prettiest artwork, sunny

Comfort & Decor: Dhurrie rugs, Delft tiles, plants, quilts. Added-on 3rd floor, high ceilings. King-bed room, rowing machine, can have private bath. Host continually freshens interior and exterior. Modest, interesting.

RATES, RESERVATIONS, & RESTRICTIONS

Deposit: 1 night; refund w/ 7-day notice

Discounts: Singles, 3rd person

Credit Cards: MC, V, AE, D

Check-in/Out: 1/11

Smoking: Restricted

Pets: Restricted

Kids: Check w/ B&B, will consider

Minimum Stay: During local college events

Open: All year

Hosts: Ms. C.C. Ledbetter
326 Benefit St.
Providence, RI 02903
(401) 351-4699
Fax: Same as phone
ccled@juno.com

HISTORIC JACOB HILL FARM, Providence

Overall: ★★★★   Room Quality: A   Value: C   Price: $95–$225

You can review an 80-page history here. Exposed corner posts date from 1722. The original servant's call box and antique wainscoting date from the Hunt Club period, 1920–1943, when the site hosted Vanderbilts, Firestones, and Grosvenors; the living room was once the men's smoking room. Because of few owners and careful use, modernizations haven't marred the expansive property. The young, enthusiastic hosts are renovating this exciting bed-and-breakfast room by room, and Bill's collection of antique toys and glass is displayed throughout. Beyond-the-call services sometimes include spontaneous tours to Newport, Boston, or Cape Cod.

SETTING & FACILITIES

Location: Rt. 114A, travel approximately 1 mi., bear right at blinking light (Old Grist Mill Tavern), follow Arcade Ave., right at Rt. 44, left on Jacob St., B&B on left at top of hill (look for black antique carriage)
Near: Antique shops, Providence; Brown University; Fall River outlets; Newport; Boston, Cape Cod
Building: Large Colonial, orig. structure from 1722; renovated in 1997
Grounds: Hilltop location oversees 40 acres; arbor, lawn games, gazebo (frequent weddings here), barn, paddock (horses boarded), hay fields, woods

Public Space: Enormous LR, den; DR; outdoor deck
Food & Drink: Full breakfast; specialties: blueberry pancakes, stuffed French toast, omelets; welcoming refreshments; afternoon cheese platters
Recreation: Seasonal berry picking, pumpkin patches, selecting Christmas trees; horseback riding, hot-air balloon rides
Amenities & Services: Kidney-shaped lighted pool, tennis court; use of gas grill, picnic table; bicycle storage, Providence shuttle, horseback riding lessons

ACCOMMODATIONS

Units: 7 guest rooms, 1 cottage
All Rooms: Bath, antiques
Some Rooms: Fireplace/woodstove, priv. porch, French doors, whirlpool, AC, TV/VCR; combine rooms to form suite
Bed & Bath: Some antique, canopy, four-posters, illusion lace canopies, sizes vary; some renovated tile baths w/ marble floors, 2-person whirlpools, bidets; some rooms will share baths if not taken as suites
Favorites: Mansion Suite—mural of farm, Gothic king bed/dresser, lace

canopy, French doors to whirlpool; Vanderbilt Suite—French country, woodstove, hand-painted furnishings, deck overlooking pool
Comfort & Decor: Farmhouse decor softened w/ imaginative and romantic touches. Rich pieces, period wallpapers. Third-floor rooms, round-topped windows, slanted ceilings. Some rooms on small side. Aptly named country cottage w/ kitchen, accommodates 2–6, for long-term stays.

RATES, RESERVATIONS, & RESTRICTIONS

Deposit: Determined at time of reservation; refund w/ 14-day notice

Discounts: 3rd person, singles, various 2-night packages, corp. weekday, extended stay (3+ days), AAA

Credit Cards: MC, V, AE, D; checks up to 10 days prior to arrival
Check-in/Out: 2/11
Smoking: Not inside; violators will be asked to leave, resp. for reserv. plus cleaning fees of $150 and future lost revenues
Pets: No
Kids: Over 12 w/ notice
No-No's: Candles or large coolers in guest rooms

Minimum Stay: 2 nights weekends; 3 nights holidays
Open: All year
Hosts: Bill and Eleonora Rezek
Box 41326
Providence, RI 02940-1326
(888) 336-9165 or (508) 336-9165
Fax: (508) 336-0951
Host@Inn-Providence-RI.com
www.inn-providence-ri.com

ADMIRAL DEWEY INN, South Kingston

Overall: ★★★½	Room Quality: B	Value: C	Price: $80–$120

Named for the hero of the Spanish-American War, The Admiral Dewey celebrated its centennial year as a guesthouse in 1998. In a fascinating photo album, you can chart the property's progress from neglected white elephant without adequate plumbing to the current pretty Victorian filled with touches of past and present. Joan and Hardy spent two years restoring the creaky, airy house—literally picking it up and moving all 137 tons to a new foundation. The big plus here is the fine beach nearby. The hosts, who also operate an antiques trade and real estate office, are heroes themselves in this impressive venture.

SETTING & FACILITIES

Location: In residential area, ocean across street
Near: Matunuck Beach across road, Point Judith, Galilee fishing village, Snug Harbor, wildlife preserves, Newport, Mystic, Block Island Ferry, Foxwoods Casino
Building: Stately 1898 Victorian, always a beach hotel
Grounds: Corner lot, veranda
Public Space: Parlor, large DR

Food & Drink: Self-serve communal cont'l breakfast; specialty: coffee cake; kitchen open for juice, teas, snacks
Recreation: Boat charters/cruises, golf, tennis, summer theater/festivals, events and county fair
Amenities & Services: Gas grill, common TV, guest refrigerator, irons, outside shower, maps, beach towels, daily paper; small meetings/weddings, pick-up from plane or train

ACCOMMODATIONS

Units: 10 guest rooms
All Rooms: Antiques, hardwood floors
Some Rooms: Bath, Block Island Sound views

Bed & Bath: Antique beds; queen, full, twin; priv. baths (8), shared (2), all showers only; some claw-foot tubs

Favorites: Honeymoon Room—3rd floor, pastel walls and bedding; Rooms 7, 8—water views
Comfort & Decor: French silk navy/rose wallpapers. Poster trundle beds, country pines, brass fixtures, inlaid oak dressers, marble-topped washstands and dressers. Ornate Gothic carved pieces, faux-painted oak. Dormers/eaves. Clean and comfy.

RATES, RESERVATIONS, & RESTRICTIONS

Deposit: 50%, refund w/ 7-day notice
Discounts: Groups, check w/ B&B for packages
Credit Cards: MC, V
Check-in/Out: 3–7/11
Smoking: On veranda only
Pets: No
Kids: Over 10

Minimum Stay: 2 nights weekends, 3 nights holidays
Open: All year
Hosts: Joan and Hardy LeBel
668 Matunuck Beach Rd.
South Kingston, RI 02879
(800) 457-2090 or (401) 783-2090 or (401) 783-8298

GREEN SHADOWS, Wakefield

| Overall: ★★★ | Room Quality: C | Value: C | Price: $75–$105 |

The friendly, well-traveled hosts literally built this little bed-and-breakfast in 1995, by completely reconstructing and redesigning their home from the ground up. Says Don, "all that was left was the foundation," and the former ranch-style residence is now a homey and attractive contemporary. All guest facilities are on the first floor; Don and Mercedes stay on the second. A half-mile from the ocean, with full breakfasts such as crunchy French toast and homebaked bread, this is a popular choice in an area with relatively few bed-and-breakfasts; the hosts recommend reserving months in advance for summer.

SETTING & FACILITIES

Location: Rt. 1 to Green Hill Beach exit, left onto Green Hill Beach Rd., in residential area; on right;
Near: Walk to Green Hill Ocean Beach, Point Judith Pond, wildlife preserves, Block Island Ferry, Newport, Old Mystic Seaport and Aquarium, Foxwoods Casino
Building: Cape Cod–style 2-story contemporary
Grounds: Landscaped and wooded priv. acre; large, priv. screened back porch overlooks pond
Public Space: Entry hall, artwork (some nude studies); library/TV room; all guests on 1st floor; porch
Food & Drink: Early riser coffee/tea; full breakfast; specialties: English tea scones, ginger pancakes, soufflé apple pancakes; refreshments
Recreation: Fishing, flea markets, summer season at Theater-By-The-Sea, Big Apple Circus, Charlestown Seafood Festival, Wickford Art Fair
Amenities & Services: Outdoor beach hot/cold shower, guest refrigerator, recipes, beach towels/supplies, pick-up from train; small priv. affairs/meetings

ACCOMMODATIONS

Units: 2 guest rooms
All Rooms: Bath, carpet
Some Rooms: Antiques
Bed & Bath: King beds, antique bed
(1); hall access w/ robes (1)
Favorites: Room w/ in-room bath

Comfort & Decor: Comfortable-sized rooms w/ attractive wallpaper, mix of contemporary and antique pieces, artwork. Comfort rather than style. Low key, informal. Good lighting.

RATES, RESERVATIONS, & RESTRICTIONS

Deposit: 1 night; refund w/ 6-day
notice
Discounts: 7 days or longer; off-season specials
Credit Cards: None
Check-in/Out: 2/11
Smoking: No
Pets: No
Kids: Over 10

Minimum Stay: 2 nights/summer
weekends
Open: All year, call in off-season
Hosts: Mercedes and Don Kratz
803 Green Hill Beach Rd.
Wakefield, RI 02879-6228
(401) 783-9752
Fax: (401) 783-0802, call first
www.virtualcities.com

WATCH HILL INN, Watch Hill

Overall: ★★★	Room Quality: C	Value: C	Price: $75–$225

Incredible bay sunsets, a casual atmosphere, and a breezy waterfront location are pluses here, along with the fact that there are few other good bed-and-breakfast properties in this part of the state. This modest inn could use a face-lift, but its relaxed, waterfront atmosphere somehow fits the salty environment. A deck seaside restaurant serves seafood, steak dinners, and outstanding clam chowder in an informal setting that has most people in shorts and tees. Old salts and families with young kids—allowed free—will be especially satisfied.

SETTING & FACILITIES

Location: Southwest tip of Rhode
Island; take Scenic Rt. 1A to Watch Hill,
or take Rt. 78 to Watch Hill, look for
signs
Near: On Bay, Marina; views of
Stonington (Conn.), Block Island; short
drive to casinos; walk to ocean
beaches; Newport, Mystic
Building: 1845 New England-style
architecture, expanded

Grounds: Bay and docked boats,
decks, windows showcase views
Public Space: Seasonal porch; DR
Food & Drink: Cont'l breakfast; lunch
and dinner daily in summer and holiday
weekends through Sept.; a specialty:
grilled pizza ("Grizza"); specialties:
seafood, steak, award-winning clam
chowder; late-night menu till midnight;
full service bar and grill; banquets

Recreation: Touring historic Watch Hill, residential "summer cottage" mansions, antique shops and art galleries, Flying Horse carousel; inn hosts local bands weekends

Amenities & Services: Beach towels; meeting, seminar, wedding and priv. party facilities

ACCOMMODATIONS

Units: 12 guest rooms, 4 junior suites
All Rooms: Bath, phone, TV, AC/heat controls, water or village views
Some Rooms: Junior suites larger: sitting area w/ pull-out sofa
Bed & Bath: Some antique, four-poster beds; some showers only, some clawfoot tubs w/ showers, not luxury baths
Favorites: Room 13—more spacious, pretty room w/ keyhole water view,

Rooms 9 and 10—most requested, direct water views
Comfort & Decor: Low-key Colonial decor. Muted, pretty floral wallcoverings. Traditional mahogany pieces, some Queen Anne–style. Some pieces could be improved w/ refinishing. Americana decor, wreaths, ceramic water pitchers. Carpet.

RATES, RESERVATIONS, & RESTRICTIONS

Deposit: 50%; refund w/ 14-day notice, full reservation payment due w/ shorter notice
Discounts: 3rd person, various packages include midweek, weekend (exclusions), full week, golf/fishing, seminars/retreats
Credit Cards: MC, V, AE
Check-in/Out: 3–6/11; late check-out charged extra day
Smoking: On porches and grounds; in restaurant/lounge
Pets: No

Kids: Welcome, no cots or cribs; young children free
Minimum Stay: 2 nights weekends; 3 nights holidays
Open: All year
Hosts: Rob DiMillio, Mary Farago, and Mark Szaro
38 Bay St.
Watch Hill, RI 02891
(800) 356-9314 or (401) 348-8912
Fax: (401) 348-6301
zorro59@aol.com
www.digiworld.com/watchhillinn

KISMET ON THE PARK, Westerly

Overall: ★★★	Room Quality: C	Value: C	Price: $75–$85

If you ever wanted to enjoy cultural events right from your own porch, you can here, including band concerts and Shakespeare plays. Wilcox Park, behind this pleasant downtowner, was modeled after Central Park. A mother-daughter team has worked long and hard to bring this once dilapidated grand house up to speed. Breakfast is light, but a short walk away are restaurants, shops, movies, and the train. The combo of urbanity and greenery is appealing.

SETTING & FACILITIES

Location: From south, I-95 to Rt. 78, Exit 3, right to fork, bear right onto High St., property on left

Near: Entrance to Wilcox Park, downtown, 2 casinos, Watch Hill, Block Island Ferry

Building: 1845 Federal-style townhouse

Grounds: Minimal in front, but backs onto large park

Public Space: Porch/balcony, public room, DR

Food & Drink: Cont'l breakfast; always open for refreshments

Recreation: Park activities and cultural events, touring Westerly, golf, tennis, beachcombing, boating

Amenities & Services: Hot tub, off-street parking for 4 cars, TV in public room, guest refrigerator, irons, kitchen privileges; meetings (20), priv. parties

ACCOMMODATIONS

Units: 3 guest rooms, I suite, I longer-stay studio apartment

All Rooms: Bath, ceiling fan, antiques

Some Rooms: Park view

Bed & Bath: Bed sizes twin and double, Early American quilts; showers only, I w/ whirlpool

Favorites: Romance Room—ruffles, whirlpool; The Apartment—full BR and

2nd BR w/ daybed and trundle, living/dining area, Americana

Comfort & Decor: Rooms bright w/ sun, white walls, and splashes of heritage colors. Lace, quilts, wicker, and early Colonial pieces. Basic but pretty. Clean and comfortable.

RATES, RESERVATIONS, & RESTRICTIONS

Deposit: I night

Discounts: Longer stays; $85 for I night, $75 each for 2 nights

Check-in/Out: 2–4/11

Smoking: On porches only

Pets: No

Kids: Over 12; apartment OK for families

Minimum Stay: 2 nights

Open: April–Dec.

Hosts: Cindy Slay & Courtney Slay
I High St.
Westerly, RI 02891
(401) 596-3237
Kismet@edgenet
www3.edgenet.net/kismet

SHELTER HARBOR INN, Westerly

Overall: ★★★½   Room Quality: C   Value: D   Price: $95–$160

Situated on busy Route 1 (with neither sea nor harbor in sight), this casual old inn is nonetheless peaceful, buffered from the highway. The low-key host, a self-described Wall Street exile, does not occupy the property, but is around if needed, often mowing the lawn. Antiques run from Stickley-craftsman to Early American, and include an enormous Hoosier hutch and a Simplex wall clock. The nearby salt pond is fun for kids, the three-mile beach is a joy to walk, and the food is tops.

SETTING & FACILITIES

Location: I-95 N to Exit 92, turn right onto Rt. 2, 1 mi. to Rt. 78, to end stoplight, Rt. 1, turn left, inn is 4 mi. on right
Near: Short drive to private-to-community barrier ocean beach, Watch Hill, Mystic, Newport, ferry to Block Island
Building: Rambling 2-story white farmhouse (built 1800–1810), some c. 1900 additions; orig. coach house and barn
Grounds: Rolling lawns, patios, gardens; paddle tennis courts, croquet
Public Space: Antique Colonial library; year-round sun porch, deck; 3 restaurant DRs

Food & Drink: Full breakfast; specialty: ginger-blueberry pancakes; restaurant open to public, 3 meals every day all year; lighter fare in veranda bar; specialties: smoked finnan haddie, other fresh seafood; full liquor license; special holiday dinners
Recreation: Ocean activities, trails, antiquing in Watch Hill, theater in Matunuck
Amenities & Services: Lawn games, roof deck, hot tub, barbecue, bike storage, cots and cribs, irons

ACCOMMODATIONS

Units: 24 guest rooms
All Rooms: Bath, seating, reading lamp, TV, phone, AC
Some Rooms: Fireplace, deck
Bed & Bath: Some four-poster beds, 1 queen or 2 doubles in rooms; most full baths, some shower only
Favorites: #9—Corner room, fireplace, priv. deck

Comfort & Decor: Comfortable, mix of authentic Victorian antiques, reproduction Colonial pieces. Muted floral bedding, window treatments. Some worn furnishings should be updated. Some Block Island views.

RATES, RESERVATIONS, & RESTRICTIONS

Deposit: 1 night; refund w/ 48-hour notice
Discounts: Children, singles, business midweek
Credit Cards: MC, V, AE, D
Check-in/Out: 2/11
Smoking: Permitted in guest rooms, bar, outside
Pets: No

Kids: Welcome
Minimum Stay: 2 nights weekends, Thanksgiving; 3 nights other holidays
Open: All year
Hosts: Jim Dey
Wagner Rd.
Westerly, RI 02891
(800) 468-8883 or (401) 322-8883
Fax: (401) 322-7907

THE VILLA, Westerly

Overall: ★★★★	Room Quality: B	Value: D	Price: $150–$225

"Land of Amore" is the way the new owners aptly describes this sensual bed-and-breakfast, and its primary purpose is romantic getaways. Locals stay here, so the place is usually full on weekends. The pool, five-seater whirlpool, and lushly landscaped patio are the focus, but fountains, flowers from the cutting garden, in-room whirlpools, soft textures, candlelit breakfast, and soft lighting all speak the "L" word. Italian-inspired room names—La Sala del Cielo, The Blue Grotto, La Sala di Verona, may indeed make you feel like Juliet, or Romeo, or both!

SETTING & FACILITIES

Location: Rt. 1 to Rt. 1A (Shore Rd.); cross Airport Rd.
Near: Watch Hill, ocean, bay, Mystic Seaport and Aquarium, Westerly, Foxwoods Casino, Newport, ferry to Block Island, ocean view golf course adjacent to property
Building: Stucco Dutch Colonial w/ Mediterranean exteriors, styled as villa
Grounds: Nearly 2 acres, 5 Euro-style gardens, fountains, statuary; pool and hot tub; decorated seasonally

Public Space: Sitting room, dining area, atrium
Food & Drink: Buffet cont'l breakfast; specialties: peach-pecan or piña colada muffins; early riser on request
Recreation: Golf, local events, deep-sea fishing, boating
Amenities & Services: Pool, games, shuttle to train or plane

ACCOMMODATIONS

Units: 6; 3 in main house, 3 in carriage house
All Rooms: Bath, carpet, compact refrigerator, TV, coffee maker, AC
Some Rooms: Skylight, fireplace, terrace/balcony; sitting area, love seat/sofa; microwave, dining tables; separate living, dining, or sitting rooms; kitchenettes; carriage house rooms: priv. entrances
Bed & Bath: Special decor beds (brass, four-poster), sizes vary; dbl. whirlpools or baths in room, some mirrored

Favorites: Blue Grotto—stone wall, ceiling fans, fireplace, dbl. whirlpool, glass doors to pool; Rosa Maiorano—four-poster, brick fireplace, dbl. bath, and separate shower; Verona—LR, DR, stereo, cathedral ceilings in sleeping area, king brass bed, skylight above dbl. whirlpool
Comfort & Decor: Rooms vary widely. Most good size. Highly romantic and sensual. Fresh greenery. Plush carpets. Not designed for reading in bed.

RATES, RESERVATIONS, & RESTRICTIONS

Deposit: 1 night or 50%; balance paid in full at check-in; must cancel 15 days in advance
Discounts: Off-season, midweek, 3rd person
Credit Cards: MC, V, AE
Check-in/Out: 1/11
Smoking: No
Pets: No

Kids: No
Open: All year
Hosts: Angela and Peter Gagnon
190 Shore Rd.
Westerly, RI 02891
(800) 722-9240 or (401) 596-1054
Fax: (401) 596-6268
villa@riconnect.com
www.thevillaatwesterly.com

WOODY HILL, Westerly

Overall: ★★★½	Room Quality: B	Value: C	Price: $92–$159

Like to talk about Walt Whitman, Nathaniel Hawthorne, and Edgar Allen Poe along with your sightseeing? Ellen has a Ph.D. in nineteenth-century American literature, and is happy to chat, so here's your chance. Her family has resided in Westerly since the 1600s, and the Early American ambiance and library full of books reflect her heritage and interests. Pretty and private, bucolic and quiet, Woody Hill is aptly named, nestled in the woods, and has a pool with a lovely view. Here's a great place to bring a book—and then discuss it.

SETTING & FACILITIES

Location: Rural setting, off busy highway
Near: Ocean, Foxwoods Casino, Mystic, Watch Hill, Newport, Ferry to Block Island, walking trails
Building: Recently constructed, authentic-looking shingle Dutch Colonial; separate guest house
Grounds: On a hilltop in the woods; 20 acres w/ gardens, pool, pool house
Public Space: Porch, front room, library; LR; keeping room

Food & Drink: Full breakfast, communal or separate; a specialty: apple crisp w/ whipped cream
Recreation: Local crafts, workshops, cultural events, antiquing, kayaking, sailing, X-C skiing
Amenities & Services: Irons, guest refrigerator, beach towels, recipes, board games; weekday discounts for tee times, lunch and dinner for Weekapaug golf course; facilities for parties, weddings, functions, meetings

ACCOMMODATIONS

Units: 4 guest rooms, I suite
All Rooms: Fresh flowers; Americana fabrics, appointments, bath
Some Rooms: Antique mahogany or cherry furnishings, TV, VCR, priv. entrance, AC, priv. roof deck; phone on request
Bed & Bath: Some canopy or bed-curtain beds; all priv. baths, I hall access, mostly showers only, I dbl. shower, I tub

Favorites: Room #3—large, windows, pretty decor, French doors, walkway to pool, can be reserved as 2-room suite; room #1—suitable for families
Comfort & Decor: Spacious rooms w/ antiques, wide-plank floors, handmade quilts. Rustic, real Early American. Suite: queen sofa bed in 2nd room. Good lighting.

RATES, RESERVATIONS, & RESTRICTIONS

Deposit: I night; refund w/ 7-day notice
Discounts: Off-season, longer stays, add'l persons, school nights; weekend

packages adjunct to area workshops (e.g., Harvest Wreath, Ballroom Dancing, Knitting, etc.)
Credits Cards: No

Check-in/Out: 2/11; guests may use facil. for day after check out
Smoking: Outside only
Pets: No; 2 cats, not allowed in guest rooms
Kids: OK; may be charged for breakfast
No-No's: Unsupervised kids at pool
Minimum Stay: 2 nights on weekends; check for 1-night availability

Open: All year
Hosts: Ellen Madison
149 South Woody Hill Rd.
Westerly, RI 02891
(401) 322-0452 or (401) 322-4003
woodyhill@riconnect.com
www.visitri.com/south/buspages/woodyhill

Connecticut

Close enough to New York to prioritize sophistication but deeply rooted in New England, the compact Nutmeg State—fewer than 60 miles from north to south and 100 miles across—features 850 lake-and-stream–filled square miles in the Quinebaug and Shetucket Rivers Valley National Heritage Corridor, as well as 250 miles of active Long Island Sound coastline.

Hartford and New Haven are centers of entertainment and cultural opportunities and famed college campuses, hilly terrain, and unspoiled Colonial villages are part of the scene. The state is still two-thirds open land, and even the busy Merritt Parkway leading to New York is a designated scenic byway, ideal for foliage splendor.

Other routes make for equally pretty drives. Route 7 runs from Litchfield County's covered Bull's Bridge north to the covered bridge in West Cornwall, near the Housatonic River, Kent, Kent Falls, and several state parks. Route 41 (in the northwest corner of the state) connects Sharon, Lakeville, Salisbury, and Bear Mountain. Route 77 from Guilford to Durham starts at the shore and runs through real countryside, passing working Dudley Farm. Shoreline. Route 146 passes through Branford and Guilford. Route 169 follows from Yankee farm areas near Woodstock to Lisbon and has been voted one of the top 10 scenic roads in the country. Route 202 passes Nepaug State Park. Route 234 is also known as the Pequot Trail and runs through Stonington.

Filled with antiques and boutiques, museums and performing arts, Litchfield, Haddam, Kent, Essex, Putnam, Norwich, Stonington, and New London are quaint, quiet areas along scenic Route 169 and much of the river valley. These towns provide ideal meandering getaways for couples, and for more excitement the nearby Foxwoods and Mohegun Sun casinos liven up the night.

Mystic, Norwalk, Lake Compounce Theme Park, Bristol, Farmington River, Bridgeport, South Norwalk, and other Connecticut towns offer steam trains, riverboat cruises, zoos and nature centers, hands-on experiments, a puppet theater, beach activities, lighthouses, professional sports, festivals, and fairs.

You can enjoy just about any activity in Connecticut except really good downhill skiing. You'll find hot-air balloon tours, swimming, boating, parasailing, diving, whitewater kayaking, skiing, fly-fishing and charter fishing, horseback riding, historical touring, antiques and outlet shopping, theater, music, dance, hiking, walking, biking, carriage rides, scenic tours, museums, and just-for-kids activities.

Bed-and-breakfasts and inns in this state tend to be romantic and historical, and many are housed in antique farmhouses. Those close to New York City, in posh Greenwich or New Canaan areas, cater to business travelers and harried weekenders, but some are just comfortable and welcome kids.

The state is also noted for dining, from the homey to the five-star sublime, with an adventurous mix of cuisines and cultures. After all, America was first introduced to pizza in Connecticut.

For More Information

Bed & Breakfast Ltd.
(203) 469-3260

Bed & Breakfast/Inns of New England
Reservation Service
(800) 582-0853

Bed & Breakfasts of Mystic Coast
(860) 892-5006

Covered Bridge B&B Reservation Service
(860) 542-5944

Destinations New England
(800) 333-INNS (all of New England)

Four Seasons International Bed &
Breakfast Reservation Service
(860) 658-2181

Mystic Country Inns
(800) 598-7116

Mystic Lodgings
(860) 536-0509 or (800) 536-6709

Nutmeg Bed & Breakfast Agency
(860) 236-6698 or (800) 727-7592
www.bnb-link.com

Connecticut Lodgings & Attractions
Association
(860) 657-2259

Connecticut Tourism
(860) 270-8080 or (800) CT-BOUND
www.state.ct.us/tourism/; www.visitconnecticut.com

Litchfield Hills Travel Council
(860) 567-4506
fax: (860) 567-5214
www.litchfieldhills.com

Ferry Information
New London to Block Island (seasonal): (860) 442-9553 or (860) 442-7891
New London to Fishers Island (year-round): (860) 442-0165 or (516) 788-7463
New London to Montauk (seasonal): (516) 668-5700
New London to Orient Point: (860) 443-5281

Zone 18
Western Connecticut

Postcard-perfect Western Connecticut is filled with steepled churches, picket fences, American flags, Colonial stone walls, and rustic barns, but has some urban areas as well. This zone starts in the northwest foothills of the Berkshires, runs south to coastal Fairfield County bordering New York, laps into Long Island Sound, and west to New Haven.

The Litchfield Hills area has been a summer retreat for more than 100 years and offers an abundance of recreational activities—antiquing, boating and lake activities, historic home tours, horseback riding, golf, tennis, hiking, snow sports, rafting, and car racing. It also is home to artistic and cultural pursuits—the hills are literally alive with music, dance, and drama. Near the Berkshires, the town of Washington is named after the man who indeed slept here and perhaps at a property where we can too. Litchfield is a classic treasure, with a clutch of great white-clapboard, black-shuttered mansions. Antique hunters and gallerygoers should stop at quaint Kent, and after scouring for bargains, enjoy the waterfalls. For authentic Americana, nearby are the Carousel Museum of New England in Bristol, and the 1841 barn-red covered bridge in West Cornwall.

Some lodgings are restored mansions with splendid period trappings. More modest accommodations may be creatively built around literary or artistic themes, and still others offer simple and cozy accommodations.

Fairfield County, the western coastal area of the state, is closest to New York and operates partially as a very upscale suburb. It offers historic homes and sites, nature centers, museums, shopping, excellent dining, and performing and fine arts in a sophisticated locale. In addition to all of that, the calm sound beaches are popular.

Westport is a creative and shopping center, with a sophisticated New York edge and prices to match. Bridgeport, a no-nonsense town with some urban ills, is home to the Beardsley Zoo and the interactive Discovery

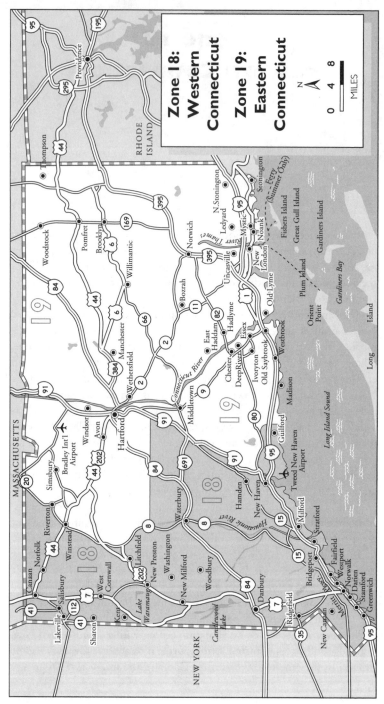

Zone 18: Western Connecticut

Zone 19: Eastern Connecticut

N

0   4   8
MILES

420

Museum. Historic Norwalk has a renowned maritime aquarium and IMAX Theatre. A ferry ride away is the 1868 Sheffield Island Lighthouse. The best bed-and-breakfasts and inns offer a quiet hideaway from New York for weekend R&R, or, conversely, a country base from which to visit the Big Apple. Business travelers are well-received, and lodgings here can be stopovers to or from an extended tour of New England.

Fishing and boating are pleasures of the Housatonic River, and low-key accommodations are nearby. The valley was the site of the second-largest Revolutionary War encampment—only Valley Forge was larger.

You can hike through American history on trails in the 183-acre Putnam Memorial State Park and gaze at contemporary works at the Aldrich Museum of Contemporary Art in Ridgefield and the Brookfield Craft Center near Candlewood Lake. Or enjoy a costumed tour of Colonial history at the Keeler Tavern Museum in Ridgefield, a center for dining, antiquing and traditional New England charm an hour's drive from NYC.

Although parts of New Haven cry out for rejuvenation, Yale's architecturally fascinating campus and renowned art museum are worth a visit. The Waterbury region has an amusement park, museums, an opera house, a railroad tour in Thomaston, and a new 10,000-square-foot, restored turn-of-the-century antiques district in Seymour. Central Connecticut features numerous pick-your-own fruit, vegetable, and pumpkin patches, Colonial walking tours, and more museums and performing arts.

For More Information

Central Connecticut Tourism District
(860) 225-3901
fax: (860) 225-0218
www.centralct.org

Coastal Fairfield County Convention &
Visitor Bureau
(203) 899-2799 or (800) 866-7925
www.visitfairfieldco.org

Fairfield Chamber of Commerce
(203) 255-1011

Greater New Haven Convention and
Visitors Bureau
(203) 777-8550 or (800) 332-STAY
www.newhavencvb.org

Housatonic Valley Tourism District
(203) 743-0546 or (800) 841-4488
www.housatonic.org

Kent Chamber of Commerce
(860) 927-1463
www.kentct.com

Litchfield Hills Visitors Bureau
(860) 567-4506
www.litchfieldhills.com

Waterbury Region Convention &
Visitors Bureau
(203) 597-9527
fax: (203) 597-8452

HOMESTEAD INN, Greenwich

Overall: ★★★★½   Room Quality: B   Value: C   Price: $130–$395+

Warm, bright owners took over this already well-regarded suburban inn in 1997. Renowned for superior cuisine (in 1998, *Esquire* named the inn's restaurant one of the best in the country), its guest quarters are catching up—slowly. The folks at the next table are probably movers and shakers on weekend R&R or local moguls dining out at their round-the-corner neighborhood favorite. Not much to do here but eat and relax in the casually elegant rooms, but for many that's quite enough, thank you. In fact, author William Inge wrote *Picnic* while staying here in the 1950s. Is it a coincidence he wrote about a meal on a lawn, just as you can enjoy on premises?

SETTING & FACILITIES

Location: I-95 to Exit 3, left at ramp end; left onto Horse Neck Ln.; left onto Field Point Rd.; inn on right, approx. .5 mi. S of I-95; I mi. from town center, in upscale Victorian-era Belle Haven residential area

Near: Historic Greenwich, museums, Pepsico sculpture gardens, Stamford Center for the Arts, Cavalier Art Gallery, commuter rail to Manhattan (45 min.)

Building: 1799 Colonial farmhouse w/ Gothic Victorian, Italianate touches

Grounds: 3 acres, gardens, stone walls

Public Space: Backgammon parlor, LR, DR, main DR, sun porch, bar, veranda

Food & Drink: Early riser coffee; breakfast, lunch, and dinner served in French style; full breakfast menu; lunch specialties: striped bass, grilled veal;

dinner specialties: Dover sole, herb-crust rack of lamb; extensive wine list
Recreation: Golf, tennis, sound-side beach, historic home tours, antiquing

Amenities & Services: Limited disabled access; beach passes; turn-down, wake-up calls; meetings, office capabilities

ACCOMMODATIONS

Units: 23 guest rooms and suites in orig. home, the Inn Between and the Cottage
All Rooms: Bath, phone/dataport, voice mail, clock/radio, TV, access to veranda, AC
Some Rooms: Desk, priv. veranda, sitting rooms
Bed & Bath: Antique beds; new baths w/ elaborate fixtures, soaking tubs, extra-large showers

Favorites: Romantic Room 23—new bath, king four-poster; Room 22—backgammon table, stunning fabrics, bath remodeled
Comfort & Decor: Superior attention to guest comfort. Rooms in orig. building, historic feel. Stencils in Robin Room from 1860. High-end, authentic-style furnishings. High-tech. Good lighting. Rooms upgraded one by one. Single rooms converting to baths for adjacent rooms.

RATES, RESERVATIONS, & RESTRICTIONS

Deposit: Credit card reservation; no charge w/ 48-hour notice for midweek, 7 days for weekends
Credit Cards: MC, V, AE
Check-In/Out: 3/noon
Smoking: Restricted
Pets: No
Kids: Over 14
Minimum Stay: 2 nights Thanksgiving/Christmas weekends

Open: All year
Hosts: Theresa Carroll and Thomas Henkelmann
420 Field Point Rd.
Greenwich, CT 06830
(203) 869-7500
Fax: (203) 869-7502
www.johansens.com

SOUND REACH, Guilford

Overall: ★★★½	Room Quality: B	Value: C	Price: $85–$95

The name Sound Reach has a double meaning, referring to the view and the music floating across the night air. Lawrence is a professional musician, and executive director of the New Haven Music School, so the house is filled with instruments, and guests are encouraged to join in for impromptu recitals. Pam lived in Denmark for six years, and her love of Scandinavian culture and aesthetics is evident. A former art editor, she currently freelances and is passionate about gardening and cooking, useful talents at this rustic, chalet-style log bed-and-breakfast. The inn is on a wooded hill, where you can catch the breeze and sometimes spot a wild turkey.

ir than in years previous. Breakfasts are especially original, with delectables ch as eggnog French toast. Kent is a center of shopping for art and tiques, an easy walk from here, yet the bed-and-breakfast is just far enough ay from the weekend crowds to allow for peaceful sleep. The site is booked ough 2002 for events at the Kent School—a pilgrimage, so to speak.

TTING & FACILITIES

cation: Follow Rt. 7 into Kent; B&B main street
ar: Walk to antiquing, Housatonic r, historic sites, Kent Falls State Park, nawk Mountain ski area, priv./board- schools, winery, 35 mi. to Danbury
lding: 1948 clapboard Colonial; ntly remodeled
unds: Summer gardens, old maples
lic Space: Entry, formal DR, sitting n

Food & Drink: Full formal breakfast; specialties: eggnog French toast, corn pancakes with crème fraiche and smoked salmon; refreshments, wine and cheese
Recreation: Antiquing, waterfall, golf, tennis, water sports, horseback riding, skiing
Amenities & Services: Phone, bicycles, car rental

COMMODATIONS

ts: 5 guest rooms
Rooms: Bath, fresh flowers, alarm /radio, AC
e Rooms: Antiques
& Bath: 1 high four-poster, bed vary; some shower-only, 1 hall ss bath, robes provided

Favorites: Garden Room—Rose wallpaper, white wicker
Comfort & Decor: Rooms currently redecorating: American country, English hunt classic, and Federal

ES, RESERVATIONS, & RESTRICTIONS

osit: Credit card holds reservation; d w/ 7-day notice, 10-day notice for ay weekends, 30-day for groups and school event weekends
ounts: 3rd person, subject to bility; singles
lit Cards: MC, V, AE, D, DC
k-In/Out: 4/10
king: No
No

Kids: Over 10
Minimum Stay: Subject to availability—check
Open: All year
Hosts: Mary Redrupp
88 North Main St.
Kent, CT 06757-0826
(860) 927-4858
Fax: (860) 927-5399
home.att.net/~chaucerbb

SEWOOD MEADOW, Kent

| all: ★★★ | Room Quality: C | Value: C | Price: $85–$105 |

mmodations are minimal in this popular town, and while a modest like this may not be outstanding in a town like Camden, Maine, or

SETTING & FACILITIES

Location: 10 min. from Guilford Green; I-95 to Exit 58; take Rt. 77 N to left turn onto Rt. 80; take next right onto Long Hill; left onto Country Rd.; B&B is 1st right onto Christmas Hill
Near: Yale, downtown New Haven, Lake Quonnipaug, Hammonasset Beach State Park, Water Authority property, lake, outlet mall, working colonial farm
Building: 1968 hilltop Swiss-style, rustic cedar log cabin; outbuildings
Grounds: 3.5 parklike, secluded acres, wooded areas; perennial and herb gardens, trails, clear-day views from Stony Creek to Long Island

Public Space: LR, loft r balconies; DR
Food & Drink: Cont'l b breakfast on request); a s home-baked breads w/ f
Recreation: Historic t mer farmers' market, an and beach activities, X-(watching
Amenities & Service Authority passes, fans a closets, refrigerator, bik gas grill, phone, daily N fax/computer services

ACCOMMODATIONS

Units: 3 guest rooms
All Rooms: Flowers, 2-phone line, candle lantern
Some Rooms: Priv. bath (1), view, writing desk
Bed & Bath: 2 rooms share 1 bath
Favorites: Double-bed room—charming, priv. bath

Comfort & Decor: painted furniture, Swe Original artworks. Ro lanterns in each room twin rooms share bat suite. Rooms at seper house, priv.

RATES, RESERVATIONS, & RESTRICTIONS

Deposit: 1 night; refund w/ reasonable notice
Discounts: Winter packages
Credit Cards: MC, V, D
Check-In/Out: By arrangement/by 10:30
Smoking: No
Pets: Check for availability
Kids: Check for availability

Minimum Stay: 2 n weekends
Open: All year
Hosts: Pam Carley a Christmas Hill Rd. Guilford, CT 06437
(203) 457-0415
Fax: (203) 457-022!
Lzucchini@aol.com

CHAUCER HOUSE, Kent

Overall: ★★★	Room Quality: B	Value: C

Warm, intelligent Mary, the new innkeeper, realized
when she took over this already pleasant white clapboa
new guest rooms and decorated all in markedly differer

Woodstock, Vermont—filled with good properties—here it can be noted. You can picnic over at Kent Falls State Park, visit the dozens of antiques shops and galleries, and peruse the collection of Early American tools at the Sloane-Stanley Museum. Sit by the stream on the grass and have afternoon tea. All civilized and pleasurable. And can you guess what Rosenbaum, the innkeepers' surname, means in German?

SETTING & FACILITIES

Location: Rt. 7 to Kent, B&B is 2.5 mi. north of the center of Kent
Near: Kent Falls State Park, quaint Kent Village
Building: 1860 white clapboard Colonial with Greek Revival touches
Grounds: 2 acres, stream, barn, terrace, rose and perennial gardens

Public Space: Den, LR, FR, DR
Food & Drink: Cont'l breakfast until 11; tea
Recreation: Hiking/walking trails, waterfalls, antiquing, restaurants
Amenities & Services: Gift shop

ACCOMMODATIONS

Units: 2 guest rooms, cottage suite
All Rooms: Bath, sitting room, decorative fireplace
Some Rooms: Cottage suite: dining area and kitchen facilities, priv. entrance, breezeway porch, TV
Bed & Bath: Double sizes, add'l beds avail., firm mattresses
Favorites: Rose Room—curved priv. staircase to pretty room w/ fireplace, priv. bath, sitting room

Comfort & Decor: Guest rooms feature hand-stenciling, Colonial painted trim. Nicely restored original floors softened w/ country needlepoint-style area rugs. Pretty artwork, some nice antiques. Some country-homey kitsch. Decorative fireplaces. One-BR cottage attached to main house; easy access for breakfast, amenities.

RATES, RESERVATIONS, & RESTRICTIONS

Deposit: 1 night; refund w/ reasonable notice
Discounts: 3rd person, long-term stays
Credit Cards: MC
Check-In/Out: 2/11
Smoking: No
Pets: No

Kids: 10 and up
Minimum Stay: 2 nights weekends
Open: All year
Hosts: Pat and Karl Rosenbaum
230 Kent Cornwall Rd.
Kent, CT 06757
(800) 600-4334 or (860) 927-4334
rosewoodmeadowb.b@snet,net

TOLL GATE HILL, Litchfield

Overall: ★★★★   Room Quality: B   Value: C   Price: $100–$200

History, history. This famed inn, three barn-red buildings, is on the National Register of Historic Places. It originally welcomed wayfarers as a stagecoach way station, hence its name. The house moved to its present site in 1923. The Tapping Reeve House and Law School and Oliver Wolcott Library, one of the first law schools in the colonies, are a part of the picture-perfect scene. The two-story ballroom with beamed ceilings has a tiny fiddler's loft, which houses dinner musicians; there's jazz on Sundays. Fireplaces glow, floorboards creak, and the food is fusion.

SETTING & FACILITIES

Location: Rt. 202, 2.5 mi. W of Litchfield Village
Near: Conservation center, Bantam Lake, art galleries, museums, crafts shops and boutiques, performing arts, Bantam art films cinema, state parks, Housatonic River
Building: Gambrel-roofed Colonial; converted schoolhouse; The Captain William Bull Tavern (c. 1745)
Grounds: 10 acres, lawns, patios, trails, woods
Public Space: Lobby; restaurant incl. formal DRs

Food & Drink: Cont'l breakfast; lunch and dinner daily in restaurant; bar/lounge, tavern-style; new American cuisine; Fri. dinner and Sun. brunch buffets (kids under 6 eat free); restaurant closed in winter, Tues., Wed.
Recreation: Antiquing, lake and river activities, picnicking, bird watching, skiing
Amenities & Services: Cribs, cots, baby-sitting; meetings, weddings, etc. (125)

ACCOMMODATIONS

Units: 15 guest rooms, 5 suites, long-term apt. avail.
All Rooms: Bath, phone, TV, AC
Some Rooms: Fireplace, deck, sitting area, VCR, mini-bar, refrigerator
Bed & Bath: Some canopy beds; queen, double, twin; 2 shower-only baths
Favorites: Room 2—mid-priced room in 1745 building, sitting area, fireplace, double canopy

Comfort & Decor: Family style. Warm colors. Lots of lighting, ottomans, comfy seating. Mid-to-quality reproduction furnishings, sturdy, attractive. Dressed up w/ fresh, contemporary/country fabrics.

RATES, RESERVATIONS, & RESTRICTIONS

Deposit: 1 night; restaurant/lodging credit w/ 10-day notice
Discounts: Corp., 3rd person, kids
Credit Cards: MC, V, AE, D, DC
Check-In/Out: 1/11
Smoking: Restricted, notice to inn
Pets: Welcome, $10 add'l charge
Kids: Welcome
Minimum Stay: 2 nights weekends,

holidays
Open: All year
Hosts: Fritz Zivic
Box 1339, Route 202 & Tollgate Rd.
Litchfield, CT 06759
(800) 445-3903 or (860) 567-4545
Fax: (860) 567-8397
www.litchfieldct.com/dng/tollgate.html

ROGER SHERMAN INN, New Canaan

Overall: ★★★½	Room Quality: B	Value: C	Price: $130–$300

Roger Sherman, this 18th-century home's namesake, was a Connecticut delegate to the Continental Congress, and the only person to sign all four documents: The Association (1774), Declaration of Independence (1776), Articles of Confederation (1777), and the Constitution (1787). Continental breakfast (no Congress) is amidst salmon-colored walls, ivy stenciling, and Tiffany "ivy" glass. Groups and the public can overrun the house at later meals, but the inn's most formal dining space out of five choices has a few candlelit tables. Alsatian handpainted wallpaper depicts American war scenes; the only similar example is in Washington, D.C.— in the White House.

SETTING & FACILITIES

Location: From I-684 take Rt. 35 E to Rt. 124 S; Inn approximately 12 mi. farther on right; 10 min. walk to village
Near: Nature center, Norwalk, aquarium, quaint shopping, IMAX Theatre, Stamford, 1 hour to NYC
Building: 1783 gabled white Colonial
Grounds: Gardens, mature trees
Public Space: Bar/lounge, 5 dining areas
Food & Drink: Cont'l breakfast; lunch, dinner, Sun. brunch, wine cellar, liquor license, contemp./cont'l menu, Swiss specialties; open 7 days except Mon. lunch; Terrace Room—most formal DR; Hunt Room; summer cocktails on porch, seasonal outdoor dining
Recreation: Maple sugar shack, 40 mi. of hiking trails; lounge piano entertainment weekend evenings; lake boating in Norwalk
Amenities & Services: Irons, hairdryers, 2 cribs. Guest laundry and dry cleaning; functions (175), in 6 connected banquet rooms

ACCOMMODATIONS

Units: 16 guest rooms, 1 2-BR suite; main house and carriage house
All Rooms: Bath, mini-bar, phone/dataport, seating, TV
Some Rooms: Balcony, decorative fireplace, sitting area, writing desk, VCR
Bed & Bath: Some sleigh, brass beds; bath sizes vary
Favorites: Room 24 (Fruit Room)— open, airy, light; Bridal Suite—queen carved bed, shutters
Comfort & Decor: Classifications: standard (smallest), superior, deluxe, junior suites, 2-BR suite. Reliable hotel-style furnishings and comfort. Early American ambiance. Quieter carriage house rooms w/ Hitchcock reproduction Colonial pieces. Some TVs in armoires. Some attractive, individually styled rooms w/ themes. Junior suites w/ balconies.

RATES, RESERVATIONS, & RESTRICTIONS

Deposit: Credit card holds reservation; refund w/ 48-hour notice
Discounts: Singles, midweek, 3rd person, some corp., infants free
Credit Cards: MC, V, AE, DC
Check-In/Out: 2/11
Smoking: Restricted to smoking lounge, outdoors
Pets: No
Kids: Welcome

Open: All year except for some major holidays, Christmas Day; check
Hosts: Thomas and Kay Weilenmann
195 Oenoke Ridge, Route 124
New Canaan, CT 06840
(203) 966-4541
Fax: (203) 966-0503
info@rogershermaninn.com
www.rogershermaninn.com

THREE CHIMNEYS INN, New Haven

Overall: ★★★½	Room Quality: B	Value: D	Price: $170

Yale is a five-minute walk away from this Victorian bed-and-breakfast, nicknamed "The Lady" for its ornate, painted facade. Sitting somewhat timidly behind an iron fence, it languished until the new innkeepers (who own a sister Three Chimneys Inn in Durham, New Hampshire) took over in 1996, refurbishing the spacious guest rooms, adding air conditioning, dataports, desks, TVs, and conference rooms. Now it is popular with Yalies, small groups, and those who prefer mounted hunt trophies and oak millwork dating from the Tall Ships era as well as fitness centers and minibars. It is the best, and one of the only, bed-and-breakfasts around this cultural mecca. Chain accommodations are your other options if you go astray.

SETTING & FACILITIES

Location: From I-95 E to downtown New Haven Exit 47, proceed to N Frontage Rd., corner of Yale St.; turn right onto York, left at 3rd traffic light onto Chapel St.; B&B 1.5 blocks on right
Near: 1 block from Yale, overlooks Chapel West museum, theater, shopping district; 1 hour to casinos, 30 mi. to Hartford
Building: 1870 Painted Lady Victorian
Grounds: Small landscaped property w/ brick carriage house

Public Space: Entry hall, dbl. parlor
Food & Drink: Full breakfast, communal or separate; refreshments; lunch and dinner by request
Recreation: Local special events, school functions, dining, performing arts, day trips
Amenities & Services: Extra beds/cots, honor bar, disabled access; concierge, laundry/dry cleaning, fax/copy services, 2 conf. facil.

ACCOMMODATIONS

Units: 10 guest rooms
All Rooms: Bath, dataport, 2-line phone, desk, TV, AC

Some Rooms: Ornamental mantel, sofa bed

Bed & Bath: Four-poster and canopy beds, queen and king; heaters, robes in some
Favorites: Room 22—Dramatic teal walls, celebrity photos, full 1920s outfits decorating walls, king four-poster
Comfort & Decor: Rooms tend toward masculine, club-room decor.

Decorated around different themes. Elegant fabrics, Oriental rugs, Edwardian bed drapes. Rich Federal wall colors. Special pieces, handcrafted armoires, club or reading chairs, rockers, Georgian furnishings.

RATES, RESERVATIONS, & RESTRICTIONS

Deposit: 1 night; refund w/ 7-day notice; payment in full for holidays, local special events, and graduations; extended cancellation policies apply
Discounts: Corp., 3rd person
Credit Cards: MC, V, AE, D
Check-In/Out: 3/11
Smoking: No
Pets: No; staff will assist in alternate pet accommodations
Kids: Over 6
No-No's: B&B will not guarantee specific room or bed type

Minimum Stay: 2 nights, holidays, local special or school events; 3 nights for graduations
Open: All year except Christmas
Hosts: Jane and Ron Peterson
1201 Chapel St.
New Haven, CT 06511
(800) 443-1554 or (203) 789-1201
Fax: (203) 776-7363
chimneysnh@aol.com
www.threechimneysinn.com

HOMESTEAD INN, New Milford

Overall: ★★★	Room Quality: D	Value: C	Price: $75–$140

Don't confuse this basic, economical bed-and-breakfast with the luxurious same-named inn in Greenwich. Low rates in an otherwise pricey area are the major plus here. Desks and good lighting in each room are a boon to laptop toters, and phones and air-conditioning are other no-nonsense bonuses. Skip the motel-like rooms in the Treadwell House section, a former restaurant space that is undistinquished. Stick to the main house, where you can play the piano by the fireplace and retire upstairs to get to work.

SETTING & FACILITIES

Location: Rt. 7 to New Milford, Rt. 202, turn left at 3rd traffic light onto Village Green (Main St.), 3 blocks to end of Green, right onto Elm St., B&B on left

Near: Village Green, shops, restaurants; state parks, New Preston, Lake Waramaug
Building: 1850 Victorian farmhouse; Treadwell House, former restaurant

Grounds: Small, perennial gardens, historic area

Public Space: Lobby, large LR

Food & Drink: Cont'l breakfast buffet; refreshments

Recreation: Golf, skiing; theater, concerts; antiquing, craft/specialty shops

Amenities & Services: Fridge, hairdryers; roll-aways, cribs

ACCOMMODATIONS

Units: 8 guest rooms in main house; 6 in Treadwell House

All Rooms: Bath, TV, phone and dataport, desk, AC

Some Rooms: Add'l bed, bay window, tin ceiling (1)

Bed & Bath: Some four-posters, bed sizes vary; some shower-only; non-allergenic bedding

Favorites: Rooms 24 and 25—Bay window

Comfort & Decor: Comfortable but basic, Early American reproductions. Waverly/Schumacher coordinates. Good setup for business travelers.

RATES, RESERVATIONS, & RESTRICTIONS

Deposit: 1 night, credited to last night's stay; refund w/ 48-hour notice

Discounts: Kids under 12, 3rd person, singles

Credit Cards: MC, V, AE, D, DC

Check-In/Out: 2/11

Smoking: No

Pets: No

Kids: Welcome

Minimum Stay: 2 nights holidays, May–Oct. weekends

Open: All year

Hosts: Rolf and Peggy Hammer
5 Elm St.
New Milford, CT 06776
(860) 354-4080
Fax: (860) 354-7046
www.homesteadct.com

THE BOULDERS INN, New Preston

Overall: ★★★★½	Room Quality: A	Value: C	Price: $295–$345

Named for the boulders incorporated into the building, the inn makes the most of nature, with lake views shimmering through expanses of glass. The best all-around active getaway closest to the Big Apple, this casually elegant inn deserves its stellar reputation for stylish comfort, with Northern California laid-back outdoorsy decor and European flair. It feels like a high-end camp for groups, sophisticates, and romantics who frolic lakeside, climb the mountain, maybe snap up an 18th-century vase or two in the pretty village, and feast on sesame-crusted sushi-grade tuna with wasabi whipped potatoes in the octagonal dining room, before climbing into the four-poster beds. Beats bunks and Kool-aid.

SETTING & FACILITIES

Location: Rt. 202 to New Preston; Rt. 45 towards lake to Inn; at foot of Berkshire Hills Pinnacle Mountain overlooking Lake Waramaug
Near: State parks, shopping, public golf course, 18th-century villages
Building: 1895 gambrel-roofed Victorian summer cottage; stone porch and chimney
Grounds: Waterfront and boathouse, barn, guest cottages
Public Space: LR; TV room, game room; octagonal DR

Food & Drink: (MAP) Full breakfast/dinner plan; creative New American dinners; specialties: smoked pheasant quesadilla, marinated venison loin; award-winning wine list; full bar
Recreation: Bird watching, golf, horses, restaurants, water/winter sports
Amenities & Services: Priv. lake beach, sailboats, canoes, paddleboats, rowboats for guest use; tennis court, trail, bicycles; special requests, gift cert.; weddings, conferences, retreats

ACCOMMODATIONS

Units: 3 guest rooms, 3 suites in main house; 3 guest rooms in carriage house; 8 duplex cottage suites
All Rooms: Bath, antiques
Some Rooms: Fireplace/wood stove, view, sitting area, deck/balcony, whirlpool, refrigerator, coffee maker, AC
Bed & Bath: Four-poster, canopy, sleigh beds; cottage baths slightly more luxurious, larger; 1 single whirlpool, 4 dbl. whirlpools; some shower-only
Favorites: Main House, Northwest Suite—lake views, sitting area, king

poster bed, full bath; Fieldstone Cottage—spacious, great views, priv. deck, fireplace, dbl. whirlpool; Carriage House Room C2—cozy, double sleigh bed, comfy sitting area, stone fireplace
Comfort & Decor: Main house: antiques and finer country pieces. Charming guest cottages: country decor. Quilts, fireplaces. Cozy carriage house rooms: French and period pieces. Cobble Cottage suites: add'l beds/rooms.

RATES, RESERVATIONS, & RESTRICTIONS

Deposit: 1 night; 50% longer stay; full payment holiday weekends; refund w/ 14-day notice (surcharge added to price holiday weekends in high season; 15% gratuity added w/ taxes)
Discounts: EP, 3rd person, midweek stays, singles
Credit Cards: MC, V, AE
Check-In/Out: 3/12
Smoking: None in main inn; restricted elsewhere
Pets: No
Kids: By special arrangement

Minimum Stay: 2 nights weekends; 3 nights holidays; check w/ inn for availability
Open: May 1–Nov., and weekends all year
Hosts: Kees and Ulla Adema
East Shore Rd. (Route 45), Box 2575
New Preston, CT 06777-0565
(800) 55-BOULD or (860) 868-0541
Fax: (860) 868-1925
boulders@bouldersinn.com
www.bouldersinn.com

LAKEVIEW INN, New Preston

Overall: ★★★½	Room Quality: B	Value: D	Price: $175–$350

Lakeview Inn was the original name of the summer lodgings on this site over 100 years ago; the hip, young owners found the original sign during renovation. Most of the tasteful public space goes to the contemporary, lakeview restaurant, complete with a star chef—and a bit of attitude brought from NYC. Fine dining and hubbub last until late evening. This largely reconstructed inn is still evolving, and plans are for a barn annex with additional suites and conference center, which would better favor guests. For now, best to enjoy the warmth and activities at The Boulders across the lake, and come here for a lunch.

SETTING & FACILITIES

Location: From center of New Preston, take Rt. 45 to stop sign (lake on left), straight to 1st left, North Shore Rd., look for inn signs
Near: Lake Waramaug, beach, winery, ski area, Kent Falls State Park, X-C skiing
Building: Turn-of-the-century clapboard, previously Inn at Lake Waramaug
Grounds: Veranda; cocktail terrace; mahogany deck; ongoing projects incl. French gardens, apple orchard, herb gardens
Public Space: Foyer, library, garden room, main dining area, small priv. DR, smoking room, bar/lounge

Food & Drink: Cont'l breakfast buffet, communal or separate; lunch, dinner avail. 5–6 days/week; open most of year; American cuisine; specialties: free-range chicken, organic salads, Maine lobster, smoked salmon
Recreation: Antiquing, moderate and advanced climbing and biking, state park boating, fly-fishing, skiing
Amenities & Services: Child play area visible from DR; games in smoking room; videos; some office support

ACCOMMODATIONS

Units: 3 guest rooms, 2 suites
All Rooms: Bath, sitting area, TVs/VCR
Some Rooms: View, kitchen, honor bar
Bed & Bath: Antique beds; full baths, some soaking tubs

Favorites: Scandanavian suite—king country pine, sitting room, wet bar w/ kitchen amenities
Comfort & Decor: Muted, stylish, rich colors in Burgundian Suite. Country themes. Reproduction furnishings. Smallish. Front rooms have noise from popular DR.

RATES, RESERVATIONS, & RESTRICTIONS

Deposit: 1 night or 50%; refund w/ 14-day notice

Discounts: 3rd person; check w/ inn
Credit Cards: MC, V, AE, DC

Check-In/Out: 3/11:30; flexible w/ notice
Smoking: Restricted
Pets: No
Kids: Over 12; check for younger kids
Minimum Stay: 2 nights weekends; 3 nights holiday weekends

Open: All year
Hosts: Dorothy and Douglas Hamilton
107 North Shore Rd.
New Preston, CT 06777
(860) 868-1000
Fax: (860) 868-2595
www.thelakeviewinn.com

ANGEL HILL, Norfolk

| Overall: ★★★★ | Room Quality: A | Value: C | Price: $150–$185 |

Feminine, gentle, caring: Mozart and mimosas, white drapes wrapped in flowers, tented ceilings, a periwinkle clapboard carriage house with a plum front door. Valentine's Day is the all-year favorite here, and no wonder. These giving innkeepers delight in surprising guests with breakfast in their room, sweets, or sweet things. And spontaneously, Donna says, "Guests leave little angels all the time." Beds and breakfasts are dreamy, and although cherubs and florals and purple tones won't appeal to all, true romantics just might find this delicate environment touched by an angel.

SETTING & FACILITIES

Location: On Rt. 44, just up the hill from town green, on right side of road in historic residential neighborhood
Near: Norfolk Chamber Music Festival, Yale Summer School of Music, state parks; Hillside Gardens, 5 acres of display gardens; Campbell waterfalls, Haystack Mountain Towers, antiquing villages, Berkshires, Lime Rock, rivers

Building: 1880 Colonial/Victorian; carriage house
Grounds: 3 acres lawns, gazebo; 8 acres gardens, woodlands, brook
Public Space: Foyer, LR, DR, library, breakfast sun porch, lounging porch
Food & Drink: Full breakfast; specialties: gingerbread waffles w/ Chantilly cream, glazed apples and sausage, edible

flowers and herbs; refreshments; carriage house guests invited weekends
Recreation: Touring, shopping, summer festivals, covered bridges, vineyards, water sports, golf, Grand Prix racing, X-C skiing

Amenities & Services: Lawn games, refrigerator, garage space for show cars; arrangements for carriage rides, massage therapy, gift baskets, flowers; beach towels, picnic baskets, breakfast in bed

ACCOMMODATIONS

Units: 2 rooms, 2 suites, 1 carriage house apt.
All Rooms: Bath, candles, stereo, breakfast table
Some Rooms: Fireplace, desk, TV/VCR, reading chair/daybed; whirlpool, AC, thermostat; carriage house: kitchen w/ gas stove
Bed & Bath: Queen, king/twin canopies; robes, full baths, 1 hall access

could be updated.

Favorites: Orchard View Room—fireplace, wrought-iron four-poster; Carriage House—treehouse retreat, queen canopy, handpainted clouds, vines,
flowers
Comfort & Decor: Dramatic beds, decor. Suites with sitting room/dressing room. Victorian Cottage Suite: dbl. whirlpool, hall access bath. Some baths

RATES, RESERVATIONS, & RESTRICTIONS

Deposit: 50%; refund with 10-day notice
Discounts: Weekdays, 2+ nights; 3rd person, off-season, weekly (Carr. House)
Check-In/Out: 3–8/noon
Smoking: No
Pets: No

Kids: Depends; check
Minimum Stay: 2 nights weekends, 3 holidays. Carr. House: 2 nights
Open: All year
Hosts: Donna and Del Gritman
54 Greenwoods Rd. East, Box 504
Norfolk, CT 06058
(860) 542-5920
Fax: (860) 542-5055
dgritman@snet.net

www.angelhill.com

MANOR HOUSE, Norfolk

Overall: ★★★★	Room Quality: A	Value: C	Price: $125–$235

Staying at this Tudor mansion feels like being in old England, not New, maybe because the original owner was the Englishman who designed the London subway system. The huge entrance gleams with cherry wood, and the 6-foot stone fireplace with flag-bearing herald reinforces the British atmosphere. Tiffany windows, high ceilings, carved arches, decorative Victorian clothing, and extensive flower gardens add interest. Beekeeper/gardener/chef Hank gives cooking demonstrations, and Diane radiates enthusiasm. The outdoor music festival in this pretty town is sublime. So is returning, perhaps by horse and carriage, to a late-night whirlpool bath under a starry skylight.

SETTING & FACILITIES

Location: Rt. 44 onto Maple Ave.; B&B between Terrace View and Laurel Way, before Maple Ave. becomes Lover's Lane

Near: Walk to Village, Yale chamber music concerts, Hillside Garden consultants, state parks, ski trails, Housatonic River, 20 mi. to Tanglewood

Building: 1898 Victorian Tudor estate mansion; renovated 1997

Grounds: 5.5 acres; gardens, walking paths, gazebo

Public Space: Entrance hall, LR, sun porch, library

Food & Drink: Full communal breakfast; specialties: orange waffles, poached eggs w/ lemon-butter-chive sauce, honey from B&B hives; refreshments avail.; BYOB; microwave

Recreation: Lime Rock car racing, water sports, vineyards, Christmas sleigh rides, carriage tours, antiquing, cultural events

Amenities & Services: Refrigerator; lake passes, books, massage therapist avail.; wedding, priv. party, corp. facil.

ACCOMMODATIONS

Units: 9 standard guest rooms, 1 single

All Rooms: Bath, antiques, seating, good lighting, ceiling fans

Some Rooms: Fireplace, balcony, whirlpool/soaking tub

Bed & Bath: Antique, brass, or illusion canopy beds, queen, king/twin, some daybeds; most, showers only; some dbl. whirlpools and soaking tubs

Favorites: Victorian—dbl. whirlpool, gas fireplace, king

Comfort & Decor: Rooms vary from ultra-luxurious to standard. Unusual artwork. Period wallcoverings. Sumptuous.

RATES, RESERVATIONS, & RESTRICTIONS

Deposit: 50%; refund w/ 10-day notice

Discounts: Promos/packages, singles, 3rd person, midweek AAA/gov't./corp.

Credit Cards: MC, V, AE

Check-In/Out: 3/11:30

Smoking: No

Pets: No

Kids: Over 12

No-No's: Kids on weekends

Minimum Stay: 2 days weekends; 3 days holidays

Open: All year

Hosts: Diane and Henry Tremblay
69 Maple Avenue
Norfolk, CT 06058
(860) 542-5690
Fax: (860) 542-5690
tremblay@esslink.com
www.manorhouse-norfolk.com/area.html

SILVERMINE TAVERN, Norwalk

Overall: ★★★½	Room Quality: C	Value: C	Price: $100–$175

Originally, women in this old crossroads town were not allowed near the bar, and the humorous host has Abigail positioned within the danger zone: a period-dressed mannequin, sporting a red cloak in winter and a print frock in warmer weather, with glass in hand. A river runs by the door and branches into a tavern mill pond, which has ducks, a waterfall, and a spacious deck above, with trees growing through it. Traditional New England cuisine is served in a dining room crammed with over 1,000 old tools and gadgets and an 1887 jukebox. A country-store annex offers old oil paintings and gadgets.

SETTING & FACILITIES

Location: I-95N/S to Exit 15, follow Rt. 7N to Exit 2, right at ramp end, 2nd light turn right, right again onto Silvermine, 2nd stop sign bear right, 1.5 mi. to tavern; on mill pond/waterfall
Near: Silvermine Art Guild and Gallery, Silvermine River, Norwalk shopping, aquarium; 5 mi. to NYC commuter, nature center; 30 min. to Danbury
Building: 1785 many-chimneyed Colonial, Jeffersonian pillared portico; restored 1998
Grounds: Summer gardens, water, brick walkway

Public Space: 2 spacious parlors
Food & Drink: Cont'l breakfast; a specialty: caramel and pecan buns; bar/lounge; DR w/ fireplace, serving lunch and dinner, seasonal outdoor dining; specialties: Oysters Country Gentlemen, scallops Nantucket
Recreation: Boating, fishing, antiquing, day trips to Manhattan, live jazz on weekends
Amenities & Services: Express check-out, phone, roll-aways; gift shop, collectibles, closed in winter; weddings, meetings, parties

ACCOMMODATIONS

Units: 10 guest rooms, 1 suite
All Rooms: Bath, seating, desk, reading lighting, clock radio, AC
Some Rooms: Sitting area, porch
Bed & Bath: Some bow-top Colonial canopy, antique beds, 1 queen room, 3 twin rooms, 7 double bed rooms; some antique soaking tubs

Favorites: Room T-2—Fairly spacious, double canopy bed, priv. porch, full bath
Comfort & Decor: Old-fashioned floral wallcoverings and fabrics, some quilts. Country colonial style. Antique and quality reproduction furnishings. Hardwood floors w/ country area rugs. Suite: sitting room, priv. deck on river.

RATES, RESERVATIONS, & RESTRICTIONS

Deposit: 1 night; refund w/ 24-hour notice weekdays, 72-hour notice on weekends

Discounts: 3rd person, corp. midweek, singles
Credit Cards: MC, V, AE, DC, CB

Check-In/Out: 4/11
Smoking: Restricted
Pets: In annex w/ prior arrangement
Kids: Welcome
Open: All year

Hosts: Frank Whitman, Jr.
194 Perry Avenue
Norwalk, CT 06850-1100
(203) 847-4558
Fax: (203) 847-9171
www.hotel-intl.com

THE ELMS INN, Ridgefield

Overall: ★★★½   Room Quality: B   Value: C   Price: $130–$190

Built by master cabinetmaker Amos Seymour on the site of the Colonial
Battle of Ridgefield, this former farmhouse became an inn in 1799. Today,
highwaymen no longer come by horse or coach; weekenders from New
York City arrive on Amtrak or by BMW, in casual-Friday dress, lured by
the reputation of the restaurant, which was rejuvenated under new owner-
ship in 1996. Dishes such as braised rabbit ravioli are typical of the original
takes on standard items, served charmingly in a stenciled dining room.
Guest rooms have also been refurbished, with some canopied beds and
four-posters, but the lodgings take a second to the food.

SETTING & FACILITIES

Location: Rt. 35 to center of
Ridgefield; inn on main street in center
of quaint village
Near: Norwalk, aquarium, museums,
historic homes, nature center, golf
course, 45 min. to Stamford, IMAX
Theatre
Building: 1760 Colonial farmhouse
Grounds: Village yard, flower gardens,
patio
Public Space: Entry hall, sitting room
Food & Drink: Cont'l breakfast; separate restaurant serving lunch, dinner;
informal tavern menu after 11:30 a.m.;
specialties: clam and corn chowder,
grilled tenderloin, bangers and mash.
Formal DRs open for lunch and dinner; creative American cuisine; specialties: seafood stew, venison, pheasant;
need reservations, closed Mon., Tues.,
Christmas
Recreation: Hiking, touring, antiquing,
shopping
Amenities & Services: Cribs, roll-
aways; long-term/corp. guest services;
meetings, functions; special bridal
packages

ACCOMMODATIONS

Units: 16 guest rooms, 4 suites
All Rooms: Bath, phone/dataport, TV,
AC
Some Rooms: Writing desk, sitting
area
Bed & Bath: Some four-poster,
canopy, brass; queen or 2 doubles; 1
shower-only, recently remodeled
Favorites: Hostess' Favorite Four-
Poster Room—Corner, quiet, sunny
Comfort & Decor: Colonial decor.
Some antiques; a few restored pieces
date to orig. construction of house.
Some rooms, add'l beds. Rooms over

restaurant, noisiest; orig., older feeling w/ hardwood floors and area rugs, others carpet. Some TVs hidden in armoires.

RATES, RESERVATIONS, & RESTRICTIONS

Deposit: 1 night incl. state tax; refund w/ 48-hour notice
Discounts: Singles, long stays w/ advance full payment, 3rd person
Credit Cards: MC, V, AE, DC, CB
Check-In/Out: 3/noon
Smoking: No
Pets: No
Kids: Welcome
Minimum Stay: 2 nights weekends

Open: All year
Hosts: The Scala Family
500 Main St.
Ridgefield, CT 06877
(203) 438-2541; (203) 438-9206
restaurant
Fax: Same as phone, call first
innkeeper@elmsinn.com
www.elmsinn.com

UNDER MOUNTAIN INN, Salisbury

| Overall: ★★★★ | Room Quality: B | Value: D | Price: $170–$210 |

This established inn is on bucolic Route 41, across from a horse farm, and the British innkeepers offer a close-as-you-can-get British experience: Dickens, *The Manchester Guardian,* travel guides, British versions of Monopoly, 160 British videos, English ales, bangers and mash or Scottish salmon, and a real English tea service. The inn, shaded by huge old trees, is historic and handsome—the bar is paneled in antique king's wood, named for its special width, and the entrance doors were solicited by the Metropolitan Museum of Art (they remain, as portals for you to enjoy).

SETTING & FACILITIES

Location: From Salisbury town, 4 mi. N on Rt. 41; look for sign
Near: Berkshire Theatre, choral/music festivals, Norman Rockwell Museum; ski resorts
Building: 18th-century Colonial farmhouse
Grounds: 3 acres, terrace, wild turkeys, front porch overlooks horse farm activities
Public Space: Library, chess/checker parlor, video lounge, pub DR

Food & Drink: (MAP) Full English breakfast; tea and shortbread; dinner; a specialty: steak & kidney pie; picnics, wine and spirits
Recreation: Lake activities, golf, tennis, antiquing, sleigh rides, white-water rafting
Amenities & Services: Refrigerator, mini-kitchen, limited disabled access, conferences (15)

ACCOMMODATIONS

Units: 7 guest rooms
All Rooms: Bath, seating, reading lighting, sherry decanters, AC
Some Rooms: Mountain, horse farm, or lake views
Bed & Bath: Canopy, brass, four-poster beds; I w/ dbl. soaking tub

Favorites: Covent Garden—huge bath, soaking tub; Buckingham Gate—king canopy; Drury Lane—view of mountains from bed
Comfort & Decor: Fabrics and wall-coverings coordinate. Wicker, antique rockers. Wide-plank floors w/ braided or Oriental rugs.

RATES, RESERVATIONS, & RESTRICTIONS

Deposit: I night; refund w/ 14-day notice
Discounts: Multiple night stays
Credit Cards: MC, V
Check-In/Out: 2/11
Smoking: No
Pets: No
Kids: Over 6
No-No's: BYOBs in common areas; early check-in

Minimum Stay: 2 nights weekends; 3 nights holidays
Open: All year
Hosts: Marged and Peter Higginson
482 Undermountain Rd., Rt. 41
Salisbury, CT 06068
(860) 435-0242
Fax: (860) 435-2379
www.innbook.com

THE WHITE HART INN, Salisbury

Overall: ★★★½   Room Quality: C   Value: C   Price: $75–$200

Edsel Ford (Henry Ford's son, who had a car named after him in the 1950s), bought this eighteenth-century inn when his son attended nearby Hotchkiss prep school. The inn hung on far longer than the car, but was in need of tune-up of its own. And happily, it's looking polished now, with a major detailing and overhaul. Car racers, including Paul Newman, flock to the area, and the pretty town has the oldest free public library in the country, so you'll have plenty to read. The staff is courteous, the new wing preferable, and although breakfast isn't included and the furnishings are reproductions, this place has the feel of a smaller property.

SETTING & FACILITIES

Location: In the center of historic Salisbury; N from the Merritt (Rt. 15), to Rt. 7
Near: Appalachian Trail, lakes, mountains; golf courses, X-C, downhill ski

areas; historic homes; Lime Rock Race Track, Skip Barber Advanced Driving School
Building: 19th-century rambling white clapboard; inn since 1810

Grounds: Lawn situated on village green, border gardens
Public Space: Lobby, front porch, DRs, banquet room
Food & Drink: No meals included in room rates; breakfast, lunch, and dinner served in 3 dining rooms—the Tap Room w/ fireplace, wainscoting paneling, old-style pub decor; American Grill and the Garden Room, award-winning wine selection, American menu

Recreation: Tap Room entertainment on Wed. evening; driving, racing and car club events/lessons; water sports; horseback riding; historic sites, art galleries, and museums; covered bridges; streams, waterfalls, trails; skiing
Amenities & Services: Cribs, cots, refrigerators, VCRs, 24-hour front desk service; gift shop, meetings, weddings

ACCOMMODATIONS

Units: 23 guest rooms, 3 suites
All Rooms: Bath, TV, phone, luggage rack, AC
Some Rooms: Decorative fireplace, priv. porch, separate sitting area, add'l bed
Bed & Bath: Some canopy, carved or four-poster; 1 hall access bath w/ robes

Favorite: Edsel Ford Room: decorative fireplace, bow-top canopy bed
Comfort & Decor: Waverly chintz floral fabrics and wallcoverings. Thomasville mahogany or Lane country-pine reproduction furnishings. Hotel-style reliability and comfort. Some smaller rooms, or rooms above restaurant may be less satisfactory.

RATES, RESERVATIONS, & RESTRICTIONS

Deposit: 1 night; refund w/ 7-day notice
Discounts: Senior midweek rates; child's cot, crib; corp. rates
Credit Cards: MC, V, AE, D, CB
Check-in/Out: 2/noon
Smoking: Restricted
Pets: Restricted, nominal fee
Kids: Welcome
Minimum Stay: 2 nights weekends

April–Nov.; 3 nights holidays
Open: All year
Host: Scott Bok, General Manager
Debra Erickson
The Village Green
Salisbury, CT 06068
(800) 832-0041 or (860) 435-0030
Fax: (860) 435-0040
innkeeper@whitehartinn.com
www.whitehartinn.com

MAYFLOWER INN, Washington

Overall: ★★★★★   Room Quality: A   Value: D   Price: $350–$750

Eleanor Roosevelt stayed here in 1933, and celebs still do. One of two Connecticut members of Relais & Chateux, this sophisticated—if self-conscious—luxury inn, is really a small country hotel. Adriana and Robert are among the top art collectors in America and own a modern-art gallery in Manhattan. The pricey inn showcases their traditional pieces, flower arrangements feature orchids, everything is placed just-so, and food is described as "Asian-Californian-meets-New England." If you enjoy close-to-perfect atmosphere, you'll enjoy this Mayflower.

SETTING & FACILITIES

Location: From Hartford take Rt. 84 W to Exit 15, Southbury; right onto Rt. 6 N, Woodbury; travel 5 mi., left onto Rt. 47 (Woodbury Rd.); Inn 8 mi. farther

Near: New Preston, Kent, Woodbury, Sharon, Housatonic River

Building: 1894 gambrel-roofed luxury mansion; outbuildings

Grounds: 28 acres, streams, trails, Shakespearean and rose gardens, statuary

Public Space: Entry hall, LR, library, game room, DR

Food & Drink: A la carte breakfast only for guests (charge); lunch and din-ner open to public; Chef Thomas Moran, Four Seasons-trained; Tap Room, weekend piano entertainment, outdoor dining, gourmet American/Cont'l menu; excellent wine list, casual dress

Recreation: Fly-fishing, golf, horseback riding, river boating, antiquing

Amenities & Services: Omni tennis court, summer heated pool, gift shop; concierges, turn-down, 24-hour room service; spa facil. (massages, facials, parafin treat., trainers, exercise classes and equip.); weddings; meetings in Tea House; new office/presentation equip.

ACCOMMODATIONS

Units: 17 guest rooms, 8 suites in 3 buildings

All Rooms: Bath, desk, 2-line phone/dataport, voice mail, TV/VCR, mini-safe, mini honor bar/refrigerator, DMX satellite music, AC; fresh flowers, orchids

Some Rooms: Fireplace, balcony; suites w/ sitting room w/ fireplace

Bed & Bath: Canopy, carved, half-canopy beds, queen/king; spacious, luxury marble baths; dbl. vanity sinks, English deep-soak tubs, walk-in show-ers

Favorites: Winslow Suite—most spacious; romantic fabrics, colors; king canopy bed, fireplace, balcony, 1.5 baths

Comfort & Decor: Indiv. decorated, often redecorated. 18th- and 19th-century antiques, or quality reproductions. Collectibles from hosts' int'l travels. English, handcrafted beds. Tabriz rugs over plush carpet, Regency stripe wallcoverings. TVs, VCRs, and mini-bars hidden in armoires.

RATES, RESERVATIONS, & RESTRICTIONS

Deposit: Credit card holds reservation; no charge w/ 21-day notice

Credit Cards: Eurocard-MC, V, AE

Check-In/Out: 3/1

Smoking: Only in Tap Room

Pets: No

Kids: 12 and up

Minimum Stay: 2 nights weekends; 3 nights holiday weekends

Open: All year

Hosts: Adriana and Robert Mnuchin

118 Woodbury Rd., Rt. 47

Washington, CT 06793

(860) 868-9466

Fax: (860) 868-1497

mayflower@relaischateaux.fr

www.relaischateaux.fr/mayflower

HILLTOP HAVEN, West Cornwall

Overall: ★★★½	Room Quality: C	Value: C	Price: $130–$155

From the tree-rimmed terrace at this unique little bed-and-breakfast atop Dibble Hill you can see, on a clear day, if not forever at least the Housatonic River below to the Catskills in New York, some 75 miles away. Guest rooms are basic, the stone library, cluttered and terrific. Since quarters are small, it's ideal for couples or families to reserve both main guest rooms. Everett lives on the property in a separate cabin and is known for his charming eccentricities and off-beat breakfasts. Character is rare, so this unusual lodging by the Appalachian Trail and perched above a picture-book village is a special joy. As Everett remarks, "Everyone seems to want to come here."

SETTING & FACILITIES

Location: Berkshire foothills; Rt. 7 to Rt. 128 (W. Cornwall), turn right to covered bridge into commercial district, call innkeeper
Near: Kent, Bantam, Hillside Garden Center, Appalachian Trail, state parks, Hill-Stead Museum, covered bridge, Oct. Scottish Festival, Mohawk Ski Area; Cooking School—The Silo
Building: 1930 hilltop retreat, cottage-style
Grounds: 63 mountainous, forested acres 800 feet above Housatonic River; terrace, great views

Public Space: Stone library, veranda, reading room, music room
Food & Drink: Full or cont'l breakfast, as requested; brunch specialties: Grand Marnier French Toast, creme brulee; evening sherry
Recreation: Sharon Audubon Center, gift shop; river activities (outfitters/guides avail.); clay court tennis, horses, golf, biking (rentals avail.)
Amenities & Services: Access to lake beach for guests, nominal fee for maps; breakfast requests

ACCOMMODATIONS

Units: 2 guest rooms, main house; 1 cabin suite (3 mi. away)
All Rooms: Bath, phone/ans. machine, AC, views, coffee pot
Bed & Bath: Sleigh, brass doubles; small full baths
Favorites: Sleigh Room—sleigh bed, woods view; Secluded Cabin—modest

log cabin in midst of nature, hot tub, woodstove, double sofa bed
Comfort & Decor: 2 main-house guest rooms, cozy. Warm, soft lighting. Eclectic furnishings, artwork. Seating and desks. Overall tone rustic, basic. Cottage truly secluded.

RATES, RESERVATIONS, & RESTRICTIONS

Deposit: Full payment by personal check
Discounts: Winter packages
Credit Cards: None

Check-In/Out: 4:30/noon
Smoking: On terrace and screened-in porch only
Pets: No

Kids: Over 14
No-No's: No walk-ins—reserv.
required
Minimum Stay: 2 nights; 3 nights
some summer holidays
Open: All year

Hosts: Everett Van Dorn
175 Dibble Hill Rd.
West Cornwall, CT 06796
(860) 672-6871
Fax: Same as telephone, call first
hilltophaven@hilltopbb.com
www.abbington.com/hilltop/hilltop.html

INN AT NATIONAL HALL, Westport

Overall: ★★★★★　　Room Quality: A　　Value: C　　Price: $200–$600

The chilly looking building was in previous incarnations a bank, shirt shop, newspaper office, and furniture store. After a total reconstruction, it reopened on its 100th birthday as one of New England's most luxurious inns, and a member of Relais & Chateaux. Fashioned after Europe's old, elite manor houses, it includes tromp l'oeil paintings on guest room walls and in the elevator, a second-floor lobby where you're greeted by name, and a charming formal staff with authentic European accents. Rooms are sumptuous, filled with fine antiques and artworks, and some have loft bedrooms. The restaurant is renowned. Prices are high, and there's not a stuffed animal around (even though one suite is named "Henny Penny").

SETTING & FACILITIES

Location: West bank, Saugatuck River, only large red brick structure in downtown Westport; visible from Post Rd.
Near: Local business district, commuter train to NYC, shops, local events, cultural activities, beach
Building: Enormous riverfront 1873 building; restored cast-iron and red-brick facade
Grounds: Small restaurant patio on river boardwalk, fountain
Public Space: Reception area, board room, elevator, downstairs classic snooker table from England

Food & Drink: Cont'l buffet breakfast; a.m. room-service delivery, beverage w/ newspaper; award-winning restaurant, Miramar, closed Mon. (Mediterranean cuisine, fine wine list); tea
Recreation: River boardwalk, beach activities, antiquing, touring
Amenities & Services: Soft drinks in room; cribs, roll-aways, list of baby-sitters, honor bar, videos/movie channels, nearby exercise facil, turn-down, meeting facil., dry cleaning; full concierge, room service

ACCOMMODATIONS

Units: 8 guest rooms, 7 suites
All Rooms: Bath, refrigerator, TV/VCR, stereo, 2-line phone/dataport, mini-vault in closet, AC, soundproofing

Some Rooms: Sitting area, desk, gas fireplace (1), hardwood floors, armoire custom-built kitchenette (1)

Bed & Bath: Canopy or four-posters, mostly king, 3 queens, king/twin split; all full baths, most w/ sep. showers, I w/ whirlpool

Favorites: Saugatuck River Suite—king canopy, river views, sep. sitting area; Turkistan Loft Suite— (once President Clinton's quarters) ornate four-poster, downstairs library w/ 2-story-high bookcases, enormous windows

Comfort & Decor: Most rooms spacious, decorated with rich silks, heavy cottons, gilded materials. Hand-painted murals. Imported English antiques, 19th-century quality reproductions. Many 18–20′ ceilings, 12′ windows. Elegant baths; four two-level suites. Equestrian Suite has fireplace, whirlpool, and kitchenette. Cameron Room is smallest, least expensive.

RATES, RESERVATIONS, & RESTRICTIONS

Deposit: I night; refund w/ 7-day notice

Discounts: Cribs free, roll-aways reduced, corp. rates

Credit Cards: MC and Euro-MC, V, AE, DC

Check-In/Out: 3/11:30

Smoking: No

Pets: No

Kids: Welcome

Minimum Stay: 2 nights, high season weekends

Open: All year

Hosts: Greenfield Partners, Gen. Mgr. Steve Schapiro
Two Post Rd. West
Westport, CT 06880
(800) NAT-HALL or (203) 221-1351
Fax: (203) 221-0276
www.integra.fr/relaischateux/nationalhall

THE FRENCH BULLDOG BED & BREAKFAST AND ANTIQUES, Winstead

Overall: ★★★½	Room Quality: C	Value: C	Price: $75–$150

The bad news: for now, you may have to share a bathroom. Lots of good news, though. This new bed-and-breakfast, and the village of Winstead—which received a $5.8 million grant—are both refurbishing. Tom, an actor on the soap "All My Children," travels for shoots and brings back collectibles. Talk TV, antiques, or travel with the hosts or just maintain your privacy. Victoriana abounds, with one of the oldest square pianos in the world, silk wallpaper, leaded-glass windows, flute background music, Ionic columns, a French Victorian etched-glass and gilt chandelier, period French phones, high teas and tea-leaf readings, and breakfast in the master suite by the piano. Good news wins.

SETTING & FACILITIES

Location: Rt. 84 to Rt. 8 N at Waterbury; travel to Winstead, when road becomes 2-lane, right onto Rt. 44; B&B is 3 blocks on left, across from Jessie's Restaurant

Near: Norfolk, Yale Summer Chamber Music School, Jacob's Pillow, Tanglewood, Hillside Garden consultants, state parks, hiking/ski trails
Building: 1895 Queen Anne Victorian, 26-room mansion; French Normandy carriage house; restoration in progress
Grounds: English gardens on the banks of Mad River, porches, summer cottage seating
Public Space: Entrance foyer, formal DR, parlor

Food & Drink: Full formal breakfast; honeymooners in master suite, breakfast in suite; refreshments
Recreation: Lime Rock car racing, vineyards, Christmas sleigh rides, historic carriage tours, cultural activities, fishing, boating, golf, shopping
Amenities & Services: Period French phones; guest kitchen, in-room refrigerator on req., antique/gift shop, historic home tours in Norfolk. Setups for BYOB; parties, meetings, fax, copier

ACCOMMODATIONS

Units: 4 guest rooms, 1 suite; carriage house luxury suite
All Rooms: Antiques
Some Rooms: Suite: large, priv. bath; 2 add'l priv. baths coming soon, fireplace
Bed & Bath: Four-poster, cannonball beds, queen/full; 4 rooms now share 1 full smallish bath and half bath, robes provided

Favorites: Master Suite—fireplace, large priv. bath w/dbl. whirlpool, priv. entrance
Comfort & Decor: Chandeliers, original maple flooring. Silk wallpapers, rich fabrics. Spacious rooms full of large antiques. Antique or quality reproduction reading lighting. Suite for families, business meetings.

RATES, RESERVATIONS, & RESTRICTIONS

Deposit: 50%; refund w/ 2-day notice
Discounts: Corp. midweek
Credit Cards: None
Check-In/Out: After 2/11 (or by arrangement)
Smoking: Porches
Pets: No

Kids: Check for availability
Minimum Stay: Open: All year
Hosts: Celia and Tom McGowan
151 Main St.
Winstead, CT 06098
(860) 738-9335
Fax: Same as telephone

Zone 19
Eastern Connecticut

Beginning quietly in the state's northeastern corner next to Massachusetts, running south along the Rhode Island line to the bustling coastal areas surrounding historic Mystic, and west through Connecticut's River Valley and National Heritage Corridor, the eastern half of the state remains largely undeveloped, despite elaborate highway systems and some business and tourist congestion.

Southeastern Connecticut is a major draw. Tiny, charming Stonington, jutting into Long Island Sound, is one of the nation's oldest authentic fishing villages. New London with its submarine shipyards is activity packed, and the southeastern corner has two of the state's three major beaches—Rocky Neck State Park and Ocean Beach Park.

But Mystic is the tourist mecca, with its enormous aquarium, Olde Mystic Village, and the Seaport, which has the largest collection of old boats and ships in the world, including a replica of the famous 1839 *Amistad*, a 77-foot schooner used to transport kidnapped slaves from Africa. Nightlife and nearby casinos add to evening excitement.

A bit farther west to the midcoastline and inland river valley are the 365 "Thimble Islands," the "beautiful sea rocks" to the Mattabec Indians. Essex, originally a ship-building center, has been ranked first in *The 100 Best Small Towns in America* guide. Old Saybrook is home to more than 400 antique dealers. Historic and quiet Guilford, with its sparkling lakes, is within commuter distance to downtown New Haven and is home to the popular Guilford Handcraft Center. Tiny Madison maintains a traditional New England village green and is near Hammonasset Beach, two miles of white sand on the sound. Quietly sophisticated East Haddam on the river, Chester, and Ivoryton are known for musical theatre, opera, and other performing arts, and have deserved reputations for fine dining.

The entire midcoast river section is dotted with nature centers and parks. Small and homey bed-and-breakfasts in this area are typically Victorian or early-American style, many showcasing restorations. There are some notable rustic exceptions worth a stay and several destination inns featuring restaurants and lodgings. A few larger facilities feature Colonial decor.

Not surprisingly, Hartford and its surrounding areas primarily serve the business traveler. But there's more: the Wadsworth Atheneum in Hartford (the first public art museum in America), the oldest statehouse in the nation, and the homes of Harriet Beecher Stowe and Mark Twain.

Simsbury, a short drive from Hartford's business district, has The International Skating Center of Connecticut, which sponsors Olympic-level exhibitions and is open for skating and lessons. The 165-foot, blue basalt tower in Simsbury's Talcott Mountain State Park affords a view of four states and the Farmington River. The mile hike to the tower is popular for hang gliders seeking a good launch. Also popular are performing and fine arts, children's activities, historic touring, shopping, and antiquing.

The northern central and corner areas of Connecticut's eastern zone are more rural. Newly opened in Windsor is a trail that follows the Farmington River. The Lt. Walter Fyler House, c. 1640, is one of the oldest frame houses in America. Stop by Woodstock to visit Roseland Cottage, a former summer retreat for many presidents and still a Gothic-Victorian charmer.

The New England Air Museum, early homesteads and historic districts replete with restored antique New England residences, natural history museums, car racing and a Colonial prison are all here in Eastern Connecticut. Herb farms flourish, and the 3,000-acre agricultural and horticultural University of Connecticut is open to the public. Don't be dismayed by the small mill sites. The quiet corner blends rural development, deliberately cultivated nature preservation, and quiet industrial work.

For More Information

Connecticut River Valley & Shoreline Visitors Council
(860) 347-0028 or (800) 486-3346
www.cttourism.org

Essex Village Tourism
email: essexct.@aol.com
www.essexct.com

Farmington Valley Visitors Association
(800) 4-WELCOME
www.farmingtonvalleyvisit.com

Norwich Tourism
(888) 4-NORWICH

New London Attractions & Tourism

(800) 510-SAND

North Central Tourism Bureau
(860) 763-2573 or (800) 248-8283
www.cnctb.org

Northeast Connecticut Visitors District
(860) 928-1228 or (888) 628-1228
email: quietcorner@snet.net
www.webtravels.com/quietcorner

Greater Hartford Tourism District
(860) 244-8181 or (800) 793-4480
www.enjoyhartford.com

Southeastern Tourism District
(860) 444-2206 or (800) TO-ENJOY
www.mysticmore.com

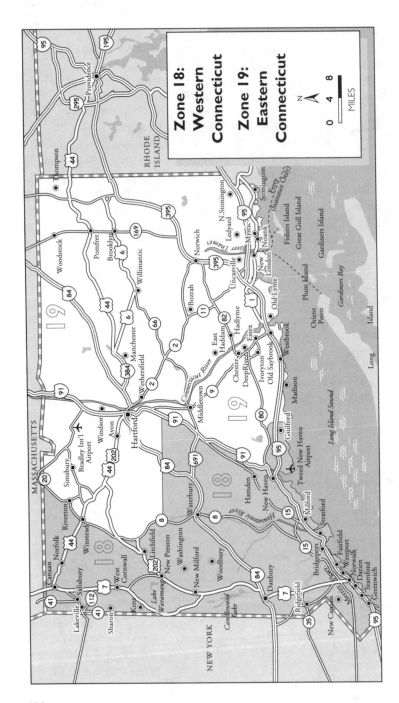

Zone 18: Western Connecticut

Zone 19: Eastern Connecticut

N

0   4   8

MILES

HEARTHSIDE FARM, Bozrah

Overall: ★★★½	Room Quality: C	Value: C	Price: $100–$150

The original, unadorned farmhouse and outbuildings here are authentic American, plain and simple, with pewter pieces, tin candle lanterns, butter churns, and a spinning wheel. Reportedly the first electrified farm in New England, it lured amazed locals, as it glowed by means of a coal-driven generator. The Gagers arrived on *The Arbells*, sister ship to *The Mayflower*, and obtained the property by a 1600s land grant. John Gager helped start New London, Olde Saybrook, and Norwich. Look for the original hidden feature in the farmhouse great room, which made Mrs. Gager the envy of her 18th-century neighbors. Luise and Michael are the first non-Gager occupants in over 200 years, but as third-generation innkeepers they have a proud heritage of their own.

SETTING & FACILITIES

Location: Rural suburb of Norwich; easy access to farm, Rt. 2 E to Exit 23; straight from ramp for .4 mile, left onto Gager Rd.; B&B 1st driveway on right (look for gates).
Near: Mystic, Thames River, baseball stadium, galleries, museums, outlets, flea market, covered bridge, historic homes, antiquing, casinos; New London Garde Art Center; Hartford
Building: Circa 1793 Georgian Colonial farmhouse
Grounds: 120 acres, state trout-stocked stream, wooded areas, patio overlooking horse paddock, outbuildings; trails connect to wildlife management area, protected state property

Public Space: Keeping room, library/orig. buttery, great room
Food & Drink: Early-riser beverages; weekday cont'l breakfast; full breakfast weekends; homemade breads
Recreation: Fishing Weekend; winery tour weekends, planting and harvesting weekends, bird dog training weekends, hay rides; carriage/sleigh rides; touring, incl. old burial grounds
Amenities & Services: Gift/antique shop, picnic table, gas grill, refrigerator stocked, in-room and portable guest phones; e-mail/message pickup; fax, dry cleaning; small weddings

ACCOMMODATIONS

Units: 3 guest rooms
All Rooms: Alarm radio, window AC
Some Rooms: Priv. baths, fireplace, wing-chair recliners
Bed & Bath: Some four-poster beds, 2 queens, 1 room w/ 2 double beds; 2 w/ priv. hall-access baths, 1 room shares hall bath w/ innkeepers, robes
Favorites: The Gager Room—

Rumford fireplace, pencil-post bed, priv. hall-access bath
Comfort & Decor: Rustic romance. Austere American antiques softened by rich woods, wreaths, local original folk art, flower garlands. New Concord Room, floral comforter and German antique collectibles, table for 2. Fairly spacious rooms.

RATES, RESERVATIONS, & RESTRICTIONS

Deposit: Credit card holds reservation; no charge w/ 7-day notice
Discounts: Midweek, corp., multiple nights; special events packages, incl. living Colonial history, open-hearth cooking, and beehive-oven baking workshops
Credit Cards: MC, V, D
Check-In/Out: 3/11
Smoking: Outdoors only
Pets: Outdoor lodgings avail. for dogs, horses w/ prior notice

Kids: Over 8
Minimum Stay: 2 nights holiday weekends
Open: All year
Hosts: Luise and Michael Ernest
15 Gager Rd.
Bozrah, CT 06334
(860) 887-4260
Fax: Same as phone
heartbnb@aol.com or info@hearthsidefarm.com
www.hearthsidefarm.com

FRIENDSHIP VALLEY INN, Brooklyn

Overall: ★★★½	Room Quality: C	Value: C	Price: $95–$150

Many trees grow in this Brooklyn area, named by Prudence Crandall, an 1830s Canterbury educator run out of town for teaching women of color in her academy. Abolitionist William Lloyd Garrison, the movement's founder, was married here, and a hidden basement entrance may be part of the Underground Railroad. The inn dates from 1708, the flag out front has 15 stars and stripes, and a dining room mantel is from the home of the founder of Cleveland, Ohio. The charming, Southern Beverly fills the historic house with music and books and indicates she would be pleased to be a guest in any of her understated, antique-filled rooms. So are we.

SETTING & FACILITIES

Location: I-395 to Exit 91, travel 4 mi. on Rt. 6 W, right at intersection of 169, travel .25 mile to B&B on right, red oval sign; faces Rt. 169, recently designated 1 of only 14 national scenic byways.
Near: Hist. center of hamlet; Putnam antique village, art galleries, fine dining, state parks; Providence, Mystic; Newport, Hartford
Building: 1740–1795 Georgian-style Colonial
Grounds: 12 wooded, wetland acres, stone walls

Public Space: Entry hall, parlors, library, colonial kitchen, formal DR, screened porch, terrace
Food & Drink: Full breakfast; tea (a reservation-only tearoom in town, operated by publisher of *Tea: A Magazine*)
Recreation: Trails; vineyard, herbery, historic sites; boating, fishing, 4-star dining, day trips
Amenities & Services: Refrigerator, guest phone, antique books, maps; very corp. friendly

ACCOMMODATIONS

Units: 4 guest rooms, suites
All Rooms: Bath, antique furnishings, reading lamps, fans avail.
Some Rooms: Ornamental fireplace, capacity to convert to suites
Bed & Bath: Antique or reproduction beds include 1 cherry step-up four-poster, antique French oak twins; 1 hall access bath w/ robes
Favorites: Prince Suite— vaulted ceiling, queen four-poster, whirlpool, priv.

entrance (limited disabled access); Kingsley Room—cozy, iron and brass double bed
Comfort & Decor: Guest rooms named for 5 previous owners of house. Original wide flooring, Oriental rugs, Colonial painted trim. Seating varies— wing-back, Victorian rockers. Relatively spacious and not overstuffed.

RATES, RESERVATIONS, & RESTRICTIONS

Deposit: 1st and last nights; refund w/ 14-day notice
Discounts: Valentine's, other packages; 3rd night 50%; check for corp., midweek
Credit Cards: MC, V, AE
Check-In/Out: After 2/11
Smoking: No
Pets: No
Kids: Over 7
Minimum Stay: No firm policy, but check during high season

Open: All year
Hosts: Beverly and Charles "Rusty" Yates
Route 169, P.O. Box 845
Brooklyn, CT 06234
(860) 779-9696
Fax: (860) 779-9844
friendshipvalley@pop.snet.net
www.friendshipvalleyinn.com

RIVERWIND, Deep River

Overall: ★★★★	Room Quality: B	Value: C	Price: $100–$185

Pigs and romance are two notable elements of this delightful, folksy house. Decorative piggies are lined on mantels and climbing stairs and shaped into biscuits and served up at breakfast as Smithfield Ham, from America's Ham Capital, where Barbara came from. (You'll be tempted to pig out at breakfast.) The romance refers to carpenter Bob, who helped Barbara remodel the abandoned estate and then married her. It's a fine, fun, sumptuous bed-and-breakfast with a mounted moose head, Mae West quotes, a garden rake handle holding a hanging mantel, and carpenters' tools for towel racks. And as a Justice of the Peace, Barbara can perform weddings.

SETTING & FACILITIES

Location: Adjacent to village green; Rt. 9 to Exit 4, left onto Rt. 154 to B&B, 1.4 mi. on right

Near: Conn. River, Canfield Woods Preserve (360 acres of trails), Essex Steam Train/Riverboat, Chester,

Goodspeed Opera House, Ivoryton Playhouse, state parks; Mystic Seaport, New Haven
Building: 1750 Colonial farmhouse w/ Victorian elements
Grounds: 1 acre, small gardens, patio
Public Space: DRs, parlor, large study, keeping room, games room, small library
Food & Drink: Early-riser coffee; Southern-style breakfast, communal or separate; specialties: Smithfield ham, biscuits, hot casseroles; refreshments
Recreation: Riverboat cruises, theatre, 4-star dining, antiquing, beach activities
Amenities & Services: 2 refrigerators, bike storage, hairdryers, special Christmas decorations, pick-up from train station

ACCOMMODATIONS

Units: 8 guest rooms
All Rooms: Bath, reading lighting, clock/radio, AC, bottled water
Some Rooms: Balcony/deck, ceiling fan
Bed & Bath: Canopy, four-poster, birds-eye maple beds; queen/double; robes, some shower-only, 1 hand-held shower w/ claw-foot soaking tub, 1 hall access bath
Favorites: Hearts and Flowers Room— French country furnishings, queen white iron and brass bed; Champagne and Roses Room— Mahogany queen pencil-post half-canopy bed, Japanese steeping tub, sep. shower, balcony, champagne.
Comfort & Decor: Rustic Americana, country and period antique furnishings, hand-artisan touches. Color schemes mirror quilts. Beautiful area rugs. Stylish, fun.

RATES, RESERVATIONS, & RESTRICTIONS

Deposit: 1 night or credit card; refund w/ 10-day notice
Discounts: 3rd person, 50% of room rate
Credit Cards: MC, V
Check-In/Out: 3–6/11
Smoking: Restricted
Pets: No
Kids: Over 12
Minimum Stay: 2 nights, April 2–Jan. 2

Open: All year
Hosts: Barbara Barlow and Bob Bucknall
209 Main St.
Deep River, CT 06417
(860) 526-2014
Fax: (860) 526-0875
www.innformation.com/ct/riverwind

GELSTON INN, East Haddam

Overall: ★★★★	Room Quality: B	Value: C	Price: $100–$225

When this cupola-topped Victorian inn opened in 1853 next door to the Goodspeed Opera House, it charged $2.50. Of course, that included a meal. Today you'll pay about 100 times that for a suite (about the same value and with a breakfast). The new owners have completely refurbished this landmark, and it sparkles again like the light on the river behind it.

Seasonal menus feature appetizers like clams tempura and entrees including grilled salmon on fennel puree with orange reduction. You can watch the river through window walls as you sup by candlelight, or opt for a Samuel Adams and a hamburger on the terrace. A plus is the theatre a few steps away; a minus is the theatre crowds, and late-night noise, a few steps away.

SETTING & FACILITIES

Location: I-91 to Rt. 9 to Exit 7, left at end of ramp; right at 1st traffic light, cross iron bridge, 2nd building on right after bridge, next to the Goodspeed Opera House on Conn. River
Near: Gillette Castle, Camelot River Cruises, incl. murder mystery theatre on river
Building: 1853 Victorian
Grounds: Rear patio w/ pavilion
Public Space: Entry, main DR, smaller DR, pub

Food & Drink: Cont'l breakfast, lunch, candlelight dinner; cont'l-style w/ Italian influences, prix-fixe creative menu, fresh lobsters; specialties: chestnut-glazed quail; roast veal; pre-theatre dinners; Sun. brunch; full liquor license
Recreation: Summer performing arts, musicals; canoeing, sailing, antiquing
Amenities & Services: Entertainment on weekends, grand piano; conf. facil.

ACCOMMODATIONS

Units: 3 guest rooms, 3 suites
All Rooms: Bath, seating, alarm clock, AC, thermostat, TV
Some Rooms: Suites w/ LR, river view
Bed & Bath: Carved headboards, all queens, roll-away beds; full baths

Favorites: Nathan Hale room—suite w/ best river view; Swan room—overlooks gardens and river
Comfort & Decor: Traditional Colonial, antique furnishings, carpet. Fresh, pretty look. Can be noisy at dinner, theatre times, late-night. Back rooms quietest.

RATES, RESERVATIONS, & RESTRICTIONS

Deposit: Credit card holds room; reasonable notice to cancel
Discounts: 3rd person
Credit Cards: MC, V, AE
Check-In/Out: 2/11
Smoking: Tavern only
Pets: No

Kids: Welcome
Open: Mid-Feb. to Jan. 2
Hosts: The Carbone Family
8 Main St.
East Haddam, CT 06423
(860) 873-1411
Fax: (860) 873-9300

GUILFORD CORNERS, Guilford

Overall: ★★★½	Room Quality: B	Value: C	Price: $110–$170

Suzie and Gary exclaim that Guilford Corners is the quintessential New England experience—the house harks back to the time when the colonies were still under sovereign rule, and the history of the house and town tell the story of New England and America. Guests love to poke into the attic and cellar, with unique architecture rarely seen outside of museum homes. The new, enthusiastic hosts enjoy explaining their antique historical maps and framed art pieces, including a favorite Lincoln lithograph. For fun, books and games are stocked in a rare built-in Guilford cupboard, and you can borrow a bicycle and pedal to the quaint village.

SETTING & FACILITIES

Location: In Guilford village, corner of State St. and Boston Post Rd.; I-95 to Exit 58, proceed south from exit ramp, left onto Rt. I, B&B entrance I block further on left

Near: Green shops, restaurants, tennis; sound-side beach; Yale, New Haven, Lake Quonnipaug, Hammonasset Beach State Park, Water Authority property, lake, outlet mall

Building: 1732 white clapboard Georgian Colonial, wraparound veranda

Grounds: Village lawns, herb and flower gardens; 1.5 blocks from Green

Public Space: Guest parlor, informal parlor, sun deck

Food & Drink: Cont'l breakfast, home-baked specialties

Recreation: Summer farmer's market, antiquing, boating, X-C skiing

Amenities & Services: Phone, refrigerator, dataport/fax hook-ups, hot tub, bikes, bike storage, lawn/board games, TVs on request, *New York Times* and *Hartford Courant,* travel services, transport to/from Guilford train station; short/long-term relocation stays; meetings, weddings, etc.; BYOB set-ups

ACCOMMODATIONS

Units: 2 guest rooms, I 2-BR suite

All Rooms: Bath, sitting area, dining area, clock radio, hot beverage kettles and set-ups

Some Rooms: Working fireplace (I), decorative fireplace (I)

Bed & Bath: Queen four-posters, suite 2nd BR w/ 2 twins; 2 shower-only baths

Favorites: Gentleman's Room—decorative fireplace, large wood-paneled full bathroom

Comfort & Decor: Rooms large (20′ x 24′) w/ high ceilings. Muted painted walls, artwork. Antique Georgian-style furnishings, fabrics and carpets. 12-over-12 windows. Original random plank flooring.

RATES, RESERVATIONS, & RESTRICTIONS

Deposit: I night; nonrefundable, credit w/ reasonable notice

Discounts: Weekly and long-term stays, 3rd person

Credit Cards: None

Check-In/Out: 4–7/11 or by arrangement

Smoking: Restricted

Pets: OK w/ prior arrangement

Kids: "Children w/ well-behaved parents welcome"

Minimum Stay: 2 nights May–Sept. weekends

Open: All year

Hosts: Suzie Balestracci and Gary Parrington

133 State St.
Guilford, CT 066437

(203) 453-4129
Fax: (203) 458-8915

COPPER BEECH INN, Ivoryton

Overall: ★★★★	Room Quality: B	Value: C	Price: $110–$180

The town is named after the early ivory trade, and this handsome clapboard inn, named after its huge copper beech tree, was originally summer home to an ivory comb and keyboard manufacturer. Carriage house rooms in the back are the quietest; noise levels can rise in rooms too near the street and popular, much-lauded dining rooms. The seasonal menu may include seared fresh duck foie gras with grilled pear, roasted loin of fresh venison with lingonberries and Grand Marnier, and white peach and champagne sorbet with cassis sauce. The conservatory is grand for after-dinner Cognac and coffee. Warning: If you don't plan to dine here, the aromas will drive you mad.

SETTING & FACILITIES

Location: 3 blocks from center; I-95 to Exit 69 to Rt. 9 N; approx. 3 mi. to Exit 3; left (W) at ramp end; inn on left; from Hartford, I-91 S to Exit 22; Rt. 9 S to Exit 3
Near: Goodspeed Opera House, Ivoryton Playhouse; Gillette Castle, Rocky Neck, and Hammonasset State Parks; sound-side beaches, Mystic, outlet malls, casinos
Building: 1880s Victorian summer cottage; glass dining additions
Grounds: 7 wooded acres, English gardens w/ thousands of spring-blooming bulbs

Public Space: Parlor, Victorian-style conservatory, 4 DRs
Food & Drink: Cont'l buffet breakfast; seasonally changing menu, French country dining; comprehensive wine list; a la carte menu, 3-course meal ($45–60); comp. soup, early evening dinner, Tues.–Fri.; restricted winter dining service.
Recreation: Summer theatre, antiquing, touring, museums, tennis, fishing, boating
Amenities & Services: Restaurant disabled access.; priv. affairs, meetings (up to 70)

ACCOMMODATIONS

Units: 4 guest rooms in main house, 9 in carriage house
All Rooms: Bath, phone/dataport, good reading lights, AC
Some Rooms: Bay window, radio in main house; Carriage House rooms: French doors to common deck, whirlpool, TV; 2 largest carriage house rooms: priv. deck

Bed & Bath: Some canopy or four-poster beds. Main house baths: antique fixtures, pedestal sinks, some claw-foot soaking tubs, some baths w/ smaller tubs only—no showers. Carriage house baths: whirlpools
Favorites: Room 1, main house—spacious, canopy, bay window; Room 219, carriage house—cathedral ceiling, canopy bed, French doors to deck

Comfort & Decor: Most rooms, spacious w/ seating areas. Main house furnishings: antique pieces, country-style fabrics, casual contemporary accessories. Pretty floral wallpapers. Carpet w/ area rugs. Converted turn-of-century carriage barn, formal-style reproduction furnishings, Chippendale, Queen Anne. Second floor carriage house rooms: cathedral ceilings, exposed beams. DR noise a factor in some main house rooms.

RATES, RESERVATIONS, & RESTRICTIONS

Deposit: 1 night, 2 nights weekends; refund w/ 5-day notice
Discounts: Midweek specials, winter packages, 3rd person
Credit Cards: MC, V, AE, D
Check-In/Out: 2/11
Smoking: Outdoors only
Pets: No
Kids: Over 10
No-No's: TVs in main house rooms

Minimum Stay: 2 nights weekends, holidays
Open: All year, except Christmas and 1st week of Jan.
Hosts: Sally and Eldon Senner
46 Main St.
Ivoryton, CT 06442
(888) 809-2056 or (860) 767-0330
Fax: (860) 767-7840
www.copperbeechinn.com

STONECROFT, Ledyard

Overall: ★★★★	Room Quality: B	Value: C	Price: $200–$320

Boating and inns are a rare combo, but here you have it. You can room in a teak yacht docked on the river and enjoy a good breakfast and dinner, too, on Villeroy and Boch china. The inn features Euro-American country ambiance, with hand-painted murals by the same artist who worked at the Inn at National Hall in Westport. The hosts seek to provide serenity, and they certainly score with aromatherapy bath salts, soft background music, and hundreds of surrounding acres of protected land, perfect for strolls and contemplation as well as horseback riding. The new Grange addition in the restored barn is rustic and elegant, with candlelight meals, guest rooms with barn flooring and angled fireplaces.

SETTING & FACILITIES

Location: I-95 to Exit 89 (Allyn St.), becomes Cow Hill Rd., then Pumpkin Hill Rd.; next to 300-acre woodland conservancy
Near: Mystic, Stonington, Rocky Neck State Park, Old Lyme, R.I. ocean beaches, Pequot Research Center and Museum, Garde Art Theatre in New London, Eugene O'Neill playwright workshop, casinos
Building: Restored 1807 Georgian Colonial; renovated barn
Grounds: 6 rural acres; gardens, terrace, meadows, trails; equestrian center next door

Public Space: Great room, Red Room, library, terrace, pergola, grange addition, lounge

Food & Drink: (MAP) Early-riser coffee/tea; candlelight cont'l breakfast; full breakfast menu, boat guests also; refreshments; breakfasts, dinners open to public

Recreation: Antiquing, fishing charters, tall ship tours, parasailing, beach

Amenities & Services: Lawn games, darts, exercise track, phone, multimedia center; transport from/to marina, Amtrak, airport; weddings, conferences

ACCOMMODATIONS

Units: 4 guest rooms, house; 4 rooms, 2 suites, The Grange; 1 unit "Boat and Breakfast" aboard docked yacht

All Rooms: Bath, sitting area, alarm clock, AC

Some Rooms: Fireplace, whirlpool; Grange rooms: dataport, terrace/deck

Bed & Bath: Some antique beds, queen, king; Grange rooms: dbl. whirlpools, walk-in showers

Favorites: The Buttery—oldest room (1704), priv. entrance/patio, white iron and brass queen, wheelchair access.

Boat—restored 40′ 1949 wooden motor yacht, teak/mahogany interior, refrigerator, coffeemaker, microwave, 2 single berths

Comfort & Decor: Some country, some romantic, Victorian. Murals, wainscoting, love seats, artist's mural, reproduction tiger maple furnishings. Grange rooms, tongue-in-groove ship-lapped ceilings. Wide range of styles, comfort. Boat not for seasick-prone (even though docked).

RATES, RESERVATIONS, & RESTRICTIONS

Deposit: 50% refund w/ 14-day notice

Discounts: B&B rates, midweek stays; off-season packages, incl. cooking classes, holistic workshops; longer stays; 3rd person

Credit Cards: MC, V, AE, D

Check-In/Out: 3–6/11

Smoking: No

Pets: No

Kids: Over 10

No-No's: Heeled shoes

Minimum Stay: 2 nights weekends; check for holiday minimums

Open: All year

Hosts: Joan and Lynn Egy
515 Pumpkin Hill Rd.
Ledyard, CT 06339-1637
(860) 572-0771
Fax: (860) 572-9161
stoncrft@cris.com or stoncrft@concentric.net
www.localnews.com/buspages/stncrft

INN AT LAFAYETTE, Madison

Overall: ★★★★	Room Quality: B	Value: C	Price: $125–$175

This newly reopened inn was the Madison Methodist Church, built of local wood by local craftsmen in 1837. Forty years later the minister was tried for murder of a parishioner, and was acquitted, but his petulant ghost reportedly lingers about the attic. The church mode is still discernable under the added portico, balcony and side awning. This old Yankee-style shoreline town is getting a big movie house and already has one of the country's favorite private booksellers, but still has few tourists. The inn centers on dining and has restructured its namesake restaurant and lightened the cuisine. It has also revamped the stylish guest rooms to support business travelers.

SETTING & FACILITIES

Location: In the center of quaint, historic Madison; I-95 to Exit 61, from west take a right onto Rt. 79 S, left onto Rt. I, inn is on left; from east take left at ramp end
Near: Long Island Sound, Hammonassett State Park and Beach; New Haven, Shubert Theatre, Yale; Mystic, casinos
Building: Landmark 1840s frame church, columned portico; inn since the 1920s
Grounds: Border landscaping, parking lot
Public Space: 2nd-floor breakfast nook/sitting area, 4 dining rooms
Food & Drink: Continental breakfast in guest rooms or breakfast nook;

restaurant serves lunch and dinner, cutting-edge, Italian lunch menu; specialties: focaccia sandwiches, grilled chicken w/ roasted peppers; dinner specialties: poached salmon in light dill sauce, fresh asparagus w/ toasted almonds; take-out lunches and dinners, hors d'oeuvres pkgs.; 3-course, prix fixe banquet features Toscana, Venezia or Milano cuisine; restaurant closed Mondays
Recreation: Historical tours, shopping, boating, hiking trails, biking, beach activities, performing arts and cultural activities
Amenities & Services: Off-street parking, irons; guest room phones w/ private lines, conference, voice mail, dataport, corp. meeting and dining facil-

ities; copying, printing and fax services

ACCOMMODATIONS

Units: 5 guest rooms
All Rooms: Bath, 2 phone lines, TV
Some Rooms: Writing desk, sitting area
Bed & Bath: King and queen four-poster beds, Egyptian cotton linens, down comforters; full marble baths, phones in baths, robes, whirlpool (1)

Favorites: Room #1 Droney Room—Most spacious room, queen, comfortable seating
Comfort & Decor: Wall-to-wall carpet. Muted color schemes. French Colonial furnishings, antiques and quality reproductions. Small-hotel feel. Good lighting, work space. Geared well for business travelers.

RATES, RESERVATIONS, & RESTRICTIONS

Deposit: Credit card holds reservation; no charge w/ 7-day notice
Discounts: 3rd person, older children in same room, corp. rates
Credit Cards: MC, V, AE, DC
Check-in/Out: 4/noon, or by prior

arrangement
Smoking: Restricted, no smoking in guestrooms
Pets: No
Kids: Over 12; check w/ inn for availability

Minimum Stay: None, but check w/ inn on holidays
Open: All year
Hosts: MRS Madison Corporation

725 Boston Post Rd.
Madison, CT 06443
(203) 245-7773
Fax: (203) 245-6256

APPLEWOOD FARMS INN, Mystic

Overall: ★★★½   Room Quality: C   Value: D   Price: $110–$300

It may not be Pebble Beach, but here you can putt on the little green in the yard, and play a bit on the chipping fairway. Clubs are available. Five generations of one family grew up in this farmhouse, and with photos and Early American objects casually placed around, it seems they are still here. The best part of this unpretentious property is the space around it. On a 33-acre former horse farm, there remains a sole horse and some sheep, but you can gaze at the neighboring herd of Arabian equines. Or just sit in the gazebo by the pond and watch the birds fly by, or relax in the hot tub—in the former corn crib. Oh, and you can bring your own horse.

SETTING & FACILITIES

Location: I-95 to Exit 89, turn onto Cow Hill Rd. (other direction is Allyn St.); left onto Col. Ledyard, and look for B&B; borders nature conservancy acreage
Near: Arabian stables, Mystic, Stonington Fishing Village; U.S. submarine base, museum; sound-side, ocean beaches, Up-Down Sawmill, Sturbridge Village; Eugene O'Neill Playwrite Workshop and events; Guard Theatre, casinos
Building: The Gallup Homestead, c.

train station

1826, center-chimney Colonial
Grounds: 33 acres, gazebo, walking trails, bird feeders, pond, horse facilities
Public Space: Parlor, keeping room, quiet sitting room
Food & Drink: Full communal breakfast in keeping room
Recreation: Fishing charters, windjammer day trips, whale watching, Newport mansions
Amenities & Services: Corn-crib spa/hot tub, USGA chipping/putting green, games; pick-up at local airport,

ACCOMMODATIONS

Units: 4 guest rooms, 1 small suite w/ priv. entrance
All Rooms: Bath, AC window units
Some Rooms: Fireplaces (4)
Bed & Bath: Some canopy, four-poster beds, some featherbeds; 1 king, others queen or double, cot avail.
Favorites: Russell Room—fireplace, queen featherbed, Victorian furniture

Comfort & Decor: Fairly spacious rooms. Walls finished w/ old-fashioned papers, hand-stenciling, white-wash. Pretty bedding, Ruffled or lace window treatments. Casual furnishings, some wicker, some antique country-style or painted pieces. Slanted ceilings and add'l bed in 2-room suite. No overhead lighting.

RATES, RESERVATIONS, & RESTRICTIONS

Deposit: Reservations paid in full in advance; refund or 8-month credit w/ 2 weeks' notice, processing fee charged per night per room
Discounts: 3rd person, children, 4+ day stay
Credit Cards: MC, V, AE, D
Check-In/Out: 3–9 p.m./11
Smoking: Restricted
Pets: Polite ones welcome, by arrangement (incl. horses!)
Kids: Over 8; by arrangement midweek, not on weekends

Minimum Stay: 2 nights weekends; 3 nights holiday weekends
Open: All year
Hosts: Frankie and Tom Betz
528 Colonel Ledyard
Mystic, CT 06339
(800) 717-4262 or (860) 536-2022
Fax: (860) 536-6015
betz@snet.net
www.visitmystic.com/applewoodfarmsinn

BRIGADOON, Mystic

Overall: ★★★	Room Quality: C	Value: C	Price: $85–$150

Scottish-born Kay imparts her own brand of traditional Scottish-style hospitality at this 15-room Victorian with an attached barn. Scones are often served for breakfast, and a Scottish flag flutters outside. The front hall has a house deed signed in the 1800s by Hancock—not John of Declaration-of-Independence fame, but Charles, possibly a relative. (Kay and Ted are researching that one.) Of the properties listed here from the Mystic area, this is the least imposing and the least expensive, and for budget travelers and families with young children, this informal bed-and-breakfast will be just fine. Just don't expect luxury or high-style.

SETTING & FACILITIES

Location: I-95 to Exit 89 (Allyn St.), left onto Allyn St. if coming from New York, right if coming from Boston; right onto Cow Hill Rd.; 4th house on left, .5 mile from highway
Near: 13 mi. to downtown Mystic, Seaport, aquarium, shopping, short drive to New London ocean beach, Rocky Neck Beach in East Lyme, Rhode Island ocean beaches
Building: Rambling 15-room farmhouse (c. 1740) w/ attached blue barn
Grounds: Over an acre, stone walls, fruit trees, summer gardens, seating under dogwood tree

Public Space: Common room, DR
Food & Drink: Full breakfast; specialties: strawberry-walnut pancakes, crepes; tea; evening wine
Recreation: Day trips, *Mystic Clipper* schooner tours, sailing, whale watching, biking trails
Amenities & Services: Movies, seasonal garden flowers, refrigerator, bike storage, games, maps; Victorian teas, seminars, family reunions

ACCOMMODATIONS

Units: 8 guest rooms
All Rooms: Bath, AC
Some Rooms: Fireplace (6), priv. deck (1)
Bed & Bath: Some iron, four-poster beds, queen/king sizes; some shower-only
Favorites: Honeymoon Suite—fireplace, king bed, priv. entrance/deck, TV

Comfort & Decor: Rooms sizes vary—small, medium, larger. Some feature orig. wide-plank or narrow white oak flooring, carpet. Furnishings mix of early-American antiques and inexpensive reproductions.

RATES, RESERVATIONS, & RESTRICTIONS

Deposit: $25; refund w/ 7-day notice
Discounts: Winter packages, midweek corp., 3rd person, kids under 14 free
Credit Cards: MC, V
Check-In/Out: 3–5/11
Smoking: No
Pets: No
Kids: Welcome
Minimum Stay: 2 nights May–Oct., all holiday weekends

Open: All year
Hosts: Kay and Ted Lucas
180 Cow Hill Rd.
Mystic, CT 06355
(860) 536-3033
Fax: (860) 536-1628
brigofdoon@aol.com
www.brigadoonofmystic.com

HOUSE OF 1833, Mystic

Overall: ★★★★½	Room Quality: A	Value: B	Price: $95–$225

Carol and Matt selected this columned Greek Revival house with pool and tennis court after reviewing 150 other potentials in 1993, and the same care continues at one of the nicest bed-and-breakfasts in Connecticut. Charming murals grace the public rooms, and guest rooms are dramatically romantic with gauzy canopies, striking color combinations, including black and mauve, and a doorway to a rooftop cupola. Matt plays piano during sumptuous, candlelight breakfasts, and sometimes in the evenings too. Not surprisingly, Winter Romance packages are popular.

SETTING & FACILITIES

Location: I-95 to Exit 90, Rt. 27 N to Old Mystic Country Store; bear right at stop, B&B approximately .5 mile on right across from steam-powered cider mill

Near: 2 mi. from Mystic Seaport, aquarium, historic sites, museums; 5 mi. to casinos; 9 mi. to Watch Hill, ocean beaches, antique shops

Building: 1833 Greek Revival mansion

Grounds: 3 country acres, gardens, pool, tennis court

Public Space: Foyer, front parlor, music room

Food & Drink: Communal breakfast; breakfast basket option; specialties: artistic fruit plate, eggs Florentine in puff pastry, honey-mustard ham, cookies and brownies

Recreation: Day trips, boat tours, sailing, whale watching tours; trails

Amenities & Services: Winter tennis avail., bikes, helmets; refrigerator, phone, bike/kayak storage; popular pkgs., gift cert.

ACCOMMODATIONS

Units: 5 guest rooms

All Rooms: Bath, fireplace/woodstove, seating, AC

Some Rooms: Sitting area, porch/balcony, soaking or whirlpool tubs

Bed & Bath: Queen brass, carved, four-poster or canopy; sinks in antique bureaus, full baths, some oversized sep. showers, whirlpools

Favorites: Peach Room—11-foot ceilings, illusion queen canopy, 2-person shower, 2-person whirlpool.

Comfort & Decor: Spacious, w/ romantic flair. Bold wallcoverings— black and deep rose tapestry fainting couch in large Oak Room. Veranda Room, antique soaking tub in front of fire. Battenburg lace in Ivy Room. Cupola Room w/ stairway to cupola sitting room. Wide pine flooring, Oriental rugs. TVs and phones deliberately excluded.

RATES, RESERVATIONS, & RESTRICTIONS

Deposit: 1 night; refund w/ 7-day notice

Discounts: Special packages and promos

Credit Cards: MC, V

Check-In/Out: 3/11

Smoking: No

Pets: No

Kids: Not on weekends

Minimum Stay: 2 nights weekends

Open: All year

Hosts: Carol and Matt Nolan

72 North Stonington Rd.

Mystic, CT 06355-0341

(800) 367-1833 or (860) 536-6325

www.visitmystic.com

OLD MYSTIC INN, Mystic

Overall: ★★★½	Room Quality: B	Value: C	Price: $105–$160+

In a prior life this red Colonial, built in 1794, was a rare-book and map store. The bed-and-breakfast replaced over 20,000 volumes, but retained many of the antique maps. Each guest room, named after a New England author, includes books by that writer, so you can choose based on literary inclinations. Also displayed is an ever-growing collection of stuffed bears. Candlelight breakfasts are served by the bay window and a roaring fireplace in winter and on the porch in summer. Peter, known as the "mayor" of Old Mystic, was an Episcopal minister, so pastoral chatter may be an option while you munch on an ever-available chocolate-chip cookie.

SETTING & FACILITIES

Location: Eastern shore; I-95 to Exit 90 onto Rt. 27 N, approximately 2 mi. to B&B on right

Near: Downtown Mystic, Olde Mystic, Mystic Seaport and aquarium, Stonington, casinos, Newport

Building: 1794 Colonial w/ turret, veranda; restored, 1986; carriage house added 1988

Grounds: .75 acre; lawn games, swingset, gazebo, old stone walls, rose gardens, perennials, picnic tables

Public Space: DR, keeping room, 2nd floor library, 3 porches

Food & Drink: Full breakfast; specialty: scrambled eggs w/crab in pastry shell w/white cheddar sauce; chocolate-chip cookies; wine and cheese party Sat. nights

Recreation: Trails, nature center, beaches; sailing and schooner tours

Amenities & Services: Bike rentals, kids' play area, portacrib, roll-away, refrigerator, phone, chocolates, ltd. disabled access. Staff member always avail.; catered weddings (up to 120); small conf., fax, copy service

ACCOMMODATIONS

Units: 7 guest rooms, 1 suite

All Rooms: Bath, small sitting area, dataport, thermostat, AC

Some Rooms: Fireplace; carriage house rooms: outdoor seating, priv. ground floor entrances; love seat sleeper sofas, 1 main house room w/ priv. porch and side entry

Bed & Bath: 3 four-poster, 5 canopy beds, queen sizes; full baths, some whirlpools

Favorites: The Herman Melville room—largest room, canopy bed, priv. porch w/ stairs to lawn; Dickinson Room—fireplace, four-poster, bay window

Comfort & Decor: Rooms named after New England authors. Telephones and TVs deliberately excluded. Carpeted rooms furnished, mix of old and reproduction Colonial. Summery wicker. Simple, country feel.

RATES, RESERVATIONS, & RESTRICTIONS

Deposit: Credit card holds reservation; no charge w/ 2-day notice
Discounts: 3rd person, incl. kids; possible midweek; corp., long stay
Credit Cards: MC, V, AE
Check-In/Out: After 2/11 or as arranged
Smoking: No
Pets: No
Kids: Over 8 in main house; all ages in carriage house

Minimum Stay: 2 nights weekends in-season
Open: All year
Hosts: Mary and Peter Knight
58 Main St., P.O. Box 634
Old Mystic, CT 06372
(860) 572-9422
Fax: (860) 572-9954
omysticinn@aol.com
www.visitmystic.com/oldmysticinn/

RED BROOK INN, Mystic

Overall: ★★★★	Room Quality: B	Value: C	Price: $100–$190

This inn offers a Colonial experience, with whale-oil lamps and iron candle stands, as well as modern comforts, including whirlpool baths. Architecture and decor are meticulously authentic, with much of the painting and renovating done by Ruth herself. On some weekends she even dresses eighteenth-century-style and cooks hearty soup in a kettle and spit-roasted meat on the open-hearth. Moving and restoring Haley's Tavern required photographing, numbering, and coding each piece, and reconstructing literally stone by stone. Ruth earned joint 1986 Transportation and President's Historic Preservation Council award, the only one bestowed on an individual that year.

SETTING & FACILITIES

Location: I-95 to Exit 89 (Allyn St.), north from ramp end, 1.5 mi. to traffic light, right (E) at Rt. 184 (Goldstar Highway), left into B&B driveway at next corner, follow arrow up hill to Haley Tavern; B&B not visible from road
Near: Mystic, Dennison Nature Center, New London, Stonington, casinos
Building: Restored c. 1740 Haley Tavern and c. 1770 Crary Homestead
Grounds: 7 acres with gardens, lawn games

Public Space: Keeping room; ladies' parlor; gentlemen's parlor; tavern
Food & Drink: Full breakfast; specialties: walnut waffles w/ sausage, pumpkin pancakes; refreshments: mulled cider, iced tea; open-hearth Colonial cooking on Thanksgiving or by arrangement
Recreation: Schooner tours, water sports, antiquing, nature trails
Amenities & Services: Fridge, phone; crib, highchair; games, TV, maps; transport to/from Mystic train station; recipes

ACCOMMODATIONS

Units: 11 guest rooms
All Rooms: Bath, antique blanket chest, candle stands, seating, AC
Some Rooms: Fireplace (7), add'l bed, writing desk
Bed & Bath: Four-poster/canopy beds, queen/double, extra beds are twins; some baths w/ large shower-only, 1-person whirlpools (2)
Favorites: Mary Virginia—fireplace, quiet corner room, 1790 carved bed;

Nancy Crary—whirlpool, hand-stenciled flooring, pencil post bed
Comfort & Decor: Romantic Colonial. Country rugs over wide board flooring. Lace canopies over Early American four-posters. Pretty handmade coverlets. Needlepoint pillows. Armoires, rare desks, tall chests. Traditional Colonial furnishings. Restored orig. woodwork.

RATES, RESERVATIONS, & RESTRICTIONS

Deposit: 1 night; refund w/ 7-day notice
Discounts: Singles, 3rd person, kids in same room free
Credit Cards: MC, V, AE, D
Check-In/Out: Noon/by 11
Smoking: No
Pets: No
Kids: "Kids who appreciate antiques" welcome

Minimum Stay: 2–3 nights weekends, holidays
Open: All year
Hosts: Ruth Keyes
Route 184 & Wells Rd., P.O. Box 237
Mystic, CT 06372
(800) 290-5619 or (860) 572-0349
Fax: Call first
redbrookin@aol.com
www.virtualcities.com

STEAMBOAT INN, Mystic

Overall: ★★★★   Room Quality: A   Value: C   Price: $110–$275

This turn-of-the-last-century warehouse is the most interesting lodging in Mystic and the only waterfront bed-and-breakfast. The location allows you to walk to shops, restaurants and galleries, avoiding parking problems and traffic, which can be terrible during summer months. The rooms, named after local schooners, are delightfully tasteful and creative, with romantic features such as whirlpools for two, wood-burning fireplaces and views of passing boats and gulls along the Mystic River. You would enjoy staying at this bed-and-breakfast even if it weren't in this historic sea town.

SETTING & FACILITIES

Location: On the Mystic River; Rt. 1 and over drawbridge, look for B&B sign
Near: Walk to Mystic Seaport Museum, restaurants, docks; seaport, aquarium, shopping village, historic

sites, museums, casinos, Fort Griswold, Stonington Village, vineyards
Building: Built 1907; B&B opened 1989
Grounds: Backyard marina, priv. dock for guest walks

Public Space: Bright common room
Food & Drink: Early riser coffee; cont'l breakfast; tea and sherry avail.

Recreation: Day trips to ocean, boat tours from B&B dock, sailing, whale watching tours
Amenities & Services: irons, books

ACCOMMODATIONS

Units: 10 guest rooms
All Rooms: Bath, sitting area, phone, dataport, hidden TV, thermostat, whirlpool
Some Rooms: Fireplace, views, sofa sleeper; dock-level rooms have wet bar w/ refrigerator, micro; French doors to small 2nd room (1)
Bed & Bath: Some canopy, four-poster beds; hairdryers, some 2-person whirlpools
Favorites: Ariadne, Room 1— most romantic, fireplace, water view, canopy

bed, 2-person whirlpool. Summer Girl, Room 5—cheery favorite, fireplace, window wall overlooks drawbridge and water
Comfort & Decor: Rooms named after famous Mystic schooners. Romantic period touches, esp. in high-end rooms. Comfortable contemporary-style seating. Antique color schemes and decorative touches, carpet. Dock-level rooms largest.

RATES, RESERVATIONS, & RESTRICTIONS

Deposit: 1 night, refund w/ 5-day notice
Discounts: Midweek corp., 3rd person, kids under 16 free
Credit Cards: MC, V, AE, D
Check-In/Out: 2/11
Smoking: No
Pets: No
Kids: In dock-level rooms only

Minimum Stay: 2 nights on weekends
Open: All year
Hosts: Diana Stadtmiller
73 Steamboat Wharf
Mystic, CT 06355-2551
(860) 536-8300
Fax: (860) 536-9528
sbwharf@aol.com
www.visitmystic.com/steamboat

PALMER INN, Noank

Overall: ★★★½   Room Quality: B   Value: C   Price: $120–$230

As the views and foghorns attest, Noank is the Native-American term for "surrounded by water." One hundred years ago, this little village was a major ship-building area, and the imposing 7,600-square-foot mansion with 30-foot entry columns and 13-foot ceilings was home to owner of the eastern seaboard's major boatyard owner. Palmers lived in the house till the 1960s, but today, despite its grandeur, its mood is mellow and the decor is fuzzy Victoriana with local artwork, family portraits, and artisans' ongoing restorations. Pat was a clinical psychologist and is an accomplished sailor, so you can talk neuroses or mainsails. She also won an apple pie contest.

SETTING & FACILITIES

Location: In quiet fishing village; at 25 Church, turn left onto Cedar Lane for parking in rear

Near: In historic fishing village; 2 mi. to Mystic, 1 block to Long Island Sound, art galleries; Watch Hill antiquing and beaches, Coast Guard Academy, casinos

Building: Circa 1900 Southern Colonial

Grounds: 1 acre on Peninsula Village, flower and herb gardens

Public Space: Main hall; library; large parlor (the "Grand Salon")

Food & Drink: Early-riser coffee, cont'l communal breakfast; specialty: granola

Recreation: Beach activities, golf, tennis

Amenities & Services: Sailing classes nearby; special occasions, holiday theme weekends (large Christmas tree-trimming party)

ACCOMMODATIONS

Units: 6 guest rooms

All Rooms: Bath, sitting/reading area, AC

Some Rooms: Fireplace (1), balcony (1), writing desk, water views, ceiling fan

Bed & Bath: Carved mahogany, brass, antique wicker; bed sizes vary; all full baths except 1 tub-only bath (claw-foot tub), hairdryers, herbal toiletries

Favorites: Balcony Room—smallest, summer favorite, antique carved bed, harbor view; Master Suite—spacious corner, balcony, harbor view, fireplace, major headboard

Comfort & Decor: 2nd and 3rd floor spacious rooms—some huge. Well-appointed. Restored original light fixtures. Hardwood flooring w/ rugs, some Oriental, hand-hooked.

RATES, RESERVATIONS, & RESTRICTIONS

Deposit: 50%; refund w/ 14-day notice

Discounts: Midweek sailing lesson packages, midweek corp. rate

Credit Cards: None

Check-In/Out: 2–6/11

Smoking: No

Pets: No

Kids: 16 and up in their own room

No-No's: No add'l people in rooms—dbl. occupancy only

Minimum Stay: 2 nights, weekends summer and foliage seasons

Open: All year

Hosts: Patricia Ann White
25 Church St.
Noank, CT 06340-5777
(860) 572-9000
www.visitmystic.com/palmerinn

ANTIQUES & ACCOMMODATIONS, North Stonington			
Overall: ★★★★	Room Quality: B	Value: C	Price: $100–$230

As in the name, the emphasis is on antiques, and as former dealers, Ann and Tom have a knack for finding marvelous furnishings and collectibles, mainly from trips to England. The kick is that you can buy many of the items, and the hosts are delighted to replace them. Change is constant, as needlepoint or Oriental rugs vary according to the host's mood, and romantic guest rooms are updated annually. This striking Victorian, with its 1820 cottage connected by gravel paths, is also known for its seasonal gardens, with 3,000 bulbs blooming in springtime. At breakfast, with flickering candlelight and classical music, you may find a pansy on your pancakes.

SETTING & FACILITIES

Location: I-95 to Exit 92, head to W 2.3 mi., bear right onto Main St., large sign announces North Stonington Village, B&B is .2 mile on right (do not go to Stonington)
Near: Groton, Stonington, hiking trails, Pawcapuck River/tributaries; 8 mi. to Mystic, 11 mi. to Watch Hill antiquing/beaches, casinos
Building: 1861 Victorian farmhouse; 1820 garden cottage
Grounds: Village yard w/ English-style gardens, patios, various seating areas

Public Space: Sitting room, formal DR
Food & Drink: Four-course, communal, candlelight breakfast; specialties: pear compote with raspberry liqueur, banana-walnut pancake, salmon omelet; sherry, refreshments
Recreation: Stonington Village Walk, historic home tours, canoeing, Mystic attractions
Amenities & Services: Canoe for experienced guests, refrigerator, cribs, roll-aways; baby-sitting arranged, fax

ACCOMMODATIONS

Units: 3 guest rooms in main house, 2 family suites in garden cottage ("1820 House")
All Rooms: Bath, TV, alarm radio, seating, AC
Some Rooms: Fireplace, sitting area; large suite in 1820 House has LR, porch, kitchen, 3 BRs; second suite: 1-BR rooms w/ baths (2) or 2-BR suite w/ 2 baths (1), common sitting room
Bed & Bath: Canopy, four-poster beds; 1 tiny bath, others full
Favorites: Jenny's Room—antique chandelier, post mahogany queen, fire-

place, antique book library; Susan's Room—teacup collection, all-white double canopy bed, bridal theme
Comfort & Decor: Airy rooms in Victorian main house, bright, spacious. Traditional American w/ touch of class. Timothy's Room—1810 Sheraton four-poster double, antiques, tiny shower-only bath. 1820 annex house tends towards country American. Creative and elegant touches. During holidays Christmas bed four-posters w/ ribbons, greens.

RATES, RESERVATIONS, & RESTRICTIONS

Deposit: Credit card holds reservation; no charge w/ 14-day notice
Discounts: Corp., long stays, midweek, kids free
Credit Cards: MC, V

Check-In/Out: 3/11 or by arrangement until noon
Smoking: No
Pets: No

Kids: Children "w/ appreciation of antiques" welcome in 1820 house
Minimum Stay: 2 nights weekends, check for availability
Open: All year

Hosts: Ann and Tom Gray
32 Main St.
North Stonington, CT 06359
(860) 535-1736
Fax: (860) 535-2613
www.visitmystic.com/antiques

BEE AND THISTLE INN, Old Lyme

Overall: ★★★½	Room Quality: B	Value: C	Price: $95–$210

Years ago when we first stayed here, Penny sang madrigals and played the guitar in the parlor, and we had peach muffins and fresh orange juice on a tray in bed. Today, you can still have breakfast in bed (alas, for a fee), and music is in the air on weekends, but the intimacy is missing a bit, as the inn has become increasingly popular with the public for lunch and dinner. On the positive side, the cottage with its decks, dock, and kitchen offers peace and privacy, and the river seems to be yours alone. And the American Impressionism paintings at The Griswold Museum are still only a few steps away.

SETTING & FACILITIES

Location: I-95 S to Exit 70, right at ramp's end; inn, 3rd house on left, in historic district
Near: Florence Griswold Museum, Goodspeed Opera House, Gillette Castle, Lyme Academy of Fine Arts, art galleries and antique shops, Essex Steam Train and Boat-Ride, state parks, Rocky Neck beaches, Mystic attractions, casinos
Building: 1756 Colonial; building moved, various additions
Grounds: 5.5 acres along Lieutenant River, broad lawns, perennial gardens, herb gardens

Public Space: 2 parlors, DR, sun porches
Food & Drink: Breakfast (fee); lounge w/ fireplace; breakfast specialties: raspberry crepes, beef-and-bacon hash; lunch: crab cakes; candlelight dinner specialties: contemp. American cuisine, venison pie, wild mushroom lasagna; tea; wine list; Sun. brunch
Recreation: Boating, tennis, golf; biking trails
Amenities & Services: Weekend entertainment; breakfast in bed option (fee)

ACCOMMODATIONS

Units: 11 guest rooms, 1 cottage
All Rooms: Bath, antiques, phone, alarm clock, AC, fan
Some Rooms: Sitting area, desk

Bed & Bath: Antique, canopy, and four-poster beds, sizes vary; some showers only

Favorites: Room 1—largest, queen fishnet lace canopy, overlooks gardens; Cottage—TV room, fireplace, brick floor, kitchen, deck and priv. dock

Comfort & Decor: Even small rooms romantic and authentically Colonial. Rich fabrics and wallcoverings. Dark woods, carved antique furnishings. Possible kitchen noise in some rooms.

RATES, RESERVATIONS, & RESTRICTIONS

Deposit: 1 night or 50%; refund w/ 10-day notice
Discounts: 3rd person in cottage
Credit Cards: MC, V, AE, D, DC
Check-In/Out: 2/11
Smoking: No
Pets: No
Kids: Over 12
No-No's: Add'l people in rooms other than in cottage

Open: All year
Hosts: The Nelson Family
100 Lyme St.
Old Lyme, CT 06371
(800) 622-4946 or (860) 434-1667
Fax: (860) 434-3402
info@beeandthistleinn.com
www.beeandthistleinn.com/lodging.html

OLD LYME INN, Old Lyme

Overall: ★★★★   Room Quality: B   Value: C   Price: $110–$150

A Winslow Homer mural graces one dining room; another, with mounted fish and wall holes from darts that missed their mark, was one of the oldest taverns in Pittsburgh. More good stuff? During the 1920s the property was a riding academy where young Jacqueline Bouvier reputedly took lessons. Even earlier, Old Lyme School Impressionist painters sat in the inn's fields and struggled with their craft. Some old-timers recall square dancing in the old barn that burned down (it stood about 300 yards behind the one still remaining). Quirkier than neighbor Bee and Thistle, it offers bottles of witch hazel in rooms and can feel like a small hotel when groups descend.

SETTING & FACILITIES

Location: I-95 S to Exit 70, right at ramp end, travel to 1st intersection, right following Rt. 1; travel to 2nd light, inn on left; check inn website for scenic drive and ferry directions
Near: Village of Old Lyme, Lyme, Hamburg, Hadlyme, Essex, Conn. River, Mystic; museums, casinos
Building: Circa 1850 Colonial farmhouse
Grounds: In-village yard (over 1 acre), gardens, outbuildings

Public Space: Entry hall, sitting room, Victorian Bar, Empire Room DR
Food & Drink: Cont'l breakfast; restaurant open 7 days; Sun. brunch, Grill Room light suppers, Italian Night Wed.; specialties: dilled carrot soup w/bay shrimp, crab cakes; Conn. rabbit; award-winning desserts and wine list; full liquor license
Recreation: River boating, nature preserves, antique shops, gallery hopping, croquet

Amenities & Services: Weekend entertainment, refrigerators, choco-lates; meetings, special occasions (2–70) w/ all support

ACCOMMODATIONS

Units: 5 guest rooms in main house; 8 north wing rooms
All Rooms: Bath, reading lights, TV, radio/alarm, phone, AC
Some Rooms: Refrigerator, writing desk (1)
Bed & Bath: Cannonball queens in main house; fishnet lace-canopy queens (7) and king/twin four-poster in north wing, some twins; shower-only bath (1); small main house baths

Favorites: Rooms 7, 11-large corner rooms, garden view, canopied queens
Comfort & Decor: North wing rooms larger, more up-to-date, w/ che-nille spreads. Main house rooms smaller, not tiny. Muted color schemes, floral wallpapers, carpet. Original art from past-turn-of-century Old Lyme School of artists. Good reproductions and genuine antiques. Two rooms w/ sleeper sofas; kids may bunk on floors in bags or portable facilities.

RATES, RESERVATIONS, & RESTRICTIONS

Deposit: $55 main house, $75 north wing per-night deposit; refund w/ 2-day notice; check for special events
Discounts: Midweek, corp., singles, group, 3rd person; kids free
Credit Cards: MC, V, AE, D, DC
Check-In/Out: 3/noon
Smoking: Restricted
Pets: Restricted
Kids: Welcome (no cots or cribs)

Minimum Stay: 2 nights at Christmas
Open: All year, check at Christmas
Hosts: Diana Field Atwood
85 Lyme St.
Old Lyme, CT 06371
(800) 434-5352 or (860) 434-2600
Fax: (860) 434-5352
olinn@aol.com
www.oldlymeinn.com

COBBSCROFT, Pomfret

Overall: ★★★½   Room Quality: C   Value: C   Price: $75–$90

Art lover, artful, or just artful at love? In any case, you'll love it here, the results of host Janet and daughter who have painted the walls, fur-niture and accessories, and watercolorist husband Tom, who sometimes gives workshops and offers artworks for sale. Typical atypical touches include metal outdoor sculptures and a well-worn needlepoint "lolling chair" (Janet can't bear to update the fabric). Antique dealers and par-ents visiting kids at the nearby prep school like to stay here, perhaps lunching at the nearby vineyard, and viewing the Tiffany windows in the local church.

SETTING & FACILITIES

Location: I-395 to Exit 93, left from ramp end onto Rt. 101, travel 6.5 mi. or so to traffic light at Rt. 169, right onto 169 N; B&B approximately 3 mi. on right, across from school
Near: Private schools, winery, Sturbridge Village, Worcester outlets and colleges; Providence, R.I. School of Design
Building: Circa 1780 farmhouse; rooms added in 1830, 1893
Grounds: Old barn w/ furniture shop, art gallery, framing shop; front-yard perennial garden w/ sculptures
Public Space: Library, living room
Food & Drink: Full communal breakfast; specialties: apple crisp, seasonal cobblers, quiche
Recreation: Trails, bird watching, bottle collecting, antiquing; day trips
Amenities & Services: On-site gift, furniture shop, art gallery; phone in library, books, games, cots, bike rentals nearby

ACCOMMODATIONS

Units: 1 guest room, 2 suites
All Rooms: Bath, orig. hardwood floors
Some Rooms: Fireplace, dressing room
Bed & Bath: Twin/king, queen, king; all full baths, 1 w/ hall access (robes)
Favorites: Bridal Suite—largest, most private, fireplace, claw-foot soaking tub; Stencil Room—hand-painted barn-door headboard, hall access bath, robes
Comfort & Decor: Airy, bright rooms. Downstairs suite good for families. Painted furniture pieces, artwork; nicely restored, small antique pieces. Oriental or hand-hooked rugs. Rather plain bedding, accessories, wallcoverings in some rooms.

RATES, RESERVATIONS, & RESTRICTIONS

Deposit: Credit card holds reservation; no charge w/ 7-day notice
Discounts: Artist's workshop packages, singles, seniors, 3rd person
Credit Cards: MC, V, AE
Check-In/Out: 2/11
Smoking: No
Pets: No
Kids: 6 and up
Open: All year
Hosts: Janet McCobb
349 Pomfret St., Route 169
Pomfret, CT 06258
(800) 928-5560 or (860) 928-5560
Fax: (860) 928-3608
info@cobbscroft.com
www.cobbscroft.com

LINDEN HOUSE, Simsbury

Overall: ★★★½	Room Quality: B	Value: C	Price: $95–$105

Opened in October 1998, after a meticulous four-year restoration, this turreted Victorian bed-and-breakfast topped by a weathervane is close to the road, and passersby sometimes stop and ask about it. (Even before it was listed as a business it was booked through word-of-mouth.) Decorated as a cherished, tasteful, private residence rather than commercial lodgings, it soon will have two more working fireplaces so that all units offer the coziness of a bedside hearth. Julia and Myles are retired and are putting in the elbow grease and amenities to upgrade already lovely rooms. Growing pains are inevitable, but check this baby out.

SETTING & FACILITIES

Location: Rt. 84 E to Exit 39 onto Rt. 4, travel .25 mile to Rt. 10 N (Hopmeadow St.); approximately 11 mi. to B&B, about 2 mi. from Entering Simsbury sign
Near: Downtown Hartford, skating, recreation and nature facilities, Farmington River
Building: Circa 1860 Victorian
Grounds: 2.5 lawn acres to Farmington River, gardens, apple trees

Public Space: Entrance foyer, large sitting room
Food & Drink: Full breakfast; tea on weekends
Recreation: 8-mi. hiking trail, horses, golf, tennis, antiquing, X-C skiing
Amenities & Services: Bike storage, telephones avail., BYOB set-ups; occasions recognized

ACCOMMODATIONS

Units: 5 guest rooms
All Rooms: Bath; 3 working, 2 ornamental fireplaces; seating, AC
Some Rooms: Small dressing areas, TV
Bed & Bath: Four-poster, sleigh, carved; king, queen, 1 room w/ twins; large baths, all full, claw-foot soaking tubs, 1 w/ whirlpool
Favorites: Hostess' favorite—smallest room, Chinese Chippendale furnishings,

fireplace; Guests' favorite—romantic four-poster king room, warm yellow walls, antique chaise
Comfort & Decor: Antique mahogany pieces, handpainted furnishings. Oriental rugs. Collectibles, artwork. Pale color schemes. Handmade quilts, bedspreads. Ornate, carved Victorian mantels. Twin room, prettiest.

RATES, RESERVATIONS, & RESTRICTIONS

Deposit: 20%; refund w/ 7-day notice
Discounts: 3rd person, corp. midweek, corp. long-term
Credit Cards: MC, V
Check-In/Out: 2–4/11 (will hold luggage)
Smoking: No
Pets: No

Kids: Over 12
Minimum Stay: 2 nights weekends
Open: All year except Christmas and a few summer days; check
Hosts: Julia and Myles McCabe
290 Hopmeadow St.
Simsbury, CT 06089
(860) 408-1321

MERRYWOOD, Simsbury

Overall: ★★★★	Room Quality: B	Value: C	Price: $130–$155

Gerlinde was an antiques dealer, and textiles and collections from around the world are draped, tossed, placed, hung, set, and framed throughout the premises. Kilims, wooden shoes, Far Eastern hats, Indian robes, and more are thoughtfully labeled, and even the antique dishes at breakfast are mix-and-match. In keeping with the creativity, you can select an original dish like the Sea-legs Omelet, filled with crab, onion, tomato, and wine. Eastern philosophical influence and laid-back comfort pervade this brick Colonial Revival, and piped-in classical music emphasizes the serenity. So do five acres of gardens and well-equipped guest rooms.

SETTING & FACILITIES

Location: Rt. 185 in Simsbury, on Rt. 10 N, right at Chart House Restaurant, travel on 185 approximately 1 mi., start up the hill, small sign on left marks B&B
Near: Farmington, downtown Hartford, priv. schools, recreation and nature facil., mountain hiking, antiquing, International World Skating
Building: Graceful Colonial Revival
Grounds: 5 landscaped, pine-treed acres; carvings, gardens, patio, walking paths

Public Space: LR, glassed-in porch, formal DR, library
Food & Drink: Full communal breakfast, guests select night before from cont'l, standard, and gourmet offerings; mimosas, espresso; specialties: German pancakes, Eierroesti (Swiss egg dish)
Recreation: Farmington River activities; horses, golf, tennis, touring, skiing, hot-air ballooning
Amenities & Services: AC, room refrigerators w/ soft drinks, beer. Special occasions recognized

ACCOMMODATIONS

Units: 2 guest rooms, 1 suite
All Rooms: Bath, small refrigerator, TV/VCR, dataport, sherry decanter
Some Rooms: Suite w/ kitchenette; priv. sound system
Bed & Bath: Queen, king/twin sizes; robes, slippers, hairdryers; 2 smallish baths—1 hall access, small sauna in suite bath

Favorites: Victorian Room—lace-canopied queen bed, antique love seat, cut-glass collection, desk
Comfort & Decor: Well-used Empire and Victorian antique furnishings. Comfortably cluttered rooms. Original artwork. Oriental influence. Suite: small BR, spacious sitting room. Refrigerators unobtrusive. Simple but creative window treatments. Soothing.

RATES, RESERVATIONS, & RESTRICTIONS

Deposit: 50%; refund w/ 14-day notice
Discounts: Singles, corp.
Credit Cards: MC, V, AE, D, DC
Check-In/Out: 2/11
Smoking: No
Pets: No
Kids: No
Open: All year

Hosts: Gerlinde and Michael Marti
100 Hartford Rd.
Simsbury, CT 06070
(860) 651-1785
Fax: (860) 651-8273
mfmarti@aol.com

SIMSBURY 1820 HOUSE, Simsbury

Overall: ★★★½	Room Quality: B	Value: C	Price: $100–$150

Formerly the Elisha Phelps House, this white-brick, many-chimneyed mansion is a mix of Georgian, Adamesque, and antebellum influences. It sits on town-owned land and is the older, smaller sibling of the nearby Simsbury Inn, a luxury 97-room resort. Meeting and recreational facilities of that modern property are available, but guests at this original property have the bonus of country ambiance, close to the capital. For groups, weddings, retreats, and those seeking a longer stay, this is an attractive combination of facilities, space, and charm. Those who seek privacy can escape to the secluded carriage house, or may want to choose another smaller inn or bed-and-breakfast.

SETTING & FACILITIES

Location: On Rt. 202 in Simsbury, hilltop site
Near: Downtown Hartford, International World Skating
Building: Built in 1822; 1890 Beaux Arts renovations; renovated 1986
Grounds: Spacious lawns, gardens

Public Space: Entry, lobby, dining room
Food & Drink: Cont'l breakfast; refreshments; lunch and dinner open to public: express lunch, contemp. American cuisine; specialties: pear and scallop bisque, lobster w/ black-bean

crepe

Recreation: Horseback riding, golf, tennis, hiking trails, X-C skiing, antiquing

Amenities & Services: Use of nearby Simsbury Inn exercise and spa facil.; party and corp. functions: ballroom (125), smaller meeting rooms

ACCOMMODATIONS

Units: 20 guest rooms in main house; 12 in carriage house

All Rooms: Bath, desk, AC, alarm clock

Some Rooms: Decorative fireplace, sitting area, sofabed, hidden TV, whirlpool

Bed & Bath: Some four-posters, queen/king; 1 room w/ 2 doubles

Favorites: Four-poster king—raised sitting area w/ sofabed, whirlpool, priv. entrance

Comfort & Decor: Hunt-country classic. Simple but elegantly furnished w/ reproductions and English period pieces. Coordinated fabrics. Luxury touches. Room sizes vary from small to quite large. Feel of smaller property in carriage house.

RATES, RESERVATIONS, & RESTRICTIONS

Deposit: 1 night

Discounts: AAA, longer stays, corp., government

Credit Cards: MC, V, AE

Check-In/Out: 3/11

Smoking: Restricted

Pets: Restricted

Kids: No

Minimum Stay: 2 nights weekends, May, June and Oct.

Open: All year

Hosts: The Brighenti Family
731 Hopemeadow St.
Simsbury, CT 06070
(800) TRY-1820 or (860) 658-7658
Fax: (860) 651-0724

LORD THOMPSON MANOR, Thompson

| Overall: ★★★½ | Room Quality: B | Value: C | Price: $100–$160 |

Wedding bells and laptops are frequently seen and heard here, as weekend weddings and weekday meetings are popular throughout the year. This 30-room stucco estate, built in 1917, was given up to the Catholic church after the Depression, and returned to its grand state in 1989, when Jackie and Andrew took over. The upstairs suites, named for horses, are choice, and one includes a rare English needle shower. A billiards room is off the imposing living room, and the breakfast area is warmed with shades of burgundy and grape. Today, much of the Frederick Law Olmsted landscaping remains on dozens of bucolic acres, perfect for strolls to close a deal (or trysts to close a deal, for that matter).

SETTING & FACILITIES

Location: From New York take I-95 to Rt. 395 N to Exit 99, right onto Rt. 200 E, B&B is 1st drive on left, watch for sign, cannot see property from road, .5 mi. driveway

Near: Antique shopping district, Sturbridge Village, casinos, Mystic

Building: 1917 Symmetrical Georgian 30-room manor, Gladding Estate

Grounds: 36 acres, old pine trees, walking paths, formal gardens designed by Frederick Law Olmsted, seating

Public Space: Entrance hall, drawing room, fully licensed wet bar, billiards room

Food & Drink: Full country breakfast; specialties: waffles, ham, Finnish pancakes; in 1998 B&B acquired nearby White Horse Inn restaurant, serving lunch, dinner, Sunday brunch

Recreation: Hiking, biking, antiquing, touring, day trips

Amenities & Services: Guest refrigerators, cots available, limited disabled access, maps, weddings; corp. meeting facilities

ACCOMMODATIONS

Units: 2 guest rooms, 4 suites

All Rooms: Writing desk, antiques, AC

Some Rooms: Priv. bath, fireplace, sitting area, phone

Bed & Bath: Sleigh, canopy, four-poster, wicker beds, down comforters, extra bedding; full original 1917 priv. baths (3); shared large shower bath (3); additional half bath (1)

Favorites: Thoroughbred Suite I— Master Suite, 1 large room, fireplace, sitting area, original paneling, ambiance lighting, rich fabrics, queen four-poster

bed, antique, English "needle shower" (only 2 or 3 in U.S.), cast iron soaking tub

Comfort & Decor: Spacious suites named for horses. Heavy mahogany furnishings, rich wood floors and carpet, fabrics. Elegant, dark tones. All original brass hardware, lighting fixtures retained and restored. Lots of romantic candles. TVs deliberately excluded from romantic rooms. Hosts set-up candlelight bubble baths, champagne, light fires for arrival.

RATES, RESERVATIONS, & RESTRICTIONS

Deposit: Credit card holds reservation; no charge w/ 7-day notice

Discounts: "Big Chill Weekend" packages, dinner packages, children, 3rd person, midweek corp. rates

Credit Cards: MC, V, AE, D

Check-in/Out: 3/11

Smoking: No

Pets: No

Kids: Welcome

No-No's: Guests may not bring their own alcohol

Open: All year

Hosts: Jackie and Andrew Silverston
Rt. 200, P.O. Box 428
Thompson, CT 06277
(860) 923-3886
Fax: (860) 923-9310
ltm@nica.com
www.lordthompsonmanor.com

CHESTER BULKLEY HOUSE, Wethersfield

Overall: ★★★½	Room Quality: C	Value: C	Price: $80–$90

Near a quiet inlet of the Connecticut River and a cluster of historic homes, this 1830 Greek Revival house slows the pace down to the era of Mr. Bulkley. Antique dolls, Oriental rugs, fireplaces, wide-board floors, and hand-carved woodwork create a fine period ambiance. Sophie's favorite antique piece is a teapot, which is kept on the low-boy designed by the founder of Tufts University. Old Wethersfield dates to 1634 and is related to a fistful of firsts: Behind the First Church of Christ, dating to the 1600s, is the landmark cemetery where America's first slave and the first commissioned Marine are buried in somewhat ironic juxtaposition.

SETTING & FACILITIES

Location: In center of historic village, amid more than 150 early 19th-century homes; I-91 to Exit 26 onto Marsh St., left onto Main St.; B&B is 4th house on left
Near: Wethersfield Cove, state parks; historic home museums; yachting cove; Hartford, oldest statehouse in America, Wadsworth Atheneum museum
Building: Pretty 1830 Greek Revival
Grounds: Village yard, brick patio w/ English gardens

Public Space: Parlor, DR, sitting room
Food & Drink: Full communal breakfast; specialties: Finnish oven-baked pancakes w/ banana, blueberry, and strawberry hot sauce, corn-flake French toast; special diets avail.; tea
Recreation: Antiquing, hiking trails, arts events, day trips
Amenities & Services: Refrigerator, cots, chocolate-covered strawberries by bed, fax/dataport, local paper, babysitters

ACCOMMODATIONS

Units: 5 guest rooms
All Rooms: Seating, phone, radio/alarm clock, A3 w/ priv. baths, writing desk
Bed & Bath: Antique, brass, carved beds, sizes vary; priv. baths; shower-only, 2 rooms share 1 full bath, robes

Favorites: Largest—king four-poster, priv. bath
Comfort & Decor: 1800s historic preservation wallcoverings. Laura Ashley and Waverly fabrics. Some carpet, some painted plank floors. Rooms sharing bath coverts to 2-BR 1-bath suite. Rear rooms most quiet.

RATES, RESERVATIONS, & RESTRICTIONS

Deposit: Credit card holds reservation; no charge w/ 7-day notice
Discounts: Midweek corp., AAA, senior, kids
Credit Cards: MC, V, AE, D

Check-In/Out: 4/11
Smoking: No
Pets: No
Kids: Welcome (no cribs)
Open: All year except Dec. 24–25

Hosts: Sophie and Frank Bottaro
184 Main St.
Wethersfield, CT 06109

(860) 563-4236
Fax: (860) 257-8266
www.choice-guide.com/ct/bulkley

ELIAS CHILD HOUSE, Woodstock

| Overall: ★★★½ | Room Quality: B | Value: C | Price: $100–$120 |

By the mid-1700s the Elias Child house was described in land records as "the mansion house." It had risen from humble one-room beginnings to include additions, outbuildings, and an "indoor outhouse," attached to the home's ell—a unique piece of Colonial history, now part of the current screened porch. Ask to see the well-preserved attic chimney smoke chamber, once used to cure and smoke meats. Veteran bed-and-breakfast hosts Mary Beth and Tony will ease you into a relaxing getaway at this still-emerging property, combining original elements—like nine fireplaces—with clean renovations. Over the years the Felice's specialty has been "peaceful romance."

SETTING & FACILITIES

Location: Rt. 171 E to West Woodstock (through Putnam and South Woodstock), turn onto Perrin Rd.; close to rural road
Near: Vineyards (luncheons by res., tours); herb farms; historic homes; living Colonial museums; Old Sturbridge Village, antiquing, flea markets, arts attractions, state parks, local fairs/events, golf; private schools; UConn, speedway, casinos
Building: 1714 symmetrical Colonial
Grounds: Over 10 acres behind house, stone walls, wooded areas

Public Space: Keeping room, reading/conversation room, stone patio, parlor, DR, screened porch
Food & Drink: Full country-style, communal breakfast; daily menu; specialties: granola, omelets, bananas Amaretto, pastries
Recreation: Walking trails; short drive to fine restaurants, biking, hiking, day trips
Amenities & Services: Summer pool, bike storage; forgotten necessities; roll-aways; BYOB set-ups, hearth-cooking demonstrations in season, bikes

ACCOMMODATIONS

Units: 2 guest rooms, 1 suite
All Rooms: Bath, fireplace, seating, reading lighting, closets
Some Rooms: Add'l beds, suite w/ sep. sitting room, decorative fireplace
Bed & Bath: Unusual antique bedsteads, double beds (suite has queen, add'l beds twin or ¾ size); shower-only, except suite

Favorites: Polly's Room—sunny southwest corner, pretty antique bed
Comfort & Decor: Sunny, spacious (18' x 14') rooms despite home's era. All rural views. Caroline's Room: double bed and ¾ bed. Suite Aimee: queen and day bed, useable antique crib. Oriental and braided area rugs. Muted colors, some hand-stenciling.

Rates, Reservations, & Restrictions

Deposit: Credit card holds reservation; no charge w/ 14-day notice
Discounts: 3rd person, 5+ night stays, check for packages
Credit Cards: MC, V, D
Check-In/Out: By arrangement/11
Smoking: No
Pets: No
Kids: Infants, or 7 and up
No-No's: Toddlers

Minimum Stay: 2 nights for local parents' weekends and graduations
Open: All year
Hosts: Mary Beth Gorke-Felice and Tony Felice
50 Perrin Rd.
Woodstock, CT 06281
877-974-9836 or (860) 974-9836
Fax: Same as main telephone
tfelice@compuserve.com

Additional Bed-and-Breakfasts and Small Inns

While our 300 profiles give you a fine range of bed-and-breakfasts and small inns, some may be fully booked when you want to visit, or you may want to stay in areas where we have not included a property. So we have included an annotated listing of 300 additional bed-and-breakfasts and small inns, spread geographically throughout New England. All properties meet our basic criteria for this guide: They have about 3–25 guestrooms, a distinct personality and individually decorated guestrooms, are open regularly, and include breakfast in the price (with a few exceptions). Prices are a range from low to high season. Most are highly recommended, but we have not visited all of these properties so we cannot recommend them across the board. We suggest you get a brochure, look on the Internet, or call and ask about some of the categories that are on the profile format to find out more. While some of these supplementals are famed and excellent, others may not be up to the level of the profiled properties.

MAINE

Zone 1: Downeast/Acadia

Bar Harbor
Bayview Inn $85–$280
(207) 288-5861 or
  (800) 356-3585

Black Friar Inn
$70–$140
(207) 288-5091

Brooklin
Lookout $60–$98
(207) 359-2188

Brooksville
Bucks Harbor Inn
$65–$75
(207) 826-8660

Calais: St. Andrews
Kingsbrai Arms
$125–$280
(506) 529-1897

Windward House
$90–$195
(207) 236-9656

Castine
Pentagoet Inn $99–$129
(207) 326-8616 or
  (800) 845-1701

Corea
The Black Duck Inn on
Corea Harbor $75–$145
(207) 963-2689

Deer Isle
Goose Cove Lodge
$90–$220
(207) 348-2508 or
  (800) 728-1963

Eastport
Todd House $45–$80
(207) 853-2328

Jonesport
Tootsies $40
(207) 497-5414

Lubec
Peacock House $70–$80
(207) 733-2403

Northeast Harbor
Harbourside Inn
$110–$190
(207) 276-3272

Maison Suisse Inn
$105–$245
(207) 276-5223 or
(800) 624-7668

Southwest Harbor
Claremont Hotel &
Cottages $95–$135
(207) 244-5036 or
(800) 244-5036

Island House $65–$85
(207) 244-5180

The Lindenwood Inn
$85–$285
(207) 244-5835 or
(800) 307-5335

Zone 2: Midcoast
Bailey Island
Captain York House Bed
& Breakfast $64–$115
(207) 833-6224

Tower Hill B&B (Orr's
Island) $70–$135
(207) 833-2311 or
(888) 833-2311

Boothbay
Hodgdon Island Inn
$75–$125
(207) 633-7474

Kenniston Hill Inn
$69–$110
(207) 633-2159 or
(800) 992-2915

Boothbay Harbor
Lawnmeer Inn $78–$168
(207) 633-2544 or
(800) 633-7645

Brunswick
Brunswick Bed and
Breakfast $87–$125
(207) 729-4914 or
(800) 299-4914

Captain's Watch B&B and
Sail Charter $95–$150
(207) 725-0979

Camden
A Little Dream $95–$225
(207) 236-8742

Maine Stay Inn $95–$140
(207) 236-9636

Nathaniel Hosmer Inn
$85–$145
(207) 236-4012

Swan House $75–$130
(207) 236-8275 or
(800) (207) 8275

Damariscotta
Brannon-Bunker Inn
$55–$75
(207) 563-5941 or
(800) 563-9225

Damariscotta Mills
Mill Pond Inn $80
(207) 453-8014

Rockland
Lakeshore Inn $105–$125
(207) 594-4209 or
(877) 783-7371

Searsport
Watchtide $80–$100
(207) 548-6575 or
(800) 698-6575

**Spruce Head (Clark
Island)**
Craignair Inn $74–$102
(207) 594-7644 or
(800) 320-9997

Vinalhaven
Fox Island Inn $55–$75
(207) 863-2122

Zone 3: Southern Coast & Greater Portland
Eliot
High Meadows $80–$90
(207) 439-0590

Freeport
Anita's Cottage Street Inn
$75–$110
(207) 865-0932 or
(800) 392-7121

Isaac Randall House
$65–$135
(207) 865-9295 or
(800) 865-9295

Kennebunk
The Waldo Emerson Inn
$85–$100
(207) 985-4250

Kennebunkport
1802 House B&B Inn
$129–$359
(207) 967-5632 or
(800) 932-5632

Captain Fairfield Inn
$89–$250
(207) 967-4454 or
(800) 322-1928

Inn at Harbor Head
$130–$315
(207) 967-5564

Phippsburg
Popham Beach $75–$150
(207) 389-2409

Portland
Inn at St. John $35–$145
(207) 773-6481 or
(800) 636-9127

West End Inn $99–$169
(207) 772-1377 or
(800) 338-1377

Saco
Crown 'n' Anchor Inn
$65–$100
(207) 282-3829 or
(800) 561-8865

York Harbor
The Admiral Olsen Inn
$125
(207) 363-1900

Inn at Harmon Park
$59–$109
(207) 363-2031

Zone 4: Inland & Lakes
Augusta
Maple Hill Farm
$55–$125
(207) 622-2708 or
(800) 622-2708

Bridgton
Noble House $74–$125
(207) 647-3733

Dedham
Lucerne Inn $59–$129
(207) 843-5123 or
(800) 325-5123

Dexter
Brewster Inn $59–$89
(207) 924-3130

Fayette
Home-Nest Farm
$60–$95
(207) 897-4125

Kingfield
Inn on Winter's Hill
$85–$150
(207) 265-5421 or
(800) 233-9687

Stratton
Putt's Place Bed &
Breakfast $50
(207) 246-4181

New Hampshire

Zone 5: Southern
Alstead
Darby Brook Farm $60
(603) 835-6624

Bedford
Bedford Village Inn
$185–$285
(603) 472-2001 or
(800) 852-1166

Chesterfield
Chesterfield Inn
$120–$195
(800) 365-5515

Dover
Highland Farm Bed and
Breakfast $90–$120
(603) 743-3399

Payne's Hill Bed and
Breakfast
$50–$65
(603) 740-9441

Durham
University Guest House
$60–$80
(603) 868-2728

East Andover
Highland Lake Inn
$85–$100
(603) 735-6426

Exeter
Inn by the Bandstand
$95–$145
(603) 772-6352 or
(877) 2EX-ETER

Greenfield
Greenfield Inn
$49–$139
(603) 547-6327 or
(800) 678-4144

Henniker
Meeting House Inn &
Restaurant
$65–$105
(603) 428-3228

Jaffrey
Benjamin Prescott Inn
$65–$130
(603) 532-6637

Portsmouth
Inn at Strawbery Banke
$85–$120
(603) 436-7242 or
(800) 428-3933

Martin Hill Inn
$80–$120
(603) 436-2287

Rindge
Grassy Pond House
$60–$70
(603) 899-5167

Sullivan
Post and Beam $45–$95
(603) 847-3330 or
(888) 3-ROMANCE

Wilton Center
Stepping Stones $60–$65
(603) 654-9048 or
(888) 654-9048

Zone 6: Central & Lakes
Canaan
Inn on Canaan Street
$75–$100
(603) 523-7310

Center Harbor
Watch Hill Bed and
Breakfast $60–$65
(603) 253-4334

Charlestown
Maplehedge Bed and
Breakfast $80–$100
(603) 826-5237 or
(800) 9-MAPLE –9

Cornish
Chase House
$105–$150
(603) 675-5391 or
(800) 401-9455

Hanover
Moose Mountain Lodge
$60–$80   (603) 643-3529

Holderness
Inn on Golden Pond
$60–$140
(603) 968-7269

Lyme
Breakfast on the
Connecticut
$106–$250
(603) 353-4444

Loch Lyme Lodge
$56–$90
(603) 795-2141 or
(800) 423-2141

Meredith
Inn at Bay Point
$129–$255
(603) 279-7006 or
(800) 622-6455

New London
Inn at Pleasant Lake
$95–$135
(603) 526-6271 or
(800) 626-4907

Northwood
Meadow Farm Bed
and Breakfast
$60–$100
(603) 942-8619

Sunapee
Inn at Sunapee
$70–$130
(603) 763-4444 or
(800) 327-2466

Wakefield
Wakefield Inn
$70–$75
(603) 522-8272 or
(800) 245-0841

West Franklin
Atwood Inn $80
(603) 934-3666

Zone 7:
Northern & White
Mountains
Bretton Woods
Bretton Arms Country Inn
$90–$199
(603) 278-1000 or
(800) 258-0330

Campton
Mountain Fare Inn
$35–$125
(603) 726-4283

Colebrook
Rooms With a View
$60–$65
(603) 237-5106
or (800) 449-5106 ext. 1

Franconia
Hilltop Inn $90–$195
(603) 823-5695 or
(800) 770-5695

Inn at Forest Hills
$90–$130
(603) 823-9550 or
(800) 280-9550

Lovett's Inn by Lafayette
Brook $100–$160
(603) 823-7762 or
(800) 356-3802

Jackson
Ellis River House
$59–$229
(603) 383-9339 or
(800) 233-8309

Paisley and Parsley
$60–$135
(603) 383-0859

Village House $75–$140
(603) 383-6666 or
(800) 972-8343

Jefferson
Jefferson Inn $80–$100
(603) 586-7998 or
(800) 729-7908

North Conway
Cabernet Inn $70–$120
(603) 356-4704 or
(800) 866-4704

Farm by the River
$85–$210
(603) 356-2694 or
(888) 414-8353

Scottish Lion Inn and
Restaurant $65–$145
(603) 356-6381 or
(888) 356-4945

1785 Inn $89–$99
(603) 356-9025 or
(800) 421-1785

Stonehurst Manor
$106–$176
(603) 356-3113 or
(800) 525-9100

Victorian Harvest Inn
$60–100 (603) 356-3548
or (800) 642-0749

Wyatt House Country Inn
$119–$175
(603) 356-7977 or
(800) 527-7978

North Woodstock
Wilderness Inn $45–$120
(603) 745-3890 or
(800) 200-WILD

Plymouth
Crab Apple Inn
$65–$100
(603) 536-4476

Snowville
Snowvillage Inn
$88–$180
(603) 447-2818 or
(800) 447-4345

Tamworth
The Tamworth Inn
$75–$105
(603) 323-7721 or
(800) 642-7352

Vermont

Zone 8: Southern

Andover
Inn at High View
$90–$145
(802) 875-2724

Arlington
Arlington Inn $70–$195
(802) 375-6784

Hill Farm Inn $65–$150
(802) 375-2269

Bennington
South Shire Inn
$105–$160
   (802) 442-3547

Chester
Madrigal Inn (and Fine
   Arts Center) $90–$120
(802) 463-1339 or
   (800) 854-2208

Night with a Native
$60–$85
(802) 875-2616

Danby
Silas Griffith Inn
$74–$109
(802) 293-5567

Dorset
Barrows House
$125–$210
(802) 867-4455 or
   (800) 639-1620

Inn at West View Farm
$80–$155
(802) 867-5715 or
   (800) 769-4903

Weddingham Farm
$120–$140
(800) 310-2010

Jamaica
Three Mountain Inn
$95–$230
(802) 874-4140

Landgrove
Landgrove Inn $85–$120
(802) 824-6673 or
   (800) 669-8466

Londonderry
Highland House
$71–$103
(802) 824-3019

Manchester
Inn at Manchester
$125–$219
(802) 362-1793 or
   (800) 273-1793

Manchester Village
Charles Orvis Inn at
   the Equinox
$569–$899
(802) 362-4747 or
   (800) 362-4747

Village Country Inn
$150–$300
(802) 362-1792

Old Bennington
Four Chimneys Inn
$100–$175
(802) 447-3500

Peru
Johnny Seesaw's
$80–$166
(802) 824-5533

Saxton's River
Inn at Saxton's River
$108
(802) 869-2110

Weston
Wilder Homestead Inn
$70–$115
(802) 824-8172

Wilmington
The White House
$108–$195
(802) 464-2135 or
   (800) 541-2135

Zone 9: Midstate/ Champlain

Bolton Valley
Black Bear Inn
$89–$132
(802) 434-2126 or
   (800) 395-6335

Chittenden
Mountain Top Inn
$225–$320
(802) 483-2311 or
   (800) 445-2100

Cuttingsville
Maple Crest Farm $75
(802) 492-3367

Fair Haven
Maplewood Inn
$70–$125
(802) 265-8039 or
   (800) 253-7729

Fairfield
Tetreault's Hillside View
Farm $50
(802) 827-4480

Goshen
Blueberry Hill $95–$120
(802) 247-6735 or
   (800) 448-0707

Killington
Mountain Meadows Lodge
$78–$115
(802) 775-1010

Peak Chalet $50–$145
(802) 422-4278

Vermont Inn $55–$200
(802) 775-0708 or
   (800) 541-7795

Mendon
Red Clover Inn
$140–$350
(802) 775-2290 or
   (800) 752-0571

Montgomery Center
Inn on Trout River
$86–$103
(802) 326-4391

Randolph
Placidia Farm Bed
& Breakfast $90
(802) 728-9883

Three Stallion Inn
$99–$112
(802) 728-5575 or
(800) 424-5575

Shrewsbury
High Pastures $50–$80
(802) 773-2087

Smuggler's Notch
Mannsview Inn $65–$95
(802) 644-8321 or
(888) 937-6266

Smuggler's Notch Inn
$60–$125
(802) 644-2412 or
(800) 845-3101

South Burlington
Willow Pond Farm Bed
& Breakfast $75–$95
(802) 985-8505

Waitsfield
Lareau Farm Country Inn
$70–$135
(802) 496-4949 or
(800) 833-0766

Zone 10: Upper Valley/Northeast Kingdom

Chelsea
Shire Inn $110–$200
(802) 685-3031 or
(800) 441-6908

Craftsbury
Craftsbury Inn &
Restaurant $140–$160
(802) 586-2848 or
(800) 336-2848

Craftsbury Common
Craftsbury Bed &
Breakfast on Wylie Hill
$60–$75
(802) 586-2206

Fairlee
Silver Maple Lodge &
Cottages $54–$79
(802) 333-4326

Greensboro
Highland Lodge
$190–$230
(802) 533-2647

Lyndonville
Branch Brook Bed &
Breakfast $60–$80
(802) 626-8316 or
(800) 572-7712

Montpelier
Inn at Montpelier
$89–$145
(802) 228-2727

North Troy
Rose Apple Acres Farms
$45–$60 (802) 988-4300

Quechee
The Queechee Inn at
Marshland Farm
$120–$200
(802) 295-3133

South Woodstock
Kedron Valley Inn
$105–$205
(802) 457-1473 or
(800) 836-1193

Stowe
Butternut Inn at Stowe
$85–$160
(802) 253-4277

Fitch Hill Inn $75–$165
(802) 888-3834 or
(800) 639-2903

Ski Inn $25–$65/person
(802) 253-4050

Taftsville
Applebutter Inn
$75–$145
(802) 457-4158

Williamstown
Autumn Harvest Inn
$79–$139
(802) 433-1355

Woolcott
Golden Maple Inn
$60–$135
(802) 888-6614 or
(800) 639-5234

MASSACHUSETTS

Zone 11: Boston Region

Andover
Andover Inn $110
(978) 475-5903

Cambridge
A Cambridge House Bed
& Breakfast Inn
$109–$250
(617) 491-6300 or
(800) 232-9989

Marblehead
Gabriella-by-the-Sea
$90–$135
(781) 631-1699

Middleborough
1831 Zachariah Eddy
House $65–$125
(508) 946-0016

Newburyport
The Morrill Place Inn
$72–$95
(978) 462-2808
or (888) 594-INNS

Rehobeth
Five Bridge Inn Bed &
Breakfast $68–$125
(508) 252-3190

Perryville Inn Bed &
   Breakfast $55–$95
(508) 252-9239

Rockport
The Captain's House
$75–$120
(978) 546-3825

Inn on Cove Hill
$60–$105
(978) 546-2701

Old Farm Inn $83–$130
(978) 546-3237

Salem
The Salem Inn
$109–$200
(978) 741-0680 or
   (800) 446-2995

Sudbury
Longfellow's Wayside Inn
$82–$132
(508) 443-1776 or
   (800) 339-1776

Zone 12:
Central/Western
Amherst
Black Walnut Inn
$105–$135
(413) 549-5649

Belchertown
Bed and Breakfast at
   Ingate Farms $69–$85
(413) 253-0440 or
   (888) INGATE-B

Mucky Duck $65–$95
(413) 323-9657

Greenfield
Brandt House Country
   Inn $90–$300
(413) 774-3329 or
   (800) 239–3329

Lee
Chambery Inn $75–$265
(413) 243-2221

Lenox
Garden Gables Inn
$95–$225
(413) 637-0193

Gateways Inn $85–$320
(413) 637-2532 or
   (888) 492-9466

The Summer White
   House $195
(413) 637-4489

Leverett
Hannah Dudley House
$125–$185
(413) 367-2323

New Salem
Bullard Farm B&B
$70–$90
 (978) 544-6959

Plymouth
Plymouth Bay Manor
$95–$110
(508) 830-0426 or
   (800) 492-1828

Richmond
Inn at Richmond
$110–$250
(413) 698-2566

South Egremont
Weathervane Inn
$95–$175
(413) 528-9580 or
   (800) 528-9580

Stockbridge
Inn at Stockbridge
$85–$260
(413) 298-3337

Ware
Wildwood Inn Bed &
   Breakfast $50–$90
(413) 967-7709 or
   (800) 860-7798

West Stockbridge
Williamsville Inn &
   Restaurant $120–$180
(413) 274-6118

Zone 13: Cape Cod
Barnstable
Ashley Manor $120–$180
(508) 362-8044

Beechwood $90–$160
(508) 362-6618

Charles Hinckley House
$119–$149
(508) 362-9924

Brewster
Bramble Inn $105–$135
(508) 896-7644

Brewster Farmhouse Inn
$95–$220
(508) 896-3910 or
   (800) 892-3910

Candleberry Inn
$90–$165
(508) 896-3300 or
   (800) 573-4769

Pepper House Inn
$89–$139
(508) 896-4389

Ruddy Turnstone Bed &
   Breakfast $80–$150
(508) 385-9871

Chatham
Captain's House
$112–$325
(508) 945-0127

Chatham Town House
$95–$285
(508) 945-2180

Cranberry Inn $99–$255
(508) 945-9232 or
   (800) 332-4667

Moses Nickerson House
$95–$179
(508) 945-5859

Dennis
Isaiah Hall B&B Inn
$85–$122
(508) 385-9928

Eastham
Penny House Inn
$110–$195
(508) 255-6632

East Orleans
Nauset House Inn
$75–$135
(508) 255-2195

Parsonage Inn $70–$135
(508) 255-8217

Falmouth
Captain Tom Lawrence
  House $83–$155
(508) 540-1445

Woods Hole Passage
$85–$145
(508) 548-9575 or
  (800) 790-8976

Hyannis
Inn on Sea Street
$85–$135
(508) 775-8030

Sandwich
Belfry Inne & Bistro
$85–$165
(508) 888-8550

Isaiah Jones Homestead
$75–$110
(508) 888-9115 or
  (800) 526-1625

West Falmouth
Inn at West Falmouth
$175–$300
(508) 540-7696

West Yarmouth
Olde Schoolhouse Bed and
  Breakfast $80–$155
(508) 778-9468

Zone 14: Martha's Vineyard/ Nantucket
Chilmark
The Inn at Blueberry Hill
$90–$650
(508) 645-3322 or
  (800) 356-3322

Edgartown
The Charlotte Inn
$225–$450
(508) 627-4751

The Daggett House
$80–$395
(508) 627-4600 or
  (800) 946-3400

Hob Knob Inn
$100–$400
(508) 627-9510 or
  (800) 696-2723

Nantucket
Cliff Lodge $65–$250
(508) 228-9480

Seven Sea Street Inn
$75–$265
(508) 228-3577

Sherburne Inn $65–$195
(508) 228-4425

The Wauwinet
$200–$750
(508) 228-0145 or
  (800) 426-8718

Oak Bluffs
The Beach Rose
$65–$100
(508) 693-6135

Vineyard Haven
Greenwood House
$109–$239
(508) 693-6150

Tuckerman House
$110–$275
(508) 693-0417

RHODE ISLAND

Zone 15: Newport & Little Compton
Newport
Admiral Farragut Inn
$50–$145
(401) 848-8000 or
  (800) 343-2863

Beech Tree Inn $69–$215
(401) 847-9794 or
  (800) 748-6565

Bluestone $75–$125
(401) 846-5408

Elliot Boss House
$75–$145
(401) 849-9425

Melville House
$100–$165
(401) 847-0640

Middletown
Inn at Shadow Lawn
$75–$185
(401) 847-0902 or
  (800) 352-3750

Lindseys' Guest House
$50–$85
(401) 846-9386

Zone 16: Block Island
Block Island
Anchor House Inn
$99–$150
(401) 466-5021 or
  (800) 730-0181

Atlantic Inn $99–$195
(401) 466-5883 or
  (800) 224-7422

Barrington Inn $75–$168
(401) 466-5510

Rose Farm Inn $75–$179
(401) 466-2034

Sasafrash $90–$120
(401) 466-5486

Zone 17: Mainland/Providence
Bristol
Rockwell House Inn
$75–$110
(401) 253-0040 or
 (800) 815-0040

William's Grant Inn
$75–$105
(401) 253-4222

Narragansett
The Canterbury $65–$80
(401) 783-0046

The Old Clerk House
$65–$115
(401) 783-8008

Windermere $70
(401) 783-0187

North Kingstown
Country House $65–$75
(401) 294-4688

The Haddie Pierce House
$80–$95
(401) 294-7674

The John Updike House
$90–$200
(401) 294-4905

Mount Maple of Wickford
$80–$110
(401) 295-4373

Providence
Old Court $90–$140
(401) 751-2002

Richmond
Country Acres $70–$80
(401) 364-9134

Inn the Woods $65–$90
(401) 539-6021

South Kingstown
Cottrell Homestead $65
(401) 783-8665

The King's Rose
$65–$120
(401) 783-5222

The Metcalfs
from $75
(401) 783-3448

VirJess Farm $65
(401) 783-3464

Wakefield
Larchwood Inn
$50–$120
(401) 783-5454 or
 (800) 275-5450

Sugarloaf Hill
$85–$125
(401) 789-8715

Warren
Nathaniel Porter Inn
$80–$99
(401) 245-6622

Warwick
Enchanted Cottage
$65–$85
(401) 732-0439

Waverly
Polly's Place
$85–$130
(401) 847-2160

White Rose Inn
$55–$85
(401) 596-9449

Westerly
Grandview $75–$95
(401) 596-6384 or
 (800) 447-6384

The White Rose Inn
$50+
(401) 596-9449

CONNECTICUT

Zone 18: Western
Bristol
Chimney Crest Manor
$85–$175
(860) 582-4219

New Preston
Birches Inn
$95–$325
(860) 868-0563 or
 (800)-LAKE-INN

Hopkins Inn
$65–$82
(860) 868-7295

Norfolk
Greenwoods Gate
$205–$245
(860) 542-5439

Ridgefield
Stonehenge $90–$200
(203) 438-6511

West Lane Inn
$125–$175
(203) 438-7323

Riverton
Old Riverton Inn
$75–$110
(860) 379-1796 or
 (800) EST-1796

Salisbury
The Earl Grey B&B at
 Chittenden House
$135–$150
(860) 435-1007

The White Hart
$99–$199
(800) 832-0041

Waterbury
House on the Hill
$100–$150
(203) 757-9901

Watertown
The Clarks $40
(860) 274-4866

Zone 19: Eastern
Bolton
Jared Cone House
$45–$70
(860) 643-8538

Bozrah
Blueberry Inn $110–$135
(860) 889-3618

Fitch Claremont House
$110–$150
(860) 889-0260

Clinton
Captain Dibbell House
$55–$105
(860) 669-1646

Coventry
Maple Hill Farm $65–$85
(800) 742-0635

Essex
The Griswold Inn
$90–$185
(860) 767-1776

Glastonbury
Butternut Farm $70–$90
(860) 633-7197

Lyme
Hidden Meadow
$95–$125
(860) 434-8360

Madison
Tidewater Inn $90–$170
(203) 245-8457

Mystic
Adams House $95–$175
(860) 572-9551

Pequot Hotel Bed &
    Breakfast $110–$155
(860) 572-0390

Whitehall Mansion
$79–$250
(860) 572-7280

New London
Queen Anne Inn
$125–$300
(860) 447-2600 or
    (800) 347-8818

North Stonington
Arbor House at Kruger's
    Old Maine Farm
$105–$145
(860) 535-4221

High Acres $100–$160
(860) 887-4355

Old Saybrook
Deacon Timothy Pratt
$100–$170
(860) 395-1229

Pomfret
Clark Cottage $65–$90
(860) 928-5741

Putnam
Felshaw Tavern $80
(860) 928-3467

Thurber House $70
(860) 928-6776

South Woodstock
Inn at Woodstock Hill
$85–$150
(860) 928-0528

Thompson
Captain Parker's Inn at
    Quinebaug $65–$125
(860) 935-5219 or
    (800) 707-7303

Tolland
Tolland Inn $70–$130
(860) 872-0800

Windsor
Charles R. Hart House
$85–$95
(860) 688-5555

Index of Profiled Bed-and-Breakfasts

Subject Index